DATE DUE			

AMERICAN SOCIAL PSYCHOLOGY
Its Origins, Development, and European Background

AMERICAN SOCIAL PSYCHOLOGY

Its Origins, Development, and European Background

BY

FAY BERGER KARPF, Ph.D.
Author of *The Psychology and Psychotherapy of Otto Rank*, etc.,

WITH A FOREWORD BY

ELLSWORTH FARIS, Ph.D.
Professor and Chairman of the Department of Sociology,
The University of Chicago

AND A NEW PREFACE BY

ROBERT C. WILLIAMSON, Ph.D.
Professor and Chairman of the Department of Social Relations,
Lehigh University

NEW YORK / RUSSELL & RUSSELL

To

M. J. K.

WITHOUT WHOSE DAY-BY-DAY STIMULATION,
COUNSEL, AND HELP THIS BOOK COULD
NOT HAVE BEEN WRITTEN

FIRST PUBLISHED IN 1932
REISSUED, 1972, BY RUSSELL & RUSSELL
A DIVISION OF ATHENEUM PUBLISHERS, INC.
BY ARRANGEMENT WITH FAY B. KARPF
L. C. CATALOG CARD NO: 78-173513
PRINTED IN THE UNITED STATES OF AMERICA

It is with considerable satisfaction that I write a preface to this reissue of Dr. Karpf's critical history of social psychology. Indeed, the reissue of this work is well overdue. There has been a regrettable tendency to ignore the origins of the discipline, as is reflected in many current social psychology texts.

Dr. Karpf's work explains with remarkable clarity and insight the theories of the nineteenth and early twentieth centuries in Europe and the United States. Since we live in an age of controversy and crisis, it is illuminating to find that two generations earlier theorists on both sides of the Atlantic were examining the motives and attitudes that might explain the events taking place in society currently. Although system builders like Ward seem excessive today, incisive analyses by Durkheim, James or Mead still have much to offer the behavioral scientist. If we find McDougall's instinct doctrine too rigid, we recall that this approach has not been completely abandoned. In other words, it is of historical value to look at social psychology as it appeared four decades ago, at what might be called the end of its classical period. However extensively the field has changed over the last generation, men like James and Dewey continue to have universal appeal.

The success of the book is of course attributable to its author. Dr. Karpf's thorough training in the methods and substantive areas of both psychology and sociology is apparent to the reader. Quite aside from her professional talents as indicated by her professional activities and her volume on Otto Rank, for example, her friendship remains a continuous inspiration to those who know her.

ROBERT C. WILLIAMSON

LEHIGH UNIVERSITY
September, 1971

PREFACE

This work had its origin in the attempt to outline the development of social-psychological thought in this country. But since this subject could not be presented significantly in isolation, the work has gradually assumed its present proportions.

The study was begun in 1921 when the need for some such survey stood out glaringly, and it was completed in its original form in 1925. Since that time, the appearance of several shorter surveys, especially the chapter by Kimball Young in *The History and Prospects of the Social Sciences*, edited by Harry Elmer Barnes, has indicated the importance of the material and encouraged its revision and elaboration to its present form.

The treatment, except for some necessary background, has been confined to the development of social psychology as social psychology. Hence no attempt has been made to extend the background survey beyond the nineteenth century crystallizations of social-psychological thought. Also, the treatment has throughout been determined by the original interest in illuminating American social-psychological thought. This consideration explains many details of emphasis and procedure which might otherwise come into question.

The method of presentation decided upon as being best adapted to the accurate handling of the task in hand, in view of the very important role which personalities still play in the social-psychological movement, is a modified form of biographical exposition organized broadly, as a matter of convenience and in order to be able to reflect the development of American social psychology upon the background of European thought, along relevant national lines. This method has certain obvious advantages in providing natural classifications, which to the author seemed determining in the present state of social-psychological development. However, it also has, as would any other method, some definite limitations. There are thus certain other possible approaches to the consideration of social psychology and especially of social psychologists. Professor Faris has undertaken to suggest in the Foreword how some of them might be followed out with profit in filling out the picture here unfolded.

No claim is made for exhaustiveness of treatment in any part of this survey and certainly not in the European background. The treatment has necessarily been selective. Others might have varied the emphasis and selection of material to be dealt with somewhat, but not materially, since the limitations of space to a single volume have made it possible to deal only with the high spots of recognized lines of influence.

Something remains to be said about the form of presentation adopted in this survey. For obvious reasons, it seemed highly desirable to present the crucial points in an author's position as far as possible in his own words. The superiority of this manner of presenting such material cannot be questioned and the method has been adhered to, in some instances even at the expense of smoothness and conciseness of exposition, especially in Part II of the survey. In Part I, it was naturally less feasible to follow out this manner of presentation consistently, but even there it was adhered to at especially important points.

The preparation of a work like this obviously places one under a many-sided obligation to authors, publishers, and others intimately connected with the work. Specific acknowledgments of indebtedness, especially in the first two connections, must necessarily be taken care of in the footnote and bibliographic references. But the author finds it necessary to make the following further acknowledgments:

First and foremost, the author is under obligation to the late Dean Albion W. Small and Professors Faris, Park, and Burgess of the University of Chicago, all of whom have at one time or another offered valuable suggestions in respect to the preparation of the manuscript. Professor Faris, in particular, has been intimately in contact with the work from the beginning. Not only was the work in the first instance carried out under his guidance, but he has maintained an unfailing interest in the material ever since. In addition, he has read the entire manuscript on two different occasions. In the course of his contact with every phase of the work, he has made many invaluable suggestions which have in one way or another been adopted. The author welcomes this opportunity to acknowledge the important part which he has had in the planning of the work.

Professor Reuter of the University of Iowa, editor of the series in which the work appears, has likewise read the manuscript twice and he, too, has made invaluable suggestions which have been incorporated in the completed work. The author is particularly under obligation to him for his critical evaluation of parts of the material and for his expert editorial advice and assistance in the final preparation of the manuscript for publication.

Professor Louis Wirth of the University of Chicago has been very helpful in respect to the section dealing with German social-psychological thought. He not only directed the author's attention from time to time to important source materials, but he also read the entire section in proof. While he did not completely agree with certain points of evaluation relevant to this section, his comments and especially references to the pertinent literature were extremely valuable.

Professor Moses J. Aronson, formerly of The Sorbonne and now of The College of the City of New York, has been similarly helpful in respect to the section dealing with French social-psychological thought. Not only did he read the entire section in proof but his comments regarding various details of treatment proved to be exceptionally helpful and encouraging.

The following graduate students of the Department of Sociology at the University of Chicago assisted in the collection of the original materials of this study during the early stages of the work: W. P. Meroney, Celian Ufford, Evalyn Cohn, Clifford Manschardt, Alison R. Bryan, William S. Hockman, Percy E. Lindley, Belle T. Pardue, Ada Davis, Frances Watson, Regena Beckmire. Grateful acknowledgment of their assistance is hereby made.

The author also wishes to acknowledge gratefully the help of Dr. Ruth Shonle Cavan of Rockford, Illinois, in assisting in the early set-up of the material and in later taking over the task of preparing the Index. Appreciative acknowledgment is also made of the assistance of Mr. George M. Wolfe, Research Assistant at The Graduate School for Jewish Social Work, who has read the entire page proof and assisted in the preparation of the bibliography. Mr. Jacob B. Lightman and Miss Ettarae Serlin, Research and Assistant Librarians at the latter institution, have likewise been helpful in the preparation and checking of the bibliography.

The author further wishes to acknowledge the courtesy of authors and publishers who have generously permitted the inclusion of quotations from their works. Acknowledgment of this is made specifically in connection with the quotations used, but the author feels this further acknowledgment is justified by the whole-hearted response of the publishers and authors involved.

Most of all the author is under obligation to Dr. M. J. Karpf for his invaluable aid in every phase of the work. No merely formal statement of indebtedness can possibly do justice to his contribution to the formulation, planning, and execution of the work.

F. B. K.

New York, N. Y.,
March, 1932.

CONTENTS

PART II

THE DEVELOPMENT OF SOCIAL-PSYCHOLOGICAL THOUGHT IN THE UNITED STATES

CHAPTER V

CHAPTER VI

CHAPTER VII

CHAPTER VIII

CHAPTER IX

FOREWORD

Social psychology is a vital and important subject of present-day discussion and investigation throughout the world, perhaps particularly in America. Attempts to designate it by special terms and to give it systematic formulation began only a little over twenty years ago, but since that time systematic treatments of it in books are found by the dozen. Other books dealing with various aspects of the field, although not necessarily bearing the title, are numbered by the hundred, while articles and special researches of a briefer character carried in the learned journals of the world are to be counted literally by the thousand. Nor is there any sign of a decrease in interest. On the contrary, more men are working in the field now than ever before. The present work of Dr. Karpf, which attempts to give the history of American social psychology, with its European background, is thus, in the highest degree, timely.

The interest in social psychology has not been confined to any one section of social science. On the contrary, workers in sociology, psychology, economics, and political science, historians, psychiatrists, and even literary men have all written important and significant books which must be classified as directly bearing on this field. The attempt to understand social psychology is obviously greater every year, and the student who tries to avail himself of the heritage is confronted with a laborious and confusing body of reading which soon makes him aware of the need of some guiding clew. It is clear then that a historical guide like the present work ought to serve a very useful purpose, besides being of general interest to the intellectual reader.

Social psychology has already accumulated a body of traditions, problems, explanations, and systems which form a broad stream whose tributaries can be traced far back in time and space. The sources offer great variety. To trace them back to a single origin is, of course, impossible, for there is not one but many. Moreover, as the stream flows on, some channels have been cut out at an angle and by a divergent path have been flowing on until they have become lost in the desiccations of the desert sand. There are other muddy currents which have refused to mingle with the main stream, being particularly resistant to the assimilating influence of the rest.

There are, of course, many ways of describing all this. The author has chosen a sort of modified biographical treatment inherited from the tradition of histories of philosophy, and by copious quotation and sympathetic condensation has set for herself the task of giving the reader the teachings of the various authors on the questions that interested them most.   French, German, and English writers pass in review before the reader, for all these have left a tradition without which the views of the Americans could not be understood.   Until the latter part of the work is reached the treatment of the Americans is roughly chronological, so that the development can be seen and the influences traced.

A history of American social psychology might be written in one of two or three ways.   It would hardly be possible to write it in all three of these ways.   The choice of the plan must obviously be left to the author. If, therefore, the reader finds certain gaps in it, that must be set down to the necessities of literary choice.   Moreover, with the clews here supplied these gaps can be filled in by sufficiently vigorous effort and sufficiently wide acquaintance with the literature.

In the first place, the student would like to know more about the place of a given author in his social and cultural setting.   The answer to this demand would tend to add to the question of what the author teaches and what he advocates the more difficult question of why he taught and advocated those doctrines.   Obviously here anyone who tries to answer is treading on slippery ground.   Just why the ardent and valiant defenders of instincts should be also in the main conservative in their philosophical, social, and political views, many of them being avowedly vocal opponents of democracy; just why the vigorous advocates of behaviorism should adopt a violently radical attitude toward religion and conventional morals with which the doctrine of behaviorism strictly defined has no more connection than it has with the politics of Mars; just why one author or one group of authors should hold that fundamental in human life is a desire for exciting and thrilling experiences, while others, perhaps because their work is more interesting, find no truth in the doctrine; why one author's work breathes sympathy with the oppressed classes, furnishes texts for economic radicals, while another's becomes a *vade mecum* for defenders of the *status quo*—all these questions are very difficult but not without their central importance.   To answer them would require a vigorous and persistent campaign in attempting to unearth the personal and biographical details of each man's life, and the result would be an interpretation so difficult to make objective that the success of such an effort would always be problematical.   Nevertheless the question is not out of order.   We know already too much about the relation of thought and reflection to action and ambition to fail to realize that we must eventually psychologize the psychologist if we are to understand his psychology.

There is another and easier and less invidious aspect of the history of social psychology which it would be interesting to know.   Each author is not merely the deliverer of a message; he is the exponent of a culture or, in our day, of some aspect of the culture of his people. For mind is not merely individual mind, nor is it merely social mind; it is, as we have been taught by Cooley, an organic whole; the individual and society are twin born. Each writer, therefore, not only writes about the group. He is also a part of a group. His ideas are generated in his group. The social forces that made and are still making social psychology are not inaccessible, and the trends of thought and sentiment if set alongside the expositions here would add much to that which we should like to know about the development of the science. Perhaps the author will be granted the leisure and have the impulse to make this account clear in a subsequent volume. It is to be hoped that she will; and if she does, she will put us all the more in her debt.

The instinct doctrine of social psychology, now rapidly dying out, did not come into existence full armed, nor do we account for it adequately when we give the arguments and statements of any particular author who is an advocate of that definite system. It is only in perspective, perhaps, that we can see how the various antecedent formulations were found increasingly difficult and how gradually this particular scheme came to be more advantageous. Moreover, when the doctrine began to lose its ascendency, it would be interesting and highly profitable to know what were the various influences, forces, and weaknesses which finally brought about the transition to something which seems to be more satisfactory. The presentation of separate authors with their separate views, while interesting and quite necessary, does not give the connection between and relation to the various points of view out of which the doctrine grew or into which it merged or which it stirred up. And there are many of these which it would be best fitting to have set forth in such a manner. The extreme reflex doctrine, starting in Russia and somewhat independently in America with the study of animals and influenced by many other forces, conspicuous among them the conflicts among the orthodox psychologies regarding the presence of imageless thought, and the firm hold that the doctrine of elements had, even for those who had rejected the instincts and which caused them to substitute a set of definite reflexes instead—all of this would be illustrative of the point that is here made. A similar tracing of the doctrine of wishes or of the neglect of physiology by the psychoanalysts or of the rejection of mental elements by the Gestaltians on the one hand and by men like John Dewey on the other, with, in each case, quite different motives and quite different outcomes— all these and other questions like them would add greatly to the interest of the story of the development of social psychology.

For we are all social psychologists enough now to know that while it is not easy to get rid of our prejudices and predilections, it is possible sometimes to know what they are, to know that we have them, to know what our friends' prejudices are, and to make allowances for both theirs and ours. The compulsive nature of social or collective thought is a factor of which we can always take account for the correcting of our data. For we are all children of our time, the scholar not least of all. Indeed, it might be contended that the scholar is most of all a child of his time. Perhaps he is the very voice of his time speaking for his group. It is the time become articulate in a single point.

This task of relating the author to his time and to his group inside the time is not so great as it might seem, for there are not so many kinds of system as there are men who write about them. There are far more books than there are classes of books, and the scholars and authors may be grouped and classified. Moreover, the groups and classes can be related to each other.

Social psychology as a definite discipline known by distinctive terms is relatively young, but it is old enough already to have many "schools." We have our partisans, our sectarian champions, our orthodoxies, and our heresies. The ancient Romans used to find amusement in making their captives fight real battles, and the crowd enjoyed it most when the slaughter was most fierce. And even in this little arena the student can witness wars of words, the annihilating phrases, and the savage battle cries which show how human scholars are. Here the alliances are across jurisdictional boundaries, and behaviorism, instinctivism, Gestaltism, and the rest seek their allies in any camp. What these schools are, what their claims are, and what shibboleths are required to membership within the company are matters not hard to learn, but their real significance requires most careful interpretation and insight.

When a science is sufficiently mature and advanced to have a clear conception of its problems and is able to organize its forces so as to attract them effectively, there are no schools. Schools of psychology are the growing pains of the science. Leaders of the schools perform the same function as fanatics in any sphere. The fanatic in religious or political or social life is one who calls attention to a neglected truth or duty by a strident exaggeration of its importance. They not only tend to become extremists, but they are also in danger of losing their scientific temper, since the search for truth is suspended by the necessity for fighting. Warfare, however, whether of attack or of defense, furnishes a pleasant excitement, an increase in loyalty, often also satisfying a certain welcome notoriety, no less satisfying for being short-lived.

For the partisan leader of a school of thought there is little hope. He usually digs into a "well-prepared position in the rear" from which security he defends himself according to his resources. But the friends of science need not be disturbed. Indeed a truly scientific mind, surely a truly scientific psychological mind, cannot allow itself to be disturbed. The extremists, like the Pharisees in the Testament, have received their reward. Fortunately life is short, and neither they nor their work shall endure.

The future is with the young who, listening to the confusing voices, will not be able or willing to continue the one-sided emphases. They will see the few grains in the heap of chaff and salvage what they can. Even the disciples and students of a pundit have been known to question his claims of infallibility in his own lifetime.

Social psychology is not only new, vigorous, rapidly growing, and greatly confused; it is also vitally important. The answers to the questions that it asks are urgently needed. The unity of our culture is broken; the confusion of tradition is by now proverbial; we are becoming aware of human nature, but we do not understand what it is. The training of children, the discipline called education, the problem of inefficiency, the control of vice, crime, poverty, and war—these problems are present in a new and dreadful form. How does our human nature come to be? Is it unchangeable, and if it can be altered, how? Whence come our motives, our ambitions, and how may these be best conceived and best directed?

We have discovered a new world, but we have not explored it yet, and our peace and success demand that we know it well. Social psychology is a name we give to this task. Dr. Karpf's book tells what men have declared when they came back from spying out the land.

Although this book was not written as a college textbook, like any thoroughly comprehensive and scholarly work in the field it will admirably serve such a purpose. Nowhere is there available any comparable survey of the contributions of modern scholarship in this field. In addition to such a use, the work will certainly find an eager audience in students of social science, particularly those interested in economics and politics who wish to understand what is going on in this field and what characterizes the leaders of thought today. Here the critical comment and comparison throw the views into sharp relief, and the historical perspective of the various authors as treated by Dr. Karpf gives meaning and significance to what might otherwise seem unrelated and isolated.

The general reader who is interested in modern thought will particularly appreciate the way in which the various trends are traced out and finally brought together in the concluding chapters. The author has brought to her task an exceptionally adequate training, a high and unwavering enthusiasm, and a thoroughness of competent scholarship which will be appreciated by all who will have the privilege of reading her work.

ELLSWORTH FARIS.

UNIVERSITY OF CHICAGO,
March, 1932.

AMERICAN SOCIAL PSYCHOLOGY

INTRODUCTION

Like most of the modern sciences of human behavior and social life, social psychology may be thought of as being both a very old and a very new field of endeavor. It may on the one hand be viewed as a very old subject with a history extending back into remotest antiquity, or at any rate into the earliest period of systematic philosophical inquiry, and on the other hand, as is more frequently the case, it may be looked upon as one of the most recent and least qualified claimants to recognition among the sisterhood of the modern sciences. There is evidently ground for both of these views. For certainly man has always concerned himself, in one way or another, with the field of inquiry with which modern social psychology seeks to deal systematically and scientifically. The practical wisdom regarding human nature and social life which custom, legend, precept, and maxim have stored down the ages of human history and the reflective theorizing about these matters which the centuries of philosophical thought record are eloquent testimony of this fact.

But certainly, again, social psychology viewed as a specialized field of scientific endeavor corresponding to the other modern psychological and social sciences is a very new development and it has as yet little to commend it that is comparable to that which the better established sciences have to offer. The very conception of social psychology as a distinct field of scientific investigation is comparatively recent as scientific development goes. In fact, it hardly extends back beyond the middle of the nineteenth century. It is, however, only with the development of social psychology in this more specialized sense that this survey is to be concerned and, more specifically, only with those aspects of the movement which have had a more or less direct bearing on the development of social psychology in this country. It is necessary to bear this limitation of treatment in mind from the outset.[1]

As stated above, the very conception of social psychology as a distinct field of scientific investigation is a comparatively recent develop-

[1] Surveys of earlier thought which have an historical interest for the social psychologist are available in the histories of both psychology and social thought. Consult, for instance, RAND, *The Classical Psychologists;* BRETT, *A History of Psychology*, vols. I, II; BOGARDUS, *A History of Social Thought*, Chaps. I–X; LICHTENBERGER, *The Development of Social Theory*, Chaps. I–IX; SOROKIN, *Contemporary Sociological Theories*, introductory sections.

ment. And naturally enough, too. For this conception had to await not only the emergence of modern naturalistic and scientific thought generally as applied to the study of human behavior but also the modern sociological movement.

For centuries, as we know, the study of mental and social life remained subordinated to other than scientific interests—metaphysical, political, religious, ethical. Such was the nature of theory concerning the subject matter of social psychology in the Greek period and throughout the middle ages. During all this time there was, of course, mental and social philosophy, but no social psychology in the sense of modern thought. And even after the study of mental and social life began to take form as distinct fields of scientific investigation within the modern scientific era, the need for a *social* psychology still remained obscured for a long time, by the development of psychology and psychological thought generally along introspective and decidedly individualistic lines.[1]

It was only as positivism and modern comparative and evolutionary thought, as reflected upon the background of nineteenth century democratic tendencies, were preparing the setting for the modern sociological movement that the need for a *social* psychology began to make itself felt. As the sociological point of view gained ground, it gradually became increasingly apparent that the conventional individualistic interpretation of human behavior was inadequate and even wholly unadapted for the explanation of the socially most significant aspects of human nature. The resulting intellectual unrest and widespread groping after more adequate conceptions and methods in the investigation of human nature and social life are well-known background in the development of modern psycho-social science. This situation, in its general aspects, is to be associated with the early stages of the modern social-psychological movement as well as with related nineteenth century scientific developments. But more specifically, it was not until, with the progress of events, modern psychology set about to ally itself definitely with physiology and to take over the point of view and experimental technique of biological science as defined in distinctly individualistic terms, and sociology likewise began to define its interest in terms of the study of objective social organization, that the essential setting for the modern social-psychological movement was completed. With this turn of events, however, social psychology, as we are to be concerned with it here, began definitely to emerge alongside of general psychology on the one hand and general sociology on the other.[2]

Because of the background of individualistic thought upon which it began to take form, modern social-psychological thought got its first

---

[1] See BRETT, *A History of Psychology*, vols. I, II.

[2] See *ibid.*, vol. II, pp. 356–360, vol. III, pp. 285–296; BALDWIN, *History of Psychology*, vol. II, pp. 126*ff.*; also McDOUGALL, *An Introduction to Social Psychology*, Chap. I.

impulse from the side of the study of social life. In fact, the modern social-psychological movement was at first, quite naturally, but a particular aspect of the larger sociological movement, with which it was on common ground in its protest against psychological individualism. The development of social psychology, as we shall see, is thus intimately bound up during the early period with the development of sociology itself, though social-psychological thought has spread out from the first from both psychological and sociological sources. It was natural that in the general groping for a more adequate approach to the study of the social aspects of human behavior, sociology should attempt to extend its scope from the study of the objective side of social organization, which was its chief concern in the first instance, to the study of the personal side, with which, it began increasingly to appear, social organization in its deeper human meaning is so intimately related. On the other hand, it was to be expected also that psychology itself, once recognizing the inadequacy of its purely individualistic approach for the study of the more complex aspects of mental life, should attempt to extend and modify its point of view and methods in accordance with the new insight.

Accordingly, modern social psychology is found developing from both of these directions and, in addition, closely connected with such other related fields of thought as social anthropology, evolutionary biology, and culture history. So far, social psychology has continued to remain, from the nature of its historical problems and its theoretical background, most intimately bound up with sociology, to the extent even of having fairly shifted the weight of emphasis in the latter science to the consideration of its own problems.[1] But this fact has not interfered with its natural association all along also with psychology and, especially during its early history, also with certain aspects of anthropology and folk psychology, which, as will appear in the early part of this survey, has in some instances amounted to the practical identification of social psychology with portions of these related fields of endeavor.

This interlinking of social psychology with related fields of scientific investigation, together with the intensely nationalistic character of nineteenth century thought generally and of psycho-social thought in particular,[2] has been favorable for the more or less particularistic cultivation of distinct angles of approach in the field and for the crystallization of those differentiated tendencies of social-psychological development, which today define the field of social psychology. So far, too, these several directions of social-psychological development have remained largely uncoordinated from the social-psychological standpoint. We

[1] For an early statement on this point, see Ellwood, *Proc. Intern. Congress Arts Sci.*, vol. 5, p. 859, 1904.

[2] See MERZ, *History of European Thought in the Nineteenth Century*, vol. IV, pp. 429–430, 447–448.

find, therefore, that each of them has been held up, and in fact continues to be held up, as *the* social psychology, more or less without regard or relation to the other claimants for this designation. This situation, as may be readily imagined, is frequently confusing, especially to the interested general reader in the field and the beginning student, who, when confronted with the several current treatises, each of them purporting to deal with the subject of social psychology without modification, are frequently at a loss to make out the connections between them and to explain their diversity of conception and material. Thus, in this country, the two best known and probably most popular works, Ross' *Social Psychology* and McDougall's, *An Introduction to Social Psychology*, seem hardly, as it has frequently been pointed out, to be concerned with the same subject matter. And those who are acquainted also with the conceptions of Cooley, Mead, Ellwood, Dewey, and Thomas, to mention only the older and more widely recognized attempts to formulate social-psychological theory in this country, know that each of these is again essentially distinct from both of the above as well as from each other.

It has been considerations of this nature and the consequent conviction that there is at the present time an urgent need in the field of social psychology for some sort of general survey, in the light of which the various current treatments and conceptions of the subject may be given place in relation to each other and to the field in its larger outlines as it has developed in its several aspects up to the present time, that have prompted this work. It is hoped that the survey of social-psychological thought which is to be followed out here will help to meet this need in a preliminary way. In particular, it is hoped that the development of American social-psychological thought will appear in significant perspective in this treatment of the subject and that, at least in so far as social-psychological endeavor in this country is concerned, it will help clear the ground for those more positive tendencies in the field which are today variously beginning to get under way here, and upon which the further advance of such a scientifically applicable social psychology as has been the objective of American social-psychological thought from the beginning must from now on squarely rest.

PART I
EUROPEAN BACKGROUND

CHAPTER I

NINETEENTH CENTURY PHILOSOPHICAL BACKGROUND

I. G. W. F. HEGEL (1770–1831)

(EVOLUTIONISM, IDEALISTIC)

It is now clear that social-psychological thought, as it will be set forth here, is essentially a product of the modern scientific movement in the field of psychological and social investigation. As such, it would seem to have little in common with the spirit of the Hegelian *a priori* and absolutistic system of thought. Because of its general position of importance in the intellectual life of the early nineteenth century, Hegelian thought is, however, an important point of reference in most of the nineteenth century psychological and social science developments and particularly in the modern social-psychological movement. Both negatively and positively, at any rate, Hegelian thought played an important role, alongside of Comtean and Spencerian thought, in defining the intellectual background of the modern social-psychological movement.[1] It must, accordingly, be given place in this connection. Nor is it, in general, disadvantageous to be obliged to project the development of modern social psychology from Hegelian thought as a starting point. For how could its developing point of view be more effectively reflected upon the background of traditional thought in this field of endeavor?

Furthermore, on the side of the conception of social-psychological interrelationship, if not on the side of general outlook and method of attack, Hegelian thought links up in an important way with the modern transition from the traditional view of the world of human events, which Hegelian thought fundamentally represented, to the more modern naturalistic and positive view, which began to gain dominance after Hegel's death. Essentially, Hegel's system represented the glorification of the traditional outlook, of course; incidentally, however, it registered, in its way, the impulse of the more modern standpoint as suggested above.[2] Hegel's relation to the modern social-psychological movement along these two directions, as may well be expected, was very different and even paradoxical. For it turned out that post-Hegelian German social-psychological thought, which was very prominent in the early period of the modern social-psychological movement, while it was directly connected with the reaction against Hegel's basic outlook and method

[1] MERZ, *History of European Thought in the Nineteenth Century*, vol. III, especially Chaps. I, III, vol. IV, especially Chaps. IX, X.

[2] *Ibid.*, vol. III, pp. 19–20, 30 *ff.*, 50–51, 386, 475; vol. IV, pp. 192 *ff.*, etc.

of approach, tended to retain the general form and pattern of the Hegelian system in so far as it seemed to bear on pertinent problems.   If we are to follow the course of modern social-psychological development as thus determined, it is thereby necessary to give at least very brief consideration to the Hegelian system of thought, as it touches on the problems of social-psychological concern.[1]

With Hegel's thought as a metaphysical system we are naturally not concerned here, except to note it as a negative influence.   In this respect, from the standpoint of social psychology as a scientific movement, Hegel was, at the time, one of the last great voices of a departing age, and he is an important figure in the development of modern social-psychological thought, if at all, rather because of the several lines of reaction which his obscure outlook and approach called forth than because of any more direct contribution.[2]

But as said above, Hegel did not merely represent a passing age of thought, even from the standpoint of social psychology viewed in modern scientific terms.   At the same time that he brought the German idealistic movement to a climax he did not remain entirely insensible to those newer impulses of the age which were groping for expression and which we associate more familiarly with such exponents of the modern scientific era in the field of psychological and social thought as Comte, Spencer, and above all Darwin.   "In the system of Hegel," says Merz, "we not only meet with the final and greatest effort to solve the philosophical problem on the basis of an idealistic or spiritual conception, we also arrive at the true center of modern thought in which many new departures have their origin."[3]   It is in this connection—that is, as a "center of modern thought in which many new departures have their origin," and particularly in connection with that tendency of modern thought which came to most fruitful expression in Darwin—that Hegel's thought, through being reinterpreted in terms of the scientific content of the latter, was able to exercise something of a determining influence on the course of the modern social-psychological movement, particularly in his own country.   These aspects of Hegel's thought, in so far as they bear on the problems of social psychology, are accordingly of more direct concern here.[4]

[1] The whole manner and spirit of Hegelian thought may, however, seem so foreign to the content of social psychology as it is at present viewed, especially in this country, that the reader who is not particularly interested in following out this aspect of the philosophical background will do well to leave this discussion of Hegel for later reference, if need be, and to begin with the discussion of Comte and Spencer instead.

[2] That there has more recently been a revival of interest in Hegel in Germany and elsewhere is not a matter of special concern at this point.   It will be considered in a later connection. See *infra*, pp. 84–88.

[3] MERZ, *History of European Thought in the Nineteenth Century*, vol. IV, p. 652.

[4] See DEWEY, *German Philosophy and Politics*, pp. 113, 120.

It is, then, of some interest to note in this connection that some few years before Comte and almost a half century before Spencer was producing his most important works, Hegel, in developing his system of thought, was giving preliminary expression to both the evolutionary and the sociological tendencies, though naturally in a very different direction from the directions in which these motives of modern thought were later embodied in the respective works of these two early exponents of the modern scientific movement in the field of social and psycho-social investigation. Hegel had a very comprehensive though decidedly mystical notion of evolution as a universal law of growth and as a universal organizing principle, especially in regard to human events. Incidentally, he also had a definite theory of society as an organic unity of component participating and self-realizing individuals. But in contrast to the biologically naturalistic formulation which these conceptions later attained in England, and the positivistic turn which they took in France, Hegel gave expression to them as a part of his idealistic philosophy.

It is impossible as well as unnecessary to go into the involved and obscure details of Hegel's complex system of thought in order to indicate the import of these features of his system from the standpoint of the modern social-psychological movement as it touches upon the development of social psychology in this country.[1] Suffice it to say here that Hegel's philosophy embodies, in characteristic manner, two basic conceptions, namely, philosophical idealism and a metaphysically postulated evolutionism. Idealism regards the world of reality as a matter of mental or spiritual essence; evolutionism, as a progressive process. These two basic motives Hegel combined in distinctive fashion in his philosophy of the Absolute Spirit. The result was a mystic picture of the world in terms of the "necessary" unity and continuity of all things and, especially, on the basis of the general principle of the unity of all mental development, of self-conscious rational thought, historical processes, and objective social forms.[2] This metaphysical conception of the unity

[1] Summary statements of systems of thought are bound to be on shaky ground, and such as are directed toward a single aspect of a system especially so. For the significance of systems inheres largely in their characteristic settings and relations, and these are usually obscured or misrepresented by one-sided emphases. In the case of Hegel these considerations are accentuated by the unfamiliarity of his terminology and thought movement, and in our case also by the very different role which his thought played in the American as compared with the German social-psychological movement. If one is not to resort to the simple expedient of ignoring important relations just because they offer difficulties of treatment, however, some such working division of treatment as the above must be arrived at for the purpose in hand, however unsatisfactory it may be when viewed from the standpoint of the system as a whole. In the case of our treatment of Hegel here, the very brevity of the discussion ought in itself to be sufficient to suggest its specialized character and its inadequacy for general purposes.

[2] MERZ, History of European Thought in the Nineteenth Century, vol. III, pp. 464 ff.; DEWEY, German Philosophy and Politics, pp. 107 ff.; TODD, Theories of Social Progress, pp. 451 ff.

and continuity of mental development has played a considerable role in nineteenth century psycho-social thought, and, especially in Germany, it has maintained itself more or less successfully in face of the Darwinian movement and the onset of more modern naturalistic conceptions. In order that its characteristic features may stand out for comparison, it is thus necessary to follow it out here in somewhat greater detail in its natural setting of Hegelian doctrine.

The world of reality, subjective as well as objective, is, according to Hegel, to be conceived of as a revelation of Absolute Reason or Idea. This principle of ultimate reality is to be thought of, further, as being "immanent" in the various phases and levels of the concrete universe and as revealing itself in a progressive process of expanding and self-realizing Absolute Purpose. In its "necessary" run of antecedents and consequents, this process constitutes for Hegel the invariable course of development in the world. Its movement may be followed out, according to him, alike introspectively and in the objective world; alike in the processes of human rational thought—which he conceived of as a dialectic of triad cycles consisting of the thesis, the antithesis, and the synthesis—and in the processes by which, according to the Hegelian conception, this dialectical movement unfolds itself in the world of externalized nature. Preeminently, however, it may be followed out in the course of human history and in the development of the objective forms and products of social life, that is, in the realm of what Hegel termed "objective mind."

In its bearing on the social-psychological process, this conception of evolution suggested the notion of a unilateral course of unfoldment, whose movement could be traced both directly through the study of the mental processes of the individual and indirectly through the study of human history and objective social life—a most confusing notion of the relation of psychology, history, and sociology, as it later proved to be. It also suggested in this connection, as the psycho-historical problem *par excellence*, the possibility of developing such a universal natural history of the mental development of mankind as later became the dominating concern not only of the folk psychologists but, with varying emphasis, to a considerable extent also of later nineteenth century psycho-social thought generally.[1]

---

[1] HEGEL, *The Phenomenology of Mind*, Preface to vol. I, trans. by Baillie; *The Philosophy of History*, especially pp. 1–103, trans. by Sibree; *Philosophy of Right*, especially pp. 240–350, trans. by Dyde; also MERZ, *History of European Thought in the Nineteenth Century*, vol. III, pp. 464 *ff.*, vol. IV, pp. 192*ff.*, 214*ff.*, 499*ff.*, etc. WINDELBAND, *A History of Philosophy*, pp. 10 *ff.*, 530, 569 *ff.*, 611 *ff.*, 646 *ff.*, trans. by Tufts; MUIRHEAD, "Hegel," *Encyclopedia Britannica* (13th ed.); ROYCE, *Lectures on Modern Idealism*, Chaps. III, VI–IX; DEWEY, *German Philosophy and Politics*, Chap. III; TODD, *Theories of Social Progress*, Chap. 30; BARNES, "Sociology before Comte," *Amer. Jour. Sociol.*, vol. 23, pp. 227*ff.*, 1917–1918.

Hegel himself, from the nature of his interest and method, was less concerned with the investigation or even with the accurate description of concrete facts than with the development of his thought in abstract form. It remained for the post-Hegelian school of German positivists in the fields of psychology, history, and social thought to attempt to work out the concrete applications of his theory and to bring it into relation with the scientific trend of thought and procedure, which began to come into its own in these fields directly after Hegel's death. His general conception, however, viewing all forms of mental phenomena as "bound together by inner necessity so as to constitute a series" in which "every phenomenon has a definite place, inasmuch as it is judged according to the amount it contributes toward the realization of the goal of the series," and in which each element in the series tends to approach that goal "by infinite stages of gradation," formed the mold into which their efforts fell.[1] Hegel's own deductive applications of his theory to the interpretation of the facts of history and social life, which he developed in his *Philosophy of History* and in his *Philosophy of Right*, could well serve as a guide in this respect.

In his *Philosophy of History*, Hegel set about to apply his theory to the interpretation of the past historical life of the race. He viewed world history, for this purpose, as a record of the successive intellectual leadership of the "genius" of one world power (regarded by him for the time as the highest embodiment of the Absolute Spirit) after another, each successive historical cycle, according to his theory, representing successive steps in the upward course of social evolution. The conception revolves about the notion that each ethnic people, in accordance with the basic principles of Hegelian thought as outlined above, embodies the Absolute in the form of an "immanent" principle of development which determines the run of its own history and its position in the larger

---

The psycho-historical problem noted above was later reinterpreted in terms of Darwinism, but as a philosophical conception it had a considerable background in German thought even before Hegel. It had been suggested by Leibnitz, for instance, and developed by later writers even in the detail of its social implications, especially by Herder in his *Ideen zur Philosophie der Geschichte der Menschheit*, 1784–1791 (DEWEY, *German Philosophy and Politics*, pp. 112*ff.*; MERZ, *History of European Thought in the Nineteenth Century*, vol. IV, pp. 211, 423). Early anthropological and philological studies in Germany were also suggestive along the same lines (see MERZ, *ibid.*, vol. III, pp. 137*ff.*, vol. IV, pp. 513–514, etc.). But Hegel did for the psycho-historical conception of evolution in Germany what Spencer did later for the biological conception in England: he brought the current of vague tendencies to a focus and gave the theory the prominence and prestige which it needed to become, for the time, the dominant mode of thought and interpretation.

[1] DESSOIR, *Outlines of the History of Psychology*, p. 181; also MERZ, *History of European Thought in the Nineteenth Century*, vol. III, p. 388; DEWEY, *German Philosophy and Politics*, p. 120.

course of world events.[1] According to this view, each great world power holds the center of the world stage until another world power, superior by virtue of the fact that it embodies the Absolute Spirit in its progressive course toward fuller self-realization and revelation on a higher plane, rises in its place. Thus, in illustration, is the course of modern world history divided by Hegel into four main periods: the Oriental, the Greek, the Roman, and the Germanic, the Germanic culture, as the most recent world bearer of the Absolute Spirit, being placed by him, in the manner that is characteristic of this type of thought, at the highest point of the process. The resulting elaboration of Hegel's thought here and his consequent glorification of the Germanic peoples, state, and culture, as supposedly the last word in progress and enlightenment, are well-known aspects of Hegelian thought. It constitutes an eminent example at once of the ethnocentricism that subjective systems of thought encourage and of their great weakness when judged by scientific standards. Hegel's theory of the mission of the Germanic peoples in the culturization of the world, through war if need be, since strife and struggle are recognized as a necessary stage of growth and progress in Hegel's scheme of thought, follows quite naturally in the wake of this logical play with the world of historical relations. Little wonder, then, that Hegel's philosophy was appropriated by a militaristically inclined age, which interpreted it to its own purposes.[2]

This conception of history, in which nations and peoples rather than individuals play the dominant role,[3] is elaborated in its more detailed social-psychological implications by Hegel's theory of the state, as reflected in his *Philosophy of Right*. Politically, as is well known, this work amounted to an apotheosis of the state, as a higher embodiment of the Absolute than the individual. Thereby Hegel provided the philosophical justification for the paternalism of the German governmental program, just as in his *Philosophy of History* he provided the philosophical justification for its imperialistic program. Theoretically, however, it meant that the individual was treated not as a separate entity, as was the common practice in psychological theory at the time, but as an organic and inseparable part of the body politic and as basically dependent upon the products and processes of social life for his mental

---

[1] This notion, in variant form and without necessarily the metaphysical implications which it carries in Hegel's philosophy, became very popular in post-Hegelian thought. It is still very widely held in theories dealing with the "spirit" and "genius" of nations and peoples.

[2] See HEGEL, *The Philosophy of History*, especially pp. 8 ff., 103 ff., 341 ff.; *Philosophy of Right*, pp. 341–350; DEWEY, *German Philosophy and Politics*, pp. 108 ff.; *Reconstruction in Philosophy*, pp. 201–202; ROYCE, *Lectures on Modern Idealism*, Preface, p. ix.

[3] "But in the history of the World [said Hegel], the Individuals we have to do with are Peoples; Totalities that are States" (*The History of Philosophy*, p. 14).

life and development. If the state is the "divine on earth," a "higher ethical principle" which the individual must not oppose, it is also the indispensable instrument of self-realization, the necessary complement to individuality, the supreme socializing institution of man.[1]

It is on this account that Hegelian thought has at times been looked upon as the direct forerunner of the modern social-psychological point of view. "Making all required allowances for changes of thought and expression," says Brett, for instance, in his historical survey of the development of modern psychology, "it can still be asserted that the 'objective mind' of Hegel's system is the true antecedent of all theories which pass beyond the individualism of earlier schools and see in the mind a reality which is not separated from other minds as one body is separated from another." According to him, therefore, it is "to the Hegelian philosophy [that] we owe the beginning of social psychology."[2]

But it is obvious, after all, that however closely Hegel's mystical conception of the unity and relation of things in the universe, including the individual and the social, may approximate our present social-psychological point of view, it is still separated from the latter by the whole length of the distance between metaphysics and science as the accepted goal.[3] The fact is that a new scientific era was dawning before which Hegel's outlook and procedure in the bordering field of psychological and social considerations were already beginning to give way even while Hegel himself was still secure in his prominent position.[4] It is on this account that despite Hegel's great popularity and influence during his lifetime, definite opposition movements against his point of view and method of approach set in along several directions of social-psychological interest almost immediately following his death. As regards the psychological problem, there was a decided shift of interest to the positive methods of experimental psychology and the so-called "scientific" psychology of Herbart and Beneke on the one hand and to the psychological approach in anthropology, ethnology, philology, and history on the other.   And as regards the social and historical problems, Schäffle,

[1] HEGEL's *Philosophy of Right*, especially pp. 240*ff.*; *The Philosophy of History*, pp. 43*ff.*; ROYCE, *Lectures on Modern Idealism*, pp. x, 52–55.

[2] BRETT, *A History of Psychology*, vol. III, pp. 38, 286.   Quotations from this work are reprinted by permission of The Macmillan Company, publishers.

[3] See in this connection, for instance, Baldwin's statement in his *Social and Ethical Interpretations*, pp. 518–522 and Appendix H; also SMALL, "Sociology and Plato's Republic," *Amer. Jour. Sociol.*, vol. 30, 1925; "General Sociology," *Amer. Jour. Sociol.*, vol. 18, pp. 200–201, 1912; DEWEY, *German Philosophy and Politics*, pp. 124–132.

[4] See MERZ, *History of European Thought in the Nineteenth Century*, vol. III, Introduction, vol. IV, Chap. X; ROYCE, *Lectures on Modern Idealism*, Chap. X; BRETT, *A History of Psychology*, vol. III, pp. 43*ff.*, 63*ff.*, 285*ff.*; BALDWIN, *History of Psychology*, vol. II, Chaps. IV–VI; SMALL, *Origins of Sociology;* BOGARDUS, *A History of Social Thought;* LICHTENBERGER, *Development of Social Theory.*

Marx, and the critical school of German historians, in divergent directions, fittingly marked the decline of Hegelian domination in the dawning age of more modern positive tendencies of thought. It was the spirit of these counter developments which, at least for the time,[1] crystallized the modern social-psychological movement in Germany as elsewhere. To get at the motivating basis of these developments, it is necessary to turn from Hegel to more modern prophets and to the progress of positive thought in the relevant fields of psychological and social inquiry generally.

II. Auguste Comte (1790–1857)

(Positivism)

In turning from Hegel to Comte, we seem to pass as from unknown to essentially familiar ground. This is in itself a significant index of the basic line of relation of social psychology as we know it in this country, for it was the spirit of positive science in human affairs that for the first time loomed large and imposingly in Comte's work. Comte stands, in fact, at the open door of the modern scientific era in the field of sociological and related theory. At any rate, whatever the discounts which critical thought may find it necessary to make of the prevalent conception that Comte was the founder of modern sociology and the initiator of the modern sociological movement,[2] his *Positive Philosophy* has come to be generally recognized at once as one of the most characteristic expressions of the developing scientific impulse of the nineteenth century in its larger aspects and as an outstanding landmark in the development of modern sociology more particularly.[3]

Referring to this broad import of the *Positive Philosophy*, Lévy-Bruhl says:

This spirit [*i.e.*, of the *Positive Philosophy*] is so intimately mingled with the general thought of our time that we scarcely notice it, just as we do not pay attention to the air we breathe. History, romance, and even poetry have reflected its influence and, being charged with it, have contributed to its diffusion.

[1] See *infra*, p. 86.

[2] See SMALL, *Origins of Sociology*, especially pp. 1, 315; "General Sociology," *Amer. Jour. Sociol.*, vol. 18, p. 200, 1912; "A Comtean Centenary," *Amer. Jour. Sociol.*, vol. 17, pp. 510–513, 1922.

[3] See MERZ, *History of European Thought in the Nineteenth Century*, vol. III, pp· 40, 80*ff.*, 192*ff.*, vol. IV, pp. 430*ff.*, 514*ff.*, 679*ff.*, etc.; BRETT, *A History of Psychology*, vol. III, pp. 246–247, 286; BALDWIN, *History of Psychology*, vol. II, pp. 43*ff.*, 71*ff.*, 127*ff.*; VILLA, *Contemporary Psychology*, pp. 30, 135–136, 321; DAVIS, *Psychological Interpretations of Society*, pp. 15–21; SMALL, *Origins of Sociology*, p. 19; *General Sociology*, pp. 65*ff.*; GIDDINGS, *Studies in the Theory of Human Society*, pp. 110*ff.*; *Principles of Sociology*, pp. 6*ff.*, 303*ff.*; PARK, "Sociology and the Social Sciences," *Amer. Jour. Sociol.*, vol. 26, pp. 401*ff.*, 1921; BRISTOL, *Social Adaptation*, Chap. I; BOGARDUS, *A History of Social Thought*, Chap. XIII; LICHTENBERGER, *Development of Social Theory*, Chap. X.

Contemporary sociology is the creation[1] of Comte; scientific psychology, in a certain degree, has also sprung from him. From all these signs it is not rash to conclude that positive philosophy expresses some of the most characteristic tendencies of the age.[2]

Whether or not the significance of Comte's positive philosophy for general thought and for the modern scientific movement in its larger aspects be viewed in precisely the above light, it is clear that for the sciences dealing with human conduct and social life, Comte's work had an altogether special significance. This is so not only because positivism, as Comte himself was at pains to point out, was more foreign to the point of view and methods of these fields than to those of the better established physical and organic sciences[3] but, in particular, because of Comte's own emphasis. For while his system of thought is a complete system of cosmology, Comte, like Spencer in England and Ward in this country, was a sociologist (in the broad sense in which he used the term sociology) by interest, emphasis, and avowed purpose. In fact, Comte undertook to develop his thought on such a large scale only because he sought by this means to bring to his theories of "social physics" the broad support and universality which seemed to him necessary to establish them upon a firm positivist basis. "If we had confined ourselves to the first and special object of the work" (the formulation of a science of society in positive terms), says he in the beginning of his work, "we should have produced merely a study of Social Physics: whereas, in introducing the second and general" (the review of what has been effected in the sciences generally), "we offer a study of Positive Philosophy, passing in review all the positive sciences already formed."[4]

These two aims, though distinct, are, however, according to Comte, inseparable. "For on the one hand," he explains, "there can be no positive philosophy without a basis of social science, without which it could not be all-comprehensive; and, on the other hand, we could not pursue social science without having been prepared by the study of phenomena less complicated than those of society, and furnished with a knowledge of laws and anterior facts which have a bearing upon social science."[5]

The general aspects of Comte's discussion as thus touched upon— his formulation of the law of the three states or stages of the development

[1] See foregoing comment on this point.

[2] Lévy-Bruhl, The Philosophy of Auguste Comte, p. 19.

[3] See Barnes, "Sociology before Comte," Amer. Jour. Sociol., vol. 23, pp. 174–247, 1917–1918; Lichtenberger, Development of Social Theory, Chaps. I–X; Bogardus, A History of Social Thought, Chaps. I–XII.

[4] The Positive Philosophy of Auguste Comte, freely translated and condensed by Harriet Martineau, vol. I, p. 8. The references to Comte's Positive Philosophy are to this translation of his work.

[5] Ibid., p. 8.

of human thought (the theological, the metaphysical, and the positive);[1] his hierarchical classification of the sciences with the newly projected science of social physics or sociology[2] as the final member of the hierarchy (the series being composed of mathematics, astronomy, physics, chemistry, biology, and sociology); his survey of the several departments of scientific knowledge from the standpoint of their progress toward positivism; his resulting argument by analogy stressing the need of a positive science of social life; and his program for the positive reconstruction of society on the basis of such a positively developed science of social phenomena—have all been made matters of common knowledge among students of psycho-social thought. We may confine ourselves here, therefore, to a review of Comte's thought as it bears more or less directly on our own special problem.

Social-psychological interest in Comte's work is centered about the principal and special aim of his work as given above, that is, about his attempt to define the basic notions and relations of the newly projected science of social physics. This is more especially the case because Comte did not include psychology in the traditional sense in his hierarchy of the fundamental positive sciences. We shall accordingly direct our attention chiefly to his consideration of this new department of knowledge. He says in this connection:

This branch of science has not hitherto entered into the domain of Positive philosophy. Theological and metaphysical methods, exploded in other departments, are as yet exclusively applied, both in the way of inquiry and discussion, in all treatment of Social subjects . . . This, is the great, while it is evidently the only gap which has to be filled, to constitute, solid and entire, the Positive Philosophy. Now that the human mind has grasped celestial and terrestrial physics,—mechanical and chemical; organic physics, both vegetable and animal, —there remains one science, to fill up the series of sciences of observation— Social physics. This is what men have now most need of: and this is the principal aim of the present work to establish.[3]

Comte says further in respect to this department of knowledge:

It would be absurd to pretend to offer this new science at once in a complete state. Others, less new, are in very unequal conditions of forwardness. But the same character of positivity which is impressed on all the others will be shown to belong to this. This once done, the philosophical system of the moderns will be in fact complete, as there will be no other phenomenon which does not naturally enter into some one of the five great categories (astronomy, physics, chemistry, biology, social physics). All our fundamental conceptions having

[1] Comte used the term "positive" for "scientific" in the sense of the natural sciences.

[2] Comte first began to use this term, which he introduced into modern psycho-social thought, in the fourth volume of his six-volume work (see *The Positive Philosophy of Auguste Comte*, vol. II, Book VI).

[3] *Ibid.*, vol. I, p. 7.

become homogeneous, the Positive state will be fully established.   It can never again change its character, though it will be forever in course of development by additions of new knowledge.[1]

Comte's program for the new science, which, as he himself recognized, was at the time necessarily limited essentially to an outline of possibilities, was very broad, his plan being to include within its scope all socially conditioned phenomena.   For our purposes here, however, we need to be concerned only with those features of his program, which touch the field of social-psychological investigation more or less specifically.

As has already been noted above, Comte did not include psychology in his hierarchy of the fundamental positive sciences.   In fact, he deliberately did not give place to the study of the individual except on the biological and sociological levels.   Comte has accordingly been criticized at times on the ground that he did not admit the possibility of a positive science of mental phenomena.   But nothing could be further from the spirit of Comte's system of thought.[2]   It was the introspective psychology, current in his day, that Comte refused to recognize in his positive scheme of the sciences but certainly not the scientific study of mental phenomena as such.   The latter was not only indispensable to his theoretical system but it was also an essential basis for such a positive science of politics as was Comte's ultimate aim.[3]

As a matter of fact, Comte devoted a good deal of space in both the *Positive Philosophy* and the *Positive Polity* to the discussion of the subject matter of psychology and to the presentation of his argument that a positive science of mental phenomena is both possible and inevitable.[4]   It is precisely because of his unconventional treatment of this field of investigation, moreover, that he was able to make a signal contribution to the impulse of the modern sociological movement as it touches upon the development of modern social psychology.

Comte did not, therefore, criticize psychology as a positive field of investigation but as a contemporary method and system of theory.[5] It was because the introspective psychology of his day appeared to him

---

[1] *Ibid.*, p. 8.

[2] *Cf.* LÉVY-BRUHL, *The Philosophy of Auguste Comte*, pp. 188*ff.*; BALDWIN, *History of Psychology*, vol. II, pp. 43–45, 70–73; BRETT, *A History of Psychology*, vol. III, pp. 247, 286; VILLA, *Contemporary Psychology*, p. 321; BODENHAFER, "Comte and Psychology," *Pub. Amer. Sociol. Soc.*, vol. 17, pp. 17*ff.*, 1922; DAVIS, *Psychological Interpretations of Society*, pp. 17*ff.*; LICHTENBERGER, *Development of Social Theory*, pp. 251–252.

[3] See Frederic Harrison's Introduction to Lévy-Bruhl, *The Philosophy of Auguste Comte*, p. xii; also *The Positive Philosophy*, vol. I, Chap. VI.

[4] See *ibid.* especially, pp. 27, 458*ff.*, vol. II, pp. 112*ff.*, 127*ff.*, 532, 543; *System of Positive Polity*, trans. by Bridges, etc., vol. I, pp. 501*ff.*, 541*ff.*, vol. II, pp. 1*ff.*, 120*ff.* The references to Comte's *Positive Polity* are to this translation of his work.

[5] See *The Positive Philosophy*, vol. I, pp. 462*ff.*

inconsistent with the requirements of positive procedure that he turned from it to emphasize the physiological and sociological approaches. He accordingly divided the content of psychology in his classification, placing part of it under biology and part of it under sociology. Comte hoped in this way to take the study of mental phenomena out of the theological and metaphysical methodologies in which, in his opinion, the introspective procedure had so long kept it to its detriment as a positive technique and to place it definitely within the scope of positive development.[1] He says on this point:

> Recurring to the first ideas of philosophical common sense, it is at once evident that no function can be studied but with relation to the organ that fulfills it, or to the phenomena of its fulfillment; and, in the second place, that the affective functions, and yet more the intellectual, exhibit in the latter respect this particular characteristic,—that they cannot be observed during their operation, but only in their results,—more or less immediate, and more or less durable. There are then only two ways of studying such an order of functions; either determining, with all attainable precision, the various organic conditions on which they depend, —which is the chief object of phrenological psychology [Comte thought of physiological psychology chiefly in terms of Gall's phrenology]; or in directly observing the series of intellectual and moral acts,—which belongs rather to natural history, properly so called: these two inseparable aspects of one subject being so conceived as to throw light on each other. Thus regarded this great study is seen to be indissolubly connected on the one hand with the whole of the foregoing parts of natural philosophy, and especially with the fundamental doctrines of biology; and on the other hand, with the whole of history,—of animals as well as of man and of humanity.[2]

Man's mental life may thus be studied positively by means of either the biological approach or the sociological approach. Biology and sociology, according to Comte's view, meet in the study of the higher levels of mental function. Hence, in his classification of the sciences, he made sociology follow biology directly without the intervention of a separate science of psychology in the conventional sense. The content matter of psychology, however, was not overlooked by Comte. On the contrary, he discussed it prominently as a part of biology on the one hand and of sociology on the other.

Comte's contribution at this point, as regards our subject, consisted chiefly not in any specific doctrine or theory, although he had some very fruitful suggestions of this nature,[3] but rather in his general recognition—

---

[1] *Ibid.*, pp. 458*ff.*

[2] *Ibid.*, pp. 461–462.

[3] In this connection may be mentioned, for instance, Comte's criticism of the current extreme intellectualism and his attempt to arrive at a more balanced point of view through emphasis on the instinctive and affective aspects of behavior or his recognition of the importance of abnormal and comparative psychology (*ibid.*, pp. 462*ff.*, 475*ff.*; *cf.* BODENHAFER, *Pub. Amer. Sociol. Soc.*, vol. 17, pp. 22*ff.*, 1922).

even if it was only from the standpoint of method primarily—that human psychology is either physiological or social. In this view, Comte was a real prophet of the modern social-psychological movement in its most fundamental and revolutionary aspects. The implications of this view for social psychology have only very gradually been developed in their more concrete bearings, and individual psychology has meanwhile elaborated a scientific procedure such as Comte could hardly have foreseen, but in one way or another this conception has remained basic to modern social-psychological activity. After half a century of social-psychological development, we find it reiterated in this country, for example, with all the added insight and assurance which the progress of modern psychological and social thought has made possible, as the basis for a renewed defense of the social-psychological standpoint and of its importance in the study of mental life.[1]

In respect to the question of the interrelation of the biological and sociological approaches which this conception brings up, Comte pointed out that not only social physics but also biological science, in so far as it is concerned with the study of intellectual and moral phenomena,[2] was still in too undeveloped a state "to have admitted, as yet, of any proper organization of the relation of the two sciences." In general, however, he suggested that

. . . from the time that the influence of former generations becomes the cause of any modification of the social movement, the mode of investigation must accord with the nature of the phenomena; and historical analysis [the method which he regarded as most characteristic of sociology] therefore becomes preponderant; while biological considerations . . . cease to be more than a valuable auxiliary and means of control.[3]

Contemplating the relation of social physics to the other sciences and what he termed "the legitimate general intervention" of its theory of social evolution, he observed:

At first sight, it appears as if this high intervention must belong to the biological theory of our nature . . . But a close examination will convince us that this universal influence must belong more to the theory of social evolution than to that of individual Man, for the reason that the development of the human mind can take place only through the social state, the direct consideration of which must therefore prevail whenever we are treating of any results of the development.[4]

[1] See DEWEY, "The Need for Social Psychology," *Psychol. Rev.*, vol. 24, pp. 266–277, 1917.
[2] See *supra*, p. 18. Comte's reference here, as already suggested, is chiefly to phrenology.
[3] *The Positive Philosophy*, vol. II, p. 114.
[4] *Ibid.*, p. 122.

Lévy-Bruhl has called attention to the fact that as Comte progressed in his thinking he increasingly stressed this sort of sociological interpretation of his position.[1] The clarification of Comte's sociological viewpoint in this respect is, in fact, quite striking if we compare his position as expressed in the *Positive Philosophy* with certain statements in his *Positive Polity*. In the earlier work he stated that "the subordination of social science to biology is evident" and that "no sociological view can therefore be admitted, at any stage of the science, or under any appearance of historical induction, that is contrary to the known laws of human nature," *i.e.*, as determined by the antecedent science of biology.[2] In so far as sociology concerns itself with the study of man's mental life, therefore, it not only begins in biology, but it must, in the nature of the situation, rest content with remaining supplementary to it and submitting to its correction.[3]

In the *Positive Polity*, however, Comte's view had progressed to the point where he was able to say that "the only part of Biology which can be regarded, from the objective standpoint, as entirely independent of the science of Humanity, is the study of the elementary or vegetal phase of life; though even this, in the subjective arrangement to be finally adopted, will be connected with it."[4] In the theory of the highest animal functions, according to his position here, the biologist has to seek instruction from sociology, "for the real laws of these phenomena can only be discovered and demonstrated by Sociology."[5] He says in this work:

Humanity succeeds to Animality, as Animality to Vegetality. This in its synthetic form, is the Hierarchy of Life; and on this triple foundation the analytical processes requisite for a more detailed view of it should rest. We shall inevitably fall into vague and useless speculations and interminable disputes, if we attempt to construct the second term, the series of animal life, independently of the first and of the final term. To do so would be to build at once without foundation and without purpose.[6]

But even in his *Positive Philosophy* Comte had definitely stated that sociology, though founded on the antecedent science of biology, was not a mere "appendix" of the latter but "a science by itself," distinct and characteristic according to his principles of hierarchical classification.[7] Biology, he felt, would leave disguised or unnoticed "the chief phenomenon in sociology,—the phenomenon which marks its scientific originality,—that is, the gradual and continuous influence of generations

[1] Lévy-Bruhl, *The Philosophy of Auguste Comte*, p. 201.
[2] *The Positive Philosophy*, vol. II, pp. 112–113.
[3] *Ibid.*, p. 113.
[4] *System of Positive Polity*, vol. I, p. 504.
[5] *Ibid.*, pp. 502–503.
[6] *Ibid.*, p. 501.
[7] *The Positive Philosophy*, vol. I, p. 27, vol. II, p. 115.

upon each other."[1] The contents of the two sciences, he maintained, "are not identical, though they are homogeneous; and it is of the highest importance to hold the two sciences separate."[2]

Emphasizing the distinctness of the two sciences from a methodological standpoint, Comte stated that in the field of social physics "the scientific spirit forbids us to regard society as composed of individuals." "The true social unit," according to him, "is certainly the family,—reduced, if necessary to the elementary couple which forms its basis."[3] Elaborating upon the implications of this point, he explained:

> This consideration [that the family is the true social unit] implies more than the physiological truth that families become tribes, and tribes become nations: so that the whole human race might be conceived of as the gradual development of a single family, if local diversities did not forbid such a supposition. There is a political point of view from which also we must consider this elementary idea, inasmuch as the family presents the true germ of the various characteristics of the social organism. Such a conception is intermediate between the idea of the individual and that of the species, or society.[4]

Both logically and psychologically, therefore, as well as methodologically, Comte was led to look upon the family as the elementary social unit. The individual he regarded as a sociological abstraction when thought of in isolation from his social setting in the family and the larger social relations of society as a whole in the sense in which the latter figured in his theory as "Humanity," this term comprehending, as he explained, "the whole of the human species, and chiefly, the whole of the white race."[5]

These aspects of Comte's theory as they touch the field of social-psychological investigation may be summed up as follows: man's mental life may be studied positively either in its physiological or in its sociological aspects. The significance of the latter approach follows from the fact that the development of the human mind can take place only through the social state. Since in the course of this process of mental development, social conditions modify the operation of physiological laws, the biological point of view with its individualistic approach becomes increasingly inadequate for the study of man's higher mental operations. To an increasing extent it needs to be supplemented by the sociological approach. Social physics, in so far as it deals with mental phenomena, though it is based on the antecedent science of biology, must build up a set of supplementary observations of its own and lead to the development

[1] *Ibid.*, vol. II, p. 114.
[2] *Ibid.*, vol. I, p. 27.
[3] *Ibid.*, vol. II, p. 132.
[4] *Ibid.*
[5] *Ibid.*, pp. 128, 508–509.

of the next step of scientific interpretation, in accordance with the principles underlying the hierarchical interrelation of the sciences.[1]

Comte recognized, in this connection, the importance of the sociologically significant facts of social cooperation, division of labor, and interdependence. In a general way, he also grasped the importance of the role which "the Union of contemporaries and the Continuity of successive generations" play in the organization of society, termed by him the "Great Being."[2] In fact, he became so impressed with this unifying aspect of social life that he made it the basis of the widely exploited notion of the "superiority" of the social organism. He says at one point respecting this matter:

The main cause of the superiority of the social to the individual organism is, according to an established law, the more marked specialty of the various functions fulfilled by organs more and more distinct, but interconnected; so that unity of aim is more and more combined with diversity of means. We cannot, of course, fully appreciate a phenomenon which is forever proceeding before our eyes, and in which, we bear a part; but if we withdraw ourselves in thought from the social system, and contemplate it as from afar, can we conceive of a more marvellous spectacle, in the whole range of natural phenomena, than the regular and constant convergence of an innumerable multitude of human beings, each possessing a distinct, and in a certain degree, independent existence, and yet incessantly disposed, amidst all their discordance of talent and character, to concur in many ways in the same general development, without concert, and even consciousness on the part of most of them, who believe that they are merely following their personal impulses? This is the scientific picture of the phenomenon: and no temporary disturbances can prevent its being, under all circumstances, essentially true. This reconciliation of the individuality of labour with cooperation of endeavours, which becomes more remarkable as society grows more complex and extended, constitutes the radical character of human operations when we rise from the domestic to the social point of view.[3]

This emphasis, coupled with his continuing metaphysical leaning in the formulation of his thought, led Comte finally in his *Polity*, when he was under the influence of a developing mysticism, to assume a sort of religious attitude toward "Society," which has antagonized many students of his otherwise widely influential system of social thought.[4] In spite of this, however, and the fact that Comte's discussion of social life is by no means free, even in his earlier work, from the metaphysical mysticism which it was his aim to eliminate from the realm of social

[1] *Ibid.*, vol. I, pp. 27, 458*ff.*, vol. II, pp. 112*ff.*, 127*ff.*, 497*ff.*
[2] *System of Positive Polity*, vol. I, p. 501.
[3] *The Positive Philosophy*, vol. II, p. 140.
[4] The practice has accordingly grown up among some students of Comte of treating his system as formulated in his *Positive Philosophy* more or less in isolation from his later work. Comte himself, however, refused to disconnect the former from his later work (see *infra*, pp. 23–24).

thought, one can readily identify in his theory some of the most characteristic conceptions of psycho-social thought as it has since developed. Comte's suggestiveness in this respect is not limited to his discussion of the purely theoretical foundations and relations of "social physics" viewed as the final member in the hierarchy of the positive sciences. Perhaps even more important, in the light of later developments, is his emphasis, as a part of his positivist position, on the close connection that should obtain between social theory and "the art of social life."

Summing up the spirit of positivism on this, from the positivist standpoint, especially important matter, Comte says:

But all Positive speculations owe their first origin to the occupations of practical life; and consequently they have always given some indication of their capacity for regulating our active powers, which had been omitted from every former synthesis. Their value in this respect has been and still is materially impaired by their want of breadth, and their isolated and incoherent character; but it has always been instinctively felt. The importance that we attach to theories which teach the laws of phenomena, and give us the power of prevision, is chiefly due to the fact that they alone can regulate our otherwise blind action upon the external world. Hence it is that while the Positive spirit has been growing more and more theoretical, and has gradually extended to every department of speculation, it has never lost the practical tendencies which it derived from its source; and this even in the case of researches useless in themselves, and only to be justified as logical exercises.[1]

The important bearing of this aspect of Comte's thought becomes immediately apparent when it is viewed in the light of the philosophical aloofness from the concrete facts and problems of practical life, which traditional thought as represented by Hegel, for instance, tended to encourage. It furthermore deserves special emphasis in contrast to the *laissez-faire* doctrine which Spencer and his followers brought into prominence in modern psycho-social theory.

Lévy-Bruhl and other students of Comte have pointed out that the *Positive Philosophy* appeared during that period following the French Revolution when the all-absorbing problem of French thought was the social reconstruction of France.[2] Comte was a product of his time in the intense interest which he displayed in the practical social affairs of the day. It was his controlling desire to contribute to the effective reordering of the disorganized social structure in which he found himself, which dominated his work throughout and prompted him to bring out the practical motive of positivist thought. He regarded his *Positive Philosophy* as merely a necessary preliminary for his *Polity*, where he was to elaborate the practical applications of his thought in the formula-

[1] *System of Positive Polity*, vol. I, p. 8.

[2] Lévy-Bruhl, *The Philosophy of Auguste Comte*, pp. 1–20. *Cf. System of Positive Polity*, vol. I, pp. 12, 47.

tion of a concrete program of social reorganization. The former was for him "the basis, and the latter the end of one comprehensive system."[1] These two aspects of what Comte looked upon as a single unified task— in more general terms, social theory and its practical applications—are, according to him, interlinked through the principle of prevision, which thus becomes central in his system of positive doctrine. The spirit of positive social theory, he stated over and over again in effect, may be concentrated, in its twofold purpose of philosophy and polity, upon a single ultimate goal—scientific prevision.[2] *Voir pour prévoir.* (See in order to foresee.) Such is the practical bearing of positive thought, according to Comte—his version of Bacon's famous dictum that "knowledge is power."[3]

If in this attempt to lay the foundation for a positive science of social life directed to the practical purposes of social control Comte was not first, he was, as has been said, up to that time "foremost."[4] With him, the notion of a positive science of social control became something more than the utopian dream it had previously been. It has ever since been a prominent interest in psycho-social thought. Later it will appear how this notion was taken up in this country, practically where Comte left it, and gradually developed as a point of departure for a distinctive emphasis in American psycho-social theory and social thought generally.

Comte's exact relation to the modern sociological and social-psychological movements in general and in this country in particular is still, however, a matter of controversy. There are those who would give him unquestioned first place in these modern developments, and again those who find his contribution overshadowed by more directly applicable if less imposing contributions, depending on whether their attention is directed at the larger conceptions of goal or the more detailed considerations of procedure and technique.[5] But, the question of the relative importance of these two types of contributions apart, it can hardly be doubted that in its general effect Comte's *Positive Philosophy* was one of the great events in the history of modern psycho-social thought. Comte could scarcely foresee the laborious scientific procedure which his conception of positive social theory involved. He was essentially a philosopher in

---

[1] *System of Positive Policy*, vol. 1, p. 1.

[2] *Ibid., The Positive Philosophy*, vol. II, p. 61.

[3] See Ward, *Dynamic Sociology*, vol. I, pp. 104, 149.

[4] PARK, "Sociology and the Social Sciences," *Amer. Jour. Sociol.*, vol. 26, p. 403, 1921.

[5] See *supra*, pp. 14, 17; also LÉVY-BRUHL, *The Philosophy of Auguste Comte.* p. 208; MERZ, *History of European Thought in the Nineteenth Century*, vol. III, p. 43, vol. IV, p. 487; DESSOIR, *Outlines of the History of Psychology*, p. 228; McDOUGALL, *An Introduction to Social Psychology*, p. 1; BODENHAFER, *Pub. Amer. Sociol. Soc.*, vol. 17, pp. 17–18, 26, 1922.

both point of view and method, a prophet and herald rather than a secure and solid builder. It remained for the new age of scientific procedure in the study of human relations, which he sought to usher in, gradually to work out the scientific implications of whatever was of value in his system of social doctrine. In the meantime, however, his preliminary formulation of the goal and spirit of positive social science has stood out as a towering guidepost on the horizon of the modern scientific movement in this field of investigation.[1] "If it cannot be said of Comte that he has created a science," said J. S. Mill, "it may be said truly that he has, for the first time, made the creation possible."[2] This critical estimate of Comte's work has in large measure been supported by the course of events since Comte's day. Peculiarly to the point, therefore, is the following observation, though it was made in another connection:

Those who first see the general importance and far-reaching power of a new movement in thought or life, are rarely those who carry it on in the most judicious manner or give the best examples and proofs of its application. Their boldness and enthusiasm leads them into error, but they nevertheless conquer in the end.[3]

Rarely is this view more strikingly exemplified than in the case of Comte and particularly in so far as his relation to later sociological and social-psychological development is concerned.

III. HERBERT SPENCER (1820–1903)

(EVOLUTIONISM, NATURALISTIC)

At times of quickened intellectual activity long strides are frequently taken in short periods. Such a period followed the appearance of Comte's *Positive Philosophy*. Comte died just two years before the appearance of *The Origin of Species*, but by virtue of the latter event, Comte had become out of date and Spencer came into prominence. For so profound was the effect of Darwinism that there was an immediate need of a reformulation of the scientific tendencies of the age and of a modernization of thought generally in accordance with the spirit of the evolutionary standpoint as given expression to it by Darwin. This, especially in the field of scientific investigation which Comte's work for the first time brought to the forefront of attention, was preeminently the work of Spencer.

[1] See MERZ, *History of European Thought in the Nineteenth Century*, vol. III, pp. 43–44, 80, vol. IV, pp. 430*ff.*, 487*ff.*; DAVIS, *Psychological Interpretations of Society*, p. 21; BALDWIN, *History of Psychology*, vol. II, pp. 73–74, 126*ff.*; BRETT, *A History of Psychology*, vol. III, pp. 247, 286; BOGARDUS, *A History of Social Thought*, p. 209; LICHTENBERGER, *The Development of Social Theory*, p. 262.

[2] See Frederic Harrison's Introduction to the 1896 (3 vol.) ed. of *The Positive Philosophy*, trans. by Martineau.

[3] MERZ, *History of European Thought in the Nineteenth Century*, vol. IV, pp. 476–477.

Spencer's position in later nineteenth century thought is thus in an important sense analogous to Comte's position in earlier nineteenth century thought.[1] As was the case with Comte, Spencer's work had particular significance for the sociological movement and for the same reasons. For Spencer, like Comte, was a sociologist first in the broad sense of early thought and a cosmologist and philosophical systematizer in consequence. And much more decidedly than Comte, Spencer impressed himself on the course of modern thought in both of these connections.[2]

Later more specialized and careful investigation in the field of the psycho-social sciences has found much to criticize in Spencer's work both on the side of method and on the side of theory. And it is naturally of the utmost importance from the standpoint of the development of a sound scientific procedure in these fields to emphasize the faults and pitfalls of Spencer's method and the resulting inconclusiveness of much of his theory. But as the counterpart to this, it should not be overlooked that later more critical and more specialized thought has built squarely upon the foundations which Spencer laid and which, in considerable measure, has made its more careful procedure possible. This fact did not always stand out in the period of violent reaction against Spencer's theory and method, which followed in the wake of justifiable scientific attack. Nor was the fact always recognized that Spencer's interest, like Comte's, was in the main frankly directed to the development of the broad import of his standpoint rather than to its detailed application in any one field of scientific investigation. In consequence, as Baldwin, for example, has pointed out, Spencer has borne the brunt of attack all the while that others have been reaping the credit for the naturalistic era of modern thought, which he helped so materially to usher in in the fields concerned with the study of human nature and social life.[3]

But the first wave of reaction against Spencer's work having passed, it is becoming possible now to view, alongside of his glaring faults of scientific procedure, also the sweeping outlines of his positive contribution to these fields of investigation. Spencer has thus been assuming a more balanced position in relation to modern developments in these fields of investigation—neither so high as seemed his due in the first blush of evolutionary enthusiasm nor so low as the reaction against him at first had set it—but above all, from the standpoint of our interest here at any rate, as an epoch-making figure in nineteenth century thought alongside of

[1] See *supra*, p. 14; also MERZ, *History of European Thought in the Nineteenth Century*, vol. III, pp. 30*ff.*, 285–286, 583; vol. IV, pp. 214*ff.*, 506*ff.* 515*ff.* 700*ff.*, etc.

[2] See *ibid.*, vol. IV, pp. 506*ff.*, 515*ff.*, 700*ff.*

[3] BALDWIN, *Fragments in Philosophy and Science*, p. 354; *History of Psychology*, vol. II, pp. 98–99; *cf.* COOLEY, *Human Nature and the Social Order*, 2d ed., p. 127; "Reflections upon the Sociology of Herbert Spencer," *Amer. Jour. Sociol.*, vol. 26, p. 129, 1920; also SMALL, "General Sociology," *Amer. Jour. Sociol.*, vol. 18, pp. 205–206, 1912.

Comte and Hegel and as a tremendously important factor in the modern sociological movement as it has affected related developments, among them modern social psychology.[1]

It has gradually become clear that it is impossible to evaluate the importance of Spencer's work for later thought, from the standpoint merely of any one of the specialized fields to which he sought to contribute and which, for the most part, have come into their own as scientific procedures since his day. For in his case particularly, it was the general effect of his work in the large, rather than his detailed theory in any one field, which constituted his greatest contribution to modern thought. And as regards the central theme of Spencer's work, his naturalistic conception of the universe in evolutionary terms, it seems hardly necessary any longer to note that, if it is viewed in broad outline and in the critical spirit made possible by the progress of scientific investigation since, this conception has established itself almost as the *sine qua non* of modern thought. In its broad universal application, furthermore, it has established itself to no small extent by way of Spencer's own preliminary formulation.

Commenting on the important role which this conception of the universe has come to play in our thinking, Merz says:

No better instance of the control—not to say the tyranny—which language exerts over our thoughts can be found than the modern use of the word Evolution. In every department of literature, scientific, philosophical, or general, systematic or unsystematic, the word occurs again and again; it seems to satisfy authors as well as their readers. By it they seem to have found the right position from which to treat or comprehend almost any subject, to have gained the right attitude of contemplation. In most cases, when the word is used on the title-pages of books, in introductions, reviews, or leading articles in the daily papers, it would be needless to ask the question what is really meant by the term; everybody is supposed to understand it; to everyone it seems to suggest a useful meaning.[2]

[1] See BALDWIN, *Fragments in Philosophy and Science*, pp. 353–359; *History of Psychology*, vol. II, pp. 98*ff.*; BRETT, *A History of Psychology*, vol. III, pp. 213–219; VILLA, *Contemporary Psychology*, pp. 38, 65, 217, etc.; DESSOIR, *Outlines of the History of Psychology*, pp. 235–238; SMALL, *General Sociology*, Chaps. VII–IX; GIDDINGS, *Principles of Sociology*, pp. 7*ff.*, 46*ff.*, 304*ff.*, etc.; *Studies in the Theory of Human Society*, pp. 3*ff.*, 111*ff.*; ROSS, *Foundations of Sociology*, pp. 42–47, 116*ff.*, 149*ff.*, etc.; PARK, "Sociology and the Social Sciences," *Amer. Jour. Sociol.*, vol. 27, pp. 1*ff.*, 1921; COOLEY, "Reflections on the Sociology of Herbert Spencer," *Amer. Jour. Sociol.*, vol. 26, pp. 129*ff.*, 1920; DAVIS, *Psychological Interpretations of Society*, pp. 21–25; BARNES, "Some Typical Contributions of English Sociology to Political Theory," *Amer. Jour. Sociol.*, vol. 27, pp. 289*ff.*, 1921; BRISTOL, *Social Adaptation*, Chap. II; BOGARDUS, *A History of Social Thought*, Chap. XVI; LICHTENBERGER, *Development of Social Theory*, Chap. XII.

[2] MERZ, *History of European Thought in the Nineteenth Century*, vol. III, pp. 30–31; also BALDWIN, *History of Psychology*, vol. II, note, pp. 98–99.

It would be difficult to overestimate Spencer's influence in respect to the formulation of the evolutionary viewpoint or the extent of the contribution which he was thereby enabled to make toward the establishment of the naturalistic and dynamic conception of the world of human phenomena. For, while Spencer was not the single-handed exponent of the general evolutionary viewpoint which he supposed himself to be, and while the scientific force of the conception in its modern form issued from Darwin's work rather than from his, Spencer's role in universalizing and popularizing some of the basic notions of naturalistic evolutionary thought, especially in the realm of psychological and social fact, stands out as unique and gives him a place of singular importance, alongside of Darwin, in the history of modern scientific developments dealing with this realm of fact.[1]

Even with respect to Spencer's uncritical method of using facts for illustrative purposes in the formulation of his theory, it must be noted that, at any rate in so far as the field of social and psycho-social thought is concerned, Spencer was able to make a notable contribution by means of it at the time.   For his work embodied thereby, in most striking form, the recognition of the need of proceeding factually in this field of endeavor. Henceforth unsupported speculation could command little respect in this as in other fields of scientific investigation.   Factual induction was established at least as an ideal, and the more careful development of the procedure was, after all, as one of Spencer's interpreters has said regarding Spencer's role in modern evolutionary thought as a whole, "only a question of time and of strength to collect and master the data."[2]

Spencer's is not merely "a system of speculative conceptions," it has been remarked significantly of Spencer's work as compared with contemporary social theory.[3]   His work represents, on the contrary, an attempt to universalize Darwin's fruitful inductive method and to carry it over, in particular, into the field of social investigation.   And while, as it appears from the results of his work, Spencer was by temperament not especially fitted for such a task,[4] his attempt in this direction was itself a contribution of importance at the time for the future development of psycho-social science.   In fact, if Comte may be said to hold first place as the prophet of the modern sociological movement, Spencer may be

---

[1] See MERZ, *History of European Thought in the Nineteenth Century*, vol. III, note, p. 30, and p. 517, vol. IV, pp. 211, 506*ff.*, 700*ff.*; also refs., *supra*, p. 27, note 1.   The universal appeal of the notion of evolution has been won largely through the appeal of suggestive shibboleths.   But it is not frequently recalled that such key phrases of modern evolutionary thought as "the survival of the fittest" and "the struggle for existence" were originally contributed by Spencer.

[2] SUMNER, "The Science of Sociology," *The Forgotten Man and Other Essays*, pp. 401–405; also PARK and BURGESS, *Introduction to the Science of Sociology*, p. 210.

[3] SMALL, *General Sociology*, p. 130.

[4] See COOLEY, *Amer. Jour. Sociol.*, vol. 26, p. 136, 1920.

said, by virtue of this contribution, to hold first place in the actual process of turning Comte's prophecy into something more than a mere promise of possibility. As a result of his work, Comte's promise began to assume something of the aspect of a definite program of scientific activity.[1]

The more important is it, however, to emphasize the faults of Spencer's procedure. The old dictum that "criticism is the life of science" has peculiar force in respect to the discussion of method. In the case of the psycho-social sciences and Spencer's work specifically, this critical attitude is especially important because of the great difficulty with which these fields of thought have gradually come to disengage themselves from the domination of philosophy, and because Spencer's work, particularly, tended to obscure essential differences of point of view and method between these two related fields of endeavor. The emphasis of scientific comment on Spencer must thus continue to fall on the defects of his mechanical, atomistic, analogical, and deductive procedure of thought, as well as on his quite general disposition to oversimplify objective facts in order to fit them into his preconceived conception of the universe and his special categories of evolutionary doctrine.[2] But this emphasis must not be permitted to bring the positive elements of Spencer's work into wrong perspective when viewed in the light of contemporary developments in the fields of our interest.

For social psychology distinctively Spencer did not have as direct a message as Comte, for Spencer, true to the tradition of British psychology, always remained essentially individualistic in his discussion of human relations. In fact, Spencer hardly took objection to the prevalent individualistic psychology, except indirectly through his study of objective social life and by possible implication from the role which the concept of "environment" plays in his theory of evolution or from his notion of the "social organism." In so far as he may be said to leave room for a social psychology outright in his system, however, it is chiefly a matter of the formal social discipline of the human individual who is primarily conceived of by him, in the manner common to individualistic thought, to be a datum in the social process. His social psychology is, furthermore, a sort of necessary evil superimposed upon the essential structure of his system rather than a fundamental aspect of his psychological and social

---

[1] See SMALL, General Sociology, pp. 130ff.; Amer. Jour. Sociol., vol. 18, pp. 205–206, 1912; GIDDINGS, Studies in Social Theory, pp. 111ff.; ROSS, Foundations of Sociology, pp. 43ff.; COOLEY, Amer. Jour. Sociol., vol. 26, p. 129, 1920; PARK and BURGESS, Introduction to the Science of Sociology, p. 210.

[2] See in this connection especially, BALDWIN, Fragments in Philosophy and Science, pp. 356ff.; BRETT, A History of Psychology, vol. III, pp. 217ff.; SMALL, General Sociology, Chap. IX; GIDDINGS, Studies in Social Theory, pp. 44ff.; ROSS, Foundations of Sociology, pp. 42ff.; COOLEY, Amer. Jour. Sociol., vol. 26, pp. 131ff., 1920; BOAS, The Mind of Primitive Man, Chap. IV; also infra, pp. 147ff., 167ff., references pp. 167ff.

theory.[1] To the actual enlargement of modern social-psychological thought specifically from the standpoint of the theory of organic evolution, Darwin himself had a more direct contribution to make than Spencer, though he is much less frequently thought of in this connection.[2] It is important to note, however, that in spite of Spencer's apparent lack of a well-founded social-psychological standpoint, his influence upon modern social-psychological thought, due to his influential position in later nineteenth century psycho-social thought generally, has been perhaps more widespread and thoroughgoing than that of any other English writer. It is essential, therefore, that we follow out in some detail the main bearing of his system as it touches the field of social psychology.

Spencer's psychological and social theories, as is well known, are integral parts of the larger scheme of his *Synthetic Philosophy*. It was Spencer's aim to develop the several parts of this scheme in such a way as to present the various orders of phenomena in an unbroken sequence of development illustrative of his theory of universal evolution. The phenomena of mental and social life were, from the standpoint of this larger program, but particular fields of interest for Spencer in which he undertook to trace out in detail the operation of the natural processes that his theory sought to establish were cosmic in scope and universal in action.[3] Like Comte, Spencer originally intended to cover all the main fields of science in his survey and to include in his *Synthetic Philosophy* a treatment of what he looked upon as the three chief kinds of evolution: inorganic, organic, and super-organic. His *First Principles* was written with this complete program in view. He finally abandoned the first part of his program, however, on the ground that "it seemed undesirable to postpone the more important applications of the doctrine for the purpose of elaborating those less important applications which logically precede them"[4] and confined himself to the development of the latter and, for him, more important parts. The *Synthetic Philosophy* includes, therefore, besides the volume on *First Principles*, two volumes on biology, two on psychology, three on sociology, and two on ethics.

Spencer thought in mechanical and physico-chemical terms, however, so that the formulation of his basic principles of thought, as worked out in his *First Principles*, suggests their applicability to the treatment of inorganic evolution much more readily than to the treatment of the organic fields in which he actually developed his theory in detail. His

[1] See Cooley's pointed observations on Spencer in this connection, *Amer. Jour. Sociol.*, vol. 26, pp. 137*ff.*, 1920.

[2] See *infra*, pp. 147*ff.*

[3] See MERZ, *History of European Thought in the Nineteenth Century*, vol. III, pp. 285–286, vol. IV, pp. 214*ff.*, 526*ff.*

[4] See *Principles of Sociology*, vol. I, p. 3.

famous definition of evolution, as he formulated it there, brings this out strikingly. It runs as follows: "Evolution is an integration of matter and concomitant dissipation of motion; during which the matter passes from an indefinite, incoherent homogeneity to a definite, coherent heterogeneity; and during which the retained motion undergoes a parallel transformation."[1]

Somewhat surprisingly also, in view of the thoroughgoing evolutionary standpoint which Spencer sought to incorporate into his work, he regarded his own conception of universal evolution as more of a break with the course of philosophical thought than it actually was. Whereas Spencer saw all phenomena as organic parts in an evolutionary process, suggests Royce, "he never learned how to regard human philosophical thought itself as an evolutionary process in which his own thinking had an organic place."[2] In point of fact, the notion of evolution had a long history, dating more or less clearly even to Greek thought. During the eighteenth century the conception took on new momentum in connection with the historical movement, and from then on it continued to hold ground in various forms and to gain force, until it became very prominent in the first half of the nineteenth century in both philosophical and scientific thought. Herder, Goethe, Hegel, Condorcet, Comte, all had made suggestive philosophical application of it in the field of social interpretation; and the new sciences of geology, embryology, anthropology, and the comparative investigation of language, culture, art, religion, etc., were bringing together a mass of supporting evidence in its favor which was becoming a serious challenge to traditional static thought in every direction. As regards the course of human history, in particular, aside from the philosophical theories of Hegel and Comte, the German school of critical historians had so far accepted the evolutionary view that they had been for some time concerning themselves, as a part of their historical technique, with the problem of its adequate methodological expression.[3] But it remained for Darwin to give the theory of evolution scientific prestige and for Spencer to give it universal formulation upon a level, as it seemed at the time, which was in keeping with the high order of Darwin's work but with the weight of his effort and influence falling in the field of the psychological and social sciences. What Spencer contributed to modern evolutionary thought, therefore, was not a new conception but its formulation in universal and scientifically suggestive naturalistic terms, at a time when such a formulation was peculiarly in a position to profit not only by his own concrete applications but also

[1] *First Principles*, p. 396.

[2] Royce, *Herbert Spencer—An Estimate and Review*, p. 48; *cf.* Merz, *History of European Thought in the Nineteenth Century*, vol. III, pp. 183–184; also Osborn, *From the Greeks to Darwin*, Chap. I.

[3] See Small, *Origins of Sociology*, Chaps. II–V.

by the prestige of Darwin's work and the accumulating testimony of a wide range of inductive investigations.[1]

But Spencer worked in isolation largely, and the effect of his viewpoint was to give the theory of evolution a distinctly biological, individualistic, and *laissez-faire* turn in application to the fields of psychology and sociology. Starting out in his *Synthetic Philosophy*, as he did, with the development of his theory in terms of a study of biological evolution, he was obliged, in accordance with his basic principle of unbroken continuity, to treat mental and social evolution as aspects of the same spontaneous, undirected, and individual process of development which seemed to him to be characteristic of evolution on the biological level. The above-mentioned characteristics of his psychological and sociological theory follow logically, therefore, from the theoretical movement of Spencer's system of thought as a whole   Behind this theoretical setting, however, were Spencer's strong emotional leaning in the direction of the practical implications of these characteristics of his psychological and sociological theory and his general tendency to view phenomena in atomistic and mechanical terms, which but came to more striking expression in these departments of his system than elsewhere.[2]

Realizing that the unity of his system would most likely be challenged at the points where his theory supposedly leads over from biological to mental and social evolution, Spencer sought the support of special devices of treatment and terminology at these points. With the aim in view of bringing his psychology and sociology into as intimate association as possible with his biology, he presented psychology outright as a special part of organic evolution and sociology in terms of "super-organic" evolution.[3] He also enlisted the aid of his well-known methods of "parallelism" in the one case and "organic analogy" in the other. In the end, despite all the criticism and opposition which his treatment of mental and social life aroused, he succeeded in impressing his biological, individualistic, and *laissez-faire* view of evolution upon English thought with such effect, that for a generation and more it successfully dominated theory dealing with these aspects of life.[4]

Spencer's detailed discussion in application of his general theory of evolution to the treatment of mental and social phenomena[5] brings into

[1] See ROYCE, *Herbert Spencer*, pp. 16*ff.*; MERZ, *History of European Thought in the Nineteenth Century*, vol. III, pp. 50–51, 183–184, 285–286, vol. IV, pp. 506*ff.*, 700*ff.*; OSBORN, *From the Greeks to Darwin*, Chaps. I, VI.

[2] *Cf.* COOLEY, *Amer. Jour. Sociol.*, vol. 26, pp. 131*ff.*, 1920; BARNES, *Amer. Jour. Sociol.*, vol. 27, pp. 301*ff.*, 1921.

[3] See *Principles of Sociology*, vol. I, pp. 3, 7; *First Principles*, pp. 316, 374.

[4] See SMALL, *Amer. Jour. Sociol.*, vol. 18, pp. 206–207, 1912–1913; *infra*, pp. 157–158.

[5] In connection with the following discussion of Spencer's more detailed treatment of mental and social evolution see *infra*, p. 40.

play his whole complex scheme of thought as it is concentrated in his definition of evolution (the persistence of force, the instability of the homogeneous, the multiplication of effects, the tendency toward segregation and equilibration, etc.).[1] In its social-psychological import, it centers, however, about his basic principle of continuity and the implications for the biological interpretation of the mental and social processes which this principle carried in his system, as already suggested above.

We get the characteristic orientation of Spencer's psychological and sociological theory as it bears on the field of social psychology at the very outset in his oft-quoted definition of life: "Life is the continuous adjustment of internal relations to external relations."[2] Already in this underlying conception of his system of organic theory, there is an indication of his one-sided emphasis on passive adaptation and his tendency to neglect the more active side of the life process which becomes so prominent in the case of man (*i.e.*, the adjustment of external relations to internal relations) and which has such deep implications for social psychology. Spencer did not completely overlook this more active side of the life process in his treatment of mental and social evolution, but he left it very much in the background. And the overwhelming emphasis of his theory as a whole was such that it left this aspect of his thought, especially in its implications for the social-psychological conception of the life process, seem quite unimportant. In his elaboration of his definition of life as given above, for instance, Spencer frequently touched upon suggestive ground from the standpoint of possible social-psychological application on the mental and social levels.[3] But he left these possibilities of application almost entirely unworked and very largely submerged by the biological orientation of his thought and his insistent individualistic emphasis.

Directed, as Spencer's work was, to the development of the larger, universal aspects of evolutionary thought and dominated, as it was throughout, by a decided individualistic leaning, it naturally did not lead out to a preoccupation with possible social-psychological implications. Rather it directed itself to the incorporation and reinterpretation from the evolutionary standpoint of the current trend of individualistic psychological and social theory, with the spirit of which Spencer was on the whole in sympathy, and of which, as it turned out, he finally became a most forceful new defender.

By way of specifically linking up his psychological with his biological theory, Spencer started out in his *Principles of Psychology* with the

---

[1] See *First Principles*, Part II, and Spencer's own summary of the basic principles of his theory in his preface to Collins, *Epitome of the Synthetic Philosophy of Herbert Spencer.*

[2] *Principles of Biology*, vol. I, p. 97; *Principles of Psychology*, vol. I, p. 293.

[3] See *Principles of Biology*, vol. I, pp. 93*ff.*; *Principles of Psychology*, vol. I, pp. 291*ff.*

"nervous shock" accompanied by the corresponding "feeling," as the elementary fact in mental life.[1] Retaining, then, the structuralistic and atomistic point of view of association psychology and proceeding in accordance with his characteristic genetic approach, he set about to build up the whole complex of psychological concepts from this primitive unit as a basis, at the same time being concerned to establish the essential thesis that the evolution of mental phenomena, through the ascending stages of mental composition involved, conforms to the laws of evolutionary development in general as they had been previously formulated by him.[2] Reflex action, instinct, emotion, sensation, memory, reason, will—these all appear, accordingly, as factors in a progressive series of mental composition and genetic development. All of them arise out of the primordial nervous shock under conditions that correspond to the general course of evolutionary development— from the simple to the complex, from the homogeneous to the heterogeneous, from the indefinite, incoherent, unintegrated and undifferentiated to the definite, coherent, integrated, and differentiated, etc. Reflex action is the result of "an integrated series of nervous shocks"; sensation is the "feeling" aspect of this process; instincts are compound reflex actions; instincts that lose their regularity of coordination result in memory and reason on the one hand and in sentiment and will on the other; and so on until the entire conceptual structure of contemporary psychology is completed.[3]

Spencer's standpoint is structuralistic and atomistic throughout and, except by possible implication in one connection or another, as already indicated, hardly more given to the social-psychological conception of mental development than that of orthodox association psychology itself. The suggestive "principle of correspondence" incorporated in his definition of life, and the concept of "environment" figure prominently in his psychological theory,[4] but their application is largely exhausted by him in biological parallelism, mechanical analogy. and bio-organic interpretation. And yet, Spencer's psychology was a definite step ahead of pre-evolutionary associationist theory from the social-psychological standpoint. For even if only in the biological sense of racial heredity, his evolutionary treatment of the subject definitely brought the social factor into view in psychology, and it even shifted emphasis from individual to racial experience as the important matter of psychological concern.[5]

[1] Principles of Psychology, vol. I, Part II, Chap. I.

[2] Ibid., Chap. II.

[3] Ibid., Parts II, IV.

[4] See ibid., pp. 291ff.

[5] See Principles of Psychology, vol. I, especially Parts II, IV; also BALDWIN, History of Psychology, vol. II, pp. 98–103; BRETT, A History of Psychology, vol. III, pp. 213–219; DESSOIR, Outlines of the History of Psychology, pp. 235–238; VILLA, Contemporary Psychology, pp. 38, 217, 267; RIBOT, English Psychology, pp. 124–197.

Spencer's phylogenetic approach and structuralistic standpoint obscured the social-psychological significance of this shift of emphasis for a time, but, as we shall see, it needed only the association of the ontogenetic point of view which Baldwin, for instance, introduced and the broader conception of organic life which characterized Darwin's thought to yield rich social-psychological results.

This was, however, essentially a matter of later reinterpretation. The immediate effect of Spencer's psychological theory was to provide a new basis of support for the individualistic rather than the social-psychological standpoint. Nor did Spencer's discussion of such topics as the "Development of Conceptions," "Language of the Emotions," "Sociality and Sympathy," "Altruistic Sentiments," etc., in his "Corollaries,"[1] which he added to the second edition of his *Principles of Psychology* with the express purpose of preparing a social-psychological foundation for his discussion of social evolution in his *Principles of Sociology*, materially alter the situation. For he not only maintained his characteristic biological standpoint also in this supplementary part of his work, but he carried it over unaltered into his study of social evolution itself, depending on his organic analogy for the transition to the consideration of the "super-organic," to which his discussion leads in his *Principles of Sociology*.[2]

Spencer accordingly passed over the whole problem of social-psychological relation with the suggestion of organic interdependence which his organic analogy carried. Otherwise, he but incorporated into his system the old-time antithesis between the individual and the social in the new form of the organic and the super-organic. He defined the relation between these parts of his system as follows:

While we are occupied with the facts displayed by an individual organism during its growth, maturity, and decay, we are studying Organic Evolution [biology and psychology]. If we take into account, as we must, the actions and reactions going on between this organism and organisms of other kinds which its life puts it in relation with, we still do not go beyond the limits of Organic Evolution. Nor need we consider that we exceed these limits on passing to the phenomena that accompany the rearing cf off-spring; though here, we see the germ of a new order of phenomena. While recognizing the fact that parental cooperation foreshadows processes of a class beyond the simply organic; and while recognizing the fact that some of the products of parental cooperation, such as nests, foreshadow products of the super-organic class; we may fitly regard Super-organic Evolution [sociology] as commencing only when there arises something more than the combined efforts of parents. Of course, no absolute separation exists. If there has been Evolution, that form of it here distinguished as super-organic must have come by insensible steps out of the organic. But we

[1] *Principles of Psychology*, vol. II, Part IX.
[2] See COOLEY, *Amer. Jour. Sociol.*, vol. 26, pp. 137*ff*., 1920.

may conveniently mark it off as including all those processes and products which imply the coordinated actions of many individuals.[1]

Passing on directly from the point where he left off in his psychology and proceeding similarly, Spencer thus starts practically anew in his sociology, with a description of primitive man, who was regarded by him as the "primitive social unit" in a sense roughly corresponding to that in which the cell was for him the "primitive unit" in biology and the nervous shock in psychology. This manner of approach, besides giving place to Spencer's wide use of anthropological and ethnological material bearing on the mind of primitive man, on the basis of which he formulated those ingenious theories of primitive mentality[2] for which his sociology became famous later, necessarily focused attention on the racial and biological aspects of social life rather than on the personal and social-psychological. It thus prepared the ground for the formulation of his biological theory of society and for the elaboration of his method of organic analogy[3] and hence, for the treatment of social evolution in objective and "super-organic" terms.

For the purposes of his discussion of this type of evolution, Spencer assumed, on the basis of his preliminary consideration of primitive man, social units as primitively conditioned "physically, emotionally, and intellectually and as thus possessed of certain early acquired ideas and correlative feelings," regarding it the function of the science of sociology "to give an account of the phenomena that result from their combined actions."[4] This problem, he then interpreted, in accordance with his conception of super-organic evolution, in terms of objective social organization. His *Principles of Sociology*, aside from the two preparatory parts dealing with the primitive mind and the organic analogy, is thus given over to a study of the course of social evolution in terms of the evolution of social institutions: domestic, ceremonial, political, ecclesiastical, professional, and industrial. The remaining six of the eight major parts into which the three volumes of his *Principles of Sociology* are divided—one for each of the above headings—are devoted to the treatment of this central problem and to the establishment in all these connections, as in his psychology, of his basic thesis asserting the applicability of his general principles of evolution to the interpretation of every level of life, social as well as individual.

In the course of his detailed survey of social evolution, Spencer made frequent formal reference to the reciprocal relation between social units and social aggregates and between mental traits and super-organic

[1] *Principles of Sociology*, vol. I, pp. 3–4. Quotations from this work are reprinted by permission of D. Appleton & Company, publishers.

[2] *Ibid.*, Part I, Chaps. IV–VII.

[3] *Ibid.*, Part II.

[4] *Ibid.*, vol. I, p. 456.

products. But here no more than in his psychology did he develop the social-psychological aspects of these suggested relations.[1] His attention was directed almost entirely to the statement of the social process, not in its own distinctive terms but in the analogical terms necessary to connect it with his treatment of organic evolution in his biology and psychology.

All in all, therefore, Spencer's sociology had a dual effect upon the modern social-psychological movement. On the one hand it did much to establish the view that the study of social life requires scientific treatment in its own right, and this view, inasmuch as it directed attention to the study of the social-environment aspect of human behavior, was indirectly of the utmost importance for the development of modern social psychology. In conjunction with the general run of Spencer's evolutionary interpretation and his organic conception of social life, this effect of Spencer's work and his sociological theory generally must accordingly be looked upon as having a decided positive significance for the furtherance of the modern social-psychological movement. On the other hand, the biological and individualistic orientation and emphasis of Spencer's thought in his sociology as in his psychology were a renewed defense of the traditional approach of individualistic psychology. And Spencer left no doubt of the very special importance which he attached to the latter aspects of his sociological theory.

Arguing by analogy from the fields of mechanics, physics, and chemistry, he maintained that his atomistic procedure, as defined by the principle "that the properties of the units determine the properties of the aggregate,"[2] was just as applicable to the study of social life as to other orders of phenomena.

Those who have been brought up in the belief that there is one law for the rest of the Universe and another law for mankind, will doubtless be astonished by the proposal to include aggregates of men in this generalization. And yet that the properties of the units determine the properties of the whole they make up, evidently holds of societies as of other things. A general survey of tribes and nations, past and present, shows clearly enough that it is so; and a brief consideration of the conditions shows, with no less clearness, that it must be so.[3]

Sociological theory clearly extends out, therefore, from the study of the individual social unit. Hence, the importance which Spencer attached to the study of primitive man in his sociology and the space

---

[1] *Cf.* COOLEY, *Amer. Jour. Sociol.*, vol. 26, pp. 137–140, 142–144, 1920; DAVIS, *Psychological Interpretations of Society*, p. 24.

[2] *The Study of Sociology*, p. 52; see also *Principles of Psychology*, vol. II, p. 509, and *Principles of Sociology*, especially vol. I, pp. 453–455. *Cf.* Comte's position, *supra*, p. 21.

[3] *Study of Sociology*, pp. 50–51. Quotations from this work are reprinted by permission of D. Appleton & Company, publishers.

which he devoted to the treatment of this subject.[1] His position on this matter is strikingly summarized in the following passage from his *Study of Sociology:*

Setting out, then, with this principle, that the properties of the units determine the properties of the aggregate, we conclude that there must be a Social Science expressing the relations between the two, with as much definiteness as the natures of the phenomena permit. Beginning with types of men who form but small and incoherent social aggregates, such a science has to show in what way the individual qualities, intellectual and emotional, negative further aggregation. It has to explain how slight modifications of individual nature, arising under modified conditions of life, make somewhat larger aggregates possible. It has to trace out, in aggregates of some size, the genesis of social relations, regulative and operative, into which the members fall. It has to exhibit the stronger and more prolonged social influences, which, by further modifying the characters of the units, facilitate further aggregation with consequent further complexity of social structure . . . [2]

These phenomena of social evolution have, of course, to be explained with due reference to the conditions each society is exposed to—the conditions furnished by its locality and its relations to neighboring societies. Noting this merely to prevent possible misapprehension, the fact which here concerns us, is, not that Social Science exhibits these or those special truths, but that, given men having certain properties, an aggregate of such men must have certain derivative properties, and which form the subject-matter of a science.[3]

Spencer became considerably more cautious in the presentation of his individualistic point of view in his *Principles of Sociology*, but the latter work represents, nevertheless, an attempt to give this program of procedure concrete and detailed elaboration.

Alongside of this individualistic movement of his thought, his organic analogy and defense of the thesis that "a society is an organism" whose attributes "are like those of a living body"[4] tended toward a sharply defined antithetical conception of the individual and society which forced the problem of social control to the forefront of attention.[5] How does the individual become an organic part of the social group of which he happens to be a member, and how does the latter, conceived of as a mere "aggregate" of "discrete" individuals, become the organic unity which he described in terms of his organic analogy? By bringing the dualism of thought represented by traditional psychology and early sociology within the compass of his own work, Spencer forced these

[1] See his *Principles of Psychology*, vol. II, Part IX; *Principles of Sociology*, vol. I, pp. 10–15, Chaps. IV *ff*.; also *supra*, p. 36.

[2] *Study of Sociology*, p. 52.

[3] *Ibid.*, p. 53.

[4] *Principles of Sociology*, vol. I, p. 467.

[5] See PARK, *Amer. Jour. Sociol.*, vol. 27, p. 5, 1921; GIDDINGS, *Studies in the Theory of Human Society*, p. 115.

problems forward as the key problems of social-psychological consideration, and social psychologists, of whatever theoretical orientation, have ever since been concerning themselves, in one way or another, with them.

The more important aspects of the progress of modern social-psychological thought in its bearing on these and related social-psychological problems will be considered as this discussion develops. At this point it may be recalled, however, that Spencer's psychological and sociological theory was itself not without possibilities of social-psychological elaboration in the interest of these basic problems. But Spencer left these possibilities undeveloped, making room in his work only for a social psychology of the more formal social integration and control of the individual, conceived of as a biological datum in social life. This process, Spencer maintained too, at least in so far as organized social action is concerned, should be reduced to a minimum, in order that the conditions of natural progress be interfered with as little as possible. The only real hope of a better condition of affairs—social as well as physical and mental—has its foundation in the slow upward course of natural development. Man can do little more than to secure the unhampered operation of the elementary processes upon which natural evolution depends and to cultivate "philosophical calm" the while he is awaiting the gradual emergence of a higher order of life.[1]

The diverse and forceful application which Spencer gave this general thesis in his discussion of all practical social questions tended to bring his *laissez-faire* position into striking contrast with Comte's program of positive social reconstruction. "It is evident," remarks a recent writer, "that in crossing the English Channel, sociology . . . suffered a sea change."[2]

But if in their practical social conclusions regarding the function of social science Comte and Spencer differed profoundly—so profoundly, in fact, that as we shall see, Ward was able to conceive of his own work as primarily an attempt to reconcile their divergent positions—in their major contentions concerning the possibility of a scientific study of social life and a naturalistic explanation of human events they were on common ground. From the standpoint of these developing tendencies of modern thought, to which their systems of theory gave epoch-making expression and on the ground of which their work takes on special significance in defining the background of the modern social-psychological movement, Comte and Spencer but reinforced each other's work, Spencer in particular standing directly in line with the course of modern scientific advance. The contribution which Comte made to these developing tendencies of

[1] See *supra*, pp. 32–33; *Study of Sociology*, pp. 384*ff.*; *Principles of Sociology*, vol. I, pp. 11*ff.*, vol. II, pp. 568*ff.*, 603*ff.*, 643*ff.*, vol. III, pp. 590*ff.*, 608*ff.*; BARNES, *Amer. Jour. Sociol.*, vol. 27, pp. 301*ff.*, 1921; BRISTOL, *Social Adaptation*, Chap. II.

[2] PARK, *Amer. Jour. Sociol.*, vol. 27, p. 1, 1921.

modern thought was in the nature of an inspiring prophecy by one who, after all, stood aloof from the actual task. Spencer, on the other hand, has seemed to many later students to speak with the authority of a great pioneer from within the ranks.[1] On this account, it might perhaps be argued with some justification that in so far as his work bears on the field of social psychology, it should have been treated in the body of the text rather than here in the philosophical background. But it was necessary to make a choice in this respect, and, on the whole, Spencer seems to belong most characteristically and properly in this section of the work rather than in the more specialized treatment of the development of social-psychological theory which follows. It will be necessary to bring his work into relation with the latter also, however, in a later part of this survey.[2]

[1] The testimony of such a critic of Spencer's point of view and method of approach as that of Cooley is of interest in this connection (see *Amer. Jour. Sociol.*, vol. 26, p. 129, 1920; *Human Nature and the Social Order*, 2d ed., note, p. 127).

[2] See *infra*, pp. 147 *ff.*, 165 *ff.* Similar considerations presented themselves in the case of Lester F. Ward, who holds something of an analogous position in American social-psychological thought to that of Comte and Spencer in France and England. Ward might logically and with justification be treated here along with Comte and Spencer. But on the whole it seemed best to discuss his work in conjunction with the special background consideration of American social-psychological thought. The close relation of his work to the movement and method of thought in this introductory section should, however, be borne in mind both at this point and in conjunction with the opening section on American social psychology.

CHAPTER II

THE DEVELOPMENT OF SOCIAL-PSYCHOLOGICAL THOUGHT IN GERMANY

I

Modern social-psychological thought, as has already been noted in a preliminary way, is a rather complex and many-sided development. It spread out from related fields of endeavor, now in one direction, now in another; these separate lines of development coming harmoniously together here, crystallizing into "schools" of thought there, and mapping out the broad present-day outlines of social psychology as a more or less clearly defined and differentiated field of investigation, only gradually and step by step. In this survey, it will of course be possible to trace out only the high spots of this development and only as it has related itself to the development of American social psychology. We shall accordingly confine this first part of our discussion to the consideration only of certain major developments of social-psychological thought in Germany, France, and England, which are intimately connected in one way or another with the development of American social-psychological thought. Then, in view of our special problem, we shall direct our attention to a more inclusive treatment of the latter.

Turning first, then, to the consideration of social-psychological thought in Germany, inasmuch as the modern social-psychological movement is most strikingly reflected there upon the background of traditional thought,[1] it seems worth while to recall here something of the setting of German post-Hegelian psychological and social thought as it was outlined in the previous section.

As was there stated, there was a distinct shift of interest in Germany after Hegel's death from the obscure metaphysical point of view and speculative method for which he stood to more objective investigation and the positive approach of natural science. The period was marked by a general restless groping for more adequate standpoints and methods in the study of human behavior and social life, some of which have a more or less direct bearing here. Herbart and Beneke, Schäffle and Marx, the critical historians and the psycho-social students of culture and the "social mind" of the day, all of these were important factors in the situation. It is, however, in connection with the development of folk psychology that we must view the new situation in its bearing upon the

[1] See *supra*, p. 7.

41

modern social-psychological movement. For it was in connection with the development of folk psychology that psychological and social thought in Germany came to a focus at this time in the first organized attempt to build up a "social" psychology in contradistinction to the individualistic general psychology which had held more or less undisputed ground until then. We accordingly turn at this point to inquire briefly into the nature of folk psychology, in so far as it sought to concern itself with what were thought to be social-psychological problems.

II. The Study of Culture History as an Approach to Social Psychology: Folk Psychology

1. Moritz Lazarus (1824–1903) and Hermann Steinthal (1823–1899)

Folk psychology is essentially a contemporaneous development with modern social psychology. Its more systematic development in Germany, in its broader psychological aspects in which it chiefly concerns us here, is often conveniently dated from the founding of the *Zeitschrift für Völkerpsychologie und Sprachwissenschaft* by the two Herbartians Lazarus and Steinthal in 1860. Certainly for our purposes here, this event is a significant point of departure for the discussion of German folk psychology in its social-psychological aspects.[1]

The term *Völkerpsychologie* has been variously rendered as "ethnic psychology,"[2] "racial psychology,"[3] the "psychology of peoples,"[4] "social psychology,"[5] "folk psychology."[6] But whatever translation is adopted for the term to which Lazarus and Steinthal set about to give scientific currency, it is obvious from an examination of their guiding principles of thought that the establishment of their review represented the crystallization of the two dominant tendencies in Germany at this time in connection with the study of mental phenomena: the positive and the social-historical. In their social-psychological bearing, these tendencies relate themselves more immediately to the Herbartian system of psychology on the one hand, and to the Hegelian conception of the relation between the individual and the social in historical development on the other.

Lazarus and Steinthal, as said above, were both Herbartians. The Herbartian school emphasized positive or, as some of them called it,

---

[1] See *infra*, p. 48.

[2] Klemm, *A History of Psychology*, p. 11.

[3] Baldwin, *History of Psychology*, vol. I, p. 20, vol. II, p. 82; Dessoir, *Outlines of the History of Psychology*, p. 242.

[4] Villa, *Contemporary Psychology*, p. 32.

[5] Judd, *Wundt's Outlines of Psychology*, pp. 10, 26, 352; *Cyclopedia of Education*, ed. by Monroe, article on "Social Psychology."

[6] Wundt, *Elements of Folk Psychology*, trans. by Schaub, for example.
Steinthal expressed a preference for the term "political ethnology" used by J. S. Mill in the sense of "the science of national character" (see his *Philologie, Geschichte und Psychologie*, note, p. 76) but this term has not established itself.

"scientific" psychology as opposed to the metaphysical psychology which was dominant under Hegel's influence. Herbart's claim to a scientific psychology was based chiefly upon his conception of psychology in terms of the statics and dynamics of mind and upon the mathematical formulation which he sought to give to his principles of mental action. In his *Lehrbuch zur Psychologie* (1816) and more elaborately in his later work on *Psychologie als Wissenschaft* (1824), he attempted to formulate a mathematically exact mechanics of mental function and so, according to his view, to found psychology upon the only basis which would enable it to become a real science. Though Herbart's mental mechanics appear highly artificial at the present time, in the Germany of his day his psychology became a tremendously influential factor in giving the weight of prestige to naturalistic attempts to explain mental phenomena.[1] These crystallized along two distinct directions in the next generation: physiological psychology and folk psychology.

Herbart's psychology played an important role in both of these developments. His suggestiveness in the latter connection, *i.e.*, in reference to folk psychology, seems to have followed from his opposition to the purely logical, deductive, and absolutistic procedure of contemporary idealistic thought in Germany and his rejection of the position of faculty psychology.[2] He believed that man is not born with fixed faculties but that his mental life is largely a product of the particular conditions of human life and experience, both physical and social. He accordingly directed attention to the "uncertainty of mental" facts and criticized faculty psychology on the ground that it tended to universalize its principles, which it arrived at from observation solely of a single level of mental operation, by overlooking "the distinguishing characteristics of the individual as well as the changing conditions of human nature."[3] The following statement is noteworthy:

The man presented by the teachers of psychology is the social, the educated man, who stands on the summit of the whole past history of his race. In this man the various functions are found apparently in combination, and under the name of mental faculties are regarded as a universal inheritance of mankind.

[1] See MERZ, *History of European Thought in the Nineteenth Century*, vol. III, pp. 204 *ff.*; Preface to Herbart's *Textbook in Psychology*, trans. by Smith, pp. vi *ff.*; RIBOT, *German Psychology of To-day*, pp. 24 *ff.*; DESSOIR, *Outlines of the History of Psychology*, pp. 210 *ff.*, 240 *ff.*; KLEMM, *A History of Psychology*, pp. 103 *ff.*; VILLA, *Contemporary Psychology*, pp. 24, 134, 319; BRETT, *A History of Psychology*, vol. III, pp. 43 *ff.*; BALDWIN, *History of Psychology*, vol. II, pp. 76 *ff.*

[2] See HERBART, *Textbook in Psychology*, pp. xxi–xxii, 36 *ff.*; BRETT, *A History of Psychology*, vol. III, p. 62; VILLA, *Contemporary Psychology*, pp. 177–178; DESSOIR, *Outlines of the History of Psychology*, vol. III, p. 62; RIBOT, *German Psychology of To-day*, pp. 26 *ff.*

[3] *Textbook in Psychology*, pp. 2–3, 37*ff.*; *cf.* BRETT, *A History of Psychology*, vol. III, pp. 54 *ff.*

Facts are silent as to whether this variety be originally found together or whether it be a manifold. The savage and the infant give us much less opportunity to admire the compass of their minds than the nobler among the brutes. Here psychologists help themselves by the evasive assumption that all higher mental activity is potentially present, not in brutes, but in children and savages, and may be regarded as undeveloped talents or as psychic faculties; and the most insignificant resemblances between the demeanor of the savage or the child, and that of the educated man, are valued by them as perceptible traces of awakening intelligence, awakening reasoning, or awakening moral sense.[1]

The limiting conditions of the observation solely of "the social, the educated man, who stands on the summit of the whole past history of his race" thus escape the faculty psychologist. "There are no universal facts," according to Herbart. "Psychological facts lie in the region of transitory conditions of individuals, and are immeasurably far removed from the height of the general notion of man in general."[2] They are functions of the fluctuating process of mental life, subject to the modifications due to stage of development, sex, temperament, physical environment, cultural history, state of mental health, etc., and they can be generalized only through a process of abstraction from these specific conditions of manifestation and variation.[3]

In spite of Herbart's continuing defense of the metaphysical basis of psychology, his critical position in regard to the current "general" psychology was both suggestive and novel, and it moreover carried decided implications for social psychology. In fact Herbart himself not only suggested the need of a social psychology incidentally as a result of his criticism of the faculty theory of mental function, but he specifically stated that "psychology will remain one-sided so long as it considers man as standing alone."[4] He suggested that persons are related to one another in society similarly to the manner in which concepts are related in the mind of the individual and that observation of the facts of social relation would make possible the formulation of a statics and dynamics of the state corresponding to the statics and dynamics of the individual mind as set forth in his psychology.[5]

Herbart's followers in this trend of thought constantly referred back to his position here as their starting point. Neither he nor they were led, however, as might perhaps be expected, to develop a social psychology in the modern sense, such, for instance, as Baldwin, starting from a

---

[1] *Textbook in Psychology*, p. 37.

[2] *Ibid.* p. 38.

[3] *Ibid.* pp. 99 *ff*.

[4] *Ibid.*, p. 190.

[5] *Ibid.*, p. 191; also his essay "Über einige Beziehungen zwischen Psychologie und Staatswissenschaft," *Schriften zur praktischen Philosophie* (*Collected Works*, vol. IX).

somewhat similar theoretical position, sought to develop in this country.[1] Such social-psychological effort as Herbart stimulated among his followers occupied itself primarily and very characteristically, both from the standpoint of his own suggested analogy and from that of the Hegelian motive which was still strongly operative in the situation, with the application of the concepts and principles of psychology, as derived from the study of the individual mind, to the problems of culture history and the interpretation of the "objective mind," their chief aim in view being the illumination of the movement of an assumed universal course of mental development, as had been suggested by Hegel. As social psychology, this procedure appears, in retrospect, to have been headed for the wrong goal from the very beginning. It was, however, not without fruit for the social-psychological movement in Germany at the time, as we shall presently see.

The new journal which Lazarus and Steinthal founded in 1860 was especially identified with two important lines of psycho-social investigation in Germany at this time: philology and anthropology. Even before Hegel had formulated his theory of historical evolution and his thesis of the unity of all mental development, the intimate bearing of philology and anthropology on psychology had received increasing attention in Germany.[2] The Hegelian system, however, reflected a new significance upon these tendencies of thought. For in the light of Hegel's theory, the study of language, institutions, religions, customs, laws, and other such elements of the "objective mind" could no longer be regarded as distinct from the study of mental phenomena as manifested in the psychological processes of the individual mind. All of these fields of inquiry represented, on the contrary, one continuous effort to lay bare the universal laws of the human mind. Anthropology and philology thus came to be looked upon more and more as important extensions of psychology and even as indispensable aids. The natural result of this conception was a quickening of interest in the psychological study of anthropological and philological material in post-Hegelian Germany.[3] The decade between 1850 and 1860 was, for various reasons, particularly fruitful in initiating activity along these lines. Besides establishing the *Zeitschrift für Völkerpsychologie und Sprachwissenschaft*, for instance, Lazarus and Steinthal brought forth several independent works dealing with special aspects of folk-psychological investigation during this period. At this time, too, Waitz began his *Anthropologie der Naturvölker* and Adolphe Bastian entered upon his extensive psycho-historical investigations into

---

[1] *Cf.* BRETT, *A History of Psychology*, vol. III, pp. 60–61.

[2] See MERZ, *History of European Thought in the Nineteenth Century*, vol. III, pp. 137 ff., vol. IV, pp. 212, 513.

[3] *Ibid.*, vol. III, p. 388, vol. IV, pp. 212–213; VILLA, *Contemporary Psychology*, p. 32.

primitive life. And these developments are but representative of many other less widely known attempts along similar lines. Viewing these attempts in their psychological aspects, Brett says:

These works form a group by reason of certain common characteristics. They all deal with what the Hegelian calls the Objective Spirit; they approach the subject under the influence of Herbart, who inspires them with psychological rather than logical methods of analysis; they are all positivist in temper and unite empirical analysis with historical synthesis. The general subject may be defined variously as collective psychology, ethnic psychology, or comparative folk-psychology.[1]

It is of significance as indicating the general trend of interest which these studies incorporated at the time that Lotze in his *Microcosmus* (1856) restated Herder's title of "Ideas towards a History of Mankind" to read "Ideas towards a Natural History of Mankind."[2] It is of significance to recall in this connection, also, that Darwin's *Origin of Species* appeared in 1859 and that Spencer had already projected the scheme of his *Synthetic Philosophy*. For while these studies were being carried out under the direct influence of Hegelian, rather than Darwinian or Spencerian, evolutionary thought, the influence of the latter in reflecting import upon this type of work must not be overlooked.

The distinctive social-psychological contribution which Lazarus and Steinthal made to this movement in connection with the founding of their journal was their attempt to define the relation between these varied efforts at the psychological study of the "objective mind" and the traditional study of mental function as carried on by general psychology. It was as an incident in this undertaking that they engaged upon the first clearly defined attempt to formulate the methodology of a *social* psychology in contradistinction to the psychology of the individual mind, with which general psychology was at the time wholly concerned.[3]

The social-psychological importance of the position which Lazarus and Steinthal thus built up, due to the hopeless involvement of their thought with the presuppositions of the Hegelian system of philosophy and its mystical notions about collective mental action, is of scarcely more than historical interest at the present time, especially from the

[1] BRETT, *A History of Psychology*, vol. III, p. 286; *cf.* VILLA, *Contemporary Psychology*, pp. 45, 156*ff*. Quotation reprinted by permission; see *supra*, p. 13.

[2] MERZ, *History of European Thought in the Nineteenth Century*, vol. IV, pp. 212, 423; see also *supra*, p. 11.

[3] See *Ztschr. f. Völkerps. u. Sprachw.*, especially vol. 1, pp. 1*ff*., vol. 2, pp. 393*ff*., vol. 3, pp. 1*ff*., vol. 17, pp. 233*ff*.

Most of the articles in the *Zeitschrift* deal with specific topics in the fields of mythology, linguistics, the history of religion, art, law, customs, etc., but there are also general discussions dealing with historical and philosophical subjects and some articles devoted specifically to the theoretical consideration of folk psychology, as, for instance, those indicated above.

standpoint of the development of social-psychological thought in this country, where folk psychology as a social-psychological movement has never struck root. And since folk psychology is best known here, in its social-psychological implications, through the work of Wundt, detailed consideration of its characteristic mode of procedure in dealing with the social-psychological viewpoint will be reserved for our discussion of this imposing representative of folk-psychological thought. It is, however, worth while to stop at this point long enough to note the purpose and program of folk psychology, as they were defined by the founders of its first common medium of scientific expression.

These aspects of their formulation may be obtained from the introductory statement which Lazarus and Steinthal published in the opening number of their journal. In this statement they addressed themselves not only to the psychologists proper of the day, whose duty, they felt, it was to reconstruct the current psychology in accordance with the new tendencies of psycho-historical thought, but likewise to all those special investigators of the "objective mind," whose aim it was, according to them, to trace the historical development of cultural phenomena in fundamental psychological terms, and who, as already noted above,[1] were so very active at this time in Germany. From both of these directions, they pointed out, as well as from the standpoint of history, especially the attempted histories of civilization, the need for such a new field of investigation as they here proposed under the name of *Völkerpsychologie* had for some time made itself felt. For both psychology and anthropology in their historical aspects, they argued, and history in its psychological aspects inevitably lead out to the concept of the *Volksgeist* or "folk mind,"[2] and it was precisely this phenomenon in its cultural manifestations and development that they proposed as the subject matter of the new field of inquiry. They therefore planned to develop folk psychology by drawing chiefly upon these three fields for information and material, *i.e.*, the psychological, the anthropological, including the very important contemporary field of linguistics, and the historical.[3]

According to their plan, folk psychology was to have two branches. It was to study the historical development of the "folk mind" in general on the one hand, and the particular "folk minds" of distinct peoples in their historical development on the other.[4] Its central aim in each case

[1] *Supra*, p. 45.

[2] Like so many of the post-Hegelian writers in Germany, Lazarus and Steinthal used this term not merely in the functional sense of later psycho-social thought but also as a metaphysical entity standing over against the individual mind. Their psychological analysis of the folk mind suggests strongly, however, aspects of later psycho-social thought, notably that of Durkheim.

[3] See *Ztschr. f. Völkerps. u. Sprachw.*, vol. 1, pp. 1-2, 25.

[4] *Ibid.*, p. 25. Two types of psychological interpretation correspond to this twofold program, represented respectively, for instance, by Fouillée, *Psychologie du peuple française*, and McDougall, *The Group Mind*.

was to be the discovery of the fundamental psychological principles which underlie the development of these phenomena. Folk psychology was to derive these fundamental principles from a basic study of the culture elements of the *Volksgeist*, that is, from a study of such phenomena as language, mythology, religion, art, literature, etc.[1] It might naturally approach the study of these phenomena from the standpoint of either one of the above described branches, but each would necessarily throw light on the other and thus contribute to the progress of folk psychology as a whole.

Of particular interest is the position which Lazarus and Steinthal assigned to this program of study in relation to general psychology. Man, they pointed out, may be studied on the level of his individual mind; this is the subject matter of *individual* psychology, or psychology as it had hitherto been conceived. But alongside of this individual psychology it is, according to them, necessary to study man as a social being, as a component element of the collective mental life of the social community of which he is a member. The psychological study of man from this latter standpoint they proposed to name *Völkerpsychologie*,[2] or "folk psychology." Their choice of this designation, as they explained at the time, was based on the thesis that the "folk" association is the fundamental form of human associated life historically and that it is always, therefore, historically implied in other forms, particularly those of civilized society (*Kulturgesellschaften*). The latter Lazarus and Steinthal regarded as derived from the folk form in accordance with the universal laws of development, which it was to be the aim of folk psychology to lay bare, and the general notion of which they took over from Hegelian thought.[3]

Man never is a member merely of mankind in general, they argued, in further explanation of their choice of the term *Völkerpsychologie*, with its emphasis upon the concept of the "folk" as over against the alternative contemporary use of the more general concepts of "society" and "humanity" in this connection, and all concrete groups in which man has existence have developed out of the folk community. The actual form which human associated life takes in history, they maintained, is separation into folk communities, so that the development of the human race generally is inevitably tied up with the development of definite historic folk communities. It is because the term *Völkerpsychologie* suggests this view that they thought it peculiarly appropriate as a designation

---

[1] *Ztschr. f. Völkerps. u. Sprachw.*, vol. 1, pp. 7, 40–67.

[2] They thereby extended and generalized the meaning of this term, for it was hitherto used, notably by Wilhelm von Humboldt, only in connection with the cultural characterization of distinct peoples through a descriptive study of their cultural life (see WUNDT, *Elements of Folk Psychology*, p. 2).

[3] *Ztschr. f. Völkerps. u. Sprachw.*, vol. 1, p. 5; also *supra*, p. 45.

for the sort of study which they had in mind. This thesis about the fundamental importance of the folk community it is, however, according to them, the special problem of folk psychology to establish both causally and historically. Suggested at the outset in explanation of the naming of the journal, it is yet, according to them, the special function of folk psychology to follow this thesis out in careful detail on the basis of concrete investigation. More specifically, as they viewed the task of folk psychology at the time, it must describe the conditions which led to the folk organization of human-kind; it must arrive at a causal explanation of this development; it must seek to indicate in what respects this form of community life was a necessary stage for further psychic development; it must establish how this stage is related to the further unfolding of the psychic process.[1]

At the very outset, therefore, Lazarus and Steinthal strike the keynote of the folk-psychological point of view, which, as will appear even in the case of Wundt, sought to build on the assumption to which Lazarus and Steinthal gave expression through their naming of the new field of investigation, namely, that the fundamental form of human association historically was that of the folk community or group and that all other forms of association have developed out of this primary form according to a universal series of stages, ascertainable from a culture-historical study of the objective products of the folk mind. From the standpoint of this thesis, the notion of the "folk" naturally loomed as the central conception about which folk psychology could build up its theory, corresponding, for instance, to the manner in which early sociology was seeking to build up its theoretical structure about "humanity" and "society" as central conceptions, or the manner in which contemporary psychology was likewise seeking to develop its theory about "consciousness" and the "soul" as organizing conceptions.[2]

Lazarus and Steinthal referred back specifically to Herbart's psychology as their point of departure in the development of their thinking on folk psychology. Herbart's conception of psychology was in very close agreement with their own, according to them, and he, they thought, would probably have become the founder of folk psychology had his efforts in this direction not been deflected to political theory.[3] They

---

[1] *Ztschr. f. Völkerps. u. Sprachw.*, vol. 1, pp. 5–6.

[2] See Steinthal's statement on the relation between folk psychology, psychology, and sociology at the time of the discontinuation of the *Zeitschrift für Völkerpsychologie und Sprachwissenschaft*, *Ztschr. d. Vereins f. Volkskunde*, vol. 1, pp. 11–17.

[3] *Ztschr. f. Völkerps. u. Sprachw.*, vol. 1, p. 69. As has already been noted, Herbart proposed a statics and dynamics of the state corresponding to his statics and dynamics of the individual mind (see *supra*, p. 44). His suggestion in this respect was followed out by the folk psychologists in one direction and by Schäffle and Lindner in another (see *infra*, pp. 67–68).

quoted his statement about the inadequacy of a purely individualistic psychology[1] as their starting point and accepted his particular system of individualistic psychology as a foundation. Since the "folk mind," they argued in this connection, exists only in the individuals who compose a folk group or people and can have no existence apart from them, it is natural to find it subject to the same fundamental psychological laws with which psychology deals in its study of the individual mind. Folk psychology is therefore concerned, according to them, with the same fundamental psychological processes with which individual psychology is concerned but in a more complicated and extended form. A people expresses its imagination in its art and literature, its emotion in its religion, its judgment in its codes of conduct, etc. The foundation of folk psychology, in the view of Lazarus and Steinthal, must thus be sought in individual psychology. Folk psychology can in fact progress as a science, according to them, only as individual psychology itself progresses and supplies it with the necessary basic concepts and principles of psychic life.[2]

This will suffice to indicate the theoretical and methodological basis upon which Lazarus and Steinthal sought to build up the structure of the new science, which they clearly recognized ought to be a "social" psychology as distinguished from individual or general psychology. Their conception, in so far as it was an attempt to bring together in one undertaking Herbart's suggestions for a "scientific" psychology and a "social" psychology, was obviously both fruitful and suggestive. But their specific program of procedure, regarded from the standpoint of social psychology as it has since developed, was quite as obviously still too much a part of Hegelian thought, with its notion of the unity of mental development and its confusing views regarding the relation of psychology, history, and sociology, to be long acceptable as a working basis of social-psychological investigation.[3] This will appear more clearly as our consideration of folk psychology continues, but it is notable here that Lazarus and Steinthal turned from Herbart to Hegel at the very point at which the former was most suggestive for social psychology, that is, in his attempt to connect psychological theory with the analysis of the concrete processes of contemporary social life. But this simply indicates that Lazarus and Steinthal remained essentially Hegelian in their outlook, and in so far as their general position is representative of early folk psychology as a whole, it also suggests why the latter has not been of more direct significance for social psychology as it has developed in this country and elsewhere outside of Germany. Not only because the early folk psychologists turned their attention primarily to anthropological

[1] *Supra*, p. 44; see *Ztschr. f. Völkerps. u. Sprachw.*, vol. 1, pp. 4, 7.
[2] *Ibid.*, vol. 1, pp. 10–11.
[3] See *supra*, p. 10.

and historical material, so that their work gradually became more closely identified with anthropology and history than with social psychology as specialized fields, but in particular because of the very decided Hegelian mysticism which they carried over into their theory of "group minds" and "folk souls," and the fact that no social psychology in any fundamental sense is at all possible if one accepts the standpoint and analogical procedure which Lazarus and Steinthal outlined and which the folk psychologists, including Wundt, in general followed, has folk psychology remained essentially apart from the main current of modern social-psychological development as it is to be followed out here.[1] Only an applied psychology of the individual mind in the field of culture history, dependent upon elaborate analogies between the *Volksgeist* and the individual mind, could result from their position, and that is precisely what folk psychology turned out to be in the main, in so far as its central approach to social-psychological considerations is concerned. It will be interesting to see how these comments apply to the important folk-psychological work of Wundt.[2]

2. Wilhelm Wundt (1832–1921)

The work of Darwin and Spencer inevitably brought support to the Hegelian conception of evolution and encouragement to the efforts of the folk psychologists. Though distinct in point of view and emphasis, the German historical and English biological views of evolution were agreed in general trend of thought, so that each in its particular sphere of influence was strengthened by the other.[3]

---

[1] Folk psychology has quite clearly affected several of the writers to be considered here, including some American writers, as will appear in the course of this section, but on the whole it represents an interesting by-current of social-psychological development from the standpoint of American social psychology.

[2] KLEMM, *A History of Psychology*, pp. 111–112; VILLA, *Contemporary Psychology*, pp. 43–45, 155–157; DESSOIR, *Outlines of the History of Psychology*, pp. 240ff.; BRETT, *A History of Psychology*, pp. 286ff., 291–293.

The *Zeitschrift für Völkerpsychologie und Sprachwissenschaft* ran from 1860 to 1890, after which it became the *Zeitschrift des Vereins für Volkskunde*. Some such outcome was inevitable as anthropology and ethnology began to extend their fields of interest to the consideration of basic psychological and social problems. See Steinthal's statement on the relation of folk psychology to the allied sciences of psychology, history, ethnology, and sociology in the opening volume of the *Zeitschrift des Vereins für Volkskunde*.

Since the war a successor to the *Zeitschrift für Völkerpsychologie und Sprachwissenschaft* has made its appearance in Germany (1925) under the name *Zeitschrift für Völkerpsychologie und Soziologie*. See the opening article by Thurnwald for a statement on its relation to its predecessor.

[3] MERZ, *History of European Thought in the Nineteenth Century*, vol. IV, pp. 515 ff.; BOAS, "The History of Anthropology," *Proc. Intern. Congress Arts Sci.*, vol. 5, pp. 470 ff.

The result for the German psycho-historical students of the "objective mind," as for the English classical school of anthropologists in a somewhat different direction and to a much more marked degree, was that evolution gradually became both a dogma and a passion with them.   In the one case as in the other, the tracing out of a particular scheme of evolutionary thought became an end in itself for a time, and the marshaling of facts for the purpose of establishing and of illustrating particular sets of preconceived notions about "origins," "stages," and "development" swept all other considerations before it.[1]   In the case of the folk psychologists, as has already been noted above, this involved the arbitrary identification of psychological, historical, and social processes. They were encouraged in this procedure, however, by the similar efforts and methods of contemporary evolutionary investigation generally and the state of feverish interest which centered about every phase of evolutionary discussion at the time.   Folk psychology was on the whole less given to the detailed schematism of English evolutionary thought, but it incorporated the general setting of contemporary evolutionary doctrine, and it is therefore not surprising to find that it in some instances led out toward parallel attempts at systematization.

This tendency is clearly reflected in Wundt's folk-psychological work.[2]   Folk psychology, as defined by Lazarus and Steinthal and the other Herbartians, was already an established fact.   As a result of the efforts of his predecessors, Wundt could fall back upon folk psychology with assurance and say, "Today, doubtless, folk psychology may be regarded as a branch of psychology concerning whose justification and problem there can no longer be dispute."[3]   His own task with respect to the new branch of psychological investigation, as Wundt saw it, was to bring it into some sort of organic relationship with the general psychology of the individual mind, especially the laboratory psychology which he had done so much to popularize in Germany.   This, Wundt felt, had never been adequately done by the folk psychologists, and this he accordingly undertook to do in his own folk-psychological work.[4]

It is highly significant from the social-psychological standpoint that Wundt, in contrast to most of the early folk psychologists, did not start with the social-historical problems of folk psychology but that he approached these problems gradually as a result of his work in experimental psychology.   Occupying, as Wundt did, a most strategic position

---

[1] See *ibid.*, p. 471.

[2] See GOLDENWEISER, "Cultural Anthropology," *The History and Prospects of the Social Sciences*, ed. by Barnes, pp. 210 *ff.*, 218–219, 230.

[3] *Elements of Folk Psychology*, trans. by Schaub, pp. 2–3.   Quotations from this work are reprinted by permission of The Macmillan Company, publishers.

[4] *Völkerpsychologie, eine Untersuchung der Entwicklungsgesetze von Sprache, Mythus und Sitte*, vol. I, p. 17.

in the development of modern experimental psychology, his recognition of the inadequacy of its individualistic approach brought a particularly strong line of support to the claims of the folk psychologists and sociologists, from within the ranks of the psychologists themselves. Wundt stands out, in consequence, as an important factor in the modern social-psychological movement, even apart from his detailed contributions in this field. The fact that he approached the problems of folk psychology by way of his experimental work in physiological psychology is of importance also in throwing light upon his particular point of view. For his point of view remained essentially individualistic in spite of his criticism of the other folk psychologists on this very ground[1] and in spite of his theory of the collective mental life of society which, he maintained, in accordance with his principle of the "creative synthesis," is not merely a summation of its component individual elements but a psychological synthesis of a new order.[2] His individualistic approach was, as we shall see, an inevitable result of his attempt to make the concepts and principles of experimental psychology (which was synonymous with physiological psychology for him) basic in the study of all psychic phenomena, even such as he himself clearly recognized were impossible of adequate study except on the social level.

Wundt's work in the field of folk psychology was thus, it appears, very closely connected with his experimental psychology, being but part and parcel of his general plan to lay the foundation for an inclusive system of positive knowledge of psychic life. It was his great aim to found the science of psychology in all its complex aspects upon the secure basis of verifiable fact. Once and for all it was necessary to put an end to the variety of attempts "to construct a psychology . . . in order that the study of experience might by degrees reveal the psychology."[3] Wundt naturally looked first and foremost to the experimental method as the means by which this purpose could best be realized. However, he became increasingly convinced that the experimental method, at any rate as he thought of it, was limited in its applicability to the study of the more simple mental processes.[4] How, then, was he to approach the study of the higher mental processes upon an equally secure positive basis? Furthermore, how could the problem of mental development, upon which he

[1] See *ibid.*, pp. 17 *ff.*

[2] See Haeberlin, "The Theoretical Foundations of Wundt's Folk-Psychology," *Psychol. Rev.*, vol. 23, pp. 279*ff.*, 1916, for a consideration of this point as well as for a rather extensive analysis of the underlying principles of Wundt's folk-psychological work generally; also Merz, *History of European Thought in the Nineteenth Century*, vol. III, pp. 396–397, vol. IV, pp. 711–713; Brett, *A History of Psychology*, vol. III, pp. 152–165, 291–293; Goldenweiser, *Early Civilization*, pp. 348–360.

[3] Brett, *A History of Psychology*, vol. III, p. 154.

[4] *Völkerpsychologie*, vol. I, pp. 21–22; *Outlines of Psychology*, trans. by Judd, pp. 26–27.

found the experimental method threw but little light, be more adequately approached?

Wundt found the answer to both of these questions in folk psychology. Man's higher mental processes, he realized, are inevitably and intimately bound up with such social products as language, myth, and custom. He accordingly decided, as had Lazarus and Steinthal before him, that the best way to study these higher mental processes upon a positive level was indirectly through the social products by means of which they come to expression. From a proper study of these phenomena, Wundt felt, the laws of the higher mental life could be deduced. Furthermore, being preserved, as Wundt believed in common with classical evolutionary thought, in a relatively permanent state in their various stages of development in the still existing cultures of the earth, it would be possible also, he decided, to trace the progress of mental evolution in these products of psychic life much more easily than in the transient states of the individual consciousness.[1] Wundt accordingly connected the "social" and "historical" with the "individual" in the study of mental phenomena, just as his predecessors in the field of folk psychology had, and so committed himself to the same confusion of these problems which characterized their essential position. This confusion of problems becomes particularly apparent in Wundt's work, furthermore, because of the systematic form which he sought to give to his folk psychology.

According to Wundt, psychology has two exact methods, like all other natural sciences: the experimental, by means of which the simpler individual processes can be analyzed; and the observational or folk psychological, by means of which the higher social processes must be investigated. These two methods are reciprocally supplementary and encompass together the whole range of psychological phenomena, "since besides the individual consciousness, whose analysis devolves upon the experimental method, and the manifestations of mental life in society, with which folk psychology deals, there exists nothing which concerns psychology as a differentiated science."[2]

The experimental method, being the more dependable scientifically, according to Wundt, should be used in so far as possible; but being also by its very nature, according to him, individualistic,[3] it is thereby not adapted to the study of the complex mental functions, which he definitely regarded as *social* both in origin and in expression. Here, Wundt felt, individual psychology needs supplementation from folk psychology, which can study these higher mental processes by the method of "pure observation." Folk psychology is thus, according to Wundt's scheme

[1] See *ibid.*, pp. 352–355.

[2] *Ibid.*, pp. 26–27; *Völkerpsychologie*, vol. 1, pp. 21–24; *Elements of Folk Psychology*, p. 3.

[3] *Völkerpsychologie*, vol. 1, p. 21.

of psychological thought, an essential part of psychology in the larger sense; it is, in fact, an indispensable aid to individual psychology, supplementing and completing it in method and problem as well as in principle.

Wundt pointed out in this connection, that the term *Völkerpsychologie* (folk psychology) only very inadequately indicated the field of study which he sought to include under this designation, for he had in mind, he tells us, a "social" psychology in the broader sense. However, he considered this term preferable to such possible alternatives as *Gemein-psychologie* (collective psychology) or *Sozialpsychologie* (social psychology), because it singled out the "folk" precisely for the emphasis which, he felt, such a field of inquiry as he had in mind should give to the most important concept with which it had to deal.[1]

The above view of the relation between individual psychology and folk psychology Wundt regarded as essentially new and radically different from that of Lazarus and Steinthal, who, he declared, accepted in common with the other Herbartians the basic principle that the relation between individual psychology and folk psychology is that of the fundamental science to its applications.[2] Among the Herbartians, according to him, the dominating position of the Herbartian individualistic and intellectualistic psychology offered resistance to the development of such a conception of the organic relationship between individual and folk psychology as he had in view.

Having, however, thus redefined the role of folk psychology and having emphasized the distinction between his conception of the organic relationship between individual and folk psychology and the conception which he attributed to the Herbartians, folk psychology remaining, according to his view, an "independent" technique,[3] Wundt nevertheless proceeded into the very individualistic involvements for which he criticized the Herbartians and on the basis of which he proposed to part company with them.

While folk psychology is the indispensable supplement to individual psychology, and indeed, as he said, "in the case of some questions the latter already finds itself obliged to fall back on the principles of folk psychology," nevertheless, it must not be forgotten "that just as there can be no folk community apart from individuals who enter into reciprocal relations within it, so also does folk psychology, in turn, presuppose individual psychology, or, as it is usually called, general psychology."[4] "Since the individual is basic to the social," he explained, "and the simple is the foundation of the complex in psychic phenomena, therefore experi-

---

[1] *Ibid.*, pp. 2–3; *Elements of Folk Psychology*, pp. 4–5.
[2] *Völkerpsychologie*, vol. I, pp. 17 *ff.*
[3] *Philosophische Studien*, vol. 1, p. 20, 1888.
[4] *Elements of Folk Psychology*, p. 3.

mental psychology has a more general and fundamental character."[1] In
the actual working out of his folk psychology, this meant that, instead of
remaining an "independent" technique, folk psychology really became, as
in the case of the other folk psychologists, merely an adjunct of individual
psychology, committed to both its individualistic conceptions and theory.[2]

From the standpoint of basic social-psychological procedure, Wundt
came out, therefore, in much the same position that Lazarus and Steinthal did, and, his objections notwithstanding, his folk psychology reduced
itself essentially to an applied individual psychology. Wundt himself
recognized this at times, but he maintained that if folk psychology be
thought of as "applied" psychology at all, it must be thought of as
applied in a special sense, since it is, according to him, a purely theoretical
science, just like individual psychology itself.[3] It is, however, in this
special sense that the folk psychology of the Herbartians was an applied
psychology, yet Wundt himself took it severely to task on the ground
that it turned out to be nothing more than an application of the principles
of individual psychology to the interpretation of certain historical products of social life.[4] In this instance, then, as so often in his case, Wundt's
keen criticism of others can be turned back in most effective criticism
of his own position.[5]

This may be disappointing in the light of Wundt's promise of a
social psychology, his criticism of the individualism of the earlier
folk psychologists, and his genuine insight into the social nature of the
more complex processes of the individual mind, but it is quite consistent
with his atomistic approach in psychology and his physiological standpoint. Wundt's entire system of psychology, despite his theory of the
"creative synthesis," is a system in which the whole is built up from the
parts and in which the former is explained as a compound of the latter,
somewhat as it is in association psychology.[6] Carrying over this approach
to the level of the psycho-social with which folk psychology was supposed
to deal, Wundt proceeded on the theory that the fundamental processes
of the individual mind are psychologically basic to the processes of the
"collective mind" and that individual psychology is therefore basic
to the study of the collective mental life of society.[7] He did not recognize
the need of explaining specifically how the former are basic to the latter
or of considering what consequences for the study of these two orders

[1] *Völkerpsychologie*, vol. I, p. 22.
[2] *Cf.* BRETT, *A History of Psychology*, vol. III, pp. 292–293.
[3] *Völkerpsychologie*, vol. I, p. 22.
[4] *Ibid.*
[5] See HALL, *Founders of Modern Psychology*, p. 419.
[6] See RIBOT, *German Psychology of To-day*, pp. 188–250; BRETT, *A History of Psychology*, vol. III, pp. 162 *ff.*; HAEBERLIN, "The Theoretical Foundations of Wundt's Folk-Psychology," *Psychol. Rev.*, vol. 23, pp. 279 *ff.*, 1916.
[7] *Völkerpsychologie*, vol. I, p. 22.

of phenomena are involved in the process of organization and integration which he assumed. We only know from his work that language is somehow intermediate between the two levels of mental phenomena in question and that they must therefore be thought of as being somehow related in terms of communication. In effect, however, we get two systems in Wundt's psychological theory: one, of the subjective individual consciousness; and the other, of the objective products of the "collective consciousness," being left very much in the dark as to just how the mystical synthesis, the "folk mind" of folk psychology, actually comes into being and how it functions.[1]

It may thus be said that Wundt's folk-psychological theory but illustrates what has been pointed out also in other connections, namely, that Wundt was a much better organizer in the field of abstract theory than in the field of concrete fact.[2] While he felt the need of bringing individual and folk psychology into organic relation theoretically as methodological procedures, he did not recognize that a similar need existed with regard to the concrete facts and processes with which individual and folk psychology were supposed to deal respectively. The latter problem was, as a matter of fact, not attacked directly by either the folk psychologists or the early sociologists. It was only gradually as the study of social life progressed and attention was gradually directed to the processes as well as the products of social interaction that this more concrete aspect of the problem of social-psychological interrelation began to come more clearly into view. But in the meantime, Wundt helped to throw light on the factors involved, both through his psychological interpretation of cultural development and through his cultural interpretation of mental development.

Accepting Wundt's folk psychology for what it is, then, rather than for what it is supposed to be, it nevertheless has importance here both on historical grounds and as an outstanding example of the folk-psychological approach to social psychology. Accordingly, we must inquire further into his conception of folk psychology and its procedure.

For Wundt, as for the other folk psychologists, folk psychology had the following chief purpose: it aimed to become "a psychological history of the development of mankind."[3] and by this phrase Wundt really meant a psychological history of the development of culture. He expressly repudiated the twofold folk-psychological program of Lazarus and Steinthal on the ground that it was the result of a confusion of thought, and he relegated the second part, *i.e.*, the study of individual

---

[1] See *ibid.*, pp. 7–11. Also Brett, *A History of Psychology*, vol. III, pp. 291–293; Haeberlin, "The Theoretical Foundations of Wundt's Folk-Psychology," *Psychol. Rev.*, vol. 23, pp. 287 *ff.*, 1916.

[2] See Hall, *Founders of Modern Psychology*, chapter on "Wundt," pp. 311–458.

[3] Subtitle of the *Elements of Folk Psychology*.

peoples,[1] to the special sciences of the collective mind, such as ethnology and philology. Folk psychology should, according to him, limit itself to the study of the general characteristics of the collective mind, just as individual psychology limits itself to the study of the general characteristics of the individual mind. Its relation to ethnology, philology, folklore, etc., though close, is like that of a general science to its materials.[2]

Wundt also emphasized the question of origins in connection with folk psychology, because it is, according to him, only in their primitive form that the mental products with which folk psychology concerns itself often reveal their true social origin. If folk psychology is to "lead us along the path of true psychogenesis," therefore, as according to him, it alone can, the problem of origins necessarily comes to be of central importance.[3]

Viewing folk psychology in these terms, Wundt looked about for the elements of the "folk mind" that would correspond to the elements of the individual mind (imagination, feeling, volition) in terms of which he built up his general psychology, in order that he might build up his folk psychology in corresponding manner.[4] He decided that they are language, mythology, and custom. In terms of these elements, the problem of folk psychology translated itself, therefore, into "a study of the developmental principles of language, mythology and custom,"[5] such related phenomena as religion, art, law, and social organization, with which his folk psychology likewise deals, being regarded by Wundt as inseparable in their origin from the three fundamental elements of the folk mind noted.[6]

In performing its task, Wundt pointed out, folk psychology, like other fields of investigation, may pursue different methods. "The course that first suggests itself," according to him, "is to single out one important phenomenon of community life after another and to trace its development after the usual pattern of general psychology in its analysis of individual consciousness." This mode of procedure is especially adapted for an intensive treatment of the subject, Wundt felt, and he therefore followed it in the *Völkerpsychologie*.[7] This intensive treatment

[1] See *supra*, p. 47.

[2] *Völkerpsychologie*, vol. I, pp. 3–5.

[3] *Ibid.*, p. 4; *Elements of Folk Psychology*, p. 4. Lazarus and Steinthal answered Wundt on this matter of the program of folk psychology (see *Philosophische Studien*, vol. I, pp. 1–29, and *Ztschr. f. Völkerps. u. Sprachw.*, vol. 17, pp. 233–264, 1887).

[4] *Völkerpsychologie*, vol. I, pp. 24–28; also BRETT, *A History of Psychology*, vol. III, p. 292; HAEBERLIN, "The Theoretical Foundations of Wundt's Folk-Psychology," *Psychol. Rev.*, vol. 23, pp. 287 ff., 1916.

[5] Subtitle of the *Völkerpsychologie*.

[6] *Völkerpsychologie*, vol. I, pp. 36–39.

[7] In this monumental work Wundt deals with language (vols. I–II), art (vol. III), mythology and religion (vols. IV–VI), social organization (vols. VII–VIII), law (vol. IX), culture and history (vol. X).

of the subject has the objection, however, according to him, "of severing mental development into a number of separate phases, whereas in reality, they are in constant interrelation," particularly in the early stages when the several phases are "so intertwined that they are scarcely separable from one another."[1] To offset this objection, he tells us, he found it necessary to supplement this intensive treatment by a synthetic survey, such as he presents in the *Elements*. Here, instead of treating successively one phenomenon after another, his procedure consists, as he tells us, "in regarding the main stages of the development with which folk psychology is concerned in their sequence, and each in the total interconnection of its phenomena," so that a connected presentation is possible. Such a connected survey, he held, is not only necessary as a supplement to the more detailed treatment of the subject matter of folk psychology, but it is really the chief purpose of folk-psychological investigation. From the standpoint of his conception, the *Völkerpsychologie* may thus be regarded as but a necessary preliminary for the synthetic survey of the *Elements*.[2] At any rate, it is to the *Elements* that we must turn to get Wundt's folk psychology in systematic form, although his larger work is actually the more valuable, for the very reason that it is more concrete and concerned with the analysis of specific problems.

In accordance with his plan of procedure in this work, as indicated, Wundt divided his discussion in the *Elements* into four psychological eras or ages, which he designated respectively the age of "primitive man," the "totemic age," the "age of heroes and gods," and the "development of humanity," the last being the age "that is coming to be."[3] These are, according to Wundt, "stages of mental development still exhibited by mankind." In its investigation of them, folk psychology "reveals well-defined primitive conditions, with transitions leading through an almost continuous series of intermediate steps to the more developed and higher civilizations." Folk psychology is thus, "in an important sense of the word, *genetic psychology*,"[4] he tells us.

If the psychological characteristics of these respective stages could once be established, Wundt held in the spirit of classical evolutionary thought, we should have an objective standard for the developmental classification of all peoples and cultures. It was his aim to begin the work of such a psychological characterization through his synthetic treatment of these periods.

While Wundt recognized more clearly perhaps than most evolutionary writers that such classification is more or less arbitrary, he felt that it was useful in much the same way as our accepted classification of the

[1] *Elements of Folk Psychology*, p. 6.
[2] *Ibid.*, pp. xiii, 7.
[3] *Ibid.*, p. 9.
[4] *Ibid.*, p. 4.

individual life into childhood, youth, and manhood. In each case, according to him, "there are certain ideas, emotions, and springs of action about which the various phenomena group themselves" and which can thereby be singled out as the basis of classification.[1]

Wundt recognized also, of course, that folk psychology, particularly in dealing with the problems of origin which his work stressed, was largely on a hypothetical level and so was forced to concern itself with matters which were chiefly in the realm of supposition and dispute. Recognizing this difficulty, he nevertheless defended the folk-psychological interest in origins. "It must not be forgotten," he said, "that folk psychology rests on precisely the same experiential basis, as regards these matters, as do all other empirical sciences." "The hypotheses of folk psychology," he explained, "never refer to a background of things or to origins that are by nature inaccessible to experiential knowledge; they are simply assumptions concerning a number of conjectured empirical facts, that for some reason or other, elude positive detection." The conjectured process, however, moves from beginning to end "on the factual plane." It is this factual basis which establishes the superiority of folk psychology over philosophy of history, he held.[2]

In accordance with the requirements of this empirical movement of folk psychology, Wundt says, he adopted the method of first describing the external facts of culture in the different periods, as they are supplied by ethnology, and only on the basis of these considering psychological implications and explanations.[3] Only in this way did he undertake to pass in review the cultural development of mankind through the four stages mentioned above, giving particular emphasis to the earlier stages and the problem of origins. Viewing his task in the large, he exclaims:

How immense is the chasm between the secret barter of primitive man who steals out of the primeval forest by night and lays down his captured game to exchange it, unseen by his neighbors, for implements and objects of adornment, and the commerce of an age when fleets traverse the seas, and eventually ships course through the air, uniting the peoples of all parts of the world into one great commercial community! We cannot undertake to delineate all aspects of this development, for the latter includes the entire history of mankind. Our concern is merely to indicate the outstanding psychological factors fundamental to the progression of the latter from that which was original, of the more perfect from the primitive, partly under the pressure of external conditions of life and partly as a result of man's own creative power.[4]

It is unnecessary and impossible to go into the details of this survey here, for the detailed consideration of Wundt's treatment of cultural

[1] *Ibid.*, p. 7.
[2] *Ibid.*, pp. xv–xvi, 519–523.
[3] *Ibid.*, pp. xiv–xvi, 7–10.
[4] *Ibid.*, p. 10.

development is, of course, essentially a matter of anthropological concern.[1] It is already sufficiently clear, however, that in so far as the general pattern of Wundt's discussion is concerned, it has much in common with classical evolutionary anthropology, so that as a system it is open to much the same sort of criticism.[2] It has been said that Wundt's folk psychology represents a heroic attempt to save philosophy of history for science, but philosophy of history is after all one thing, and social psychology, in the stricter sense of recent thought, quite another. In any event, whatever may be said for Wundt's folk psychology as a system of anthropology, ethnology, and history, it is certainly not social psychology in the usual understanding of the latter field of investigation, except as Wundt incidentally touches on the subject and as he incidentally incorporates the social-psychological perspective in the treatment of specific problems.[3] In this respect, however, Wundt's work is of very considerable social-psychological importance. This is strikingly brought out in his discussion of language, which by way of illustration, will accordingly be considered here briefly in its social-psychological import.

Emphasizing the problem of origins in connection with the phenomenon of language, as elsewhere, Wundt related it to emotional expression and other elementary forms of social gesture. Human language, according to his treatment of the subject, is neither a special creation nor the result of the conscious desire to communicate the results of intellectual reflection, as had so long been held by psychology, but a highly evolved and conventionalized form of natural gesture, which is intimately related to such other forms of communicative gesture as emotional cries, animal calls, the gesture language of deaf-mutes, child language, etc. The characteristic which distinguishes human language from lower forms of communicative gesture, according to Wundt, is its ideational content. By virtue of this associated ideational content, movements expressive of emotions come to be expressions also of ideas; the communication of an individual's experience to others results in an exchange of thought as well as in an exchange of emotional attitudes, and the effect is language with its rich psychological and cultural setting, instead of gesture merely.[4]

Wundt saw clearly that this characteristic of human language gives it a peculiarly social significance. Language is not only the basic instru-

---

[1] See in this connection GOLDENWEISER, *Early Civilization*, pp. 348–350, 359; "Cultural Anthropology," *The History and Prospects of the Social Sciences*, ed. by Barnes, pp. 218–219, 230.

[2] See *infra*, pp. 123*ff*., 166*ff*.; also BRETT, *A History of Psychology*, vol. III, pp. 291*ff*.; HAEBERLIN, *Psychol. Rev.*, vol. 23, pp. 295*ff*., 1916; GOLDENWEISER, *Early Civilization*, pp. 20*ff*., 348*ff*.

[3] *Cf.* BRETT, *A History of Psychology*, vol. III, pp. 292–293.

[4] *Elements of Folk Psychology*, pp. 53*ff*.; *Völkerpsychologie*, especially vol. I, Introduction, and Chaps. I, II, III, vol. II, Chap. IX; JUDD, *Psychology*, pp. 209*ff*., 2d ed., 1917; article on "Language" (Psychology of), *Cyclopedia of Education*, ed. by Monroe; *The Psychology of Social Institutions*, Chap. X.

ment through which the higher mental processes of the individual develop
and express themselves, but it is at the same time preeminently a social
act. It is both the means and the product of social life. In consequence
of language, according to Wundt, the human group becomes something
more than a mere herd; it develops precisely into a *human* horde or
community, welded together through a "community of language."[1]
Language is thus of fundamental importance for the understanding of
both the individual mind as well as of the "social mind." Accordingly,
in Wundt's system of psychological thought, it is in language that
individual and folk psychology most conspicuously overlap. This is,
however, as far as Wundt got in his social-psychological theory. Language is the necessary medium for man's mental development and function, and language being social in origin and nature, man's mental life is
necessarily linked up with his social environment and the collective mind.
That man's mental life itself is thereby made a social product and that
this fact has methodological consequences of broad social-psychological
import is a step ahead which Wundt's work variously suggested, but
which it did not in any sense actually encompass.

That language has come to be recognized as so very important a
factor in mental development and social life is nevertheless in no small
measure due to Wundt's work. The trend of thought which Wundt
developed in his discussion of language was not new in its elements but
it was new and compelling in its organization. German philologists and
folk psychologists had for some time maintained that language is very
closely interlinked with mental development and unified social life,[2] and
the comparative evolutionary literature of the day was consistently
arguing continuity of development in every phase of what seemed to be
distinctly human culture. But it was left for Wundt to bring the
Darwinian point of view to bear upon the problem of language in such a
way as to suggest the fundamental connection which exists between the
mental life of the individual, language as a communicative gesture, and
the development of group unity and culture.

Wundt's analysis of the other elements of culture is similar in its
social-psychological implications. Throughout, the effect of his argument, if it is disconnected from its evolutionary setting, is the establishment of an intimate connection between the mental processes of the
individual, the cultural life of the social group, and the unification of
the human community.[3]

[1] *Elements of Folk Psychology*, pp. 2–3, 52–53; *Völkerpsychologie*, vol. I, pp. 19–25,
43–50.

[2] The study of language was from the first a very strong interest in folk psychology.

[3] See, *Völkerpsychologie*, vol. I, pp. 19–25, 36–43, vol. III, pp. 5–12, vol. IV, pp.
3–7, etc.; *Elements of Folk Psychology*, pp. 2–5, 50–53, 94ff., etc.; JUDD, *The Psychology of Social Institutions*, Preface and Chap. I; GOLDENWEISER, *Early Civilization*,
pp. 348–360.

In all this, Wundt was of course on fundamental social-psychological ground, and frequently he was clearly on the way to conceiving the human mind in fundamental social-psychological terms.   Nevertheless his work did not net social-psychological theory except in the incidental manner indicated above.[1] For he was deflected from a direct attack upon the social-psychological problems of relation which his work touched upon, just as the other folk psychologists had been, by the philosophical setting which defined the outlook of this school of thought and by the conditions which he assumed were basic to the social-psychological process.

While Wundt apparently recognized clearly enough, then, the need of supplementing the psychological study of the individual mind by a study of culture and social life, and while he recognized clearly enough, also, that the latter is intimately interlinked with the former in human life, he very largely overlooked the social-psychological importance of the process of functional interrelationship which binds these two levels of psychic phenomena and unites them into a single functional whole, and which has its methodological implications, as we now know, for the study of the one order of psychic fact just as surely as for the other. In other words, whatever may be said of Wundt's folk-psychological work in other connections, as social psychology, it still very largely fell short of the more direct methods of approach and conception of functional relationship between the individual and the social, which we gradually get, especially in French and American social-psychological thought. Instead, like the other German folk psychologists of the period, Wundt passed this problem over by leaving the Hegelian notion vaguely in the air that the process of individual mental development is, in its social aspects, somehow identified with the evolution of the "objective mind," remaining thereby content with his basically individualistic analysis of human psychic phenomena, both personal and social.[2]

Accordingly, though it cannot be questioned—as exponents of other than the folk-psychological school of thought have sometimes been tempted to question[3]—that Wundt and the other folk psychologists were concerning themselves, in their way, with some of the basic considerations of social psychology and that, for reasons already indicated, they have, in fact, played a considerable role in the modern social-psychological movement, social psychology, especially as we know it in this country, still remains something quite distinct in conception, approach, and content from the historical evolutionism and analogical mysticism with which folk psychology, as represented alike by Wundt and the earlier folk psychologists, met the social-psychological aspects of its field of interest.   Looking

[1] See *supra*, p. 61.
[2] *Cf.* BRETT, *A History of Psychology*, vol. III, pp. 292–293.
[3] See TOSTI, "Social Psychology and Sociology," *Psychol. Rev.*, vol. 5, p. 352, 1898.

back upon the efforts of the folk psychologists from the modern social-psychological standpoint in this country, Dewey, for instance, says:

I shall avoid engaging in the disputed question of the value of an introspective psychology. But it seems almost self-evident that even if introspection were a valid method in individual psychology, so called, it could not be of use in the investigation of social facts, even though those facts be labelled social mind or consciousness. Yet one has only to look at the writings of the Austrian and German School of "folk-psychologists" (say of Wundt, obviously the most important) to see how this treatment has been affected by an assumed need of making the method and results of social psychology conform to the received categories of introspective psychology.[1]

According to this view, the persistence of the analogical procedure of folk psychology in the field of social-psychological investigation is one of the chief causes of the backwardness of modern social psychology.[2] And yet, as we have already seen, folk psychology has not been without its distinct fruitfulness for the modern social-psychological movement. For aside from its specific contribution to social-psychological thought, which, as in the case of Wundt's analysis of language, was considerable, folk psychology brought support in an important way to the growing dissatisfaction with psychological individualism and to the resulting interest in the study of psychic phenomena from more adequate social standpoints. In particular it stimulated the psychological study of culture with this interest in view, and, incidentally in this connection, it forced to the forefront of attention various aspects of the "group-mind" theory of social life, through its attempt to establish the cultural significance of such phenomena as it designated by the terms "folk," "people," "folk mind," "social consciousness," "group will," etc. Important, also, is the fact that folk psychology stressed the psychological standpoint in the study of social phenomena at a time when the tendency was toward a one-sided overemphasis of the biological standpoint. These were contributions which were reflected indirectly even in this country, through Wundt's American followers and students in the field of psychology—through whom Wundt's psychology, and through it German psychological thought generally, became an increasingly important factor in American thought—as well as through German sociological, anthropological, and philosophical thought.[3]

More direct influence of folk-psychological theory on social psychology in this country is, however, not easily traceable. Folk psychol-

---

[1] "The Need for Social Psychology," *Psychol. Rev.*, vol. 24, pp. 270–271, 1917.

[2] See *ibid.*

[3] Hall and Cattell in the field of psychology, Judd in the field of educational psychology, Small in the field of sociology, and Boas in the field of anthropology reflect this influence prominently. James, Baldwin, Dewey, and Mead represent it less directly. These names are sufficient to suggest the importance of this direction of influence. See *infra*, pp. 245*ff.*, 266*ff.*

ogy as a social-psychological movement never struck root here for several reasons. In the first place, as has already been noted, the historical approach of folk psychology tended to link this field of endeavor chiefly with anthropology rather than with social psychology as specialized fields of investigation.[1] Then, too, folk psychology was already superseded by more spectacular social-psychological developments when social-psychological thought in this country began to come into its own. Again, American psycho-social thought in its early development, when we are most concerned with folk psychology as a general social-psychological movement, was tied up more directly with French and English influences than with German. The latter became an important factor only gradually as a result of the close contact with German thought which followed in the wake of the movement toward study in German universities toward the close of the nineteenth century. And even then, contact with German psycho-social thought followed chiefly through the older fields of psychological and social science on the one hand, and through German philosophy on the other, rather than through folk psychology. By this time, furthermore, distinct tendencies of social-psychological thought were already in the process of formation here, so that such German influences as were thus being introduced were necessarily reinterpreted in the light of the local situation and the previously organized intellectual background of American psychological and social thought. It is in this reinterpreted form that German thought is reflected, for instance, in Baldwin's work and, through him, in most of the social-psychological work which has since appeared in this country.[2]

---

[1] See *supra*, pp. 50–51.

[2] A notable recent example of the more direct influence of German and especially Wundt's folk psychology in this field of thought is to be had in JUDD, *Psychology of Social Institutions* (1926). The foundations of his thinking in this work, Judd tells us, were laid by the teachings of Wundt, "whose lectures and volumes on social psychology constitute the most elaborate contribution which has ever been made in this field." Preface, p. v. See in this connection also comment on Hall and section on Mead, *infra*, pp. 267, 318.

Since the war there has been a revival of interest in the social-psychological aspects of folk psychology in Germany. The *Zeitschrift für Völkerpsychologic und Soziologie*, vol. I (1925), represents this interest prominently. See the opening article by Thurnwald for a statement of its relation to the earlier *Zeitschrift für Völkerpsychologie und Sprachwissenschaft;* see also his succeeding articles in this journal, as well as an article in the *Kölner Vier. f. Soziol.*, vol. IV, pp. 32–43, 1924, for a statement on the more recent status of folk psychology in German thought and its relation especially to the developing social-psychological interests of German sociology. Thurnwald is on much the same ground as are an increasing number of American writers in emphasizing the cultural aspects of social psychology. See in this connection *infra*, pp. 267 and 380 *ff*. But this development, along with other recent developments in German psychological and social thought, has as yet scarcely had any noticeable effect upon American social psychology.

III. Social-psychological Aspects of German Sociology

From the standpoint of modern social psychology, folk psychology was one of the important results growing out of the dissatisfaction with the individualistic approach of traditional psychology in later nineteenth century German thought, and the development of modern sociological theory was the other. Folk psychology identified itself from the first chiefly with the field of historical and anthropological source material and the special problems of culture history and culture origins. For the most part it did not interfere, therefore, with the parallel development alongside of it in Germany and Austria of modern sociology, although it naturally determined the latter field to some extent on the ground of division of labor. But at any rate, unlike the situation in England, where evolutionary anthropology and the evolutionary treatment of social phenomena practically preempted the field of psycho-social investigation for some time following the early work of Darwin and Spencer, we have in Germany and Austria, developing alongside of and parallel with modern anthropology and folk psychology, also the social-economic and social-political analysis of social life, especially in terms of the study of the modern state, by such followers in the tradition of Comte and Spencer, as Schäffle, Gumplowicz, Ratzenhofer, Simmel, etc.[1] As in the case of folk psychology, this treatment of social life has certain notable social-psychological bearings which it is necessary to touch upon briefly here, although in keeping its view focused chiefly on the objective aspects of social organization to the practical disregard of its subjective psychological aspects, German sociological thought remained, at any rate during its early development, more closely identified with social psychology as it is at present understood, in name and general tendency as over against the individualistic approach in the study of human phenomena, than in specific viewpoint and distinctive interest.

The close association and partial identification of social-psychological and sociological thought which we find at the present time have come

[1] In a general way folk psychology represents the historical approach in the study of culture and social life, and sociology the analytical approach, but inasmuch as the relation between these two approaches in the field of psycho-social thought has been a subject of much controversy especially in Germany (see *infra*, pp. 76ff., 81ff.), it is but natural to find these fields overlapping and merging into each other at times, as appears strikingly in the case of such German writers as Gumplowicz (see *infra*, pp. 71–72), Vierkandt, *Naturvölker und Kulturvölker, ein Beitrag zur Sozialpsychologie* (1896), and Thurnwald (see references to the *Ztschr. f. Völkerps. u. Soziol., supra*, p. 65, note 2). Recently such overlapping has become much more pronounced, in consequence of the renewed theoretical defense which has been made of the culture-historical approach in Germany. This, however, is an aspect of the developing reaction against positivism in German psycho-social thought which has a somewhat different basis and hence will be dealt with in another connection (see *infra*, pp. 84 *ff.*).

about through the rise into prominence of psychological sociology, and while German sociological thought has made some important contributions to this trend of sociological development, as will presently appear, it has been French and American sociology which have stood out most prominently in this respect. Still, even the earlier work of the German and Austrian sociological students of society has features of social-psychological interest which cannot be passed by here. This is more especially the case because the background of individualistic thought upon which modern social psychology began to take form, made social-psychological progress largely dependent on the previous sociological preparation of the ground and on the balancing effect which its emphasis on the objective social-environment aspect of human life introduced, as over against the individualistic emphasis of general psychology.[1] It is in this respect primarily that some of the following writers assume importance here.

1. Albert Schäffle (1831–1903)

It is of interest to note here, therefore, that the eminent German follower of Comte and Spencer, Albert Schäffle, in his *Bau und Leben des socialen Körpers* (first, four-volume edition, 1875–1878), devoted a whole section of more than three hundred pages to the treatment of what he termed "The Psychic Facts of Social Life in Their General Bearing or the General Phenomena of the Folk-mind," under the explanatory heading of "Outline of Social Psychology."[2] In the second edition of his work (two-volume edition, 1896), this section was naturally condensed, but it still appears as one of the main divisions of his treatment of social life, and the term "social psychology" still appears alongside of "social morphology" and "social physiology" as a basic concept in his analogical scheme of social thought.[3]

Schäffle's treatment of "the mental life of society," developed for the most part in terms of an objectively interpreted super-individualistic psychology of "social cognition, feeling, and will" as applied to the description of objective social organization, was an attempt to carry out Herbart's suggestion for a supplementary "social" psychology in another direction from that which folk psychology sought to follow out.[4] Depending avowedly on analogical elaboration, which, moreover, was in large part biological rather than psychological in orientation, it resulted in little that was immediately an advance upon the social-

[1] See *supra*, p. 3.

[2] Vol. I, Part IV, pp. 392–730.

[3] Vol. I, Part V, pp. 176–266. A reproduction of the scheme of the second edition of Schäffle's work is to be found in SMALL, *General Sociology*, Part III; see also SMALL and VINCENT, *Introduction to the Study of Society*, the organization of which definitely reflects Schäffle's influence.

[4] See *supra*, p. 49.

psychological aspects of folk psychology, except that Schäffle's work supplemented the latter in the study of present-day social life and that it connected up directly with the whole trend of nineteenth century sociological thought and criticism of psychological individualism. Apart from the fact that it brought the term "social psychology" conspicuously into use in this connection,[1] Schäffle's work is notable here, therefore, chiefly as an elaboration and variation of the Spencerian biological standpoint as applied to the interpretation of social life, and especially of the method of organic analogy as it was introduced by Spencer through his *Principles of Sociology*.[2]

Schäffle, it is true, emphasized function more than Spencer in his system of social analogy, and he remained sufficiently under the domination of the Hegelian trend of thought to give a much more important place to the psychological, group, and purposive aspects of social life. In consequence, he recognized the need of a "social psychology" in common with the folk psychologists, while Spencer did not, except in a very incidental manner. But potentially suggestive as was this conception in the general setting of Schäffle's work as a whole, his own procedure did not carry him very far in giving it concrete expression, for the simple reason that his approach was not easily adaptable to the purposes of this part of his system.[3] The method of organic analogy, even in Schäffle's hands, netted little more for social psychology, in fact, than a crudely realistic emphasis on the notion of mental interrelation and social unity in human society and a more concrete description of some of the known facts of psycho-social interdependence.

---

[1] A still earlier use of this term in a similar connection to that in which Schäffle used it is to be found in Lindner, *Ideen zur Psychologie der Gesellschaft* (1871). Lindner sought to carry out the parallelism between the psychology of the individual mind and the psychology of the state in strict conformity with the suggestion which Herbart made for a statics and dynamics of the state corresponding to his statics and dynamics of the individual mind. Taking issue with the folk psychologists, Lindner maintained that the modern state is a much more fruitful field for the study of the social aspects of mind than the folk community, and he applied himself to the task, accordingly, of outlining the general form which such a psychological study of the state should take. To differentiate his work, too, from the current *Völkerpsychologie* he, like Schäffle, proposed to name the new field of investigation *Sozialpsychologie*. But aside from the historical interest which might attach to this use of the term "social psychology," Lindner's work can have little social-psychological significance at the present time, since it is developed on purely deductive lines outlining the social applicability of the Herbartian introspective psychology. In so far as American social psychology is concerned, furthermore, the writer has found no reference to it directly or indirectly of importance here.

[2] See *supra*, pp. 36 *ff.*; also SMALL, *General Sociology*, Chap. XI.

[3] See PARK and BURGESS, *Introduction to the Science of Sociology*, pp. 28–29; DAVIS, *Psychological Interpretations of Society*, pp. 39–40; SMALL, *General Sociology*, Chap. XI; BOGARDUS, *A History of Social Thought*, Chap. XVI.

Social psychology may be said to begin only where the bio-organic analogy fails. In frankly directing his attention to the elaboration of the latter, therefore, Schäffle, like Spencer and the other representatives of the bio-organic school of social thought, was accordingly more successful in preparing the ground for social-psychological investigation than in building up what might reasonably be regarded as social-psychological theory itself.[1] In this respect, however, Schäffle's work had some notable results for social-psychological thought in Germany and elsewhere, and it is necessary to indicate some of them here.

In the first place, Schäffle turned sharply from the mere historico-evolutionary treatment of psycho-social phenomena that was so popular in Germany at the time and directed his attention primarily to the analysis of present-day social life in terms of the modern state.[2] While recognizing the importance of the historical approach and seeking to round out his analysis through a theoretical consideration of the essential facts of social and cultural evolution,[3] his basic method was nevertheless definitely directed to the study of the social process through its functional analysis in present-day social life. The social-psychological importance of this feature of Schäffle's work consisted in the fact that, however artificial his own treatment of social life was, it helped to shift attention from the inferential subject matter with which the evolutionary social studies of the day were so largely concerned and to direct it instead to the investigation of social life in more easily accessible and directly verifiable form. As a result of this shift of attention, Schäffle's work became an important factor in bringing about the gradual differentiation of the social-psychological from the historical problem and in helping to liberate social-psychological thought from the unrelieved confusion of historical involvement in which contemporary evolutionary and folk-psychological theory had for the time left it.

Then, too, Schäffle's work, not unlike that of Comte and Spencer, with which he primarily sought to link it, contributed materially to the spread of the naturalistic conception of psychic phenomena. The very association of the term "social mind," for instance, with Schäffle's biological approach in the description of the "social body" was itself an unfavorable setting for some of the historical mysticism with which Hegelian and folk-psychological thought had surrounded this concept and social-psychological thought relating to it generally in Germany.

[1] Folk psychology as it has been considered here was on analogical ground too in its assumption of the applicability of the concepts and principles of introspective psychology to the study of the "social mind," as we have seen. But it was not as conspicuously and systematically so, and, in addition, this aspect of its thought was in large part overshadowed by its historical outlook and its interest in concrete historical and anthropological material.

[2] See BRISTOL, *Social Adaptation*, p. 126.

[3] See SMALL, *General Sociology*, pp. 160–163.

Taken in conjunction with his detailed analysis of objective social organization in the modern state and his attempt to present psycho-social function in terms of the institutional instruments of present-day social and intellectual life as well as in the more usual folk-psychological terms of language and culture, this was a most important feature of Schäffle's work. Notable here especially is the fact that it brought Schäffle's work into more direct relation with the course of social-psychological events outside of Germany than was the case with a great deal of German folk psychology, so that his work has played something of a role in the modern social-psychological movement even in this country.[1]

Again, in Schäffle's work the social group plays a distinctly important methodological role as over against the individual. And while this emphasis upon the social group did not lead to very fruitful social-psychological results in Schäffle's own case, for the reasons already indicated, it was a definite step ahead, following Comte and Spencer, in the sociological challenge of the prevalent individualistic mode of thought and procedure, which was bound to bear social-psychological fruit in the long run.

It is of interest to note in these connections that Schäffle, like the folk psychologists, made his departure in his conception of a "social psychology" from Herbart, who had entertained the conception of a social psychology, Schäffle felt as had Lazarus and Steinthal, but just missed developing one.[2] Modern social-psychological thought in Germany, despite its more or less distinct folk-psychological and sociological directions of development, thus flows from Herbart as the common and important point of departure alongside of Hegel. Schäffle deliberately chose to designate the new field of investigation "social psychology" in preference to the alternative "folk psychology," because he felt that the mystical fashion in which the folk psychologists had been using the term "folk mind" had made their distinctive designation of the field undesirable for his purposes, and because he was eager to differentiate his work from theirs on that account.[3] Wundt, on the other hand, as we have seen, found the term social psychology inapplicable to his work, because it was associated by Schäffle, and following him increasingly by other sociologists, with the analysis of the social process in present-day

---

[1] See *supra*, pp. 50–51, 65. Schäffle's treatment of the subject of social psychology was reinterpreted along with other parts of Schäffle's social theory and introduced into the literature of American psycho-social thought by Small and Vincent in their *Introduction to the Study of Society* (1894), where, following Schäffle, they devoted one of the five main sections of their work to "social psychology." This appears to be the earliest conspicuous use of this term in American thought. With the appearance of Baldwin's *Social and Ethical Interpretations* (1896), this treatment of the subject was, however, very soon overshadowed (see *infra*, p. 278).

[2] *Bau und Leben des Socialen Körpers*, 1st. ed., pp. 392, 421, 427*ff*.

[3] See his *Abriss der Soziologie*, pp. 70, 156.

social life.[1]   The progress of social-psychological development, especially outside of Germany, has for the most part run clear of the differences which separated Wundt's and Schäffle's work, but it has, on the whole, supported Schäffle's choice rather than Wundt's and left his designation largely in possession of the field of thought to which, in their respective ways, both of these two writers aimed in notable fashion to contribute.[2]

2. Ludwig Gumplowicz (1838-1909) and Gustav Ratzenhofer (1842-1904)

The general theories of these two writers and the contributions which they made to the advance of psycho-social thought have been made common knowledge in this country, in the one case by Ward who regarded Gumplowicz's race-conflict theory as the most important contribution to sociological theory since Comte and Spencer,[3] and in the other case by Small who placed a similarly high estimate upon Ratzenhofer's theory of interests.   Small also built up his own sociological theory, which links up in more than one direction with the development of American social-psychological thought, about Ratzenhofer's theory of interests and about a reinterpretation of his analysis of the social process in terms of this theory.[4]   It is thereby necessary to indicate only the specific social-psychological bearings of their work here in continuation of our discussion of the direction of influence represented by Schäffle.

Gumplowicz and Ratzenhofer did not direct special attention to the new field of social-psychological investigation, as did the other writers so far discussed here, but their work, especially that of Ratzenhofer, has some notable social-psychological bearings from our standpoint, nevertheless. In the case of Gumplowicz, this followed more or less incidentally in consequence of his more decisive influence along similar lines to those of Schäffle: his more decided social determinism and general emphasis on the social group as the basic unit of interpretation in sociology;[5] his more critical treatment of social life in terms of specific social groups and processes rather than in terms of the vague conceptions of "society" and "humanity as a whole" which give the setting of Comte's and Spencer's and to a lesser degree also of Schäffle's work; his clearer conception of the function of sociology as a natural science; the more definite methodology of social analysis which his work incorporates; and so on.

[1] See *supra*, p. 55.

[2] For a further discussion of Schäffle's sociological theory, see SMALL, *General Sociology*, Part III; JACOBS, *German Sociology*, pp. 7, 18, 38, 73; BRISTOL, *Social Adaptation*, pp. 123*ff.*; BOGARDUS, *A History of Social Thought*, pp. 271*ff*; SOROKIN, *Contemporary Sociological Theories*, pp. 200*ff.*

[3] *Pure Sociology*, pp. 203 *ff.*

[4] *General Sociology*, pp. 189 *ff*.

[5] Gumplowicz regarded LeBon's sociological point of view, in consequence, as an improvement upon that of folk psychology (see his *Outlines of Sociology*, trans. by Moore, p. 214).

In other respects, Gumplowicz's sociological work is closely related to the work of the folk psychologists, as he himself indicated.[1] Like them, Gumplowicz was interested chiefly in the historical and evolutionary treatment of the social process—in a "natural history of mankind or civilization," that is—and like them he largely fell back, in consequence, on the field of anthropological and historical source material.[2] But in his general approach and emphasis, Gumplowicz chiefly followed along the sociological lines of Comte and Spencer rather than along those of the folk psychologists. The characteristic race-struggle and group-conflict theory of the social process which he thereby arrived at suggests strongly the Marxian class-struggle theory and, back of it, the whole Hegelian as well as the Spencerian and Darwinian schemes of evolutionary thought, with its emphasis on ethnic "peoples" as the instruments of world progress and the principle of evolution through the progressive synthesis of unlike elements, which is thus brought to mind.[3] It represents one of the notable modern attempts to formulate the "conflict" theory of social life and to interpret the "survival-of-the-fittest" principle in terms of collectivistic social thought.

This theory seemed more important a few decades ago when interest centered, as it did with Ward, about the application of the evolutionary theory to the realm of psycho-social interpretation. At the present time it, and Gumplowicz's work as a whole in so far as it centers about the elaboration of this theory, can have place only alongside of the many other particularistic conceptions and treatments of the social process, including, of course, such as have stressed the opposite tendency, namely, cooperation. Historically, however, Gumplowicz's work operated as an important counterbalancing factor to the individualistic interpretations of the social process, such as Spencer's work, for instance, popularized.[4] In conjunction with other influences tending in the same direction, especially French collectivistic sociology, it played a conspicuous role in leading over to the more balanced standpoint regarding the interplay of individual and social elements in the social process, which is, in general, characteristic of modern social-psychological thought. Among modern social theorists only Durkheim pushed his emphasis upon the dynamic importance of the social factor more insistently than did Gumplowicz.[5]

---

[1] See his Foreword and Chap. I in *Der Rassenkampf;* also *supra,* p. 66, note 1.

[2] *Cf.* JACOBS, *German Sociology,* pp. 12, 59.

[3] See *Der Rassenkampf,* especially Part IV; *Outlines of Sociology,* pp. 110 *ff.*

[4] Gumplowicz quite reversed the usual psychological approach in social interpretation and maintained that the individual is to be understood through the social group instead of the group through its component individuals (see his *Outlines of Sociology,* Part IV).

[5] For a further discussion of Gumplowicz's sociological theory see SMALL, *General Sociology,* pp. 86–87, 600–602; JACOBS, *German Sociology,* pp. 7, 28, 50, 57, 63; BRISTOL, *Social Adaptation,* pp. 162–170; BOGARDUS, *A History of Social Theory,* pp. 338–341;

Gumplowicz's analysis of the social process in terms of group conflict and group interest was supplemented by Ratzenhofer's theory of personal interests. In conjunction with this aspect of his theory, as Small has pointed out with careful detail, Ratzenhofer, for the first time in German sociological thought, deliberately shifted emphasis from the objective facts of social organization as the important phenomena of sociological concern to persons and personal motives.[1] Thereby he took an important step for the advance of German as well as general sociological theory along the lines of modern psychological development, which naturally brings it into much more intimate interrelation with social psychology. In consequence of this shift of emphasis, in fact, Ratzenhofer placed himself more directly in line with the approach of modern social psychology than any of the German sociologists of the older school, excepting only, perhaps, Simmel.

By combining the Hegelian, Comtean, and Spencerian trends of social thought with the standpoint of the Austrian psychological school of economics[2], Ratzenhofer arrived at a theory of human interests as the basic facts of social interpretation which was very similar to Ward's theory of human desires, as a comparison with the latter in Part II of this survey will readily reveal and as Ward himself recognized.[3] Ratzenhofer's theory appeared in a less challenging general theoretical setting than did Ward's, but it gained in significance from the social-psychological standpoint, because it was associated with the group approach which Ratzenhofer, in common with the other German sociologists, incorporated into his work, and which, in various ways, has played such an important role in the modern social-psychological movement.[4]

Of course, neither Ward nor Ratzenhofer used the theory of desires, wants, and interests critically from our modern standpoint, for neither had the background of information necessary for the critical development of such a theory of the basic springs of human action as each felt the need for. But in view of the social-psychological importance which was later attached to the approach of instinct psychology, their theories take on a direct significance here, in that they offered an alternative orientation to that of modern instinct theory and indirectly, also, a basis of sociological criticism of the latter theory.

LICHTENBERGER, *Development of Social Theory*, Chap. XV; SOROKIN, *Contemporary Sociological Theories*, pp. 480–487.

[1] See SMALL, *General Sociology*, pp. 188 *ff*.

[2] See SMALL, *Origins of Sociology*, note, p. 157, pp. 303–304.

[3] *Pure Sociology*, pp. 21–22.

[4] For a discussion of the important role which this approach has played in American social thought see BODENHAFER, "The Comparative Role of the Group Concept in Ward's *Dynamic Sociology* and Contemporary American Sociology," *Amer. Jour. Sociol.*, vol. 26, pp. 273, 425, 588, 716, 1920–1921.

Ratzenhofer's interest theory, as he himself developed it, was intimately bound up with his monistic philosophical conception of the universe and his metaphysics of "original power" (*Urkraft*), looked upon by him as the basic creative principle of life. Interest, according to him, is the organic embodiment of this basic creative principle. He thought of man as being physiologically endowed with a single general interest that is expressive of this "original power," and he regarded all specific human interests, in the form in which we know them in the world of concrete human motive, as developments of this innate general interest, in consciousness and under the influence of the specific environment. As thus specifically constituted, human interests are desires subjectively and needs or wants objectively. Under the stress of the inner feeling of necessity that characterizes them and expresses their relation to "original power," they become the drives to activity that is calculated to satisfy them, and thereby they determine the run of attention, purpose, will, and human conduct generally.

Ratzenhofer presented a logical classification of human interests by dividing the innate general interest into five specialized classes as follows: (1) the sex interest, (2) the physiological interest (the interest in keeping alive), (3) the individual interest, (4) the social interest, (5) the transcendental interest.[1] He also worked out detailed classifications of the concrete social interests which are operative in the modern political state and, more particularly, in the Austrian state at the time.[2] In these more specific forms, he applied his interest theory systematically in the interpretation of the social process, viewing it as a product of the complex interplay of human motives as thus defined by him.[3]

But as developed by himself, Ratzenhofer's theory gained only a limited influence in German sociological thought, and it attracted very little attention outside of Austria and Germany.[4] In this country, however, it was stripped of its philosophical encumbrances and reinterpreted and developed by Small, who, as said above, built up his own system of sociological thought largely around it and the group approach with which it is linked in Ratzenhofer's sociology.[5] In this reinterpreted form, Ratzenhofer's theory has entered into the stream of American psycho-

---

[1] *Die sociologische Erkenntniss*, pp. 56 *ff.*

[2] See SMALL, *General Sociology*, especially pp. 252, 393.

[3] See *Die sociologische Erkenntniss;* also SMALL, *General Sociology*, Parts IV–V; JACOBS, *German Sociology*, pp. 68–69; BRISTOL, *Social Adaptation*, pp. 170 *ff.*; LICHTENBERGER, *Development of Social Theory*, pp. 438 *ff.*

[4] JACOBS, *German Sociology*, p. 8.

[5] See SMALL, *General Sociology*, especially Chaps. XIV, XV, XXXI; also JACOBS, *German Sociology*, note, p. 68, p. 70.

The classification of human interests which Small arrived at on the basis of a consideration of Ratzenhofer's work is as follows: (1) health, (2) wealth, (3) sociability, (4) beauty, (5) knowledge, (6) rightness (see his *General Sociology*, pp. 425 *ff.*).

sociological thought as an important factor.   It connects up more or less directly, for instance, with Thomas' theory of the wishes and attitudes[1] and with much of the criticism of the individualistic approach in social psychology that has come forth from the side of sociological thought in this country.[2]

3. Georg Simmel (1858-1918) and More Recent Developments

Of the group of older German sociological writers whose influence upon modern social-psychological thought in this country and elsewhere is more or less directly traceable only Simmel's sociological theory will still be considered here in detail.   While seemingly very novel, Simmel's formulation of sociological theory really brings to a head important aspects of the sociological trend of influence which have been traced out in this section, and at the same time it provides essential background for the consideration of more recent developments.   This is so not only because with Simmel sociology definitely becomes psychological sociology so that it reflects back directly even on social psychology conceived of narrowly as the study of the social aspects of individual behavior, in which sense Simmel himself gave it place as a part of general psychology rather than of sociology,[3] but also because his conception of sociology is itself important background from the standpoint of social psychology, inasmuch as it deals with subject matter which has been identified as a part of social psychology by other writers in the field.[4]   In addition, Simmel's formal treatment of sociology tends to bring conspicuously into view certain notable general conditions of German psycho-social

---

[1] See Park and Burgess, *Introduction to the Science of Sociology*, Chap. VII, pp. 436 *ff.*

[2] For a further discussion of Ratzenhofer's sociological theory, see Small, *General Sociology*, Parts IV *ff.*; Jacobs, *German Sociology*, pp. 8, 32, 43, 66; Bristol, *Social Adaptation*, pp. 170–178; Bogardus, *A History of Social Theory*, pp. 357 *ff.*; Lichtenberger, *Development of Social Theory*, Chap. XV; Sorokin, *Contemporary Sociological Theories*, pp. 642 *ff.*

[3] See his *Soziologie*, pp. 21, 556–563.   In this Simmel departed from the more common sociological practice of regarding social psychology as the "lower story of sociology" rather than the "top story of psychology" (see Ross, *Foundations of Sociology*, p. 8).   From the latter standpoint, Simmel's sociology would only with difficulty, if at all, be distinguishable from social psychology (see Ellwood, *Introduction to Social Psychology*, Chap. IV, especially p. 84; Woodworth, *Dynamic Psychology*, p. 179).   We are here obviously face to face with the situation that the same problems have historically been dealt with as psychology, sociology, and social psychology. The important consideration for us, however, is the fact that Simmel was one of the first German writers to direct attention to the "interrelational" in human behavior as over against the merely objectively "social" and "cultural" on the one hand and the subjectively "individual" on the other and that a recognition of the "interrelational" is basic to any sort of real social psychology.

[4] See, for example, Bogardus, *Fundamentals of Social Psychology* (1924); *infra*, p. 398.

thought which it is necessary to consider here briefly in their historical bearing upon German social psychology. The development of psycho-social thought in Germany has, to a much larger extent than elsewhere, been associated with the logical and methodological differentiation of its several specialized fields from one another and from related thought. In this process, Simmel's sociological work has played an outstanding role, and in consequence it reflects this aspect of the situation with special clearness.[1]

Seeking to define sociology in distinctive sociological terms so as to set it off clearly from the other psychological and social sciences on the one hand and from philosophy of history, social philosophy, etc., on the other, with which this field had remained so persistently linked in German thought, Simmel attempted to carry over the delimiting standpoint and methodology of mathematics and formal logic to the field of sociology. The resulting conception of the function of sociology as a science which Simmel arrived at is necessary background for the consideration of his detailed sociological analyses and important background for the consideration of German psycho-social thought as a whole.[2] In particular it is illuminating as an introduction to the consideration of more recent psycho-social thought in Germany. It will accordingly be followed out here sufficiently to give the characteristic setting of Simmel's thought. Because of the novelty of Simmel's views and the unfamiliarity of his basic standpoint, the usual summary statement will not suffice in his case. It is necessary to develop his position to some extent in his own terms.

Simmel thought of sociology as the science of the *forms* of association[3] in contrast to the *content*, which constitutes the subject matter of the

[1] See PARK and BURGESS, *Introduction to the Science of Sociology*, pp. 8–12; JACOBS, *German Sociology*, pp. 6, 12ff., 54 ff.; SPYKMAN, *The Social Theory of Georg Simmel*, pp. 257 ff.; ABEL, *Systematic Sociology in Germany*, pp. 6–8.

[2] See JACOBS, *German Sociology*, p. 8; SMALL, *General Sociology*, p. 498; PARK and BURGESS, *Introduction to the Science of Sociology*, pp. 286, 331, 341, etc.; SPYKMAN, *The Social Theory of Georg Simmel*, pp. xiv, 257ff.; ABEL, *Systematic German Sociology*, Preface.

[3] The importance of this conception for social psychology follows from the fact that Simmel thought of these forms in functional psychological terms and, moreover, in the distinct social-psychological terms of personal interaction. It might then perhaps be asked, as Simmel himself suggested, whether sociology so conceived is not, after all, concerned with "but chapters of psychology, or at most of social psychology" ("The Problem of Sociology," *Amer. Jour. Sociol.*, vol. 15, p. 313, 1909–1910). The answer, it is evident, is a matter largely of definition and standpoint, and Simmel himself, as already noted, was not of this view (*supra*, p. 75). Interested, as he was, in keeping sociology clear of all related fields of endeavor, including social psychology, he defined social psychology in terms of the individualized approach of general psychology so that it necessarily fell within the scope of psychology rather than sociology. Its special problem, according to him, is the study of the modifications which the mental processes of the individual undergo under the specific conditions of social interaction. On the other hand, the study of social interaction from the unifying

special social sciences—history, anthropology, economics, political science, etc.—as the science, that is, of the patterns of association, considered in abstraction from the specific conditions of historical occurrence that give association concrete reality in time and place. Sociology, according to his conception, is no more concerned with the *content* of these social forms than geometry is concerned with the content of geometric forms.[1] As distinct sciences, both geometry and sociology are concerned with the universal, the typical, and the constant relations of form abstractly considered, not with the concrete, the unique, and the variable factors that attach to the particular content of their actual historical occurrence.[2]

Thus [explains Jacobs in illumination of Simmel's conception] a circle is a circle to the geometrician, whether it encompass water, air, or paper, or whether it be a mere abstraction. So to the sociologist, a group of students is the same in social form regardless of whether it contains a certain race of men, or men of a particular religion, or only men of a certain economic status. The number, the conflicts within the group, the spatial expansion, the psychological connections—these would interest the sociologist and would form the subject matter

---

standpoints of the products and processes of association is the subject matter of the special social sciences on the one hand and of sociology on the other in accordance with the distinction developed above. Group psychology is thereby a part of sociology rather than social psychology, according to Simmel's standpoint.

This division of subject matter may appear highly artificial and entirely too disregardful of the facts in the case to have much weight, but it indicates that Simmel's conception of sociology has a direct bearing not only on social psychology regardless of how it is defined but on all science dealing with human phenomena. For it reflects an emphasis on social interaction which brings the study of human phenomena into quite a different social perspective from that in which traditional individualistic thought left it. Whether the investigation of human phenomena from this standpoint be labeled psychology or sociology is of little importance. What is of importance, in so far as the development of social psychology is concerned, is the standpoint itself, and in the appreciation of the social-psychological significance of this standpoint, Simmel was as farsighted as any social theorist of the day (see *Amer. Jour. Sociol.*, vol. 15, pp. 308*ff.*, 1909–1910; *Soziologie*, pp. 21*ff.*, 556*ff.*; *Spykman, The Social Theory of Georg Simmel*, Chap. III).

[1] For a criticism of this conception see SMALL, *Amer. Jour. Sociol.*, vol. 15, running footnote comment pp. 295 *ff.*, 1909–1910; HAYES, "Sociological Construction Lines," *Amer. Jour. Sociol.*, vol. 11, pp. 31*ff.*, 1905–1906; ROSS, *The Foundations of Sociology*, pp. 4*ff.*; ELLWOOD, *Sociology in Its Psychological Aspects*, pp. 6, 149–150, 341*ff.*; SOROKIN, *Contemporary Sociological Theories*, pp. 495 *ff.*

[2] See his *Soziologie* and the translated sections in the *Amer. Jour. Sociol.*, vols. 2, 5, 8, 11, 15, 16; also JACOBS, *German Sociology*, pp. 8, 29, 47, 55, 70; PARK and BURGESS, *Introduction to the Science of Sociology*, pp. 10, 286, 331, 341, etc.; HAYES, "Sociological Construction Lines," *Amer. Jour. Sociol.*, vol. 11, pp. 26–48, 1905–1906; ELLWOOD, *Sociology in Its Psychological Aspects*, Chap. XVI; SPYKMAN, *The Social Theory of Georg Simmel*; ABEL, *Systematic Sociology in Germany*, Chap. I; SOROKIN, *Contemporary Sociological Theories*, Chap. IX; VON WIESE, "Current Sociology," *Sociol. Rev.*, vol. 19, 21–25, 1927.

of sociology. These are elements of form, as opposed to the elements of content given above. The content is of no interest to sociology, except in so far as it has an effect on the form of the group.[1]

Being basic to his sociological theory, Simmel himself took pains to illustrate and explain this conception in various connections:

With reference to *competition*, for example, we meet it in countless varieties in the most varied connections; in politics and in economic management, in the history of religion and of art, etc. The point is to determine from these facts what competition means as a pure form of human behavior, under what circumstances it comes into existence, how it develops, what modifications it undergoes through the peculiar character of its object, through what contemporary formal and material delimitations of a society it is intensified or the reverse, how competition between individuals differs from that between groups—in short, what sort of relationship between persons competition is, inasmuch as it may involve all sorts of contents, yet by the likeness of its appearance along with great variety of contents it proves that it belongs to a sphere governed by its own laws, a sphere which may with propriety be abstracted from other spheres.[2]

It is important, according to Simmel, to distinguish two meanings of the term "society" in this connection: first, the broader meaning which includes, according to him, "the sum of all the individuals concerned in reciprocal relations, together with all the interests which united these interacting persons"; and, second, the narrower meaning which he sought to establish, and indicating, in his words, "the society or association as such; that is, the interaction itself which constitutes the bond of association, in abstraction from its material content." Sociology, he maintained, is concerned with society only in the latter restricted sense.[3]

By way of illustration, again, Simmel said in another connection:

We designate as a cube on the one hand any natural object in cubical form; on the other hand the simple form alone, which made the material contents into a "cube" in the former sense, constitutes of itself, independently and abstractly considered, an object for geometry. The significance of geometry appears in the fact that the formal relations which it determines hold good for all possible objects formed in space. In like manner it is the purpose of sociology to determine the forms and modes of the relations between man, which although constituted of entirely different contents, material, and interests, nevertheless take shape in formally similar social structures.[4]

[1] JACOBS, *German Sociology*, pp. 48–49.

[2] "The Problem of Sociology," trans. by Small, *Amer. Jour. Sociol.*, vol. 15, p. 305, 1909–1910. Quotations from *The American Journal of Sociology* are reprinted by permission of The University of Chicago Press, publishers.

[3] "Superiority and Subordination as Subject-Matter of Sociology," trans. by Small, *Amer. Jour. Sociol.*, vol. 2, p. 167, 1896–1897.

[4] *Ibid.*, p. 168.

It is clear that this conception brings up the problem of sociological technique in an important way. Precisely how is one to proceed to study "society or association as such" or "interaction itself . . . in abstraction from its material content"? Simmel held that this technique would take on definiteness and precision gradually as the actual analysis of social forms is carried on. In the meantime, he was obliged to remain content with a general statement of objectives and with an appeal "to a special direction of insight" in putting them into effect.[1] He said:

We gain knowledge of the forms of socialization by bringing together inductively the manifestations of these forms which have had actual historical existence. In other words we have to collect and exhibit that element of form which these historical manifestations have in common, abstracted from the variety of material—economical, ethical, ecclesiastical, social, political, etc.,—with respect to which they differ.[2]

We can reach an understanding of these relationships only by casting the sum of a great number of real historical cases; that is, by leaving out of consideration the differences in the material content of these relations, and by making only the forms of these relations, in all their modifications, crossings, and complications the object of our investigations, just as logic becomes a science when we disregard all defined and specific contents of thought and consider only the forms in which single representations are so combined as to form truths.[3]

What is necessary, according to Simmel, is to raise the similar elements of form in social situations "into prominence as by a cross-section," by allowing the dissimilar elements of content to become "reciprocally paralyzed," in order that the essential aspects of association may be lifted out for consideration apart from the distortion of variable factors.[4]

The desideratum is to discern in the countless historical groupings the principle of group formation as such, in order that we may approximate the laws of the influences which human beings exert upon each other in their reciprocal contacts,—laws which in themselves are not affected by the material causes or purposes of these contacts, although the different contents of socialization will, of course, lead to various combinations, different degrees of strength, and different courses of development in these forms of contact. And as we reach a science of religion by turning our attention away from all other interests of life except religion, or at least by treating them merely as accidents, as we gain a science of language by abstracting language and its immediate psychological conditions from everything that lies beyond, although as a matter of fact there would never have been utterance without the excluded concrete motives, so we shall gain a sociology by seeking to recognize the laws, forms and developments of socialization (*Vergesellschaftung*) which to be sure in reality determine life only together

[1] "The Problem of Sociology," *Amer. Jour. Sociol.*, vol. 15, p. 308, 1909–1910.
[2] "Superiority and Subordination," *Amer. Jour. Sociol.*, vol. 2, p. 168, 1896–1897.
[3] *Ibid.*, p. 189.
[4] "The Problem of Sociology," *Amer. Jour. Sociol.*, vol. 15, p. 305, 1909–1910.

with other functions and forces, which nevertheless can constitute the subject matter of a distinct science only in abstraction from these other factors.[1]

One more passage interrelating the foregoing aspects of Simmel's theory will suffice for our purposes:

The subject matter of sociology is, therefore, the forms or ways in which human beings exist beside, for, and with each other. The purposes for the sake of which these socializations came into being—economic and social, religious and criminal, sexual and military, political and ethical, etc.—will be treated by other sciences. Since now socialization only occurs among human beings for the sake of such purposes, we shall discover the laws of social forms only by collecting such societary phenomena of the most diverse contents, and by ascertaining what is common to them in spite of their diversity. In this way the diverse contents of the forms of socialization multiply each other, and that which is formally the same, the societary form as such, must clearly appear. For instance, we observe the formation of parties on political and artistic, on religious and economic ground. By searching for that which is common in these phenomena, in spite of wide variation of purpose and interests, we discover the laws and species of party formation as such, as a form of the coexistence of human beings in general. By this method we discover, for example, as such forms, superiority and inferiority, the erection of hierarchies, competition, division of labor, imitation, representation, and countless other types of human socialization.[2]

Reduced to the lowest terms, Simmel's position, as so far developed, may be briefly summarized as follows:

Sociology as a separate science has as its subject matter the study of the forms, types, or patterns of association.[3] In the fundamental sense of Simmel's thought, these are basic features of social life in general. They are to that extent independent of specific cultural content and particular conditions of historical occurrence. In its attempt to arrive at its subject matter, sociology must direct its attention to the common, the typical, and the constant factors of association, to the exclusion of its historically unique and variable factors. In order to do this, it is necessary for sociology to subject the concrete reality of social life to a process of abstraction on the basis of its own interest. Sociology can do this by balancing examples of specific instances of association over against each other in such a manner that the unique and variable features cancel each other and only the permanent and essential features—in Simmel's words, "the forms of association as such"—are left for consideration. It is in this sense that sociology is, from Simmel's standpoint, concerned with the pure *forms* of association in abstraction from their concrete

---

[1] "Superiority and Subordination," *Amer. Jour. Sociol.*, vol. 2, p. 415, 1896–1897.

[2] "The Persistence of Social Groups," trans. by Small, *Amer. Jour. Sociol.*, vol. 3, p. 663, 1897–1898. Simmel's *Soziologie* consists primarily of sample studies of such social forms (see *infra*, pp. 82–83).

[3] *Cf.* HAYES, "Sociological Construction Lines," *Amer. Jour. Sociol.*, vol. 11, p. 31, 1905–1906.

conditions of historical occurrence—in abstraction, that is, from what he termed their material *content*.

In a sense this is unquestioned ground in all science that aims to arrive at general laws and principles. Simmel simply sought to formulate the generalizing procedure of modern science and to apply it to the complex field of social investigation in defining its relation to the timeless, general laws and principles on which all applicable science depends. And this attempt to clarify social-science procedure was the more important because it came at a time when there was much confusion of thought on this matter, especially in Germany, where emphasis on the historical approach tended to obscure essential differences of relation to applicable science, between history and the historical sciences of culture and social life (as represented by folk psychology, for instance) on the one hand and psychology, sociology, and social psychology (conceived of as generalizing sciences) on the other.[1]

This being readily granted, it nevertheless remains that few have been able to follow Simmel in his logical division of the field of psychosocial investigation and in his conception of sociology and sociological procedure.[2]   Other sciences are just as interested as sociology in building up general laws and principles, but they do not on that account rule out of their realm of interest the detailed description and investigation of the concrete facts on which this generalizing aspect supposedly rests. In other words, while it may be important to recognize—and Simmel has been conspicuous in the attempt to make this clear in the field of psychosocial thought—that science, in so far as it is concerned with the discovery of laws and principles, necessarily deals with the general, the typical, and the representative aspects of the situations which it seeks to describe, it is most important to recognize also that, as science, it deals with the latter only as expressions of the concrete facts which alone can give them validity.   Unfortunately Simmel built up his position chiefly on the basis of analogy from the field of mathematics, and the

[1] See JACOBS, *German Sociology*, pp. 6*ff.*, 12, 54*ff.*; PARK and BURGESS, *Introduction to the Science of Sociology*, pp. 6–12; SPYKMAN, *The Social Theory of Georg Simmel*, especially pp. 257, 267, 270–271.

[2] See SMALL, review of Simmel, *Soziologie*, *Amer. Jour. Sociol.*, vol. 14, pp. 544–545, 1908–1909, and footnote comment *ibid.*, vol. 15, pp. 295*ff.*, 1909–1910; also *supra*, p. 77, note 1.   From the standpoint of social psychology for instance, it is notable that Simmel's conception of sociology neglects entirely certain problems which have been regarded as essential parts of sociological theory by some, for example, the problem of the motivation of social behavior, upon which many sociologists since the time of Ratzenhofer and Ward have laid stress.   Simmel's view of sociology leaves these problems to the individualistic interpretation of psychology.   It has accordingly appeared particularly inadequate from the standpoint of the more unified development of sociology and social psychology which the course of social-psychological events has fostered in this country (*cf.* Ross, *Foundations of Sociology*, pp. 4*ff.*; ELLWOOD, *Sociology in Its Psychological Aspects*, pp. 6, 149–150, 341 *ff.*).

mathematical procedure is in this respect very different from the procedure of natural science generally. Suggestive as his formal sociological theory is, therefore, in conjunction with the attempt which was made in Germany, under the influence of such writers as Windelband and Rickert, to free psycho-social science viewed as generalizing science for development apart from confusing entanglement with the fields of history and the special historical studies of culture and social life, it nevertheless seems to be fragmentary and one-sided in its emphasis at best, and it has been held to be definitely misleading at its worst.[1]

From the standpoint of inductive scientific procedure, it is artificial, to say the least, to attempt to divide a field of study with respect to *form* and *content* as Simmel did. In the case of sociology it is particularly objectionable, inasmuch as it seems to justify the abstract theorizing which has so long obscured the need for a factual approach in this field.[2] Fortunately, it is not at all necessary to interpret Simmel's theory literally in this respect, and the refusal to accept this part of his theory does not invalidate his discriminating thought about sociology and psycho-social science generally in other respects. In fact, the real import of Simmel's formal sociological theory appears only in relation to a thoroughgoing inductive and factual approach such as modern scientific procedure demands. Some of Simmel's followers and interpreters have accordingly taken the logical next step of attempting to work out the implications of his point of view in a concrete program of sociological investigation. It has been the suggestiveness of Simmel's theory when thus interpreted which has given him place in the foremost rank of modern social theorists in Germany and a general importance, according to his followers and defenders, which should be much more widely recognized.[3]

As so often happens in the history of thought, Simmel was led into an extremist position in defining the function of sociology as a science that aims to arrive at general laws and principles, for the sake of emphasis. For in his own sample treatment of actual forms of association—superiority and subordination, conflict, secrecy, poverty, cooperation, division

---

[1] See references *supra*, p. 77, note 1.

[2] See SMALL, review of Simmel, *Soziologie, Amer. Jour. Sociol.*, vol. 14, pp. 544–545, 1908–1909; HAYES, "Sociological Construction Lines," *Amer. Jour. Sociol.*, vol. 11, p. 33, 1905–1906; ELLWOOD, *Sociology in Its Psychological Aspects*, pp. 6, 149, 341; SOROKIN, *Contemporary Sociological Theories*, pp. 495 *ff.*; ABEL, *Systematic Sociology in Germany*, pp. 48–49.

[3] Simmel has had a strong following in Germany for some time, including, among others, such diverse writers as Leopold von Wiese, Alfred Vierkandt in his more recent works, and Max Scheler.   There is much in common, too, between Simmel's sociology and *gestalt* psychology (see SPYKMAN, *The Social Theory of Georg Simmel*, p. xxviii; SOROKIN, *Contemporary Sociological Theories*, pp. 488–489; also references *infra*, p. 83, note 5).   In this country some of the members of the Department of Sociology of the University of Chicago have been considerably influenced by Simmel's work.

of labor, etc.[1]—presented, though his analyses were, in illustration of his formal theory,[2] Simmel by no means held to his purely formal views. The strength of his sociological analyses lies precisely in the fact that he in large measure disregarded the limitations of his formal theory in them and directed himself to an all-round descriptive treatment of certain basic psycho-social processes and relations.[3] Nevertheless, it remains that Simmel's procedure as he himself sought to describe and illustrate it reduces itself essentially to an abstract discussion of certain categories of social relationship. Illuminating and keen as are his sociological analyses (and of this even a chance reading of any of his sample exhibits will convince one) and valuable as they have been in indicating fruitful lines of further inquiry, they have, accordingly, like so much of German psycho-social investigation, not proved to be entirely acceptable to the developing strictly scientific interest in this field, which has found it necessary, above all else, to seek to free psycho-social science from the domination of the abstract philosophical approach. For they but prove that Simmel sought to give first place to abstract concepts rather than to concrete facts.[4] Only those who have been able to view Simmel's work in the light of the peculiar controversial atmosphere which has surrounded German psycho-social thought[5] and in application to the concrete approach of present-day inductive scientific procedure, have thus been able to appreciate the important contributions for the clarification of psycho-social thought which his work embodies.

That Simmel's thought reflects local conditions so much has naturally limited his influence outside of Germany, where interest in abstract methodological discussion is not as general as there. Particularly difficult has it been to arouse any sustained interest in Simmel's work in this

---

[1] See his *Soziologie* and his translated articles in the *Amer. Jour. Sociol.*, vols. 2, 3, 4, 5 *ff.* Simmel made no attempt to treat sociology systematically; he felt that it was still too much of a pioneer endeavor for that (see *supra*, p. 80, note 2).

[2] See *Amer. Jour. Sociol.*, vol. 15, pp. 309, 320, 1909–1910.

[3] As Simmel himself noted (see his note on the Table of Contents in his *Soziologie*), much appears in these sample studies of social forms that would ordinarily not be suggested by the titles, certainly not as interpreted in terms of his formal theory. The more important of his analyses have been translated by Small in the *Amer. Jour. Sociol.*, vols. 2 *ff.*

[4] *Cf.* SPYKMAN, *The Social Theory of Georg Simmel*, pp. 3, 33, 38*ff.*, and references *supra*, p. 82, note 2.

[5] See *supra*, p. 81, note 1; WIRTH, "Topical Summaries of Current Literature: Modern German Conceptions of Sociology," *Amer. Jour. Sociol.*, vol. 32, pp. 461–470, 1926; WALTHER, "The Present Position of Sociology in Germany," *Jour. Appl. Sociol.*, vol. 10, pp. 229–238, 1925–1926; VON WIESE, "Current Sociology: Germany," *Sociol. Rev.*, vol. 19, pp. 21–25, 1927; BRINKMAN, "The Present Situation of German Sociology," *Pub. Amer. Sociol. Soc.*, vol. 21, pp. 47–56, 1927; also KLÜVER, "Contemporary German Psychology" in Murphy, *An Historical Introduction to Modern Psychology;* and section on German thought, especially on "Psychology," in *Philosophy Today,* ed. by Schaub.

country, not merely because of the abstract character of much of his discussion, but more especially because his emphasis so frequently seems to run counter, though it actually does not, to the dominant emphasis of American psycho-social thought, with its deep-lying interest in the concrete and the practical motives of science.[1]

All in all Simmel's work thus brings to a focus what has appeared over and over again in our review of the social-psychological bearings of German folk-psychological and sociological theory, namely, that in so far as these two fields represent German social-psychological thought, and in the absence of any considerable more specialized social-psychological literature, these two fields have been outstandingly active in the revolt against the individualistic approach of traditional psychology and in the attempt to establish a "social psychology" alongside of it in Germany,[2] they reflect quite a different setting from that which is associated with social-psychological thought elsewhere and especially in this country. The German leaning toward speculation and theoretical discussion has kept thought in these and related fields occupied to no small degree with abstract discussions of definition, scope, method, purpose, etc., and preoccupied with questions of the relation between

[1] *Cf.* JACOBS, *German Sociology*, pp. 70*ff.*; SMALL, review of Spykman, *The Social Theory of Georg Simmel*, *Amer. Jour. Sociol.*, vol. 31, pp. 84, 87, 1925; also references *supra*, p. 77, note 1, and p. 82 note 2.

Simmel's sociological theory has been popularized in this country to some extent by Small through his translations of parts of Simmel's work and by Park and Burgess through the reinterpretation of aspects of Simmel's theory which they have worked into their broadly conceived program of sociological research (see PARK and BURGESS, *Introduction to the Science of Sociology*). Recently a simplified presentation of Simmel's theory has been made available to English readers by Spykman (*The Social Theory of Georg Simmel*) and the Society for Social Research of the University of Chicago through its publication of a simplified version of Simmel's lectures (*Soziologische Vorlesungen von Georg Simmel*). What effect these new attempts to gain attention for Simmel's sociological theory in this country will have remains, of course, to be seen. But it is of interest to note here also, by way of indicating the more usual attitude toward Simmel's work in this country, that a somewhat similar, though differently orientated, view regarding the function of sociology was arrived at independently in this country in the beginning of the century by Hayes (see his articles in *Amer. Jour. Sociol.* on "Sociological Construction Lines," vols. 10–11). His comment on this is exceptionally revealing:

"Professor Georg Simmel defines sociology as a study of the forms of social relations. This definition has seemed particularly barren, uninteresting, unpromising, and capable of eliciting protracted toil only from one who is willing to devote himself to intellectual gymnastics, and it is somewhat startling to have emerged from this discussion at a point so close to his position" (*Amer. Jour. Sociol.*, vol. 11, p. 33, 1906).

[2] It is notable in this connection that the new journal of *Völkerpsychologie und Soziologie*, to which attention has already been directed in the section on folk psychology (see *supra*, pp. 51 and 65), seeks, as one of its objectives, to coordinate these two chief sources of social-psychological development in Germany.

them and bordering fields. Even now, when these issues are no longer matters of serious concern elsewhere, in Germany thought is apparently involved anew in earnest dispute as to whether sociology, for instance, as one of the fields intimately associated with the development of social psychology, is essentially history, philosophy of history, social philosophy, or a positive scientific technique and, in either case, whether it ought to remain an appendage and under the tutelage of one or the other of the older and better established fields such as psychology, history, economics, political science, anthropology, and so on or to develop as a distinct discipline in its own right.[1] The situation as regards psychology, in so far as psychology is associated with social interpretation, as it notably is in the case of folk psychology, is not far different.[2]

In developing in this intellectual atmosphere, social-psychological thought in Germany has naturally involved itself in this complex theoretical setting.[3] In very striking manner, it has thereby handicapped its development as an independent field of investigation. Social-psychological thought in Germany has so far on the whole tended to enrich related fields of investigation at the expense of its own advance and scientific progress. It remains a fragmentary and incidental matter, an aspect of many fields of related thought rather than a distinct field of scientific endeavor, as it is beginning to be viewed more and more elsewhere, and especially in this country. If the distinction be permitted in this connection, one might say that there is a great deal of social psychologizing in Germany but as yet very little social psychology or distinctively social-psychological developments such as loom up more conspicuously on the horizon of modern French, English, and American thought, at any rate from the standpoint of social psychology as it has developed in this country, and this is naturally of central importance here.

It is thereby difficult to know just where to stop in presenting the social-psychological aspects of modern German thought as background for the consideration of American social psychology. One could go on from one field that touches upon social-psychological problems to the

---

[1] See JACOBS, German Sociology, pp. 9 ff., 53ff., 85ff.; also references supra, p. 83, note 5. A well-known early work which strikingly reflects this controversial atmosphere in Germany is Barth, Die Philosophie der Geschichte als Soziologie (1897). Another more recent work is Vierkandt, Gesellschaftslehre, Hauptprobleme der philosophischen Soziologie (1922). It is illuminating to compare these positions with those of Thurnwald, "Probleme der empirischen Soziologie," Ztschr. f. Völkerps. u. Soz., vol. 3, 1927, and Von Wiese, Allgemeine Soziologie, Beziehungslehre (1924). It is notable, also, that all of these positions relate themselves, in one way or another, to Simmel's work.

[2] See references supra, p. 83, note 5.

[3] It is significant that the only extensive German work which has so far appeared under the title of social psychology (Stoltenberg, Sozialpsychologie, 1914, 1922) is given over chiefly to a theoretical discussion of the interrelations of psychology, social psychology, and sociology.

other almost indefinitely, considering significant social-psychological aspects of German thought, until one came to such recent developments as the *Gestalt* movement in modern German psychology which seems to hold out special promise for social psychology, on the side of investigational procedure at any rate.[1] For very remotely, at least, many of these aspects of German thought would have a connection with American social psychology. Little would be gained, however, from such a complication of our background material, inasmuch as the more important of these connections, historically considered, have already been followed out and even these seem quite remote and far-fetched at times. And this would in some respects be even more strikingly the case since the period of Simmel's influence in sociology and Wundt's in psychology. For since then a strong reaction movement against positivism in the psychological and social sciences has come to the fore in Germany,[2] which has had the effect at once of further diffusing German social-psychological thought and setting it off even more so than heretofore from the corresponding field of thought in this country.

This, together with the isolation of the war period, has made for a distinct break in the interplay of German influence upon American social-psychological thought. Since the war it has been the unfamiliarity of German social and psychological thought which has been attracting most attention here. It may be necessary for American thought to pass through a period of orientation not unlike that of a generation ago before the pre-war contact with German social and psychological thought is reestablished. Meanwhile, it has been largely through *Gestalt* psychology, which has been expounded here during the last few years by its own exponents, that this contact has been maintained. This movement being, however, still very new even in the study of the simpler aspects of mental life and as yet hardly directed to the consideration of the complex field of social-psychological phenomena, its effect upon American social psychology still remains very uncertain, and hence it is unnecessary to give it any sort of detailed treatment here as yet in so far as background considerations are concerned. Much the same may be said regarding certain other recent German developments, such as the beginnings, along similar lines to those which have recently

---

[1] The literature on *Gestalt* psychology is for the most part quite recent. The following may be consulted: KOFFKA, "Perception, An Introduction to the Gestalt Theory," *Psychol. Bull.*, vol. 19, 1922; *The Growth of the Mind*, An Introduction to Child Psychology, trans. by Ogden (1925); KÖHLER, *The Mentality of Apes*, trans. by Winter (1925); *Gestalt Psychology* (1929); HELSON, "The Psychology of Gestalt," *Amer. Jour. Psychol.*, vols. 36, 37, 1924–1925; KOFFKA and KÖHLER in *Psychologies of 1925* and *Psychologies of 1930;* also FOLLETT, *Creative Experience* (1924), Chap. V; Murphy, *An Historical Introduction to Modern Psychology* (1930), pp. 243, 426 *ff.*; WOODWORTH, *Contemporary Schools of Psychology* (1931), Chap. IV.

[2] See *supra*, p. 83, note 5.

been coming prominently to the fore in this country,[1] of what might be described as the extension of the older laboratory technique to the realm of social-psychological and sociological observation.[2] Recognizing the fact, then, that there are many interesting recent developments in German thought of possible significance for American social psychology, though as yet of comparatively little actual background importance,[3] we may just as well leave off considering German background influences at this point and turn our attention again to the consideration of more directly important background influences, in so far as the actual development of American social psychology is concerned.

It is on the surface a most striking fact that with the social perspective which is characteristic of the modern social-psychological approach deeply ingrained in German thought and firmly rooted in its idealistic philosophy, and in the fragmentary manner noted above perhaps more widely and variously cultivated in Germany than anywhere else, social psychology as a specialized field of endeavor should not have made greater progress in establishing itself there than it has.[4] Among the many considerations which suggest themselves in explanation of this fact, the following appears to be of determining importance. German thought stands apart from the main current of modern social-psychological development as it is to be followed out here in that, while social-psychological thought outside of Germany is very largely orientated in the natural-science approach, German thought, as we have already had frequent occasion to note, has definitely opposed the spread of a thoroughgoing naturalism and positivism in the fields with which its social-psychological thought is most intimately associated. It has sought rather, on the whole, to keep these fields in close touch with history and

[1] Reflected prominently, for example, in ALLPORT, *Social Psychology* (see *infra*, p. 404).

[2] The following works are notable in this connection: MOEDE, *Experimentelle Massenpsychologie* (1920); BÜHLER, *Kindheit und Jugend* (1928); HELLPACH, *Sozialpsychologische Forschungen*, vol. 1 (1922).

[3] One might mention further, for example, the "personalism" of William Stern (*Die Psychologie und der Personalismus*, 1917); the "typology" of Eduard Spranger (*Lebensformen*, 1922, Eng. trans. *Types of Men*), Max Scheler (*Wissensformen und die Gesellschaft*, 1926), and Max Weber (*Gesammelte Aufsätze zur Religionssoziologie*, 1922–1923); the developmental theory of Felix Krueger (*Entwicklungspsychologie*, 1916); etc.

[4] "In the case of Germany," says a recent German writer, "it is as yet impossible to speak of social-psychological investigation—although there is a series of works at hand dealing with the subject-matter of social psychology—also foreign works on social psychology are still for the most part unknown" (Geck, *Sozialpsychologie im Auslande*, p. vi). Recognizing this situation, this writer has set about in the above-mentioned work to acquaint German thought with developments in the field of social psychology outside of Germany. More recently he has also outlined some corresponding developments in German thought (see his two articles on "Social Psychology in Germany," *Sociol. and Soc. Res.*, vols. 13, 14, 1929).

philosophy.   The partial reaction against this situation, which came to expression in the form of a reaction against Hegelianism in the early part of the modern social-psychological movement and which brought German thought for a time into closer relation with social-psychological thought outside of Germany, has more recently been overshadowed by a revival of interest in the historical and metaphysical approaches. German thought is thus, in important respects, more at variance with the spirit of social-psychological thought outside of Germany today than it was in the early period of modern social-psychological development. This very striking fact overshadows for the time the common inductive ground of German psychological, sociological, and folk-psychological thought.   It remains for the coming period of social-psychological development to bring these important aspects of the situation into greater prominence.[1]   For it will undoubtedly be on the basis of this common ground that the firmest bonds between German and American social-psychological thought will ultimately be established.

In the meantime, it is necessary to turn now, as in the philosophical background, to the consideration of French and English background influences, which have been much more directly interlinked with the development of American social psychology, especially during the first period of its differentiation and emergence.

---

[1] It is interesting to note that as this volume goes to press there has just appeared an imposing survey of the field entitled *Experimental Social Psychology*, by Murphy and Murphy, which goes a long way in this direction in so far as experimental subject matter is concerned.

CHAPTER III

THE DEVELOPMENT OF SOCIAL-PSYCHOLOGICAL THOUGHT IN FRANCE

I

One of the striking features about the modern social-psychological movement which comes into view in such a survey as this is the distinctive and yet supplementary character of its chief lines of development. The movement advanced, it appears, not only as a many-sided investigation of concrete social and psychic life but also as a complex of basic outlook and approach. The abstract philosophical orientation of German social-psychological thought, for instance, is supplemented by a striking closeness to the concrete reality of social life in France; the collectivistic emphasis of the latter is supplemented by the individualistic setting of social-psychological thought in England; the dualism of standpoint and procedure thus brought into view is supplemented by the synthetic point of view introduced by American social-psychological thought; and so on.

Each of these lines of development has contributed in its own characteristic manner to the modern social-psychological movement and to the product which has come to be known as "social psychology." But the spectacular role which French thought has played in this development has from the first been a thing apart. Comte, Tarde, Durkheim, Le Bon, these are outstanding names in the modern social-psychological movement, and in so far as the development of American social-psychological thought in particular is concerned, the importance of French thought as represented by these writers will come clearly into evidence in several distinct connections in the second part of this survey.

German thought, it seems necessary to note here again, has been an important factor in the modern social-psychological movement, but in the case of American social-psychological thought in particular, it has for the most part played an indirect rather than a direct role. French thought, on the other hand, has been a direct factor in the situation from the first. It has been directly incorporated into the stream of American social-psychological thought at several important points and it has operated all along as a most important factor alongside of the basic flow of English influence. In turning from German to French social-psychological thought, we thus come not merely upon another major chapter of modern social-pychological development which is of the utmost significance in itself but upon one also which has a special significance here as background for the presentation of American social-pychological theory.

The outstanding figure in French thought, following Comte, from the standpoint of the modern social-psychological movement, is Gabriel Tarde. Between Comte and Tarde, there are, however, a series of events of social-psychological significance, some of which it is necessary to touch upon briefly here before attempting to consider Tarde's theory in detail.

Comte's influence in France, in so far as the study of human behavior and social life is concerned, did not assert itself as immediately and as directly as did the corresponding influence of Spencer in England and Hegel in Germany. In fact, Comte's influence became an important factor in French psycho-social thought only after it was reinterpreted in terms of English naturalism on the one hand and modified by contact with German idealism on the other, and only by way of the popularization which his theories underwent in the works of such of his early followers as Littré, Renan, and Taine.[1] Dominated by the general notion of positivism without the specific content to make it scientifically effective, Comte's thought inevitably laid itself open to reinterpretation and restatement in terms of these related developments. This situation had decided advantages from the standpoint of the development of French social-psychological thought, for unlike the situations in the two other countries, it permitted the infusion of varied impulses into the stream of French thought before it began to crystallize into definite directions of effort. French social-psychological thought presents, in consequence, a somewhat broader base than the corresponding German and English trends of thought; it was not dominated to the same extent by a single theoretical motive and directed to a single decisive course of development—all in all a wholesome condition when a new field of investigation is just beginning to take form.

Directly in line with the above and entering as a specific factor in the determination of French social-psychological thought was the close contact of French thought, following Comte, with the development of psychology in Germany and England. After the discredit which introspective psychology suffered at the hands of Comte, the popularization of English and German psychology through the works of Taine and Ribot[2] and the reflection of the accompanying tendencies of social-

---

[1] See MERZ, *History of European Thought in the Nineteenth Century*, vol. III, p. 43, vol. IV, pp. 234–236, 502*ff.*

[2] TAINE, *De l'Intelligence* (1870); RIBOT, *La psychologie anglaise contemporaine* (1870), trans. as *English Psychology; La psychologie allemande contemporaine* (1879), trans. by Baldwin as, *German Psychology of To-day;* see MERZ, *History of European Thought in the Nineteenth Century*, vol. III, pp. 269*ff.*

psychological development in these countries,[1] brought about a unique situation. As far as the basic trend of French social-psychological development was concerned, the Comtean collectivistic and positivistic standpoint made the uncritical acceptance of either the English or German genetic psychology as a substitute for the investigation of the complexities of social behavior as manifested in the concrete occurrences of contemporary social life impossible. However, German and English psychology entered as distinctly recognizable factors into the stream of French social-psychological thought at this time, as is evidenced by such attempted harmonizations of theories as Taine's threefold formula of "race, epoch, and milieu"[2] and Fouillée's theory of "idea-forces."[3] The net result of this preliminary intermingling of theoretical motives for French social-psychological thought was a thoroughgoing reinterpretation and a decided enrichment of the main current of Comtean influence as regards its effect upon social and psychological investigation.[4]

Of paramount importance also in determining social-psychological thought in France was the development of French psychological interest in the pathological manifestations of human mental behavior, an aspect of psychological investigation the importance of which traditional psychology tended to obscure. This interest in the pathology of mental behavior dates back in France to the early nineteenth century, when Pinel directed the attention of science to the serious study of insanity and Itard similarly directed attention to the mentally defective.[5] Somewhat earlier even, Mesmer had created something of a sensation through his psychotherapeutic activities and his theory of animal magnetism, as a result of which interest was also aroused in this related field of investigation. These events initiated a period of growing scientific interest and activity in the fields of psychopathology and psychiatry in France. It was only, of course, with Taine, Ribot, and Binet on the one hand and Bernheim, Charcot, and even Janet and Freud on the other that the full significance of the facts revealed by the study of psychopathological behavior for the understanding of normal human behavior began to be definitely established. Sociological interest was, however, directed rather early to this field of inquiry in France, first on positive

[1] In the work of Taine, Fouillée, etc.; for instance, FOUILLÉE, La science sociale contemporaine, 1885 (see BRETT, A History of Psychology, vol. III, pp. 242–254; MERZ, History of European Thought in the Nineteenth Century, vol. IV, pp. 514ff.).

[2] Illustrated in his Historie de la littérature anglaise (1863), trans. by Van Laun as, The History of English Literature.

[3] Developed in his Evolutionnisme des idée-forces (1890) and his La psychologie des idées-forces (1893).

[4] See BRETT, A History of Psychology, vol. III, pp. 247ff.; MERZ, History of European Thought in the Nineteenth Century, vol. IV, pp. 502ff.

[5] See WOODWORTH, Dynamic Psychology, pp. 13–16, 167ff.; Contemporary Schools of Psychology, pp. 126ff.; BRETT, A History of Psychology, vol. III, pp. 245–246, 305–308; MURPHY, An Historical Introduction to Modern Psychology, Chaps. VIII, XIX.

grounds in connection with the criticism of introspective psychology, as was the case with Comte,[1] and later because the facts revealed, especially in connection with the study of hypnosis, appeared to have a direct bearing on the problem of socialization.[2] It is not altogether surprising, therefore, to find Tarde turning to the facts of psychopathology in his effort to lay bare the mechanism of social behavior.

Still another factor which merits mention here, and which appears of ever increasing importance as the demands for scientific fact and precision are beginning to make themselves felt in the field of psycho-social thought, was the introduction of the statistical and the monographic methods of presenting and treating social facts by the Belgian statistician and social theorist Quetelet (1796–1874) and his French contemporary LePlay (1806–1882).[3] While modern psycho-social thought has come by the social-statistical and the monographic and case-study methods, more by way of psychiatry, social work, modern ethnology, and such more .recent followers of Quetelet and LePlay as Booth, Rowntree, Galton, Pearson, etc., rather than directly by way of the work of these pioneers in the use of these investigational methods, and while at the time, the deductive methods of Comte and Spencer quite overshadowed the more inductive procedures for which Quetelet and LePlay stood, it is nevertheless important to note here that each of these was, in his way, sowing the seed of more careful inductive procedure, much as was Darwin in another and more spectacular way. The significance of the work of Quetelet and LePlay, from the standpoint of social-science technique, as differentiated from the specific theoretical settings of their work as a whole, has come to be recognized only very gradually. Nevertheless, even Comte himself was to some extent influenced by Quetelet's mathematical approach, and the detailed monographic procedure of the LePlay school has continued all along to exert a recognizable influence on Comte's followers.[4]

[1] The Positive Philosophy of Auguste Comte (Martineau), vol. I, pp. 381, 393.

[2] See TARDE, The Laws of Imitation, note 1, p. 76; also SIDIS, The Psychology of Suggestion; BECHTEREW, Die Bedeutung der Suggestion im socialen Leben; STOLL, Suggestion und Hypnotismus in der Völkerpsychologie; PARK and BURGESS, An Introduction to the Science of Sociology, Chap. VI.

[3] QUETELET, Sur l'homme et le développement de ses facultés, un essai de physique sociale (1835); Du système sociale et des lois qui le régissent (1848); L'Anthropométrie ou mesure des différentes facultés de l'homme (1870); LEPLAY, Les ouvriers européens (1855).

[4] See HANKINS, Adolphe Quetelet; also "Individual Differences: The Galton-Pearson Approach," Social Forces, vol. 4, pp. 272–281, 1925; SMALL and VINCENT, An Introduction to the Study of Society, pp. 47–50; ELLWOOD, "The LePlay Method of Social Observation," Amer. Jour. Sociol., vol. 2, pp. 662–680; articles on the LePlay school in Sociol. Rev., vol. 11, 1918; BRISTOL, Social Adaptation, pp. 43–46; BOGARDUS, A History of Social Thought, pp. 480–482; SOROKIN, Contemporary Sociological Theories, pp. 63ff., 252; also DAVY, "Sociology," Philosophy Today, collected and ed. by Schaub, pp. 289–309.

These influences, as was suggested above, came upon the basic background of Comtean thought, which gave general direction to modern French social-psychological effort just as definitely as did the Hegelian and Spencerian systems of thought in Germany and England. Because of its characteristic Comtean standpoint, social-psychological thought in France has tended to develop along lines which have been variously designated as "collective," "mass" or "group" psychology, and, in the case of Tarde, "inter-psychology," in contradistinction to the social psychology which centers its operations in the study of the social individual, and it has been formulated chiefly as a part of sociological rather than psychological theory, as was the case in the two other countries.[1] Indeed, modern *psychological* sociology (so-called to differentiate it from the objective approach of the sociological students of social organization) was in the first place largely a product of this trend of social-psychological development. Tarde, who is to be considered first in this connection, seems to focus attention on the individual, it is true, but it is the individual as the converging point chiefly rather than as the unit in the social process, as will presently appear. The general effect of his work, therefore, was in the same direction as that of French psycho-social thought as a whole, though it did incorporate a somewhat different emphasis.

II. The Study of Imitation as an Approach to Social Psychology: Inter-psychology

1. Gabriel Tarde (1843-1904)

Tarde was in the first place a jurist, criminologist, and statistician; he was a sociologist only indirectly and by way of these major professional activities. His interest in the general problems of human behavior and social life was an outgrowth of his reflections upon the specific problems with which he was called upon to deal daily in connection with his work as a magistrate. This is significant as an indication of the close relation between social thought and the practical affairs of social life, which the positivist tradition fostered in France.

Imbued, by way of Cournot[2] and otherwise, with the spirit of Comtean sociology, Tarde could not accept the current theories of the Lombrosian school of criminology.[3] Crime, being a social phenomenon, it must have a social explanation. With this outlook as a basis, Tarde observed and

---

[1] TARDE, *Études de psychologie sociale* (1898), is an illustration (see MERZ, *History of European Thought in the Nineteenth Century*, vol. III, p. 193, vol. IV, pp. 436, 502ff.; BALDWIN, *History of Psychology*, vol. II, pp. 43-45, 126ff.; BRETT, *A History of Psychology*, vol. III, pp. 242-254; also DUPRAT, *La psychologie sociale*, Chap. I).

[2] *The Laws of Imitation*, trans. by Parsons, Preface to the 1st ed., p. xi.

[3] See his *Penal Philosophy*, trans. by Howell, especially the Author's Foreword, the Editorial Preface, and Chap. VI; also, BRETT, *A History of Psychology*, vol. III, p. 308.

reflected upon not only the specific manifestations of criminal behavior, which were his immediate concern, but also the larger problems involved of human motive and social conduct generally. Gradually his criminological views began to shape themselves into definite theories which attracted world-wide attention. Gradually also the larger significance of his theories for a science of social behavior began to take shape in his mind. And thus Tarde prepared himself for the formulation of a new system of social theory.[1]

As is well known, Tarde's social theory centers about the principle of suggestion-imitation. In looking about for a social explanation of crime, the mysterious inter-influence of minds brought to light in the study of hypnotism attracted his attention. The play of mental interaction in hypnosis was a striking and challenging fact to him as to other students of human behavior. It was a source of concrete support, seemingly, for attempted social explanations of conduct. Here socio-psychic inter-influence was manifest almost in palpable form. The social factor as a determinant in human behavior was undeniable, observable clearly at least under the conditions attendant upon the hypnotic relation.[2]

It was but a step, as Giddings has suggested,[3] for Tarde to attempt to apply this principle to the facts of criminal conduct. His observations relating to crime "waves" and "epidemics" encouraged him in this direction of thought, for these phenomena frequently seemed to offer very startling evidence of the play of suggestion-imitation. And when these baffling mysteries of criminal conduct appeared to give way before the new principle of explanation, Tarde naturally did not stop with criminal conduct. If suggestion-imitation plays such an important role in abnormal conduct and in criminal behavior, is it likely that its place in normal conduct is not equally important, even if its manifestations are less striking and tangible? Both the results of psychopathological investigation, which had already successfully undermined the notion that a sharp line of demarcation separates the abnormal from the normal in human behavior,[4] and the theory of psychic continuity, which was in the air at the time in connection with contemporary evolutionary thought, urged the necessity of a favorable reply to such a question. It is little wonder, therefore, that Tarde felt he was on the trail of a great discovery and that he was lured on by an overwhelming

[1] MERZ, *History of European Thought in the Nineteenth Century*, vol. IV, p. 562; GIDDINGS, Introduction to Tarde, *The Laws of Imitation*, pp. iii *ff.*; DAVIS, *Psychological Interpretations of Society*, p. 84.

[2] *Social Laws*, trans. by Warren, see note, p. 30.

[3] Introduction to TARDE, *The Laws of Imitation*.

[4] It is notable that more recently there has been an attempt in French psychological thought to draw this distinction much more sharply (see BLONDEL, *La conscience morbide*, 1914; also *infra*, p. 131).

enthusiasm to push his theory to the utmost of its logical possibilities as an explanation of social behavior.

"Very rapidly," says Giddings, "M. Tarde's ardent mind ranged over the field of history, followed the spread of Western Civilization, and reviewed the development of language, the evolution of art, of law, and of institutions. The evidence was overwhelming that in all the affairs of men, whether of good or of evil report, imitation is an ever-present factor." To a philosophical mind such as Tarde's, he adds, the implication was obvious, "that there must be psychological or sociological laws of imitation, worthy of most thorough study."[1] When, therefore, in the light of Tarde's developing scheme of relations, imitation began finally to loom, not merely as an ever-present but as the *distinctive* factor in social life, the essential basis of his theory emerged clearly into view and the key principle of his entire system was definitely revealed.[2]

Tarde's imitation theory was not new in conception, for imitation as a factor in social life had been set forth in various connections by previous writers—Cournot, Espinas, Romanes, Bagehot, etc.;[3] but it was new by emphasis. Instead of giving imitation *a* place in his thought, as has been noted, Tarde gave it *the* place.[4] With him the principle of imitation became the center of a complete system of social theory and eventually also of a comprehensive system of cosmic theory.

The conviction gradually grew upon Tarde that the theory of imitation was "the key to the social mystery,"[5] the elementary principle which would transform the chaos of history and social fact into order, and in general do for social science what the discovery of the cell theory did for biology or the theory of molecular movement did for physics.[6] In it, he felt, he had arrived at "the fundamental social fact" and so had put the foundation under the all-important science of sociology, which, he pointed out, remained in a most unstable condition of scientific development as long as the fundamental fact in terms of which its valid scientific generalizations could be set up remained undiscovered.[7] Once ascertained, however, sociology was thereby securely placed in the way of orderly development, for henceforth its progress as a science was but a matter of following out the operation of this elemental social

[1] Introduction to TARDE, *The Laws of Imitation*, p. iv. Quotations from this work are reprinted by permission of Henry Holt and Company, publishers.

[2] *Ibid.* p. xvi.

[3] See DAVIS, *Psychological Interpretations of Society*, pp. 109 *ff.*; PARK, *Masse und Publikum*, Chap. II; PARK and BURGESS, *Introduction to the Science of Sociology*, Chap. VI.

[4] DAVIS, *Psychological Interpretations of Society*, p. 113.

[5] *Social Laws*, p. 47.

[6] *The Laws of Imitation*, p. 11; *Social Laws*, pp. 53 *ff.*; DAVIS, *Psychological Interpretations of Society*, p. 85.

[7] *Social Laws*, pp. 28, 55 *ff.*

fact in the detail of its application to the various aspects and processes of social life.[1]

Tarde's ideal of procedure for this purpose was the detailed monographic method which the LePlay school was popularizing in France.[2] Such detailed study of the social process at various points and in various concrete connections, Tarde felt, could not but lead to valuable sociological generalizations. But lacking such a basis of detailed social investigation, he fell back upon his own observations and on such available records of social life as were at hand in history, economics, existing accounts of the development of culture, art, law, etc., for detail material to support and illustrate his theories. Then, to establish their wider applicability as a cosmic scheme of thought, he finally resorted to the method of elaborate analogy from every sphere of scientific inquiry.

It is of course undeniable that the fact of imitation being admitted on as general a scale as it was by Tarde, his theory proved to be a remarkably effective organizing medium in the field of psycho-social thought. It bridged the gap between the individual and the social realms more successfully than any principle so far set forth, and it introduced a dynamic view of the social process which seemed for the first time to provide an adequate psychological foundation for sociology. Much that the folk psychologists and the organic sociologists suggested but left vague and unintelligible—the relation between subjective and objective mental phenomena, the nature of group unity and psycho-social interdependence, the play of individual and social factors in the social process, etc.—seemed to take on definite meaning when regarded from the standpoint of imitation. Furthermore, it seemed to Tarde that the theory of imitation provided once and for all a secure basis for the differentiation of social from biological science. Neither Comte nor Spencer had adequately differentiated sociology from biology, Tarde felt. The theory of imitation, however, made this distinction clear: all that is the result of hereditary transmission in social phenomena is biology; all that is the result of imitation is sociology.[3] Beyond this, Tarde followed Comte: man's mental life is a matter of biology or sociology, and it is the latter on the side of content.[4]

Tarde's interest was naturally centered in the latter aspects of mental life. In individual psychology as such, Tarde was hardly more interested

[1] *Ibid.*, pp. 3, 9 *ff.*, 47.

[2] *Ibid.*, pp. 198–199, see note.

[3] *The Laws of Imitation*, pp. 14, 50.

[4] *Ibid.*, pp. 145 *ff.*; *Social Laws*, pp. 38–39; "Inter-psychology," trans. by Page, *Intern. Quar.*, vol. 7, pp. 64 *ff.*, 1903; see Dewey's comment on this position, *Psychol. Rev.*, vol. 24, p. 267, 1917. Like Comte, Tarde practically reversed the traditional approach of individualistic thought here. "The psychological," he stated, "is explained by the social just because the social sprang from the psychological" (*The Laws of Imitation*, note, p. xiv).

than Comte. But Tarde did not disregard individual psychology, as did Comte. Instead, he suggested the need, for the purposes of social theory, of reinterpreting its principles so as to bring out their social significance. In his own social theory he sought to do this by making belief and desire figure as the fundamental psychological elements and motivating forces of social life.[1]

Having then arrived, in the manner indicated, at the conviction that imitation is the all-important principle in social life, the next question of importance for Tarde was, What is it that is being imitated? The answer to this question was in a sense but the logical corollary to his main thesis and hence simple by comparison and readily forthcoming. People imitate the novel and the striking, that is, the inventions and discoveries that appear from time to time at every point in the social process.[2] This answer gave Tarde the other half of his formula and at the same time it suggested the solution to the important problem as to how change is effected in a social world in which the basic process is, as he maintained, a matter of imitation. Imitation in itself could account for social uniformity only; it left social variation unexplained. In its two-fold aspect of invention-imitation, however, the principle covered both of these fundamental aspects of social life. In this form, the theory accordingly appeared to be both adequate and complete.

"Socially," says Tarde, "everything is either invention or imitation."[3] To the extent that social life is a matter of new and individual "initiatives," it is invention; to the extent that it is a matter of traditional continuities, it is imitation. From the cyclic interplay of these two factors, all of the variety and complexity of social life comes into being. In its twofold formulation, the principle of imitation thus encompasses the whole social process for Tarde, as to both process and product; all that is of social significance in human association and in social organization.[4] With much justification, therefore, he felt that he had discovered "the key to almost every lock" in the social mystery.[5] And having reached this view, he set about the task of developing his theory through a process of elaboration, illustration, application, and eventually also of universalization, in the approved contemporary manner.

[1] In Tarde's scheme of thought, belief and desire occupy a place similar to that of sensations in association psychology. Sensations, he maintained, being non-communicable, are purely individual phenomena and hence of no significance as a basis for the study of social life (see, *The Laws of Imitation*, pp. xvi, 145 *ff*.; *Social Laws*, pp. 28–34; "Inter-psychology," *Intern. Quar.*, vol. 7, pp. 70 *ff*., 1903; also DAVIS, *Psychological Interpretations of Society*, pp. 99 *ff*.).

[2] *The Laws of Imitation*, pp. 2, 7.

[3] *Ibid.*, pp. 3, 144.

[4] See DAVIS, *Psychological Interpretations of Society*, pp. 88–89.

[5] *The Laws of Imitation*, p. ix.

In the course of this expansion of his thought, Tarde developed his theory in many articles and in volume after volume. In its essential aspects it appears, however, in his first and best known sociological work, *Les lois de l'imitation* (1890), the two later companion volumes of his principal sociological series, *La logique sociale* (1895) and *L'opposition universelle* (1897), being elaborations chiefly of aspects of his original theory which appeared to need more emphasis and clarification. But these three works do not present Tarde's system of thought in logical order. Such an orderly presentation he first brought forth in his *Les lois sociales* (1898). Here his theory is developed in terms of the three universalized processes of *repetition*, *opposition*, and *adaptation*, with which, according to Tarde, all science is concerned. Of these, he pointed out in accordance with his basic position, repetition, taking the form of undulation in the physical world, heredity in the biological world, and imitation in the social world, is the most fundamental. Opposition is but an intermediary process between repetition and adaptation, and adaptation itself but marks the initiation of a new cycle of repetition. Applied to the field of social phenomena, this meant, in effect, that imitation, the social form of repetition, is basically the beginning, the end, and the all of the social process —from its point of origin in individual invention, through its precipitation as social tradition, and leading on again, in the form of the socially inherited elements and conditions of thought, to a new invention and a new cycle of imitation. Conflict, and especially invention, the social forms respectively of opposition and adaptation, are important factors, to be sure, but in so far as they have social significance, they are to be regarded as functions of imitation, necessary intermediate stages, as, in their endless cyclic flow, wave upon wave of imitation passes on through the social medium.[1]

From the very outset, in reading Tarde, we realize that we are in a rather novel atmosphere of social thought. "Why," asks Tarde in the opening pages of his *Laws of Imitation*, "is the science of society still unborn, or born but recently, among all its adult and vigorous sister sciences"?

The chief reason is, I think, that we have thrown away the substance for its shadow and substituted words for things. We have thought it impossible to give a scientific look to *sociology* except by giving it a biological or, better still, a mechanical air. This is an attempt to light up the known by the unknown. It is transforming a solar system into a non-resolvable nebula in order to understand it better.[2]

For in social subjects, according to him, we are exceptionally privileged in having "veritable causes, positive and specific acts, at first hand,"—a

---

[1] *Social Laws*, especially pp. 7-8, 133 *ff*., 212-213.
[2] *The Laws of Imitation*, p. 1.

condition which is wholly lacking in every other subject of investigation. "It is unnecessary, therefore," in his view, "to rely for an explanation of social facts upon the so-called general causes which physicists and naturalists are obliged to create under the name of force, energy, conditions of existence, and other verbal palliatives of their ignorance of the real groundwork of things."[1]

Striving after the scientific, Tarde goes on to point out, we bind ourselves to contrive causes for social change "on the type of those useful fictions which are elsewhere imposed upon us, and we congratulate ourselves upon being able at times to give an entirely impersonal colour to human phenomena by reason of our lofty, but, truly speaking, obscure point of view." "Let us ward off this vague idealism," urges he. "Let us likewise ward off the vapid individualism which consists in explaining social changes as the caprices of certain great men."[2] Instead, he proceeds to outline his own approach as follows:

On the other hand, let us explain these changes through the more or less fortuitous appearance, as to time and place, of certain great ideas, or rather, of a considerable number of both major and minor ideas, of ideas which are generally anonymous and usually of obscure birth; which are simple or abstruse; which are seldom illustrious, but which are always novel. Because of this latter attribute, I shall take the liberty of baptising them collectively *inventions* or *discoveries*. By these two terms I mean any kind of an innovation or improvement, however slight, which is made in any previous innovation throughout the range of social phenomena—language, religion, politics, law, industry, or art. At the moment when this novel thing, big or little as it may be, is conceived of, or determined by, an individual, nothing appears to change in the social body—just as nothing changes in the physical appearance of an organism which a harmful or beneficent microbe has just invaded—and the gradual changes caused by the introduction of the new element seem to follow, without visible break, upon the anterior social changes into whose current they glided. Hence arises the illusion which leads philosophers of history into affirming that there is a real and fundamental continuity in historic metamorphoses. The true causes can be reduced to a chain of ideas which are, to be sure, very numerous, but which are in themselves distinct and discontinuous, although they are connected by the more numerous acts of imitation which are modelled upon them.[3]

This is Tarde's own statement of his theory reduced to its simplest terms: individual innovation spread and organized socially through imitation; or, more accurately, since imitation is the fundamental social fact, according to Tarde—imitation and hence socialization of individual innovation. He says:

Our starting-point lies here in the re-inspiring initiatives which bring new wants, together with new satisfactions, into the world, and which then, through

[1] *Ibid.*
[2] *Ibid.*, pp. 1–2.
[3] *Ibid.*, p. 2.

spontaneous and unconscious or artificial and deliberate imitation, propagate or tend to propagate, themselves, at a more or less rapid, but regular, rate, like a wave of light, or like a family of termites . . . I confess that this is an extremely difficult analysis . . . but in holding to it boldly and unreservedly, in exploiting it from the most trivial detail to the most complete synthesis of facts, we may, perhaps, notice how well fitted it is to bring into relief all the picturesqueness and, at the same time, all the simplicity of history, and to reveal historic perspectives which may be characterized by the freakishness of a rock-bound landscape, or the conventionality of a park walk. This is idealism also, if you choose to call it so; but it is the idealism which consists in explaining history through the ideas of its actors, not through those of the historian.[1]

But this bare skeleton of Tarde's theory does not in itself carry much meaning or do justice to the breadth of appeal of the imposing system of theory and illustration which he built up. For the purposes of social psychology particularly, it is necessary to follow Tarde in his detailed analysis a little in order to see how he brings invention and imitation, the individual and the social together in a functionally interacting and dynamically unified social-psychological process.

From Tarde's definition as given in the previous quotation, it is apparent that invention may take place in any aspect of social behavior. Wherever it occurs, however, it is always a function of belief and desire, the two psychological "quantities" which are at bottom, according to Tarde, "the substance and the force" of social phenomena.[2] As indicated above,[3] belief and desire are the meeting point of the biological and the social in Tarde's system. The organic substratum of belief and desire, existing as potential tendencies toward activity, is biological; the content in terms of which this organic substratum is given concrete direction is social, that is, obtained through imitation.[4] Invention, being a product of belief and desire, is neither wholly biological nor wholly social but, according to Tarde, a "happy" combination of these two contributing factors. "It arises from the intersection of an individual genius, an intermittent and characteristic racial product, the ripe fruit of a series of happy marriages, with the currents and radiation of imitation which one day happened to cross each other in a more or less exceptional brain,"[5]—a combination of circumstances which is to some extent a matter of chance, according to Tarde, and hence reducible only to a system of pseudo-laws, as compared with the real laws of imitation.[6]

[1] *Ibid.*, pp. 2–3.
[2] *Ibid.*, pp. 144–145.
[3] See *supra*, p. 97.
[4] *The Laws of Imitation*, pp. 24, 44*ff.*, 146.
[5] *Ibid.*, p. xxii; *cf.* pp. xiv, 43 *ff.*, 382; *Social Laws*, pp. 137*ff.*, 169; DAVIS, *Psychological Interpretations of Society*, pp. 89–94.
[6] *The Laws of Imitation*, pp. 13, 142.

But inventions are regarded by Tarde, despite the part which, according to him, imitation plays in their appearance, as individual products until they repeat themselves through imitative radiation. An invention that is not imitated is, from his point of view, "socially non-existent."[1] Since, then, as he pointed out, "given one hundred different innovations conceived of at the same time . . . perhaps ten will spread abroad, while ninety will be forgotten,"[2] the social significance of inventions beyond the point of their appearance becomes entirely a matter of the process of imitation. The center of interest accordingly shifts in Tarde's theory, with the assumption of the appearance of inventions, to the process upon which their social fate depends, *i.e.*, to the socially all-important process of imitation.[3]

Every invention tends to expand in its social environment through imitation, according to Tarde, similarly to the circling which takes place when a stone falls into water or when waves of light or sound are set in motion. The well-known laws of Malthus and Darwin on the tendency of the individuals of a species to increase in geometrical progression are, according to him, true laws of radiation through imitation. It is by just such a process of geometrical progression, for instance, that a local dialect, spoken only by certain families, gradually becomes a national idiom through imitation.[4]

Such expansion of an invention in regular geometrical progression can take place, however, only if a perfectly homogeneous environment is presupposed and no hindrances arise to its spread. But usually discoveries and inventions encounter obstacles of various kinds, so that this tendency often proves abortive in varying degrees or even completely.[5] Because of these complicating factors, the most important of which is the competing spread of other inventions, the problem of whether an invention will spread by imitation at all and, if it does, what course it will follow and what progress it will make thus becomes a complex affair. Viewing the situation in intellectualistic terms, Tarde sought to describe it as a matter of logic, as a play of individual and social "logic" or "dialectic,"[6] the chief social aspects of which have already been suggested above in connection with our mention of Tarde's three chief sociological works.[7]

---

[1] *Ibid.*, p. 150; *Social Laws*, p. 40.

[2] *The Laws of Imitation*, pp. 45*ff.*, 140.

[3] Tarde's more extensive treatment of invention in relation to imitation is to be found in his *La logique sociale* (see especially Chap. IV).

[4] *The Laws of Imitation*, p. 17; *Social Laws*, pp. 61 *ff.*

[5] *Tne Laws of Imitation*, pp. 17*ff.*, 140*ff.*, 165*ff.*; *Social Laws*, pp. 63–64.

[6] These phrases, used in reference to Tarde's theory of imitation, suggest the similar reference of Baldwin's "dialectic of personal and social growth," though Baldwin himself objected to the association (see *Social and Ethical Interpretations*, Prefaces to 1st and 2d ed.).

[7] *Supra*, p. 98; *The Laws of Imitation*, pp. 150*ff.*, 168; DAVIS, *Psychological Interpretations of Society*, pp. 94*ff.*

Two outstanding tendencies are distinguishable in the process, according to Tarde, "the one creative, the other critical, the one abounding in combinations of old *accumulable* inventions and discoveries, the other in struggles between *alternative* inventions or discoveries."[1] He says:

When two waves, two *physical* things which are pretty much alike, and which have spread separately from two distinct centers, meet together in the same physical *being*, in the same particle of matter, the impetus of each is increased or neutralized, as its direction coincides with, or is diametrically opposed to, the direction of the other. In the first case, a new and complex wave sets in which is stronger than the others and which tends to propagate itself in turn; in the second, struggle and partial destruction follow, until one of the two rivals has the better of the other . . . In the same way, when two beliefs or two desires, or a belief and a desire, in short when two social things (in the last analysis all social facts are beliefs or desires under the different names of dogmas, sentiment, laws, wants, customs, morals, etc.), have for a certain time travelled their separate roads in the world by means of education or example, *i.e.*, of imitation, they often end by coming into mutual contact. In order that their encounter and interference may be really psychological and social, co-existence in the same brain and participation in the same state of mind and heart is not only necessary, but in addition, one must present itself either in support of, or in opposition to the other, either as a principle, of which the other is a corollary or as an affirmative, of which the other is the negative.[2]

The social process thus consists for Tarde, essentially of a flux of logical *alliances* and logical *combats*, logical *unions* and logical *duels*.[3] Hence, his emphasis on opposition and adaptation as the complementary processes of repetition and imitation. These being, however, after all, only secondary developments—really, only especially notable aspects in the main movement of imitative radiation—the latter, in the inclusive sense, represents the social process in its entirety for him. This is the significance of his epigrammatic statement that socially "everything, *even the desire to invent*," has the same imitation origin.[4] "What is society?" asks Tarde, in order to epitomize his theory. "I have answered: Society is imitation."[5]

Coming, then, to the more detailed study of the laws of imitation, "which are to sociology," according to him, "what the laws of habit and heredity are to biology, the laws of gravitation to astronomy, the laws of vibration to physics,"[6] Tarde notes that the imitative spread of an invention is determined by both physical and social factors. But consistently

[1] *The Laws of Imitation*, p. 154.
[2] *Ibid.*, pp. 24–25; *cf. Social Laws*, pp. 99*ff.*, 133*ff.*
[3] *The Laws of Imitation*, pp. 149, 154*ff.*, 173*ff.*
[4] *Ibid.*, p. 150; *Social Laws*, pp. 40–41.
[5] *The Laws of Imitation*, p. 74; *Social Laws*, pp. 39, 47.
[6] *Ibid.*, p. 61.

with his intention "to unfold the purely sociological side of human facts,"[1] he passes the first order of factors by with their mention and confines himself to the treatment of the latter order. He distinguishes two kinds of social influences, the logical and the extra-logical.

"Logical causes operate whenever an individual prefers a given innovation to others because he thinks it is more useful or more true than others, that is, more in accord than they are with the aims or principles that have already found a place in his mind."[2] Such considerations precipitate the *logical duel* and the *logical union* as psychological and social processes. Extra-logical causes are concerned with such matters as the time, the place, the social prestige, and the rhythm of imitation. Imitation, Tarde states, in consideration of these factors, proceeds from within without, from the socially superior to the socially inferior, from epochs of "custom imitation" to epochs of "fashion imitation" and back again.[3]

This has probably been the most popular part of Tarde's theory. The simplicity and comparative finality of his formulation of these considerations in the form of social laws and the striking manner in which he illustrated their operation in the different aspects of social life—in the fields of language, religion, government, legislation, political economy, morals, and art—made a tremendous impression on the psychological and social thought of the day, especially as regards the social-psychological implications of his views and general position.[4]

But what, more specifically, according to Tarde, is the nature of the all-important process of imitation?[5] What is imitation in his sense? As already noted, it was primarily with the social manifestations of imitation that he was concerned. The analysis of imitation as a psychological process he regarded as essentially a psychological problem which the sociologist should yield to the psychologist.[6] But psychology, Tarde pointed out, was as yet able to throw little light on the operation of this phenomenon in normal mental and social life.

What is the essential nature of the suggestion which passes from one cerebral cell to another and which constitutes mental life? We do not know. Do we

---

[1] *The Laws of Imitation*, pp. xv, 140–141.

[2] *Ibid.*, p. 141.

[3] *Ibid.*, Chaps. VI *ff.*

[4] See references *infra*, p. 107.

[5] In his original edition of *Les lois de l'imitation*, Tarde nowhere formally defined imitation, but after his use of the term had been challenged, he replied in defense in the preface to the second edition with the following statement: "I have always given it a very precise and characteristic meaning, that of the action at a distance of one mind upon another, and of action which consists of a quasi-photographic reproduction of a central image upon the sensitive plate of another brain . . . By imitation I mean every impression of an interpsychical photography, so to speak, willed or not willed, passive or active" (*The Laws of Imitation*, Preface to 2d ed., p. xiv).

[6] *Ibid.*, p. 74.

know anything more about the essence of the suggestion which passes from one person to another and which constitutes social life? We do not; for if we take this phenomenon in itself, in its higher state of purity and intensity, we find it related to one of the most mysterious of facts, a fact which is being studied with intense curiosity by the baffled philosophic alienists of the day, *i.e.*, somnambulism.[1]

Accordingly, Tarde turned to the literature of contemporary psychopathology, and with something of an apology for adopting the terminology of the students of hypnotism, he tells us that it need not appear fanciful to think of the social man "as a veritable somnambulist."[2] He justifies his use of this analogy on the ground that in the hypnotic state, we get the social tie in its purest and simplest form. With this justification, he goes on to say that "the social like the hypnotic state is only a form of dream, a dream of command and a dream of action"[3] and to develop an elaborate and detailed analogy on this basis.

The child, according to Tarde, is unquestionably a true somnambulist. It lives constantly in a magnetized state of respect and admiration for parents, teachers, and associates of prestige. But neither is the adult, whether in primitive or civilized society, ever wholly demagnetized. Whether it is through the reciprocal suggestion and imitation which come into play among equals or through the unilateral polarization which comes into play as a result of social prestige and which more closely parallels the hypnotic relation; whether it is in the form of "custom-imitation" or "fashion-imitation," unconscious or deliberate imitation, the adult, like the child, is ever held in some manner under the spell of social hypnotism.[4]

"Suppose," says Tarde, "a somnambulist should imitate his medium to the point of becoming a medium himself and magnetising a third person, who, in turn, would imitate him, and so on indefinitely. Is not social life this very thing?"[5] His reply was unqualified. "Society is imitation and imitation is a kind of somnambulism."[6] Being challenged in this view later, he explained: "If we observe that wherever there is a social relation between two living beings, there we have imitation in this sense . . . we shall have to admit that a sociologist was justified in taking this notion as a look-out post."[7]

While in association, according to him, we can never escape imitation even enough to make invention possible. "To innovate, to discover, to

[1] *Ibid.*, pp. 75–76. It should be recalled that Tarde first wrote this in 1884 (see *The Laws of Imitation*, note 1, p. 76).

[2] *Ibid.*, p. 76.

[3] *Ibid.*, p. 77; also "Inter-psychology," *Intern. Quar.*, vol. 7, p. 69, 1903.

[4] *The Laws of Imitation*, pp. 77 ff.

[5] *Ibid.*, p. 84.

[6] *Ibid.*, p. 87.

[7] *Ibid.*, p. xiv.

awake for an instant from his dream of home and country" the individual must escape, for the time being, from his social surroundings and become "super-social rather than social."[1]

Such, in essence, is Tarde's social theory. "In following this cycle from invention through imitation and back again, with all the logical and psychological appurtenances," says M. M. Davis in his summary of Tarde's theory, "we can see, also, how and why Tarde has so insistently and consistently clung to imitation as the distinctive sociological stage, the distinctively social factor . . . Invention is an individual product, belief and desire are individual, and logical conflicts are at bottom conflicts in individual minds."[2] How are these individual facts transformed into social facts? Tarde was one of the first psycho-social theorists to face this problem squarely, and his answer was clear and challenging. We reach the social stage through imitation. The social stage appears, according to him, when an invention spreads through imitation from its center in the mind of a creative individual to other individuals. Thereby it takes on an inter-cerebral instead of a merely intra-cerebral character and so becomes a social instead of a merely individual fact. "Like many other sociologists," says Davis, "Tarde has sought for the quintessence of society, for that single aspect or process of our complex common life which makes it what it is, by distinguishing it from everything else under the sun. He finds this to be Imitation." Upon imitation as the foundation, he accordingly sought to construct his system of social theory.[3]

What importance has this theory for social psychology? Tarde was inconsistent and faltering in the application of the social-psychological implications of his theory. Despite his attempts to reinterpret individualistic psychology, he continued all along to be held down by its individualistic view of mental life. His whole approach rests on the assumption that the individual is somehow basic in human life and that the social must have some distinguishing characteristic which will lift it out from the enveloping setting of individual fact. Nevertheless, his position as developed in terms of the theory of imitation was a long and decisive step in advance of the conventional dualism of thought about the subjective-individual and the objective-social aspects of human life. And it was obviously an advance also, from the social-psychological standpoint, over the attempted biological and historical syntheses of organic sociology on the one hand and folk psychology on the other—so decisive an advance, in fact, that along with some other important events

---

[1] *Ibid.*, pp. 87–88.

[2] See DAVIS, *Psychological Interpretations of Society*, pp. 105–106.

[3] *Ibid.*, p. 105; *The Laws of Imitation*, pp. 74*ff.*; "Inter-psychology," *Intern. Quar.*, vol. 7, pp. 60 *ff.*, 1903; *La logique sociale*, Chap. I; *Études de psychologie sociale*, Chap. I; DAVIS, *Psychological Interpretations of Society*, pp. 105–106.

of the day leading in the same direction, notably Ward's emphasis on the psychic factors in evolution, Tarde's work definitely marks a new era of social-psychological interest and activity.

Disregarding the extravagance of Tarde's somnambulistic analogies and the pseudo-scientific nature of his "laws," the twofold thesis which stands out boldly above everything else in his system of social thought— if we can but disentangle it from the specific theory in terms of which Tarde developed it and which later investigation has proved to be faulty in the main,[1]—is that human social life is essentially a psychical process and human psychic life largely a social process. This much in itself was a considerable clarification of the atmosphere of psycho-social thought at a time when biological conceptions and the confusing historical point of view predominated in the field.[2] But Tarde did much more: he illumined each part of this fundamental social-psychological thesis by bringing it into functional relation with the other in a common process of psycho-social interaction. And by further defining this process of interaction in terms of the more concrete process of suggestion-imitation, he brought a reality to the notion of "social" psychology which all the vague theory about the place of the social factor in human mental development and cultural evolution was powerless to reflect. Also, Tarde's work was a distinct step ahead in the direction of the triumph of direct analysis over deduction and analogy in social psychology. In combination, these features acted as a veritable leaven in stimulating social-psychological thought and investigation. Tarde's very extravagance and inconsistency acted as a scientific challenge in this respect, it appears.

To say that "society is a continuing process of interaction between individuals, in which their initiatives become mutually influential and are harmonized and correlated into useful cooperative action," says Davis, would be "not only more true" of the social process than Tarde's "Society is imitation," but it would also "represent more closely what Tarde's sociological theory really is, as we gather it from his work as a whole."[3] However, it would have been much less effective, and Tarde, as Davis notes, was enough of a *littérateur* to know the effective and to appreciate its value even in the field of science.

In the long run, the effective was perhaps also the fruitful at a time when the spectacular was needed to attract attention to the field of

---

[1] See FARIS, "The Concept of Imitation," *Amer. Jour. Sociol.*, vol. 32, pp. 369–378, 1926. In this country, Thorndike's experimental work on imitation had a determining effect in undermining the theory of imitation in the broad sense of Tarde's use. See THORNDIKE, *The Original Nature of Man*, Chap. VIII.

[2] See *The Laws of Imitation*, p. iv; "Inter-psychology," *Intern. Quar.*, vol. 7, pp. 62 *ff.*, 1903.

[3] DAVIS, *Psychological Interpretations of Society*, p. 141.

social-psychological investigation. But however that may be, there can be little doubt but that Tarde's influential position in modern social-psychological thought can be traced to his literary boldness almost as much as to his scientific suggestiveness. And all in all, Tarde was probably the most influential figure in modern sociological theory from the standpoint of its effect upon modern social psychology since Comte and Spencer. We can probably therefore follow at least part way those of his defenders who point to Tarde's work as the chief source from which modern social psychology leads out.[1] For from whatever combination of circumstances, Tarde's work was certainly a very notable factor in ushering in the modern era of intensive social-psychological activity.[2] The bridge between general psychology and general sociology which modern social psychology has gradually built up has of course come about as a cooperative work of several fields, chiefly psychology and sociology. But because of the individualistic background of modern social-psychological thought, the sociological direction of approach has been particularly important—and few can lay claim to greater importance in this respect than Tarde. However much later thought has found it necessary to discount in Tarde's social theory, therefore—the artificiality of his system, the faulty basis of his specific theory of socialization, the over-simplification and pseudo-scientific nature of his so-called "laws"— it thus remains that Tarde is one of the outstanding figures in the modern social-psychological as well as sociological movements. In this country, as we shall see, Tarde's work figured both directly and indirectly in stimulating social-psychological thought. For besides the general effect of his work, as indicated above, his specific theory was taken over and incorporated into the stream of American social-psychological thought, notably through the work of Ross but less conspicuously also through the work of other writers, such as Baldwin, Giddings, and Ellwood.[3]

[1] See TOSTI, "Social Psychology and Sociology," *Psychol. Rev.*, vol. 5, pp. 352*ff.*, 1898; also ROSS, *Social Psychology*, Preface.

[2] *Cf.* BOGARDUS, *A History of Social Thought*, pp. 379–380; also DEWEY, "The Need of a Social Psychology," *Psychol. Rev.*, vol. 24, pp. 266–276, 1917.

[3] For a further discussion of Tarde's social theory, see, besides the foregoing references, BRISTOL, *Social Adaptation*, pp. 185–192; BOGARDUS, *A History of Social Thought*, pp. 372–380; LICHTENBERGER, *Development of Social Theory*, Chap. XIV; BARNES, "The Philosophy of the State in the Writings of Gabriel Tarde," *Phil. Rev.*, vol. 28, pp. 248–279, 1919; SMALL, *General Sociology*, Chap. XXXIX; Review of *Social Laws*, *Amer. Jour. Sociol.*, vol. 4, pp. 395–397, 1899; ROSS, *The Foundations of Sociology*, *passim*; ELLWOOD, "The Theory of Imitation in Social Psychology," *Amer. Jour. Sociol.*, vol. 6, pp. 721–741, 1901; *Sociology in Its Psychological Aspects*, pp. 294–308; GINSBERG, *The Psychology of Society*, pp. 23 *ff.*; SOROKIN, *Contemporary Sociological Theories*, pp. 634–640; see also DUMAS *et al.*, *Traité de psychologie*, chap. on 'L'Interpsychologie"; Matagrin, *La psychologie sociale de Gabriel Tarde*, especially Chaps. I, VI; also *infra*, pp. 117*ff.*, 121*ff.*, and general references, p. 122, note 4.

III. The Study of "Collective Representations" as an Approach
to Social Psychology: Collective Psychology

1. Émile Durkheim (1858–1917)

Alongside of Tarde as a foremost representative of modern psycho-sociological thought in France and in a sense at the opposite sociological extreme from Tarde in his emphasis on the individual factor in social causation stands Emile Durkheim. As over against Tarde's approach by way of invention, which he regarded as private and individual until it spread by imitation, Durkheim emphasized the importance of the group factor in the social process. Durkheim's standpoint, just as Tarde's, is nevertheless thoroughly psychological.[1] He started out, however, at the other pole of the socio-psychical complex with which social psychology is concerned compared to Tarde and worked more or less against the current of Tarde's mode of thought, a procedure which tended to bring their respective theories into striking contrasts and, incidentally, to play up the dualism of emphasis which necessarily follows in the wake of the conventional approaches from the opposite look-out posts of the "individual" and the "collective" in social life.

Tarde was so impressed with the reality and importance of the individual factor in the social process that he made the individual his center of operations and kept his attention fixed upon the individual mind to the almost complete disregard of the collective aspect of social life. Durkheim, on the other hand, was equally impressed with the reality and importance of the collective factor. Accordingly, he made the social group his center of operations, with the result that he came out at the other extreme of having practically ignored the individual factor.[2] In this difference of approach, Tarde and Durkheim epitomized at close range the antagonism of standpoint which traditional individualistic and collectivistic thought embodied. Individualistic thought, as represented by traditional psychology, approached the problems of human behavior and social life from the subjective and individualistic standpoint. Collectivistic thought, as represented especially by early sociology in its study of social organization but also by anthropology in its study of objective culture, approached these problems from their objective and collectivistic standpoint. Social psychology arose as a result of the effort which nineteenth century thought made to bridge the gap between these two systems of theory. However, this difference of approach was carried over also into the new field of inquiry, and at any rate in so far as the development of social psychology from the side of sociology is

[1] See Gehlke, *Emile Durkheim's Contributions to Sociological Theory*, p. 79.
[2] *Cf.* Davis, *Psychological Interpretations of Society*, p. 133; Gehlke, *Emile Durkheim's Contributions to Sociological Theory*, p. 44.

concerned, as represented by Tarde and Durkheim, this difference of approach is clearly associated with what has been suggestively termed the "nominalistic" and "realistic" positions in modern sociology. Tarde and Durkheim stand at opposite poles in this classification.[1]

But however opposed Tarde and Durkheim are in sociological approach, they are both sociologists, and as such they hold common social-psychological ground over against biological and psychological individualism. From the standpoint of social psychology, it is accordingly just as important to note the fundamental agreement of their positions in their common emphasis on the social factor in the organization of human mental life as it is to note the equally fundamental disagreement of their positions with regard to their respective theories as to the nature of this social factor and the process in which it arises.

Durkheim's theory of social behavior centers about his definition of social phenomena in terms of "exteriority" and "constraint." These properties figure as the criteria of *sociality* in his scheme of social thought, just as imitation figures in Tarde's scheme. They are the distinctive characteristics of the social process and the key to social interpretation, according to him—not "imitation," as Tarde maintained.[2] The theoretical defense of this conception is to be found in Durkheim's theory of "collective representations" and "social mind," which it is accordingly necessary to develop briefly here, in order to get at the characteristic setting of his views.

Unlike Tarde, Durkheim did not seek to produce a systematic treatment of sociological theory. He felt, with Simmel[3] and others, that in its present stage of development sociology was not yet ready for systematic treatment. His theory must therefore be pieced together, in some form, from his chief works, among which the following are especially important: De la division du travail social (1893), Les règles de la méthode sociologique (1895), Le suicide (1897), Les formes élémentaires de la vie religieuse (1912). The first of these presents the concrete background of his theory; the second develops certain of its methodological and theoretical implications more formally; the other two are applications of his point of view to the investigation of specific social phenomena. The social-psychological basis of his characteristic position Durkheim formulated most systematically in his article on "Représentations indi-

---

[1] See Park and Burgess, *Introduction to the Science of Sociology*, pp. 27ff.; Brett, *A History of Psychology*, vol. III, pp. 288–289.

[2] Cf. *Les règles de la méthode sociologique*, Chap. I; *Le suicide*, Chap. IV, and Tarde, *Laws of Imitation*, Chap. III; *Études de psychologie sociale*, Chap. II.

[3] Durkheim's theory presents striking similarities to the sociological theories of Simmel and some of the German social-economic students of social organization (see Gehlke, *Emile Durkheim's Contributions to Sociological Theory*, p. 83; also *infra* pp. 120, 121, note 3).

viduelles et représentations collectives,"[1] but it is to be found in fragmentary form also in the above-mentioned works.

In general, représentations collectives, as used by Durkheim, may be said to stand for the re-presentations, in imagination and memory, of common group experiences. They are the ideas and concepts "which embody the objectives of group activity"; the psychic symbols of common social life and experience.[2] In Durkheim's own words, "they correspond to the way in which this very special being, society, considers the things of its own proper experience."[3] But such formal definitions have even less value in the case of Durkheim than in the case of Tarde. To understand what Durkheim really meant to convey by this conception and what significance he attached to it as a tool of social analysis, it is necessary to view it in relation to his psycho-social system as a whole, for Durkheim's social theory is, even more than Tarde's, all of a piece with his psychological views and largely incomprehensible apart from them.

Durkheim was an intellectualist and an interactionist psychologically. He thought of mental life as consisting essentially of représentations. This term as it has been used by the Durkheim school is generally carried over into English in its French form, since our nearest analogues —ideas, images, concepts—do not adequately render it in the broader sense in which it has been used by the representatives of this school of social thought.[4] There are, according to Durkheim, two orders of representations: those constituting the individual mind and those constituting the collective mind. The latter, that is, the collective representations, are, according to him, compounds of individual representations. Individual representations, in turn, Durkheim assumed to be compounds of sensations. And sensations themselves were referred by him, in orthodox interactionist fashion, to basic neural elements. Though related in a hierarchical series, these several levels of psychological phenomena are, Durkheim maintained, distinct and characteristically different orders of facts, explainable only in terms of their own properties and not reducible one to the other. This all follows logically from Durkheim's theory regarding the nature of the process of compounding and combination which separates each level of this series. It is a process in the course of which, according to him, in consequence of a sort of chemical action and synthesis which takes place when chemical elements are in interaction, a totally new product is created. The latter is distinct and independent of the elements that enter into its composition in so far as its characteristics and properties are concerned, much as

---

[1] DURKHEIM, "Représentations individuelles et représentations collectives," Revue de mét. et de mor., vol. 6, pp. 273 ff., 1898, repr. in Sociologie et philosophie, 1924.

[2] See DURKHEIM, Elementary Forms of Religious Life, trans. by Swain, pp. 10, 18, 432; also PARK and BURGESS, Introduction to the Science of Sociology, pp. 164–165.

[3] Elementary Forms of Religious Life, p. 435.

[4] Cf. GEHLKE, Emile Durkheim's Contributions to Sociological Theory, p. 17.

water, the chemical compound of hydrogen and oxygen, is distinct and independent of its component elements in respect to the characteristics and properties which it manifests.[1]

Durkheim laid a great deal of stress on this theory of the compounding of psychological elements. He relied upon it to explain the why and the wherefore of his characteristic views and methodological position. It follows from this theory, he pointed out, that sensations, though they have as their primary basis neural elements, are not explainable in terms of the latter; they are a new synthesis *sui generis* from the nature of the process which produces them. Likewise are individual representations a new synthesis *sui generis* and hence not explainable in terms of the sensations which enter as basic elements into their composition. Finally collective representations, and thereby also the system of social life which they reflect, are a new synthesis *sui generis* and so cannot be explained in terms of the individual elements which constitute their basic substratum. This was Durkheim's objective from the first, of course, the point to which he sought to lead up naturally through his discussion of the compounding of sensations and individual representations. And having led up to it step by step in this way, he sought to make the most of the analogies in support of his social theory, which his broad discussion of his underlying principle of the compounding of elements made possible.[2]

In the social as in the biological field, according to him, association creates "new phenomena" whose germ it is impossible to find in any of the associated elements. In either case, "the whole is not identical with the sum of the parts, it is something else with different properties than those which the parts present of which it is composed."[3] He stated by way of elaboration:

By virtue of this principle society is not a mere sum of individuals, but a system formed by their association representing a specific reality which has its own proper characteristics. Without doubt, collective life cannot be produced if the individual consciousnesses are not given; but this necessary condition is not sufficient. It is necessary further that these consciousnesses be associated, combined, and combined in a definite manner; it is from this combination that social life results and, in consequence, it is this combination which explains it. By aggregating, interpenetrating, fusing, the individual minds give birth to a being, psychic if you will, but which constitutes a psychic individuality of a new kind. It is

[1] *Revue de mét. et de mor.*, vol. 6, pp. 273*ff.*, 1898; *Les règles de la méthode sociologique*, pp. 15*ff.*, 125*ff.*; GEHLKE, *Emile Durkheim's Contributions to Sociological Theory*, pp. 19*ff.*, see especially summary, p. 32, and criticism, p. 96; also article on "Sociologie" by Fauconnet and Mauss in *La Grande Encyclopédie*.

[2] See *Revue de mét. et de mor.*, vol. 6, pp. 293*ff.*, 1898; *Les règles de la méthode sociologique*, Chap. I, pp. 125*ff.*, 136; *Elementary Forms*, pp. 15–17, 424*ff.*; GEHLKE, *Emile Durkheim's Contributions to Sociological Theory*, pp. 19*ff.*, Chap. II.

[3] *Les règles de la méthode sociologique*, p. 126.

therefore in the nature of this individuality, not in that of its component units, that one must set about to search for the decisive and determining causes of the facts to which it gives rise. The group thinks, feels, and acts quite differently from the manner in which its members would act, were they isolated. If then one start from the latter, he cannot understand anything of what transpires in the group. In a word, there is in the case of psychology and sociology, the same break in continuity as between biology and the physico-chemical sciences. Accordingly, whenever a social phenomenon is directly explained by a psychological phenomenon, one may be sure that the explanation is false.[1]

Durkheim realized, of course, that he was here on highly controversial ground in attempting to apply to the field of social life the principle that "the whole is not identical with the sum of its parts."[2] He accordingly sought to proceed very cautiously. He thus explained:

Society has for its substratum the ensemble of the associated individuals. The system formed by their union, which varies according to their number, their disposition over the surface of the territory, the nature of and the number of ways of communication, constitutes the base upon which the social life arises. The representations which are the woof [trame] of it are derived from the relations established between the individuals thus combined, or between the secondary groups that are intercalated [intercalé] between the individual and the whole society. Now if one sees nothing extraordinary in the fact that these individual representations, produced by the interactions of neural elements, should not be inherent in these elements, what is there surprising in the fact that collective representations, produced by the interactions of the elementary consciousnesses of which society is made, should not be derived directly from these latter, and, as a result, should extend beyond them [les débordent]? The relation which, in this conception, unites the social substratum to the social life, is at all points analogous to that which one must admit [to exist] between the physiological substratum and the psychic life of the individual, if one does not desire to negate all that which is properly called psychology.[3]

The same break in continuity and the same methodological consequences follow in the one case as in the other, and they are, according to Durkheim, even more immediately apparent in the latter instance than in the former. Collective representations are a distinct order of phenomena because they are derived from the union or fusion (concours)

[1] Ibid., pp. 127–128.

[2] Ibid., p. 126; Revue de mét. et de mor., vol. 6, pp. 295 ff., 1898. This principle is similar, in its social and psychological implications, to Wundt's principle of the "creative synthesis." In fact, Durkheim's whole system of psychological thought runs more or less parallel to Wundt's (see GEHLKE, Emile Durkheim's Contributions, pp. 25–26, 80). It is in their methodological applications of this principle that they differ.

[3] Revue de mét. et de mor., vol. 6, pp. 293–294, 1898, trans. quoted from GEHLKE, Emile Durkheim's Contributions to Sociological Theory, pp. 28–29. Quotations from this work are reprinted by permission of Columbia Studies in History, Economics, and Public Law.

of individuals in association. That collective representations cannot be studied mediately through the primary individual elements which enter into their composition (the individual representations) follows inescapably, according to him, from the fact that the latter, as he maintained, are altered and transformed in the process of psycho-social synthesis which separates the two levels of mental phenomena under consideration. He thus explained further:

> Doubtless, in the elaboration of the common result each [individual] bears his due share; but the private sentiments do not become social except by combining under the action of the forces *sui generis* which association develops. As a result of these combinations, and of the mutual alterations which result therefrom, *they* [the private sentiments] become something else [*autre chose*]. A chemical synthesis results, which concentrates, unifies, the elements synthesized, and by that very process transforms them . . . The resultant derived therefrom extends then beyond [*déborde*] the individual mind as the whole is greater than the part. To know really what it is, one must take the aggregate in its totality. It is this that thinks, that feels, that wills, although it may not be able to will, feel or act save by the intermediation of individual consciousnesses. This explains also why the social phenomenon does not depend on the personal nature of the individuals. It is because in the fusion through which it evolves, all the individual characters, being divergent by definition, are mutually neutralized and cancelled. Only the most general properties of human nature remain unsubmerged; and because of their extreme generality they would not be able to account for the very special and complex forms which characterize collective facts.[1]

Such is the relation and the distinction which Durkheim set up between the individual and the social factors in mental life. Collective representations are compounds of individual representations, and they are to that extent dependent upon them. But they are at the same time separated from these individual elements by a process of fusion and synthesis which constitutes them a new order of phenomena, an *autre chose*, which is distinct from its basic individual substratum and not understandable in terms of it. In this insistence upon the sharp distinction between what is individual and what is social in human psychology, Durkheim but followed out to the logical extreme the dictum upon which conventional individualistic and collectivistic thought built, namely, that "man is double"[2] in his mental life. And refusing to take the conventional path of harmonization through deriving in some fashion the one factor from the other, he insisted instead upon the necessity of maintaining their essential methodological separation. Whatever the difficulties which this position led Durkheim into, it did emphasize most

---

[1] *Revue de mét. et de mor.*, vol. 6, p. 295, 1898, trans. quoted from GEHLKE, *Emile Durkheim's Contributions to Sociological Theory*, pp. 29–30.

[2] *Elementary Forms of Religious Life*, p. 16.

dramatically the importance and the concrete reality of the social factor in human conduct. Durkheim's is perhaps the most persistent defense of the group approach in modern psycho-social theory. Alongside of it, the collectivistic emphasis of German psycho-social thought, except in the case of such a writer as Gumplowicz, was weak and wavering. Durkheim's work was thus an outstanding factor in establishing that balance of collectivistic and individualistic tendencies of thought which finally led to the synthetic social-psychological standpoint as it has been developed more especially in this country.

Having set up this sharp distinction between the individual and the social in mental life, Durkheim accounted for the fact that he was concerned only with the latter order of phenomena (collective representations, social facts, the social mind) on the ground that sociology is an autonomous science, quite as distinct from and independent of individual psychology as the subject matter with which the latter field supposedly deals (individual representations) is distinct from and independent of the subject matter with which the former field deals (collective representations).[1] Passing, then, to the description of collective representations, Durkheim emphasized in particular, as already noted above,[2] two of their distinctive characteristics: their "exteriority" with reference to the individual mind and their "constraining power."

Exteriority refers to the property which collective representations have of coming to the individual mind *as from outside it.* This property comes to them of necessity from the fact, according to Durkheim, that they are "the product of collective elaboration"[3] and hence cannot be of any one mind. Such phenomena as religious beliefs, social usages, moral concepts, scientific symbols and categories readily illustrate this property. As they are the product "of no particular mind" but of many minds in interaction, no individual mind can encompass them as its own. Hence they present themselves to the individual mind as from the outside and as exterior to it.[4]

The significance of this property of exteriority appears especially when taken in conjunction with another property of collective representations which Durkheim makes much of, namely, their "superiority" as compared with the representations constituting the individual mind. By this notion Durkheim meant that in consequence of the extension in

---

[1] *Les règles de la méthode sociologique,* pp. 8, 120, 176–177; GEHLKE, *Emile Durkheim's Contributions to Sociological Theory,* pp. 78–80.

[2] *Supra,* p. 109.

[3] *Revue de mét. et de mor.,* vol. 6, p. 295, 1898; *Elementary Forms of Religious Life,* p. 434.

[4] *Revue de mét. et de mor.,* vol. 6, pp. 294–295, 1898; *Elementary Forms of Religious Life,* pp. 16, 432; GEHLKE, *Emile Durkheim's Contributions to Sociological Theory,* pp. 32–33.

time and space, which collective representations attain, they gather a force over and above that of individual representations.[1]

Collective representations are the result of an immense cooperation which stretches out not only in space, but into time as well; to make them a multitude of minds have associated, united and combined their ideas and sentiments; for them long generations have accumulated their experience and knowledge. A special intellectual activity is therefore concentrated in them which is infinitely richer and more complex than that of the individual.[2]

This characteristic is concretely symbolized in the "constraining power" of social phenomena, the invariable obligatoriness with which they present themselves to the individual mind and before which, according to Durkheim, the latter necessarily bows in submission.[3] In conjunction with each other, then, these properties of collective representations provide the basis for Durkheim's definition of social facts and phenomena in terms of "exteriority" and "constraint."

The importance of emphasizing these characteristic properties of collective representations appears readily when we realize that though they constitute distinct psychic systems, according to Durkheim, individual and collective representations coexist as "two beings" within the mind of the individual.[4] It thus becomes a most important matter of sociological methodology to differentiate one system of representations and its relations from the other, in the most definite terms possible. The properties of exteriority and constraint, since they are, from Durkheim's standpoint, *peculiarly* and *distinctively* characteristic of social phenomena and ought to be, according to him, "immediately discernible," thus take on a practical utility as differentiating criteria of "socialness."[5] Hence the value, from Durkheim's point of view, of his definition of social facts and phenomena in terms of these distinguishing criteria. "They [social facts] consist," he says, "in ways of acting, thinking, and feeling, exterior to the individual and endowed with a power of coercion, by virtue of which they impose themselves upon him."[6]

It is in the description of the "social" or "collective" mind, by which Durkheim tells us he meant nothing more than the stream of collective representations considered as a unity (a conception which corresponded

---

[1] *Revue de mét. et de mor.*, vol. 6, p. 299*ff.*, 1898; GEHLKE, *Emile Durkheim's Contributions to Sociological Theory*, pp. 36*ff.*

[2] *Elementary Forms of Religious Life*, p. 16.

[3] *Les règles de la méthode sociologique*, pp. 6, 128–129, 150; *Elementary Forms*, pp. 16–18, 206*ff.*, 432*ff.*; GEHLKE, *Emile Durkheim's Contributions to Sociological Theory*, pp. 36–38, 62.

[4] *Revue de mét. et de mor.*, vol. 6, p. 295, 1898; *Elementary Forms of Religious Life*, pp. 16, 432*ff.*; GEHLKE, *Emile Durkheim's Contributions to Sociological Theory*, pp. 41*ff.*

[5] See *ibid.*, pp. 59–60.

[6] *Les règlesde la méthode sociologique*, p. 8.

to his conception of the individual mind as constituting the stream of individual representations considered as a unity,[1] and which, he thus felt, had the same justification and usefulness as a descriptive tool as the analogous conception of the individual mind), that Durkheim concentrated these criteria of the social. It is "exterior" and "superior" to the individual mind and thereby characteristically "coercive" upon individual behavior. Durkheim elaborated upon the implications of these characteristics of the collective mind in various connections, and he sought to illustrate their concrete significance in the consideration of various aspects of social life.

The property of exteriority, he pointed out, is readily observable on every side. The various systems of collective representations which constitute the collective mind: science, morality, religion, custom, fashion, language, law, in fact the whole content of the social mind—its ideas, habits, judgments, emotions—come to the individual, according to Durkheim, as from the outside, i.e., more or less as finished products which are without the compass of individual experience.[2] As regards the superiority of the collective mind, this property is clearly symbolized in the process of education, which Durkheim regarded from the social standpoint as essentially a process of impressing the collective ways of thinking, feeling, and acting (these being, of course, according to him, basically distinct from the ways in which the individual thinks, feels, and acts) upon the individual mind.[3] Again, the resulting power of coercion and constraint which the collective mind should exert is illustrated in its clearest form in the moral, religious, and legal systems of society, for through them "the voice of the larger mind" becomes most conspicuously evident in its function as an instrument of control.[4]

It is these properties of the social mind, summed up in the characteristic "coerciveness" of social facts, that insure the social conformity of the individual and the unity of the social group. The individual conforms from an inner feeling of necessity; he is literally whipped into line socially by processes over which he has no control and from which there can be no escape, since his own mind becomes the instrument by which he is controlled.[5] He is led in this way to submerge his individual ends and

[1] Revue de mét. et de mor., vol. 6, p. 287, 1898; Les règles de la méthode sociologique, note, pp. 127–128; GEHLKE, Emile Durkheim's Contributions to Sociological Theory, pp. 17, 32, 45, 105.

[2] Les règles de la méthode sociologique, pp. 8ff.; GEHLKE, Emile Durkheim's Contributions to Sociological Theory, pp. 32–33, 60–62.

[3] Les règles de la méthode sociologique, pp. 11, 128; GEHLKE, Emile Durkheim's Contributions to Sociological Theory, pp. 36ff.

[4] Les règles de la méthode sociologique, pp. 14, 128, 150; Elementary Forms of Religious Life, pp. 206ff., 223, 434; GEHLKE, Emile Durkheim's Contributions to Sociological Theory, pp. 38–39, 62.

[5] Elementary Forms of Religious Life, pp. 16–18, 424.

purposes in the larger ends and purposes of the group and to adopt the latter as the most potent motives of his conduct. This, the "coerciveness" of social facts, is for Durkheim above all, therefore, the characteristic social criterion.[1] And aside from his, as it would seem, rather extremist statement of his theory,[2] judging from the trend of recent sociological thought, which has tended increasingly to emphasize the problem of social control as a central consideration,[3] Durkheim hit upon a most fruitful viewpoint in this principle. However, he could not follow it out freely and with balance, because despite his extreme collectivistic leanings in some directions, he, like Tarde, was definitely held down by the prepossessions of an individualistic psychology which, on the whole, he accepted uncritically. It was largely because of this definitely dualistic orientation of his thought, in fact, that Durkheim was forced into his extremist collectivistic assertions.

It may seem somewhat paradoxical in this connection that Tarde, standing, as he did, for emphasis upon the individual factor in the social process, should have refused to accept sensations as the psychological basis of sociology, on the ground that sensations are purely subjective and individual phenomena which can have no sociological significance; while Durkheim, though he leaned toward an extreme collectivistic standpoint, should have accepted sensations as basic psychological elements without criticism. The explanation is to be found, however, in their diverse theories of the nature of the social process.

According to Tarde, as we have seen, the social process is essentially a process of repetition by imitation. The result is an increase of human uniformities and similarities through the constantly increasing reproduction of socially effective models. As such, Tarde was obliged to set out with some socially significant individual fact to begin with, for the social process, according to his point of view, can only multiply this fact and not change it. According to Durkheim's conception, in contrast, the social process is a sort of chemical process in the course of which individual elements are transformed and fused to produce a totally new product, which is characteristically social and distinct in its properties from its component elements. The result, according to him, is not greater uniformity but greater interdependence and unity, not the growth of individual similarities and likenesses but the production of "new things," common products and group purposes, collective representations.[4] With such a theory, Durkheim was not dependent upon a

---

[1] *Les règles de la mét᠎ ᠎de sociologique*, p. 126; *Elementary Forms of Religious Life*, p. 434.

[2] See *infra*, pp. 119–120.

[3] See PARK and BURGESS, *Introduction to the Science of Sociology*, pp. 34, 42; GEHLKE, *Emile Durkheim's Contributions to Sociological Theory*, p. 183.

[4] See PARK and BURGESS, *Introduction to the Science of Sociology*, pp. 33–34.

socially significant psychological basis as a starting point; his theory of the nature of the social process in itself led him directly over from the individual to the social reality.

Durkheim, as already noted,[1] based his theory on the, from his point of view, eminently significant social fact of economic division of labor. This phenomenon, he sought to point out, following the lead of Comte in this,[2] has a sociological and psychological significance over and above its merely economic and biological significance.   The psycho-social correlatives of division of labor, according to Durkheim, are differentiation of function, supplementary cooperation, interdependence, participation in common motives and purposes, solidarity.   And these processes, it seemed to him, are at the very base of social life and personal development.   In this view, Durkheim felt, history bore him out, for historically, according to him, the social process has been a process of developing social solidarity based chiefly on functional diversity and interdependence, rather than on the growth of social uniformities and likenesses, as Tarde affirmed.   Social evolution has been characteristically tending, from Durkheim's standpoint, toward the gradual displacement of a primitive mechanical type of social solidarity, based on authoritative pressure and like-mindedness, by a functional or organic type, based on the functional interdependence and organization of society.   Parallel to this development of organic social solidarity and acting both as a cause and an effect of it have proceeded alike the complementary development of personal individuality and the realignment of social groupings from a kinship to a territorial and finally to a functional or occupational basis.   Further socialization and personal development must of course lie along the same path: continued social incorporation and unification, through further division of labor and still greater differentiation of social function.   The social process is essentially not a matter, therefore, of the progressive growth of social resemblances, as Tarde's theory suggested.[3]

As has frequently been pointed out,[4] Durkheim and Tarde are not necessarily in conflict in their conceptions here, despite the seeming opposition of their views.   For it is entirely possible to become subjectively more similar in the Tardean sense at the same time that we become functionally more differentiated and interdependent in Durkheim's sense. But behind this merely reconcilable difference of emphasis lies, as indi-

[1] Supra, p. 109.

[2] Comte, The Positive Philosophy, trans. by Martineau, vol. II, Chap. V.

[3] De la division du travail social, see especially Preface, Introduction, Chap. I; also MERZ, History of European Thought in the Nineteenth Century, vol. 1V, pp. 558ff.; PARK and BURGESS, Introduction to the Science of Sociology, pp. 714–718; GEHLKE, Emile Durkheim's Contributions to Sociological Theory, pp. 157ff.

[4] See ROSS, Foundations of Sociology, pp. 268–269; GIDDINGS, Principles of Sociology, pp. 15–16.

cated above,[1] a more or less real difference of sociological standpoint and approach—a difference, however, which the social-psychological outlook is gradually minimizing if not eliminating.

Durkheim's social application of his general principle that "the whole is not the same as the sum of its parts" necessarily involved a complete repudiation of the individualistic approach in sociology. The latter, from the nature of its method, is, according to Durkheim, "a contradiction in terms"—a point which he took particular pains to emphasize in connection with his criticism of the sociological approaches of Tarde and Spencer. According to Durkheim's view, it is methodologically neither possible to explain the whole by the parts nor to explain the parts by the whole. Each order of phenomena must be explained in terms of its own distinctive facts: social facts in terms of society and individual facts in terms of the individual.[2]

This is seemingly simple enough as a theoretical statement. From the standpoint of application, however, it does little more than to push the problem back a step, for everything then depends upon the definition of the "social" and the "individual." And upon this latter question, Durkheim's position is neither always clear nor consistent. In general, he agreed with Comte and Tarde in regarding everything socially caused which is not of a purely biological nature and origin.[3] The difference between Durkheim and Tarde at this point is mainly one of terminology, though it eventually carries over to their different conceptions of the social process. Tarde called inventions, to which he ultimately reduced everything social, individual products, despite his theory as to the important role which the social process plays in their appearance.[4] Durkheim was logically more consistent than Tarde in regarding everything that is not individual in the biological sense as social, as a matter of collective representations. But he obtained this greater logical consistency at the expense of having practically negated the reality of the individual as a factor in social behavior.[5]

It is sometimes suggested that Durkheim's rather extreme position on this matter reflects a confusion of thought regarding content and process.[6] It is questionable, in the light of recent developments in social psychology, whether this is an entirely successful basis of criticism of

[1] See *supra*, pp. 108–109.

[2] *Revue de mét. et de mor.*, vol. 6, pp. 297–298, 1898; *Les règles de la méthode sociologique*, pp. 124*ff.*, 135.

[3] *Cf.* GEHLKE, *Emile Durkheim's Contributions to Sociological Theory*, pp. 44–45, 53–54.

[4] *Supra*, p. 101.

[5] See *Elementary Forms of Religious Life*, pp. 424*ff.*; GEHLKE, *Emile Durkheim's Contributions to Sociological Theory*, pp. 43*ff.*

[6] See GINSBERG, *The Psychology of Society*, pp. 53–54, 58; BRETT, *A History of Psychology*, vol. III, p. 289.

Durkheim's theory, but it is certainly true that, from the nature of his basic premises, Durkheim was interested chiefly in the products and forms of social life and that he concerned himself very little with psychological processes.[1] But whatever may have been the basis of Durkheim's rather extreme collectivism, he could not maintain it consistently because it was incompatible with his underlying individualistic psychological presuppositions and constantly came into conflict with them. And finally, his views led him into an inescapable theoretical dilemma. "If the scope of the individual mind be confined to the narrow limits given by our author, where are the individual representations out of which, by a process of fusion and blending, the social representations are to be compounded?" asks Gehlke in calling attention to this conflict in Durkheim's theory. "Is it fair to call such an elementary complexus of psychic processes [as Durkheim leaves in the realm of individual psychology] a 'mind,' in the sense of a system of representations?"[2]

But despite this seeming difficulty and despite the atmosphere of vagueness which surrounds much of Durkheim's discussion and which at times recalls the somewhat similar discussion of Simmel, in its general implications his theory was a contribution to social-psychological thought of the first importance. His point of view, as he and his associates have worked it out, has proved to be not only very illuminating theoretically and important as a corrective of the still dominant purely individualistic interpretation of social phenomena but most fruitful in application.[3] However, Durkheim was so anxious to defend his position and to establish the reality of the collective mind that he sometimes permitted himself to sacrifice scientific accuracy for rhetorical effect to a dangerous degree. In the end, not unlike Comte and others before him, he fell prey to something of a religious idealization of the all-important social reality which he was trying to describe. Society becomes the "supreme" reality, a "superior" moral authority which dominates the individual because it "surpasses" and "transcends" him. In conflict, the social is the "sacred" and the individual is the "profane." Deity itself is nothing but this supreme moral authority apotheosized, society personalized. He speaks of the autonomy of the collective mind; of its independence of the nature of the individuals that constitute the social collectivity; of the existence of social facts in themselves independently of their individual manifestations; and in general, by his vagueness and mysticism,[4] offends the scientific mind which does not interpret these

---

[1] See GEHLKE, *Emile Durkheim's Contributions to Sociological Theory*, p. 44.

[2] *Ibid.*, p. 45. More recently an attempt has been made to throw new light on this aspect of Durkheim's thought (see DUMAS *et al.*, *Traité de psychologie*, vol. II, articles by Dumas, Blondel, and Delacroix).

[3] See *infra*, p. 123.

[4] *Elementary Forms of Religious Life*, pp. 16, 37, 206, 229, 347, 422, 437; *Les règles de la méthode sociologique*, pp. 9–10, 37, 125ff., 136; *Revue de mét. et de mor.*, vol. 6,

phrases sympathetically. Little wonder that many have regarded the collectivistic approach in social theory with suspicion!

In consequence, Durkheim called forth an almost unparalleled run of criticism, the serious charge being leveled against him that he sought to introduce an atmosphere of mediaeval realism into sociological theory.[1] Of his critics none was more severe than Tarde, who quoted him almost to absurdity as follows: "Eliminate the individuals and society remains."[2] Durkheim, as already quoted above, was of course not entirely undeserving of this criticism, and he further encouraged it by the abstract and formal manner in which he outlined his theory.[3] His interest, however, was thoroughly positivist in the scientific sense: he always looked to the test of the practical applicability of his views, and it was his strength that he constantly aimed to hold them down to the concrete facts of social life in detailed social investigation.[4]

It was in this latter respect that Durkheim's position was stronger than that of Tarde, who was disposed to rest content with the purely theoretical elaboration of his theory. In the formal statement of his position, Durkheim seems unnecessarily extremist and belabored from our present standpoint, it is true, but it was precisely because of this that his theory had so much value at the time, as a counterbalance against the one-sided individualistic approach which persisted methodologically, as we have seen, alike in psychology and sociology, despite theoretical criticism and a growing interest in the social-psychological standpoint. This was largely a period of particularistic theory in the development of modern psycho-social thought in any event, and among the rival positions in the field, Durkheim's influence was on the whole a most wholesome one. Durkheim felt very strongly that the individualistic approach "denatured" social facts,[5] and his counter to the criticism

---

pp. 295, 299, 1898; GEHLKE, *Emile Durkheim's Contributions to Sociological Theory*, pp. 32, 38–39, 62, 84, 156*ff.*

[1] See MERZ, *History of European Thought in the Nineteenth Century*, vol. IV, p. 561; GEHLKE, *Emile Durkheim's Contributions to Sociological Theory*, pp. 84*ff.*, 93*ff.*

[2] *La logique sociale*, Preface p. vi, pp. 1*ff.*; *Études de psychologie sociale*, pp. 64*ff.*; see also criticisms of TOSTI and LEUBA, *Amer. Jour. Sociol.*, vol. 3, pp. 464*ff.*, vol. 4, pp. 171*ff.*, vol. 19, pp. 333*ff.* and references, *infra*, p. 122, note 4.

[3] Durkheim felt that sociology was greatly hindered in its development as a differentiated science by the lack of a formulated scientific logic. He, like Simmel, with whom he and others of the school obviously have much in common, therefore set about to write its needed charter of scientific freedom (see Introduction, *Les règles de la méthode sociologique*, and *Revue de mét. et de mor.*, vol. 6, p. 301, 1898). Hence, the formal character of much of his discussion and his constant emphasis on what seemed to him to be the essential nature of the sociological method.

[4] *L'Année sociologique*, which is notable as a record of the investigations and activities of the Durkheim school, is a concrete expression of these positivist interests. See also "Sociologie" by Fauconnet and Mauss in *La Grande Encyclopédie*.

[5] *Les règles de la méthode sociologique*, pp. 120*ff.*

which was leveled against his approach by Tarde and others was the statement quoted above, namely, that "whenever a social phenomenon is directly explained by a psychological phenomenon, one may be sure that the explanation is false."[1]

As so frequently happens in the history of human thought, time has tended to balance these extreme points of view against each other, and modern social psychology, particularly, has tended to steer a middle course between them. In this process of social-psychological balancing, Tarde and Durkheim have for the most part been thrown together as representing the sociological approach, rather than over against each other. But where their theories have been played against each other, as on the question of the nature of the socialization process and collective social action, criticism and controversy have on the whole and in the large favored Durkheim's point of view in balanced perspective rather than Tarde's, at least to the extent that there has been an increasing emphasis on the social "control" motive in recent psycho-social thought and on the group and culture aspects of mental life.[2] This result has to some extent come about not because Durkheim's position was less easily assailable than Tarde's but because it led out toward detailed social investigation and the development of a "school" which has certainly become one of the most influential and productive schools of recent sociological thought.[3] These are nevertheless matters regarding which there is as yet no unity of opinion, and in the meantime both positions require consideration, not only from the standpoint of the historical balance of perspective but also as a basis of necessary orientation for more critical procedure in the field of psycho-social investigation.[4]

[1] *Ibid.*, p. 128; *cf.* p. 135, where he says: "*La cause déterminante d'un fait social doit être cherchée parmi les faits sociaux antécédents, et non parmi les états de la conscience individuelle*"; see also *Le suicide*, Chap. IV.

[2] *Cf.* Park and Burgess, *Introduction to the Science of Sociology*, pp. 27–43; see Gehlke, *Emile Durkheim's Contributions to Sociological Theory*, pp. 54–57, 183.

[3] Tarde did not develop a "school" of thought in the same sense, but the effect of his work has none the less been epoch making (see *supra*, pp. 106–107), as is evident even in the case of the more recent work of the Durkheim school itself.

[4] For a further discussion of Durkheim's social theory, see, besides the foregoing references, Bristol, *Social Adaptation*, pp. 138–145; Barnes, "Durkheim's Contribution to the Reconstruction of Political Theory," *Pol. Sci. Quar.*, vol. 35, pp. 236–254, 1920; Ginsberg, *The Psychology of Society*, pp. 54ff.; Goldenweiser, *Early Civilization*, pp. 360–380; "Current Sociology—The Durkheim School in France," *Sociol. Rev.*, vol. 19, pp. 15–20, 1927; Sorokin, *Contemporary Sociological Theories*, Chap. VIII; also *Sociological Papers*, vol. I; *Amer. Jour. Sociol.*, vol. 10, pp. 134, 256, 1904–1905; *Sociol. Rev.*, vol. 11, pp. 54, 77–82, 1918; and especially sections on psychology and sociology in France, in *Philosophy of Today*, collected and ed. by Schaub; Dumas *et al. Traité de psychologie*, vol. II, chap. on "La sociologie"; Bouglé, "The Present Tendency of the Social Sciences in France," *The New Social Science*, ed. by White; Blondel, *Introduction à la psychologie collective*, Part I.

2. Lucien Lévy-Bruhl (1857)

Along with Durkheim must be mentioned his co-worker and interpreter Lévy-Bruhl, who sought to apply the theory of collective representations to the interpretation of primitive mentality. This aspect of
Lévy-Bruhl's work is of interest here not only because it illustrates
the type of constructive application of the theory of collective representations in which the Durkheim school has now for some time been engaged,[1]
following Durkheim's own attempt at application in his treatment of
primitive religion, suicide, and education,[2] but in particular because of
the attention which Lévy-Bruhl's work has attracted as a further formulation of the Durkheim point of view and because of the far-reaching
criticism of the point of view and methodology of classical anthropology
which it incidentally incorporated. This criticism applies equally, of
course, to other fields of social investigation in so far as they are on
common ground with classical anthropology in standpoint and approach,
and hence the more general importance of Lévy-Bruhl's work.

Nineteenth century evolutionary philosophy established a very close
connection between social psychology and the study of primitive life.
This connection has never been broken, but its basis has gradually shifted
from the assumption of relationship posited by evolutionary philosophy
to a recognition of the value of the comparative approach, in the more
critical sense of modern thought, *per se* in social-psychological investigation. The Durkheim school has been a very important factor in bringing
about this change of outlook and more critical viewpoint. While it in
general accepted the basic premise of relationship between primitive
and civilized mentality postulated by nineteenth century evolutionary
philosophy, namely, that primitive and civilized mentality are genetically
related in a progressive scale of development, it did not entirely accept
the biological and historical explanations of this relationship which
classical English anthropology and German folk psychology attempted
to work out. Instead of these theories of primitivity, following respectively from the prevalent biological and historical conceptions of development, the Durkheim school sought a more distinctively social explanation.
Anthropologically considered, it may thus be regarded as representing
an alternative standpoint of interpretation to that of the classical English
and German schools. Lévy-Bruhl's contribution, at any rate, has run

[1] Among the other members of the Durkheim group one may mention Bouglé,
Davy, Fauconnet, Mauss, and Halbwachs, who have worked out important appli-
cations of Durkheim's theory respectively to the subjects of value, law, responsibility,
primitive exchange, memory. Similar applications are at present being worked out in
French psychology (see Dumas *et al.*, *Traité de psychologie*, vol. II, especially articles by
Dumas, Blondel and Delacroix; also Duprat, *La psychologie sociale*, Chaps. I, VII–VIII).

[2] See *supra*, p. 109. Durkheim's works in the latter field have been published
posthumously: *Education et sociologie* (1922); *L'Education morale* (1925).

decidedly in this direction; that is, it has chiefly been a contribution to the methodology of handling and interpreting existing accounts of primitive mentality, rather than a contribution toward first-hand investigation of primitive life itself.

Lévy-Bruhl made his departure from classical anthropology directly in terms of the theory of collective representations as it was being worked out by Durkheim and his collaborators.[1] This theory, as we have seen, definitely correlated mentality with social *milieu*. It directed attention, in the search for explanations of mental phenomena, to a study of the social situations of which they are supposedly a function. Applied to the problem of primitive mentality, this involved a shift of emphasis from the prevailing approaches in terms of the biological and historical conceptions of development to a study of primitive man's social *milieu* as the determining factor. The line of reasoning is clear: Human mentality is essentially a social product, a matter of collective representations. These, since they depend upon and reflect the specific social setting in which they arise, naturally vary as the social *milieu* varies. The social *milieu* of primitive[2] man is fundamentally different from that of civilized man. Hence his system of collective representations and mental organization must be fundamentally different from that of civilized man.[3] It is the concrete application and illustration of this thesis that Lévy-Bruhl undertook in his important work *Les fonctions mentales dans les sociétés inférieures* (1910) and in his two elaborations of this work *La mentalité primitive* (1922) and *L'âme primitive* (1927).[4]

Methodologically, the theory of collective representations implies that psycho-social phenomena must be studied *in situ* socially, that is, in relation to the social system of which they are a part. Classical anthropology was, of course, conspicuously disregardful of this methodological principle, and Lévy-Bruhl accordingly started out with a criticism of its methodology. For this purpose he singled out for special mention the English anthropological school as represented by Tylor, Frazer, Hartland, Lang, etc., both because of the important contributions which

[1] See LÉVY-BRUHL, *Les fonctions mentales dans les sociétés inférieures*, pp. 1–2, 27ff. (*How Natives Think*, pp. 13–14, 35ff.); *Primitive Mentality*, pp. 5–6, 32–33. This section was written before the English translation of *Les fonctions* appeared. The references to this work are therefore to the French edition. The corresponding references to *How Natives Think* have, however, been appended for convenience and the longer citations have been made to correspond to the authorized translation.

[2] By this term Lévy-Bruhl did not mean "earliest" man but merely "members of the simplest societies known to us" [*Les fonctions mentales dans les sociétés inférieures*, note p. 2 (*How Natives Think*, p. 13)].

[3] See GEHLKE, *Emile Durkheim's Contributions to Sociological Theory*, pp. 35–36, 139; LÉVY-BRUHL, *Les fonctions mentales dans les sociétés inférieures*, pp. 19ff., 37ff. (*How Natives Think*, pp. 27ff., 43ff.); *Primitive Mentality*, p. 78.

[4] English translations by Lilian A. Clare: *How Natives Think* 1927; *Primitive Mentality* 1923; *The Soul of the Primitive* (1928).

this school made to modern anthropology and because its representatives were such prominent offenders against the methodological implications of the theory of collective representations.[1]

The procedure of these representatives of classical anthropology, Lévy-Bruhl pointed out, rests on the basic assumption of the psychic unity of mankind and the resulting erroneous theory that primitive man thinks as we do.[2] In accordance with this theoretical orientation, accepted by these anthropologists as axiomatic and as too obvious to need proof or even formal statement and consideration, according to Lévy-Bruhl, they employed the method of superimposing upon the facts of primitive mentality the criteria and measuring devices of their own logic—a procedure which is to be condemned on two major counts, from Lévy-Bruhl's standpoint: first, because it neglected the important principle that mental organization is a function of social organization and so varies with it; and, second, because the principles of mental function upon which the English school built are in themselves the products of a faulty, too rationalistic, and too individualistic psychology. Classical anthropology as represented by the English anthropologists of the Spencerian period is thus criticized by Lévy-Bruhl not only because it attempted to apply principles which in the nature of the social situations involved could not be applicable to the study of primitive mentality but also because these principles were in the first place erroneous. The theory of animism, which the English anthropological school popularized, is cited by Lévy-Bruhl as a striking example of its faulty methodology. It is, according to him, a product of the superimposition of British association psychology upon the facts of primitive mentality rather than a natural outgrowth of the objective study of these facts themselves. It describes the primitive mind not as it really functions but as the "white, adult and civilized" mind of later nineteenth century England assumed it ought to function.[3]

More specifically, Lévy-Bruhl criticized the English anthropologists for wrenching social facts indiscriminately from their natural social settings and fitting them artificially into their own preconceived conceptions and hypotheses; for attributing a questioning attitude to the primitive mind with respect to matters which it does not question; for overemphasizing the superficial anthropological resemblances of social facts and disregarding their fundamental differences; for taking over a highly abstract and somewhat questionable psychology and attempting to apply it uncritically to a totally different type of mentality and a totally

[1] *Les fonctions mentales dans les sociétés inférieures*, pp. 4 *ff.* (*How Natives Think*, pp. 15 *ff.*).

[2] *Ibid.*, pp. 7, 27 (*How Natives Think*, pp. 18, 35).

[3] *Ibid.*, pp. 2, 7*ff.*, 81*ff.* (*How Natives Think*, pp. 13–14, 18*ff.*, 80*ff.*); see review by Goldenweiser, *Amer. Anthrop.*, n.s., vol. 13, pp. 121*ff.*, 1911.

different social situation. The sum and substance of Lévy-Bruhl's position on this matter was that the classical English school of anthropology made an outstanding contribution to scientific anthropology, through the accumulation of an invaluable mass of concrete information about primitive life, but that its interpretations and explanations were faulty and rather reflected the uncritical application of the doctrines of Spencerian evolutionary philosophy and British associationist psychology than the objective scientific treatment of the facts of primitive life themselves.[1]

In contrast to the theoretical orientation of classical anthropology, Lévy-Bruhl proposed in the spirit of the theory of collective representations that it is methodologically faulty to search *our* logic for the principles governing the behavior of the primitive mind, because primitive mentality must have laws of its own which are peculiar to it and from the standpoint of which it can be studied positively and not merely negatively, as classical anthropology tended to study it, in terms of "less" and "lower."[2] It is, according to him, one of the chief tasks of anthropology and sociology to discover these laws through an objective study of primitive mentality viewed in relation to its own proper social and intellectual setting. And in the preliminary manner in which the existing information about primitive life made the task possible, he proposed to apply himself to the study of the primitive mind from this standpoint.[3]

Summarizing his approach, Lévy-Bruhl contrasted it with that of classical anthropology as follows:

Instead of imagining the primitives whom we are studying to be like ourselves and making them think as we should do in their places—a proceeding which can only lead to hypotheses, at most merely probable, and nearly always false— let us on the contrary endeavor to guard against our own mental habits, and try to discover, by analyzing their collective representations and the connections between these, what the primitives' way of thinking would be.

As long as we assume that their minds are orientated like our own, that they react as ours do to the impressions made upon them, we assume, by implication, that they *should* reason and reflect as ours do with regard to the phenomena and entities of the known world. But we agree that as a matter of fact they neither reason nor reflect thus, and to explain this apparent anomaly we make use of a

---

[1] *Les fonctions mentales dans les sociétés inférieures*, pp. 5*ff.*, 81*ff*. (*How Natives Think*, pp. 16*ff*., 80*ff*.); *Primitive Mentality*, pp. 59, 93, 440; *cf.* BOAS, *The Mind of Primitive Man*, Chap. VII; see also GOLDENWEISER, *Amer. Anthrop.*, vol. 13, pp. 121*ff*., 1911; also reviews of *Les fonctions mentales* in *Amer. Jour. Sociol.*, vol. 16, pp. 420–423, 1910–1911 and DURKHEIM, *Les formes élémentaires de la vie religieuse*, *Amer. Jour. Sociol.*, vol. 18, pp. 843–846, 1912–1913.

[2] *Les fonctions mentales dans les sociétés inférieures*, pp. 13–14, 68, 111 (*How Natives Think*, pp. 27–29, 69, 105).

[3] *Ibid.*, pp. 2–3, 20–21, 425 (*How Natives Think*, pp. 14–15, 29, 361).

number of different hypotheses, such as the feebleness and torpidity of their minds, their perplexity, childlike ignorance, stupidity, etc., none of which take the facts sufficiently into account.

Let us abandon this position and rid our minds of all preconceived ideas in entering upon an objective study of primitive mentality, in the way in which it manifests itself in the institutions of uncivilized races or in the collective ideas from which these institutions are derived. Then we shall no longer define the mental activity of primitives beforehand as a rudimentary form of our own, and consider it childish and almost pathological. On the contrary, it will appear to be normal under the conditions in which it is employed, to be both complex and developed in its own way. By ceasing to connect it with a type which is not its own, and trying to determine its functioning solely according to the manifestations peculiar to it, we may hope that our description and analysis of it will not misrepresent its nature.[1]

Lévy-Bruhl started out in his *Les fonctions mentales* with a brief description of collective representations, developed in terms of the following characteristics, as his actual point of departure from classical anthropology:

The representations which are termed collective, defined as a whole without entering into detail, may be recognized by the following signs. They are common to the members of a given social group; they are transmitted from one generation to another; they impress themselves upon its individual members, and awaken in them sentiments of respect, fear, adoration, and so on, according to the circumstances of the case. Their existence does not depend upon the individual; not that they imply a collective unity distinct from the individuals composing the social group, but because they present themselves in aspects which cannot be accounted for by considering individuals merely as such. Thus it is that a language, although, properly speaking, it exists only in the minds of the individuals who speak it, is none the less an incontestable social reality, founded upon an ensemble of collective representations, for it imposes its claims on each one of these individuals; it is in existence before his day, and it survives him.[2]

A very important consequence, upon which the sociologists have justifiably insisted and which has escaped the anthropologists, follows from the above, according to Lévy-Bruhl, namely "that in order to understand the mechanism of institutions (especially in primitive societies) it is necessary in the first place to dispossess oneself of the prejudice which consists in the belief that collective representations in general, and those of primitive societies in particular, obey the laws of psychology arrived at on the basis of an analysis of the individual mind." "Collective representations," he pointed out, "have their own proper laws, which

[1] *Primitive Mentality*, pp. 32–33. Quotations from this work are reprinted by permission of The Macmillan Company, publishers.

[2] *Les fonctions mentales dans les sociétés inférieures*, p. 1 (translation quoted from *How Natives Think*, p. 13). Quotations from this work are reprinted by permission of George Allen Unwin, Ltd., publishers.

it is impossible to discover—especially in the case of primitives—from the study of the 'white, adult, and civilized' individual." It is rather, according to him, the study of primitive collective representations that can throw light on the genesis of our own thought processes. Of this, Durkheim and his collaborators had already brought forth some striking illustrations, according to Lévy-Bruhl. It was with the aim in view, he tells us, of coordinating and synthesizing their work in this respect and of applying their point of view more systematically that he undertook his own more general study of primitive mentality.[1]

Basing himself on the earlier work of the Durkheim school and on the investigations of anthropologists, ethnologists, and sociologists in the field of primitive mentality generally, therefore, Lévy-Bruhl proceeded to develop his mode of approach further. According to the commonly accepted terminology of ordinary psychology, a "representation," he pointed out, is generally thought of as *par excellence* an intellectual or cognitive phenomenon. We cannot, however, according to him, view the collective representations of primitives from this standpoint. For their mental activity is too little differentiated for us to be able to regard their ideas or images of objects apart from the sentiments, emotions, and passions which evoke them or are evoked by them. With them "the emotional and motor elements are *integral parts* of the representations." In order to retain this term in the study of primitive mentality, it is thereby, according to him, necessary to modify its accepted meaning so as to make it applicable to the conditions of primitive life.[2]

By this state of mental activity in primitives, we must understand something which is not a purely or almost purely intellectual or cognitive phenomenon, but a more complex one, in which what is really "representation" to us is found blended with other elements of an emotional or motor character, coloured and imbued by them, and therefore implying a different attitude with regard to the objects represented . . .

The collective representations of primitives, therefore, differ very profoundly from our ideas or concepts, nor are they their equivalent either. On the one hand, as we shall presently discover, they have not their logical character. On the other hand, not being genuine representations, in the strict sense of the term, they express, or rather imply, not only that the primitive actually has an image of the object in his mind, and thinks it real, but also that he has some hope or fear connected with it, that some definite influence emanates from it, or is exercised upon it. This influence is a virtue, an occult power which varies with objects and circumstances, but is always real to the primitive and forms an integral part of his representation. If I were to express in one word the

---

[1] *Ibid.*, pp. 1–3, 440*ff.* (*How Natives Think*, pp. 12–15; 374*ff.*); *Primitive Mentality*, pp. 5–6.

[2] *Les fonctions mentales dans les sociétés inférieures*, p. 28 (*How Natives Think*, pp. 35–36).

general peculiarity of the collective representations which play so important a part in the mental activity of undeveloped peoples, I should say that this mental activity was a *mystic* one. In default of a better, I shall make use of this term— not referring thereby to the religious mysticism of our communities, which is something entirely different, but employing the word in the strictly defined sense in which "mystic" implies belief in forces and influences and actions which, though imperceptible to sense, are nevertheless real.[1]

Proceeding, then, from the standpoint of the theory of collective representations as thus defined, Lévy-Bruhl examined the pertinent information bearing on the function of primitive mentality as it manifests itself in primitive institutions, customs, and beliefs.[2] He arrived at the conclusion that the behavior of the primitive mind is so far different in orientation from our own that by comparison he felt justified in characterizing it as essentially "mystical" and relatively "prelogical."[3] While we are chiefly governed in our mental behavior by the law of contradiction, the primitive mind is, according to Lévy-Bruhl, chiefly governed by the law of participation. Primitive man is above all in a continual state of *participation* with the mystic "preconnections" of his group representations. His mental life is so far dominated by the latter, in fact, that he is in consequence relatively "impervious" to individual experience and "insensible" to logical contradiction. Accordingly, objective personal experience, which in our case constitutes the basis upon which the law of contradiction operates, does not so function in the case of primitive man. "The reality in which primitives live is itself mystical," according to Lévy-Bruhl. Sense perception and individual experience are in themselves therefore transfigured by the mystic content of primitive collective representations. Where our logic would expect a critical attitude, the primitive mind accordingly remains undisturbed. Its worlds of sense impression and tribal mysticism continue to flow harmoniously together as a unified stream of experience.[4]

The basic principle of primitive man's mentality—participation—it thus appeared to Lévy-Bruhl, is in essential conflict with our logic in that it is relatively indifferent to the law of contradiction, the corresponding principle of civilized man's mentality. Accordingly, retaining here the classical practice of setting up our own mentality as the criterion, he characterized primitive mentality as "mystical" and "prelogical." The logical attitude of civilized man is separated out from the complex pre-logical attitude of primitive man, according to Lévy-Bruhl, by a process of dissociation, in the course of which man gradually learns to

---

[1] *Ibid.*, pp. 28–30 (translation quoted from *How Natives Think*, pp. 36–38).

[2] *Ibid.*, p. 22 (*How Natives Think*, p. 30); *Primitive Mentality*, pp. 11–12, 436.

[3] *Les fonctions mentales dans les sociétés inférieures*, p. 78 (*How Natives Think*, p. 78).

[4] *Ibid.*, pp. 30, 75, 114, 425 (*How Natives Think*, pp. 30, 75, 108, 361).

distinguish what is objectively real in the mystic complex constituting the primitive conception. It is a sort of logical "precipitate" of primitive man's attitude toward the world.[1]

Lévy-Bruhl recognized, of course, that the distinction between primitive and civilized mentality which he thus set up is not absolute: primitive thought is not entirely mystical, as primitive man's ability to pursue natural ends in his practical life proves; nor is our own thought entirely free from the mystical attributes of primitive thought. But even in this crossing of mental attitude, the distinction to which he directed attention persists, according to him. The most uneducated members in our social life differentiate between the natural and the supernatural. Primitive man does not. For him there is only one reality, and it is its mystic relations which appeal as most important to him. The difference between our mental life and that of primitive man is thus not a matter merely of degree. Primitive mentality is to be regarded not as a lower type of civilized mentality, as classical anthropology led us to believe, but as essentially a different kind of mentality, intelligible only in terms of its own organization and social background.[2] It is, says Lévy-Bruhl: " . . . not only mystic, that is, at all times orientated to occult forces: it is not only prelogical, that is, indifferent as a rule to the law of contradiction: it is more than this; the causality it pictures to itself is of a type differing from that familiar to us, and this third characteristic is indissolubly bound up with the other two."[3]

The following additional quotation will bring these points out more clearly:

Primitives perceive nothing in the same way as we do. The social *milieu* which surrounds them differs from ours, and precisely because it is different, the external world they perceive differs from that which we apprehend. Undoubtedly they have the same sense as ours—rather more acute than ours in a general way, in spite of our persuasion to the contrary—and their cerebral structure is like our own. But we have to bear in mind that which their collective representations instil into all their perceptions. Whatever the object presented to their minds, it implies mystic properties which are inextricably bound up with it, and the primitive, in perceiving it, never separates these from it . . .

To him there is no phenomenon which is, strictly speaking, a physical one, in the sense in which we use the term. The rippling water, the whistling wind, the falling rain, any natural phenomenon whatever, a sound, a colour—these things are never perceived by him as they are by us, that is, as more or less compound movements bearing a definite relation to preceding and to subsequent

[1] *Ibid.*, especially Chaps. I, II, III, IX; *Primitive Mentality*, especially Chaps. I, II, XIV; see GOLDENWEISER, *Early Civilization*, pp. 380–389.

[2] See *Les fonctions mentales dans les sociétés inférieures*, pp. 40–41, 66–67, 111*ff.* (*How Natives Think*, pp. 46, 67–68, 105*ff.*).

[3] *Primitive Mentality*, pp. 89–90.

movements. His perceptive organs have indeed grasped the displacement of a mass of material as ours do; familiar objects are readily recognized according to previous experience; in short, all the physiological and psychological processes of perception have actually taken place in him as in ourselves. Its result, however, is immediately enveloped in a state of complex consciousness, dominated by collective representations. Primitives see with eyes like ours, but they do not perceive with the same minds . . .

The profound difference which exists between primitive mentality and our own is shown even in the ordinary perception or mere apprehension of the very simplest things. Primitive perception is fundamentally mystic on account of the mystic nature of the collective representations which form an integral part of every perception. Ours has ceased to be so, at any rate with regard to most of the objects which surround us. Nothing appears alike to them and to us . . .

It is not correct to maintain, as is frequently done, that primitives associate occult powers, magic properties, a kind of soul or vital principle with all the objects which affect their senses or strike their imagination, and that their perceptions are surcharged with animistic beliefs. It is not a question of *association*. The mystic properties with which things and beings are imbued form an integral part of the idea to the primitive, who views it as a synthetic whole . . .

In the same way, we shall find ourselves in a blind alley, whenever we propound a question in such terms as: How would the primitive's mind explain this or that phenomenon? The very enunciation of the problem implies a false hypothesis. We are supposing that his mind apprehends these phenomena like our own. We imagine that he simply perceives such facts as sleep, dreaming, illness, death, the rise and decline of the heavenly bodies, rain, thunder, etc., and then, stimulated by the principle of causality, tries to account for them. But to the mentality of undeveloped peoples, there are no natural phenomena such as we understand by the term. Their mentality has no need to seek an explanation of them; for the explanation is implied in the mystic elements of the collective representations of them. Therefore problems of this nature must be inverted. What we must seek is not the logical process which might have resulted in the interpretation of phenomena, for this mentality never perceives the phenomenon as distinct from the interpretation; we must find out how the phenomenon became by degrees detached from the complex in which it first found itself enveloped, so that it might be apprehended separately, and how what originally was an integral part of it should later on have become an "explanation" . . . [1]

The sharp distinction between primitive and civilized mentality which Lévy-Bruhl set up[2] centers about his specialized use of the term "collective representations." Lévy-Bruhl emphasized the mystic tribal aspects of primitive mentality in connection with his use of this term. In effect, if not by specific enunciation, he contrasted the collective character of primitive mentality with the individualized logic of civilized

[1] *Les fonctions mentales dans les sociétés inférieures*, pp. 37–40 (translation quoted from *How Natives Think*, pp. 43–45); see also *Primitive Mentality*, pp. 431*ff.*

[2] Under the influence of his work, an attempt has been made to draw a similar distinction between morbid and healthy mentality (see Blondel, *La conscience morbide*, 1914).

mentality.   While the germ of this contrast is to be found in Durkheim's work, the particular form in which it was formulated by Lévy-Bruhl appears to be decidedly antagonistic to the larger implications of Durkheim's theory of collective representations.[1]   In the spirit of the latter, as Lévy-Bruhl himself incidentally suggested, our own thought is to be regarded not so much as less collective in character than primitive thought, as differing in its collective nature, in consequence of the fact that our collective representations are different from those of primitive man and our mental integration takes place under different conditions of social and cultural organization.   This is of course the more consistent as well as the more suggestive conception.   In specializing the use of the term collective representations as he did, Lévy-Bruhl no doubt gained in emphasis for the particular point which he set out to make, namely, that the primitive mind is a product of its own peculiar social *milieu* and is understandable only in connection with it, but he lost ground from the standpoint of the theory of collective representations in its broader aspects.   According to the latter, the mental organization of civilized man, no less than that of primitive man, must be referred to his social *milieu*, so that if the methodology implied by the theory of collective representations is valid at all, it is just as applicable in the study of civilized as of primitive mentality.

But even apart from these considerations, Lévy-Bruhl undoubtedly pushed his contrast between primitive and civilized mentality farther than, according to present-day critical investigation of the subject, the facts appear to warrant.[2]   The distinction which he set up in connection with his characterization of primitive mentality as "mystic" and "prelogical" is a distinction which modern thought has, on the whole, found very useful, but it is to be interpreted as a difference in degree rather than in kind, as Lévy-Bruhl tended to interpret it.   We are, after all, according to the testimony of modern psychological and social thought, much more "prelogical" in Lévy-Bruhl's sense, and primitive man, it would seem, is much more "logical" than his theory would seem to indicate.   What his thesis about the difference between primitive and civilized mentality reduces to, therefore, is that in primitive society more of life is mystically controlled and in civilized society more is logically and scientifically controlled; but the two mental attitudes coexist side by side in both cases and the relative proportion of the one

[1] See *Elementary Forms of Religious Life*, p. 439; Gehlke, *Emile Durkheim's Contributions to Sociological Theory*, pp. 49, 56–57; Goldenweiser, *Early Civilization*, p. 377.

[2] *Cf.* Boas, *The Mind of Primitive Man*, Chaps. IV, VIII; Goldenweiser, *Early Civilization*, pp. 386–389; Rivers, *Psychology and Ethnology*, pp. 37–47; Thurnwald, *Zeitschr. f. Völkerpsychol. u. Soziol.*, vol. 4, pp. 324–330, 1928; Baldwin, *History of Psychology*, vol. I, pp. 21*ff.*   Also, Radin, *Primitive Man as Philosopher* and Essertier, *Les formes inférieures de l'explication*.

to the other is in neither case fixed nor constant. In our own society, as Lévy-Bruhl himself recognized, all grades of combination of the mystical and the logical attitudes are represented, and for all of us the proportion varies with the occasion and the situation. As developed by him, Lévy-Bruhl's theory of primitive mentality represents a similar exaggeration of an aspect of primitive man's mental life to the one for which he criticized the British anthropological school, though in the opposite direction; that is, Lévy-Bruhl tended to overemphasize the differences between primitive and civilized mentality just as classical anthropology tended to overemphasize their similarities. In defense of his treatment, it may of course be pointed out that it was his aim to orientate the Western European mind with respect to what appears strange and unintelligible to it in the behavior of primitive mentality and that he therefore emphasized differences from rather than similarities to our own mode of mental activity, intentionally on that account.[1] But it nevertheless remains that his treatment leaves one with almost as one-sided a view of primitive mentality, if it is taken apart from the classical point of view which he criticized, as does the latter.

This, as said before, was a period of reaction against conventional psychological and social thought, especially in France, and under the circumstances a tendency to lean to the other extreme from the one toward which the period was directed was to be expected. We have had occasion to note the effect of this tendency in the case of Tarde and Durkheim, and now we note it again in the case of Lévy-Bruhl. In his own way, he was quite as extremist in pushing his point of view as were Tarde and Durkheim in theirs.

But if, on the one hand, the effect of Lévy-Bruhl's work was to narrow the application of the concept of collective representations in one direction, as indicated above, it, on the other hand, enriched its application as a result of the emphasis which it laid on the affective, motor, and unconscious aspects of primitive mental life.[2] It thus brought the concept into closer agreement with the general trend of modern psychological thought, which has been steadily drifting away from the intellectualism that Durkheim's theory reflected to a recognition of the role which the emotional, the unconscious, and the motor factors play in human behavior. Lévy-Bruhl combined the impulses which Durkheim represented in sociology with those which Ribot represented in psychology[3] and thus arrived at a more representative social-psychological

---

[1] *Les fonctions mentales dans les sociétés inférieures*, pp. 1–2, 20–21, 425 (*How Natives Think*, pp. 13–14, 29, 361); *Primitive Mentality*, pp. 11–13, 444.

[2] See *Les fonctions mentales dans les sociétés inférieures*, pp. 27*ff.*, 111*ff.* (*How Natives Think*, pp. 35*ff.*, 105*ff.*); *Primitive Mentality*, pp. 444–447.

[3] *Les fonctions mentales dans les sociétés inférieures*, pp. 2–3 (*How Natives Think*, pp. 14–15).

viewpoint.   Combined with the broader sociological scope which Durkheim's work embodied and the more balanced perspective which modern psychology has fostered, this enriched conception of the nature of collective representations has provided a very illuminating standpoint of investigation, corresponding to an aspect of psycho-social life which was largely neglected by previous thought.[1]

It is worth while noting in this connection that while German and English psycho-social thought of the day was drawing primitive and civilized man closer together psychologically, French thought, through Lévy-Bruhl, was setting up a sharp distinction between them, just as in different form, through Tarde and Durkheim, it was setting up a sharp distinction between the individual and the social factors in mental life.   As we have seen, French psycho-social thought as represented by these writers tended to be extremist in this tendency, but it thereby brought into action a balancing process, the inevitable result of which was to lead to a more representative and a more discriminating point of view in the investigation of the problems of human conduct and social life.[2]

IV. The Study of Crowd Behavior as an Approach to Social Psychology: Crowd Psychology

1. Gustave Le Bon (1841–1931)

The novelty of point of view and approach which, as we have seen, characterized the work of Tarde, Durkheim, and Lévy-Bruhl was carried forward into still another important field of observation and analysis by Le Bon in his *Psychologie des foules* (1895)[3].   Le Bon was considerably influenced by both Tarde and Durkheim, but in general, being directed toward an interest in group psychology, and especially in his study of the crowd, he rather tended to support Durkheim's view of social life.   In his definition of the crowd, he carried out Durkheim's analogy between the functional unity of the biological organism and that of the social collectivity, as well as his view that the social process may be described as a sort of chemical interaction and synthesis of individual elements.[4] He speaks of the organized collectivity as "a single being,"[5] of the formation of "a collective mind,"[5] and of the creation of "new character-

---

[1] See Park and Burgess, *Introduction to the Science of Sociology*, pp. 37–38, 164–165, 894–895.

[2] *Cf. supra*, pp. 67, 89, 133.

[3] Eng. trans. *The Crowd*.   Some of Le Bon's other notable works are *Lois psychologiques de l'evolution des peuples*, 1894 (Eng. trans. *The Psychology of Peoples*); *La révolution française et la psychologie des révolutions*, 1912   (Eng. trans. *The Psychology of Revolution.*)

[4] *The Crowd*, p. 30.

[5] *Ibid.*, p. 26.

istics very different from those of the individuals composing it"[1] in much the same sense as Durkheim did and with the added significance of specific reference to the conditions of collective behavior in the crowd.

Le Bon was, however, not as consistent in maintaining this position as Durkheim.   In fact, his work presents an unsynthesized conglomeration of most of the important sociological theories of the day, especially those of Tarde and Durkheim, superimposed on a basic conception of racial constitution, in which both the English biological view and the Hegelian notion of the "genius" of peoples figure prominently.[2]   Sociologically, he accordingly stands somewhere between Tarde and Durkheim in their respective emphasis on the individual and the group factors in social life. Accepting the notion of the individual with tendencies as observable under ordinary social conditions as one basic aspect of social reality, and the social aggregate acting as a functional unity as the other, he set about to describe, in concrete and characteristic terms, the relation between the two and the conditions under which the former enters as a component element to form the latter under the influence of crowd excitement.   His description, as said above, gives clear evidence of both Tarde's and Durkheim's influence, but on the whole it rather tends in the direction of Durkheim's theory of social action.   In fact, in its own special way, it is even more challenging in its collectivistic views and references than the latter.   Le Bon's thought also incorporates a characteristic current of racial mysticism and a definite anti-democratic bias.[3]   He is frequently quite carried away, for instance, by his distrust of the masses and his dislike of the "philosophy of number,"[4] and yet he stands in awe of the "mysterious forces" which, according to him, at times seem to guide crowds, in the form of nations at any rate, in the performance of superior social functions.[5]   His analysis of group behavior is therefore not always as objective and dependable as might be.   On the other hand, his observations have a closeness to reality and a suggestiveness of the concrete, which make him not only one of the most readable of the French school of psycho-social theorists but seemingly, also, one whose theory has a particularly direct bearing on the practical problems of social life.

It is because of these latter characteristics that Le Bon's study of the crowd has made such a wide appeal and aroused so much interest. It has attracted attention because of its vividness and suggestiveness rather than because of its scientific accuracy and objectivity.   Since the

---

[1] *Ibid.*

[2] See *ibid.*, pp. 5, 6–7, 9; also review in *Amer. Jour. Sociol.*, vol. 2, pp. 612–614, 1896–1897.

[3] See *The Crowd*, pp. 8–10, 15 *ff.*

[4] *Ibid.*, p. 19. Le Bon tended to identify "the crowd" with "the masses," for he thought of the latter as actual, or at least potential, crowds.

[5] *Ibid.*, p. 9.

appearance of Le Bon's work, a considerable body of literature on the crowd has grown up, much of it more carefully discriminating and critical than Le Bon's study, and some of it more accurately illustrative because of the use of case material;[1] but Le Bon's work continues to hold its own as the most suggestive general treatment of the subject that we have. In fact, a good deal of what has since been done in this field of investigation has been a product largely of the elaboration and refinement of the observations which appear in preliminary but very striking form in Le Bon's work.[2] Discussion of the subject of crowd behavior accordingly continues to center about his classic analysis.

Le Bon's study of the crowd also has a more general social-psychological interest than is at first likely to appear if it is viewed merely as a description of a special aspect of social life. For besides being one of the earliest attempts at the sociological treatment of crowd behavior in itself, Le Bon's work also initiated the study of social behavior generally from the standpoint of what has since come to be known as "crowd psychology."[3] Incidentally, it introduced a new emphasis into the collectivistic theory of social causation by directing attention, especially in this connection, to the study of social control in the concrete forms in which it manifests itself under the influence of collective excitement.[4]

With these general considerations in view, we turn to Le Bon's more detailed description and analysis. He says by way of general introduction to his subject:

The whole of the common characteristics with which heredity endows the individuals of a race constitute the genius of the race. When, however, a certain number of these individuals are gathered together in a crowd for purposes of action, observation proves that, from the mere fact of their being assembled, there result certain new psychological characteristics, which are added to the racial characteristics and differ from them at times to a very considerable degree.[5]

It is with the investigation of these "new psychological characteristics" that Le Bon is primarily concerned. Having thus indicated their relation to the more permanent racial characteristics of man, he accordingly proceeds to describe the conditions of their appearance in greater detail.

[1] See PARK and BURGESS, *Introduction to the Science of Sociology*, Chap. XIII.

[2] See *infra*, pp. 142–143.

[3] Earlier attempts to describe the crowd in sociological terms, but from the criminological standpoint chiefly, were made by Sighele (*La folla delinquente*, 1891) and Tarde (*Philosophie penale*, 1890). See LE BON, *The Crowd*, pp. 19, 20; Ross, *Foundations of Sociology*, pp. 19 *ff.*; PARK and BURGESS, *Introduction to the Science of Sociology*, note, pp. 867–868; PARK, *Masse und Publikum*, pp. 4–15.

[4] PARK and BURGESS, *Introduction to the Science of Sociology*, pp. 33*ff.*, 867.

[5] *The Crowd*, pp. 5, 29–31. Quotations from this work are reprinted by permission of The Macmillan Company, publishers.

Under certain given circumstances, and only under those circumstances, an agglomeration of men presents new characteristics very different from those of the individuals composing it. The sentiments and ideas of all the persons in the gathering take one and the same direction, and their conscious personality vanishes. A collective mind is formed, doubtless transitory, but presenting very clearly defined characteristics. The gathering has thus become what, in the absence of a better expression, I will call an organized crowd. It forms a single being, and is subjected to the *law of the mental unity of crowds.*[1]

It is, according to Le Bon, not by the mere fact of a number of individuals finding themselves accidentally side by side that they acquire the character of an organized crowd. "A thousand individuals accidentally gathered in a public place without any determined object in no way constitute a crowd from the psychological point of view," he says. "On the other hand, an entire nation, though there may be no visible agglomeration, may become a crowd under the action of certain influences." All depends upon the presence or absence "of certain predisposing causes."[2]

The first of these, according to him, is "that the individual forming part of a crowd acquires, solely from numerical considerations, a sentiment of invincible power which allows him to yield to instincts which, had he been alone, he would perforce have kept under restraint. He will be the less disposed to check himself," says Le Bon, "from the consideration that, a crowd being anonymous, and in consequence irresponsible, the sentiment of responsibility which always controls individuals disappears entirely."[3]

The second of these predisposing causes which he mentions is contagion. "In a crowd," says Le Bon, "every sentiment and act is contagious, and contagious to such a degree that an individual readily sacrifices his personal interest to the collective interest." This is a characteristic which he regards very contrary to the individual's usual behavior. Man is scarcely capable of it, according to him, "except when he makes part of a crowd."[4]

The third and, in Le Bon's opinion, by far the most important of these predisposing causes making for the appearance of the special characteristics of crowd behavior is "that suggestibility of which . . . the contagion mentioned above is neither more nor less than an effect." In explanation of this important point he says:

To understand this phenomenon it is necessary to bear in mind certain recent physiological discoveries. We know today that by various processes an individual may be brought into such a condition that, having entirely lost his con-

[1] *Ibid.*, p. 26.
[2] *Ibid.*, pp. 26–27.
[3] *Ibid.*, p. 33.
[4] *Ibid.*, p. 34.

scious personality, he obeys all the suggestions of the operator who has deprived him of it, and commits acts in utter contradiction with his character and habits. The most careful observations seem to prove that an individual immerged for some length of time in a crowd in action soon finds himself—either in consequence of the magnetic influence given out by the crowd or from some other cause of which we are ignorant—in a special state, which much resembles the state of fascination in which the hypnotised individual finds himself in the hands of the hypnotiser. The activity of the brain being paralysed in the case of the hypnotised subject, the latter becomes the slave of all the unconscious activities of his spinal cord, which the hypnotiser directs at will. The conscious personality has entirely vanished; will and discernment are lost. All feelings and thoughts are bent in the direction determined by the hypnotiser.

Such also is approximately the state of the individual forming part of a psychological crowd. He is no longer conscious of his acts. In his case, as in the case of the hypnotised subject, at the same time that certain faculties are destroyed, others may be brought to a high degree of exaltation. Under the influence of a suggestion, he will undertake the accomplishment of certain acts with irresistible impetuosity. This impetuosity is the more irresistible in the case of crowds than in that of the hypnotised subject, from the fact that, the suggestion being the same for all the individuals of the crowd, it gains in strength by reciprocity. The individualities in the crowd who might possess a personality sufficiently strong to resist the suggestion are too few in number to struggle against the current. At the utmost, they may be able to attempt a diversion by means of different suggestions. It is in this way, for instance, that a happy expression, an image opportunely evoked, have occasionally deterred crowds from the most bloodthirsty acts.[1]

When these predisposing causes are in operation, we get the formation of what Le Bon terms an "organized" or a "psychological" crowd, subjected to the *law of the mental unity of crowds*, and the appearance of the special characteristics referred to above: "the disappearance of the conscious personality, the predominance of the unconscious personality, the turning by means of suggestion and contagion of feelings and ideas in an identical direction, the tendency to immediately transform the suggested ideas into acts."[2] This occurs, according to Le Bon, regardless of the character of the individuals that compose the crowd, and this, in turn, he regards as "the most striking peculiarity presented by a psychological crowd."

Whoever be the individuals that compose it, however like or unlike be their mode of life, their occupations, their character, or their intelligence, the fact that they have been transformed into a crowd puts them in possession of a sort of collective mind which makes them feel, think, and act in a manner quite different from that in which each individual of them would feel, think, and act were he in a state of isolation.[3]

[1] *Ibid.*, pp. 34–35.
[2] *Ibid.*, pp. 26, 35–36.
[3] *Ibid.*, pp. 29–30.

The "collective mind" thus formed in the crowd, Le Bon takes pains to point out, is in no sense a mere "summing-up of or an average struck between its elements," as Spencer, for instance, thought. "What really takes place," according to him, "is a combination followed by the creation of new characteristics, just as in chemistry certain elements, when brought into contact—bases and acids, for example—combine to form a new body possessing properties quite different from those of the bodies that have served to form it."[1] The result is "a provisional being formed of heterogeneous elements, which for a moment are combined, exactly as the cells which constitute a living body form by their reunion a new being which displays characteristics very different from those possessed by each of the cells singly."[1]

To produce this "provisional being," the individuals composing it undergo, according to Le Bon, not a mere superficial change that attracts the attention of the observer of crowd behavior but a fundamental transformation. "It is not only by his acts that the individual in a crowd differs essentially from himself," he says. "Even before he has entirely lost his independence, his ideas and feelings have undergone a transformation, and the transformation is so profound as to change the miser into a spendthrift, the skeptic into a believer, the honest man into a criminal, and the coward into a hero."[2] When the crowd attains complete organization, the individual "is no longer himself, but has become an automaton who has ceased to be guided by his will."[3]

This change, just as in the case of the hypnotized individual, involves a decided lowering of intellectual level, according to Le Bon. He says:

Moreover, by the mere fact that he forms part of an organized crowd, a man descends several rungs in the ladder of civilisation. Isolated, he may be a cultivated individual; in a crowd, he is a barbarian—that is, a creature acting by instinct. He possesses the spontaneity, the violence, the ferocity, and also the enthusiasm and heroism of primitive beings, whom he further tends to resemble by the facility with which he allows himself to be impressed by words and images —which would be entirely without action on each of the isolated individuals composing the crowd—and to be induced to commit acts contrary to his most obvious interests and his best-known habits. An individual in a crowd is a grain of sand amid other grains of sand, which the wind stirs at will.[3]

In fact, crowd action is necessarily on a low intellectual plane, according to Le Bon. This is so, according to him, because the crowd can act only on the level of the qualities possessed in common by the individuals in the group by virtue of their common biological heredity, that is, on the level of those "general qualities of character, governed by forces of

---

[1] *Ibid.*, p. 30.
[2] *Ibid.*, p. 37.
[3] *Ibid.*, p. 36.

which we are unconscious, and possessed by the majority of the normal individuals of a race in much the same degree."[1]   In crowds, Le Bon stated, "the intellectual aptitudes of the individuals, and in consequence their individuality, are weakened.   The heterogeneous is swamped by the homogeneous, and the unconscious qualities obtain the upper hand."[1]

This fact, "that crowds possess in common ordinary qualities,"[1] explains, according to Le Bon, why they can never accomplish acts demanding a high degree of intelligence.   "The decisions affecting matters of general interest come to by an assembly of men of distinction, but specialists in different walks of life, are not sensibly superior to the decisions that would be adopted by a gathering of imbeciles," says Le Bon.   "The truth is they can only bring to bear in common on the work in hand those mediocre qualities which are the birthright of every average individual.   In crowds it is stupidity and not mother-wit that is accumulated."[2]

The conclusion to be drawn from all this, according to Le Bon, is "that the crowd is always intellectually inferior to the isolated individual, but that, from the point of view of feelings and of the acts these feelings provoke, the crowd may, according to circumstances, be better or worse than the individual.   All depends on the nature of the suggestion to which the crowd is exposed."[3]   In this view Le Bon claimed to have gone a long step beyond previous thought on the subject of crowd action, inasmuch as the hitherto meager consideration of this subject was, according to him, entirely dominated by the criminal point of view and directed to the study only of "the crimes crowds are capable of committing."[4]   He says in elaboration of this point:

Without a doubt criminal crowds exist, but virtuous and heroic crowds, and crowds of many other kinds, are also to be met with.   The crimes of crowds only constitute a particular phase of their psychology.   The mental constitution of crowds is not to be learnt merely by a study of their crimes, any more than that of an individual by a mere description of his vices.[5]

In further elaboration of this point, he says again:

It is crowds rather than isolated individuals that may be induced to run the risk of death to secure the triumph of a creed or an idea, that may be fired with enthusiasm for glory and honour, that are led on—almost without bread and without arms, as in the age of the Crusades—to deliver the tomb of Christ from the infidel, or, as in '93 to defend the fatherland.   Such heroism is without doubt

[1] *Ibid.*, pp. 31–32.
[2] *Ibid.*, p. 32.
[3] *Ibid.*, p. 37.
[4] *Ibid.*, pp. 20, 37.
[5] *Ibid.*, p. 20.

somewhat unconscious, but it is of such heroism that history is made. Were peoples only to be credited with the great actions performed in cold blood, the annals of the world would register but few of them.[1]

What, then, more specifically, is the role of the crowd as viewed by Le Bon in the economy of the social process?

In the crowd, according to him, the old is destroyed so that it may be replaced by the new. "History tells us," he says, "that when the moral forces on which a civilization rested have lost their strength, its final dissolution is brought about by those unconscious and brutal crowds known, justifiably enough, as barbarians . . . When the structure of a civilization is rotten, it is always the masses that bring about its downfall."[2] In the exercise of this function the masses act, according to Le Bon, "like those microbes which hasten the dissolution of enfeebled or dead bodies." Deplorable though the conditions attendant upon the advent to power of crowds seemed to him, they were thus, he felt, necessary accompaniments of social reorganization and progress. Such "periods of confused anarchy," he stated, "seem always destined to precede the birth of every new society."[3]

However, it is only at such junctures, according to him, that "the philosophy of number seems the only philosophy of history." The positive elements of civilization and the re-creation of the social order he regarded as essentially the work of the few intellectually *élite*. "Civilizations as yet," he declared, "have only been created and directed by a small intellectual aristocracy, never by crowds."[4]

This was the position which Le Bon maintained in general, and his concern over the spreading "reign of the masses" led him to bolster it up at some cost to the integrity of his social theory, in view of his thesis regarding the importance of crowds in the economy of the social process. However, his method of lumping all kinds of group aggregations under the term "crowd" and of attributing to them the characteristics which he derived from observation of the more spontaneous and transitory social groupings made it difficult for him to be consistent in this estimate of the social function of crowds.[5] "What, for instance," he asks in one connection, "can be more complicated, more logical, more marvellous than a language? Yet whence can this admirably organized production have arisen, except it be the outcome of the unconscious genius of crowds? The most learned academies, the most esteemed grammarians do no more than note down the laws that govern languages; they would be

[1] *Ibid.*, pp. 37–38.
[2] *Ibid.*, pp. 18–19.
[3] *Ibid.*, p. 18.
[4] *Ibid.*, p. 19.
[5] *Ibid.*, pp. 6, 27, 177*ff.*

utterly incapable of creating them." And even with respect to the ideas of great men, he asks again, "are we certain that they are exclusively the offspring of their brains? No doubt, such ideas are always created by solitary minds, but is it not the genius of crowds that has furnished the thousands of grains of dust forming the soil in which they have sprung up?"[1] Le Bon's unrefined analytical procedure prevented him from following out these suggestions more systematically, as did Tarde and Durkheim, but in this incidental manner, at least, he gave expression to the more positive aspects of his theory of collective behavior.

While very suggestive in so far as it applies, Le Bon's description of crowd behavior must thus be viewed critically in its more general implications for collective behavior. Every social aggregation, from a street mob to a religious sect and a parliamentary assembly, is a crowd within the limits of his usage.[2] But such a broad conception of the crowd is hardly compatible with the characteristics of crowd behavior which he presents. These, as suggested above, were apparently generalizations arrived at on the basis of a study of the more spontaneous forms of social aggregation, the applicability of which Le Bon then extended uncritically. The result was the crystallization of a paradox in psycho-social theory not unlike that noted in the discussion of Spencer.[3] As stated by McDougall, writers like Le Bon emphasize the view that "participation in group life degrades the individual," whereas writers like Durkheim insist that only "by participation in group life does man fully become man."[4] The attempt to resolve this paradox has defined a good part of further thought and investigation on the subject.

Recognizing that it is, after all, more confusing than enlightening to speak of the "vanishing of the conscious personality" in a deliberative assembly or a jury in any such sense as in the mob, the caste, or the sect, as Le Bon in effect does, an attempt has been made by later writers to refine his handling of the subject and to bring it into relation with other studies of group life. A most significant step in advance was taken by Tarde, who made the important distinction between the crowd and the public.[5] The crowd, according to him, is a product of physical contact; its limits are determined by the length to which a voice will carry and the distance which an eye can survey. The public, on the other hand, has no such physical limitations. It is the product of the printing press and other long-range media of communication which can produce "contagion without contact." This, it is evident, is a distinction of fundamental significance involving most important consequences for the

[1] *Ibid.*, p. 9.

[2] See *ibid.*, pp. 177*ff.*

[3] See *supra*, p. 38.

[4] See *infra* p. 192.

[5] *L'Opinion et la foule* (1901).

study of each of these types of social grouping.[1]   Another significant
distinction has been made by McDougall in his emphasis on the distinguishing importance of *organization* in the study of collective behavior.[2]

The effect of these distinctions and refinements of analysis has been
to limit the implications of Le Bon's discussion rather than to discredit it.
In so far as the treatment of crowd behavior itself is concerned, therefore,
Le Bon's work remains the accepted basis of analysis.   Other well-
known treatments of the subject, including those of Tarde, Ross, McDougall, and the psycho-analytic treatment of crowd behavior,[3] are notable
chiefly as departures from the analysis which Le Bon developed or as
reinterpretations from the peculiar standpoints in question of the observed
characteristics of crowd action which he originally reported.   This will
appear in our further discussion of the subject, especially in connection
with the consideration of McDougall's *Group Mind* and Ross's *Social
Psychology*.[4]

The importance of the writers considered in this chapter of our survey
has been such that their influence in the modern social-psychological
movement remains a determining factor in the situation not only in
France but also in this country and generally.   As was noted at the
outset of the chapter, French psycho-social thought has been incorporated directly into American social-psychological theory at several
points of strategic importance.   And indirectly, too, its influence has
been very prominent.   There is, therefore, a close connection between
this part of our discussion and Part II of our survey, as will appear in
some detail in the course of our elaboration of the latter.   Nor has there
been any such a decided break in the continuity of this connection during
and since the war as was noted in the case of German thought.   No
doubt the time is past in this country for the wholesale importation
of social-psychological thought currents, such as marked the earlier period
of American social-psychological development as represented by Ross's
work, for example.   But in the normal interflow of related movements
and tendencies, French psycho-social thought, as represented by the
writers considered in this chapter, remains a highly significant factor
in the situation.   At this time, as in the earlier period, it is however

[1] See PARK and BURGESS, *Introduction to the Science of Sociology*, pp. 868–869.
[2] See *infra*, p. 193.
[3] Ross, *Foundations of Sociology*, Chap. VI; *Social Psychology*, Chaps. III, IV, V;
McDOUGALL, *The Group Mind*, Part I; MARTIN, *The Behavior of Crowds*.
[4] For a further discussion of Le Bon's theory of crowd behavior see PARK and
BURGESS, *Introduction to the Science of Sociology*, Chap. XIII; GINSBERG, *The Psychology of Society*, Chap. IX; BRISTOL, *Social Adaptation*, pp. 133–138; BARNES, "A
Psychological Interpretation of Modern Social Problems and of Contemporary History," *Amer. Jour. Psychol.*, vol. 21, pp. 333–369, 1920.

only in terms of the basic background of American social-psychological thought to be followed out in the next chapter and developed in Part II of our survey that this factor may be adequately viewed.   In any event, this part of our discussion leads naturally into the next chapter and the remaining sections of our survey.   For in conjunction with them, it traces an essential aspect of the intimate setting of American social-psychological thought.

CHAPTER IV

THE DEVELOPMENT OF SOCIAL-PSYCHOLOGICAL THOUGHT IN ENGLAND

I

The situation in England as regards the development of modern social-psychological thought marks a new stage in the modern social-psychological movement from the standpoint of the progress of thought as it has been traced out so far here. Social-psychological thought, as we know it today, is a product which is deeply rooted in both the study of social life and in that of individual behavior. Our survey so far, and especially as developed in the previous chapter, has emphasized the former direction of development chiefly. In the case of English social-psychological thought, however, we get a definite shift of emphasis to the latter direction of development. The importance of this shift of emphasis, from the standpoint of American social-psychological thought, will appear only gradually as this chapter leads over into Part II of this survey. But in the meantime it is necessary, in view of the close connection which has existed between English and American psychological and social thought generally, to follow out the basis for this shift of emphasis in some considerable detail.

From the time of Hobbes and Locke on, and especially during the pre-evolutionary period, English thought was the stronghold of the individualistic approach. Psychological and social theory was consistently individualistic and *laissez-faire*, the product of the atomistic approach of association psychology and the conception of the inevitableness of natural law which was carried over into classical economic and political theory from the developing fields of physics and mechanics, chiefly under the influence of Newton's work.[1] In addition, discussion in the bordering field of psychological and social problems during the early period of modern social-psychological development was directing

---

[1] Reflected in much of the psychological and social theory of the eighteenth and early nineteenth centuries, this approach persisted as a part of individualistic thought in England until it reached its climax in the utilitarian "calculus of pleasures and pains" and the Spencerian conception of evolution (see ROGERS, *English and American Philosophy since 1800*, pp. 49*ff.*; BARNES, "Some Typical Contributions of English Sociology to Political Theory," *Amer. Jour. Sociol.*, vol. 27, pp. 289–292, 1921; "Some Contributions of American Psychology to Political Theory," *Sociol Rev.*, vol. 13, p. 153, 1921; BOGARDUS, *History of Social Thought*, pp. 173*ff.*, 367 *ff.*; BALDWIN, *History of Psychology*, vol. II, pp. 43 *ff.*, 126*ff.*).

itself increasingly to the consideration of practical matters, especially such as related themselves more or less directly and immediately to the nineteenth century program of English humanitarian reform. Investigation in the field of human conduct and social life, such as could conceivably lead to the reconstruction of basic psychological and social conceptions along social-psychological lines, was thus at a minimum. Economics and politics as the complements of individualistic psychology, rather than psycho-social analysis, were long the central interests in England, and English economics and politics have been notably individualistic in their emphasis and approach.[1]

There was, of course, in the background of late English nineteenth century psychological and social thought, Hume's well-known analysis of sympathy as a socializing force in his *Treatise of Human Nature* (1739–1740); and following Hume along the same line, Adam Smith's famous treatise on *The Theory of Moral Sentiments* (1759). Hume and Adam Smith have both in consequence been held to be highly important landmarks in the history of the modern social-psychological movement.[2] Notable in this connection, too, is Buckle's imposing attempt to treat the problems of social development in terms of geography and statistics in his *History of Civilization in England* (1857–1861), and one should perhaps mention here also, the echo of Comtean thought which made itself felt in the positive and social motives of later English utilitarian philosophy and ethics, chiefly through the agency of J. S. Mill and G. H. Lewes.[3]

But even these variations from the prevailing run of English psychological and social thought were essentially orthodox in their underlying individualistic presuppositions as regards human conduct. The emphasis on sympathy and altruism as the primary socializing forces, for instance, as has recently been pointed out in connection with the criticism of instinct psychology, in itself indicates an individualistic view of human conduct, based usually on an assumption of prior or natural individualism.[4]

---

[1] See MERZ, *History of European Thought in the Nineteenth Century*, vol. III, pp. 43*ff.*, vol. IV, pp. 427*ff.*, 446*ff.*; ROGERS, *English and American Philosophy since 1800*, pp. 1*ff.*, 49*ff.*, 128*ff*; McDOUGALL, *Introduction to Social Psychology*, pp. 4*ff.*; *The Group Mind*, pp. 3*ff.*; BARNES, "The Fate of Sociology in England," *Pub. Amer. Sociol. Soc.*, vol. 21, pp. 26–46, 1927.

[2] See BOGARDUS, *Social Psychology*, pp. 20–21; *History of Social Thought*, pp. 185, 369–371; PATTEN, *Development of English Thought*, p. 215; GIDDINGS, *Principles of Sociology*, Preface; BRETT, *A History of Psychology*, vol. II, pp. 356*ff.*; BALDWIN, *History of Psychology*, vol. II, p. 127.

[3] See MERZ, *History of European Thought*, vol. IV, pp. 494, 510, 515; ROGERS, *English and American Philosophy since 1800*, pp. 64, 130, 166, 189; BRETT, *A History of Psychology*, vol. III, pp. 219*ff.*; BALDWIN, *History of Psychology*, vol. II, p. 63; BOGARDUS, *History of Social Thought*, pp. 217*ff.*; Bristol, *Social Adaptation*, pp. 105*ff.*

[4] See COOLEY, "Reflections upon the Sociology of Herbert Spencer," *Amer. Jour. Sociol.*, vol. 26, p. 138, 1920.

And as regards the other trends of thought mentioned above, they were clearly even less positive in their social-psychological bearing as they were worked out in England.

On the whole, therefore, English thought experienced very little of the restless groping after more adequate approaches and standpoints related to the social-psychological which characterized the rise of modern social-psychological consciousness in France and Germany, at least until the time of Darwin and Spencer.[1] And even then, we get a social-psychological movement in England not as a well-defined movement in its own right but only as an expression of the larger evolutionary movement, from which social-psychological thought led out, at first at least, only as an incidental by-product. It was in the first place only that, with the formulations of Darwin and Spencer, the evolutionary motive became so strong as practically to impose its viewpoint on every field of scientific and intellectual endeavor of the day. But it was precisely because of this that English social-psychological thought became such an important factor in the modern social-psychological movement and that it has played such an important role in the development of our modern social-psychological conceptions. The individualistic orientation of English thought gave a peculiar force and significance to its social-psychological leanings and a unique direction to its social-psychological theory, as did also the fact that the latter emerged merely as an extension of its general evolutionary approach.[1]

It is thus, perhaps, the more important to follow out the development of English social-psychological and related thought because of these seemingly unfavorable considerations. From the standpoint of our primary purpose here, at any rate, it seems more important to follow out this direction of social-psychological development than any other, since American social psychology emerged, as might reasonably be expected, more or less as the natural outgrowth of its English background, and particularly the evolutionary standpoint as it was defined by Darwin and Spencer.

II. The Background of English Evolutionary Doctrine

1. Charles Darwin (1809–1882) and Herbert Spencer (1820–1903)

With Darwin and Spencer we enter upon a new era in English thought along several lines of direct interest to us here. First and foremost, of course, Darwin and Spencer came to represent an attitude of mind which marked the triumph of naturalism, in the realm of mental and social as well as biological thought. When the tumult of passionate dispute

---

[1] See McDougall, *The Group Mind*, pp. 3*ff.*; Brett, *A History of Psychology*, vol. III, pp. 202*ff.*, 213*ff.*, 224*ff.*; Baldwin, *History of Psychology*, vol. II, pp. 43*ff.*, 70*ff.*, 126*ff.*

which the publication of *The Origin of Species* first stirred to action began to subside, it left evolution, Darwinian evolution, the scientific watchword of the age. "A new generation of writers," says Brett, "began by assuming what their fathers disputed, and then proceeded to carry on the work of Darwin, both to amplify and to correct it."[1] In the course of this activity Darwinism and naturalism were placed on an unshakable foundation as guiding principles in modern thought, not only in the biological but also in the psychological and social sciences.

Then, as already suggested, Darwin and Spencer mark a definite departure from the crude individualism of early nineteenth century English thought. Darwin's work is particularly notable in this respect, for Spencer rather tended to redirect evolutionary thought along traditional individualistic lines, despite the emphasis which his work placed on sociological investigation and which doubtless ranged his influence on the side of the modern social-psychological movement in the long run.[2] Darwin's approach was, of course, frankly biological. Therein lay the power of his position. The weight of his influence accordingly went toward the development of a biological point of view. But it was not the one-sided biological view which was later frequently attributed to him. Later thought came to associate Darwin's name chiefly with his first great work, but it must be recalled, as one of the early exponents of social-psychological thought in this country has pointed out, that "the *Origin of Species* was followed by the *Descent of Man*" and that "Darwin the zoologist is Darwin the humanist as well."[3] And these two epoch-making works were furthermore followed by *The Expression of the Emotions* and by the unpretentious but very suggestive "Biographical Sketch of an Infant" (published in *Mind*, vol. 2, 1877).[4] All of these later products of Darwin's investigations have important social-psychological implications. Incidentally, Darwin laid the foundation in these works for the behavioristic and comparative movements in modern psychology and to some extent, also, for the modern child-study movement, all of which have been intimately bound up in one way or another, as we shall see, with the development of modern social-psychological thought.[5]

---

[1] BRETT, *A History of Psychology*, vol. III, p. 225; see also BALDWIN, *History of Psychology*, vol. II, pp. 94*ff*., 126*ff*.; GIDDINGS, *Studies in the Theory of Human Society* pp. 4*ff*.; LICHTENBERGER, *Development of Social Theory*, pp. 274–279; BRISTOL, *Social Adaptation*, pp. 58–68.

[2] See *supra*, pp. 35, 71; *infra*, p. 158.

[3] BALDWIN, *Darwin and the Humanities*, pp. 1, 7*ff*., 39*ff*.

[4] Darwin's observations in his "Biographical Sketch of an Infant" are in some respects extremely suggestive from the social-psychological standpoint. See especially his section on the "Moral Sense" and on "Means of Communication."

[5] See BALDWIN, *History of Psychology*, vol. II, pp. 94*ff*.; BRETT, *A History of Psychology*, vol. III, pp. 173, 224*ff*., 296, 300. Spencer's article on "The Comparative

Again, and here Darwin's work must definitely be kept distinct from Spencer's—though the influence of the latter was by no means a negligible factor in the establishment of the final result[1]—Darwin stood for just those qualities of scientific attitude and patient objective research which were and still are the outstanding need in the field of psychological and social investigation. Philosophical speculation about human conduct was age-old. What was needed most at this time for progress, not only in the field of social psychology but in all of the psychological and social sciences, was to pull the level of thought about human affairs up the laborious path of rigid scientific procedure. Darwin's example in this respect was for a long time overshadowed by the Spencerian vogue.[2] In the field of the psycho-social sciences, it is, in fact, only at the cost of much wasteful effort that the difference between Darwin and Spencer in this regard is gradually coming into evidence. Nevertheless, Darwin's work stood out all along as a disquieting criticism of unverified generalization and careless methodological procedure, until time and experience are at length definitely establishing the inductive method as a conscious objective also in this field of investigation. And now this aspect of Darwin's work stands out the more challengingly because it was for a time so completely overlooked in this field of investigation.[3]

Finally, Darwin and Spencer were the signal in England for a widespread extension of interest toward the more detached investigation of the facts of human behavior and social development.[4] Much of this investigation was in the first place, as we now know, essentially of the nature of illustration rather than research, but the general advance of interest in the scientific investigation of psycho-social phenomena which it represented, and which the evolutionary impulse stimulated along so many diversified lines, could not but accrue, in the long run, to the

---

Psychology of Man" (published in *Mind* vol. I, 1876) must also be noted as having been highly suggestive in these connections.

[1] See *supra*, pp. 28 *ff.*

[2] One very notable exception should be mentioned here in this connection, and that is the work of the Galton school. While consistently biological rather than social-psychological in their interpretation of Darwinian thought, their contributions in the field of method, especially statistical method, have been epoch-making for social psychology as for all psychological and social science. The fact that these contributions are chiefly affecting social-psychological investigation indirectly through other activities than those of the Galton school does not alter this major consideration. On the side of method, it may fairly be said, it was Galton along special lines in his study of heredity and individual differences (*Hereditary Genius*, 1869; *Inquiries into Human Faculty and Its Development*, 1883; *Natural Inheritance*, 1889) rather than Spencer, who most significantly supported Darwin's work. (See *supra*, p. 92.)

[3] See, in this connection, Osborn, *From the Greeks to Darwin*, Chaps. I, VI; also references, pp. 28, 148, 167.

[4] See *supra*, p. 146.

advantage of modern social psychology, as to all related fields of psychological and social science.[1]

The specific theories of Spencer, in so far as they have had a direct bearing on the modern social-psychological movement, have already been previously outlined and commented upon.[2] It will therefore not be necessary to repeat that part of our survey here. We need only to recall in this connection the dual effect which Spencer's work as a whole has had on modern social-psychological thought: positive in that it gave place and prestige to the study of the social-environment factor in human life; negative in that it provided a powerful defense of traditional individualistic and *laissez-faire* thought by restating it in modern evolutionary terms. The reader can fill in the detailed discussion leading to this conclusion by referring back to the section on Spencer at this point. We pass on directly here, therefore, to the more detailed consideration of Darwin's work from the standpoint of its bearing on modern social-psychological thought.

In the development of Darwinian influence, *The Origin of Species* (1859) was of course the event of greatest importance, but *The Descent of Man* (1871) and *The Expression of the Emotions* (1872) were doubtless of greater immediate significance as regards the fields of our interest here. After the first wave of intellectual excitement following upon the publication of *The Origin of Species* had spent itself, it began to appear as if Darwinism was after all stayed at the door of the so-called higher human faculties. In Darwin's first work, natural selection appears as a process resulting from a ruthless biological struggle between animal forms for mere physical existence. The implication as regards human development in its higher manifestations was there, but it was overshadowed by the weight of emphasis on the purely physical aspects of animal adjustment.

Darwin had rested content at the time with the statement that by this work "light would be thrown on the origin of man and his history."[3] He did not indicate just how his theory of natural selection bore on the special problems presented by the human species. He tells us that though he had been collecting notes on the descent of man for many years at the time, it was his intention not to publish them, because, as he puts it, "I thought that I should thus only add to the prejudices against my views."[4] Later events during the twelve years between the publication of *The Origin of Species* and *The Descent of Man* were such, however (the notion of natural selection having meanwhile attained wide support

---

[1] See BALDWIN, *History of Psychology*, vol. II, pp. 127ff.
[2] See *supra*, pp. 25ff.
[3] See *The Origin of Species*, p. 473; *The Descent of Man*, p. 1.
[4] *Ibid.*, p. 1.

among biologists), that he was encouraged to put together his notes "so as to see how far the general conclusions arrived at in my former works were applicable to men."[1] The result, as all the world now knows, was a death blow to conventional thought about human matters, which was as decisive in its effect upon the psychological and social sciences as Darwin's first work had been upon the biological sciences. The impassable wall which theology and metaphysics had set up between man and the rest of the animal world crumpled irreparably and, along with it, theological and metaphysical domination in the realm of what was now protectively termed "the distinctly human." Human phenomena, like the phenomena of life generally, were once and for all conquered, as Dewey says, "for the principle of transition" and freed for the application of the modern scientific method.[2] The way was thus for the first time definitely laid open for the positive investigation of mental and social life.

In the field of the biological sciences, Darwin's point of view was not entirely new; it was rather his method of presenting his point of view which was revolutionary. But in the field of the mental and social sciences, Darwin's point of view came as a veritable whirlwind of destruction to the established order of thought. And adjustment in the latter field, embodying, as it does, the values we prize most highly, was much more difficult and painful. Accordingly, Darwin's later works, his *Descent of Man* and his *Expression of the Emotions*, precipitated an even more feverish storm of intellectual agitation than did his *Origin of Species*. It was the violent opposition which these works met with, in fact, which finally became the most effective medium for the spread of Darwinian thought.

A general acquaintance with Darwin's application of his theory of natural selection in his *Descent of Man* must here be assumed, for the incidental references to this work which can be made here are in themselves entirely inadequate to convey the spirit of his exposition. A previous acquaintance with Darwin's general exposition being therefore assumed, the chief points of his discussion as regards the traits of our greatest interest here may be briefly outlined.

Man, it appears from observable evidence, bears in his bodily structure clear traces of his descent from some lower form.[3] In the evolutionary view of things, it is not even clear at just what point in the development of organic forms one ought to begin to apply the term "man." "In a series of forms graduating insensibly from some ape-like creature to man as he now exists," says Darwin in a famous passage, "it would be impossible to fix on any definite point when the term 'man' ought to be used."[4] Nor is this a matter of great importance from Dar-

---

[1] *Ibid.*, p. 2.

[2] *The Influence of Darwin on Philosophy and Other Essays*, p. 3.

[3] *The Descent of Man*, p. 65.

[4] *Ibid.*, p. 184.

win's point of view, since the fixing of any such point of demarcation must necessarily depend on the definition which is employed. But as we now know him, man owes his superiority over the rest of the animal world to his more highly developed intellectual faculties, to his social habits, and to his corporeal structure. "The supreme importance of these characters," says Darwin, "has been proved by the final arbitrament of the battle for life."[1]

Of particular interest to us here is Darwin's discussion of the "paramount importance" of the first two sets of these factors, which he, with characteristic insight, treated in relation to each other.

Through man's power of intellect, articulate language has been evolved; and on this, according to Darwin, has man's wonderful advancement mainly depended. Man has invented and learned to use various weapons, tools, traps, etc. He has made rafts or canoes for fishing or crossing over to neighboring fertile islands. He has discovered the art of making fire, by which hard and stringy roots can be rendered digestible, and poisonous roots or herbs innocuous.[2] Furthermore, man is a social animal and his destiny as an individual has been inseparable from the destiny of his tribe. Hence, he has developed characteristics which are beneficial to the social group as a whole.[3] He has learned to be helpful to his fellow-men, to anticipate future events, and to practice division of labor; to be sociable, sympathetic, loyal and above all, sensitive to praise and blame.[4]

Through these various means man has developed a remarkable power of adaptability. The lower animals must have their bodily structure modified in order to survive under greatly changed conditions.[5] If they fail to be thus modified, they cease to exist. But the case of man is widely different. After he had partially acquired those intellectual and moral faculties which distinguish him from the lower animals, man would have been but little liable to bodily modifications through natural selection or any other means, since man's mental faculties and social habits enable him "to keep with an unchanged body in harmony with the changing universe."[6] It is these mental and moral qualities, therefore, which are of predominant importance in the case of human development, and it is these which have been chiefly perfected and advanced through natural selection. The biological process of natural selection thus gives place, in the case of man, chiefly to a psychological and social

[1] *Ibid.*, p. 48.
[2] *Ibid.*
[3] *Ibid.*, p. 63.
[4] *Ibid.*, Chap. V.
[5] *Ibid.*, p. 130.
[6] *Ibid.*, p. 129.

process, as the basis for the natural development of man's higher intellectual and social nature.[1]

But the difference in mental power between man and the higher animals, great as it is, is one of degree only and not of kind.[2] Language itself, though it has justly been considered the chief path of departure along which man has proceeded to his position of preeminence, is not to be regarded as the peculiar possession of man.   In fact, it still bears the stamp of its gradual evolution in the animal world.[3] It is to be related to the expressive emotional movements, gestures, and vocal ejaculations, which man shares in common with the lower animals.[4] So also with the senses and intuitions, the various emotions and higher intellectual faculties such as love, memory, attention, curiosity, imitation, reason, etc., of which man has boasted special possession, as well as with his social and moral qualities.   All of these are found in an incipient or even sometimes in a well-developed condition in the lower animals.[5]

Summing up this naturalistic view of man, Darwin says:

> If no organic being excepting man had possessed any mental power, or if his powers had been of a wholly different nature from those of the lower animals, then we should never have been able to convince ourselves that our high faculties had been gradually developed. But it can be shown that there is no fundamental difference of this kind. We must also admit that there is a much wider interval between one of the lowest fishes, as a lamprey or lancelot, and one of the higher apes, than between an ape and man; yet this interval is filled up by numberless gradations.[6]

What more natural, therefore, than to expect that the same is true for the higher reaches of the evolutionary process?   Furthermore, there are gradations of differences also in moral disposition and intellect between the highest men of the highest races and the lowest savages. Differences here, as elsewhere in the evolutionary scale of forms, are connected by fine gradations, and it is possible, suggests Darwin, "that they might pass and be developed into each other."[7]

Thus is the theory of evolution by natural selection brought to bear with full force by Darwin in naturalistic explanation of those very characteristics which were at the time still supposed to be the distinctive endowments of human nature: language, reason, the higher emotions and

[1] *Ibid.*, pp. 130–132. Herein lies the superiority of Darwin's position over Spencer's from the social-psychological point of view. Spencer never worked out such a fundamental conception of mental and social adaptation (see Cooley, *Amer. Jour. Sociol.*, vol. 26, p. 140, 1920).

[2] *The Descent of Man*, p. 128.

[3] *Ibid.*, pp. 48, 128.

[4] *Ibid.*, pp. 85–86 (*cf. supra*, p. 62).

[5] *Ibid.*, p. 128.

[6] *Ibid.*, pp. 65–66.

[7] *Ibid.*, p. 66.

sentiments, morality, etc.   The biological process which figured almost exclusively in *The Origin of Species* is supplemented in *The Descent of Man* by a psychological and social process; the struggle for existence between individual forms becomes here chiefly a struggle between groups; natural selection operates especially on the level of the intellectual and the moral —and eventually man stands out, in all his complexity, seemingly just as much a natural product as the forms of the animal world and in close relationship to them.

At the time of the publication of *The Origin of Species*, applicability of the principle of natural selection to man's mental and social life appeared questionable even to Darwin's mind; at any rate the direction of its applicability was not then clear even to him.[1]   In *The Descent of Man*, for the first time, were the psychological and social implications of the principle of natural selection for human development clearly presented by Darwin and their significance for mental and social science indicated.   The chief aspects of his discussion as there developed have been schematized by Giddings in terms of the following four major considerations: (1) the importance of group or tribal cohesion as a factor of success in intertribal struggle; (2) the importance of sympathy as a factor in group cohesion; (3) the importance of mutual fidelity and unselfish courage; and (4) the great part played by sensitiveness to praise and blame in developing both unselfish courage and fidelity. "In terms of these four facts," Darwin found an answer, says Giddings, "to the question, how, within the conditions fixed by a struggle for existence, social and moral qualities could tend slowly to advance and to be diffused throughout the world."[2]   This seeming paradox explained, the issue between the old and new points of view, as regards human development, stood forth clearly for the first time as an inescapable challenge to psychological and social thought.[3]

In *The Expression of the Emotions*, Darwin carried his thesis forward in greater detail with respect to the investigation of a single problem. In its general bearing, this work is a part of *The Descent of Man*.   Darwin tells us that he at first planned to include it in the latter volume but that because of the proportions to which the book had grown, he thought it best to publish his essay on emotion separately.   It is to be regarded, however, as a particular study bearing closely on the thesis which he developed in more general outline in his earlier work.

Darwin points out that his attention was called to the subject of human emotion by the theory of a prominent biologist which held that man is endowed with certain muscles solely for the sake of expressing

[1] See GIDDINGS, *Studies in the Theory of Human Society*, pp. 4–5.

[2] *Ibid.*, p. 7.   Quotations from this work are reprinted by permission of The Macmillan Company, publishers.

[3] See *ibid.*, pp. 4–5; BRETT, *A History of Psychology*, vol. III, pp. 224*ff*.

his emotions. "As this view is obviously opposed to the belief that man is descended from some other and lower form," says he, "it was necessary for me to consider it."[1] In attacking the problem, Darwin brought to bear upon it his characteristic comparative and genetic approach. The result was an epoch-making treatment of the subject of emotion, supporting his general thesis as developed in *The Descent of Man* and of the same far-reaching significance for psychological and social thought.

"No doubt," says Darwin, "as long as man and all other animals are viewed as independent creations, an effectual stop is put to our natural desire to investigate as far as possible the causes of Expression. By this doctrine, anything and everything can be equally well explained; and it has proved as pernicious with respect to Expression as to every other branch of natural history . . . [But] he who admits on general grounds that the structure and habits of all animals have been gradually evolved, will look at the whole subject of Expression in a new and interesting light."[2] In the case of mankind, in fact, according to him, some expressions, "such as the bristling of the hair under the influence of extreme terror, or the uncovering of the teeth under that of furious rage, can hardly be understood, except on the belief that man once existed in a much lower and animal-like condition." Likewise, such apparently unexplainable phenomena as "the community of certain expressions in distinct though allied species, as in the movements of the same facial muscles during laughter by man and by various monkeys," are rendered more intelligible if they are viewed from the standpoint of common descent.[3]

Surveying, therefore, the facts of emotional expression as they present themselves in a comparative description of the manner of expression in man and the higher animal forms, from the evolutionary point of view, Darwin derived his famous three principles of naturalistic explanation: the principle of serviceable associated habits, the principle of antithesis, and the principle of direct nervous discharge.[4] These three principles appeared to him to account for most of the emotional expressions and gestures used by man and the lower animal forms. "It appears to me," said Darwin at the time, "that so many expressions are thus explained in a fairly satisfactory manner, that probably all will hereafter be found to come under the same or closely analogous heads."[5] These principles of explanation, especially the last two, have, as a matter of fact, come into considerable dispute, but the general setting of Darwinian thought in which they are incorporated has nevertheless provided at once the

---

[1] *The Descent of Man*, p. 4.
[2] *The Expression of the Emotions*, p. 12.
[3] *Ibid.*, p. 12.
[4] *Ibid.*, Chaps. I, II, III.
[5] *Ibid.*, pp. 27–28.

stimulus and the indispensable groundwork for later investigation of the subject of emotion.[1]

Aside from the evolutionary and naturalistic approach which Darwin introduced into the discussion of emotion, his survey brought in an important innovation .in the methodological treatment of the subject. In order that he might be able to study emotion comparatively in man and the lower animals, Darwin departed from the established practice of dealing with emotion in terms of "states of mind" and he approached the subject instead from the standpoint of "expression." This procedure not only enabled him to make his principles generally applicable alike to man and the lower animals, but it incidentally introduced the practice "of taking emotion out of the soul and the mind, and putting it into the body and the muscles," where it could be observed on a large scale and described in objective terms. According to Brett, Darwin thereby "to a great extent inverted the common view of the subject," since he regarded "expression" as the significant and relatively permanent element in emotion, inherited and fixed in organic structure, and consciousness as a comparatively insignificant concomitant element. Emotion thus became primarily an inherited reaction pattern of the organism and only secondarily a conscious state.[2] While this approach from the standpoint of "expression" was not entirely original with Darwin,[3] it took on general psychological significance only in connection with the evolutionary standpoint as developed by him. For this reason *The Expression of the Emotions* was a highly important event in the development of the modern behavioristic movement in psychology, especially, in view of Darwin's work as a whole, in its extensions into modern social and social-psychological theory.[4]

Darwin's treatment of emotion is notable here particularly, however, because of its more direct social-psychological bearing. Emotion is a significant fact socially, the Darwinian view suggests, first, because it implies an original social situation as a genetic and evolutionary background. Anger, for instance, is a social phenomenon implying interaction with another form. Then, again, emotion becomes socially significant in individual development through the meaning which attaches to it in terms of the response called forth. Finally, emotion is of social significance because it functions as an agency of social communica-

---

[1] See BALDWIN, *Darwin and the Humanities*, pp. 7–8; *History of Psychology*, vol. II, pp. 139*ff.*; BRETT, *A History of Psychology*, vol. III, pp. 173, 225, 300; also ALLPORT, *Social Psychology*, p. 210*ff*; *Feelings and Emotion: The Wittenberg Symposium*, ed. by Reymert, pp. 27–29.

[2] BRETT, *A History of Psychology*, vol. III, pp. 225–226.

[3] See his own citation of references in *The Expression of the Emotions*, Chap. I.

[4] See BRETT, *A History of Psychology*, vol. III, pp. 226, 288, 295; BALDWIN, *History of Psychology*, vol. II, pp. 95*ff.*, 128*ff.*; *Darwin and the Humanities*, Chaps. I, II; MURPHY, *Historical Introduction to Modern Psychology*, Chaps. VII, XVI, XVIII.

tion—because it is, in fact, the primal medium of social communication and intercourse.[1]

From the standpoint of its own genesis as well as from the standpoint of its relation to personal growth and the development of the human race as a whole, therefore, emotion has a distinct social-psychological significance. The inherited mechanisms of emotional expression ("the language of the emotions") are the primal media for the operation of the basic social-psychological processes of communication and control. The movements of expression, says Darwin in a very suggestive passage, "serve as the first means of communication between the mother and her infant; she smiles approval, and thus encourages her child on the right path, or frowns disapproval," and is likewise effective in discouraging it from the wrong path.[2] And on the other side, he suggests that, "even infants, if carefully attended to, find out at a very early age that their screaming brings relief, and they soon voluntarily practice it" as a means of communication and control of environment.[3] In another connection, as already pointed out,[4] Darwin related emotional expression and language genetically in racial development. Language, he suggested, stands in intimate reaction with more elementary forms of communication, such as expressive emotional movements, gestures, and vocal ejaculations.

The social-psychological implications of these suggested lines of relation appear to be most far-reaching. They have so far, however, been worked out only inadequately in social-psychological literature, especially in England itself, where, as we shall see, Darwinism was until recently given a distinctly individualistic turn by what Baldwin has well termed "Spencer's ambitious pre-emption of the field of social science with a construction motivated by individualism and founded on association."[5] The ascendency of the Spencerian individualistic conception of evolutionary doctrine was followed by a veritable tyranny of Spencerian influence as regards method. The development of social-psychological thought from this point therefore proceeds from the level at which Spencer left it rather than from the level at which Darwin left it.

It is one of the necessary conditions of Spencer's contribution to modern thought that it cost in terms of Darwin, and from the standpoint of social psychology the cost has perhaps been considerable. No doubt it remains, however, that nineteenth century psychological and social thought was ready for Spencer and not wholly for Darwin and that

---

[1] These leads to the social-psychological conception of emotional expression have been incorporated into American social-psychological theory especially by George H. Mead (see *infra*, p. 318).

[2] *The Expression of the Emotions*, pp. 365–366.

[3] *Ibid.*, p. 356.

[4] See *supra*, p. 153.

[5] BALDWIN, *History of Psychology*, vol. II, p. 128; *cf. supra*, p. 35.

Spencer did, after all, prepare the ground for a fuller appreciation of Darwin in the field of the psychological and social sciences. At any rate, it was largely the individualistic and *laissez-faire* attitude of traditional British psychological and social thought which Spencer reestablished with renewed vigor under the guise of the new evolutionary doctrine; and his construction of evolutionary thought remained dominant in England for a generation and more after the first formulation of the Darwinian theory.[1]

2. Walter Bagehot (1826–1877)

The development of the Darwinian theory in its broader psychological and social aspects links up in a very intimate manner with the work of Bagehot. In fact, the demonstration of the applicability of the theory of natural selection to the realm of man's higher development, and the actual extension of the theory from the point at which Darwin left it in his *Origin of Species* to the field of social interpretation, was first worked out, contrary to popular impression, by neither Darwin nor Spencer but rather by their, in this respect, less widely known contemporary, Walter Bagehot. His thought on this subject first appeared in a series of articles which he later republished as his *Physics and Politics* (1872). In commenting on this point, Giddings says:

> It was not until the publication of *The Descent of Man*, in 1871, when controversy over *The Origin of Species* had raged through twelve years of intellectual tempest, that the full significance of natural selection for the doctrine of human progress was apprehended by the scientific world. Mr. Spencer saw it when *The Origin of Species* appeared. Mr. Darwin himself had perceived that he must offer a credible explanation of the paradox that a ruthless struggle for existence yields the peaceable fruits of righteousness. But it was neither Mr. Spencer, nor Mr. Darwin, who first recognized the specific phase of the life struggle in which the clue to the mystery might be sought. The gifted thinker who made that discovery was Walter Bagehot, editor of the London *Economist*, whose little book on *Physics and Politics* or *Thoughts on the Application of the Principles of Natural Selection and Inheritance to Political Society*, was published first as a series of articles in *The Fortnightly Review*, beginning in November 1867 . . . Revised and put together in book form they made a volume of only two hundred and twenty-three small pages in large type, but no more original, brilliant or, as far as it goes, satisfactory examination of the deeper problems of social causation has ever been offered from that day until now. It anticipated much that is most valuable in later exposition.[2]

This it was able to do, of course, because of its relation to Darwinian thought. Darwin himself pronounced Bagehot's articles "remarkable,"

[1] See *supra*, pp. 32 *ff.*, 147; BALDWIN, *History of Psychology*, vol. II, pp. 128 *ff.*; SMALL, *Amer. Jour. Sociol.*, vol. 18, pp. 206 *ff.*, 1912–1913; BARNES, *Amer. Jour. Sociol.*, vol. 27, pp. 291–292, 314*ff.*, 442, 1921–1922.

[2] GIDDINGS, *Studies in the Theory of Human Society*, pp. 4–5.

and there can be little doubt but that they were an important factor in bringing to a head his own thoughts on human development.[1]

Bagehot, not unlike the German folk psychologists and some of the French and German sociologists of the period, was impressed with the cooperative and integrative aspect of group life—particularly in his case, in accordance with his political and legislative interest, with the cooperative and integrative aspect of the political and law-making functions of the modern state. Also, in common with most of the forward-looking scientific thinkers of the day in England, Bagehot was impressed with the value of the Darwinian approach and the concept of natural selection. He then took the step in advance in his treatment of the political and law-making functions of the state of linking together these two notions of the cooperativeness and unifying quality of group life on the one hand and natural selection on the other. He thereby arrived at the concept of group struggle in contrast to the individual struggle which Darwin had described in his *Origin of Species* and at an extension of the applicability of the principle of natural selection, which seemingly made it as useful an instrument of interpretation in the realm of social as it had already been found to be in the realm of organic facts. The result was an evolutionary survey of the political development of the modern state from the Darwinian standpoint, which is of historical interest here not only as a first attempt to apply the principle of natural selection to the field of social interpretation and as an early indication of the persistent interests and tendencies of English evolutionary thought as applied to the field of social theory, but also because it incorporates in preliminary form so many of the important concepts and principles of later psychosocial analysis. For despite his predominantly political interest, and despite the fact also that Bagehot was sufficiently under the influence of the biological approach to retain both the framework and the terminology of biological thought, he recognized clearly that the social process is essentially psychic in nature, so that his analysis is in large measure developed on the psychological level. In this respect Bagehot differs conspicuously from Spencer and he falls in line rather with the later school of psycho-social theorists. He may be said to have been one of the first of the modern group of evolutionary writers to outline a predominantly socio-psychological interpretation of social evolution.[2]

Like Comte before him, though from a notably different angle of approach and with a different purpose in view, Bagehot singled out three

[1] *Ibid.*, pp. 6–7; see *The Descent of Man*, Amer. repr. from 2d Eng. ed., 1874, p. 147, also pp. 132, 150, 208.

[2] See GIDDINGS, *Studies in the Theory of Human Society*, p. 212; BARNES, *Amer. Jour. Sociol.*, vol. 27, p. 574, 1922.

stages or, as he called them, "ages" of development: (1) the preliminary or custom-making age,[1] during which, according to him, imitation is the important principle of social life and the development of what he termed the "cake of custom,"[2] the dominant social process; (2) the nation-making age,[3] during which struggle and war become the important social principles, and the conflict and competition of "cakes of custom" the predominant social process; and (3) the age of discussion,[4] during which government by discussion gradually loosens the strangle hold of custom by placing a premium on the cultivation of reason, tolerance, and deliberate choice.

For the student of evolutionary thought proper, this scheme of evolutionary stages offers an interesting basis of comparison with those of later evolutionary thought in England and elsewhere. Here it is enough to take note of it as an early indication of a tendency toward schematization which became widely characteristic of post-Darwinian social theory. Passing on directly, then, to the development of Bagehot's analysis in terms of the fundamental social principles and processes involved, we come upon some very interesting anticipations of some of the key-note theories about which later psycho-social thought has centered.[5]

Bagehot starts out with the basic principle that man can progress only in cooperative groups. "The first principle of the subject," he says, "is that man can only make progress in 'co-operative' groups; I might say tribes and nations, but I use the less common word because few people would at once see that tribes and nations are co-operative groups, and that it is their being so which makes their value."[6] Going a step further in his analysis, he arrives at the theory that in the struggle between groups, the unified social group has a determining advantage over the loosely organized group. "Unless you can make a strong co-operative bond," he says, "your society will be conquered and killed out by some other society which has such a bond." This implies, according to him, "that the members of such a group should be similar enough to one another to co-operate easily and readily together"—a condition which depends, in turn, "on a *felt union* of heart and spirit" that

---

[1] *Physics and Politics*, No. 1.

The social-psychological significance of Bagehot's theory appears strikingly when it is compared with the biological emphasis given to Darwinian thought in the work of the Galton school.

[2] *Ibid.*, p. 27.

[3] *Ibid.*, Nos. III, IV.

[4] *Ibid.*, No. V.

[5] See GIDDINGS, *Studies in the Theory of Human Society*, pp. 5 *ff.*; BARNES, *Amer. Jour. Sociol.*, vol. 27, pp. 579*ff.*, 1922.

[6] *Physics and Politics*, p. 213. Quotations from this work are reprinted by permission of D. Appleton and Company, publishers.

can come into being only "when there is a great degree of real likeness in mind and feeling, however that likeness may have been attained."[1]

Continuing his analysis, Bagehot goes on to say that "this needful co-operation and this requisite likeness I believe to have been produced by one of the strongest yokes (as we should think if it were to be reimposed now) and the most terrible tyrannies ever known among men—the authority of 'customary law.'"[2] The latter it is, according to his scheme of thought, the chief function of "the preliminary age" to develop, and upon its efficient functioning in unifying the primitive group, as it seemed to him, depends the fate of primitive communities in the elemental struggle for existence which characterizes this period. In explanation of this elementary custom-making process itself, Bagehot outlined a theory of imitation which is strikingly suggestive of Tarde's theory of imitation as it was later developed, even as to detail.[3]

The process, according to Bagehot, is somewhat as follows: a sort of "chance predominance" of behavior becoming a social model, an invincible attraction, "the necessity which rules all but the strongest men to imitate what is before their eyes,"[4] secures the spread of this accepted model and eventually also of its precipitation as custom. Once established, variation from such a customary practice comes under the control of the strongest social sanctions. By social proscription and reward it becomes firmly cemented and fixed. In the "preliminary age" when "cakes of custom" are forming, everything which interferes with this process is considered dangerous and treated accordingly. "And the instinct of early ages," Bagehot suggests, "is a right guide for the needs of early ages," for "the living spectacle of an admitted unbelief destroys the binding authority of religious custom and snaps the social cord" during this primitive period of social integration.[5]

But the early food of social progress becomes its later poison, according to Bagehot.[6] Hence stagnation is the rule in the primitive world and progress is the rare exception which history demonstrates it to be. The customary control which in the preliminary stage is necessary to the life of the social community becomes, by the very principle which gives

---

[1] *Ibid.*, also note 3 below.

[2] *Physics and Politics*, p. 213.

[3] *Physics and Politics*, pp. 31*ff.*, 97*ff.* Bagehot's analysis as thus outlined, it will be apparent to anyone who has a reading acquaintance with modern psycho-sociological literature, is, in varying degrees, also suggestive of the distinctive positions which were later developed by Gumplowicz, Ratzenhofer, Giddings, Sumner, Ross, and others. See GIDDINGS, *Studies in the Theory of Human Society*, pp. 5–6, 18, 191; BARNES, *Amer. Jour. Sociol.*, vol. 27, pp. 579–580, 1922.

[4] *Physics and Politics*, pp. 36, 92.

[5] *Ibid.*, pp. 50*ff.*, 146, 214–215.

[6] *Ibid.*, pp. 41*ff.*, 74.

it value in the beginning, a barrier to further progress.[1] Custom makes for conformity and continuity, while progress, according to the Darwinian theory, requires also variation. And nature provides for the latter, it was suggested by Bagehot, through a persistent tendency toward variability.[2] In most early societies the yoke of custom becomes so unyielding, however, according to him, that this natural variability is killed off almost at birth. "Uncongenial minds become first cowed, then melancholy, then out of health, and at last they die," he says.[3] The natural means of further progress being thus ruthlessly destroyed in the germ so to speak, social stagnation is the inevitable result, followed by the natural penalty of eventual defeat in the struggle for existence and elimination from the scene of history.[4]

It is necessary in order to safeguard a healthy pace of progress, it thus appeared to Bagehot, to break the "mummy-like imitation" which custom rule fosters, so as to reintroduce the principles of competition and selection. This is the function of the second age, the nation-forming age, during which conflict replaces imitation as the dominant principle of social life, with the resulting impact and competition of customs and the final elimination or reorganization of the less fit.[5] The military principle, once it brings about the organization of powerful national groups and firmly established national customs, becomes in turn, however, a barrier to further progress. Conflict hardens the competing "cakes of custom" and the successful groups are left, even more rigidly dominated by the tyranny of customary authority than in the previous age.[6] Proportionally the more difficult does it become, according to Bagehot, to break through this firmly integrated customary authority and to set in operation again the mechanism of further development, so that progress may go on to the next stage. "The great difficulty which history records is not that of the first step, but that of the second step," he says. "What is most evident is not the difficulty of getting a fixed law; not of cementing . . . a cake of custom, but of breaking the cake of custom; not of making the first preservative habit, but of breaking through it and reaching something better."[7]

This "something better" is government by discussion, with the premium which it places on the cultivation of reason, tolerance, and deliberate choice. These are the processes which are brought increasingly into play, according to Bagehot, during the third age of development—the

---

[1] *Ibid.*, pp. 57*ff.*, 64, 157–158.
[2] *Ibid.*, p. 54.
[3] *Ibid.*, p. 146.
[4] *Ibid.*, No. II.
[5] *Ibid.*, pp. 44, 81*ff.*, 215*ff.*
[6] *Ibid.*, pp. 51 *ff.*
[7] *Ibid.*, pp. 53*ff.*

age of discussion.[1] The great majority of national groups are, according to him, powerless to take this next step forward. They thus range themselves on the losing side of the advancing tide of progress and become, in the course of time, material for the story of "arrested civilizations."[2] Advance to this stage is possible only "in those happy cases where the force of legality has gone far enough to bind the nation together, but not far enough to kill out all varieties and destroy nature's perpetual tendency to change,"[3] and only to those nations which have learned to put the principle of variability to social use. This requires a fine balance of antagonistic tendencies, of conformity and non-conformity, of nation *making* and nation *changing*, which has limited this further step ahead only to a comparatively few progressive nations of history. "Only a few nations, and these of European origin, advance," says Bagehot, while "a large part, a very large part, of the world seems to be ready to advance to something good—to have prepared all the means to advance to something good,—and then to have stopped, and not advanced."[4]

Among the nations which have advanced, the English peoples are especially notable, Bagehot felt, for the qualities which characterize this age of development. In particular they excel, so he claimed, in the possession of that most useful quality of the mind which he termed "animated moderation." This is a quality which it is, according to him, not easy to describe exactly. It is a subtle "union of life with measure, of spirit with reasonableness . . . of spur and bridle, of energy and moderation," characteristic of the greatest literature, the best thought, the most successful statesmanship, the most fruitful practical endeavor.[5] He says:

There is an infinite deal to be laid against us, and as we are unpopular with most others, and as we are always grumbling at ourselves, there is no want of people to say it. But, after all, in a certain sense, England is a success in the world; her career has had many faults, but still it has been a fine and winning career upon the whole. And this on account of the exact possession of this particular quality . . . if you ask for a description of a great practical Englishman, you will be sure to have this, or something like it, "Oh, he has plenty of go in him; but he knows when to pull up." He may have all other defects in him; he may be coarse, he may be illiterate, he may be stupid to talk to; still this great union of spur and bridle, of energy and moderation, will remain to him. Probably he will hardly be able to explain why he stops when he does stop, or why he continued to move as long as he, in fact, moved; but still, as by a rough

[1] *Ibid.*, pp. 65, 114, 156*ff.*, 200*ff.*
[2] *Ibid.*, pp. 42, 53*ff.*, 150*ff.*
[3] *Ibid.*, p. 64.
[4] *Ibid.*, pp. 42, 53, 57, 77.
[5] *Ibid.*, pp. 161*ff.*, 200*ff.*; also BARNES, *Amer. Jour. Sociol.*, vol. 27, p. 578, 1927.

instinct, he pulls up pretty much where he should, though he was going at such a pace before.[1]

Bagehot's survey ends with his famous discussion of "Verifiable Progress Politically Considered"[2] and with a comparison of the English nation and the so-called primitive social groups of the outlying districts of the world, in the spirit which was made so familiar by nineteenth century thought, both German and English.   He says in this connection:

> Let us consider in what a village of English colonists is superior to a tribe of Australian natives who roam about them.   Indisputably in one, and that a main sense, they are superior.   They can beat the Australians in war when they like; they can take from them anything they like, and kill any of them they choose . . . Nor is this all.   Indisputably in the English village there are more means of happiness, a greater accumulation of the instruments of enjoyment, than in the Australian tribe.   The English have all manner of books, utensils, and machines which the others do not use, value, or understand.   And in addition, and beyond particular inventions, there is a general strength which is capable of being used in conquering a thousand difficulties, and is an abiding source of happiness, because those who possess it always feel that they can use it.
>
> If we omit the higher but disputed topics of morals and religion, we shall find, I think, that the plainer and agreed-on superiorities of the Englishmen are these: first, that they have a greater command over the powers of nature upon the whole . . . Secondly, that this power is not external only; it is also internal . . . Thirdly, civilized man not only has greater powers over nature, but knows better how to use them, and by better I here mean better for the health and comfort of his present body and mind . . . Much, if not all, of these three ways may be summed up in Mr. Spencer's phrase, that progress is an increase of adaptation of man to his environment, that is, of his internal powers and wishes to his external lot and life.[3]

Bagehot's relation to later psycho-social thought, because of the connection which his work had with the development of Darwin's own views, really extends the boundaries of his own direct influence, which was itself quite extensive.   His analysis of social life, like Spencer's, is in fact relatable, on this account as well as because of the suggestive character of his special principles of analysis as already indicated above,[4] to most post-Darwinian psycho-social theory, and even more than Spencer's work it is remarkable as an early example at once of the rich possibilities which Darwinian thought held out for social interpretation and the faults with which it has so frequently been associated.   This will become clearer in so far as social-psychological thought is concerned, it is hoped, in the course of the next two sections of this survey.[5]

[1] *Physics and Politics*, p. 201.

[2] *Ibid.*, Chap. VI.

[3] *Ibid.*, pp. 207–208.

[4] See *supra*, pp. 159, 161, note 3.

[5] For a further discussion of Bagehot's social theory see GIDDINGS, *Studies in the Theory of Human Society*, pp. 5ff., 191, 211ff.; BRISTOL, *Social Adaptation*, pp. 177–

3. English Evolutionary Anthropology

We have dwelt on Bagehot's work at this length because it reflects so well some of the characteristics of classical English evolutionary thought which it is necessary to follow out here further in several important connections.

Events such as Darwin and Spencer represent in the history of scientific thought do not define themselves in an atmosphere of critical moderation. Copernicus, Galileo, Newton, Darwin, these became the epoch-making figures which the history of modern thought reveals them to have been not merely by virtue of the magnitude of their own personal achievement. To a very large extent their importance attaches to the fact that the discoveries which are associated with their names gripped the imagination of their respective generations and inspired them with a faith and an enthusiasm that did not stop to evaluate critically but sought expression in a quickening wave of unusual intellectual activity and accomplishment. Such a period followed upon the work of Darwin and Spencer. The first few years of questioning discussion gave way gradually to a period marked by an unbounded faith in the possibilities of the evolutionary approach. The magic terms "origin" and "development" seemed to meet every difficulty and to solve every problem. Thought was held spellbound for a time. In every field of biological, psychological, and social inquiry the older analytical method with its problems of structure and relation was being superseded by the newer genetic method, with its considerations of "trend," "process," and "stages." The age-old query with respect to any phenomenon of What is it? was for the time being completely overshadowed by the seemingly all-important question of Where does it come in the evolutionary scheme of things?[1] And an unparalleled productivity in all these fields of endeavor gave evidence of the vitalizing influence which the new approach had become.

No phase of inquiry reflected the effects of the new point of view more strikingly than the still practically uncultivated field of the naturalistic consideration of man himself, and especially man in his higher mental and social relations.[2] Here, as has already been noted, the advent of

---

180, 185; BARNES, "Some Typical Contributions of English Sociology to Political Theory," *Amer. Jour. Sociol.*, vol. 27, pp. 573–581, 1922; GINSBERG, *The Psychology of Society*, pp. xiii, 22–23; LICHTENBERGER, *Development of Social Theory*, pp. 279–284, 405–407.

[1] See BRETT, *A History of Psychology*, vol. III, pp. 217, 225; BALDWIN, *History of Psychology*, vol. II, pp. 96–97; ROGERS, *English and American Philosophy since 1800*, p. 128; GIDDINGS, *Studies in the Theory of Human Society*, pp. 3ff.

[2] See MERZ, *History of European Thought in the Nineteenth Century*, vol. IV, pp. 515ff.; GIDDINGS, *Studies in the Theory of Human Society*, chap. I; BRETT, *A History of Psychology*, vol. III, pp. 224ff.

Darwinism, in addition to establishing the evolutionary approach with full vigor, was the signal for a fundamental redirection of outlook and endeavor and for a tremendous heightening of interest in more detached scientific investigation.[1] It was a period of very earnest scientific activity, therefore, which applied itself to the solution of the problems which Darwinism defined in connection with the study of man's mental and social life. The importance which attached to the genetic and comparative methods of Darwin and Spencer reflected particular significance on the points of view represented by modern animal, comparative, and genetic psychology (both individual and racial) on the one hand and by evolutionary anthropology and ethnology on the other. It is, in fact, to the impulse of the Darwinian movement that these fields of inquiry chiefly owe the inspiration which has energized their remarkable modern development.[2]

In England itself the emphasis of scientific effort with respect to these fields of investigation fell chiefly in the direction of comparative and genetic psychology and thence in the direction of the development of instinct psychology on the one hand and evolutionary anthropology and ethnology on the other. The first of these directions of inquiry concerned itself with man as a biological organism and with his biological relation to the rest of the animal world; the second, with his developmental history as a human being. The aim in the one connection was to attack the problem of man's animal nature in an effort to draw him closer to the other animal forms and to preserve thereby the continuity of the evolutionary scheme on the side of animal life; and in the other, frequently by what today appears to be a highly artificial cultural grading of races, to carry this evolutionary scheme forward also on the level of social and cultural development.

Turning to the latter field of investigation first here as background for the more detailed consideration of the former, and in continuity of the foregoing discussion of Bagehot, it is notable that for a time this field of investigation was the common meeting ground of several present-day fields of specialized endeavor—of sociology, for instance, as well as of anthropology and ethnology. The evolutionary approach tended to merge psycho-social thought in England and to concentrate it upon the problem of tracing out mental and cultural development. This concentration of effort resulted in the emergence of that impressive galaxy of evolutionary writers who compose the classical school of English anthro-

---

[1] *Supra*, p. 146.

[2] BRETT, *A History of Psychology*, vol. III, pp. 213*ff.*, 224*ff.*; BALDWIN, *History of Psychology*, vol. II, pp. 94*ff.*, 103*ff.*; VILLA, *Contemporary Psychology*, pp. 38, 42*ff.*; McDOUGALL, *The Group Mind*, pp. 5*ff.*; BOAS, "History of Anthropology," *Proc. Intern. Congress Arts Sci.*, vol. 5, pp. 470*ff.*, 1904.

pology, besides Spencer—Tylor, Frazer, Lang, McLennan, Hartland, Lubbock, etc.[1]

The work of this school is not directly a part of social-psychological thought in the strict sense, for it definitely incorporated the individualistic approach of association psychology. Nor is it even as directly concerned with the problems of social-psychology as some of the related developments in nineteenth century thought which have been touched upon here in our survey of French and German social-psychological thought. Indirectly it was however a most important factor in the modern social-psychological movement, in that, like folk psychology and early sociology but more dramatically perhaps than either, it was bringing into view and giving concrete content to the social-environment aspect of human behavior, alongside of the individualistic aspect which contemporary biology and psychology were stressing. In this way it was helping conspicuously to prepare the ground for the more direct attack of modern social psychology. It must accordingly be given place here alongside of the other nineteenth century developments which stand out as important factors in defining the background of modern social-psychological thought, and especially social-psychological thought as it is to be developed in this chapter.

The faults and failings of English evolutionary anthropology are a matter of common knowledge at present to all who have an interest in the field of social investigation; likewise also its important position in the history of modern anthropological and ethnological thought as well as social thought generally.[2] That its representatives were biased by an axiomatic acceptance of the presuppositions of evolutionary philosophy and association psychology; that their work shows a lack of discrimination between "illustration" and "research"; that they too often "fitted" rather than "followed" their facts; that their method of citing cultural examples out of content and context was in itself basically faulty methodology; and that they were in general not essentially explorers of fact but supporters of a system of thought—all this has been gradually established

---

[1] Among American writers the work of L. H. Morgan and G. G. Brinton might be said to represent this period of anthropological development conspicuously.

[2] See *ibid.*, pp. 470*ff.*, 1904; *The Mind of Primitive Man*, Chap. VII; HADDON, *History of Anthropology*, pp. 13*ff.*; BARNES, "The Development of Historical Sociology," *Pub. Amer. Sociol. Soc.*, vol. 16, pp. 17–50, 1921; "Psychology and History," *Amer. Jour. Psychol.*, vol. 30, pp. 337–396, 1919; GOLDENWEISER, "Four Phases of Anthropological Thought," *Pub. Amer. Sociol. Soc.*, vol. 16, pp. 50–70, 1921; *Early Civilization*, pp. 20–27, 330–348; "Cultural Anthropology," *The History and Prospects of the Social Sciences*, ed. by Barnes, Chap. V; BRETT, *A History of Psychology*, vol. III, pp. 285*ff.*; VILLA, *Contemporary Psychology*, pp. 43*ff.*; BOGARDUS, *A History of Social Thought*, Chap. XVIII; ELLWOOD, "Recent Developments in Sociology," *Recent Developments in the Social Sciences*, ed. by Hayes, Chap. I; WISSLER, "Recent Developments in Anthropology," *ibid.*, Chap. II.

with the advance of anthropological knowledge and the progress of more careful investigation, and it is now frequently held up in striking illustration of the dangers of bias and presupposition in science. In general, much of the justifiable scientific criticism which has been leveled against Spencer[1] applies also in varying degrees to this whole school. The work of its representatives suffered greatly from the lack of a functional social-psychological point of view, which English thought, being at this time under the almost tyrannical domination of the biologically individualistic approach of Spencer, was just then particularly powerless to provide. The fact remains, however, that, like Spencer himself, this school of pioneer workers in modern social and evolutionary theory as a whole, did conspicuous service in helping to establish the naturalistic treatment of human phenomena on a firm and unshakable basis, and that it provided not only an inspiring foundation for the modern development of anthropological and ethnological thought but also necessary background for the development of all modern thought about human conduct and social life. In this general way English evolutionary anthropology has been a factor in the modern social-psychological movement, and it is necessary to consider from this general standpoint its relation to allied factors in the background of modern social-psychological development.

Not unlike some of the German folk psychology of the period, such as Wundt's,[2] though from a different orientation of evolutionary doctrine, English evolutionary anthropology directed its attention chiefly to the solution of the problem of mental and cultural evolution. Much more energetically than the former students of the problem, as was to be expected from the importance which was attached to the evolutionary approach in England at the time, it applied itself to the task of tracing out "stages" of development, and particularly "origins," in the various departments of culture: with respect to religion, mythology, art, custom, morals, technology, social organization and specific social institutions, etc.—in fact, with respect to all aspects of culture that seemed to offer promise of illuminating mental and social evolution.

In this undertaking it was dominated by the view, in the notable words of Boas, "that one definite system can be found according to which all culture has developed; that there is one type of evolution from a primitive form to the highest civilization, which is applicable to the whole of mankind; that notwithstanding many variations caused by local and historical conditions, the general type of evolution is the same everywhere."[3] Basic to this conception was the theory of the psychic unity

[1] See *supra*, pp. 29*ff.*

[2] See *supra*, pp. 41*ff.*

[3] *Proc. Intern. Congress Arts Sci.*, vol. 5, p. 472, 1904; also *The Mind of Primitive Man*, p. 175; *cf.* RIVERS, *Psychology and Politics*, pp. 112 *ff.*; *Psychology and Ethnology*, pp. 121*ff.*

of the human mind and the assumption of essential unimportance of the environmental conditions of cultural development. The conception seemed to imply, according to Boas, "that the different groups of mankind started at a very early time from a general condition of lack of culture; and owing to the unity of the human mind and the consequent similar response to outer and inner stimuli, they have developed everywhere approximately along the same line, making similar inventions and developing similar customs and beliefs."[1]

Holding that it is still possible to trace out the essential stages of this system of evolution from a study of the existing cultural groups of the world,[2] evolutionary anthropology applied itself with energy to this task. In the light of its outlook, the essential task of anthropology stood forth clearly. Boas says:

The multiplicity and diversity of curious customs and beliefs appeared as early steps in the evolution of civilization from simple forms of culture. The striking similarity between the customs of remote districts was the proof of the uniform manner in which civilization had developed the world over. The laws according to which this uniform development of culture took place became then the chief problem which engrossed the attention of anthropology.[3]

This theoretical setting of English evolutionary anthropology is most clearly reflected in Tylor's work. He says at the outset of his epoch-making work on *Primitive Culture* (1871):

The condition of culture among the various societies of mankind, in so far as it is capable of being investigated on general principles, is a subject apt for the study of laws of human thought and action. On the one hand, the uniformity which so largely pervades civilization may be ascribed, in great measure, to the uniform action of uniform causes; while on the other hand its various grades may be regarded as stages of development or evolution each the outcome of previous history, and about to do its proper part in shaping the history of the future.[4]

It was to the investigation of these two great principles, with special consideration of the civilization of the lower tribes as related to the civilization of the higher nations, that Tylor chiefly devoted his work, as he tells us, and his statement on this matter may be regarded as formulative of the central purpose of classical English evolutionary anthropology as a whole.[5]

In the working out of its problems, English evolutionary anthropology was obliged, particularly with regard to the all-important problem of

[1] *The Mind of Primitive Man*, p. 181.

[2] *Ibid.*, p. 176; also GOLDENWEISER, "Cultural Anthropology," *The History and Prospects of the Social Sciences*, ed. by Barnes, p. 221.

[3] *Proc. Intern. Congress Arts Sci.*, vol. 5, p. 472, 1904; *The Mind of Primitive Man*, pp. 175ff.; see also RIVERS, *Psychology and Politics*, pp. 112–113; *Psychology and Ethnology*, p. 121.

[4] P. 1.

[5] See BOAS, *The Mind of Primitive Man*, pp. 175ff.; also RIVERS, *Psychology and Politics*, pp. 107–137; *Psychology and Ethnology*, pp. 120–140.

origins, upon which adequate factual evidence is usually lacking, to fall back upon inference and speculation on the basis of so-called "vestiges" or "survivals."[1] These it interpreted, in accordance with its evolutionary outlook and general theoretical standpoint, in terms of the achievements of nineteenth century Western Europe, or rather England. The "subjective valuation" which usually enters into evolutionary systems, as has been brought out with dramatic effect, by the Durkheim school in France and the Boas school in this country,[2] thus became a basic part of the very foundation upon which English evolutionary anthropology sought to build its system of theory. Upon it rests squarely its characteristic pattern of discussion, variously tracing out stages "from savagery through barbarism to civilization, or from an assumed pre-savagery through the same stages to enlightenment,"[3] for all the array of fact which evolutionary anthropology frequently marshaled in proof of this basic structure. This is the source, too, of the purely negative attitude which it maintained toward primitive man. The notion, made famous by Spencer's well-known statement, that so-called primitive man is, as he put it, "on the average less than man as we know him,"[4] is more or less characteristic of the point of view of English evolutionary anthropology. Its whole theory of primitive mentality has been attacked by later students on the ground of subjective bias, and the more careful and detailed investigation of the facts of primitive life is gradually bringing about its reconstruction along fundamental lines.[5]

Such is the background upon which must be reflected the imposing productions of the school of thought under consideration. The whole field of evolutionary theory in the realm of culture and social fact was left, by its ambitious but premature attempts at classification and systematization, very much in need of revision and reinterpretation. And this has been a matter of concern not only to subsequent thought in the fields of anthropology and ethnology but also of all related thought, including social psychology, since the progress of psycho-social science as a whole in the modern period has been so intimately tied up with the clarification of our evolutionary views and conceptions.[6]

[1] See BOAS, The Mind of Primitive Man, p. 176; GOLDENWEISER, Pub. Amer. Sociol. Soc., vol. 16, p. 52, 1921; "Cultural Anthropology," The History and Prospects of the Social Sciences, ed. by Barnes, p. 220.

[2] See supra, p. 123; infra, p. 267.

[3] BOAS, Proc. Intern. Congress Arts and Sci., vol. 5, pp. 473–474; The Mind of Primitive Man, p. 181.

[4] Principles of Sociology, vol. I, p. 52.

[5] See supra, pp. 123ff.; also references p. 167 and infra, p. 267.

[6] See GOLDENWEISER, Pub. Amer. Sociol. Soc., vol. 16, pp. 59ff., 1921; BARNES, ibid., pp. 25, 27 ff.; OGBURN, ibid., pp. 74 ff. The development of American social-psychological thought, as will be seen, presents a striking illustration of this point.

As regards light upon the problems of social psychology in particular, the work of this school was only indirectly a contribution, in the nature of the situation as outlined above. It offered only the bare facts of primitive life, such as could be disentangled from its carefully woven scheme of relations, and incidentally, a broadened perspective and the comparative outlook. These have however proved to be indispensable factors in the social-psychological movement, especially in England, where the modification of individualistic thought along social lines has fallen chiefly to the lot of cultural anthropology.[1]

It was evolutionary philosophy which, in both Germany and England, intimately associated the social-psychological and the anthropological problems. With the abandonment of the search for a single grand system of mental and social evolution, however, and the gradual differentiation of the social-psychological and anthropological problems in terms of specialized investigation, the intimate relation which early evolutionary philosophy had set up between these two fields began to lose hold, and social-psychological interest in anthropological theory accordingly lagged.[2] Social psychology began increasingly to turn from the historical problems of anthropological concern to the study of psychosocial interaction as it is observable in present-day social life. However, as the careful study of specific problems has gradually replaced the earlier interest of anthropology in speculative evolutionary reconstruction, social psychology has begun to discover a new basis of interest in anthropological and ethnological investigation, growing out of the recognition that the historical and comparative methods have a value for the study of human nature in themselves and quite apart from the early interest in evolutionary reconstruction. It is the feeling of a growing number of students at the present time, in view of these considerations, that much more direct contributions for the social-psychological study of human behavior can reasonably be expected from anthropological and ethnological investigation than have hitherto appeared from this source. It is the conviction of some investigators, in fact, that the only remedy for those ethnocentric tendencies which the study of human nature in relation to culture usually brings forth in one form or another is its careful observation under widely diverse cultural conditions; and in this connection the importance of the so-called "primitive" or "pre-literate"[3] peoples as objects of comparative study with each other and with civilized

---

[1] The influence of sociology which is so much in evidence elsewhere in this connection, for instance, has been largely lacking in England. For sociology as a separate field of endeavor has never gained a footing there, despite the epoch-making sociological work of Spencer. For explanations see SMALL, "General Sociology," Amer. Jour. Sociol., vol. 18, pp. 200–214, 1912–1913; BARNES, "The Fate of Sociology in England," Pub. Amer. Sociol. Soc., vol. 21, pp. 26–46, 1927.

[2] See BARNES, Pub. Amer. Sociol. Soc., vol. 16, pp. 47ff., 1921.

[3] See Amer. Jour. Sociol., vol. 30, pp. 710–712, 1925.

peoples can certainly not easily be overlooked.[1] The significance of this view, as a check upon hasty generalization, has been emphasized especially in connection with the "instinct psychology"[2] which developed as a part of the other direction of investigation mentioned above relating to the evolutionary study of man in England, namely, that which attacked the problem of man's animal nature and his relation, psychically and socially as well as biologically, to the rest of the animal world. And it is with the latter, as the characteristic approach of English social-psychological thought, that we are chiefly concerned here.

In England as elsewhere, this more critical view of the relation between social psychology and cultural anthropology has been emerging gradually in conjunction with the criticism and the reconsideration of the underlying presuppositions of classical evolutionary theory, but in England especially, it has remained intimately a part of the latter. While this view has so far not been very aggressively stated in its specific social-psychological implications in England, it is more or less clearly projected, at least in so far as anthropological thought is concerned, in the more recent works of such writers as W. H. R. Rivers and R. R. Marett,[3] so that English cultural anthropology is gradually tending toward a position which closely approaches that of the Boas school in this country, as regards the social-psychological effect of its modification of classical evolutionary theory.[4] And in the case of English thought in particular, as stated above, it is necessary to keep the developing social and historical point of view of modern anthropological investigation in mind as an offsetting influence of the one-sided biological approach of instinct psychology. For in the practical absence of a psychological sociology as something distinct from cultural anthropology in England, the developing social and historical approach of modern

[1] BOAS, "Psychological Problems in Anthropology," Amer. Jour. Psychol., vol. 21, pp. 371–384, 1910; GOLDENWEISER, "History, Psychology and Culture," Jour. Phil., Psychol. Sci. Meth., vol. 15, pp. 589–607, 1918; "Psychology and Culture," Pub. Amer. Sociol. Soc., vol. 19, pp. 15–36, 1925; OGBURN, "The Historical Method in the Analysis of Social Phenomena," Pub. Amer. Sociol. Soc., vol. 16, pp. 70–83, 1921; KROEBER, "The Possibility of a Social Psychology," Amer. Jour. Sociol., vol. 23, pp. 633–650, 1917; ELLWOOD, "Cultural Theories of Evolution," Amer. Jour. Sociol., pp. 779ff., 1918; "Mental Patterns in Social Evolution," Pub. Amer. Sociol. Soc., vol. 17, pp. 88–100, 1922; FARIS, "Ethnological Light on Psychological Problems," Pub. Amer. Sociol. Soc., vol. 16, pp. 113–120, 1921; "The Subjective Aspect of Culture," Pub. Amer. Sociol. Soc., vol. 19, pp. 37–46, 1925; RIVERS, "Sociology and Psychology," Sociol. Rev., vol. 9, pp. 1–13, 1916.

[2] See FARIS, "Ethnological Light on Psychological Problems," Pub. Amer. Sociol. Soc., pp. 116ff., 1921.

[3] RIVERS, Psychology and Politics (1923); Psychology and Ethnology (1926); MARETT, Psychology and Folklore (1920); also BARTLETT, Psychology and Primitive Culture (1923).

[4] See BARNES, "The Fate of Sociology in England," Pub. Amer. Sociol. Soc., vol. 21, p. 39, 1927.

anthropological investigation stands out, together with the broadening viewpoint of evolutionary theory, as the chief social counterparts of the individualistic approach of instinct psychology.[1]

III. The Study of the Instinctive Basis of Social Behavior as an Approach to Social Psychology: Instinct Psychology

Instinct psychology as a factor in the modern social-psychological movement, as said above, had its center, very naturally, in the biological standpoint which modern animal and comparative psychology represent, as these fields of investigation were defined in post-Darwinian thought. Interest in the phylogenetic approach and emphasis on the biological continuity of evolutionary forms, tended to bring animal and comparative psychology into prominence as the natural transition steps leading over into the province of human psychology.[2]

This tendency to approach the study of human behavior on the level of animal and comparative psychology was revolutionary in at least two directions: first, because it naturally resulted in the extension of the behavioristic outlook to the province of human psychology; and, second, because it consequently brought into prominence the instinctive and emotional aspects of mental life as against the older intellectualism which had set up an almost impassable wall between human and animal behavior, on the ground that the former is explainable chiefly in terms of reason while the latter is essentially a matter of instinct.

The evolutionary approach as represented by animal and comparative psychology could naturally not accept any such separation of human from animal modes of behavior. It proceeded on the assumption, rather, that man being but a unit in the progressive series of evolutionary forms, his behavior tendencies must be looked upon as essentially continuous with the behavior tendencies manifested by the rest of the series. If, then, instinct is the key to animal behavior, this instrument of explanation must have a position of comparable importance in the world of human conduct. Again, if reason is a prominent characteristic of human behavior, this fact must in itself be regarded from the evolutionary point of view and its antecedent manifestations in the animal world established.[3] Accordingly, comparative psychology began to develop in two directions corresponding to these two lines of reasoning: the one emphasizing the importance of instinct in human behavior; the other

---

[1] See *supra*, p. 171.

[2] Ginsberg, *The Psychology of Society*, p. xiii; Baldwin, *History of Psychology*, vol. II, pp. 103*ff.*; Brett, *A History of Psychology*, vol. III, pp. 226, 299*ff.*

[3] The works of Lloyd Morgan, *Animal Life and Intelligence*, 1891; *Introduction to Comparative Psychology*, 1894 and of G. J. Romanes, *Mental Evolution*, 1878; *Animal Intelligence*, 1882; *Mental Evolution in Animals*, 1883; *Mental Evolution in Man*, 1883 are notable in this connection (see Brett, *A History of Psychology*, vol. III, pp. 300–301).

emphasizing the play of reason in animal behavior. Early English evolutionary thought emphasized the former attack particularly, thus preparing the stage for the development of modern instinct psychology as an explanation of human conduct and social events.[1]

Instinct psychology as an explanation of human behavior and social life has enjoyed wide popularity from the first. The whole subject of instinct in human psychology has nevertheless remained a storm center of violent controversy all along: first, because with its growing popularity, conservative opposition to the naturalistic view of human conduct tended to concentrate its attack on instinct psychology; and, more recently, because the progress of psychological and social thought has brought forth a great deal of criticism of its peculiar biologically individualistic standpoint. Nor is agreement on this matter immediately in sight even now. The controversy about the role of instinct in human conduct has, if anything, been gathering new momentum lately. Modern students of human behavior, who have been anxious to rescue psychological and social theory from the confusion and inconsistency in which the instinct theory of human conduct has seemingly involved itself, have turned their attention toward a critical reexamination of the implications of instinct psychology and as a result have begun to challenge the very foundation on which instinct psychology as an instrument of human conduct explanation appears to rest. And instinct psychology, supported in striking manner by the presuppositions of modern psychoanalytic and psychiatric theory and by certain exponents of such other important developments as the conditioned reflex doctrine, has seemed to some of its adherents to be stronger than ever in its basic position.[2]

---

[1] See BALDWIN, *History of Psychology*, vol. II, pp. 105*ff.*; McDOUGALL, *An Introduction to Social Psychology*, pp. 3, 10, 14*ff.*; *The Group Mind*, pp. 7–8.

[2] See, for instance, in this connection, DUNLAP, "Are There Any Instincts?" *Jour. Abnor. Psychol.*, vol. 14, 1919; BERNARD, "The Misuse of Instincts in the Social Sciences," *Psychol. Rev.*, vol. 28, 1921; and especially his recent work, *Instinct—A Study in Social Psychology*, Chaps. II–IV; KANTOR, "A Functional View of Human Instincts," *Psychol. Rev.*, vol. 27, 1920; FARIS, "Are Instincts Data or Hypotheses?" *Amer. Jour. Sociol.*, vol. 27, 1921; KUO, "Giving Up Instincts in Psychology," *Jour. Phil.*, vol. 18, 1921; ALLPORT, "Behavior and Experiment in Social Psychology," *Jour. Abnor. Psychol.*, vol. 14, 1919; WATSON, *Psychology from the Standpoint of a Behaviorist*, Chaps. VI–VII; DEWEY, *Human Nature and Conduct*, Chaps. VI–VII; also McDOUGALL, "The Use and Abuse of Instincts in Social Psychology," *Jour. Abnor. Psychol. Soc. Psychol.*, vol. 16, 1921–1922; "Can Sociology and Social Psychology Dispense with Instincts?" *Amer. Jour. Sociol.*, vol. 29, 1924; *An Introduction to Social Psychology*, rev. ed. suppl. Chap. IV; and presentations in *Psychologies of 1925* and *Psychologies of 1930*. Several very suggestive all-round treatments of the subject have recently appeared—for example, the above-mentioned work by Bernard, and JOSEY, *The Social Philosophy of Instinct*. See also WOODWORTH, *Contemporary Schools of Psychology*, Chap. VI and MURPHY, *An Historical Introduction to Modern Psychology*, Chap. XX.

It is inevitable that our views of the mechanisms of human conduct should be clarified as a result of this many-sided controversy. It has gradually come to be recognized that both the defenders of instinct psychology and its critics need the support of verifiable fact and investigation, so that interest is necessarily tending toward that direction of activity. This is obviously a net gain for social psychology whatever the outcome of such investigation may be. And in the meantime, however well-considered some of the present-day criticism of instinct psychology appears to be, there can be no question that it has played a tremendously important role in modern social-psychological thought and that it in large part remains at the basis of our conceptions of impulse, drive, and motivation in human behavior. Many streams of thought converge upon our modern views of human nature, as we have in some measure already seen, but none is more intimately a part of our whole modern outlook than the biological and evolutionary emphasis which has expressed itself most distinctively and effectively in the field of social-psychological thought through instinct psychology.

But the fact remains, nevertheless, that considering the dogmatism and special claims to scientific validity with which instinct theories of human conduct have frequently been presented, there is as yet surprisingly little agreement even on the more elementary aspects of the subject. There are at one extreme, for instance, those who, interpreting the struggle for existence narrowly, admit only a minimum number of instincts—usually only such as appear to be an absolute logical necessity for mere biological survival. At the other extreme, again, there are those who use the term so loosely as to cover any seemingly persistent tendency of human conduct. Between these two extremes there are all sorts of intermediate positions even among writers identified with the field of social psychology.[1] McDougall, for instance, emphasizes certain so-called "principal" instincts which have an individual survival value, but he gives place also to other more general tendencies, which presumably have only a secondary or social value. Trotter lays stress on the special importance of the gregarious instinct, alongside of the orthodox array of instincts which he seeks to include under the three major categories of self-preservation, food, and sex. Other writers again, such as Bagehot and Tarde, have appealed especially to what McDougall has termed the "pseudo-instincts" of imitation, suggestion, and sympathy. And so on.[2]

Very little more can seemingly be entered on the side of any considerable agreement than the general conception, which becomes extremely vague and uncertain in application in the case of man, namely, that by

[1] For a thorough-going survey of these varying usages, see BERNARD, *Instinct,* especially Chaps. II–IV.

[2] See MCDOUGALL, *An Introduction to Social Psychology,* pp. 93 *ff.*

the term instinct we mean to indicate "certain more or less complicated strains of movement which are adapted to certain ends useful to the race, which are congenitally determined and are independent of previous experience by the individual organism."[1] Beyond this general conception the writers on the subject of instinct appear to be unable to agree on any of the elementary essentials involved in the application of the instinct theory to the interpretation of human behavior, such as the number, the criteria, the specific nature of human instincts, or their relation to other than merely instinctive types of activity.[2] There are, as a matter of fact, almost as many systems of instinct theory as writers in the field of instinct psychology, the differences of treatment being at times most spectacular.[3] Such being the case, the subject has attached to itself much loose and biased thinking. This condition of affairs has effectively played into the hands of the critics of instinct psychology, and they have accordingly been successful, for the time being, in reflecting a certain measure of scientific distrust on the instinct theory of human behavior. At any rate, they have succeeded in forcing instinct psychology as a theory of human conduct to assume a definitely defensive position lately.[4] But this latest chapter of the career of instinct psychology as an aspect of social-psychological thought, as has already been suggested above, is still in large part to be written, and meanwhile the importance of the subject and the recent concentration of social-psychological interest and controversy about it make it especially important to follow out this section of our survey.

1. William McDougall (1871)

In the field of social psychology, discussion of the instinct theory of human conduct usually centers about McDougall's *Introduction to Social Psychology* (1908), not only because of the popularity of McDougall's treatment of the subject and the fact that his work sought to present instinct psychology systematically for the first time in its social implications, but in particular because McDougall so deliberately associated his work with the field of social psychology and because his work has in consequence played such an important role in modern social-psychological thought. McDougall's work has in fact held place as one of the two

---

[1] GINSBERG, *The Psychology of Society*, p. 1; see also McDougall, *An Introduction to Social Psychology*, pp. 23–24.

[2] See GINSBERG, *The Psychology of Society*, pp. 1ff.; McDougall, *An Introduction to Social Psychology*, pp. 24–25.

[3] See BERNARD, *Instinct*, Chap. IV.

[4] See in this connection, for instance, McDougall, "The Use and Abuse of Instinct in Social Psychology," *Jour. Abnor. Psychol. Soc. Psychol.*, vol. 16, pp. 285–333, 1921; "Can Sociology and Social Psychology Dispense with Instincts?" *Amer. Jour. Sociol.*, vol. 29, pp. 657–673, 1924; *An Introduction to Social Psychology*, rev. ed. suppl. Chap. IV.

pioneer systematic treatises on social psychology, the other being Ross's simultaneous work on *Social Psychology* (1908). And whatever modification of this generally accepted view a consideration of the historical development of the subject matter of modern social psychology may make for, it is an established fact that these two works have been outstanding influences in the modern social-psychological movement and in the gradual differentiation, especially in this country, of social-psychological from related and better established fields of endeavor. It is accordingly necessary to examine McDougall's position with some considerable detail here.

McDougall, not unlike Wundt,[1] approached the problem of social psychology by way of physiological psychology, and his point of view has remained, in consequence, as was the case with the latter, basically individualistic throughout.[2] As was the case with Wundt, also, McDougall recognized when he came to the study of social life that social groupings present themselves for study as functioning psychological unities, and as a result he was forced, as Wundt had been, into a dualism of social-psychological position which it has been difficult to defend. This dualism of position was made necessary, in either case, by the individualistic foundations upon which both Wundt and McDougall sought to build. But McDougall's standpoint, even as regards the study of the individual, was a considerable step ahead of the associationist standpoint which dominated English psychological thought in the preceding period, in the direction of what Merz has termed the *vue d'ensemble*.[3] For McDougall's evolutionary approach recognized, as the latter did not, that the social environment is not a negligible factor in psychology and certainly not in social psychology.

A "very important advance of psychology toward usefulness," says McDougall, "is due to the increasing recognition that the adult human mind is the product of the moulding influence exerted by the social environment, and of the fact that the strictly individual human mind, with which alone the older introspective and descriptive psychology concerned itself, is an abstraction merely and has no real existence."[4] McDougall, however, gave the current biological interpretation to this view. In his actual procedure, his broadened social standpoint reduced itself chiefly, therefore, to a recognition of the importance of the social factor in racial rather than in personal development.[5]

[1] See McDougall's reference to Wundt's work in *The Group Mind*, pp. xiii–xiv.

[2] *Cf.* GINSBERG, *The Psychology of Society*, pp. 11*ff.*, 16*ff.*

[3] *History of European Thought in the Nineteenth Century*, vol. III, pp. 192 *ff.*, vol. IV, pp. 422, 434*ff.*, 502*ff.*; also McDOUGALL, *The Group Mind*, pp. 3, 6.

[4] *An Introduction to Social Psychology*, p. 16. Quotations from this work are reprinted by permission of John W. Luce and Company, publishers.

[5] See GINSBERG, *The Psychology of Society*, pp. 11*ff.*; WOODWORTH, *Dynamic Psychology*, pp. 93*ff.*

McDougall nevertheless started out, in both his *Introduction to Social Psychology* and his *Group Mind*, with a round criticism of the older psychology on the ground that it had failed to provide a useful basis for social interpretation.[1] He says in his earlier work:

The department of psychology that is of primary importance for the social sciences is that which deals with the springs of human action, the impulses and motives that sustain mental and bodily activity and regulate conduct; and this of all the departments of psychology is the one that has remained in the most backward state, in which the greatest obscurity, vagueness, and confusion still reign.[2]

Until the later decades of the nineteenth century, McDougall explains, psychology continued to concern itself with such problems as "the proper classification of conscious states, the analysis of them into their elements, the nature of these elements, and the laws of the compounding of them," and these problems, according to him, have but little bearing upon the social sciences. The same may be said, he points out further, "of the ranges of problems connected with the relations of soul and body, of psychical and physical process, of consciousness and brain processes; and also of the discussion of the more purely intellectual processes, of the way we arrive at the perception of relations of time and place or of likeness and difference, of the classification and description of the intellectual process of ideation, conception, comparison, and abstraction, and of their relations to one another."[3]

Not these processes themselves, but only the results or products of these processes—the knowledge or system of ideas and beliefs achieved by them, and the way in which these ideas and beliefs regulate conduct and determine social institutions and the relations of men to one another in society are of immediate importance for the social sciences. It is the mental forces, the sources of energy, which set the ends and sustain the course of all human activity—of which forces the intellectual processes are but the servants, instruments, or means—that must be clearly defined, and whose history in the race and in the individual must be made clear, before the social sciences can build upon a firm psychological foundation.[4]

Since it was McDougall's aim to help make good the deficiencies of the older psychology in this respect, he applied himself specifically to the consideration of these "more socially important problems."[5]

Progress in this department of psychological inquiry, however much it was to be desired, was impossible, according to McDougall, before the modern development of biological theory. "It is only comparative and

---

[1] *An Introduction to Social Psychology*, pp. 1*ff.*; *The Group Mind*, pp. 3*ff.*
[2] *An Introduction to Social Psychology*, pp. 2–3.
[3] *Ibid.*, p. 3; *The Group Mind*, pp. 3–4.
[4] *An Introduction to Social Psychology*, p. 3.
[5] *Ibid.*, pp. 4, 17–19.

evolutionary psychology," he suggests, "that can provide the needed basis; and this could not be created before the work of Darwin had convinced men of the continuity of human with animal evolution as regards all bodily characters, and had prepared the way for the quickly following recognition of the similar continuity of man's mental evolution with that of the animal world."[1]   Only then did it, according to him, begin to appear that instead of usually acting according to the laws of reason, as the older psychology assumed, men are in truth moved "by a variety of impulses whose nature has been determined through long ages of the evolutionary process without reference to the life of men in civilized societies"; and only as a result of this view did the psychological problem of providing a full and accurate account "of those most fundamental elements of our constitution, the innate tendencies to thought and action that constitute the native basis of the mind," present itself for solution.[2]

Accepting, then, the standpoint of comparative and evolutionary psychology, McDougall nevertheless felt the need of explaining why he organized his work as he did, under the title An Introduction to Social Psychology.   It might be said, he tells us, that the description of these innate tendencies of the mind "is not properly a part of a social psychology."   It is, however, according to him, "an indispensable preliminary of all social psychology," and, since no consistent and generally acceptable treatment of the subject was available, it was necessary, he felt, to attempt to furnish the needed basis of discussion.[3]   "It may even be contended," he states further, that this subject "deals with the fundamental problem of social psychology."   "For social psychology has to show how, given the native propensities and capacities of the individual human mind, all the complex mental life of societies is shaped by them and in turn reacts upon the course of their development and operation in the individual."   Of this task, he suggests, "the primary and most essential part is the showing how the life of highly organised societies, involving as it does high moral qualities of character and conduct on the part of the great mass of men, is at all possible to creatures that have been evolved from the animal world, whose nature bears so many of the marks of this animal origin, and whose principal springs of activity are essentially similar to those of the higher animals."   "That is to say," he explains, "the fundamental problem of social psychology is the moralisation of the individual by the society into which he is born as a creature in which the non-moral and purely egoistic tendencies are so much stronger than any altruistic tendencies."[4]

[1] Ibid., p. 5.
[2] Ibid., pp. 10, 16.
[3] Ibid., pp. 17–18.
[4] Ibid., p. 18; see also BRETT, A History of Psychology, vol. III, p. 295; WOODWORTH, Dynamic Psychology, pp. 199 ff.

This is a conception of the problem of social psychology from the standpoint of evolutionary theory in its Spencerian biologically individualistic interpretation. In the light of it, the preliminary part of McDougall's analysis, that dealing with "the principal instincts and the primary emotions of man" as "the mental characters . . . of primary importance for his life in society," shone forth as the really significant aspect of his work. In any event, discussion has centered about this part of his analysis. Attention will accordingly be directed chiefly to this part of the work.

McDougall states his position aggressively at the very outset of his discussion:

The human mind has certain innate or inherited tendencies which are the essential springs or motive powers of all thought and action, whether individual or collective, and are the bases from which the character and will of individuals and of nations are gradually developed under the guidance of the intellectual faculties. These primary innate tendencies have different relative strengths in the native constitutions of the individuals of different races, and they are favoured or checked in very different degrees by the very different social circumstances of men in different stages of culture; but they are probably common to the men of every race and of every age. If this view, that human nature has everywhere and at all times this common native foundation, can be established, it will afford a much-needed basis for speculation on the history of the development of human societies and human institutions. For so long as it is possible to assume, as has often been done, that these innate tendencies of the human mind have varied greatly from age to age and from race to race, all such speculation is founded on quicksand and we cannot hope to reach views of a reasonable degree of certainty.

The evidence that the native basis of the human mind, constituted by the sum of these innate tendencies, has this stable unchanging character is afforded by comparative psychology. For we find, not only that these tendencies, in stronger or weaker degree, are present in men of all races now living on the earth, but that we may find all of them, or at least the germs of them, in most of the higher animals. Hence, there can be little doubt that they played the same essential part in the minds of the primitive human stock, or stocks, and in the pre-human ancestors that bridged the great gap in the evolutionary series between man and the animal world.[1]

Having then indicated, in this preliminary way, the general orientation and widespread significance of his projected study, he passes on directly to the psychological analysis of these basic tendencies of the human mind. They are grouped by him for analysis in two main classes as follows:

1. The specific tendencies or instincts;
2. The general or non-specific tendencies arising out of the constitution of mind and the nature of mental process in general, when mind and mental process attain a certain degree of complexity in the course of evolution.[2]

[1] *An Introduction to Social Psychology*, pp. 20–21.
[2] *Ibid.*, p. 21.

In the first class belong seven so-called principal instincts, the excitement of which yields the most definite of the primary emotions. He gives these principal instincts and their associated primary emotions in corresponding array as follows: (1) the instinct of flight and the emotion of fear; (2) the instinct of repulsion and the emotion of disgust; (3) the instinct of curiosity and the emotion of wonder; (4) the instinct of pugnacity and the emotion of anger; (5-6) the instincts of self-abasement (or subjection) and of self-assertion (or self-display), and the emotions of subjection and elation (or negative and positive self-feeling); and (7) the parental instinct and the tender emotion.[1] In this class belong also a few human instincts, which do not have such well-defined associated emotions as the seven instincts grouped above, but which are of very great importance for social life. Such, according to McDougall, are the instinct of reproduction, the gregarious instinct, the instinct of acquisition, and the instinct of construction.[2]

"The instincts enumerated above," says McDougall, "together with a number of minor instincts, such as those that prompt to crawling and walking, are, I think, all that we can recognise with certainty in the constitution of the human mind."[3] Lightly to postulate an indefinite number and variety of human instincts is, according to him, a cheap and easy way to solve psychological problems and is an error "hardly less serious and less common than the opposite error of ignoring all the instincts."[4] How often, for instance, asks McDougall, do we not hear of a religious instinct! Much has been written also, he points out, of the instincts of imitation, sympathy, and play. And yet, he declares, there exists no sufficient justification for the postulation of any of these instincts. He is also unfavorably inclined toward admitting an instinct of emulation or rivalry into his scheme of specific innate tendencies, as was done by James. "It would, I think," he says, "be difficult to make out any good case for the existence of such an instinct in the animal world."[5]

But precisely because such commonly postulated tendencies do not, according to McDougall, fit into the class of specific instincts, it is neces-

[1] *Ibid.*, pp. 51*ff.*

[2] *Ibid.*, pp. 84*ff.*

[3] *Ibid.*, p. 91. In his more recent *Outline of Psychology* (1923), McDougall changed this list. He mentions here, besides the six minor instincts which are concerned with the vegetative functions of the body, thirteen primary instincts. These are the Parental or Protective Instinct, the Instinct of Combat, the Instinct of Curiosity, the Food-seeking Instinct, the Instinct of Repulsion, the Instinct of Escape, the Gregarious Instinct, the Instinct of Primitive Passive Sympathy, the Instincts of Self-Assertion and Submission, the Mating Instinct, the Acquisitive Instinct, the Constructive Instinct, the Instinct of Appeal (see Chap. V).

[4] *An Introduction to Social Psychology*, p. 91.

[5] *Ibid.*, pp. 91-92.

sary to allow for a second class of more complex native tendencies, termed by him "the general or non-specific innate tendencies." In this class of "pseudo-instincts," as he suggests they might be called, he mentions, first, that commonly associated trio of social impulses: suggestion, imitation, and sympathy; then, the tendency to play and, in connection with it, the impulse to rivalry; also that "universal tendency of the mind, which is so familiar as to run the risk of being neglected," namely, "the tendency for every process to be repeated more readily in virtue of its previous occurrence and in proportion to the frequency of its previous repetitions"—in other words, the tendency toward habit formation; and finally, altogether in a class by themselves, innate temperamental tendencies.[1]

These tendencies, McDougall explains, have an innate basis, but they are not ascribable to special instincts, for they do not have the specific characters which genuine instincts, according to him, have. They are rather "of a many-sided and general nature" and for that reason, in his opinion, properly classed apart from the more definite instinctive tendencies of man, as given above.[2]

"Are then, these instinctive impulses," asks McDougall with a view to emphasizing his basic position, "the only motive powers of the human mind to thought and action? What of pleasure and pain, which by so many of the older psychologists were held to be the only motives of human activity, the only objects or sources of desire and aversion?"[3] In reply to the first of these questions, he brings up the subject of habit: "It must be said that in the developed human mind there are springs of action of another class, namely, acquired habits of thought and action. An acquired mode of activity becomes by repetition habitual, and the more frequently it is repeated the more powerful becomes the habit as a source of impulse or motive power." Few habits can, however, he declares, "equal in this respect the principal instincts." Furthermore habits are "in a sense derived from, and secondary to, instincts; for, in the absence of instincts, no thought and no action could ever be achieved or repeated, and so no habits of thought or action could be formed. Habits," says McDougall, "are formed only in the service of the instincts."

His reply to the second question is similar: "Pleasure and pain are not in themselves springs of action, but at the most of undirected movements; they serve rather to modify instinctive processes, pleasure tending to sustain and prolong any mode of action, pain to cut it short." Under their prompting and guidance are effected, according to him, "those modifications and adaptations of the instinctive bodily movements"

[1] *Ibid.*, pp. 93*ff.*
[2] *Ibid.*, p. 93.
[3] *Ibid.*, p. 44.

which are variously brought about in the course of experience and development.[1] He thus states his position in summary, therefore:

We may say, then, that directly or indirectly the instincts are the prime movers of all human activity; by the conative or impulsive force of some instinct (or of some habit derived from an instinct), every train of thought, however cold and passionless it may seem, is borne along towards its end, and every bodily activity is initiated and sustained.   The instinctive impulses determine the ends of all activities and supply the driving power by which all mental activities are sustained; and all the complex intellectual apparatus of the most highly developed mind is but a means toward these ends, is but the instrument by which the instinctive impulses seek their satisfactions, while pleasure and pain do but serve to guide them in their choice of the means.

Take away these instinctive dispositions with their powerful impulses and the organism would become incapable of activity of any kind; it would lie inert and motionless like a wonderful clockwork whose mainspring had been removed or a steam-engine whose fires had been drawn.   These impulses are the mental forces that maintain and shape all the life of individuals and societies, and in them we are confronted with the central mystery of life and mind and will.[2]

This is McDougall's essential thesis.   The rest of his discussion is directed to the psychological elaboration of this thesis and to its varied application in the analysis of specific human facts and situations.   There are, however, certain aspects of McDougall's more detailed treatment of the subject of human instinct which it is necessary to take note of here in view of the course of later discussion of the subject.   Particularly notable is his view that instinct has the threefold aspect (cognitive, affective, and conative) commonly, according to him, ascribed to other mental processes and, in this connection especially, his close association of instinct and emotion; his suggested use of this principle of association in the determination of the primary emotions and principal instincts; and his treatment of sentiment.

His definition of instinct runs as follows:

We may, then, define an instinct as an inherited or innate psycho-physical disposition which determines its possessor to perceive, and to pay attention to, objects of a certain class, to experience an emotional excitement of a particular quality upon perceiving such an object, and to act in regard to it in a particular manner, or at least, to experience an impulse to such action.[3]

This definition, McDougall felt, besides avoiding many of the difficulties which commonly arise in consequence of the usual insistence that

[1] *Ibid.*, pp. 44–45, 31*ff.*

[2] *Ibid.*, pp. 45–46; see also GINSBERG, *The Psychology of Society*, Chaps. I, II; WOODWORTH, *Dynamic Psychology*, Chaps. III, VIII; BARNES, *Amer. Jour. Sociol.*, vol. 27, pp. 742*ff.*, 1922; BERNARD, *Instinct*, Chap. IV.   There is a very interesting autobiographical statement on the origin of this theory in *A History of Psychology in Autobiography*, ed. by Murchison, vol. I, p. 208.

[3] *An Introduction to Social Psychology*, p. 30.

instinctive action is action performed without experience, or that it is necessarily action performed without awareness of the end toward which it tends, differs from most definitions of instinct and instinctive action in that the latter usually take account only of the conative or motor tendencies by which instincts manifest themselves. Instincts are more than merely tendencies to certain kinds of movement, according to him.[1] He says on this point:

There is every reason to believe that even the most pure instinctive action is the outcome of a distinctly mental process, one which is incapable of being described in purely mechanical terms, because it is a psycho-physical process, involving psychical as well as physical changes, and one which, like every other mental process, has, and can only be fully described in terms of, the three aspects of all mental process—the cognitive, the affective, and the conative aspects; that is to say, every instance of instinctive behaviour involves a knowing of some thing or object, a feeling in regard to it, and a striving towards or away from that object.[2]

These three psychic aspects of instinct are associated by McDougall respectively with the afferent, central, and motor parts of the neural mechanism constituting the neural basis of the instinctive process.[3] Instinct thus becomes, in neural terms, an inherited organization of these several parts of the neural structure, determining function in the manner manifested by the instinctive activity.[4]

In the case of the higher animals, according to McDougall, one is justified in assuming distinct cognitive and affective aspects as part of the instinctive process. On this level of behavior, however, and especially in the case of man, in consequence of his more highly developed intelligence and adaptability, great complications of instinctive processes are brought about—complications so great, in fact, "that they have obscured until recent years the essential likeness of the instinctive processes in man and animals."[5] Now it is the afferent and motor parts of the instinctive disposition, according to him, which are subject to modification in the course of the life history of the individual; while the central part persists throughout life as the essential unchanging nucleus of the disposition. In the case of man, then, the cognitive aspect through which the instinctive process is initiated and, even more so, in the view of McDougall, the bodily movements by which the instinctive process achieves its end become immensely modified; while the emotional excitement with its accompanying nervous activities of the central part of the disposition is the part of the instinctive process that retains its specific character and remains common to all individuals and all situations in which the instinct

---

[1] *Ibid.*, note, pp. 30–32.
[2] *Ibid.*, p. 27.
[3] *Ibid.*, pp. 33–34.
[4] *Ibid.*, p. 30; *cf.* GINSBERG, *The Psychology of Society*, pp. 4–5.
[5] *An Introduction to Social Psychology*, pp. 32–33.

is excited. "It is for this reason," he says, "that authors have commonly treated of the instinctive actions of animals on the one hand, and of the emotions of men on the other hand, as distinct types of mental process, failing to see that each kind of emotional excitement is always an indication of, and the most constant feature of, some instinctive process."[1]

It is his theory that each mental process resulting from the excitement of an instinct has always, accompanying it, an affective aspect the nature of which depends upon the constitution of that most stable and unchanging of the three parts of the instinctive disposition noted above, namely the central part.[2] In the case of the simpler instincts, according to him, this affective aspect of the instinctive processes is not well defined. Hence we have no special names for them. But in the case of the principal powerful instincts, the affective quality of each instinct is specific and peculiar to it; and language thereby provides special names for them. They constitute, in fact, according to McDougall, the most definite of the primary emotions: anger, fear, curiosity, etc.[3] "Each of the principal instincts," he says, "conditions, then, some one kind of emotional excitement whose quality is specific or peculiar to it; and the emotional excitement of specific quality that is the affective aspect of the operation of any one of the principal instincts may be called a primary emotion."[4] In order to emphasize this point, McDougall associated the primary emotions with their corresponding principal instincts, as already indicated above.[5]

This principle of association, which McDougall regarded as a notable contribution to the subject of instinct theory and which is epitomized in the popularized concept of "instinct-emotion,"[6] is of great value, according to him, in the analysis of the complexities of emotional and instinctive experiences with which we are confronted on the level of human behavior. In connection with it, he formulated the following very important statement of guiding principles for the application of the instinct theory of human conduct:

In considering the claim of any human emotion or impulse to rank as a primary emotion or simple instinctive impulsive, we shall find two principles of great assistance. First, if a similar emotion and impulse are clearly displayed in the

[1] *Ibid.*, pp. 34–35.

[2] *Ibid.*, p. 48.

[3] *Ibid.*, pp. 48–49.

[4] *Ibid.*, pp. 49–50.

[5] See *supra*, p. 181. In his *Outline of Psychology*, McDougall gives a more complete list of emotions corresponding to his list of instincts, but he no longer attempts to associate specific instincts and emotions (see his *Outline of Psychology*, p. 324).

[6] Among others, McDougall recognized James's contribution to this conception. "Professor James," he says, "who treats of the instincts and the emotions in successive chapters, comes very near to the recognition of the principle laid down above, without, however, explicitly stating it" (*An Introduction to Social Psychology*, note, p. 50).

instinctive activities of the higher animals, that fact will afford a strong presumption that the emotion and impulse in question are primary and simple; on the other hand, if no such instinctive activity occurs among the higher animals, we must suspect the affective state in question of being either a complex composite emotion or no true emotion.   Secondly, we must inquire in each case whether the emotion and impulse in question occasionally appear in human beings with morbidly exaggerated intensity, apart from such general hyper-excitability as is displayed in mania.   For it would seem that each instinctive disposition, being a relatively independent functional unit in the constitution of the mind, is capable of morbid hypertrophy or of becoming abnormally excitable, independently of the rest of the mental dispositions and functions.   That is to say, we must look to comparative psychology and to mental pathology for confirmation of the primary character of those of our emotions that appear to be simple and unanalysable.[1]

The definite enunciation of these guiding principles must be regarded as a most important contribution to the clarification of the instinct theory of human conduct and as a distinct advance upon the vague and undefined standpoints of most treatments of the subject.   And the principles themselves are of interest here because they indicate clearly the tendency of instinct psychology to look upon the distinctly "human" characteristics as something derived and secondary, as a sort of recently acquired "veneer" beneath which it is necessary for the psychologist to probe in order that he may get at what, from the point of view of instinct psychology, are the basic facts of conduct—the facts, that is, which are continuous with the facts of animal nature.

This, it appears from the standpoint of instinct psychology, can best be done not by studying human conduct itself as it is observable under normal conditions of social life but, as has been said somewhat flippantly but nevertheless tellingly by opponents of the instinct theory of human conduct, "by turning to the menagerie and the insane asylum"; the implication here being not a criticism of the importance which instinct psychology attaches to these fields of investigation in themselves but of the relation which, basing itself on the presuppositions of evolutionary philosophy, it axiomatically assumes to exist between these fields of inquiry and human psychology generally.   "One can understand present human behavior," says a recent defender of the viewpoint of instinct psychology, "only if one constantly looks beneath the surface appearance of responses acquired through the educative influences of civilized society and sees the ever-present background of behavior characteristic of man's savage and animal ancestry."[2]   This point of view, it has seemed to an increasing number of critical students, is subject to the leveling-down fallacy, sponsored by early evolutionary doctrine as interpreted by Spencer.   As it concerns the study of human phenomena,

[1] *An Introduction to Social Psychology*, pp. 50–51.

[2] WELLS, "The Value for Social Psychology of the Concept of Instinct," *Jour. Abnor. Psychol. Soc. Psychol.*, vol. 16, pp. 335–336, 1921.

it has come to be increasingly challenged recently. This challenge, it should be noted, is a challenge of the basic foundations of instinct psychology and not merely of some incidental detail in it. In fact, it strikes at the very core of the social-psychological controversy which has recently centered about the instinct theory of human conduct. McDougall and other exponents of instinct psychology and the biological approach proceed on the assumption that it is possible and profitable to attempt to separate out of the complex of concrete human behavior the biologically individual factor and that knowledge of the latter is a necessary basis of social-psychological analysis and interpretation, while the social critics of this approach maintain that observable human behavior on the level of social conduct, at any rate, is always an indivisible compound of biologically innate and socially acquired factors, so that any attempt to arrive at either of these factors in pure form, as a starting point in analysis, must be made on the basis of some sort of unverifiable abstraction. Instinct psychology, according to this view, thus tends to become a metaphysical dogma, no better than other types of unverifiable theorizing about human conduct but much more dangerous because of its peculiar claim to scientific validity and reliability. By shifting attention from concern with the concretely verifiable facts of human behavior to preoccupation with abstractly oversimplified elements and relations, it is maintained, instinct psychology really operates as an obstacle to the positive development of a real science of human conduct.[1]

But returning now to McDougall's discussion, it is necessary also for us to consider the third distinctive feature of his treatment of the subject of human instinct mentioned above.[2] In connection with his treatment of the subject of emotion, McDougall, following Shand, undertook the differentiation of emotion and sentiment and the analysis of the latter as "an organized system of emotional tendencies centered about some object."[3] This, by the way, is the part of McDougall's discussion which the progress of social-psychological thought has left most secure and which he himself has regarded as of the greatest importance; and the fact that it is based on Shand's work[4] would seem to argue the social-psychological superiority of Shand's approach[5] over his

---

[1] See references p. 174 and especially FARIS, "Ethnological Light on Psychological Problems," *Pub. Amer. Sociol. Soc.*, vol. 16, 1921; "Are Instincts Data or Hypotheses?" *Amer. Jour. Sociol.*, vol. 27, 1921; DEWEY, *Human Nature and Conduct*, Part II; BERNARD, *Instinct*, Chap. II; DUNLAP, "The Foundations of a Social Psychology," *Psychol. Rev.*, vol. 30, 1923; ALLPORT, *Social Psychology*, Chap. III; KANTOR, "The Institutional Foundation of a Scientific Social Psychology," *Amer. Jour. Sociol.*, vol. 29, 1924; COOLEY, *Human Nature and the Social Order*, 1922 ed., Introduction.

[2] *Supra*, p. 183.

[3] *An Introduction to Social Psychology*, Chaps. V, VI.

[4] See *ibid.*, pp. 126*ff.*

[5] Developed in his *Foundations of Character* (1912).

own. But as a matter of fact, Shand's approach is open to much the same social-psychological objections as instinct psychology in general.[1] His differentiation of emotion and sentiment on the ground of complexity of organization and his analysis of the process of sentiment development in human experience and of its function in character formation were important contributions to psychological theory, however,[2] and McDougall, in taking this part of Shand's work over and giving it place and significance in his own more popular treatment of instinct psychology, succeeded not only in establishing this useful conception but also in suggesting the complex basis of his own interpretation of human volition and character.[3] However, in order to follow out this more complex basis of interpretation consistently, it would have been necessary for McDougall to build up his instinct approach in some such manner as Shand did.

It should be noted, therefore, that Shand did not stop with the notion of simple innate emotional disposition in his analysis of human character. Instead, he passed on to develop the concept of sentiment and to speak of character as a hierarchy of these complexly organized and experientially conditioned systems of emotional tendencies. While basing his theory on the same biological oversimplification of human behavior that McDougall's instinct theory builds upon, Shand thus went beyond it in his analysis. His concept of sentiment has accordingly proved to be a much more acceptable tool of social-psychological analysis than McDougall's basic concept of instinct.[4] To rise to the same level of analysis on the basis of his own characteristic instinct approach, McDougall would have been obliged to invent a corresponding term to express the notion of instinctive behavior with corresponding social implications that the term "sentiment" has as over against the simpler types of emotional behavior. "Habit," "attitude," "want," "desire," "interest" have, in fact, been suggested at various times and in various connections to cover precisely this situation, and, as we shall see, recent social-psychological criticism of instinct theory has to no small extent centered around these suggestions. The combination "sentiment-attitude," in particular, has been proposed as a corresponding conception to the conception of "instinct-emotion" upon which McDougall's analysis ultimately rests.[5] For while immediately McDougall's analysis of concrete behavior is usually carried on in terms of complexly organized sentiments and tendencies, ultimately these are themselves resolved into the primary emotions and principal instincts, so that the latter remain the real

[1] See BERNARD, *Instinct*, pp. 454ff.

[2] See McDOUGALL, *An Introduction to Social Psychology*, pp. 126ff.

[3] See *ibid.*, Chaps. VII–IX; GINSBERG, *The Psychology of Society*, pp. 38ff.

[4] See McDougall's own estimate of this contribution (*Jour. Abnor. Psychol. Soc. Psychol.*, vol. 16, p. 332, 1921).

[5] See *infra*, pp. 238, 333, 380; *supra*, p. 74.

foundation stones of his theory. His analysis of the development of parental behavior may be noted as an illustration of the procedure.

McDougall's *Introduction to Social Psychology*, as has been said above, has been widely popular and it has maintained a good deal of that popularity, despite the fact that more recently it has also been very widely criticized.[1] Representing, as his work does, the biological approach and the individualistic view of human behavior, it has in general appealed more strongly to students of psychology than to students of sociology, although the "architectural simplicity"[2] of McDougall's scheme and the authoritative manner in which it is presented have not failed to gain for it popularity also in the latter field.[3] The feeling has been growing, however, on both sides, and not without support from McDougall himself, that whatever may be said for his scheme as psychology, it is certainly very little "social."[4] Moreover, even from the standpoint of his own biological approach, it has seemed, as one critic of McDougall's theory has pointedly put it, according to McDougall himself, that he does "a great deal of packing in preparation for a journey on which he never starts."[5]

McDougall took up this challenge in his work on *The Group Mind* (1920), declaring that this statement exactly describes his earlier work and that that was precisely its aim. "I found myself," he says, "like so many of my predecessors and contemporaries, about to start on a voyage of exploration of societies with an empty trunk, or at least with one very inadequately supplied with the things essential for successful travelling. I decided to avoid the usual practice of starting without impedimenta and of picking up or inventing bits of makeshift equipment as each emergency arose; I would pack my trunk carefully before starting."[6] "That other work was designed," he tells us at this time, "merely as a propaedeutic; it aimed merely at clearing the ground and laying the foundations for Social Psychology, while leaving the topic itself for subsequent treatment."[7] Social psychology itself, as the situation

---

[1] McDougall has recently expressed the view that his work has "withstood the fires of criticism remarkably well" (*An Introduction to Social Psychology*, rev. ed. p. 473).

[2] See GINSBERG, *The Psychology of Society*, p. 7.

[3] In the field of psychology, McDougall's work definitely initiated a new era of interest in social psychology, certainly in this country and in England. According to Woodworth, "it created social psychology as a branch of psychology, whereas previously it had been treated almost exclusively by sociologists" (*Contemporary Schools of Psychology*, p. 192).

[4] See McDougall's own statement (*Introduction to Social Psychology*, p. 18; *The Group Mind*, pp. xi, 2); *cf.* BRETT, *A History of Psychology*, vol. III, p. 295.

[5] See *The Group Mind*, p. xi.

[6] *Ibid.*, Preface, p. xi. Quotations from this work are reprinted by courtesy of G. P. Putnam's Sons, Publishers, New York and London.

[7] *Ibid.*, pp. ix, 2.

now appeared to McDougall,[1] consists of two divisions: the one dealing with the life of groups; the other, with the influence which this group life exerts on the growth and activities of the individual.[2] In *The Group Mind*, he concerns himself with the first of these two divisions. This leaves the latter, the division which has gradually come into the foreground in this country, as the core of the social-psychological problem, presumably as the subject matter of a third companion volume.[3]

Having, however, disposed of the formal aspects of the situation in the above manner, the fact still remains that McDougall's instinct approach in social psychology is unchanged. For "general" or "social" psychology, his *Introduction to Social Psychology* remains for him the essential basis of his system of social-psychological theory.[4]

And yet McDougall's procedure, once he is launched on his "voyage of exploration" in the field of what he now regarded as social psychology proper, is tantamount to an admission that he found his carefully planned equipment quite inadequate and even more or less useless for the purpose in hand, for he leaves most of it behind without much ado and sets about to work his way along in much the same sort of makeshift fashion that characterized the work of most of his predecessors in this field of thought. Impressed with the fact, as stated above,[5] that social groupings present themselves for study as functional psychological unities, he is obliged to leave his equipment of individualistic categories, which he was at so much pains to establish in his preliminary work, and to start practically anew. We accordingly discover that the "group mind" is not only not a matter merely of those elementary instinctive tendencies which figure in McDougall's introductory treatise, but that it is even something beyond "the mere sum of the mental lives of its units existing as independent units," *i.e.*, something beyond the organization of those elementary instinctive impulses which the individual units in isolation could achieve, were that in itself, as McDougall says, conceivable.[6] "The group as such is more than the sum of the individuals," we are told; it

---

[1] *Cf. supra*, pp. 179–180.

[2] This view of the subject, it is apparent, tends to bring social psychology into closer relation with sociology than with psychology. Generally, however, the conception of the subject which is attributed to McDougall is the one which he seemed to have in view when he wrote his *Introduction to Social Psychology*.

[3] *The Group Mind*, pp. 2, 8. McDougall projected his *Group Mind* as the first part of what was to be his *magnum opus*. But the course of later developments and his feeling that the title of this work was unfortunate in that it crystallized opposition to the book, have left the plan somewhat uncertain. (See *A History of Psychology in Autobiography*, ed. by Murchison, vol. I, p. 211.)

[4] See his more recent expression on this point in his *Outline of Psychology*, p. 128.

[5] *Supra*, p. 177.

[6] *The Group Mind*, pp. 10, 14–15.

"has its own life proceeding according to laws of group life," and these "are not the laws of individual life."[1]

In fact, McDougall defends the collectivistic view of social life generally in his *Group Mind*. He also inclines toward some modification of his instinct standpoint as previously stated.[2] But in any event, we are here introduced to the need of studying "unities," "organic wholes," and "potentialities," and these, we are told repeatedly, are not deducible from a study of isolated individuals merely.[3]

Consistently with this new emphasis, McDougall gives a more decided social setting to his criticism of the older psychology. "Until the later decades of the nineteenth century," he says, "psychology continued to concern itself almost exclusively with the mind of man conceived in an abstract fashion, not as the mind of any particular individual, but as the mind of a representative individual considered in abstraction from his social setting as something given to our contemplation fully formed and complete."[4] It was, according to him, the genetic and synthetic interests in psychology which led out from this abstract and individualistic conception into the broadening view of modern social psychology. His statement on this point is of interest here in that it seeks to bring out the social motive of English evolutionary thought. He says:

The general growth of interest in genetic problems, stimulated so greatly by the work of Darwin, turned the attention of psychologists to the problem of the genesis of the developed human mind,—the problem of its evolution in the race and its development in the individual. Then it at once became apparent that both these processes are essentially social; that they evolve, and at every step are determined by, interactions between the individual and his social environment; that, while the growth of the individual mind is moulded by the mental forces of the society in which it grows up, those forces are in turn the products of the interplay of the minds composing the society; that, therefore we can only understand the life of individuals and the life of societies, if we consider them always in relation to one another. It was realized that each man is an individual only in an incomplete sense; that he is a unit in a vast system of vital and spiritual forces which, expressing themselves in the form of human societies,

[1] *Ibid.*, p. 17; *cf. Introduction to Social Psychology*, pp. 18–19. A more consistent position on the part of McDougall in respect to the study of group life, in so far as his *Introduction to Social Psychology* is concerned, would probably have led him to a view not unlike that of Allport, who has approached the subject of social psychology from a somewhat similar starting point and who has consistently opposed group theories of social life (see *infra*, p. 407).

[2] McDougall has gradually broadened his viewpoint in a direction similar to that outlined in the section on Hobhouse.

[3] See *The Group Mind*, pp. 9–10. For a thoroughgoing criticism of this view and McDougall's reply, see MacIver, "What Is Social Psychology?" *Sociol. Rev.*, vol. 6, pp. 147–160, 1913; *The Group Mind*, pp. 12 *ff*. See also section on Allport, *infra*, p. 401.

[4] *The Group Mind*, p. 3.

are working towards ends which no man can foresee; a unit whose chief function it is to transmit these forces unimpaired, which can change or add to them only in infinitesimal degree, and which, therefore, has but little significance and cannot be accounted for when considered in abstraction from that system. It became clear that the play of this system of forces at any moment of history is predominantly determined by conditions which are themselves the products of an immensely long course of evolution, conditions which have been produced by the mental activities of countless generations and which are but very little modified by the members of society living at any one time; so that as has been said, society consists of the dead as well as of the living, and the part of the living in determining its life is but insignificant as compared with the part of the dead.[1]

No better statement of the grounds for the social-psychological conception of human nature is necessary. That this broadened social outlook did not react to revolutionize McDougall's individualistic approach as developed in his *Introduction to Social Psychology* is a seeming inconsistency of his social-psychological theory which, in so far as his own work to date is concerned, remains largely unexplained.

McDougall's elaboration of his theory of the group mind does not require the detailed consideration here that his earlier work required. For the importance of *The Group Mind*, as McDougall himself pointed out,[2] consists chiefly in the fact that it seeks to reconcile previous thought on the subject, which has to some extent already been covered here, especially in the sections on French and German social-psychological theory. His treatment is novel in its attention to the more formal aspects of associated life which had hitherto remained chiefly the domain of general sociological theory, but apart from this and the characteristic evolutionary and instinctivist setting which he throughout works into his discussion, it contains little that is an advance on the previous literature bearing on the subject of the group mind.[3] Also, McDougall's discussion, like most discussions in this field of thought, leaves much to be desired in the way of scientific balance and objectivity.[4] We pass on directly, therefore, to the consideration of the special feature of his work to which McDougall calls attention, namely, his attempt to work out a synthesis of thought bearing on the subject of group psychology.

Existing literature on the subject of the group mind presents a strikingly paradoxical divergence of view, according to McDougall. There are on the one hand, he points out, the crowd psychologists, who have concerned themselves chiefly with the task of describing "how participation in the group life degrades the individual, how the group feels and thinks and acts on a much lower plane than the average plane of the

[1] *Ibid.*, pp. 7–8.
[2] *Ibid.*, pp. 27–28.
[3] *Cf.* GINSBERG, *The Psychology of Society*, pp. 60*ff.*; also BARNES, *Amer. Jour. Sociol.*, vol. 27, pp. 748*ff.*, 1922 and *supra* p. 143.
[4] See, for instance, his Preface, pp. xii *ff.*

individuals who compose it"; and on the other hand, the many writers who "have insisted on the fact, that it is only by participation in the life of society that any man can realize his higher potentialities; that society has ideals and aims and traditions loftier than any principles of conduct the individual can form for himself unaided; and that only by further evolution of organized society can mankind be raised to higher levels."[1] We thus seem to stand before a most confusing paradox, according to McDougall:

> Participation in group life degrades the individual, assimilating his mental processes to those of the crowd, whose brutality, inconsistency, and unreasoning impulsiveness have been the theme of many writers; yet only by participation in group life does man become fully man, only so does he rise above the level of the savage.[2]

The resolution of this paradox contributes the essential theme of *The Group Mind*. It is his theory that the answer to the puzzle is to be sought in the phenomenon of group organization. About this theory as a point of departure, McDougall therefore develops his discussion. This appears clearly from his own outline of the chief points of his discussion. *The Group Mind*, he says, "examines and fully recognizes the mental and moral defects of the crowd and its degrading effects upon all those who are caught up in it and carried away by the contagion of its reckless spirit. It then goes on to show how organization of the group may, and generally does in large measure, counteract these degrading tendencies; and how the better kind of organization renders group life the great ennobling influence by aid of which alone man rises a little above the animals and may even aspire to fellowship with the angels."[3]

Starting out, then, with a description of behavior in the loosely organized crowd[4] along the lines of Le Bon's classical study, as exemplifying the lowest level of group behavior, McDougall passes on to a corresponding description of behavior in the highly organized army,[5] as exemplifying the other extreme of group behavior from that of the crowd. The discussion thus leads on to a consideration of the factors which, in social groupings of higher organization, enter in to raise the level of behavior and to modify the elementary characteristics which appear in the crowd.

McDougall mentions five conditions which he regards as of fundamental importance: group continuity, group self-consciousness, group interaction, the development of group traditions and customs, and group organization for the performance of differentiated and specialized func-

---

[1] *The Group Mind*, p. 27.
[2] *Ibid.*, pp. 27–28.
[3] *Ibid.*, p. 28.
[4] *Ibid.*, Chap. II.
[5] *Ibid.*, Chap. III.

tions.[1] These conditions working together with the basic conditions of collective life operative in the crowd tend, McDougall feels, toward the development of a "group-spirit" (that is, of a sentiment of loyalty and devotion for the group as a group on the part of its members); and toward the organization of a collective mental life or "group-mind" that is expressive of the group as a whole as over against the individual minds of its constituent members.[2]

The consequence for the individual in such a group is that his egoistic nature is brought into harmonious relation with the defined motives of organized group life. He becomes identified with the aims and purposes of his group so that "he is moved to desire and to work for its welfare, its success, its honor and glory, by the same motives which prompt him to desire and to work for his own welfare and success and honour."[3] The individual, according to McDougall, "wills the common end; and, believing that the choice of means to that end is best effected by the appropriate part of the whole organisation, he accepts the means chosen, makes of them his proximate end, and wills them."[4]

This is a two-edged process, securing at the same time the individual's highest expression and the most effective functioning of collective group life.[5] McDougall says:

This is the essential character of the effective organization of any human group; it secures that while the common end of collective action is willed by all, the choice of means is left to those best qualified and in the best position for deliberation and choice; and it secures that co-ordination of voluntary action of the parts which brings about the common end by the means so chosen. In this way the collective actions of the well-organized group, instead of being, like those of a simple crowd, merely impulsive or instinctive actions, implying a degree of intelligence and of morality far inferior to that of the average individual of the crowd, become truly volitional actions expressive of a degree of intelligence and morality much higher than that of the average member of the group; *i.e.*, the whole is raised above the level of its average member; and even by reason of exaltation of emotion and organized co-operation in deliberation, above that of its highest members.[6]

Group life naturally exists in all degrees of organization, but the group mind of a highly organized social group that has enjoyed long life presents itself, according to McDougall, as "an organized system of forces which has a life of its own, tendencies of its own, a power of moulding all its component individuals, and a power of perpetuating itself as a self-identical system, subject only to slow and gradual change." It is a

[1] *Ibid.*, pp. 68*ff.*
[2] *Ibid.*, pp. 12, 25, Chap. IV.
[3] *Ibid.*, pp. 110–111.
[4] *Ibid.*, p. 73.
[5] *Ibid.*, pp. 27–28, 70*ff.*
[6] *Ibid.*, pp. 73–74.

system which can "think and will and feel and act" in a sense that corresponds to the sense in which the individual mind does these things; and it may become "something indefinitely greater, more powerful, more comprehensive" than any one individual or any mere sum of the individuals that compose the group.[1]

In explanation of this frequently challenged view, McDougall has the following to say:

We may fairly define a mind as an organized system of mental or purposive force; and, in the sense so defined, every highly organized human society may properly be said to possess a collective mind. For the collective actions which constitute the history of any such society are conditioned by an organisation which can only be described in terms of mind, and which yet is not comprised within the mind of any individual; the society is rather constituted by the system of relations obtaining between the individual minds which are its units of composition. Under any given circumstances the actions of society are, or may be, very different from the mere sum of the actions with which its several members would react to the situation in the absence of the system of relations which render them a society; or, in other words, the thinking and acting of each man, in so far as he thinks and acts as a member of a society, are very different from his thinking and acting as an isolated individual.[2]

This conception McDougall was much concerned to differentiate from the collectivism of German idealistic thought.[3] It was his aim, he tells us, to preserve the truth of both collectivism and individualism in social theory and in the light of this better balanced view to present a systematic exposition of group psychology.[4] It is, however, not easy to follow McDougall in this attempt at differentiation. At any rate, the differences, such as they are, are less in evidence than the similarities.[5] Nevertheless, as a serious attempt to synthesize the conflicting views of collective psychology and to present a systematic treatment of the subject, his work is a definite contribution to the literature of this field of thought and, in so far as English psycho-social thought is concerned in particular, a considerable departure also from established views and conceptions. One need only compare his treatment of the subject with that of Le Bon to appreciate the step in advance which McDougall's work represents.[6]

So much for the part of McDougall's work which deals with the general principles of group psychology. The greater part of his work is devoted to the application of this background of theory to the interpre-

---

[1] *Ibid.*, pp. 12, 14, 16.
[2] *Ibid.*, p. 13.
[3] *Ibid.*, pp. xii, xv, xvi.
[4] See *ibid.*, pp. xv–xvi, 23*ff.*, Chap. XII.
[5] *Cf.* GINSBERG, *The Psychology of Society*, pp. 61–63.
[6] *Ibid.*, 61*ff.*; BARNES, *Amer. Jour. Sociol.*, vol. 27, pp. 754*ff.*, 1922.

tation of the nation-state as "the most interesting, most complex and most important kind of group mind" and to an evolutionary survey of the nation-making process somewhat along the lines of Bagehot's survey in his *Physics and Politics*. This part of McDougall's discussion, like so much related literature, is of a semi-popular nature and need, therefore, not occupy us in detail. It is notable, however, that his survey ends with a defense of social telesis, such as inevitably calls to mind the classic defense of this thesis by Auguste Comte and Lester F. Ward.[1] It thus appears that McDougall reflects two new motives in his later work: the collectivistic motive in the sense in which it figures in French and German sociological thought; and the social control motive, so conspicuously a part especially of American sociological thought. These two motives gradually entered, first to challenge and finally to modify the characteristic biologically individualistic and *laissez-faire* point of view of Spencerian evolutionary thought in England, as we shall presently see.

In the case of McDougall, however, these motives appear as a somewhat inconsistent superimposition upon his basic conception of human behavior as outlined in his *Introduction to Social Psychology*. The theory that men are essentially moved by "non-moral and purely egoistic" impulses "whose nature has been determined through long ages of the evolutionary process without reference to the life of men in civilized societies"[2] does not after all leave much room for the collectivistic view of human behavior or for conscious social control as a fundamental social-psychological principle. Except in so far as social control can influence the biological factors operative in the future, it is altogether a matter of secondary importance in the drama of human life. The logical complement to this conception of human nature, therefore, is not an aggressive faith in social telesis in the sense of Comte's and Ward's views but in the sense of the Galton school, in the sense, that is, of the eugenics movement to which it gave rise in England, as the outstanding contribution of biological evolutionary doctrine to a program of practical social reform.[3]

2. Wilfred Trotter, Graham Wallas, Leonard T. Hobhouse

The above-mentioned doctrines have nevertheless come to play an increasingly important part in English psycho-social thought, and some

---

[1] See *supra*, p. 16; *infra*, p. 222; *cf.* BARNES, *Amer. Jour. Sociol.*, vol. 27, p. 755, 1922.

[2] See *Introduction to Social Psychology*, pp. 10, 18; *supra*, p. 179.

[3] See BRISTOL, *Social Adaptation*, pp. 92–99; BOGARDUS, *A History of Social Thought*, Chap. XIX; also BARNES, "Some Typical Contributions of English Sociology to Political Theory," *Amer. Jour. Sociol.*, vol. 27, pp. 748–757, 1922; "The Fate of Sociology in England," *Pub. Amer. Sociol. Soc.*, vol. 21, pp. 26–46, 1927.

of the other recent writers on the instinct theory of human conduct in England have sought to depart from the orthodox position of instinct psychology sufficiently to enable them to incorporate the relevant theories more consistently as organic parts of their social-psychological thinking. Of these, we have selected Trotter, Wallas, and Hobhouse for brief consideration here, as representing further the development of social-psychological thought in England.

It is therefore notable in the above connection, that Trotter, in his *Instincts of the Herd in Peace and War* (1916)[1] has set about to criticize the characteristic individualism of orthodox instinct theory. The commonly accepted individualistic instincts, which he classifies under the categories of self-preservation, nutrition, and sex,[2] cannot, according to him, adequately cover the known facts of human behavior. Man is moved by the promptings of these primary instincts sufficiently, he states, so that "the temptation to declare that all human behavior could be resumed under them was irresistible." It was, however, inevitable, according to him, that "these early triumphs of materialism" should finally begin to be troubled by doubt. For no amount of "sophistry" can suffice, in his opinion, to squeeze the behavior of man as a gregarious animal into these categories of explanation without the aid of an additional category. This indispensable additional category of explanation, Trotter argues, is gregariousness or, as he prefers, the herd instinct.[3]

As used by Trotter, this category of explanation is merely a biological device to enable him to take account of the social and the intellectual factors in human behavior more directly than is commonly done by instinct psychology. His point of departure from the position which he attributes to orthodox instinct theory in this respect appears readily from his objection to the prevalent instinct conception of gregariousness. He says:

Gregariousness seems frequently to be regarded as a somewhat superficial character, scarcely deserving, as it were, the name of an instinct, advantageous

---

[1] The two chief articles of this work had already previously appeared in *Sociol. Rev.*, 1908–1909.

[2] Trotter criticizes the practice of ascribing many separate instincts to man. "Very little consideration of most of these propositions," says he, "shows that they are based upon too lax a definition or a want of analysis." Most of the activities referred to special instincts are, according to him, derivatives of the great primal instincts which are common to or very widely distributed over the animal kingdom. Such, according to his particular scheme, are the instincts of self-preservation, nutrition, and reproduction and, in addition in the case of gregarious animals, what he terms "the herd instinct" (*Instincts of the Herd in Peace and War*, pp. 96–97).

[3] *Ibid.*, pp. 16–17. Quotations from this work are reprinted by permission of The Macmillan Company, publishers.

it is true, but not of fundamental importance or likely to be deeply ingrained in the inheritance of the species.[1]

This view is entirely unjustified by the facts, in Trotter's opinion. "A study of bees and ants," he points out, "shows at once how fundamental the importance of gregariousness may become . . . The individual in such communities is completely incapable, often physically, of existing apart from the community, and this fact at once gives rise to the suspicion that even in communities less closely knit than those of the ant and bee, the individual may in fact be more dependent on communal life than appears at first sight."[2]

Accordingly he proceeds to a reconsideration of the place and importance of gregariousness in the case of man. By way of introduction, he says:

The conception of man as a gregarious animal is, of course, extremely familiar; one frequently meets with it in the writings of psychologists and sociologists, and it has obtained a respectable currency with the lay public. It has, indeed, become so hackneyed that it is the first duty of a writer who maintains the thesis that its significance is not even yet fully understood, to show that the popular conception of it has been far from exhaustive. As used hitherto the idea seems to have had a certain vagueness which greatly impaired its practical value. It furnished an interesting analogy for some of the behavior of man, or was enunciated as a half serious illustration by a writer who felt himself to be in an exceptionally sardonic vein, but it was not at all widely looked upon as a definite fact of biology which must have consequences as precise and a significance as ascertainable as the secretion of the gastric juice or the refracting apparatus of the eye. One of the most familiar attitudes was that which regarded the social instinct as a late development. The family was looked upon as the primitive unit; from it developed the tribe, and by the spread of family feeling to the tribe the social instinct arose.[3]

As against this conception, Trotter proposes the view instead "that gregariousness may be regarded as a fundamental quality of man."[4] The relevant facts of comparative psychology and general evolutionary doctrine seem to leave no room for doubt in this matter, according to him. In defense of this position, he appeals to such considerations as the following:

From the biological standpoint the probability of gregariousness being a primitive and fundamental quality in man seems to be considerable. As already pointed out . . . it would appear to have the effect of enlarging the advantages of variation. Varieties not immediately favorable, varieties departing widely

[1] *Ibid.*, p. 19; *cf.* McDougall's treatment of the gregarious instinct (*Introduction to Social Psychology*, pp. 86–90).
[2] *Instincts of the Herd in Peace and War*, pp. 19–20.
[3] *Ibid.*, p. 21; *cf.* McDougall, *An Introduction to Social Psychology*, pp. 68*ff.*, 86*ff.*, 271*ff.*
[4] *Instincts of the Herd in Peace and War*, p. 23.

from the standard, varieties even unfavourable to the individual may be supposed to be given by it a chance of survival. Now the course of the development of man seems to present many features incompatible with its having proceeded amongst isolated individuals exposed to the unmodified action of natural selection. Changes so serious as the assumption of the upright posture, the reduction in the jaw and its musculature, the reduction in the acuity of smell and hearing, demand, if the species is to survive, either a delicacy of adjustment with the compensatingly developing intelligence so minute as to be almost inconceivable, or the existence of some kind of protective enclosure, however imperfect, in which the varying individuals were sheltered from the direct influence of natural selection. The existence of such a mechanism would compensate losses of physical strength in the individual by the greatly increased strength of the larger unit, of the unit, that is to say upon which natural selection still acts unmodified. A realization, therefore, of this function of gregariousness relieves us from the necessity of supposing that the double variations of diminishing physical and increasing mental activity always occurred *pari passu*. The case for the primitiveness of the social habit would seem to be still further strengthened by a consideration of such widely aberrant developments as speech and the aesthetic activities . . .[1]

Reasoning upon this thesis of "the primitiveness of the social habit" in man,[2] therefore, Trotter proceeds to the elaboration of the psychological and social consequences of his view and to the demonstration of its value for the interpretation of human conduct. His discussion thus follows along with the aim in view of giving place, in terms of his new category of explanation, to such facts of social control and group domination as modern crowd psychology and sociological analysis have brought to light, through the works of such writers as Tarde, Ross, Durkheim, Sumner, Le Bon, and others, and to certain relevant psychoanalytic considerations connected with the concepts of conflict and repression.[3]

The herd instinct, as above viewed, introduces a tremendously complicating factor into the run of human mental processes, according to Trotter. For it operates to give an instinctive sanction, approaching

[1] *Ibid.*, pp. 22–23.

[2] Whatever may be said in criticism of Trotter's herd theory, it has the merit at least, over most discussions of instinct theory, that Trotter frankly admits it to be the product chiefly of a process of deductive reasoning and that he calls attention to the need of applying a more exact method of investigation (see *ibid.*, pp. 8, 42–43).

[3] This attempt to appropriate psychoanalytic theory for social interpretation has been followed up in England especially by Rivers (see his *Psychology and Politics*, Chap. III). More recently McDougall has likewise directed his attention to this task (*Outline of Abnormal Psychology*). Psychoanalytic and instinct theory being so nearly on common ground as regards the biological conception of human nature, it is natural that there should be a strong bond of sympathy between them, especially in face of criticism of this conception (*cf.* Bernard, "Instinct and Psychoanalysis," *Jour. Abnor. Psychol. Soc. Psychol.*, vol. 17, pp. 350–366, 1923; also BARNES, *Amer. Jour. Sociol.*, vol. 8, note, pp. 203–204, 1922).

the potency of any other instinct, to the varied influences of social constraint and herd suggestion.[1] Any herd impulse may thereby assume the characteristics and the emotional drive of genuine instincts. The consequence of this for social life is that the power of the herd instinct. in the absence of proper social direction, may range itself on the side of social disadvantage in various ways.[2] It may even happen that the herd instinct should come into conflict with the operation of the other primary instincts (self-preservation, nutrition, and reproduction). In that case the stage is biologically set for the appearance of those disturbing phenomena of social stress and mental conflict in human life which have come to figure so prominently in modern thought and which psychoanalytic theory particularly has so insistently held up before us.[3]

The remedy for these threatening effects of herd suggestion would seem to lie, according to Trotter, in making certain that suggestion always acts on the side of reason and human welfare. "If rationality," he says, "were once to become really respectable, if we feared the entertaining of an unverifiable opinion with the warmth with which we fear using the wrong implement at the dinner table, if the thought of holding a prejudice disgusted us as a foul disease, then the dangers of man's suggestibility would be turned into advantages."[4] Theoretically, at any rate, the herd instinct provides us with a most powerful instrument of constructive social life. It is up to man to learn how to use it in the interest of his welfare and progress.[5]

In this way Trotter seeks to overcome the sharp dualism of position with respect to instinct and intelligence and the "individual" and the "social," into which orthodox instinct psychology usually leads, and to provide a more hopeful basis of social control than seems consistent with the position of the latter. According to him, the herd instinct can confer the marks of instinctive sanction on any belief or action that presents itself with the authority of herd suggestion.[6] All that is necessary, therefore, is to enlist the power of herd suggestion on the side of human advantage.[7] What we need is a technique for directing the emotional drive of the herd instinct in the path of rationality. Trotter recognizes, of course, that the problem of developing an adequate technique for this purpose is a very difficult one. But he maintains that upon its effective solution depends the hope of harmonious social life and personal development. Upon man's ability thus to enlist in his favor the tide of forces operative in herd suggestion, in fact, according to him, depends not

[1] *Instincts of the Herd in Peace and War*, pp. 47*ff.*
[2] *Ibid.*, pp. 47–48.
[3] *Ibid.*, pp. 16*ff.*
[4] *Ibid.*, p. 45.
[5] *Ibid.*, pp. 17, 29*ff.*, 42*ff.*
[6] *Ibid.*, pp. 30–31.
[7] *Ibid.*, pp. 60*ff.*

only his future welfare and progress but "his very tenure" on the face of the earth. "Living as he does in a world," says Trotter, "where outside his race no allowances are made for infirmity, and where figments however beautiful never become facts, it needs but little imagination to see how great are the probabilities that after all man will prove but one more of Nature's failures, ignominiously to be swept from her work-table to make way for another venture of her tireless curiosity and patience."[1] Rational social control is thus not a matter of choice or expediency merely; it is a matter of determining importance in man's elemental struggle for existence. Man dare not leave uncontrolled the tremendous forces of herd suggestion, lest by so doing he find himself some day helplessly and hopelessly overwhelmed by them and the con-flicts which they introduce into his life.[2]

Wallas, in his *Great Society* (1914) has resorted to a more drastic method than Trotter's of meeting the difficulties of instinct psychology in the field of social interpretation. In this work Wallas definitely retreats from his previous thoroughgoing support of instinct psychology as developed in his *Human Nature and Politics* (1908), where he took a position not unlike that of McDougall in his *Introduction to Social Psychology*. He attacks especially the extreme anti-intellectualism which he attributes to conventional instinct theory.[3]

In criticising "the Intellectualism of the Utilitarians," modern social psychologists of the instinct school, points out Wallas, are apt to fall into a kind of anti-intellectualism which involves a curiously similar fallacy to the one from which they aim to free psychological thought.[4] Of the two fallacies, in fact—the extreme intellectualism of the utilitari-ans of the nineteenth century and the loose anti-intellectualism of the instinct psychology of the twentieth century—he feels that the latter, representing as it does thought "as the mere servant of the lower passions and a cynical struggle for life as the only condition which answers to the deeper facts of our nature" may prove to be infinitely the more dangerous.[5]

Wallas holds, as against the latter view, that "Intelligence in its simplest forms is as 'natural' to us, as much due to inherited disposition, as the working of any one of the usual list of instincts." It "is as truly a

[1] *Ibid.*, p. 65.

[2] *Ibid.*, pp. 64–65; see also GINSBERG, *The Psychology of Society*, pp. 19–22; BARNES, "Some Typical Contributions of English Sociology to Political Theory," *Amer. Jour. Sociol.*, vol. 28, pp. 49–66, 1922.

[3] *Cf.* GINSBERG, *The Psychology of Society*, p. xv.

[4] *The Great Society*, pp. 39*ff.*

[5] *Ibid*, Preface, pp. 42–44. Quotations from this work are reprinted by permission of The Macmillan Company, publishers.

part of our inherited nature and as independent a cause of human action."[1] "We are born with a tendency, under appropriate conditions, to think," he says, "which is as original and independent as our tendency, under appropriate conditions, to run away."[2] Furthermore, in the case of the higher animals and man, memory and experience play an ever increasing and to some extent even a determining role.

Not long, therefore, after birth, man, and apparently also the other higher vertebrates, begin to live in an atmosphere of organized ideas, of memory that is to say, association and imagination. An Esquimaux or Indian hunter, and, to a less degree, perhaps, an experienced old wolf, follows, it is true, an imperious instinct in seeking game, but he does so with an ever-growing memory of earlier hunts, with an exact conception of what he is going to do next, and with some prevision of the probable result.

In the case of man, this irradiation of instinctive action by intelligence shades into processes in which intelligence acts as an independent directing force. Instead, for instance, of a purely instinctive impulse to hunt being made more effective by intelligence, our decision to hunt may itself be due to a preliminary process of reflection upon our future wants and the possible ways of satisfying them.[3]

Wallas accordingly objects to the common opposition which is set up by instinct theory between instinct and intelligence on the ground that the former is more elemental to our nature than the latter. He cites C. S. Meyers[4] with approval to the effect "that the psychology and physiology of instinct are inseparable from the psychology and physiology of intelligence" and that "we ought to speak not of instinct and intelligence but of instinct-intelligence, treating the two as one indivisible mental function which in the course of evolution has approached now nearer to so-called instinct, now nearer to so-called intelligence."[5] He also suggests the use of the term "disposition" to designate this more complex view of the inherited basis of behavior.[6]

Wallas, it is thus clear, has sought to attach to intelligence, thought, and reason something of the elemental instinctive sanction which Trotter, through the agency of his herd instinct, attached to sociality. Thought is not, according to Wallas, merely a subordinate mechanism acting in the service of instinct, as McDougall maintained in his *Introduction to Social Psychology;* it is "a true natural disposition," as "original and independent" as is instinct itself.[7] It may become an "independent

[1] *Ibid.,* pp. 36, 45.

[2] *Ibid.,* p. 40.

[3] *Ibid.,* pp. 35–36.

[4] From "Symposium on Instinct and Intelligence," *Brit. Jour. Psychol.,* vol. 3, p. 267, 1910.

[5] See *The Great Society,* note, pp. 42–43.

[6] *Ibid.,* pp. 20, 42–43, 53. In connection with his discussion of the maladjustments of modern industrial life, Wallas also popularized the term "balked disposition."

[7] *Ibid.,* pp. 40, 48, 176, 218. "We inherit biologically . . . an instinctive impulse to think," says Wallas (*Our Social Heritage,* p. 15).

cause of human action" and be brought to bear as a directive force leading to the conscious control of human conduct and social life. This, in fact, is precisely the function of thought in the economy of the human life process, as Wallas views the situation in his later work.[1]

"Thought," says Wallas, "may be late in evolution, it may be deplorably weak in driving power, but without its guidance no man or organization can find a safe path amid the vast impersonal complexities of the universe as we have learnt to see it."[2] Especially important is it for man to utilize this directive power of thought, for the guidance of his conduct in the growing complexity of modern life in the "Great Society." Instinctive action on any considerable scale is not only impossible here but it is unadapted to the demands of a rapidly changing situation.[3] Thought, then, is the only safe guide. In its increased and more effective application, both in his personal life and in his social planning, lies man's chief hope to welfare and progress in the present-day social order.[4]

In *Our Social Heritage* (1921), Wallas developed this thesis further from the standpoint of social tradition. Because of man's flexible instinctive equipment and his increasing reliance on thought as an instrument of adjustment, social tradition comes to have quite a unique place in human life, according to him.[5] He says:

The process of social inheritance is, as far as I know, not necessary for the existence of any wild non-human species or variety. But the most important and progressive of the human race would probably, if social inheritance were in their case interrupted, die out altogether . . .[6]

Man has been increasingly dependent on his social heritage since the beginning of conventional language and of the art of flint-chipping, that is to say, for perhaps half a million years. This fact has brought about important modifications in our biologically inherited nature. We have become biologically more fitted to live with the help of social heritage, and biologically less fitted to live without it. We have become, one may say, biologically parasitic upon our social heritage.[7]

The problem of bringing about the effective functioning and transference from one generation to the other of man's rapidly expanding social tradition is thus a matter of the utmost importance for his welfare. As the complement to his inquiry into the biological basis of human behavior in his *Human Nature*, Wallas is thus led in *Our Social Heritage* to a consideration of those expedients—political, economic, and social—whereby social tradition can be made to function more effectively in meeting the

[1] *The Great Society*, pp. 36, 45, 176, 224*ff*.

[2] *Ibid.*, p. 45.

[3] *Ibid.*, pp. 224*ff*.

[4] *Ibid.*, Chaps. X–XI; see also BARNES, *Amer. Jour. Sociol.*, vol. 28, pp. 189*ff*., 1922.

[5] *Our Social Heritage*, pp. 15–16.

[6] *Ibid.*, pp. 16–17.

[7] *Ibid.*, p. 19.

changing needs of our life as described in *The Great Society*.[1]   These three works accordingly reflect the development of Wallas' thought from a predominantly biological to a broadening social and cultural orientation.

But it is in the work of Hobhouse, of course, that these newer tendencies of English evolutionary thought have found most complete expression.   Only in the restatement of evolutionary theory which Hobhouse's work incorporates, furthermore, has the newer point of view attained formulation on a level of philosophical prestige and breadth of application to offer anything like an effective challenge to the earlier Spencerian conception.

This is not the place for a detailed consideration of the many-sided implications of Hobhouse's conception of evolution, both because his conception has so far not impressed itself noticeably on American social psychology and because the newer elements of thought which it incorporates and which are especially significant for the development of this exposition are better treated elsewhere in this survey, particularly through the work of such writers as Auguste Comte and Lester F. Ward.[2]   Suffice it to note here, then, that in consequence of his own research and deliberation on the subject and the spread of Hegelian influence in England, Hobhouse was led, especially in his later works, to formulate a restatement of the older biological conception of evolution in terms of mind, rational purpose, and conscious control.[3]   In place of Spencer's conception of evolution as a mechanical, spontaneous, and unconscious process, Hobhouse submits the view "that the evolutionary process can be best understood as the effect of a purpose slowly working itself out under limiting conditions which it brings successively under control."[4]   He also maintains as against the Spencerian view that evolution is a single, continuous, and uninterrupted movement, that, at least in so far as organic life is concerned, " . . . the facts of growth when disinterestedly studied do reveal changes which we ought to regard as changes of kind, and indeed of a kind very material to the interpretation of evolution, of the position of mind in reality, and of the future possibilities of man."   He states:

The sum and substance of these changes is to effect a complete revolution in the position which the older theory of evolution assigned to mind as it exists in living beings.   Coming into existence as the biologist has told us as a means of securing the permanence of the species it never loses that function, and indeed comes to perform it more efficiently.   But it ceases to be limited by the conditions

[1] *Ibid.*, Chaps. III*ff.*

[2] See Hobhouse's own references to these writers: *Mind in Evolution*, Preface; *Development and Purpose*, pp. xix, 10.

[3] *Ibid.*, pp. xv*ff.*; *Mind in Evolution*, Chap. I.

[4] *Development and Purpose*, p. xxvi.   Quotations from this work are reprinted by permission of The Macmillan Company, publishers.

of its genesis. It becomes self-determining, is guided, that is to say, by values which belong to its own world, and finally it begins to master the very conditions which first engendered it. In the end, when we have fairly taken the measure and grasped the condition of its growth, we are led to regard the development of mind not as a side product of natural selection [as the older biological conception usually pictured it] but as the central fact of the history of life upon the earth.[1]

From this changed standpoint, the study of mental development naturally falls into two main divisions, according to Hobhouse:

In examining the emergence of intelligence as a factor in the life of the lower organisms, in measuring its growing importance in the behavior of the higher mammals, and in estimating the qualitative changes which mark the transition from animal to human mentality, we are dealing in the main with the functions or capabilities of the individual mind. But as soon as we begin to follow the track of the higher developments of mind in man the nature of the enquiry changes. The forces to be considered are now social rather than psychological, or, more accurately, are matters of social rather than individual psychology.[2]

This is so, he explains, not because we have to do, in the case of man, with the emergence of any new faculty or with any essential change in the structure of the brain and in the sum of hereditary dispositions and capacities, but rather because this part of the survey is concerned "with what we may call the social mind, understanding by that term, the order formed by the operation of mind on mind, incorporated in a social tradition handed on by language and by social institutions of many kinds, and shaping the ideas and the practice of each new generation that grows up under its shadow." This is an enquiry, according to Hobhouse, "into institutions, into creeds, into social relations, rather than an enquiry into the consciousness of individual human beings" and is thereby rather sociological than psychological in character.[3]

A survey of mental evolution, could it ever be fully carried out, would thus, according to Hobhouse, proceed through the following steps:

. . . it would begin with the most rudimentary germs of mental activity discoverable in the lowest organisms; it would trace the successive stages of mental growth in the higher orders of the animal creation till it reached the beginning of human intelligence; and thence proceeding essentially by the same method, but concerning itself now for the most part with social forces and social products, it would follow the successive stages in the movement of human thought from its first beginnings to that phase of development in which we live and in which we share.[4]

The data for such an inquiry, Hobhouse points out, "are not and perhaps never will be complete." Our conception of the lowest phases

[1] *Ibid.*, pp. 10–12.
[2] *Ibid.*, p. 12; also *Mind in Evolution*, Preface, p. v.
[3] *Development and Purpose*, pp. 12–13.
[4] *Ibid.*, p. 13.

of mind is necessarily inferential and our knowledge of early societies is scanty and at some points altogether wanting. But in this we suffer no more, according to him, than biology suffers from the imperfection of the geological record. "Though we may never be able to paint an accurate picture of mental evolution as a whole," he says, "there is no reason why we should not endeavor to seize such salient points as may serve to determine its trend and measure the length and direction of the path along which it has moved."[1]

This is a conception of the task of psychological and social-psychological investigation which is not radically different from other historical conceptions, such for instance, as that of German folk psychology. As elaborated by Hobhouse in such of his works as *Mind in Evolution* (1901), *Morals in Evolution* (1906), *Development and Purpose* (1913), *Social Development* (1924), etc., it however relates itself significantly to the work of Spencer and to the psychological and social theory which based itself on Spencer's interpretation of evolutionary doctrine, and it is in this connection chiefly that Hobhouse's standpoint has important social-psychological bearings here.

Hobhouse departed from Spencerian thought as it bore on the study of human life, chiefly along two directions: in his greater emphasis on the rational and the purposive aspects of mental development and in his greater emphasis on the importance of the social factor.[2] This difference of standpoint and emphasis did not prevent him as might perhaps be expected, from accepting instinct psychology, as presented by McDougall, as the basis of his psychological and social thought, though, like Trotter and Wallas, he has introduced certain modifying considerations which it is important to note here. The nature of these will appear from the following short statement giving Hobhouse's view of the role of instinct and the hereditary element in human life.

We find, then, a certain raw material of our conscious life, which arises in direct and uncomplicated response, determined by the hereditary structure, to outward objects, or from physical changes of the internal structure. Furthermore, heredity lays the foundation of our entire mental life. We inherit not only capacities for sensation and emotion, but also capacities for distinguishing, analysing and combining them. We have opposed intelligence as the work of the individual to instinct as the product of heredity, but intelligence, as a capacity is also hereditary. The propensity to inquire, and the methods of analysing

[1] *Ibid.*, pp. 13–14.

[2] See, for instance, *Mind in Evolution* (1915 ed.), Chaps. I, XIII; *Development and Purpose*, Chaps. I, XI; *Morals in Evolution* (1919 ed.), Part I, Chap. I, Part II, Chap. VIII; *Social Development*, Chaps. VI–VIII; *Social Evolution and Political Theory*, Chaps. II, IV. These departures appear readily even when Hobhouse's work is compared with the work of such a writer as Westermarck, whose *Origin and Development of Moral Ideas* (1906–1908) and *History of Human Marriage* (1894) may be said to represent a very popular intermediate position.

and comparing used in inquiry, all have a foundation in the hereditary structure . . . We cannot, therefore, in classifying the works of the mind place
heredity and acquirement in two perfectly separate portions. Our division is
analytical. It is a separation of functions which in working are combined, and
an attempt in resolving a joint product to assign to each what is its due. This
must be borne in mind in any attempt to estimate the part played by instinct
in human life.

     . . . The older psychology expressed the contrast between the human and the
animal mind in terms of the opposition between intelligence and instinct. Recent
psychology has emphasised the part of instinct in human nature. But to begin
with, it must be clear that in human nature there is very little that is pure instinct.
Man is always capable of reflection. Even if instinct sets him the aim he can
appreciate it, distinguish what is essential from what is indifferent, and vary
the means that he uses indefinitely. Nor is this all. As a rational being he is
capable of criticising the instinctive interest, if such we are to call it, itself. He
brings it in relation to his life as a whole and to the lives of other people. It is
modified by the social atmosphere in which he grows up. It takes its particular
shape from the traditions of his society, his class, his school, his family. It never
governs him as long as he remains mentally and morally sane, but is merged in
that moral organism of many interacting parts which is called the self . . . Nor
is the behavior determined by the kind of interests popularly called instinctive
specifically defined and fixed, prior to experience . . . What is hereditary in
man is capacity, propensity, disposition, but the capacities are filled in, the
propensities encouraged or checked, the dispositions inhibited or developed
by mutual interactions and the pervading influence of the circumambient atmosphere. Elements of true instinct remain, but in a state of dilapidation. Heredity does not operate by itself in human nature, but everywhere in interaction
with capacity to assimilate, to foresee, and to control.[1]

    The main question [adds Hobhouse in a note to this passage] is whether the
fundamental elements of human nature are of the nature of separate units which
interact like independent powers, or whether what is inherited is an abstraction
and what is acquired another abstraction, the two together forming the concrete
whole of actual behaviour. In the main I believe the latter account to be true
of human nature, the former to be true of the lowest and partly true of the higher
animals, and it is this increasing unity of the organism as a whole which I take
to be one of the distinguishing marks of the human as compared with the animal
mind.

Hence the link between the study of human mental and social development, according to Hobhouse, and the importance of keeping distinct the
treatment of human mentality, in the manner outlined above.

    Hobhouse tells us that his conception of evolution represents a syn-
thesis of Hegelian and Spencerian thought so as to bring them into
agreement with Comtean positivism.[2] The resulting view which he
arrived at, he felt, was in closer agreement with that of Lester F. Ward

---

[1] *Mind in Evolution*, (1915 ed.) pp. 103–105. Quotations from this work are
reprinted by permission of The Macmillan Company, publishers.

[2] See *Development and Purpose*, pp. xv–xx.

than any other.[1] But despite broad points of similarity, Hobhouse's whole outlook and approach are quite distinct from Ward's and also from American psycho-social thought, which has in a large measure followed in the lead of Ward's work, generally. Hobhouse's thought is Hegelian in form and philosophical in standpoint and interest, and these characteristics serve to set his work off from most of the corresponding material with which we shall be concerned in our treatment of American psycho-social theory. In addition, his work is still intimately a part of that whole complex of English evolutionary doctrine, which we have been outlining here, and from which American psycho-social thought has departed radically along several directions of deep social-psychological import. This appears more in the applications which Hobhouse has made of his theory in the treatment of specific problems than in the general formulation of his position as such. An examination of the four volumes constituting his so-called "Principles of Sociology"—*The Metaphysical Theory of the State* (1918), *The Rational Good* (1921), *The Elements of Social Justice* (1922), *Social Development* (1924), for example, since Hobhouse, like Spencer, identified himself with this field of thought particularly, is sufficiently indicative of this point.[2]

But the real significance of the departure from English evolutionary doctrine which American social-psychological thought incorporates can appear only on the basis of the detailed presentation of American social-psychological thought in the following sections of this survey. It is necessary to note here only what has already been suggested previously,[3] namely, that American social-psychological thought represents not only a departure from but in a real sense also a continuation of the direction of social-psychological development which we have been outlining here. The next section thus follows along, in the first place, almost as an extension of the background of English evolutionary thought as it has been developed in this part of our treatment of the subject. It will be our purpose now to follow out this, from our standpoint, very important extension of social-psychological thought and to indicate the developing basis of its divergencies of outlook, viewpoint, and conception.

[1] *Mind in Evolution*, p. vi.

[2] See in this connection SMALL, reviews of *Social Evolution and Political Theory* and *Social Development, Amer. Jour. Sociol.*, vol. 17, pp. 546–548, 1912; vol. 30, pp. 216–220, 1924; BARNES, "Some Typical Contributions of English Sociology to Political Theory," *Amer. Jour. Sociol.*, vol. 27, pp. 442–485, 1922; "The Fate of Sociology in England," *Pub. Amer. Soc. Sociol.*, vol. 21, pp. 43 *ff.*, 1927; CARTER, *The Social Theories of L. T. Hobhouse*, especially Chaps. I, IV.

[3] See *supra*, p. 147.

PART II

THE DEVELOPMENT OF SOCIAL-PSYCHOLOGICAL
THOUGHT IN THE UNITED STATES

CHAPTER V

BACKGROUND AND BEGINNINGS

I

The modern social-psychological movement, as it is being followed out here, is as a whole of such recent origin comparatively that the balanced perspective which time and verification lend is necessarily in large measure still lacking as a basis for the consideration of its course of development. Hence one must stand ready to see some significant turn of events change the complexion of occurrences very radically all along the line. Such being the case, little can be lost and certainly much may be gained from such an attempted array of forces, for the most part still in active operation, as a survey of American social-psychological thought necessarily involves. For American social-psychological thought, certainly as a distinctive product, is a matter almost wholly of the present generation. That is, the considerable body of social-psychological literature which this country has produced and for which it has become notable if not predominant in this field of thought has been a contribution of very recent date—so recent, in fact, that all but one or two of its pioneer exponents are still alive and still actively affecting the situation.

It was, as a matter of fact, not until the last decade or two of the nineteenth century that notable evidence began to appear on the horizon of American thought indicating that an American social-psychological movement as a distinctive product was beginning to take shape and form. For, from the standpoint of the developing conditions of American social-psychological thought, as indeed it may be said quite generally in regard to the conditions of American thought until that time, this country remained very largely a European if not merely a British colony. America was notable intellectually until then chiefly as a reflecting ground for European thought currents, such as could be fitted in consistently with the pious and pioneer setting of early life in this country, the predominant influence being, of course, English. Thus, for a century or so beyond her formal attainment of political independence, this country continued to remain so intimately a part of English and European thought, at least in the fields most closely related to modern social psychology, as to produce little in the way of a constructively differentiated and intellectually self-conscious expression of her own developing outlook and standpoint.[1]

In the field of psychology, for instance, according to Brett, the influence of Locke and Berkeley was followed after an interval by "that career of domination" of the Scottish school of Reid, Dugald Stewart, and Brown, which, as he says, "lasted down to 1890."[2] Throughout this period, according to him, originality of psychological thought in this country "is the feature most conspicuous by its absence."[3] Much the same may be said for sociology in so far as one may speak of sociology at this early date in this country, and very largely for social thought in general until 1883[4] and thereabouts. Here until that time the theological interest and the precedent of classical English economic, political, and social theory held sway until the conflict between evolutionism and supernaturalism left Spencerian thought, as in England, in a position of domination. It was not until toward the close of the nineteenth century that the spell of this domination began to give way, so that a fresh start could be made.[5]

But neither from the standpoint of the special fields which are directly of concern here nor more generally was this early period merely a negative period of American thought in so far as more distinctive later developments are concerned. It was rather a period of preparation during which the material was being matured wherewith the new product was in due time to be constructed.[6] And it was, of course, inevitable that such a period of intellectual preparation should have elapsed before "American" thought in any field, and especially in the fields intimately related to social psychology, could crystallize into definitely expressible form. The thought of a people is necessarily an attainment of slow growth, and American thought in the fields intimately related to social

---

[1] See RILEY, *American Philosophy*, Chap. I; *American Thought*, Chaps. I-VII; ROGERS, *English and American Philosophy since 1800*, pp. 39, 198, 213, etc.; BRETT, *A History of Psychology*, vol. III, pp. 255 ff.; BALDWIN, "Psychology Past and Present," *Psychol. Rev.*, vol. 1, pp. 363 ff., 1894; SMALL, "Fifty Years of Sociology in the United States," *Amer. Jour. Soc.*, vol. 21, pp. 721 ff., 1915–1916; "General Sociology," *Amer. Jour. Soc.*, vol. 18, pp. 207 ff., 1912; *Origins of Sociology*, Chap. XIX. Also PARRINGTON, *Main Currents in American Thought*, vol. I, Introduction.

[2] The date of the publication of James' *Principles of Psychology*.

[3] BRETT, *A History of Psychology*, vol. III, p. 256; also BALDWIN, "Psychology Past and Present," *Psychol. Rev.*, vol. 1, pp. 363–364, 1894.

[4] The date of the publication of Ward's *Dynamic Sociology*. The date is notable also as marking the opening of the first psychological laboratory in this country (see BRETT, *A History of Psychology*, vol. III, p. 267; MURPHY, *An Historical Introduction to Modern Psychology*, pp. 181–182; also *infra.*, p. 266).

[5] See *infra*, pp. 215 ff.; SMALL, *Amer. Jour. Sociol.*, vol. 21, pp. 748 ff., 1915–1916; ODUM, *American Masters of Social Science*, Chaps. I, III; RILEY, *American Thought*, Chap. VII; BERNARD, *Encycl. Soc. Sciences*, vol. I, pp. 324–340.

[6] See references note 1, above.

psychology, from the nature of the national situation here during the early period of American history, both practical and theoretical, particularly so. For, besides the unyielding pressure of the practical problems of adjustment in early American life and the unfavorable theological atmosphere which surrounded the discussion of all matters relating to human conduct, there was here all along, as already noted above, such a closeness of British contact and influence in the field of psychological and social thought, as to direct even such energy as could extricate itself from this pressure of practical and theological considerations into the characteristic channels of English precedent and example.

It is not to be wondered at, therefore, that only gradually, with the deepening of national problems and issues which followed in the wake of the second war with England, and particularly as an accompaniment of the national events that led over into the Civil War and the troubling conditions resulting therefrom, did an American intellectual self-consciousness begin to assert itself in the fields directly of significance for social psychology. The bearing of these national events as important factors in the situation has been frequently and variously commented upon. The growing practice of study abroad and, in conjunction with this broadening of intellectual perspective, the extension of psychological and social science activities generally at the time, are other important considerations in the situation.[1] But in any event, the fact remains that the period following the Civil War was an altogether unusual period in American thought from the standpoint of developments significant for the emergence of American social psychology.[2]

And whatever may have been the importance of other factors operative in the situation, it cannot be overlooked that the Civil War period in this country was such as to stimulate thought along directions of significance for social psychology. People "whose thought-world had been stirred to its depths by the war found themselves in 1865," says Small in describing the period, "star-gazing in social heavens that had never looked so confused nor so mysterious."

[1] See BODENHAFER, Amer. Jour. Sociol., vol. 26, pp. 273 ff., 1920; BRETT, A History of Psychology, vol. III, pp. 258–261; SMALL, Origins of Sociology, pp. 325–326; Amer. Jour. Sociol., vol. 21, pp. 724–725, 1915–1916; GILLIN, "The Development of Sociology in the United States," Pub. Amer. Sociol. Soc., 1927; also RILEY, American Thought, Chaps. VI–IX; ROGERS, English and American Philosophy since 1800, Chap. VII; DEWEY, "The Development of American Pragmatism," Studies in the History of Ideas, ed. by Dept. of Philosophy, Columbia University, vol. II, pp. 351–377.

[2] For a somewhat detailed survey of important social science developments at this time see SMALL, Amer. Jour. Sociol., vol. 21, pp. 773 ff., 1915–1916; and for the development of the social background at this time see BODENHAFER, Amer. Jour. Sociol., vol. 26, pp. 273 ff., 1920; also, LICHTENBERGER, Development of Social Theory, pp. 355–357; ODUM, American Masters of Social Science, Chap. I; BRETT, A History of Psychology, vol. III, pp. 258 ff; BERNARD, Encycl. Soc. Sciences, vol. I, pp. 324–340.

At the close of the war [he explains], the intelligent people of the country were more sophisticated than at its beginning. They realized in part that the country was not the primitive, simple affair which it had been when all its inhabitants were pioneers. They had been jostled a good deal in the fondest of American illusions that a constitution and laws enacted in pursuance thereof would automatically produce human welfare. They became acutely aware that life in the United States was not altogether a success. They perceived more or less distinctly that work was ahead to bring American conditions into tolerable likeness to American ideals.[1]

This country, it gradually began to appear, was still, as a matter of fact, socially if not politically on trial before the world, and upon the successful solution of the complex problems of social relation in which it had involved itself depended in very large measure its future security and that of the principles upon which it was founded. As in the corresponding case of French thought at the time of Comte, this condition of intellectual unrest and social insecurity was close upon the heels of a growing appreciation of the significance of the social-psychological as over against the traditional individualistic outlook on human problems. For certainly social Darwinism in its prevalent mode of interpretation, upon which the most progressive social thought of the day was so intently focused, had little to offer that bore encouragingly on the situation. The biological conception of human nature was of questionable avail in face of the fact that this nation was composed of elements from every strain and section of the earth. Also, traditional psychological and social theory with its individualistic emphasis and its association with *laissez-faire* doctrine had little to offer that seemed relevant. *Laissez-faire* doctrine and traditional individualism were alike intolerable as a refuge to those who continued to hold fast to the hope of seeing the professed American ideal of the state as a government "of the people, by the people, and for the people," with its pledge of equal opportunity for "life, liberty and the pursuit of happiness," attain a reasonable degree of realization in fact.   In face of the situation here at the time, therefore, conventional theory about human nature and social life seemed bankrupt and an inescapable challenge to the socially and scientifically minded of the day.[2]

It was inevitable that this condition of bankruptcy should finally be recognized and that the challenge inherent in the situation should have been met in some fashion. And so American thought set out on a new venture of promise in the field of psychological and social theory, proclaimed almost simultaneously from the side of both sociology and psychology. This it is which attaches more than a merely local significance to the early events of the American social-psychological move-

---

[1] SMALL, *Amer. Jour. Sociol.*, vol. 21, pp. 724–725, 1915–1916.
[2] See WARD, *Dynamic Sociology*, Preface, pp. v *ff*.

ment. For Ward and James as the spokesmen of this movement in American psychological and sociological thought, and along with them its other early representatives in this country,[1] mark not only the opening chapter of American social psychology but also an important new chapter in modern social-psychological thought generally.[2]

The first notable event here in point of time, and the most important event perhaps from the standpoint of its revolutionizing effect in so far as the general setting of American social-psychological thought is concerned, was the appearance of Ward's *Dynamic Sociology*. In point of more immediate influence and importance from the standpoint of the definition of the specific trend of later social-psychological thought in this country, perhaps James' *Principles of Psychology* or even Dewey's early work, his *Psychology* (1886), should take precedence. But the question of chronological order and relative importance is of little account here. What does matter for our purpose is recognition of the fact that these works, and close upon them, also Small and Vincent's *Introduction to the Study of Society* (1894), Baldwin's *Mental Development in the Child and the Race* (1895), and Giddings' *Principles of Sociology* (1896), appeared at this time in this country to echo and reecho a change in American psychological and sociological thought which was widely significant for social psychology. Coming upon the social and intellectual background as outlined above, these works initiated a period of accelerated development of social-psychological thought in this country, which it will be most interesting to envisage upon the background of related developments as they have been traced out here so far.

We shall consider Ward's *Dynamic Sociology* and James' *Principles of Psychology* as prominently representative of this opening period of American social-psychological thought. In particular, we shall consider Ward's work at some length, because in no other way could the general setting of American social-psychological thought be outlined as well. It should be recalled in this connection, however, that, as was stated in the opening chapter of this survey,[3] Ward could very properly have been treated there in the philosophical introduction, along with Comte and Spencer. But on the whole it seemed best to consider his work in the present connection. The close relation of Ward's work to the movement and method of thought outlined in that part of our survey should nevertheless be recalled at this point. For only in relation to the other systems

[1] See note 2 below.

[2] In the absence of any single representative of American thought corresponding to the position of Hegel, Comte, and Spencer, we have chosen for intensive consideration here, for the purposes of background, two classic products of early American social and psychological thought: Ward's *Dynamic Sociology* and James' *Principles of Psychology*. These works should, however, be viewed in relation to other supporting contemporary developments to be considered here alongside of these works.

[3] See *supra*, p. 40, note 2.

of thought considered there does the significance of his work for American social psychology appear.

II. LESTER F. WARD (1841–1913) AND OTHER EARLY AMERICAN SOCIOLOGICAL INFLUENCES

Ward's position in the modern social-psychological movement, in the more limited scope of his influence, is not unlike that of Comte and Spencer, his chosen models and acknowledged predecessors. Certainly Ward's relation to the social-psychological movement in this country is analogous to the relation of Comte and Spencer to the social-psychological movements in their respective countries. In each case, that relation was primarily a matter of general effect on contemporary thought as a whole, rather than of specific contribution to the detail of social-psychological theory as such, and in each case, therefore, insight into the characteristic tendencies of thought for which Comte, Spencer, and Ward respectively stood is of the first importance as background from which to view the more specific social-psychological events that followed. In the case of Ward this is particularly true. His *Dynamic Sociology* not only develops the setting of American psycho-social thought very illuminatingly in relation to its European background, but it also gives striking preliminary expression to some of those gathering motives of American thought generally which the American social-psychological movement, among other developments, was in due time to incorporate in characteristic form. We shall find it profitable, therefore, to examine certain aspects of Ward's social theory in some detail here, despite the fact that it may at times seem to be rather distant from the specific body of social-psychological theory as it has since been built up in this country, and despite the fact also that in some of its underlying assumptions regarding the mechanisms of social conduct it was seemingly on shaky ground even at the time.

Ward gives evidence in his *Dynamic Sociology* of having been profoundly influenced by only his two above-mentioned predecessors in the field of social thought—Comte and Spencer. At any rate, his system of thought as there outlined is a product which rests squarely on the thought systems of these two pioneer sociologists.[1] And Ward, as has been pointed out by later students, while he later took occasion to acknowledge numerous other workers in the field of his special interest,[2] never really shifted in any essential respect from his position as originally outlined in his *Dynamic Sociology*.[3] It is Comte and Spencer essentially, therefore, that we get in Ward, though in new form and combination, and in novel relation to the remaining world of thought, such as enters in to

---

[1] See *Dynamic Sociology*, vol. I, pp. 142–143.

[2] *Cf. ibid.*, Prefaces to 1st and 2d ed.

[3] See SMALL, *Amer. Jour. Sociol.*, vol. 21, p. 752, 1915–1916; also, *Amer. Jour. Sociol.*, vol. 19, pp. 75–78, 1913–1914.

fill out Ward's sweeping vision of cosmic organization and social reconstruction. This is the only claim to originality which Ward himself
makes for his work. He says in this connection:

It has been found sufficiently difficult in any age to contribute anything new
to the thought of the world. In the present age, with its accumulations of
learning and its intense intellectual activity, such an attempt would, indeed, be
presumptuous. Henceforth it can be only in the direction of improved methods,
and new forms of presenting old truths, that novelty and successful innovation,
in any but the domain of original scientific research, are to be expected. The
only positive claim here made is of this nature—that while the world's present
stock of known truth, the generous tribute of many great minds, has been fully
but appreciatively employed, it has been woven into a unique fabric, and one by
which [as it seemed to him at the time] society may be completely rehabilitated.[1]

But this contribution was, as later events proved, because of its
"significant timeliness,"[2] a contribution of the first importance, comparable in some sense even to the inspiring contributions of Ward's
avowed models, the glamor of whose work so completely possessed
his imagination. For with Ward we enter upon a change of evolutionary
perspective the quickening effect of which on psycho-social thought can
be measured only in terms of the important role which the doctrine of
social control has come to play in recent social theory as over against
the doctrine of *laissez-faire*. The general direction and import of Ward's
influence we have already had occasion to indicate in connection with our
review of recent English psycho-social thought,[3] but its detailed significance will be brought out only gradually in this part of our survey.
It is with some justice, however, as we shall see, that Ward has been
termed "the last of the great trio of sociological giants of the nineteenth
century"[4] and that he is usually given place in the company of Comte
and Spencer in the treatment of modern psycho-social theory.

The prominent position for which Ward singled out Comte and
Spencer in his thought, as he says, was due not so much to an assumed
preeminence of these two writers over all others as to the fact that "they
alone, of all the thinkers of the world, have the merit of having carried
their generalizations from the phenomena of inorganic nature up to those
of human action and social life." Such a grand monistic and synthetic
conception of the universe, he felt, was "the final crown of human
thought." Naturally enough, therefore, in building up his own system
of thought, he turned to the work of those whom he recognized as predecessors in this conception.[5]

[1] Preface to *Dynamic Sociology*, 1st ed., p. vii.
[2] SMALL, *Amer. Jour. Sociol.*, vol. 21, p. 755, 1915–1916.
[3] See *supra*, pp. 196, 207–208.
[4] ELLWOOD, *Amer. Jour. Sociol.*, vol. 19, pp. 61–78, 1913–1914.
[5] See *Dynamic Sociology*, vol. I, pp. 142–143.

Ward regarded the works of Comte and Spencer, in relation to his own thought, somewhat as follows: Comte, according to him, was a genuinely great mind permitted to see a great vision of fundamental truth but wedded almost inextricably to only less fundamental error. The essential basis of Comte's reasoning Ward regarded as not only sound, progressive, and new but of the very essence of fundamental truth. On the other hand, the framework through which Comte had sought to give detailed expression to his vision of truth he looked upon as obtrusively and challengingly steeped in error.[1]

This rare characteristic of weaving upon a warp of truth a woof of error Comte everywhere manifests in his work, according to Ward, so that he continually throws into strange contrast "the iron consistency of his general logic" and "the flimsy fallacies that fill out its framework, and stare at the astonished reader from every page." Comte, says Ward, "is a great general in the army of thinkers, but, when he descends, as he continually does, to meddle with the brigades, regiments, and platoons, he throws them into confusion by the undue severity and amazing stupidity of his commands."[2]

It is, however, in the opinion of Ward, "the misfortune of all truly great minds to be wedded to errors as well as truths." While Comte's errors were, therefore, according to him, both very numerous and obtrusive, and adhered to in his writings, as Ward says, "with all the pertinacity, emphasis and iteration to which the French language is capable of vigorous expression," nevertheless, by virtue of the great service which, according to him, Comte rendered to future thought, as the propounder of the positive philosophy and the "unquestioned founder" of the science of sociology, he was impelled to give him first place in developing the background of his own system of social theory.[3]

And it is, of course, a very striking fact that in the practical import of his theories, Ward followed Comte closely as the master who had seen the light. Throughout, in his social theory, it is the spirit of the *Positive Philosophy* that is reflected from the pages of Ward's work. Most of the characteristic features of Comte's social theory, in fact, reappear in both spirit and terminology in Ward's system: the utilitarian view of science, the doctrine of social meliorism, the teleological conception of social progress, the division of sociology into social statics and social dynamics and the emphasis in connection with the latter on prevision and foresight as epitomized in the popularized dictum "see in order to foresee," the opposition to *laissez-faire*, the faith in universal education, and so on.[4]

[1] *Ibid.*, pp. 82 *ff.*
[2] *Ibid.*, pp. 129–130. Quotations from this work are reprinted by permission of D. Appleton and Company, publishers.
[3] *Ibid.*, pp. 82–85.
[4] *Ibid.*, Chap. I, especially p. 81.

Comte, according to Ward, had recognized "in its entire length and breadth the science of sociology, to which he gave its name." He overlooked "neither the statical, the passive dynamical, nor the active dynamical class of social phenomena." In regard to the last-named class of phenomena especially (the central interest for Ward as for Comte and, according to them, the end for which all the rest exists as a means), Comte expressed himself, says Ward, "in an unmistakable manner." While, therefore, Comte's system with its cumbersome details and faulty framework deserved and has received, according to him, "the fate of all its class," the basic principle of the positive control of social phenomena upon which Comte built continued to remain secure. This principle, declared Ward by way of his own emphasis, "must reappear again and again until the increase of knowledge shall crown it with success."[1]

Such, in essence, was Ward's estimate of Comte and his feeling of kinship with the general aim and purpose of the *Positive Philosophy*. It was his own chief aim to help create the intellectual atmosphere in which the "crowning with success" of the basic principle of Comte's social theory would be increasingly realizable in fact.

Spencer, on the other hand, Ward felt, was above all else a careful builder of the detailed framework of his thought; strong in the very features in which Comte most needed correction. Spencer "has received, and probably deserves," says Ward, "the title of England's greatest philosopher; and, when we reach England's greatest in any achievement of the mind we have usually also reached the world's greatest."[2]

To Spencer's lot it thus fell, according to Ward, to improve and perfect Comte's system of positive thought, a task for which, as it seemed to him, Spencer was eminently qualified. Spencer had, Ward pointed out, the two great essentials for the successful performance of this task: a comprehensive knowledge of the field of science and unusual coordinating abilities—a combination of faculties which, he believed, the history of human thought had proved very rare.[3] The resulting system of detailed theory which Spencer built up Ward regarded as one of the most inspiring feats of the human mind. In respect to the detailed structure of his thought, then, Ward regarded Spencer as a vast improvement and a decided advance on Comte.[4] But Spencer's system, he held, however perfect in structure, was incomplete; it lacked the reach and promise of Comte's vision of social betterment, the final and crowning step, according to Ward, in any complete system of thought. Spencer, he declared, continued persistently to cling "to the pure and better

[1] *Ibid.*, p. 150.
[2] *Ibid.*, p. 139.
[3] *Ibid.*, p. 142.
[4] *Ibid.*, pp. 142 *ff*.

established statical aspects of the subject treated, rarely rising into the passively dynamic, and never into the actively dynamic, or applied, department."[1] Notwithstanding the claims of *The Synthetic Philosophy* to rank as a system, therefore, according to Ward, "it is not itself in strictness such," certainly not in the true sense in which, according to him, Comte's *Positive Philosophy* is a system.[2] Spencer's *Synthetic Philosophy* presents, as it seemed to Ward, "a somewhat systematic, and certainly very able coordination of the greater part of all known truth," but as compared with Comte's *Positive Philosophy*, it is merely expository, whereas the latter is also constructive. This purely expository nature of *The Synthetic Philosophy* gives it a character "of great solidity and respectability," Ward held, but it leaves Spencer's work unfinished at the point of greatest interest from his standpoint. At this point, then, Spencer falls decidedly short of Comte, according to Ward.[3]

In explanation of this shortcoming of Spencer, Ward suggests that all true systems "necessarily involve much that the world calls chimerical," inasmuch as "it is impossible to construct a logical and symmetrical edifice of thought without going both below and above the familiar range of common experience, and enunciating propositions, whether true or false, which the popular mind, or even the general sentiment of the most enlightened portion of the community, will refuse to accept, and will pronounce Utopian."[3] Spencer, however, "steadfastly declined to be drawn by his logic into anything that even the most incredulous could call a vagary," in the opinion of Ward. "No man," he says, "probably ever wrote as much as he has written without saying more that the average judgment of mankind could not indorse as soon as presented." This Ward attributed "to the firm manner in which his [Spencer's] reason was enthroned, and the all-sided and practical wisdom with which his extensive information enables him to survey every problem." It is precisely these qualities, however, that render Spencer "un-systematic, non-constructive and non-progressive," according to Ward. "Paradoxical as it may sound and whether it be construed as complimentary or otherwise," he says, "Mr. Spencer had too much good sense and too much real knowledge to build a perfect system of philosophy." In particular, he found it impossible, according to Ward, to "go back to the initial steps in the aggregation of ultimate atoms, or on, to revel in dreams of future social perfection in a millennial age."[3]

What Spencer gave to the world, therefore, was something altogether different. "He has taken," says Ward, "the materials which the world already possessed and made the most of them." "He accepted the estate which human thought and labor have bequeathed," he goes on to say

[1] *Ibid.*, p. 217.
[2] *Ibid.*, pp. 217–218, 141.
[3] *Ibid.*, p. 218.

in a notable passage of tribute to Spencer, "and fitted it up for the occupancy of a higher and nobler race of beings."[1] Writing, as he later tells us,[2] under the influence of the biological movement with which the age appreciatively connected Spencer's name, Ward was inclined to rate this accomplishment very highly; not so highly, however—and herein is the starting-point of his own contribution—as to overshadow the essential non-constructiveness and non-progressiveness of Spencer's thought. It was his vigorous criticism of these characteristics of Spencer's work, in fact, that defined his own line of departure from the latter.

If, then, Ward regarded Comte's system as glaringly imperfect, he considered Spencer's as just as glaringly incomplete. But Comte and Spencer were in these respects, according to him, mutually complementary and hence combinable in a larger synthesis such as would preserve the virtues of each. It was his task as their successor, this being the relation in which Ward saw himself and the next step forward in the development of social theory, as he viewed the situation, to work out the manner of this new synthesis. The result of his attempt to accomplish this task was the *Dynamic Sociology* with its Spencerian framework of evolutionary theory and its Comtean spirit of positivism in social science.

Thus it is that Ward made his own important contribution to social theory and that his work stands out, especially as a landmark in the development of American social thought. For by combining the evolutionary grasp of things with which Darwin and Spencer fired the imagination of the modern world, and the inspiring promise of the positivist view of science, Ward worked into his thought the two most powerfully energizing conceptions of the developing scientific movement as it touched the field of social investigation. With considerable justification, therefore, he set himself up at once as the most recent prophet and the latest defender of the possibilities of psycho-social science.

The distinctive feature of Ward's work, in view of the Spencerian background upon which the *Dynamic Sociology* made its appearance, was, of course, its reinterpretation of the Comtean positivist spirit in the field of psycho-social thought. But Ward was able to make this spirit count at the time, it must not be overlooked, only because of the Spencerian setting in which he embodied it and which was seemingly an essential requisite of a respectful hearing in the biological atmosphere of later nineteenth century social thought in this country and in England.[3] It was precisely because Ward was a biologist of the evolutionist school, points out Small in commenting on Ward's work, and the presumption of

[1] *Ibid.*, p. 219.

[2] *Ibid.*, Preface to 2d ed., p. ix.

[3] See Barnes, *Sociol. Rev.*, vol. 14, p. 202, 1922; Small, *Amer. Jour. Sociol.*, vol. 21, pp. 755 *ff.*, 1915–1916.

bias in his case was rather against such a teleological interpretation of society in terms of psychic forces as he presents, that so much significance attached to his work.[1] The fact stands out strikingly, however, that in his social theory, Ward turned sharply from the characteristic *laissez-faire* position of Spencer to reecho, in modern form and with added strength, the positive spirit of Comte. All the more revolutionary does Ward's position in this respect appear because, coming upon the background of contemporary social thought in this country, his work necessarily took the form of a revolt against the popularized position of Spencer. Because of the deep significance of this aspect of his theory for later psycho-social thought in this country, it is worth while to follow Ward's position through at this point in greater detail. It should perhaps be added here that his argumentation at this point is still a vital issue in the field of psycho-social thought.

Ward tells us that it was a growing sense of the essential sterility of the prevailing Spencerian type of social science, which, he pointed out, not only fails to apply to data which it arrives at but persists, in addition, "in teaching that no application of them can be made," that provided the chief incentive for the preparation of his own work.[2] Not that the results attained by this class of social science are without value, he explained, but that its value "is thus far potential only, and can not be converted into actual value until truer views shall prevail respecting the nature of social phenomena and social forces." In accordance with this insight and standpoint, Ward naturally came to regard these "truer views" as the primary need of the contemporary stage of social-science development. It is with the aim of bringing them into proper perspective, therefore, that he wrote.

"Just as Comte could with justice complain that the philosophy of Hobbes, Locke and Voltaire was negative, so," says Ward in this connection, "it may now be maintained that the school of Mill, Spencer and Fiske is also negative." From the purely statical stage of the former, he goes on to explain, the latter has advanced only to the passively dynamic stage, which recognizes only the changes wrought by nature, unaided by art. Before the science of society can be truly founded, however, according to him, another advance must be made, and the actively dynamic stage reached, "in which social phenomena shall be contemplated as capable of intelligent control by society itself in its own interest."[3]

Thus, in bold outline, does Ward give preliminary expression to his intention of carrying over into the post-Darwinian *laissez-faire* atmosphere, which Spencer's work had fostered, the spirit of Comtean positivism. Touching more directly upon the status of evolutionary thought

[1] *Ibid.*, p. 755; *General Sociology*, p. 55.
[2] *Dynamic Sociology*, Preface to 1st ed., p. v.
[3] *Ibid.*, pp. v–vi.

in the field of social investigation at the time, Ward goes on to state that so far the indictment of sterility has held against it, as it has held against other great systems of thought, because, while justly claiming social science, evolutionary thought has so far fallen short "of admitting its complete homology with other sciences," and, while demonstrating the uniformity of social as of physical phenomena, it has so far denied to the former "that susceptibility to artificial modification which, applied to the latter, constitutes the only practical value that science has for man."[1]

Sociology (and Ward conceived sociology broadly in the sense of Comte and Spencer), having developed under the influence of this negative standpoint, has been reproached, he explains, even by those who admit its legitimacy, "with being impracticable and fruitless." The prevailing methods of treating sociology, including those employed by its highest living advocates, to a great extent justify this charge, according to him. "There are," he says in an impressive passage in this connection, "dead sciences as well as dead languages. The real object of science is to benefit man. A science which fails to do this, however agreeable its study, is lifeless. Sociology, which of all sciences should benefit man most, is in danger of falling into the class of polite amusements, or dead sciences." It was his object in the *Dynamic Sociology*, he tells us, "to point out a method, by which the breath of life may be breathed into its nostrils."[2]

The means for bringing about this rejuvenation was already sufficiently at hand, according to Ward, in the utilitarian conception of science which Comte held. What was necessary was its harmonious incorporation into the structure of evolutionary thought as formulated by Spencer. This, as we have seen, Ward regarded as his particular task and contribution to the advance of social theory.

In his own system of theory, then, Ward sought to build on the basic conceptions of Comtean and Spencerian thought with a view to supplementing each in terms of the other, thus to arrive at a more workable outlook than was characteristic of either of these two of his predecessors, as he viewed them. Equipped "with the principle of evolution as a law and guide, and with the doctrine of 'meliorism' as an incentive and motive-power," the two cardinal principles which, by virtue of the work of Comte and Spencer, were, according to Ward, made available in combination for the first time to his generation, he set about his chosen task of reconstruction. The result, as already noted, was a new system of cosmic philosophy developed about the evolutionary conception of the universe in Spencerian form but in Comtean spirit.[3]

[1] *Ibid.*, p. vi.
[2] *Ibid.*, p. vii.
[3] See *ibid.*, vol. I, pp. 8–9.

More specifically, Ward organized his own system of theory about the notion of aggregation as a unifying principle. In terms of this principle as "the great law of progress in the universe,"[1] he presents the several orders of phenomena for consideration as levels of aggregation, much as Spencer presented them in his *First Principles* as levels of evolution. Thus, he treats the world of physical and chemical phenomena under the classification "primary aggregation";[2] the world of organic phenomena, including the genesis of mind and man, under the category "secondary aggregation";[3] and the world of social phenomena, the genesis of society, the place of the family, the function and mode of operation of the so-called "social forces," etc., under the designation "tertiary aggregation."[4] The world of social phenomena accordingly appears, as in the case of Spencer's treatment, merely as a higher order of development in a unitary process of cosmic change, differing from the other orders chiefly in degree of complexity of organization. It represents, says Ward, "the last and highest step with which we are acquainted of this long, unbroken series of cosmical aggregations leading from the ultimate material atom up to the social aggregate."[5] Largely after the manner of treatment in Spencer's *First Principles*, Ward thereby provides the setting for the naturalistic view of social as of other orders of fact, and for that extension of the utilitarian conception of science which, he felt, would breathe "the breath of life" into contemporary social thought, and especially into the newly established science of sociology.

The consideration of the world of social phenomena, *i.e.*, "tertiary aggregation," was of course Ward's goal in view from the first. The other orders of phenomena are considered, as in Comte's system of theory, merely for the purpose of completeness and necessary background from which to reflect the standpoint which it was Ward's as well as Comte's aim to carry over into the field of social thought. "Tertiary aggregation," therefore, constitutes the bulk of his discussion, occupying all of the second volume and a large portion also of the first volume of the *Dynamic Sociology*.

Ward starts out in this part of his theory from the position that man was originally solitary and that only as the result of a long process of evolutionary development and growing mentality did he arrive at his present social state.[6] He builds, therefore, like Spencer and Spencerian evolutionary thought generally, on the theory of primitive individualism.

[1] *Ibid.*, pp. 247–249.
[2] *Ibid.*, Chap. III.
[3] *Ibid.*, Chaps. IV–VII.
[4] *Ibid.*, Chaps. VII *ff.*
[5] *Ibid.*, p. 451.
[6] *Ibid.*, Chap. VII.

In this individualistic evolutionary approach, with some necessary modifications growing out of the special aspects of his theory considered below, Ward persists throughout.[1] The conception of the social nature of human personality, for which American social psychology characteristically stands, and the use of the group concept as a tool of sociological analysis in this country were a later development and find little place, therefore, in Ward's system of thought.[2] In other words, Ward's basic approach was hardly more adequate from the social-psychological standpoint than Spencer's. But in the practical import of Ward's theory, this fact is overshadowed by the inspiring vision of "social telesis" which Ward, following Comte, unfolds before the reader and by his suggestive treatment, in this connection, of the social importance of education on the one hand and scientific knowledge applied to the direction of the so-called "social forces" or human desires on the other, the latter, according to him, constituting the basic springs of human action and the dynamic elements operative in society. It is these aspects of Ward's work that are the outstandingly important ones from the standpoint of the American social-psychological movement, and it is upon these aspects of his work, therefore, that we shall concentrate our further analysis. Ward's argument in defence of this part of his theory is both drawn out and laborious, but in view of its central significance in defining his system of thought and the background of later more specialized psycho-social endeavor in this country, we proceed to follow it through in some detail nevertheless.

Ward, like Comte whom he follows rather closely in respect to his doctrine of social telesis, seeks to bring to this part of his argument the weight and prestige of his whole theoretical system, which, having been developed in Spencerian form, reflects upon Ward's position the same broad basis of supporting modern evolutionary doctrine on which Spencer himself had built. In other words, Ward turns its own weapons upon the prevalent biological approach, a performance for which he, it has been pointed out, as "a recognized evolutionist and a professed Darwinian," was especially well equipped.[3]

His approach here is by way of the positivist conception of human progress, as measurable in terms of the positive control which man succeeds in obtaining over the forces of nature and the distinction which, in familiar form, he set up between biological and social evolution in the dictum that "the environment transforms the animal, while man transforms the environment."[4] "It is natural selection," he says in introducing this view, "that has created intellect; it is natural selection

[1] See BODENHAFER, Amer. Jour. Sociol., vol. 26, pp. 292 ff., 1920.

[2] Ibid., p. 292.

[3] See SMALL, Amer. Jour. Sociol., vol. 21, pp. 755–756, 1915–1916.

[4] Pure Sociology, p. 16.

that has developed it to its present condition, and it is intellect as a product of natural selection that has guided man up to his present position. The principle of artificial selection which he has been taught by nature, and has applied to other creatures, more as an art than as a science, to his immense advantage, he has not yet thought of applying to himself." Not until he does this, however, according to Ward's detailed argument as outlined below, not until man begins to emancipate himself from the play of accident and the tremendous waste which is incident to the uncontrolled operation of the processes of natural selection in his own life, can he claim any true distinction from other animals or any greater security of position in nature.[1]

Man's progress, argues Ward, like all "natural progress," has so far been a purely cosmic process, the result of accident or, at least, of the operation of uncontrolled and unknown laws of nature. "There has been progress in civilization," he says, "just as there has been progress in organic life, because the highest and best [in the natural, not necessarily in the human sense[2]] has been selected and preserved, and the lowest and poorest has perished." It is simply, according to him, "that man, as a progressive animal before the human period, and before the historic period, did not cease to be a progressive animal after reaching these periods. His progress has been the progress of nature, a secular and cosmical movement, not the progress of art, the result of foresight and intelligent direction."[3] It is, he says again, that "only progressive or at most stationary societies can survive. All others (and they may have been many) have disappeared." The most that can thus be said "is that society exists because it is not retrogressive. And this explains," he challengingly adds, "in the only scientific way why it is progressive."[4]

The kind of social progress of which man stands most in need, however, according to Ward, is "teleological" progress, by which he means, as he tells us, social progress such as man in his social capacity seeking to improve society could effect "by the exercise of an intelligent foresight, in seizing upon the laws of nature and directing them to the ends which his reason, combined with his acquaintance with those laws, teaches him to be those certain to secure the advantage of society."[5] The slow and imperceptible genetic or natural progress which society has thus far made, declares Ward, is barely sufficient to keep pace with the increase of population. Its entire increment toward improving the condition of society is neutralized, he points out, by the rapid multiplication of individuals which it enables the race to carry on. There can thus

[1] *Dynamic Sociology*, vol. I, pp. 15–16, 80–81, vol. II, Chap. X.
[2] *Ibid.*, vol. I, p. 21.
[3] *Ibid.*, p. 15.
[4] *Ibid.*, pp. 80–81.
[5] *Ibid.*, p. 28.

follow in consequence of this type of progress very little perceptible amelioration of the condition of society at large. He says in an eloquent passage:

The world does, indeed, enjoy thousands of material blessings which this unorganized progress has scattered over it; but when we consider the proletariat, when we look into great cities or out on large plantations, or visit those immense centers of production, the factories, we realize that, while the intellectual and material condition of society has reached almost giddy heights, the moral or emotional condition of man has scarcely advanced at all. There still remain the overworked millions on the one hand, and the unemployed millions on the other. There are still all the depths of ignorance, poverty, drudgery, and nameless misery that have ever been the baneful concomitants of human civilization. I am aware that it will be said that all this is a necessary evil, that it arises out of the inherent depravity, the idleness, or the perversity of human nature in some of its phases, and that it is incurable. This, however, is precisely the issue. There are some who think it quite unnecessary and the result of the wholly unorganized state of society itself—that these wretched ones are simply the unfortunates who, in the great soulless struggle for existence and scramble for gain, are crowded to the wall. There are those who believe that the organization of society on such a basis as shall put these evils in the way of immediate mitigation and ultimate removal is not a chimera.[1]

Almost every one, without admitting it, entertains notions more or less definite of this kind, according to Ward, despite the fact that the failure of attempts in this direction has led to an avowal of much skepticism of this conception in recent times. All moral and religious systems, for instance, he points out, have been nothing more than so many notable attempts to realize a teleological progress. And government, too, he maintains, with all its usurpations and oppressions, has always avowed and still avows as one of its primary functions the temporal advancement of its citizens and subjects. It thus expressly declares, according to him, for the feasibility of the teleological improvement of society. That these attempts have so far, says Ward, "almost without exception failed to realize the results claimed has not prevented nearly all mankind, not in the past only but in the present, from giving in their adhesion to this doctrine, so that even those who repudiate it in the case of religious institutions generally accept it in the case of political ones."[2]

It could hardly be otherwise, according to him. Nature, he argues in a now famous and oft-repeated passage, is nowhere so jealously preservative of her creations that man can overlook the possibility that at any time the slow pace of natural progress may come to an abrupt end. He says:

[1] *Ibid.*, pp. 29–30.
[2] *Ibid.*, pp. 30–31.

Let no one . . . be deluded by the thought that this cosmical progress, even in its own slow way, can continue forever. It will . . . be shown . . . that this swarming planet will soon see the conditions of human advancement exhausted, and the night of reaction and degeneracy ushered in, never to be again succeeded by the daylight of progress, unless something swifter and more certain than natural selection can be brought to bear upon the development of the psychic faculty, by which alone man is distinguished from the rest of the fauna of the earth and enabled to people all parts of its surface. The resources of the globe [continues Ward in grave warning which calls to mind similar passages from the later works of such writers as Trotter and Wallas] are not inexhaustible unless zealously husbanded by the deliberative foresight of enlightened intellect.[1]

But the era of teleological or artificial social progress has, according to him, not yet begun. "It may," he says, "never begin, but until it does so, society is as liable to succumb to an adverse wave of reaction, and suffer extinction, as is any race or species of animals or plants; and we know that this is constantly occurring."[2]

Ward realized, of course, that his position here involved him in an outright challenge of *laissez-faire* doctrine and he entered upon the task with courage. Let us take up this doctrine of *laissez-faire*, says he in effect. "Indeed, let us expand this notion beyond the limits usually assigned to it, and embrace not only the question whether human government can rightfully or successfully undertake, to initiate and conduct reformatory and progressive measures, but with this the wider one, whether society, no matter by what means, whether through political, moral, religious, or any other system of institutions, regulations or measures, can, either rightfully or successfully, prosecute any plans having the improvement of its own condition for their object."[3]

The question of right can, according to him, be disposed of with a word, if it is not complicated by the metaphysical conception of "abstract right," and unless it is thus uncomplicated, he holds, one is unprepared to discuss the problem of man's progress, "conceived of as capable of accomplishment by his own efforts," intelligently; for here, as everywhere in man's dominion over nature, from Ward's standpoint, it is simply a case of "might *makes* right."[4]

The question of *laissez-faire* resolves itself, therefore, for Ward, purely into a question of the ability of society successfully to become the arbiter of its own destiny, and this question can, according to him, be discussed profitably only in the abstract, since, as he says, "there is, on the one hand, nothing in the experience of the past to teach us the possibility of the ultimate success of teleological measures, while, on the

[1] *Ibid.*, p. 16.
[2] *Ibid.*, p. 81.
[3] *Ibid.*, p. 31.
[4] *Ibid.*, pp. 31–32.

other hand, the short-sighted and profoundly mistaken character of nearly all such measures as have thus far been tried renders them wholly useless as signals either to follow or to shun."[1] Accordingly, he proceeds to develop an elaborate analogy between teleological action on the level of individual behavior and social life. "If we rise a step higher," he says, "and expand our term teleology one circle wider, so as to make it embracè the acts of the individual members of society performed solely for their own benefit, and without conscious application to the good of society, we find that all the increment which mere 'natural selection' has produced in the direction of human advancement has come from this source"; i.e., it has been the result "of the discovery and application to human needs, each individual for himself, of certain valuable materials and laws which existed in nature." This process, he explains, proves on analysis "to be simply a higher form of natural or genetic development; for, given a being with the degree of organization possessed by man at the time he began this new sort of development, including the cerebral, such a result must take place as a purely natural process." Nothing more than this can, according to him, be said of the last and greatest of discoveries and inventions. And nothing more than this is required as a basis for the application of human teleology to the realm of social life.[2]

A machine, for instance, Ward goes on to elaborate, is nothing but a collection of material substances so formed and adjusted by human foresight (i.e., teleologically) as to perform valuable service for the inventor. In fact every invention is simply such an "anthropo-teleological" direction of nature's forces into channels which carry benefit to man. "These natural forces," says Ward, "always exist. They operate according to fixed and invariable laws. They can neither be created nor destroyed, but they can be controlled." All the material civilization which man has achieved has resulted, according to him, from just this kind of successful teleological control of the forces of nature. This is not alone true of what are called mechanical or physical forces, although of these, he points out, man controls some of the most subtle and inscrutible—light, heat, electricity, etc. For man also takes advantage of what are generally distinguished as vital laws. The domestication of animals, for instance, Ward calls to mind here, no less than the cultivation of plants, is a simple application of human teleology in the field of vital law. And the high degree of refinement to which man's control of the vital forces of nature has been brought is strikingly attested, he recalls further, by the skill attained by both breeders and horticulturists in artificially improving animals and plants. "Man even controls emotional and intellectual forces," says Ward, by way of driving to the point of his

[1] Ibid., p. 33.
[2] Ibid., pp. 33–34.

analogy. "In the training of animals, he does this to a limited extent. He does the same in governing those of his own race. He does nothing else when he governs himself."[1] Summarizing his position here, he declares further:

We see that by the aid of a more or less powerful intellect put in possession of a greater or less number of natural truths man has succeeded in so directing his own vital or muscular movements as to regulate, in a greater or less degree, the external physical or mechanical movements of the material objects around him, and by obstructing their advance here, intensifying their velocity there, and forcing them into harmless or useful channels in other places, he causes nature first to leave him unmolested, and then actually to serve him in the most advantageous ways. It is in this alone that civilization consists. It is by extending this dominion over other higher and yet unsubdued forces that all progress in the future must be secured.[2]

Returning, then, to the direct consideration of the doctrine of *laissez-faire* on the basis of the ground thus prepared, Ward continues:

Society is simply a compound organism whose acts . . . whether individual or collective, obey fixed laws. Objectively viewed, society is a natural object, presenting a variety of complicated movements produced by a particular class of natural forces. The question, therefore, simply is, Can man ever control these forces to his advantage as he controls other, and some very complicated, natural forces?[2]

And in another eloquent passage which has become famous, Ward gives his reply as follows:

Is it true that man shall ultimately obtain the dominion of the whole world except himself? I regard society and the social forces as constituting just as much a legitimate field for the exercise of human ingenuity as do the various material substances and physical forces. The former have been investigated and subjugated. The latter are still pursuing their wild, unbridled course. The former still exist, still exhibit their indestructible dynamic tendencies, still obey the Newtonian laws of motion, still operate along lines of least resistance. But man, by teleological foresight, has succeeded in *harmonizing these lines of least resistance with those of greatest advantage to himself*. He has made the winds, the waters, fire, steam, and electricity, do his bidding. All nature, both animal and inanimate, has been reduced to his service. One field alone remains unsubdued. One class of natural forces still remains the play of chance, and from it, instead of aid, he is constantly receiving the most serious checks. This field is that of society itself, these unreclaimed forces are the social forces, of whose nature man seems to possess no knowledge, whose very existence he persistently ignores, and which he consequently is powerless to control.[3]

[1] *Ibid.*, p. 34.
[2] *Ibid.*, p. 35.
[3] *Ibid.*, pp. 35–36.

But, suggests Ward, bringing forward a possible *laissez-faire* objection, we have said that the very systems, moral, religious, political, of which mention has been made, are but so many direct attempts to control society and improve its conditions. "True," he answers, "and they failed to accomplish their object because they did not recognize the very laws and forces which they sought to control." They recall, according to him, the misdirected efforts and hopeless dreams of the inventors of "perpetual motion," and, as attempted inventions, they have failed for the same reason. "These complicated machines have not worked, because they were contrived in ignorance of the forces they were expected to control." Not *laissez-faire*, then, but quite another lesson can be drawn from these misdirected attempts to control society, according to him. "The extraordinary influence which they have, in fact, exerted," says he, "shows how great would have been the result had they really been directed in channels of human advantage."[1]

However, the defenders of *laissez-faire* will object, suggests Ward further, "that society has always done better when let alone; that all efforts to improve the moral or material condition of society by legislation and kindred means have not only been inoperative, but have in the majority of cases done positive harm, often to the very cause they were intended to serve." In answer he counters again: "If it could be proved that they had always been absolutely inoperative, the case would, perhaps, be somewhat discouraging: but, if they can be shown to have had an evil effect, this is all we can hope or desire. For if they can do *harm*, they can do *something*, and nothing is left but to make them do *good*." Legislation, Ward explains, using the term in its most general sense, "is nothing else but invention. It is an effort so to control the forces of a state as to secure the greatest benefits to its people." As matters have thus far been, according to him, government, in so far as the improvement of society is concerned, has been to a great extent a failure. "But why," asks he, "has it failed as a promoter of the social welfare to which it has laid such special claims? Because," he replies, "legislators, as inventors, have proved mere bunglers; because they have known nothing of the laws of society; because they have been ignorant of the forces over which they have sought to exercise control."[2]

Success in invention must be limited by the acquaintance of the inventor with the forces that are to propel his machine. Man rarely stumbles by mere chance upon any great invention. Art is measured by science; and a comparison of its progress since the scientific epoch began with that of the ages that preceded that epoch proves incontrovertibly that all progress in practical art must be preceded by progress in science. Before science taught man the nature of physical laws, all attempts at invention, except of the simplest kind, were just

[1] *Ibid.*, p. 36.
[2] *Ibid.*, pp. 36–37.

such wretched miscarriages as attempts at progressive legislation are today, and for the same reason, *viz.*, that the inventors possessed no science of the field of natural forces over which they sought to exert an influence. Before progressive legislation can become a success every legislature must become, as it were, a polytechnic school, a laboratory of philosophical research into the laws of society and of human nature . . . Every true legislator must be a sociologist, and have his knowledge of that most intricate of all sciences founded upon organic and inorganic science . . . How utterly incompetent, from this ideal standpoint, are the men who have always held and still hold the reins of power in society! And what wonder that all their short-sighted efforts to promote its material welfare have proved abortive, and that their schemes so often react upon themselves and "return to plague the inventor"![1]

We are still living, declares Ward, in the "stone-age" of the art of government, and we shall not emerge from it until the principle of "attractive legislation" (*i.e.*, legistation which would take advantage of the forces of human nature and direct them planfully on the basis of scientific knowledge into channels of social welfare), being thoroughly understood and applied, takes the place of the wasteful and ineffectual coercive type of legislation to which society has so far, according to him, almost exclusively resorted.[2]

The existing laws on almost all subjects, Ward points out, are nearly all prohibitory, compulsory, penal. They appeal to the fear of punishment as the sole deterrent. They forbid such acts and fix such penalties. Whether the citizen choose to perform the act and pay the penalty or to refrain from the act and escape the penalty, he necessarily loses something. A portion of his liberty is abridged and some of his desires fail of gratification. This is a loss, however viewed, according to Ward, and when the principle of attractive legislation is understood, it will be seen that it is also in large measure an unnecessary loss. He proceeds in his argument:

If it be said that the activities thus arrested were injurious ones, and were better suppressed than exercised, the reply is, that so much force has been lost by equilibration, and this should have been saved and conducted into useful channels. And if it be further insisted that it could not have been so conducted, the answer is, that this is precisely the issue. The sociologist who really believes there is such a science has a right to claim that all the social forces may be utilized as the physical ones have been. He classes those who maintain the contrary along with those who once believed that the thunders were only engines of destruction, the winds powers of evil, and the gases demoniacal spirits. Evil is only relative. Whatever produces injury is evil. But in the physical world we find nearly all the forces producing both good and evil, according to the degree to which man has placed them under control and subjected them to his service. The vast benefits and injuries wrought by fire form a striking illustration

[1] *Ibid.*, pp. 37–38.
[2] *Ibid.*, pp. 40–41.

of this. But the elements—the waters, steam, electricity, and even light—are also examples. If any one imagines that any social forces exist which are wholly bad, it is because he has not considered these facts in the light of the history of science.[1]

The social forces need only to be investigated as the rest have been, according to him, in order to discover ways in which their utility can be demonstrated. "Here," he urges, "is a vast field of true scientific exploitation as yet untracked." To what extent it will yield to the scientific approach it is as yet, according to him, impossible to predict, but if, he suggests, "the domain of social phenomena is as completely one of law as that of physical phenomena—and between this and total absence of law there can be no intermediate condition—then may we logically expect the same measure of success, in proportion as these laws are known, which marks the progress of human supremacy in the material world."[2]

Such a degree of social progress simply bewilders the mind, Ward admits, but not more so than our material civilization bewilders the mind of the savage; and in the art of politics, he maintained, "we are still savages."[2]

The history of human thought shows, he declares by way of illustration, that to the untutored mind nature presents itself as an unbroken series of inscrutible paradoxes which beguile and mislead it.[3] Only as appearances have been made to give way to realities, whether it be in the domain of physical, vital, or psychic laws, has mankind been able to make any material progress, and only when the same shall have been done in the domain of social law will social progress except as a cosmic process become possible. As yet, he points out, little has, however, been done in the domain of social law to make appearances give way to realities and facts. In consequence, social progress as an art is still impossible, and such attempts in this direction as have been made have necessarily for the most part ended in dramatic failure.

But why lay so much stress on these crude failures at invention, due to the absence of science? [asks Ward]. Why point to them as permanent warnings against all future attempts to regulate society? Why cry *"Laissez-faire!"* as if society would ever work out its own progress? As well say to all inventors: Cease trying to control nature, let it alone and it will control itself; it will, if left undisturbed, work out, in its own good time, all the cotton-gins, reaping-machines, printing-presses, and sand-blasts that are needed. Why not, because the first telegraph line and the first ocean cable failed, cry down the Wheatstones and the Fields, and say, Let these matters alone, they will regulate themselves?[4]

[1] *Ibid.*, pp. 42–43.
[2] *Ibid.*, p. 43.
[3] *Ibid.*, pp. 45 *ff*.
[4] *Ibid.*, pp. 52–53.

In point of fact, he suggests in reply to these queries, there were many who did so exclaim; and while they could not claim that nature would ever do these things itself, they insisted that they could never be done. But despite them, the *"retardataires,"* as Ward calls them, man has, according to him, gone on to develop his knowledge and to extend his control of the physical forces of nature and to reap thereby immeasurable benefit. Let us, then, approach the domain of the social forces in the same spirit! "Let us admit," says he, "as candor dictates, that almost everything that has been said by the advocates of *laissez-faire* about the evils of governmental interference is true, and that there is much more that has not been said which should be said on the same subject. Let us only take care not to admit the principle in its abstract essence." For amid all the past failure, according to him, the principle of positive control in the domain of social law remains as unshaken as in the domain of physical law, and faith in its applicability "the only hope there is for the ultimate establishment of a teleological progress in society," against which the only alternative left "is to allow the race to drift on under purely natural influences, and reach any stage to which the conditions found on the planet may be capable of carrying it."[1]

It is needless further to illustrate the emphasis and eloquence with which Ward outlines his position on the positive control of society. Ward's name has come to stand for the theory of positive social control, just as Spencer's has for *laissez-faire.* The very title of his epoch-making work, *Dynamic Sociology,* and the term "social telesis" which Ward coined in the formulation of his theory, have become by-words of positive social-control doctrine. Revolutionary in his day, Ward's position in its general aspects has gradually become a commonplace of current social thought, especially in this country, where it has been a tremendously important factor in giving distinctive direction to the developing field of sociology and, supported by the work of other writers to be considered presently, also to the emerging field of social psychology. Viewing the general effect of Ward's work in this light, we accordingly pass on to the consideration of the two subsidiary points of emphasis in his social theory which are of interest here, namely, his plea, on teleological grounds, for universal education and his suggestive treatment of the "social forces."

The teleological control of society—besides being necessarily dependent on the preparation of an adequate scientific background, to which

---

[1] *Ibid.*, pp. 16, 54–55. For estimates of the importance for social theory of Ward's position here see *Amer. Jour. Sociol.*, vol. 19, pp. 61–78, 1913–1914; also, SMALL, *Amer. Jour. Sociol.*, vol. 21, pp. 755 *ff.*, 1915–1916; BRISTOL, *Social Adaptation*, pp. 236 *ff.*; BARNES, *Amer. Jour. Sociol.*, vol. 25, pp. 155 *ff.*, 1919–1920; *Sociol. Rev.*, vol. 14, pp. 202–205, 1922; BOGARDUS, *A History of Social Thought*, pp. 277 *ff.*; GIDDINGS, *Studies in the Theory of Human Society*, p. 293; LICHTENBERGER, *Development of Social Theory*, pp. 382 *ff.*

it is related as is art to science—is dependent, further, Ward contends, upon the ability of the mass of humanity to cooperate in the common end. Its advance as a social program is thus, according to him, doubly complicated and difficult, and it is the more important to analyze the process by which it may be furthered.[1]

In the first place, he points out, we are here faced with the necessity of adopting an entirely different method of spreading the gospel from that which has been employed in advancing social doctrines in the past. "No amount of exhorting, of proselyting, of missionary work, of war, or of persecution, would in the least avail for this purpose." An entirely new element, according to him, must be added to the emotional force which past doctrines have mustered—the guidance of intellect. For it is upon intellect as a directive force of human emotion, the latter being, as he held, the fountain source of human action, that the success of a program of teleological social progress must depend.[2] And to bring this element into effective operation, Ward felt, nothing short of the universal diffusion of knowledge will suffice. Only thus, it seemed to him, could such a program be protected from the evils attendant upon the selfish utilization of the emotional forces of society, to which it might otherwise be peculiarly exposed. But the difficulties of this task, he suggests, with the view of emphasizing the importance of this point, may be deemed wholly insuperable. His reply is characteristic:

If so, then the proposed system must be given up. For it would be impossible to carry it on, and insure the object which it has in view, in a state of society where the directive force was confined to an oligarchy who simply managed the operations of an impelling force residing in the passions of the masses. Not that wisdom, if properly applied to emotion, no matter where either should reside, might not secure the benefits sought; but because, from the constitution of man, it can never be properly applied where the two are vested in different individuals.[3]

The fundamental law of human nature, Ward goes on to explain, "is that all men will, under all circumstances, seek their greatest gain." In consequence, "where the intellectual and moral forces of a great social movement are separated, the temptations to self-aggrandizement on the part of those wielding the former are wholly irresistible." To secure the success of a program of social telesis, therefore, "every individual

[1] *Dynamic Sociology*, vol. I, p. 18.

[2] Ward was one of the earliest evolutionary writers to elaborate the theory of intellect as the guide of impulse, with the end in view of bringing the doctrine of impulse and intellect into harmony rather than into antagonism as in the case of the anti-intellectualism of instinct psychology (see *supra*, pp. 207–208, 196, also *infra*, p. 241). He mentions the contrast which his social theory makes between feeling as the motive force and intellect as the directive force in human action as one of the five original points in his system (see *Dynamic Sociology*, Preface to 1st ed., p. viii).

[3] *Ibid.*, vol. I, pp. 18–19; also *Applied Sociology*, Preface, p. iv.

must be both a force and a rein for himself."[1] The problem, according to him, is to apply to a truly progressive system such as can succeed in accomplishing the desired end the vast emotional forces which are ever striving to improve society but failing for want of proper intellectual guidance. "The intellect alone can do this," he says, "intelligent mind, fortified with knowledge," and knowledge, as he explains, of a dynamic sort, *i.e.*, of the laws and forces of nature. Knowledge of this sort is, thus from his standpoint, "the prime necessity" and its diffusion among the masses of mankind "the only hope we have of securing any greater social progress than that which nature itself vouchsafes through its own process of selection."[2]

The knowledge here referred to, he points out, "is just that which is embraced in the word *science*, and the diffusion of it is the process which goes by the name of *education*." Therefore, "the first element of a truly progressive system is *popular scientific education*."[3] Furthermore, of the two elements combined in this proposition, education is, in the present condition of affairs, the more important, inasmuch as man, according to Ward, obedient to the strictly biological law of natural selection has already "brought to light a vast mass of truth, sufficient, if properly distributed, to place society on the highway to permanent prosperity." The great drawback to the effective social utilization of this available mass of truth, he held, is the fact that, conditions being what they are, the great majority of people never even learn of the existence of this rich fund of knowledge and very few get any inkling of its value. The situation is such, says Ward, "that not one-hundredth part of the facts which original research has already brought forth are today obtainable by the one-hundredth part of the members of society, so that not one truth in ten thousand is fully utilized." It would not be difficult to demonstrate, he adds, "that this constant accumulation of materials for progress so far beyond the capacity of society to utilize them, or even to become conscious of their existence, exerts along with some direct benefits a large amount of indirect evil to society itself." It is, he declares, "like gorging the stomach to repletion in the hope that thereby nutrition may be increased." In the present complex state of social life, it results in "a dangerous chasm between the intelligent few and the ignorant many which cannot," according to him, "fail to accomplish the aggrandizement of the former at the expense of the latter."[4]

"To this influence, if I mistake not," says Ward, "is to be ascribed the greater part of the evils of which modern society complains."[5] Knowl-

---

[1] *Dynamic Sociology*, vol. I, p. 20.
[2] *Ibid.*, p. 21.
[3] *Ibid.*, p. 22.
[4] *Ibid.*, pp. 22–23.
[5] *Ibid.*, p. 23.

edge is power, he recalls in this connection, and power has ever been wielded for self-aggrandizement and will continue to be thus wielded until it is held in check and balanced by the equal distribution of the *means* of intellectual power in the form of universal dynamic education. It is thus more important for the general social welfare, from his standpoint, that the data of intelligent action shall be in possession of all than that a great amount of intelligence shall exist. The former situation is in the first place socially less dangerous, he felt, and in the second place not so difficult of correction, under proper conditions, as might easily be supposed.[1]

Ward was the more encouraged in this belief because he had great faith in the possibilities of the average run of human being. The great differences of intellectual power at present observable, he felt, were more an effect of our system of unequal opportunity than a necessary consequence of difference in native ability. Given opportunity, the great bulk of humanity could become scientifically productive and certainly "amply capable of taking care of themselves" intellectually as well as in regard to other matters. Such differences as would persist under a system of equal opportunity, it was his contention, would be recognized to be not the artificial differences fostered by an unjust system of unequal advantage, but the result of natural variability and genuine merit to which none could then reasonably object, so that they would thereby become socially more useful.[2] From the standpoint of the absolute increase of the fund of human knowledge as well as from the standpoint of its effective functioning in social life, Ward accordingly felt justified in emphasizing universal education as the first great need of modern society. "If, by the term *education*," he says, "there can be constantly implied the two adjuncts, *scientific* and *popular;* if the word can be made to embrace the notion of imparting a knowledge of the *materials and forces of nature to all the members of society*, there can be no objection to the employment of this word *education* as the embodiment of all that is progressive."[3]

Thus understood education becomes, then, the crown of Ward's system. It is, he says, "the available means of setting the progressive wheels of society in motion"; it is, "the lever to which the power must be applied," if the ultimate end of teleological progress, which Ward as an adherent of philosophical hedonism defined in terms of the increase of human happiness, is to be most effectively secured. "Give society education, strictly held within the assigned limits," he says, "and all things else will be added."[4] The whole dynamic series of proximate

---

[1] *Ibid.*, vol. II, pp. 596, 602.
[2] *Ibid.*, pp. 598 *ff.*; also, *Applied Sociology*, pp. 7, 23–24, 115, etc.
[3] *Dynamic Sociology*, vol. I, p. 26.
[4] *Ibid.*, Preface, p. viii, vol. I, p. 26, vol. II, Chap. XIV.

ends and means which he gives as the epitome of his doctrine of social progress—education, knowledge, dynamic opinion, dynamic action, progress, happiness—will be set into operation. In the end the ultimate goal—the increase of human happiness—will thereby be most economically reached.[1]

On this broad basis of social theory does Ward make his plea for universal education. Not merely on humanitarian and economic grounds as ordinarily understood, though these motives too appear,[2] but on the ground of the social cost of ignorance in terms of possible social progress does he chiefly base his argument. It would be difficult, it has been justifiably pointed out, to find a more eloquent defense of the principle of universal education on social grounds in all literature.[3] Not even Dewey, that forceful expounder of the social role of education in American life, is in this respect more compelling in his treatment of the subject.[4]

But the foundation stone of both social telesis and education as the first important step in its realization, and Ward's central interest as scientist after all, is the other primary element in his basic proposition regarding the social importance of *popular scientific education*, namely, *science*—knowledge of the laws and forces operative in society. Here the *Dynamic Sociology*, as has been appreciatively suggested by Small, having been by way of introduction a cosmic philosophy, turns out to be in its more specific purpose a thesis in social psychology.[5] And while Ward's social psychology, if such it may broadly be called, was social in purpose chiefly rather than in essential conception and approach,[6] it is nevertheless of interest here as an important point of reference and comparison with later social-psychological developments in this country. What is especially of interest for us in connection with this part of Ward's work, which involves the varied elaboration of his utilitarian doctrine of action and his theory of psychological hedonism, the two principles which appeared psychologically basic from his standpoint, is his well-known analysis and classification of human desires as the motive forces of social action. These are the basic "social forces" upon a knowledge of which, according to Ward, all social science and all social action must build.[7]

There are first, according to him, the primary preservative and reproductive forces. These correspond, he suggests, to the two primary objects

[1] *Ibid.*, vol. II, pp. 108–110, 542 *ff.*

[2] *Ibid.*, vol. II, pp. 589, 593 *ff.*

[3] See Barnes, *Amer. Jour. Sociol.*, vol. 25, p. 167, 1919–1920.

[4] *Cf. Democracy and Education*, especially Chaps. VII–VIII; see also *infra*, p. 243.

[5] Small, *Amer. Jour. Sociol.*, vol. 21, pp. 754–755, 1915–1916.

[6] See *supra*, pp. 224–225.

[7] *Cf.* Ratzenhofer's theory of interests (*supra*, pp. 73–74); also such a more recent psychological formulation of the basic importance of desire in social behavior as Dunlap, "The Foundations of Social Psychology," *Psychol. Rev.*, vol., 30, pp. 81–102, 1923.

of nature in the organic world, *viz.*, the preservation of the individual and the continuance of the species or race, which in sentient beings are secured by the two powerful classes of desires connected with the gustatory and sexual appetites. As they are, from a logical standpoint, absolutely essential to life, Ward terms them the "essential forces." He also recognizes, however, as operative in the developed state of mankind what he terms by contrast the "non-essential forces." In the latter group, he takes account of, first, the forces relating to the aesthetic life; second, the forces relating to the moral life; and, third, the intellectual forces.[1] This scheme of "social forces" Ward presents in well-known diagrammatic form as follows:[2]

Social forces	Essential forces	Preservative forces	Positive, gustatory (seeking pleasure)
			Negative, protective (avoiding pain)
		Reproductive forces	Direct. The sexual and amative desires
			Indirect. Parental and consanguineal affections
	Non-essential forces	Aesthetic forces	
		Emotional (moral) forces	
		Intellectual forces	

The importance of these desires as social forces follows from their manner of expression in social life. Desires, according to Ward, arise in consequence of ungratified natural appetites. They constitute painful bodily states which induce action on the part of the organism following, as he held, the utilitarian principle of action and calculated to bring about a more pleasurable state through gratification. This is the mechanism, according to him, of all voluntary action, *i.e.*, as he explains, of all action except spontaneous physical motion. It is, of course, with action of this order, with action that thus has its incentive in desire, that social science is primarily concerned. The study of desire is thus a matter of fundamental importance for its purposes.[3]

Ward's detailed analysis of desires as social forces is worked out, as already noted, on a background of utilitarian philosophy and hedonistic theory which it is at this time unnecessary to follow out here. His contribution at this point, which incorporates the important distinction between desire and feeling as the dynamic agent and intellect as the directive agent in human life,[4] as in general, lay not in the validity of his detailed analysis but rather in the general implications of his position, which, in consequence of the forceful challenge his comparative emphasis on the psychic nature of the social process offered to the dominant biological approach of conventional evolutionary theory, were most

---

[1] *Dynamic Sociology*, vol. I, pp. 468 *ff.*

[2] *Ibid.*, p. 472.

[3] *Ibid.*, pp. 461–462, 468 *ff.*, vol. II, pp. 89 *ff.*, 133 *ff.*, 320 *ff.*; see also *Psychic Factors in Civilization*, Chap. IX; *Pure Sociology*, Chap. VI.

[4] See *supra*, p. 173.

far-reaching in their significance along the lines already outlined above. In effect, Ward presented an alternative to the biological interpretation of instinct psychology, which was just beginning to gain popular favor.

Ward's challenge of the Spencerian rendering of evolutionary doctrine, with its fatalistic implications and its tendency to concentrate attention on the physical and vital elements involved at the expense of the psychic and social, and his assertion "that there are social forces in addition to the merely impersonal cosmic forces—that human initiative, as distinct from purely physical causation, is a reality and not an illusion," did not, of course, suggests Small in his estimate of the historical importance of this part of Ward's work, amount to a solution of all or any of the problems which his theory of the social forces brought into view. It did, however, he points out, add a powerful new impulse to the psychological study of the social process, and that was all-important at the time. "With the aid of that study, if at all," Ward maintained, "the mysteries of the action of the psychic forces, which are the social forces, must be resolved."[1] In this view we have the parting of the ways between English and American psycho-social thought and certainly one of the important points of departure of American social psychology.

Ward's restatement of prevalent evolutionary doctrine in the field of social thought in such a way as to center attention upon the psychic factors, resulting as it did in the stimulation of interest in the psycho-social as over against the purely biological approach, was a contribution comparable in some sense to the importance which was attached to the evolutionary approach at the time. From the standpoint of social psychology, it was an event of major significance alongside of those related developments in France, Germany, and England, already commented upon here, which marked the opening of the modern era of psychological interpretation of social phenomena in those countries.[2] Ward's own attempt to analyze the psychic factors operative in society was in this respect only a starting point, as he himself realized.[3] His own position as developed in his *Dynamic Sociology* was later strengthened by his admission that in this work he was still too much under the dominant influence of the biological movement and the Spencerian tradition to give due emphasis to the psychic aspects of his theory. This deficiency, as he tells us, he sought to correct by following up his earlier work

[1] Small, *Amer. Jour. Sociol.*, vol. 21, pp. 757–758, 1915–1916; *General Sociology*, p. 82.

[2] See Small, *Amer. Jour. Sociol.*, vol. 21, pp. 754 ff., 1915–1916; *General Sociology*, pp. 82 ff.; Ellwood, *Amer. Jour. Sociol.*, vol. 19, p. 72, 1913–1915; Barnes, *Sociol. Rev.*, vol. 14, pp. 222 ff., 1922; Bristol, *Development of Social Theory*, p. 222 ff.; Bogardus, *A History of Social Thought*, pp. 279 ff.; Lichtenberger, *Development of Social Theory*, pp. 377 ff.

[3] Small, *Amer. Jour. Sociol.*, vol. 21, p. 758, 1915–1916.

with *The Psychic Factors of Civilization* (1893).[1] But his general conception of desire as the basic datum of social behavior, when interpreted in the light of his social theory as a whole, was itself, like Ratzenhofer's similar conception of human interests,[2] a very stimulating conception which provided important background for later social-psychological thought. It offered possibilities of psycho-social elaboration which the biological conception of instinct did not, and thereby it suggested points of criticism of the latter which finally led out to some very fruitful social-psychological results, as we shall see. And meanwhile his classification of the fundamental human desires presented a challenging basis of comparison with the various classifications of instincts which, with the appearance of McDougall's *Introduction to Social Psychology*, seemed to be so crucial for social psychology.[3]

It should, however, be recalled here again that Ward's chief contribution to modern psycho-social thought, just as that of Comte and Spencer with whom he must be ranked in this connection, lay in his large grasp of cosmic processes and relations which loomed so all-important in the evolutionary atmosphere of the day and in his inspiring general outlook rather than in his detailed theory which, especially his theory of social forces, was on much too shaky ground as regards basic assumptions to be more than passingly suggestive. Nor need this estimate of Ward's historical importance from the standpoint of social psychology be materially altered in consequence of any of his later more specialized works, which, for instance, his *Pure Sociology* (1903), his *Applied Sociology* (1904), and even his *Psychic Factors* (1893), already mentioned above, are little more than elaborations of his basic theory as outlined in his *Dynamic Sociology*.[4]

In closing, it may, therefore, be well to summarize the essential aspects of Ward's position in the large. This has been done in inimitable fashion by another pioneer American sociologist, and his statement accordingly is quoted in this connection:

Throughout all Ward's work there runs one dominating and organizing thought. Human society, as we who live now know it, is not the passive product of unconscious forces. It lies within the domain of cosmic law, but so does the mind of man; and this mind of man has knowingly, artfully, adapted and readapted its social environment, and with reflective intelligence has begun to shape it into an instrument wherewith to fulfill man's will. With forecasting wisdom man will perfect it, until it shall be at once adequate and adaptable to

[1] See *Dynamic Sociology*, Preface to 2d ed., p. ix.
[2] See *Pure Sociology*, pp. 21–22, 34, 60–61, 108, etc.; also *supra*, p. 73.
[3] See *supra*, pp. 187–188; also HOUSE, "The Concept 'Social Forces' in American Sociology," *Amer. Jour. Sociol.*, vol. 31, pp. 145 ff., 347 ff., 507 ff., 1925; PARK and BURGESS, *Introduction to the Science of Sociology*, Chap. VII.
[4] SMALL, *Amer. Jour. Sociol.*, vol. 21, p. 752, 1915–1916; vol. 19, pp. 77–78, 1913–1914.

all its uses. This he will do not by creative impulse evolving in a void, but by constructive intelligence shaping the substantial stuff of verified scientific knowledge. Wherefore, scientific knowledge must be made the possession of mankind. Education must not merely train the mind. It must also equip, and store, with knowledge.

This great thought, he says, Ward "apprehended, expressed, explained, illuminated, drove home to the minds of all who read his pages, as no other writer, ancient or modern, has ever done. It is his enduring and cogent contribution to sociology."[1]

In its essential effect, according to Small's historical perspective, this thought was a generation ahead of social thought in England. In any event, according to him, it saved America "the long wandering in the wilderness of misconstrued evolution" in which English social thought was for the time engaged. It thereby freed American thought for other interests, among them the distinctive development of American sociology and on the side of the latter, at least, also the distinctive development of American social psychology.[2]

Ward's influence on the social-psychological movement in this country was naturally part and parcel of his influence on the field of sociology and social thought in general. It is by reason of the new meaning and value which his conception of social evolution reflected upon the social-psychological approach generally and upon his own attempts at psychic interpretation of social phenomena in particular, in consequence of which he helped so prominently to bring about that intensification of social-psychological interest which has given impetus to the recent rapid course of social-psychological development in this country, that Ward stands out as one of the important figures in the background of modern social-psychological thought. If he looms here somewhat less imposingly than in the field of sociology itself, it is because of the psychological current of influence in the same direction with which his own influence united. But certainly social-psychological theory as it developed from the side of sociological thought in this country is a product which is deeply rooted in Ward's influence.

Ward took generously from Comte and Spencer, it should be recalled finally in this connection, and generously acknowledged his debt to them. It is amply evident now, however, that he did not

---

[1] GIDDINGS, *Amer. Jour. Sociol.*, vol. 19, pp. 67–68, 1913–1914; also *Studies in the Theory of Human Society*, p. 293.

[2] See SMALL, *Amer. Jour. Sociol.*, vol. 21, pp. 755 *ff.*, 1915–1916; vol. 19, p. 77, 1913–1914; also BARNES, *Amer. Jour. Soc.*, vol. 25, pp. 150–170, 1919–1920; *Sociol. Rev.*, vol. 14, pp. 202–205, 1922; BOGARDUS, *A History of Social Thought*, p. 267, Chap. XVII; BRISTOL, *Social Adaptation*, pp. 221–244; LICHTENBERGER, *Development of Social Theory*, Chap. XIII; DEALEY, "Lester Frank Ward," *American Masters of Social Science*, ed. by Odum, Chap. III.

merely give Comte and Spencer back in original form but that, on the contrary, he contributed much to the product that was his own as spokesman of the developing intellectual temper in this country in the field of psycho-social thought. What, in fact, could be more representative of the latter, or better evidence of its emergence as a distinctive product, than the pioneer expression of optimism in the possibilities of human effort to order the universe to its satisfaction and the democratic profession of faith in the principle of equality of opportunity as an essential factor in the process, that we get as underlying motives in Ward's social theory.[1]

The extent to which Ward departed from current evolutionary doctrine in his social theory appears strikingly from a comparison of his basic position with that of such recognized exponents of Spencerian social thought in this country at the time, as for instance Fiske and Sumner, both of whom he took occasion specifically to mention in criticism.[2]

[1] It is hardly necessary to suggest here that it is in the pragmatic philosophy of Dewey and his followers, which is sometimes termed *"the* American philosophy," and which is so intimately interlinked through the work of Dewey, Mead, etc., with the development of social psychology in this country, as we shall see, that these crucial doctrines of Ward's theory have received fullest expression (see in this connection *supra*, references pp. 212, 213; also OTTO, "Instrumentalism," *Philosophy Today*, ed. by Schaub, pp. 37–54) and *infra*, p. 238.

[2] See *Dynamic Sociology*, Preface to 1st ed., p. v; *Psychic Factors of Civilization*, note, pp. 100–101.

John Fiske (1812–1901) was the recognized interpreter of the spirit of Spencer's social theory in this country at the time, and Ward, accordingly, coupled his name with that of Spencer in his general attack on the then current *laissez-faire* doctrine which they represented (*Dynamic Sociology*, Preface to 1st ed., p. 2). It is true that Fiske departed from Spencer in one important respect, and that like Ward he sought to emphasize the psychic nature of the process of social evolution. In this connection, he sought to point out some of the sociological implications of the important fact of "the prolongation of human infancy" as a factor in human development (see *Outlines of Cosmic Philosophy*, vol. II, pp. 286, 342 ff.). But in the light of the spiritualistic and religious interpretation which Fiske gave his theory, this feature served but to change the form of Spencer's *laissez-faire* theory without altering its essential implications.

Thus Fiske, like Spencer, speaks of human progress and adaptation only in what Ward termed the passive sense, and he emphasizes, like Spencer, the descriptive phase of social science rather than the prediction and control phases which Ward emphasized (see *Cosmic Philosophy*, especially vol. I, Chaps. IX, X, vol. II, Chap. VI). According to him, human progress is essentially a process of religious adaptation to the evolving cosmic order, and the ultimate salvation of mankind is to be wrought "by obedience to his religious instinct," under the guidance of which it becomes increasingly possible for man to discover God's will as it is revealed in the process of evolution and to conform to it (*Cosmic Philosophy*, vol. II, pp. 502 ff.). All such attempts at scientific prediction and positive control of the social process for which Ward argued Fiske condemned outright. "We are not autocrats, but servants and interpreters of nature," says he (*ibid.*, vol. II, p. 507; *cf.* WARD, *Dynamic Sociology*, vol. II, p. 11). The whole Comtean conception of positive social reconstruction, with the spirit of

To a young people, fired by the zeal of achievement, Ward's point of view came as a welcome relief from the Spencerian "philosophy of despair," as he termed it.[1] It is not surprising, therefore, that American thought should on the whole have followed Ward's lead in holding to the scientifically aggressive approach which he mapped out.[2] Thus it is that the main current of psycho-social thought in this country began to separate itself from the corresponding current of English thought.

---

which Ward felt such close kinship, Fiske regarded as an "insane" attempt to inject human foresight and control where in the nature of the processes involved, according to him, only natural development can avail; and hence—"save as a warning for future thinkers—so much labour thrown away," since, as he has it, "society grows, but is not made," and "man cannot be *taught* a higher stage of civilization, but can only be *bred* into it" (*Cosmic Philosophy*, vol. II, pp. 492, 489; also Bristol, *Social Adaptation*, pp. 214–217).

William Graham Sumner (1840–1910) was even more boldly outspoken in his defense of *laissez-faire*. The following very famous passage presents his attitude strikingly:

"If this poor old world is as bad as they say, one more reflection may check the zeal of the headlong reformer. It is at any rate a tough old world. It has taken its trend and curvature and all its twists and tangles from a long course of formation. All its wry and crooked gnarls and knobs are therefore stiff and stubborn. If we puny men by our arts can do anything at all to straighten them, it will only be by modifying the tendencies of some of the forces at work, so that, after a sufficient time, their action may be changed a little and slowly the lines of movement be modified. This effort, however, can at least be only slight, and it will take a long time. In the meantime spontaneous forces will be at work, compared with which our efforts are like those of a man trying to deflect a river, and these forces will have changed the whole problem before our interferences have time to make themselves felt. The great stream of time and earthly things will sweep on just the same in spite of us. It bears with it now all the errors and follies of the past, the wreckage of all the philosophies, the fragments of all the civilizations, the wisdom of all the abandoned ethical systems, the débris of all the institutions, and the penalties of all the mistakes. It is only in imagination that we stand by and look at and criticize it and plan to change it. Everyone of us is a child of his age and cannot get out of it. He is in the stream and swept along with it. Therefore the tide will not be changed by us. It will swallow up both us and our experiments. It will absorb the efforts at change and take them into itself as new but trivial components, and the great movement of tradition and work will go on unchanged by our fads and schemes. The things which will change it are the great discoveries and inventions, the new reactions inside the social organism, and the changes in the earth itself on account of changes in the cosmical forces. These causes will make of it just what, in fidelity to them, it ought to be. The men will be carried along with it and be made by it. The utmost they can do by their cleverness will be to note and record their course as they are carried along, which is what we do now, and is that which leads us to the vain fancy that we can make or guide the movement. That is why it is the greatest folly of which a man is capable, to sit down with a slate and pencil to plan out a new social world" (from "The Absurd Effort to Make the World Over," *War and Other Essays*, pp. 208–210; also *infra*, pp. 247, 313, note 3).

[1] *Applied Sociology*, p. iii.

[2] See SMALL, *Amer. Jour. Sociol.*, vol. 21, pp. 755 ff., 1915–1916; BARNES, *Amer. Jour. Sociol.*, vol. 25, p. 170, 1919–1920.

The practical import of this departure soon began to make itself felt. It is directly reflected in the early work of the other pioneer American sociologists, and less directly it also provides necessary setting for the psychological current of influence on American social-psychological thought. From the standpoint of social psychology, therefore, the stage was set by Ward's work for the appearance of America's contribution; indeed, the first chapter of American social-psychological thought was already begun, and Ward himself stands out as a notable figure in connection with it.

With Ward, "systems" of thought suffered a loss of prestige in this country and attention in the fields of his influence turned rather to more specialized inquiry and discussion. But it was upon the background of his work that this more specialized investigation crystallized and thrived. In fact, his own work, with its central emphasis on dynamic knowledge and scientific social control, led naturally over into it.

At this point it is, however, necessary to note here more specifically some of the supporting activities, during the formative period of Ward's work, of the other early American sociologists. Ward's pioneer reinterpretation of the field of sociological thought in this country was followed shortly by the early attempts to establish the subject academically—at Yale by Sumner, at Columbia by Giddings, at the University of Chicago by Small. The first two of these proceeded chiefly from English sources, the latter from German, but altogether and in conjunction with Ward, these pioneer sociologists achieved something of the balanced perspective which James more conspicuously achieved for American psychology at the time. It is this more complex sociological background which comes to play an increasingly important rôle in the American social-psychological movement and, in combination with the psychological background influences presently to be considered here, is reflected in the first really distinctive formulations of American social-psychological thought, as represented, in the first instance, more especially by the work of Baldwin, Cooley, and Ross.

In particular, it is necessary to mention here, as supporting Ward's emphasis on the psychic factors in social life, Small and Vincent's *Introduction to the Study of Society* (1894) and Giddings's *Principles of Sociology* (1896). The first-mentioned of these works presents an analogical analysis of social life, developed as a brief adaptation of Schäffle's scheme of social analysis, and, as a part of this treatment of social life, a section entitled "Social Psychology"[1] which corresponds to the same section in

[1] See *supra*, p. 70; *infra*, p. 278. In conjunction with this work, Small began that popularization of German background sources which he continued throughout his professional career as a sociologist. In his later work and especially in his *General Sociology* (1905), which links up in a general way with the social psychology of W. I. Thomas and others of the group associated with him, as has already been noted in the

Schäffle's work and which represents the first notable use of this term in this country. In both Germany and this country, therefore, the term "social psychology" first came into use in connection with the analogical method as it had established itself at the time in the field of sociology and in the former case also, it will be recalled, in the field of folk psychology. It is notable here that Baldwin's use of the term stands ín close relation with this usage and the German background influences to which it in the first place refers, though, as we shall see, he incorporated it in a different setting of psychological and evolutionary thought, which was profoundly significant for social psychology and which defined the main current of later social-psychological development in this country.

But as was noted in the case of Schäffle, real progress in the field of social-psychological thought on the sociological side depended upon a more direct analysis of the social process, and this we do not in general get either in Schäffle's work or in Small and Vincent's adaptation but most conspicuously, in the first place, in the work of the French sociological writers beginning with Tarde. It is in this connection that Giddings's above-mentioned work takes on historical significance here, in that it attempted to approach the analysis of social life more directly after the manner of these writers. Taking his cue in the first instance from Adam Smith's analysis of sympathy[1] and later from Walter Bagehot's treatment of political evolution,[2] Giddings set forth the view that "the original and elementary subjective fact in society is *consciousness* of *kind,*" by which he meant "a state of consciousness in which any being, whether low or high in the scale of life, recognizes another conscious being as of like kind with itself."[3] He thereby outlined an analysis of social life in terms of this basic principle, both as a criticism of and as a substitute for similar attempts at analysis, notably that of Tarde in terms of the popular theory of imitation.[4] In the end, Giddings reached a position not unlike that of Tarde in emphasizing *like mindedness* as a basic social fact, though he differed with him in so far as the further sociological analysis of this fact is concerned and especially in the general

---

section on Ratzenhofer (see *supra*, pp. 74–75), he stressed particularly Ratzenhofer's sociological theory and especially the latter's theory of interests, as a point of departure for his own sociological thinking. It was in the first place primarily through his efforts, too, that American sociological thought, and through it American social-psychological thought, has to some extent become familiar with Simmel's sociology. See *supra*, p. 84.

[1] See *supra*, pp. 146*ff.*; GIDDINGS, *Principles of Sociology*, Preface to 3d ed., pp. x–xi.

[2] See *supra*, p. 161; GIDDINGS, *Principles of Sociology*, pp. 322, 357, 389; *Studies in the Theory of Human Society*, Chap. I.

[3] *Principles of Sociology*, p. 17, Preface, p. v.

[4] *Ibid.*, pp. 10–16, 18, 103.

setting of Spencerian evolutionary doctrine in which he incorporated his theory.[1]

Both of the above-mentioned works were important influences on the border line of American social-psychological thought during its early period of development, and they did not become more specifically influential in this connection only because of the more definite concentration of social-psychological interest at the time about the work of James, Baldwin, and Cooley on the one hand and Ross on the other. And in the latter connection, strangely enough in view of his well-known position as already outlined, Sumner's sociological work as represented by his *Folkways* (1906), which is notable here both as a very important concrete study of social control and as introducing in this country the use of ethnological material in the treatment of such problems,[2] stands in more intimate relation than either of the above-mentioned works. But this work, in which Sumner passes over into a social determinism approaching in some respects that of the Durkheim school, will be commented upon again in a later connection.[3] At this point our discussion leads us back to a consideration of the psychological background of American social-psychological thought corresponding to the sociological background, as it has been traced out so far.

III. WILLIAM JAMES (1842–1911) AND OTHER EARLY AMERICAN PSYCHOLOGICAL INFLUENCES

It is a fact of the utmost significance, it should be recalled at this point, therefore, from the standpoint of the more detailed consideration of American social-psychological thought during its early period of development, that the psychic emphasis of Ward's social theory had its counterpart in an expanded social outlook in American psychology at the time. This is not only because Ward's theory was weak in its psychological foundations and very much in need of reenforcement at this point but also because Ward did not readily take root in this country. It was, in fact, only after he had attained the recognition of a govern-

[1] After this early work, particularistic explanations of social life began to lose ground rapidly in this country, and Giddings turned his attention to other problems, especially to the statistical development of sociology. In this later effort of his, we have one of the sources of the recent movement toward measurement and quantitative procedure in American social psychology. We shall note other sources presently (see *infra.*, pp. 266, 384).

[2] Despite the seemingly very close connection between American anthropology and social psychology at the present time, this connection was in the first place largely indirect only, being most conspicuously in evidence in such works as Sumner's *Folkways* and W. I. Thomas' early works, especially his *Source Book for Social Origins*, 1909 (see *infra*, pp. 353*ff.*). The more direct influence of American anthropology began to come in with Boas' *Mind of Primitive Man*, 1911 (see in this connection also *infra*, p. 267).

[3] *Infra*, p. 313.

mental prohibition abroad that Ward began to attract attention in this country even in the developing field of sociology. And Ward's influence though profound was always rather limited.[1] Thus it is that from the standpoint of more immediate effect upon the social-psychological direction of thought in this country the psychological trend of development might appear more decisive, James' *Principles of Psychology* (1890) especially, though it actually appeared somewhat later than Ward's *Dynamic Sociology*,[2] presenting itself as an event not only of the utmost but also of prior significance.

At any rate, the psychological side of the situation is extremely important. Dewey's *Psychology* (1886) with its activistic emphasis (this was a point of emphasis with Ward and James also) and its leaning toward the synthetic view of mental life, as supported by both English and German contemporary thought, marked, as Brett says, "the first grey dawn of that to-morrow" which James more definitely ushered in. It was, according to him, "the proclamation of a new era" in American psychology and, by possible implication, an event of the first importance also for American social psychology.[3] But since Dewey developed the social-psychological implications of his psychological position specifically and in some detail later, after it had matured under the growing influence of James' psychology, we can postpone consideration of his work to its due order in the latter connection and turn here to the further development of the background of American social-psychological thought through a consideration of James' *Principles of Psychology*, which will best fill out the picture as so far presented in terms of Ward's *Dynamic Sociology* and the other early American background influences on the sociological side.

We accordingly come to the consideration of another classic of early American thought in defining the background of American social-psychological development. More strikingly even than is the case with Ward's *Dynamic Sociology*, because of its more specific character, James' *Principles of Psychology* has a unique place of importance in the early history of American social-psychological thought. Temperament, training, broad interest, and rare literary ability apparently all combined to make this work a thing apart in American psychological literature and to raise James generally to a position of importance from the standpoint of

---

[1] See *Dynamic Sociology*, Preface to 2d ed., pp. x–xxiv; SMALL, *Amer. Jour. Sociol.*, vol. 21, pp. 788 *ff.*, 1915–1916; DEALEY, "Lester Frank Ward," *American Masters of Social Science*, ed. by Odum, p. 74.

[2] It should be noted that preliminary installments of James' work, notably his important chapters on "The Stream of Thought" and "Habit," had appeared in periodical form before their appearance in final form in 1890.

[3] See BRETT, *A History of Psychology*, vol. III, pp. 256, 259 *ff.*; also BALDWIN, *Social and Ethical Interpretation*, 3d ed., p. 595; *infra*, p. 266.

the later course of American psychological and related endeavor, which is peculiarly his own.

"Of all the scientific works ever produced," says Brett in attempting to place James historically, "James' *Principles of Psychology* is most deserving to be called a 'phenomenon.'" "For those who have not read all or part of the *Principles of Psychology*," he suggests, "a description of its rubrics would be worse than useless; those who have read it know why such a proceeding is to be avoided." But today, according to him, "America is most widely known [in so far as its psychology is concerned] for two assets, experimental psychology and William James."[1] With this somewhat striking but essentially not unrepresentative statement as an introduction, it will suffice to recall here that it has become something of a tradition not only to date the modern period of psychological development in this country from James' famous work but also to refer to it, as a sort of first cause, almost every advance in American psychological thought which has since come into view. Nor is this without good ground, it would seem, in view of the prestige and popularity which James reflected even upon the byways of his influence.[2]

From the first James was, and to many he still remains, "the eminently readable psychologist."[3] It is hardly necessary any longer, according to a recent writer, "to dwell upon James' contributions to psychology," inasmuch as the most important of them "have entered into current thought, on its popular as well as on its more professional side."[4] This fact must be borne in mind when considering James' relation to later American thought in any of the departments which his work touched upon. From the standpoint of social psychology, for instance, the importance of James' position attaches in no small measure to this consideration, to what Dewey has in this connection termed "the depth and breadth of the influence of James," and viewed in the light of it, his real and many-sided social-psychological suggestiveness assumes a significance which is one of the very notable features of early American social-psychological thought—and this despite the altogether incidental character of James' treatment of social-psychological material.[5]

Like Ward, James started out equipped with an intimate knowledge of biological science through early training. In that period, when scientific thought was so largely centered in the theory of biological

[1] Brett, *A History of Psychology*, vol. III, p. 262.

[2] See *ibid.*, vol. III, pp. 261 *ff.*; WOODWORTH, *Dynamic Psychology*, pp. 18–19; MURPHY, *Historical Introduction to Modern Psychology*, Chap. XII.

[3] BRETT, *A History of Psychology*, vol. III, p. 265.

[4] ROGERS, *English and American Philosophy since 1800*, p. 369.

[5] BRETT, *A History of Psychology*, vol. III, pp. 261 *ff.*; DEWEY, "The Need for Social Psychology," *Psychol. Rev.*, vol. 24, p. 267, 1917; BARNES, "Some Contributions of American Psychology to Modern Social and Political Theory," *Sociol. Rev.*, vol. 13, p. 157, 1921. Also COOLEY, *Human Nature and the Social Order*, 2d ed., note, p. 125.

evolution, this was not merely an advantage; it was a necessary part of one's equipment. At any rate it served James well, as it had served Ward well, in encouraging him, like Ward, to carry over the naturalistic and positive view of contemporary biological thought to the study of human nature.[1] This was the step in advance beyond his predecessors who held to the spiritualistic approach of the Scottish school of thought, which James made bold to take. And so important a step did it loom at the time, that it overshadowed in James' mind every other feature of his work.

Whatever other ample grounds for the claim of originality which others might find in James' work, therefore, it is the only ground, as he tells us, on which he himself felt tempted to make such a claim. "I have kept close to the point of view of natural science throughout the book," says James in describing his point of departure in his *Principles of Psychology*.[2] This is the feature of his work which he sought to emphasize above every other, and which he did emphasize in various ways throughout the detailed structure of his theory.

In accordance with his expressed purpose to keep close to the point of view of natural science and to steer clear of metaphysics in his psychology, he started out, in opposition to both the current Scottish and the contemporary British association psychology, by considering the basic data of psychology as constituting "the science of finite individual minds." These he gives as " (1) *thoughts and feelings*, and (2) *a physical world* in time and space with which they coexist and which (3) *they know*."[3] He says in this connection:

This book, assuming that thoughts and feelings exist and are vehicles of knowledge, thereupon contends that psychology when she has ascertained the empirical correlation of the various sorts of thought or feeling with definite conditions of the brain, can go no farther—can go no farther, that is, as a natural science. If she goes farther she becomes metaphysical. All attempts to *explain* our phenomenally given thoughts as products of deeper-lying entities (whether the latter be named "Soul," "Transcendental Ego," "Ideas" or "Elementary

---

[1] James, it is worth while noting here, not only accepted the naturalistic and evolutionary view of mental activity, but he was led to do some preliminary psychological experimentation even before Wundt opened his laboratory. That he gradually became less hospitable to experimental psychology was due to the fact that its approach in the hands of its early exponents seemed to him to be both irrelevant and inconsistent with his own more organic view of mental life. It is hardly necessary to suggest that it is this characteristic of his work which makes it especially significant for us here (see WOODWORTH, *Dynamic Psychology*, pp. 9, 18; BRETT, *A History of Psychology*, vol. III, p. 267; MURPHY, *Historical Introduction to Modern Psychology*, pp. 182, 218; also *infra*, p. 266).

[2] *Principles of Psychology*, Preface, p. v. Quotations from this work are reprinted by permission of Henry Holt and Company, publishers.

[3] *Ibid.*, Preface, pp. v–vi.

Units of Consciousness") are metaphysical. This book consequently rejects both the associationist and the spiritualist theories; and in this strictly positivist point of view consists the only feature of it for which I am tempted to claim originality.[1]

Baldwin has taken occasion to indicate his disagreement with James' judgment here. Others, including himself,[2] he points out, were similarly engaged at this time in the task of producing a positive psychology in this country. James' greatest originality, therefore, according to him, "is not where he claims it—in the point of view" but rather "in his theoretical construction of data—in matters of interpretation."[3] Perhaps, in the case of James, these two aspects of his work ought not to be separated. However, it is the latter aspect of his work which, taken in conjunction with the former, stands out most strikingly here alongside of Ward's imposing endeavor in the interest of positivism as applied to the investigation of human behavior.

James, as already suggested above, presents no specialized treatment of social psychology as such. American thought had not yet become sufficiently self-conscious of the social-psychological point of view to give it specialized consideration. His significant social-psychological theory appears, therefore, more or less as an incidental by-product of his discussion of such relevant topics as "habit," "instinct," the "stream of thought," and, more specifically, the "social self." But James' suggestiveness from the standpoint of social psychology is not limited to his discussion of these specific topics, for some of the deepest social-psychological implications of his work hang rather upon his general outlook and procedure than upon his specific theory.

It is most significant from the social-psychological standpoint, for instance, that James, in aiming to hold strictly to the empirical approach, is led, unlike traditional psychology, to treat his subject matter analytically rather than synthetically. He accordingly starts out with habit and the stream of thought as the basic facts in psychology. The dual basis of procedure in terms of these two psychological facts, as James explains, corresponds to the objective and introspective methods in psychology, the task of psychology being thereby approached respectively from the outer and the inner points of view. Habit, then, appears as the starting point when mental behavior is regarded from the standpoint of its outer manifestations, and the stream of thought likewise is the starting point when mental behavior is viewed from within.

In explanation of this procedure, James says in connection with the latter mode of approach, which was the first to be formulated by him:[4]

[1] *Ibid.*, Preface, p. vi.
[2] In his *Handbook of Psychology* (1889–1891).
[3] BALDWIN, *Fragments in Philosophy and Science*, p. 373.
[4] See *Principles of Psychology*, vol. I, note, p. 224.

Most books start with sensations, as the simplest mental facts, and proceed synthetically, constructing each higher stage from those below it. But this is abandoning the empirical method of investigation. No one ever had a simple sensation by itself. Consciousness, from our natal day, is of a teeming multiplicity of objects and relations, and what we call simple sensations are results of discriminative attention, pushed often to a very high degree. It is astonishing what havoc is wrought in psychology by admitting at the outset apparently innocent suppositions, that nevertheless contain a flaw. The bad consequences develop themselves later on, and are irremediable, being woven through the whole texture of the work. The notion that sensations, being the simplest things, are the first things to take up in psychology is one of these suppositions. The only thing which psychology has a right to postulate at the outset is the fact of thinking itself, and that must first be taken up and analyzed. If sensations then prove to be amongst the elements of the thinking, we shall be no worse off as respects them than if we had taken them for granted at the start.[1]

"*The first fact for us, then, as psychologists,*" says James, "*is that thinking of some sort goes on.*" Explaining that he uses the term thinking for every form of consciousness indiscriminately, he suggests that if we could say in English "it thinks," as we say "it rains" or "it blows," we should be stating the fact most simply and with the minimum assumption. As we cannot, we must, according to him, "simply say that *thought goes on.*"[2]

Relating this view further to the traditional view of component psychological elements which are held together in some form through association, James points out significantly that this elementary thought process "does not appear to itself chopped up in bits." He says: "Such words as 'chain' or 'train' do not describe it fitly as it presents itself in the first instance. It is nothing jointed: it flows. A 'river' or a 'stream' are the metaphors by which it is most naturally described." "*Let us call it,*" he suggests, "*the stream of thought, of consciousness, or of subjective life.*"[3]

The social-psychological consequences of this new outlook and approach are far-reaching and they begin to take on something of a specific reference when James proceeds to discuss the characteristics of this thinking process and to point out, first and foremost, that thinking is always personal; *i.e.,* it is an expression of a personal mind and belongs always to a personal self, so that every thought is, as he says, "owned."[4]

It thus seems, he points out, as if the elementary psychic fact for psychology is not merely *thought,* or even *this thought* or *that thought,* but rather *my thought.* In fact, according to him, "the personal self rather than the thought might be treated as the immediate datum in

[1] *Ibid.,* p. 224.
[2] *Ibid.,* pp. 224–225.
[3] *Ibid.,* p. 239.
[4] *Ibid.,* pp. 225 *ff.*

psychology." But in any event, the universal conscious fact, he declares, "is not 'feeling and thought exist,' but 'I think' and 'I feel.' "[1]

The personal self being always a product of time, place, and social condition, as later social-psychological theory definitely established and as James himself clearly indicates in his discussion of the subject,[2] the social-psychological suggestiveness of this view is immediately apparent. However, James practically left the subject at this point in so far as its social-psychological implications are concerned. He made no attempt to follow through consistently the social-psychological aspects of his new approach or even to point out definitely specific lines of social-psychological applicability. This was a task which naturally fell to the later development of social-psychological thought in this country, as will presently appear.

Similarly suggestive from the social-psychological standpoint is James' objective approach from the side of habit, although he does not in this connection indicate the methodological consequences of his change of standpoint as clearly as in the previous connection. However, he orientates his objective approach in the following significant manner:

When we look at living creatures from the outward point of view, one of the first things that strikes us is that they are bundles of habits. In wild animals the usual round of daily behavior seems a necessity implanted at birth; in animals domesticated, and especially in man, it seems to a great extent, to be the result of education. The habits to which there is an innate tendency are called instincts; some of those due to education would by most persons be called acts of reason.[3] It thus appears that habit covers a very large part of life, and that one engaged in studying the objective manifestations of mind is bound at the very outset to define clearly just what its limits are.[4]

Habit, then, is the important fact in terms of which James proceeds in his objective analysis of mental life. And habit being, according to his conception, a broadly inclusive psychological term touching instinctive behavior on the one hand and acts such as "would by most persons be called acts of reason" on the other, the emphasis of the discussion relating to this wide range of psychological fact is thrown naturally on the notion of *plasticity* as the characteristic quality of organic life upon which, according to James, habit depends. James' objective approach thereby again stands over against the corresponding approach of contemporary psychology, which, as we have seen in the case of English post-Darwinian

[1] *Ibid.*, p. 226.

[2] *Ibid.*, Chap. X.

[3] Whatever the difficulties of this view, it is decidedly suggestive from the social-psychological standpoint, as will appear from Dewey's later elaboration of the psychology of habit (see *infra*, p. 334).

[4] *Principles of Psychology*, vol. I, p. 104.

psychological theory, tended to place emphasis rather on the notion of biological determinism.[1]

Plasticity is defined broadly by James in this connection in mechanistic terms as meaning "the possession of a structure weak enough to yield to an influence, but strong enough not to yield all at once."[2]   Such a structure permits facility of readjustment without disruption.   "Organic matter, especially nervous tissue, seems endowed with a very extraordinary degree of plasticity of this sort," says James.   We may, according to him, "without hesitation lay down as our first proposition the following, that *the phenomena of habit in living beings are due to the plasticity of the organic materials of which their bodies are composed.*"[2]

This makes habit, for James, in the first instance, a chapter in physics.[3]   But it is a chapter of broad psychological and social consequences as he views it, especially on the level of human life, since habit is, of course, particularly applicable as a tool of analysis to human behavior.   There is essential truth, James felt, in the French formula *La fonction fait l'organe*,[4] and the quoted statement that "*our nervous system grows to the modes in which it has been exercised*" seemed to him to be generally acceptable as an expression of the philosophy of habit in a nutshell.[5]

The social or, as James has it, the ethical consequences of this theory of habit are, according to him, "numerous and momentous."   "Habit a second nature!   Habit is ten times nature," he quotes with approval the Duke of Wellington as having said.[6]   In a famous passage he elaborates upon this view as follows:

> Habit is thus the enormous fly-wheel of society, its most precious conservative agent.   It alone is what keeps us all within the bounds of ordinance, and saves the children of fortune from the envious uprisings of the poor.   It alone prevents the hardest and most repulsive walks of life from being deserted by those brought up to tread therein.   It keeps the fisherman and the deck-hand at sea through the winter; it holds the miner in his darkness, and nails the countryman to his log-cabin and his lonely farm through all the months of snow; it protects us from invasion by the natives of the desert and the frozen zone.   It dooms us all to fight out the battle of life upon the lines of our nurture or our early choice, and to make the best of a pursuit that disagrees, because there is no other for which we are fitted, and it is too late to begin again.   It keeps different social strata from mixing.   Already at the age of twenty-five you see professional mannerisms settling down on the young commercial traveller, on the young doctor, on the young minister, on the young counsellor-at-law.   You see the little lines of cleavage running through the character, the tricks of thought, the prejudices,

---

[1] See *ibid.*, pp. 104 *ff.*
[2] *Ibid.*, p. 105.
[3] *Ibid.*, p. 107.
[4] *Ibid.*, p. 109.
[5] *Ibid.*, p. 112.
[6] *Ibid.*, p. 120.

the ways of the "shop," in a word, from which the man can by-and-by no more escape than his coat-sleeve can suddenly fall into a new set of folds. On the whole, it is best he should not escape. It is well for the world that in most of us, by the age of thirty, the character has set like plaster, and will never soften again.[1]

Such, according to James, is the broad scope of social implication of the law of habit, as he conceived it. The round of daily behavior in man, he had said at the outset, "seems to a great extent, to be the result of education."[2] And education—what could it be from his point of view but essentially a process of habit formation? Hence the broad import of the following exhortation addressed to youth:

> Could the young but realize how soon they will become mere walking bundles of habits, they would give more heed to their conduct while in the plastic state. We are spinning our own fates, good or evil, and never to be undone. Every smallest stroke of virtue or of vice leaves its ever so little scar. The drunken Rip Van Winkle, in Jefferson's play, excuses himself for every fresh dereliction by saying, "I won't count this time!" Well! he may not count it, and a kind Heaven may not count it; but it is being counted none the less. Down among his nervecells and fibres the molecules are counting it, registering and storing it up to be used against him when the next temptation comes. Nothing we ever do is, in strict scientific literalness, wiped out. Of course, this has its good side as well as its bad one. As we become permanent drunkards by so many separate drinks, so we become saints in the moral, and authorities and experts in the practical and scientific spheres, by so many separate acts and hours of work. Let no youth have any anxiety about the upshot of his education, whatever the line of it may be. If he keep faithfully busy each hour of the working-day, he may safely leave the final result to itself. He can with perfect certainty count on waking up some fine morning, to find himself one of the competent ones of his generation, in whatever pursuit he may have singled out. Silently, between all the details of his business, the *power of judging* in all that class of matter will have built itself up within him as a possession that will never pass away. Young people should know this in advance. The ignorance of it has probably engendered more discouragement and faint-heartedness in youths embarking on arduous careers than all other causes put together.[3]

But here, again, James left the subject further undeveloped from the social-psychological standpoint. Except for some passing suggestions made in this connection or that, the far-reaching social-psychological import of this emphasis upon the psychology of habit is first brought clearly into view in Dewey's recent social-psychological work, where, as we shall see, the psychology of habit is followed out in its social-psychological bearings more or less systematically and in considerable detail.[4]

[1] *Ibid.*, p. 121.
[2] See *supra*, p. 253.
[3] *Principles of Psychology*, vol. I, p. 127.
[4] See *infra*, p. 334.

James' theory of habit leads over naturally into his discussion of instinct, for instinctive tendencies constitute, according to him, the basis upon which habits are grafted and by which they become displaced in the economy of human mental organization. And here we come upon a chapter of James' psychological theory which, in the course of psychological and social-psychological events since, has attracted even more attention than the foregoing ones. Since James wrote his now famous chapter on "Instinct," the problem of the role of instinct in human behavior has attracted an ever growing interest on the part of many students of human nature, and many, both here and abroad, have sought to carry forward James' treatment of the subject. Despite this expanding interest and activity, however, the subject has remained a conspicuous nucleus of controversy and contention, and at the present time, as we have already seen in a previous connection, it is seemingly more of a storm center of discussion, certainly in so far as social-psychological thought is concerned, than ever.[1] The more important does it appear to follow out James' treatment of the subject here as background upon which to reflect the consideration of this controversial situation as it has developed in this country.

James accepted what he held was the usual definition of the term instinct, "*as the faculty of acting in such a way as to produce certain ends, without foresight of the ends, and without previous education in the performance.*"[2]

That instincts, as thus defined, exist on an enormous scale in the animal kingdom needs no proof, according to him. They are generally viewed as "the functional correlatives of structure"[3] in the case of animal behavior. When one comes to human behavior, however, he points out, "nothing is commoner than the remark that Man differs from lower creatures by the almost total absence of instincts, and the assumption of their work in him by 'reason.'"[4] This was, of course, the basically implied assumption of rationalistic psychology and the point of the popular dualism represented by the phrase "instinct and intelligence." A fruitless discussion, James suggests, might be waged on this subject by two theorizers who, as he says, "were careful not to define their

---

[1] See *supra*, pp. 174, 186–187.

[2] *Principles of Psychology*, vol. II, p. 383.

[3] *Ibid.*, p. 383. Emotions are also, of course, "functional correlatives of structure," according to James. He suggested in connection with his treatment of the latter subject that a very close relation exists between instinct and emotion (Chap. XXV). His oft-quoted passage that "an emotion is a tendency to feel, and an instinct a tendency to act, characteristically, when in the presence of a certain object in the environment" (p. 373) is especially notable in view of the emphasis which McDougall later placed upon this theory (*cf.* ENGLISH, "Emotion as Related to Instinct," *Psychol. Bull.*, vol. 21, pp. 309–326, 1924; *supra.*, p, 185).

[4] *Principles of Psychology*, vol. II, p. 389.

terms." It is, however, necessary to avoid a quarrel about words, and the facts of the case are, according to him, tolerably clear.[1]

Man really has, James held, "a far greater variety of *impulses* than any lower animal; and any one of these impulses, taken in itself, is as 'blind' as the lowest instinct can be; but, owing to man's memory, power of reflection, and power of inference, they come each one to be felt by him, after he has once yielded to them and experienced their results, in connection with a *foresight* of these results." In this condition, according to him, "an impulse acted out may be said to be acted out, in part at least, *for the sake* of its results," for, he declares, "it is obvious that *every instinctive act, in an animal with memory, must cease to be 'blind' after being once repeated,* and must be accompanied with foresight of its 'end' just so far as that end may have fallen under the animal's cognizance."[2] He says in respect to this point:

It is plain, then, that, *no matter how well endowed an animal may originally be in the way of instincts, his resultant actions will be much modified if the instincts combine with experience,* if in addition to impulses we have memories, associations, inferences, and expectations, on any considerable scale.[2]

By way of explanation, he suggests:

Wherever the mind is elevated enough to discriminate; wherever several distinct sensory elements must combine to discharge the reflex-arc; wherever, instead of plumping into action instantly at the first rough intimation of what *sort* of a thing is there, the agent waits to see what *one* of its kind it is and what the *circumstances* are of its appearance; wherever different individuals and different circumstances can compel him in different ways; wherever these are the conditions—we have a masking of the elementary constitution of the instinctive life.[3]

This holds, of course, equally in the whole realm of animal behavior, but it is conspicuously descriptive of its higher reaches and more especially of human behavior.

In an inimitable passage James elaborates upon this point as follows:

Nature, in them [the lower animals], has left matters in a rough way, and made them act *always* in the manner which would be *oftenest* right. There are more worms unattached to hooks than impaled upon them; therefore on the whole, says Nature to her fishy children, bite at *every* worm and take your chances. But as her children get higher, and their lives more precious, she reduces the risks. Since what seems to be the same object may be now a genuine food and now a bait; since in gregarious species each individual may prove to be either the friend or the rival, according to the circumstances, of another; since any entirely unknown object may be fraught with weal or woe, *Nature implants contrary*

[1] *Ibid.*, pp. 389–390.
[2] *Ibid.*, p. 390.
[3] *Ibid.*, pp. 390, 392.

impulses to act on many classes of things, and leaves it to slight alterations in the conditions of the individual case to decide which impulse shall carry the day. Thus, greediness and suspicion, curiosity and timidity, coyness and desire, bashfulness and vanity, sociability and pugnacity, seem to shoot over into each other as quickly, and to remain in as unstable equilibrium, in the higher birds and mammals as in man. They are all impulses, congenital, blind at first, and productive of motor reactions of a rigorously determinative sort. *Each one of them, then, is an instinct* as instincts are commonly defined. *But they contradict each other*—"experience" in each particular opportunity of application usually deciding the issue. *The animal that exhibits them loses the "instinctive" demeanor* and appears to lead a life of hesitation and choice, an intellectual life; *not, however, because he has no instincts*, rather because he has so many that they block each other's path.[1]

Referring to human behavior more specifically he continues:

Thus, then, without troubling ourselves about the words instinct and reason, we may confidently say that however uncertain man's reactions upon his environment may sometimes seem in comparison with those of lower creatures, the uncertainty is probably not due to their possession of any principle of action which he lacks. *On the contrary, man possesses all the impulses that they have, and a great many more besides.* In other words, there is no material antagonism between instinct and reason. Reason, *per se*, can inhibit no impulses; the only thing that can neutralize an impulse is an impulse the other way. Reason may, however, make an *inference which will excite the imagination so as to set loose the impulse the other way;* and thus though the animal richest in reason might be also the animal richest in instinctive impulses too, he would never seem the fatal automaton which a *merely* instinctive animal would be.[2]

This is the case, according to James, with respect to the question of instinct in human behavior. In explanation of the striking lack of uniformity of conduct which man under varying circumstances displays, as compared with the essential uniformity of behavior on other than the human level, he sets forth the two special principles of *the inhibition of instincts by habits* and *the transitoriness of instincts*, in addition to the principles already implied in the foregoing statement, namely, "that the same object may excite ambiguous impulses or *suggest* an impulse different from that which it *excites*, by suggesting a remote object." Taken in conjunction with the latter, the above two principles can explain, according to him, "any amount of departure from uniformity of conduct, without implying any getting out of gear of the elementary impulses from which the conduct flows."[3]

The first of these principles—that concerned with the inhibition of instincts by habits—is formulated by James as follows: "*When objects*

[1] *Ibid.*, pp. 392–393.
[2] *Ibid.*, p. 393.
[3] *Ibid.*, pp. 393–394.

of a certain class elicit from an animal a certain sort of reaction, it often happens that the animal becomes partial to the first specimen of the class on which it has reacted, and will not afterward react on any other specimen."[1] Thus, according to him, "the selection of a particular hole to live in, of a particular mate, of a particular feeding-ground, a particular variety of diet, a particular anything, in short, out of a possible multitude, is a very widespread tendency among animals, even those low down in the scale." "The limpet will return to the same sticking place in its rock, and the lobster to its favorite nook on the sea-bottom. The rabbit will deposit its dung in the same corner; the bird makes its nest on the same bough." But each of these preferences, he suggests, "carries with it an insensibility to *other* opportunities and occasions—an insensibility which can only be described physiologically as an inhibition of new impulses by the habit of old ones already acquired."

On the human level, according to him, "the possession of homes and wives of our own makes us strangely insensible to the charms of those of other people. Few of us are adventurous in the matter of food; in fact, most of us think there is something disgusting in a bill of fare to which we are unused. Strangers, we are apt to think, cannot be worth knowing, especially if they come from distant cities, etc." The original impulse which got us homes, wives, dietaries, and friends at all, he explains, "seems to exhaust itself in its first achievements and to leave no surplus energy for reacting on new cases." It thus comes about "that, witnessing this torpor, an observer of mankind might say that no *instinctive* propensity toward certain objects existed at all." It existed, he observes, but "*miscellaneously*, or as an instinct pure and simple, only before habit was formed," for "a habit once grafted on an instinctive tendency, restricts the range of the tendency itself, and keeps us from reacting on any but the habitual object, although other objects might just as well have been chosen had they been the first-comers."[2]

The principle of the inhibition of instincts by habits may also operate in another way, according to James. "Another sort of arrest of instinct by habit is where the same class of objects awakens contrary instinctive impulses. Here the impulse first followed toward a given individual of the class is apt to keep him from ever awakening the opposite impulse in us. In fact, the whole class may be protected by this individual specimen from the application to it of the other impulse." Animals, for example, he points out, awaken in a child the opposite impulses of fearing and fondling. "But if a child, in his attempts to pat a dog, gets snapped or bitten, so that the impulse of fear is strongly aroused, it may be that for years to come no dog will excite in him the impulse to fondle again. On the other hand, the greatest natural ene-

[1] *Ibid.*, p. 394.
[2] *Ibid.*, pp. 394–395.

mies, if carefully introduced to each other when young and guided at the outset by superior authority, settle down into those 'happy families' of friends which we see in our menageries."[1]

The principle of transitoriness, again, is formulated by James in terms of the observation that "*many instincts ripen at a certain age and then fade away.*" A consequence of this principle is, he points out, "that if, during the time of such an instinct's vivacity, objects adequate to arouse it are met with, a *habit* of acting on them is formed which remains when the original instinct has passed away; but that if no such objects are met with, then no habit will be formed; and, later on in life, when the animal meets the objects, he will altogether fail to react, as at the earlier epoch he would instinctively have done."[2]

To turn to human life directly, we see this principle corroborated on the widest scale, according to James, by the alternation of different interests and passions as human life goes on. "With the child," he says, "life is all play and fairy-tales and learning the external properties of 'things'; with the youth, it is bodily exercise of a more systematic sort, novels of the real world, boon-fellowship and song, friendship and love, nature, travel and adventure, science and philosophy; with the man, ambition and policy, acquisitiveness, responsibility to others, and the selfish zest of the battle of life." If, then, he points out by way of illustration, "a boy grows up alone at the age of games and sports, and learns neither to play ball, nor row, nor sail, nor ride, nor skate, nor fish, nor shoot, probably he will be sedentary to the end of his days; and, though the best of opportunities be offered him for learning these things later, it is a hundred to one but he will pass them by and shrink back from the effort of taking these necessary first steps the prospect of which, at an earlier age, would have filled him with eager delight." Even the sexual passion, the most nearly perfect of the human instincts, expires after a protracted reign, he calls to mind. It is also well known, according to him, that its peculiar manifestations in a given individual depend almost entirely on the habits he may form during the early period of its activity, these early habits having established the mode of expression to the practical exclusion of other modes, in accordance with the principle under consideration.[3]

The natural conclusion to draw from this principle of transiency, says James, "is that *most instincts are implanted for the sake of giving rise to habits, and that, this purpose once accomplished, the instincts themselves, as such have no raison d'être in the psychical economy, and consequently fade away.*" That occasionally an instinct should fade before circumstances permit of a habit being formed or that, if the habit be formed, other factors than the pure instinct should modify its course need not,

[1] *Ibid.*, p. 395.
[2] *Ibid.*, p. 398.
[3] *Ibid.*, pp. 400–402.

then, surprise us, according to him. "Life," he remarks, "is full of the imperfect adjustment to individual cases, of arrangements which, taking the species as a whole, are quite orderly and regular. Instinct cannot be expected to escape this general risk."[1]

All this is in explanation of the variability of human behavior as compared with animal behavior despite the fact that, as James maintains, far from having no instincts or fewer instincts than the lower animals, man has in reality many more—so many, in fact, that they most frequently block each other's path and thereby make it appear that man acts chiefly by choice and reason.

"But specifically what instincts do exist in man?" asks James. What kind of motor reactions upon objects shall we count as instincts, in view of the consideration that human instincts are so frequently masked and man's conduct is so variable? James was one of the few post-Darwinian writers who recognized the difficulties of the methodological problem involved here, and in striking contrast to the dogmatic attitude which has been assumed by some of his successors, he frankly admits that the answer to the above questions is "a somewhat arbitrary matter." Instincts fall, according to him, somewhere in between reflexes and habits, and since it is very hard to draw an exact line of demarcation between these types of activity, it is, on the whole, he suggests, "best to be catholic" and to call all kinds of activity instinctive, "so far as it may be *naturally* provoked by the presence of specific sorts of outward fact."[2]

With this preliminary statement as an introduction, James proceeds to develop his well-known list of human instincts. It includes, besides such elementary actions as sucking, biting, clasping, crying, smiling, etc., the following more complex actions: imitation, emulation or rivalry, pugnacity, anger and resentment, sympathy, the hunting instinct, fear, appropriation or acquisitiveness, constructiveness, play, curiosity, sociability and shyness, secretiveness, cleanliness, modesty, shame, sexual love, jealousy, and parental love.[3]

Summarizing his views regarding these activities, he says:

These are the most prominent of the tendencies which are worthy of being called instinctive in the human species. It will be observed that *no other mammal, not even the monkey, shows so large an array.* In a perfectly-rounded development, every one of these instincts would start a habit toward certain objects and inhibit a habit toward certain others. Usually, this is the case; but, in the one-sided development of civilized life, it happens that the timely age goes by in a sort of starvation of objects, and the individual then grows up with gaps in his psychic constitution which future experiences can never fill. Compare the accomplished gentleman with the poor artisan or tradesman of the city: during

[1] *Ibid.*, p. 402.
[2] *Ibid.*, pp. 393, 403.
[3] *Ibid.*, pp. 404 *ff.*

the adolescence of the former, objects appropriate to his growing interests, bodily and mental, were offered as fast as the interests awoke, and, as a consequence, he is armed and equipped at every angle to meet the world. Sport came to the rescue and completed his education where real things were lacking. He has tasted of the essence of every side of human life, being sailor, hunter, athlete, scholar, fighter, talker, dandy, man of affairs, etc., all in one. Over the city poor boy's youth no such golden opportunities were hung, and in his manhood no desires for most of them exist. Fortunate it is for him if gaps are the only anomalies his instinctive life presents; perversions are too often the fruit of his unnatural bringing up.[1]

James' own striking comment on his attempt to describe the chief human instincts is extremely interesting. He says:

Some will, of course, find the list too large, others too small. With the boundaries of instinct fading into reflex action below, and into acquired habit or suggested activity above, it is likely that there will always be controversy about just what to include under the class-name. Shall we add the propensity to walk along a curbstone or any other narrow path, to the list of instincts? Shall we subtract secretiveness, as due to shyness or to fear? Who knows? Meanwhile our physiological method has this inestimable advantage, that such questions of limit have neither theoretical nor practical importance. The facts once noted, it matters little how they are named.

He is accordingly little concerned with the consideration that, as he points out, most authors give a shorter list than his, while some would include tendencies which he did not include, or again that instinct is at times very broadly conceived on the side of physiological function on the one hand and on the side of complex intellectual processes on the other.[2]

In this frank recognition of the fact that classifications of instincts are something of an arbitrary matter, James could well stand as a model for the instinct school of social psychology, which has come into prominence since his day. It is also, of course, clear that with him the emphasis, even in his discussion of instinct, remains upon habit, where it was first placed, and in this respect, too, he is in line with the later development of social-psychological thought. In fact, as already noted, James goes a long way in the direction of that theory of habit which Dewey has recently developed in greater social-psychological detail.[3] This appears especially in what James says regarding the sex impulse, the strongest of the human instinctive impulses, according to him. He says:

Of all propensities, the sexual impulses bear on their face the most obvious signs of being instinctive in the sense of blind, automatic, and untaught. The teleology they contain is often at variance with the wishes of the individuals

[1] *Ibid.*, pp. 440–441.
[2] See *ibid.*, note.
[3] See *supra*, p. 334.

concerned; and the actions are performed for no assignable reason but because Nature urges just that way. Here, if ever, then, we ought to find those characters, of fatality, infallibility, and uniformity, which, we are told, make of actions done from instinct a class so utterly apart. But is this so? The facts are just the reverse: the sexual instinct is particularly liable to be checked and modified by slight differences in the individual stimulus, by the inward condition of the agent himself, by habits once acquired, and by antagonisms of contrary impulses operating on the mind. One of these is the ordinary shyness recently described. Another is what might be called the *anti-sexual instinct*, the instinct of personal isolation, the actual repulsiveness to us of the idea of intimate contact with most of the persons we meet, especially those of our own sex. Thus it comes about that this strongest passion of all, so far from being the most "irresistible," may, on the contrary, be the hardest one to give rein to, and that individuals in whom the inhibiting influences are potent may pass through life and never find an occasion to have it gratified. There could be no better proof of the truth of that proposition with which we began our study of the instinctive life in man, that irregularity of behavior may come as well from the possession of too many instincts as from the lack of any at all.[1]

James did not have the "culture" outlook and tools of explanation which have been placed at the disposal of later social-psychological theory. But he clearly recognized that the sex motive in the case of human beings is something more than an expression of instinctive impulse merely. He speaks, significantly enough from the social-psychological point of view, of *habits*, formed under the influence of *example*, as the important consideration in regard to human irregularity of conduct here as in other aspects of human life and of the principle "that the direction of the sexual instinct towards one individual tends to inhibit its application to other individuals" as the basis upon which, as he says, "though it suffers many exceptions, the whole *régime* of monogamy is based."[2]

James' psychological theory reaches something of a climax from the social-psychological standpoint in his discussion of the "social self," a conception which, even in the restricted sense of his own preliminary application, is highly suggestive in its implications for social psychology. The social self, according to him, is one of the four fundamental aspects of personal selfhood in the more inclusive sense in which this conception figures in his discussion of the personal nature of thought,[3] the three others being the "material self," the "spiritual self," and the "pure ego."[4] He defines the self in this more inclusive sense as follows:

In its widest possible sense, a man's self "*is the sum total of all that he CAN call his*, not only his body and his psychic powers, but his clothes and his house, his wife and children, his ancestors and friends, his reputa-

---

[1] *Principles of Psychology*, vol. II, pp. 437–438.
[2] *Ibid.*, p. 439.
[3] See *supra*, pp. 252–253.
[4] *Principles of Psychology*, vol. I, p. 292.

tion and works, his lands and horses, and yacht and bank-account"[1]—a fluctuating material, as he points out, varying with specific condition and circumstance.

The part of this larger self which constitues, according to James, "a man's Social Self is the recognition which he gets from his mates."[2] As elsewhere in his theory, he relates this aspect of personality with its organic basis. "We are," he explains, "not only gregarious animals, liking to be in sight of our fellows, but we have an innate propensity to get ourselves noticed, and noticed favorably, by our kind."[2]

Properly speaking, according to him, "*a man has as many social selves as there are individuals who recognize him* and carry an image of him in their mind." However, as the individuals who carry the images fall naturally into classes, we may practically say "that he has as many different social selves as there are distinct *groups* of persons about whose opinion he cares."[3] One generally shows a different side of himself to each of these different groups. Thus, according to him, "many a youth who is demure enough before his parents and teachers, swears and swaggers like a pirate among his 'tough' young friends." And in general, "we do not show ourselves to our children as to our club-companions, to our customers as to the laborers we employ, to our own masters and employers as to our intimate friends." There thereby results, according to James, "what practically is a division of the man into several selves"; and this, he points out, may be a discordant splitting, as where one is afraid to let one set of his acquaintances know him as he is elsewhere; or it may be a perfectly harmonious division of labor and correspond normally to the varied aspects of our social life.[3]

Fame, good or bad, and honor or dishonor, are names for such special social selves, according to him. The particular social self of a man called *his honor* "is his image in the eyes of his own 'set' which exalts or condemns him as he conforms or not to certain requirements that may not be made of one in another walk of life." To illustrate, "a layman may abandon a city infected with cholera; but a priest or a doctor would think such an act incompatible with his honor. A soldier's honor requires him to fight or die under circumstances where another man can apologize or run away with no stain upon his social self. A judge, a statesman, are in like manner debarred by the honor of their cloth from entering into pecuniary relations perfectly honorable to persons in private life."[4]

What may be called "club-opinion," he declares, is one of the very strongest forces in life. "The thief must not steal from other thieves; the gambler must pay his gambling-debts, though he pay no other debts

[1] *Ibid.*, p. 291.
[2] *Ibid.*, p. 293.
[3] *Ibid.*, p. 294.
[4] *Ibid.*, p. 295.

in the world"; in fashionable society, "you must not lie in general, but you may lie as much as you please if asked about your relations with a lady; you must accept a challenge from an equal, but if challenged by an inferior you may laugh him to scorn," etc.[1] These are examples both of the meaning and of the importance of the social self as conceived of by James.

It is evident that James comes very close here to the general conception of the social nature of personality which was later worked out in much greater and more concrete detail by American social psychology but only, as in the case of the other social-psychological aspects of his theory, in a very limited sense and from a still very uncertain and quite incidental social-psychological standpoint. It was the task of the more systematic investigation of social behavior which followed in this country, both psychological and sociological, to clothe James' germinal social-psychological suggestions, particularly as they were reflected upon the background of the wider social setting of Ward's thought, with more specific and more concrete content, and it is largely in consequence of this later work that his suggestions appear now so significant. Viewed in the light of this later work, however, James' germinal suggestions loom very important. "Big books," says Dewey, "have been written since which are hardly more than an amplification of the suggestions" found in James.[2] It will be our purpose in the following chapters to trace out the course of this later development of American social-psychological thought so that the connections with as well as departures from its background as so far outlined will appear.

It should be noted here in this connection that James marks, even more than Ward, the final breakdown of the earlier provincialism of American psychological and social thought. The influence of French thought was at the time well established in this country along with the continuing influence of English thought (it is prominently reflected in both James' work and Ward's),[3] and the influence of German thought began to come in full force with the growing practice of German university training in the eighties.[4] In James we get this interinfluence of thought currents notably. English, French, and German elements and approaches were combined by him into a new and well-balanced point of view. "All in all," remarks Woodworth in commenting on James' psychological position, "he was evidently a good internationalist in his science, as

[1] *Ibid.*, pp. 295–296.

[2] Dewey, "The Need for Social Psychology," *Psychol. Rev.*, vol. 24, p. 266, 1917.

[3] Just as Ward reflected the influence of French thought through his attempt to reconcile Spencer and Comte, so James reflected the influence of French thought through his numerous quotations and statements of indebtedness to Renouvier and other French writers (see especially his dedications in his *Principles of Psychology* and in *Some Problems in Philosophy*; also *The Will to Believe*, p. 143).

[4] See *supra*, pp. 64–65, 213.

indeed every good psychologist must be."[1]   This broadening of intellectual perspective in American psychological and social thought will be markedly evident in the work of some of the followers of James and Ward in the field of social-psychological thought and must be kept in view here as a factor of increasing importance in the American social-psychological movement.

At this point, however, as in the case of Ward, it is necessary to note some of the other early developments, on the side of psychology, which are important in defining the background of American social-psychological thought. It is necessary to mention again in particular, as supporting James' work in its social-psychological implications on the side of theoretical construction, Dewey's early *Psychology* (1886) and, less immediately, Baldwin's early formulation of psychological theory, both of which have already been referred to here in relation to James' psychology.[2] On the side of method, it is necessary to note as a most important development in American psychology generally at the time, but ultimately of importance also for American social psychology, the opening of the first psychological laboratories in this country by the early American students of Wundt, notably by Hall and Cattell in 1883 and 1888 respectively. For the time being, it was inevitable that theoretical construction should take precedence over considerations of method in the still very new field of social psychology, especially the method of early psychological experimentation, which, under the influence of Wundt's own work, was both individualistic and physiological in its bearing,[3] whereas social psychology was still very largely identified with social investigation. Hence, experimental psychology was for a time only indirect in its influence upon social psychology. But ultimately, and especially in conjunction with the turn which social-psychological thought began to take in the work of Baldwin and Cooley, the development under consideration here was obviously of great import for the eventual establishment of social psychology as a field of scientific investigation. In the hands of Cattell, in particular, experimental psychology as popularized by Wundt was gradually combined with the statistical and testing techniques as they were being developed by Galton and Binet, so that at that early date the gradual extension of these techniques was begun, which has more recently brought them within the scope of definite social-psychological interest and application.[4]

[1] WOODWORTH, *Dynamic Psychology*, pp. 18–19.

[2] See *supra*, pp. 215, 248, 251.

[3] It will be recalled that Wundt considered experimental psychology the method of individual psychology, to be supplemented on the social-psychological side by the historical method of folk psychology (see *supra*, pp. 52 *ff*).

[4] See in this connection MURPHY, *Historical Introduction to Modern Psychology*, pp. 173*ff.*, 181–182; also *Experimental Social Psychology*, especially Chap. I.

Hall exerted himself in other directions of significance for social psychology. In the first place, he was outstandingly instrumental in establishing and popularizing child psychology in this country, and this field of investigation, as will appear in some detail in the next section of our survey, links up directly with the next step of social-psychological development as it is to be followed out here.[1] In conjunction with his interest in this field of investigation, he was instrumental also in advancing other fields intimately related to social psychology, for example, anthropology and psychoanalysis. Hall's interest in anthropology should especially be mentioned in this connection. Viewing anthropology and folk psychology, after the manner of Wundt, as indispensable supplements to psychology in the study of mental life,[2] Hall established the first department of anthropology in this country as a part of his program for the development of child and genetic psychology. It is in conjunction with this part of his program that Franz Boas began his academic career, and in a preliminary way that plan of study which has so profoundly affected modern anthropology on the side of method as well as outlook and conception and which in the course of time became so profoundly significant for the critical reconsideration of classical evolutionary theory, including the assumptions upon which Hall himself seemed so securely to build.[3]

[1] See *infra*, pp. 270, 272 *ff.*; also BRETT, *A History of Psychology*, vol. III, pp. 267, 297; BARNES, *Sociol. Rev.*, vol. 13, pp. 163, 204, 1921; MURPHY, *Historical Introduction to Modern Psychology*, pp. 181–182, 280–283, 333.

[2] See *Adolescence*, Preface and Chaps. X, XVIII.

[3] As was stated in the section on English evolutionary thought, the whole field of evolutionary theory in respect to culture and social fact was left, by the ambitious attempts at generalization and systematization in which classical evolutionary anthropology engaged, very much in need of revision and reinterpretation. It is to this task that Boas, among other recent investigators, applied himself. Realizing that the technical questions which classical evolutionary anthropology precipitated, such as the crucial questions of independent origin and parallel development, could be resolved only through the intensive study of specific situations, Boas directed his attention increasingly to this approach, conceiving a program of intensive investigation gradually which has been epoch-making in its importance for anthropology and ultimately also for all related thought, including social psychology. For some time, Boas' work and that of his associates was so technical and specific that it remained the special concern of anthropology and affected social psychology for the most part only indirectly. More recently, and especially since the publication of Boas' *The Mind of Primitive Man* (1911), this school of thought has, however, entered upon a period of more general formulation of their point of view and procedure which has brought them into closer relation with social psychology. This is more especially the case because their position has brought them into conflict with some of the assumptions underlying biological and psychological individualism, so that they have become involved in the recent criticism of instinct psychology (see, for example, KROEBER, "The Possibility of a Social Psychology," *Amer. Jour. Sociol.*, vol. 23, pp. 633–650, 1917; "The Superorganic," *Amer. Anthrop.*, vol. 19, pp. 163–213, 1917; LOWIE, "Psychology and Sociology," *Amer. Jour. Sociol.*, vol. 21, pp. 217–229, 1915; WALLIS, "The Independence of Social Psychology," *Jour. Abnor. Social Psychol.*, vol., 20,

Hall's role in associating psychoanalysis with conventional psychology in this country was likewise dramatic. It was in considerable measure under his sponsorship that both Freud and Jung were in the first place introduced to American academic psychology.[1] What the total effect of this sponsorship has been, it is difficult to say, but the fact remains that it is from this period that the recent developing emphasis upon the psychoanalytic strain in American psychological and social thought dates.[2] Psychoanalysis fitted in peculiarly with Hall's underlying psychological conceptions. His feeling of kinship for it was therefore natural and to be expected.

Hall's own pioneer work in the field of child and genetic psychology, important as it was in its own ways, was chiefly negative in its social-psychological implications, as will appear in the next few pages. It was for the most part only indirectly through his many-sided activities in the interest of child and genetic psychology that his views were frequently realized in their more positive social-psychological bearing. But these activities are necessary background for the further course of our discussion and for the consideration of the social-psychological interpretation of mental development, more particularly as it comes to view in the next section of our survey. Also, certain aspects of his theory provide an illuminating basis of comparison with the latter. They will be briefly indicated in this connection in the next chapter.

---

pp. 147–150, 1925; GOLDENWEISER, "Diffusionism and the American School of Historical Ethnology," *Amer. Jour. Sociol.*, vol. 31, pp. 19–38, 1925. Also *supra*, pp. 166*ff.*, 171, 247). The effect of this closer connection with social psychology is reflected in the emphasis upon "culture" in many of the recent formulations of American social psychologists and, in the case of such a writer as Allport, also in the heated criticism of this viewpoint (see *infra*, p. 403).

[1] See FREUD, "The Origin and Development of Psychoanalysis, *Amer. Jour. Psychol.*, vol. 21, pp. 181–218, 1910; JUNG, "The Association Method," *ibid.*, pp. 219–269. Also Hall's Preface to FREUD, *A General Introduction to Psychoanalysis.*

[2] See MURPHY, *Historical Introduction to Modern Psychology*, pp. 332–335; BARNES, *Sociol. Rev.*, vol. 13, pp. 163–167, 1921.

CHAPTER VI

SOCIAL-PSYCHOLOGICAL THOUGHT AS AN EXTENSION OF PSYCHOLOGICAL AND SOCIOLOGICAL THEORY

I. James M. Baldwin (1861)

The directions of development which we have been tracing out here first came together with very significant social-psychological results in the work of Baldwin, who approached social-psychological thought from the side of child psychology regarded as a part of genetic psychology in the broad sense of contemporary evolutionary thought. In order to bring this approach into proper social-psychological perspective, it is necessary to consider it briefly from the standpoint of its natural setting in contemporary psychological and social theory as the latter has been developed so far.

Baldwin's approach is deeply rooted in the notion of "the social growth of personality," a conception which he brought into prominence in this country in conjunction with his well-known formulation of "the dialectic of personal growth." This conception had two distinct sources in American thought: the philosophical analysis of the self, emanating chiefly from German idealistic thought of the Hegelian strain and introduced into psychology in this country especially by James and Dewey but also by such a representative of this direction of thought itself as Josiah Royce;[1] and child psychology in its more inductive aspects, which, like so many other scientific movements of the day, took its modern impulse chiefly from Darwinism and in connection with which Hall, as has already been noted, stands out in this country as a notable pioneer figure.[2]

It was the latter field of inquiry which, in conjunction with the progress of contemporary sociological and anthropological investigation, brought to this conception of personal growth the factual support and concrete significance that it needed to establish itself as a contribution to modern scientific theory, for the former direction of thought, while it

[1] See *infra*, p. 290.

[2] See Brett, *A History of Psychology*, vol. III, pp. 296 *ff.*; Davis, *Psychological Interpretations of Society*, Chap. IV; Hall, *Adolescence*, Chap. X; *Life and Confessions of a Psychologist*, pp. 354 *ff.*; Baldwin, *Mental Development in the Child and the Race*, Preface, notes pp. 339, 346, etc.; *Social and Ethical Interpretations in Mental Development*, note p. 15, p. 523, etc.; Barnes, *Sociol. Rev.*, vol. 13, pp. 163 *ff.*, 204 *ff.*, 1921. *Supra*, pp. 13, 65, 165–166, 267.

held the germ of interpretation which the conception incorporates, was itself dependent on the facts brought forth by the above fields of investigation for its concrete meaning and value. To the modern development of child psychology as reflected upon the background of Darwinian evolutionary doctrine, therefore, we owe the chief scientific impulse behind the conception of "the social growth of personality" as it has been developed by American social psychology beginning with Baldwin. This is the claim made by Baldwin himself, who acknowledged both sources of influence, at the same time taking pains to establish the point that his theory rests on the observed findings of psychogenesis and especially in the "direct observation of children," a field of inquiry which tended to bring, according to him, inductive confirmation of the conception of the self which had been deductively arrived at by the German trend of idealistic thought, as noted above.[1] In defense of this emphasis on the positive approach in the study of mental development, in which respect, it will be recalled, he was notably at one with the emphasis incorporated in the work of Ward and James, Baldwin says:

The advantage of the psychological genetic method is that it is constantly based upon observed facts and may be controlled by them. Psychological observations of the child fall within the range of positive science; and their value consists in the possibility of their repeated corroboration. The theoretical inferences of the work are thus made more secure; and they may be supported, moreover, by a corresponding appeal to the facts of social life for confirmation.[2]

It is especially necessary, therefore, to follow out in greater detail the orientation of Baldwin's approach in child psychology.

This field of investigation, as suggested above, received its chief impulse in the modern period from Darwinian evolutionary doctrine. It was another one of those scientific by-products which took on renewed vigor in the atmosphere of modern evolutionary thought, with its emphasis on the genetic point of view and the phenomena of development.[3]

There were, of course, spasmodic attempts at child study before Darwin's day,[4] but in general the older psychology did not foster the display of special interest in the child mind as a particularly significant

[1] See *Mental Development in the Child and in the Race*, Preface, notes pp. 339, 346; *Social and Ethical Interpretations in Mental Development*, pp. 15, 518–522.

[2] *Ibid.*, p. 3.

[3] See *supra*, pp. 165–166; GINSBERG, *The Psychology of Society*, p. xii; BRETT, *A History of Psychology*, vol. III, pp. 296 *ff.*; WADDLE, *Introduction to Child Psychology*, Chap. I; BALDWIN, *History of Psychology*, vol. II, pp. 103, 94 *ff.*; *Story of the Mind*, Chap. IV.

[4] See BRETT, *A History of Psychology*, vol. III, p. 296; VILLA, *Contemporary Psychology*, pp. 48, 154; WADDLE, *Introduction to Child Psychology*, pp. 15–17; STERN, *Psychology of Early Childhood*, pp. 26–34; MURPHY, *Historical Introduction to Modern Psychology*, Chap. XVII.

field of psychological investigation. Like all other levels of mental phenomena, the child mind was supposed to be explainable in terms of the universal principles of mental action with which this psychology concerned itself and which, it was held, could best be studied where they were most perfectly manifested, namely, in the adult mind of civilized man. The child mind was thus measured up to the adult mind, just as the so-called "primitive" mind was measured up to the civilized mind, the adult mind of modern man remaining always the standard and basis of procedure.[1]

Modern evolutionary doctrine fairly reversed this psychological outlook. From its standpoint the child mind, the animal mind, and the mind of primitive man came into their own as important aspects of psychological investigation both on their own account and as preliminary to an understanding of the adult mind of civilized man, which came to be looked upon as the highest link in the evolutionary chain of mental development. Hence the growing interest in the genetic approach and, as one aspect of it, the growing emphasis on child study which are reflected in modern psychological theory.[2]

For the general problem of mental development which evolutionary thought brought into view, it will be recalled here, resolved itself into several differentiated fields of investigation and methods of attack. Thus in England, as we have seen, it was mainly by way of instinct psychology, with its tendency to link the study of animal and human mentality, and comparative evolutionary anthropology, with its interest in grading and classification, that the genetic approach was chiefly cultivated. In Germany, again, evolutionary thought interpreted from the idealistic standpoint brought culture history chiefly into prominence. All of these directions of inquiry concerned themselves primarily with the racial aspects of the problem of the mental development. The other aspect of the problem, *i.e.*, the mental development of the individual, was for the time comparatively neglected, and this despite the fact that Darwin himself had recognized the importance and set the example of investigation in this field from the standpoint of the new perspective introduced by modern evolutionary doctrine, as he had in so many other directions.[3] Only, in fact, as the findings of embryology began to reflect scientific support on the notion which, in a vague way, had for some time been current in evolutionary thought of the historico-philosophical type,

[1] See BALDWIN, *Mental Development in the Child and the Race*, pp. 1 *ff.*; HALL, *Life and Confessions of a Psychologist*, pp. 360–361; KING, *The Psychology of Child Development*, pp. 2*ff.*; *Cyclopedia of Education*, ed. by Monroe, articles on "Child Psychology" and "Child Study."

[2] See *supra*, pp. 165–166; BRETT, *A History of Psychology*, vol. III, p. 297; VILLA, *Contemporary Psychology*, pp. 153–154; BALDWIN, *Mental Development in the Child and the Race*, pp. 2*ff.*; *History of Psychology*, vol. II, p. 103; *Story of the Mind*, Chap. IV.

[3] In his "Biographical Sketch of an Infant," *Mind*, vol. 2, 1877; see supra, p. 166.

namely, that the individual in his growth in some way passes through the main stages of development through which the race had passed, as implied by the recapitulation theory[1] (thus suggesting a new source of confirmation for the theory that a very close relation exists between the study of individual development and the larger aspects of the problem of mental evolution with which the thought of the day was chiefly concerned), did this other aspect of the problem of mental development also begin to take on importance in the scheme of contemporary genetic thought.[2] And appropriately enough, it would seem, both from the standpoint of the division of labor on this problem in nineteenth century social and psychological thought and in view of the intellectual situation here at the time, as it was outlined in the opening section of this part of our survey, it was in this country that this approach took most vigorous root after its first period of Darwinian cultivation abroad.

The publication of Darwin's "Biographical Sketch of an Infant" was followed in the next few years by a number of similar reports, including Wilhelm Preyer's famous study *Die Seele des Kindes* (1881). This work, the first of these studies, according to Brett, to reach "the dimensions of a book on the subject," though it was largely physiological in character, is usually looked upon as the real initiating event of modern child psychology.[3] The more recent period of widespread interest in this field of investigation was, however, not ushered in until child study began to be popularized in this country chiefly in the first place, as was stated above,[4] through the efforts of G. Stanley Hall and his immediate associates and followers. Under Hall's influence, whatever one may say of specific aspects of his detailed procedure and characteristic point of view, child study began to take on such an importance, both theoretical and practical, that it has ever since remained one of the most active fields of psycho-genetic investigation.[5] Most important for us here, in

[1] This theory was vaguely a part, for instance, of both Comte's and Hegel's systems of thought. It became more specific in the culture-epoch theory of the folk psychologists on the one hand and in the biological doctrine of recapitulation on the other.

[2] See BRETT, *A History of Psychology*, vol. III, p. 297; BALDWIN, *Mental Development*, pp. 12 ff.; *History of Psychology*, Preface, pp. vi–vii, vol. I, pp. 6 ff., vol. II, Chap. VIII; HALL, *Adolescence*, Preface, Chap. X; *Life and Confessions of a Psychologist*, pp. 354ff., 369 ff.

[3] See BRETT, *A History of Psychology*, vol. III, p. 296; VILLA, *Contemporary Psychology*, pp. 48, 154; STERN, *Psychology of Early Childhood*, pp. 26 ff.; WADDLE, *Introduction to Child Psychology*, pp. 17, 35; KING, *The Psychology of Child Development*, p. xii.

[4] *Supra*, p. 267.

[5] BRETT, *A History of Psychology*, vol. III, pp. 297–299; BALDWIN, *History of Psychology*, vol. II, pp. 124–125; DAVIS, *Psychological Interpretations of Society*, p. 53; KIRKPATRICK, *Fundamentals of Child Study*, Preface p. viii; BARNES, *Sociol. Rev.*, vol. 13, pp. 163–167, 1921; HALL, *Life and Confessions of a Psychologist*, pp. 378–379; also *Aspects of Child Life and Education*, by Hall etc., p. v.; MURPHY, *Historical Introduction to Modern Psychology*, Chap. XVII.

this connection, is the fact that child study in this country assumed a definitely social-psychological trend in some of its aspects and that in the case of some writers more particularly, beginning with Baldwin, it resolved itself into deeply significant social-psychological results.[1] It is with these aspects of its development, naturally, that we are chiefly concerned here, and we thus come in the first instance to the consideration of Baldwin's work in its social-psychological bearings.

It is necessary only to indicate more definitely, in passing, the role which Hall's pioneer exploitation of the field of genetic psychology in this country has played in this development. It was through his efforts in the first place in this country that such key terms of modern child and genetic psychology as "infancy," "childhood," "puberty," "adolescence," "youth," and along with them more recently also "maturity" and "senescence" began to take on concrete meaning and definite psychological and social significance. These terms form a series by means of which Hall sought to give concrete content and meaning to the vague evolutionary conception of the continuity of mental development, which had so long remained in need of more concrete elaboration along the lines of its application to the study of the individual. Thereby Hall did much to bridge the gap that was created by the early studies of childhood, such as under the influence of Darwin had increasingly begun to appear on the one hand, and conventional adult psychology on the other. It is in this respect that his work helped to prepare the ground for the social-psychological interpretation of mental development, as we are to be concerned with it in this part of our survey. At any rate, it is illuminating to bear the general setting of Hall's work in view here, especially in conjunction with the following discussion of Baldwin's genetic theory.[2] For it is as a departure from Hall's biological approach and physiological emphasis in the study of mental development, which link his work with Spencer's rather than with Ward's interpretation of evolutionary doctrine, and with the standpoint of instinct psychology in its extremer biological forms, rather than with the broader psychological standpoint of James' position, as outlined above, that the social-psychological aspects of Baldwin's genetic theory can be most significantly presented here. It is by way of offering a basis of comparison for this purpose that Hall's general position is illustrated below.[3]

[1] See, for instance, COOLEY, *Human Nature and the Social Order*, (2d ed.), pp. 56 *ff.*, 81 *ff.*, 97 *ff.*, 189 *ff.*

[2] See bibliography of Hall's early articles on childhood in WILSON, *G. Stanley Hall*, pp. 119–144; Hall, *Life and Confessions of a Psychologist*, pp. 597–616; also his *Adolescence*, especially Preface and Chap. X; *Youth*, Chaps. I, VI; PARTRIDGE, *The Genetic Philosophy of Education*, especially Chap. IV; O'SHEA, review of *Adolescence, Psychol. Bull.*, vol. 2, pp. 121–138, 1905.

[3] Believing "that we are influenced in our deeper more temperamental dispositions by the life-habits and codes of conduct of we know not what unnumbered hosts of

Like Hall, Baldwin sought to build his genetic theory on a foundation of recapitulation doctrine, thereby to tie up his theory of individual

---

ancestors, which like a cloud of witnesses are present throughout our lives, and that our souls are echo-chambers in which their whispers reverberate" (*Adolescence*, vol. II, p. 61), Hall maintained that "the best and only key to truly explain mind in man is mind in the animals he has sprung from and in his own infancy, which so faintly recapitulates them" (*ibid.*, vol. II, p. 65). "We have to deal," he said, "with the archeology of mind, with zones or strata which precede consciousness as we know it, compared to which even it, and especially cultured intellect, is an upstart novelty" (*ibid.*, vol. II, p. 61).

The following characteristic passages will illustrate this position in the more concrete terms in which Hall developed it in his *Adolescence:*

"The years from about eight to twelve constitute an unique period of human life . . . Everything, in short, suggests the culmination of one stage of life as if it thus represented what was once, and for a very protracted and relatively stationary period, the age of maturity in some remote, perhaps pigmoid, stage of human evolution, when in a warm climate the young of our species once shifted for themselves independently of further parental aid. The qualities now developed are phyletically vastly older than all the neo-atavistic traits of body and soul, later to be superimposed like a new and higher story built on to our primal nature . . . Thus the boy is father of the man in a new sense in that his qualities are indefinitely older and existed well compacted untold ages before the more distinctly human attributes were developed" (*ibid.*, Preface, pp. ix–x).

"Rousseau would leave prepubescent years to nature and to these primal hereditary impulsions and allow the fundamental traits of savagery their fling till twelve. Biological psychology finds many and cogent reasons to confirm this view if only a proper environment could be provided. The child revels in savagery, and if its tribal, predatory, hunting, fishing, fighting, roving, idle, playing proclivities could be indulged in the country and under conditions that now, alas! seem hopelessly ideal, they could conceivably be so organized and directed as to be far more truly humanistic and liberal than all that the best modern school can provide. Rudimentary organs of the soul now suppressed, perverted, or delayed, to crop out in menacing forms later, would be developed in their season so that we should be immune to them in maturer years, on the principle of the Aristotelian catharsis for which I have tried to suggest a far broader application than the Stagirite could see in his day" (*ibid.*, Preface, p. x).

"Adolescence is a new birth, for the higher and more completely human traits are now born. The qualities of body and soul that now emerge are far newer. The child comes from and harks back to a remoter past; the adolescent is neo-atavistic, and in him the later acquisitions of the race slowly become prepotent. Development is less gradual and more saltatory, suggestive of some ancient period of storm and stress when old moorings were broken and a higher level attained" (*ibid.*, Preface, p. xiii).

"Psychic adolescence is heralded by all-sided mobilization. The child from nine to twelve is well adjusted to his environment and proportionately developed; he represents probably an old and relatively perfected stage of race-maturity, still in some sense and degree feasible in warm climates, which, as we have previously urged, stands for a long-continued one, a terminal stage of human development at some post-simian point. At dawning adolescence this old unity and harmony with nature is broken up; the child is driven from paradise and must enter upon a long viaticum of ascent, must conquer a higher kingdom of man for himself, break out a new sphere, and evolve a more modern story to his psycho-physical nature" (*ibid.*, vol. II, p. 71).

development with the broader aspects of evolutionary thought with which scientific interest of the day was so largely concerned.[1] But because of his particular conception of the mental and social bearing of the evolutionary process, he was much more cautious than was Hall in the application of its suggested biological analogies. The development of the recapitulation parallelism was nevertheless with Baldwin, as it was with Hall, a major interest, and his dependence upon it, superficial though it is, helps to give his work a more out-of-date air than it would otherwise have. This, in the light of more recent inquiry, is true again in regard to Baldwin's emphasis on imitation as the chief mechanism of personal and social growth, even though he redefined imitation in broad organic terms.[2] But these features of Baldwin's theory, important as he regarded them at the time, have come to be looked upon as incidental details in the formulation of his point of view as a whole, which in its larger social-psychological aspects may be said to mark the real beginning of social-psychological thought in this country as well as an important new phase of social-psychological thought generally.

The significance of Baldwin's point of view for social psychology consisted in the fact that he grasped the social implications of the process of personal growth and that he was able, in consequence, to work out a synthetic view of the process, which seemed to harmonize the positions represented by biological and psychological individualism on the one hand and sociological collectivism on the other and in large part to overcome their most troubling and, as it had hitherto appeared, irreconcilable oppositions.[3] Baldwin gives us the following details of the origin of his point of view and the basic doctrines in terms of which he first formulated it in his *Mental Development in the Child and the Race* (1895):

This work, he tells us, was begun as a series of articles reporting observations on infants. In the prosecution of this purpose, he found it necessary constantly to enlarge his scope, "for the entertainment of a widened genetic view." This need came to clearer consciousness, according to him, in the treatment of the child's imitations, especially in the treatment of the relation of imitation to volition. "The farther study of this subject," he says, "brought what was to me such a revelation of the genetic function of imitation that I then determined—under the inspiration, also, of the small group of writers lately treating the subject—to work out a theory of mental development in the child, incorporating

---

[1] See his *Mental Development in the Child and the Race*, pp. 14 *ff.*; *Social and Ethical Interpretations in Mental Development*, pp. 197 *ff.*; *History of Psychology*, Preface, Chap. I.

[2] See *History of Psychology*, pp. 110 *ff.*; *Mental Development in the Child and the Race*, pp. ix *ff.*, Chaps. IX–XI; also *infra*, p. 276, note 2.

[3] *Cf.* BRETT, *A History of Psychology*, vol. III, pp. 297–298; DAVIS, *Psychological Interpretations of Society*, p. 53.

this new insight."[1] It is thus in connection with the "revelation of the genetic function of imitation" that Baldwin's view of the social nature of individual mental growth has root, imitation in the sense in which he used this term[2] being, according to him, the specific mechanism by means of which the social integration of mental growth is accomplished. And this revelation, though it is suggestive of the similar emphasis on imitation in the previous works of Bagehot and Tarde, was apparently, at least in the first instance, an independent position arrived at chiefly on the basis of observations of the mental processes of children.[3] This is of some importance here, for it gives the distinctive orientation of Baldwin's social-psychological thought, even though Baldwin later followed the example of previous writers in attempting to generalize his observations on the mental development of children. In any event, we have here a statement on the relation between Baldwin's social-psychological point of view and his observations in the field of child psychology—and, incidentally, the origin of one of the central conceptions of his theory, for us the more important one, namely, imitation.

The other conception—recapitulation—Baldwin tells us, came as a result of his conviction, which followed upon an additional period of thought on the subject, "that no consistent view of mental development in the individual could possibly be reached without a doctrine of the race development of consciousness,—i.e., the great problem of the evolution of the mind" in general. On the basis of this new insight, according to him, he fell to reading again the literature of biological evolution, "with a view of a possible synthesis of the current biological theory of organic adaptation with the doctrine of the infant's development, as my previous work had led me to formulate it." The result, as he points out, was a new attack upon the problem of Spencer and Romanes carried on from the standpoint represented by child study. This new approach, he suggests, "accounts for the preliminaries and incidents of treatment which make my book so different in its topics and arrangement from theirs and from any work constructed from the start with a 'System of Genetic Psychology' in view."[4]

[1] *Mental Development in the Child and the Race*, p. vii.

[2] Baldwin thought of imitation as a process of "circular reaction." The process, according to him, has a basic physiological aspect in which an individual imitates himself because of a tendency "to maintain, repeat, and reproduce" movements and acts to which the organism has once been attuned. With him imitation thus becomes the basis of motor as well as mental and social development and, unlike the case with most writers on the subject, a fundamental principle of individual as well as social psychology (see *Mental Development in the Child and the Race*, Chap. IX; PARK and BURGESS, *Introduction to the Science of Sociology*, pp. 390, 423–424; also *A History of Psychology in Autobiography*, ed. by Murchison, vol. I, p. 4).

[3] See Prefaces to 1st, 2d, and 3d ed. of his *Social and Ethical Interpretations in Mental Development*.

[4] *Mental Development in the Child and the Race*, pp. vii–viii. Quotations from this work are reprinted by permission of The Macmillan Company, publishers.

Baldwin first formulated his theory of mental growth, which, it has been suggested, sought to bring together "the biological, sociological and psychological trends of thought" on the subject at the time, in his *Mental Development*. "The success of this book," says Brett, "which has been considerable both in its English and its German form, may be regarded as a proof that it provided for many readers the synthesis of ideas which time had prepared them to expect."[1] Folk psychology, he proceeds to point out, had made familiar the idea of a continuous evolution of the content of thought as well as of the processes of thought which could contain the ever increasing complexity of content-material. The same general view appeared in varied form and with renewed emphasis in the English literature of biological evolution, which also brought new support to the theory of recapitulation and additional incentive for child study. Contempory sociological and anthropological thought again was stressing in a variety of indirect ways the dependence of human thought on cultural level and social environment. The background for Baldwin's theory was thus quite complete. He needed only to take the step beyond of bringing these thought currents to bear on the specific problem of individual as over against racial mental growth, and of tying them up with the facts of child psychology as he himself was confronted with them and as they were beginning increasingly to appear in the contemporary detailed reports on child development. His own contribution consisted chiefly of the characteristic synthesis of these elements of thought and investigation which he worked out in preliminary form in his *Mental Development* and in more elaborate form in his *Social and Ethical Interpretations* (1897).[2]

From the standpoint of social psychology, Baldwin's *Mental Development* is thus merely introductory to his later volume on *Social and Ethical Interpretations*, in which the social implications of his theory of individual mental growth are developed. Baldwin's earlier volume had indicated the social nature of the process of mental growth and projected the later work in which this aspect of the theory was to be elaborated, but it was itself chiefly concerned with those aspects of the theory that, according to him, fall within the field of individual rather than social psychology. The specific reference which Baldwin there made to his later work is interesting. He says:

There are certain other great provinces, besides, which I find capable of fruitful exploration with the same theoretical principles. Of course, genetic psychology ought to lay the only solid foundation for education, both in its method and its results. And it is equally true, though it has never been adequately realized, that it is in genetic theory that social or collective psychology must find both its root and its ripe fruitage. We have no social psychology,

[1] BRETT, *A History of Psychology*, vol. III, pp. 297–298.
[2] *Cf. ibid.*, p. 298.

because we have had no doctrine of the *socius*. We have had theories of the *ego* and the *alter;* but that they did not reveal the *socius* is just their condemnation.[1]

These social-psychological aspects of the subject Baldwin proposed to take up "in another work, already well under way, to bear the same general title as this volume, but to be known by the sub-title *Interpretations: Educational, Social, and Ethical,* in contrast with the *Methods and Processes,* by which this book is described more particularly on the title-page."[2] This later work, he explains, "will endeavor to find a basis in the natural history of man as a social being for the theory and practice of activities in which his life of education, social co-operation, and duty involves him."[3]

It is interesting to note that by the time Baldwin came to the actual publication of his *Social and Ethical Interpretations,* his social-psychological point of view had apparently so far crystallized as to influence him to change the title of the work as given above so as to include the subtitle "A Study of Social Psychology." This is usually taken to be the first prominent use of the term "social psychology" in this country.[4] As a matter of fact, as we have already seen, three years earlier Small and Vincent had designated a section of their *Introduction to the Study of Society* as "Social Psychology," presenting under it a discussion modeled on Schäffle's treatment of the subject.[5] This was apparently the first notable use of the term "social psychology" in this country, over-shadowed though it very quickly was by Baldwin's more suggestive approach and presently, especially by Ross' popular treatment of the subject.

Baldwin starts out in his *Social and Ethical Interpretations* with the following widely quoted passage from his earlier work describing the chief steps in the emergence of selfhood, the self being, as he maintained

---

[1] *Mental Development in the Child and the Race,* p. ix.

[2] The relation between these two works is clearly indicated here by the subtitles "Methods and Processes" and "Interpretations." It is evident that Baldwin's later work, though grounded in the observations reported in the earlier volume, is itself considerably removed from the inductive basis of fact upon which that work rests. It is essentially a theoretical elaboration of certain conclusions which Baldwin arrived at there and a logical extension of contemporary evolutionary doctrine into a new field of interpretation.

Like James (see *supra,* p. 250), Baldwin was disappointed with the showing which early experimental psychology was making and accordingly he turned his attention increasingly to the problems of mental development defined by the Darwinian evolutionary viewpoint. It was thus that he became more and more interested in the fields of genetic and social psychology, (see his statement in *A History of Psychology in Autobiography,* ed. by Murchison, vol. I, pp. 4ff).

[3] *Mental Development in the Child and the Race,* pp. ix–x.

[4] See SMALL, Article on "Sociology," *Encyclopedia Americana;* BOGARDUS, *A History of Social Thought,* p. 386.

[5] SMALL and VINCENT, Book V, pp. 305–366; see *supra,* pp. 70, 245–246.

with much greater emphasis and elaboration than James, a *social* product. Since it is in this way that Baldwin himself chose to indicate the relation between his two above-mentioned works, and since this passage is basic to all of his later social-psychological theorizing, we shall quote it here as a whole.[1]

"One of the most interesting tendencies of the very young child in its response to its environment is the tendency to recognize differences of personality. It responds to what have been called 'suggestions of personality.' As early as the second month it distinguished its mother's or nurse's touch in the dark. It learns characteristic methods of holding, taking up, patting, and adapts itself to these personal variations. It is quite a different thing from the child's behavior toward things which are not persons. I think this is the child's very first step toward a sense of the qualities which distinguish persons. The sense of uncertainty grows stronger in its dealings with persons. A person stands for a group of experiences quite unstable in its prophetic as it is in its historical meaning. This we may, for brevity of expression, assuming it to be first in order of development, call the *projective* stage in the growth of the child's personal consciousness.

"Further observation of children shows that the instrument of transition from such a projective to a subjective sense of personality is the child's active bodily self, and the method of it is the *function of imitation*. When the organism is ripe for the enlargement of its active range by new accommodations, then he begins to be dissatisfied with 'projects,' with contemplation, and starts his career of imitation. And of course he imitates persons.

"Further, persons are bodies which move. And among these bodies which move, which have certain projective attributes, a very peculiar and interesting one is his own body. It has connected with it certain intimate features which all others lack—strains, stresses, resistances, pains, etc., an inner felt series added to the new imitative series. But it is only when a peculiar experience arises which we call effort that there comes that great line of cleavage in his experience which indicates the rise of volition, and which separates off the series now first really *subjective*. What has formerly been 'projective' now becomes 'subjective.' This we may call the *subjective* stage in the growth of the self-notion. It rapidly assimilates to itself all the other elements by which the child's own body differs in his experience from other active bodies—all the passive inner series of pains, pleasures, strains, etc. Again it is easy to see what now happens. The child's subject sense goes out by a sort of return dialectic to illuminate the other persons. The 'project' of the earlier period is now lighted up, claimed, clothed on with the raiment of selfhood, by analogy with the subjective. The subjective becomes *ejective;* that is, other people's bodies, says the child to himself, have experiences *in them* such as mine has. They are also *me's;* let them be assimilated to my me-copy. This is the third stage; the ejective, or social self, is born.

"The 'ego' and the 'alter' are thus born together. Both are crude and unreflective, largely organic. And the two get purified and clarified together by this twofold reaction between project and subject, and between subject and eject.

[1] Quotations from Baldwin's *Social and Ethical Interpretations in Mental Development* are reprinted by permission of The Macmillan Company, publishers.

My sense of myself grows by imitation of you, and my sense of yourself grows in terms of my sense of myself. But *ego* and *alter* are thus essentially social; each is a *socius* and each is an imitative creation."[1]

"This give-and-take between the individual and his fellows, looked at generally," says Baldwin, "we may call the *Dialectic of Personal Growth.*" It serves, he tells us, as the point of departure for the main positions developed in his *Social and Ethical Interpretations.*[2]

With this statement of the process of social give-and-take attendant upon the growth of selfhood, as formulative of the basic core of his theory, Baldwin proceeds, in somewhat disconnected topical form, to develop the more detailed implications of his position by bringing it into relief over against the background of current biological, psychological, and sociological theory in the reconsideration of various topics which bear directly on the problem of personal development. He thus leads into a discussion and a reinterpretation, from the standpoint outlined, of such relevant topics as invention and imitation, instinct and emotion, intelligence, sentiment, personal and social sanction, the social forces, social matter, process, and progress. The result is the elaboration of a social-psychological position which borders on the Tardean in its emphasis on imitation as the specific socializing process, but which is for the first time definitely directed to the problem of integrating the individual and the social as reciprocally interacting factors in a common process of personal and social development. The latter is thus presented by Baldwin in the twofold aspect of "the dialectic of personal growth" and "the dialectic of social growth," corresponding respectively to the particularizing and generalizing functions of the process.[3]

The points of view of psychological individualism and sociological collectivism, in their historical forms, are alike criticized by Baldwin on the ground that they are both one-sided and unreal abstractions from the concrete give-and-take of the actual process of development outlined. Through emphasis upon such unifying conceptions as "the social person,"[4] "the social self," "the socius," Baldwin sought to bring these

[1] *Social and Ethical Interpretations in Mental Development*, pp. 13–15, quotation from *Mental Development in the Child and the Race*, pp. 334–339; see also *ibid.*, pp. 17–18. This position Baldwin regarded as being essentially in accord with the position arrived at independently in this country from a purely philosophical standpoint by Josiah Royce (see *Mental Development in the Child and the Race*, notes pp. 330 and 339; *Social and Ethical Interpretations in Mental Development*, pp. viii, 15, 518 *ff.*, Appendix H).

[2] *Social and Ethical Interpretations in Mental Development*, p. 15; also *Mental Development in the Child and the Race*, p. 339.

[3] See *Social and Ethical Interpretations in Mental Development*, pp. 13 *ff.*, 27 *ff.*, 539, 570.

[4] This term has taken on a peculiarly distinctive social-psychological significance through the later work especially of Cooley, Thomas, and the group of writers

points of view into relation with each other and with his own distinctive standpoint in a most challenging manner. In fact, some of the most striking passages of his work are formulated in these connections.[1] He says at one point, for instance, in his discussion of the developing personality of the child:

I do not see, in short, how the personality of this child can be expressed in any but social terms; nor how, on the other hand, social terms can get any content or value but from the understanding of the developing individual. This is a circle in the process of growth; and that is just my point. On the one hand, we can get no doctrine of society but by getting the psychology of the "socius" with all his natural history; and on the other hand, we can get no true view of the "socius" at any time without describing the social conditions under which he normally lives, with the history of their action and reaction upon him.[2]

And at another point he says again:

All our thought has led us to see that one of the historical conceptions of man is, in its social aspects, mistaken. Man is not a person who stands up in his isolated majesty, meanness, passion, or humility, and sees, hits, worships, fights, or overcomes, another man, who does the opposite things to him, each preserving his isolated majesty, meanness, passion, humility, all the while, so that he can be considered a "unit" for the compounding processes of social speculation. On the contrary, *a man is a social outcome rather than a social unit.* He is always, in his greatest part, also some one else. Social acts of his—that is, acts which may not prove anti-social—are his *because they are society's first;* otherwise he would not have learned them nor have had any tendency to do them. Everything that he learns is copied, reproduced, assimilated, from his fellows; and what all of them, including him,—all the social fellows,—do and think, they do and think because they have each been through the same course of copying, reproducing, assimilating, that he has. When he acts quite privately, it is always with a boomerang in his hand; and every use he makes of his weapon leaves its indelible impression upon the other and upon him.[3]

It is on the basis of this new insight, according to Baldwin, that the theory of the individual and of society must be gradually built up, and only the complete neglect of the basic facts which support it can, according to him, account for the state of conventional discussion dealing with such overdrawn dualisms of thought as are indicated by the phrases "heredity and environment," "ego and alter," the "individual and the social," the "selfish and the ethical," and the like, all of which rest, as he maintained, on the erroneous position of historical individualism. Could we once free ourselves from the view, suggests Baldwin, "that

intimately associated with the latter (see PARK and BURGESS, *Introduction to the Science of Sociology,* p. 55, Chap. II, pp. 488–490; also *infra,* pp. 380–381).

[1] See *Social and Ethical Interpretations in Mental Development,* pp. 27 *ff.*; also *The Individual and Society,* Chap. I.

[2] *Social and Ethical Interpretations in Mental Development,* p. 27.

[3] *Ibid.,* p. 97.

man is not two, an ego and an alter, each of which is in active and chronic protest against a third great thing, society; could we once dispel this hideous un-fact, and with it the remedies found by the egoists,—back all the way from the modern Individualists to Hobbes," the main barrier to the successful understanding of man and his social relations would be removed.[1]

Particularly insistent in this respect was Baldwin's criticism of the "naïve" biological approach in the study of human relations. At the same time, he had great faith in the applicability of the Darwinian trend of thought to the fields of psychological and sociological interpretation,[2] and he set about consistently in connection with his doctrine of "the social person" to adapt the formulas and main conceptions of evolutionary thought, as the latter was reflected in the contemporary literature of biological evolution, for more significant social and psychological use. The concepts of "social heredity," "social environment," "social variation and selection," and "social accommodation," in particular, were thus reinterpreted by him and introduced prominently into his theory.[3] Baldwin felt the need more especially in this connection, however, definitely to set his point of view in the use of these concepts off from the individualistic and anti-intellectualistic point of view of English post-Darwinian evolutionary thought. The latter was prominently represented at the time by Kidd's *Social Evolution* (1894), which retained in bold outline the tendency of English evolutionary thought to present society and the individual in sharply defined antagonistic terms, though it deviated somewhat from the extremer type of anti-intellectualism of some of the earlier formulations of evolutionary doctrine. Baldwin accordingly took this work under consideration in this connection, and he says with respect to it:

Perhaps no better illustration of the point of view which I wish to leave prominently in the reader's mind can be reached than to cite its contrast with that of the recent book by Mr. Kidd on *Social Evolution*. His whole conception hinges on the view that the individual can get no "rational sanction" for social life. He must then either rebel against society or strangle his "reason." According to Mr. Kidd he does the latter and, by espousing a supernatural sanction found in some religious systems, acts—by inference—*irrationally*.

"But why," asks he in challenging this position, "are his selfish and anti-social impulses the only rational part of the man? Does not the most superficial consideration of the origin of man, to say nothing of the

[1] *Ibid.*, pp. 96–97.

[2] See his *Darwin and the Humanities*, Chaps. I, II.

[3] *Mental Development in the Child and the Race*, Chaps. VII, VIII, XVI; *Social and Ethical Interpretations in Mental Development*, Chap. II; *The Individual and Society*, pp. 9–10, Chap. II; *History of Psychology*, vol. II, pp. 129 ff.; *The Story of the Mind*, Chap. IX.

teaching of the first principles of psychology, show that the indulgence of these impulses is in many instances irrational?"[1]   And again, does it not show, that very frequently "action on his real, most complex, richest thought, is rational?"[2]

And if the antagonism be set, as it more commonly is in the biological interpretation of evolutionary thought, between the instinctive and the acquired rather, or between heredity and environment, Baldwin again has serious objections to offer.   In the first place, heredity as well as environment, according to him, is social in reference, and in a double sense: first, because heredity reflects past socially useful tendencies; and, second, because it is dependent on social environment for its present expression.[3]   Again, the contrast of factors suggested is artificial, from Baldwin's point of view, in that a person's equipment presents itself in reality always as a matter of both factors in combination.[4]   In any event, the factor of "social heredity" is quite as definitely determining in the development of the child, according to him, as is the factor of "physical heredity."   He says:

It is as inexorably his [the child's] as the color of his eyes and the shape of his nose.   He is born into a system of social relationships just as he is born into a certain quality of air.   As he grows in body by breathing the one, so he grows in mind by absorbing the other.   The influence is as real and as tangible; and the only reason that it is variable in its results upon different individuals is that each individual has his physical heredity besides, and the outcome is always the outcome of the two factors—natural temperament and social heredity.[5]

Baldwin accordingly says regarding the above-mentioned contrast of factors:

If that contrast is to be made and if it be a question of the division of a man's equipment into two parts, one due to his endowment or physical heredity, and the other due to his environment, there is no question of a third category.   It supposes that these two agencies are opposed forces, and that each element of the man's entire character must be due to one or the other of them.   The alternative, that *most of the man's equipment is due to both causes working together*, is not recognized; and the resulting dualism or strife between the two supposed influences at work has no way of reconciliation.[6]

It is precisely this alternative, however, that he sought to emphasize. Our views about the relation of heredity and environment must all be reconstructed, according to him, in the light of the new insight into mental development which issues from the study of personal growth on

[1] *Social and Ethical Interpretations in Mental Development*, pp. 97–98.
[2] *Ibid.*, p. 92, Chap. IX, 420–421.
[3] *Ibid.*, pp. 68, 74 *ff.*, 86–87.
[4] *Ibid.*, pp. 66 *ff.*, 74, 77 *ff.*
[5] *Ibid.*, pp. 69–70.
[6] *Ibid.*, pp. 76–77.

the one hand and of the complex problem of "social heredity" on the other. It is this new insight which he sought to concentrate in the formulation of his "dialectic," viewed as a twofold movement of personal and social integration.

In his *History of Psychology*, Baldwin attempted to bring his position as here outlined more definitely into historical perspective, and it is illuminating to note how he projects it upon the background of related psychological and social thought. Like other related fields, modern psychology, he there points out, has reflected the collectivistic tendency generally noticeable in late nineteenth century thought. This tendency became potent in psychology, according to him, both in consequence of the direct criticism of theories based on the concept of the isolated individual and because the need of a social psychology was more indirectly brought into view from the side of the developing social sciences. The need was thus put in evidence, he points out, for a genetic and social psychology, which would reveal the state of the individual mind in given social conditions and thus relate psychological individualism with the world of objective social facts that were being brought to light by sociology.[1] Put in Kantian form, according to him, the question of social psychology as it thus emerged was this: "How is a social subject or self possible? Is he a socialized individual self, or is he an individualized social self?"[2]

His own answer to these hypothetical questions is significantly formulated as follows:

> The outcome of social psychology until now points plainly to a negative answer to the first, and a positive answer to the second, of these questions. It thus reverses the point of view of historical individualism, and gives collectivism its *point d'appui* in the processes of mental development itself.[3]

The larger results upon the basis of which Baldwin arrived at this verdict are presented by him for consideration in this connection and they are of sufficient significance in orientating his general point of view to make it worth while to follow them out in some detail here.

The matter of "tradition" has, according to him, been cleared up with the recognition of the role which social heredity plays in development. He says in respect to this point:

> . . . a true social heredity is to be recognized among animals, running parallel to physical heredity and supplementing it. In human groups this is enormously developed in what we call "culture," a body of beliefs, usages, and sanctions

[1] *History of Psychology*, vol. II, pp. 126–128; also *The Individual and Society*, Chap. I.
[2] *History of Psychology*, vol. II, pp. 128–129. Quotations from this work are reprinted by courtesy of G. P. Putnam's Sons, Publishers, New York and London.
[3] *Ibid.*, p. 129.

transmitted entirely by social means, and administered to growing individuals by example, precept, and discipline. This constitutes the social store, the collective wealth of the group, its moral heritage. It constitutes the *milieu*, a body of influences which are necessary to the development of the individual mind. Such functions as language, spoken and written, play and art; such inventions as fire, building, and weaving, are not only conveniences of life; they are necessary means of growth.[1]

Applying this insight more specifically to his own characteristic mode of approach in terms of the genesis of the social individual, Baldwin continues:

The society into which the child is born is, therefore, not to be conceived merely as a loose aggregate, made up of a number of biological individuals. It is rather a body of mental products, an established network of psychical relationships. By this the new person is moulded and shaped to his maturity. He enters into this network as a new cell in the social tissue, joining in its movement, revealing its nature, and contributing to its growth. It is literally a tissue, psychological in character, in the development of which the new individual is differentiated. He does not *enter into it* as an individual; on the contrary, he is only an individual when he *comes out of it*—by a process of "budding" or "cell-division," to pursue the physiological analogy. Society is a mass of mental and moral states and values, which perpetuates itself in individual persons. In the personal self, the social is individualised.[2]

From this, according to Baldwin, the more specific task of social psychology appears.

It is that of tracing out the internal development of the individual mind, its progressive endowment with individuality, under the constant stimulation of its *entourage*, and with nourishment drawn from it. A constant give-and-take process—a "social dialectic"—is found between the individual and his social fellows. By this process the materials of selfhood are absorbed and assimilated. The "self" is a gradually forming nucleus within the mind; a mass of feeling, effort, and knowledge. It grows in feeling by contagion, in knowledge by imitation, in will by opposition and obedience. The outline of the individual gradually appears, and at every stage it shows the pattern of the social situation in which it becomes constantly a more and more adequate and competent unit. This process the social psychologist has patiently traced out; and apart from details, on which opinions differ, it constitutes a positive gain to our knowledge.[3]

The social aspects of this developmental process are brought into relation with the individual here in an especially suggestive manner. Baldwin says:

The consciousness of the self, thus developed, carries with it that of the "alter"-selves, the other "socii" who are also determinations of the same social

[1] *Ibid.*, pp. 129–130.
[2] *Ibid.*, pp. 130–131.
[3] *Ibid.*, pp. 131–132.

matter. The bond, therefore, that binds the members of the group together is reflected in the self-consciousness of each member. The external social organization in which each has a certain *status* is reinstated in the thought of the individual. It becomes for each a psychological situation constituted by selves or agents, in which each shares the duties and rights common to the group. Upon the background of commonness of nature and community of interests the specific motives of reflective individuality—self-assertion, rivalry, altruism—are projected; but they are fruits of self-consciousness, they are not the motives that exclusively determine its form. All through its history, individualism is tempered by the collective conditions of its origin.

When the self has become a conscious and active person, we may say that the mental individual as such is born. But the individual remains a part of the whole out of which he has arisen, a whole that is collective in character and of which he is a specification. He lives and moves and has his being still in a system of collective facts and values. He is a "socius," an element in a social network or situation; only by this can his individuality and independence become possible or have any meaning. In this new sense is the Aristotelian dictum confirmed—"man is a social animal." But we may express the whole truth more adequately by saying that man is *a society individualised;* for in the new individual society comes always to a new expression of itself.[1]

"Once introduced, the inch develops into the ell," says Baldwin. The social strain, once it began to come into view in these connections, has been made out in the normal working of most of the mental functions of man. Thus:

Biological intimations of social conditions have been pointed out in bashfulness, organic sympathy, gregarious impulses, etc. Apart from the specific means by which the processes of socialising and training go on—contagion, imitation, play, sympathy, obedience, language, moral sense, etc.—the element of "community" has been found to extend to the operations considered by earlier thinkers the most individualistic. Self-love is never free from the colouring of sympathy, invention rests upon imitation, rebellion involves the recognition of the rights of others, rivalry is a form of co-operation. Thought no less than life is shot through with the motive of collectivism. Opinion is formed on social models, social authority preceded logical validity, private judgment is never really private. Even in the processes of deductive reasoning, fundamental social conditions of genesis are never wholly concealed; the "proposition" is a social "proposal" or suggestion; the conclusion is held to be valid for all persons as well as for all cases; even the constructive categories of thought are founded on racial experience ingrained in individual endowment. There is a synnomic force in all reflective thought, in all science.[2]

Baldwin's more detailed elaboration of these points in his *Social and Ethical Interpretations,* of which the above is a summary statement, is carried out in an involved manner of presentation and in a heavy literary

[1] *Ibid.*, p. 133.
[2] *Ibid.*, pp. 134–135.

style which it is difficult to illustrate by quotation.   At times his exposition meets dogmatism with dogmatism so that it hardly seems to be an advance, from the standpoint of scientific balance, upon the positions which it seeks to criticize, synthesize, and displace.   Remotely at least, however, as has already been noted, his general outlook is supposedly grounded in the "direct observation of children,"[1] and to that extent, his work marked a new era in the modern social-psychological movement in that it linked social psychology with a field of most fruitful and, as it seemed, easily verifiable observation which had hitherto been practically neglected by it.   In fact, Baldwin's work was doubly suggestive in this respect, since, as we have seen,[2] it had a definitely positivist as well as social-psychological bearing.   And this consideration is further enhanced by the attempt which Baldwin made to pin his discussion down also to the concrete facts of social life, although his theory is naturally much weaker on the social than on the psychological side. Thus, he presents for our consideration "the young hero of the nursery," placed very suggestively in a family of children and brought into relation with his father, his mother, his brothers and sisters, his nurse, the members of the larger family circle, the school, the play group, etc.[3]   This approach, as readily appears, leads out in a widening circle of concrete social relations which, in the form of "social heredity," reflect back upon "the dialectic of personal growth" and link it with "the dialectic of social growth" quite in the manner demanded by Baldwin's description of the circular give-and-take of the process.[4]   It remained, of course, to follow out these important relations in more concrete detail, but this was a task for later social-psychological effort in this country and elsewhere.   Meanwhile Baldwin's work reflected such a significance on the social-psychological approach applied to the study of personal development as to put social psychology, conceived of in his terms, definitely in the way of its recent course of popularization and development.

The deep-lying implications of his theory for social psychology have been stated by Baldwin most simply and compactly in his more recent work *The Individual and Society* (1911), which constitutes, as he tells us, a sort of popular résumé of his two earlier works.[5]   The following passage in particular is of interest here, at once as a summary of his essential position in its more detailed elaboration and as an important introduction to the further consideration of American social-psychological thought. We accordingly quote it at some length.

[1] *Social and Ethical Interpretations in Mental Development*, pp. 2–3; *Mental Development in the Child and the Race*, p. vii.

[2] See *supra*, p. 270.

[3] *Social and Ethical Interpretations in Mental Development*, pp. 22 ff.

[4] *Ibid.*, pp. 27, 34, 459 ff., 537 ff.

[5] *The Individual and Society*, p. 8.

The individual comes into the world with the impulse of the history of the race behind him. He has few perfect instincts, such as many of the animals show. He is, on the contrary, plastic and educable. But his development is nevertheless to be a compromise between the two tendencies which throughout all his life represent individualism and collectivism. He has distinctly egoistic and individualistic impulses but with them he has also positive predispositions to social life. These two germinal tendencies are to receive their more perfect adjustment, or at least a working relation, in his education and training in the habits and usages of the social group.

It is not necessary to dwell upon the more individualistic factor, in his heredity; it is summed up in the word "appetite." He has a mass of tendencies which are necessary to the preservation and advancement of his vegetative and animal life. These are of necessity direct, strong, and self-seeking.

But over against these we find certain positive impulses which are of a quasi-social or gregarious sort, ready soon after birth to develop the other side of his nature. Bashfulness, shame, jealousy, are some of the more fundamental tendencies rooted in the organic structure of the human babe, which seem to reveal ancestral conditions of collective life and habit.

With these go, in a more positive sense, certain great motives of action which, natural as they are and quasi-instinctive, become the tools of "socialization according to nature" very early in the individual's personal history. *Play* and *imitation*, twin brothers in the scheme of the child's hereditary impulses, come to assume, each alone and both together, a very extraordinary role.

By play the young animal and the child alike come into the most fruitful social relations with one another. The meaning of the varied situations of life is learned in play, under conditions free from the storm and stress of actual serious life; and thus the functions playfully exercised are developed. The great activities of later utility in the struggles of life, and in the varied social conditions of existence, are thus made ready. In play we find one of the great meeting places of the forces of individualism and collectivism.

Imitation is another great socializing function. The child naturally falls to imitating, and when once this has begun he is a veritable copying machine, turning out acts, opinions, decisions, which are based with more or less correctness upon models found in his social environment.

By imitation he gets the "feel" of things that others do, and so learns to value the safe and sane; by imitation, he tries on the varied ways of doing things and so learns his own capacities and limitations; by imitation he actually acquires the stored up riches of the social movements of history; by imitation he learns to use the tools of culture, speech, writing, manual skill, so that through the independent use of these tools he may become a more competent and fruitful individual; finally, it is by imitation in the way of varied and effortful trial that he succeeds in being original and inventive . . .

Armed with these impulses, the weapons of competition as well as of co-operation, the young hero of the nursery begins his personal development, as a centre of considerate and purposeful action. The nucleus of personality, to the outsider, is the bodily self; it is a sort of social unit; but to the individual himself, the distinction between persons as minds and persons as mere bodily presences soon springs up and takes on greater and greater significance. For this is not an inborn distinction. The sense of self is not a ready-made and perfect gift; it is a slow growth, the stages of which show in a most interesting way the interaction of the individualistic and social factors.

It begins, probably, when the child notes the capricious and seemingly lawless actions of persons, in contrast with the more regular and mechanical actions of things, such as the swinging of the pendulum, the opening and closing of the door, the rolling of the ball upon the floor. Persons do the most unexpected, the most inconsistent things. And it is these things that attract attention and call out the impulse to imitate. The child imitates the acts of persons.

Thus he is admitted to the inside of the other's mind, as it were, and discovers that bodies are not, as minds are, centers of feeling, will, and knowledge. He makes very quickly the discovery that his own personality is likewise two-sided; that he, too, is a mind on the inside, and that that which others see of him on the outside is not the mind, but merely the physical person. He goes through a series of distinguishable processes of interpretation, all worked out in detail by the psychologist, which are of momentous significance for the evolution of personality.[1]

His reference here is to the steps of the "dialectic" as given in the opening quotation from his *Mental Development*[2] and as developed by him in terms of the growing sense of self. This process leads to the following outcome:

Other persons are thought of then in just the same terms as the private self; and the private self in the same terms as other persons; it is impossible to distinguish them, so far as the meaning in subjective terms is concerned. The thought of self is of a *larger self which includes personalities* in general; and the different persons, in all that which is not singular or characteristic of each, *are fundamentally the same.*[3]

The significance of this outcome for the study of social personality thus appears. Baldwin says:

It is impossible for anyone to begin life as an individualist in the sense of radically separating himself from his social fellows. The social bond is established and rooted in the very growth of self-consciousness. Each individual's apprehension of his own personal self and its interests involves the recognition of others and their interests; and his pursuit of one type of purposes, generous or selfish, is in so far the pursuit of the other also.[4]

For social psychology in general the significance of this outcome resides "in the fact," according to Baldwin, "that it shows the true basis of social relationships; they are rooted in the normal psychic processes of individual growth." He says by way of conclusion in this connection:

---

[1] *Ibid.*, pp. 18–24. Quotations from this work are reprinted by permission of Richard G. Badger, publisher.

[2] See *supra*, pp. 279–280; also *The Individual and Society*, pp. 24–26.

[3] *Ibid.*, pp. 25–26.

[4] *Ibid.*, pp. 26–27.

We may then consider as answered the question as to how the individual is able to be social. He does not have to consider the question at all, nor do we, for he is simply social by the same right that he is personal. He grows in personality and individuality by growing also in sociality. He does not have two lives, two sets of interests, two selves; one personal and the other social. He has but one self, which is personal and social in one, by right of the essential and normal movement of his growth.[1]

This conception of the relation between the individual and society, which finds expression in the common meeting ground of psychology and sociology in the social-psychological point of view, particularly as he defined it, Baldwin regarded as the most notable outcome of the development of modern social theory. He says in respect to this point:

It is to my mind, the most remarkable outcome of modern social theory—the recognition of the fact that the individual's normal growth lands him in essential solidarity with his fellows, while on the other hand the exercise of his social duties and privileges advances his highest and purest individuality. The movements are one, although the sciences, from their necessary difference in point of view, must treat them as if they were two."[2]

Baldwin's social-psychological theory as thus outlined, like Tarde's, with which it is most frequently associated in respect to its importance in extending the social-psychological viewpoint as well as in respect to its specific theory of socialization, has precipitated a great deal of comment and discussion. And this indirect popularization of the social-psychological viewpoint, as was the case with Tarde, has not been the least of Baldwin's contributions to the development of social psychology.[3] It should be noted in this connection, however, that Baldwin took serious objection to the practice of lumping his theory indiscriminately with Tarde's "without proper distinction." His position in the matter was that despite important points of agreement relating to their common emphasis upon imitation, the two theories are so far different that, according to him, "it is well-nigh impossible for any one to treat M. Tarde's views and my own together without seriously misrepresenting one writer or the other."[4]   "In spite of the large place which I assign to Imitation in the social life," he said, "I should prefer to have my theory known as the 'Self' or the 'Self-thought' theory of social organization."[5]

Whether Baldwin was entirely justified in this position or not, in conjunction with which he testified to "a more fundamental agreement" with the views of Josiah Royce and the idealistic trend of thought which

[1] *Ibid.*, pp. 27–28.
[2] *Ibid.*, p. 16.
[3] See his reply to some of these comments and criticism, *Social and Ethical Interpretations*, Prefaces to 1st, 2d, 3d ed., pp. 3–9, Appendix K.
[4] *Ibid.*, p. xviii.
[5] *Ibid.*, Preface to 1st ed., p. viii.

the latter represented in this country generally,[1] it did define an important point of emphasis in his theory which, largely by way of his work, has become central in American social-psychological thought. In any event, the "self" emphasis which he so prominently introduced runs through most of the social-psychological theory still to be considered in this part of our survey.

Like the direction of thought with which he identified his position, Baldwin's formulation of his theory was highly intellectualistic, and to that extent it was not altogether in harmony with the developing tendencies of American social-psychological thought as outlined in the foregoing chapter. In a general way, however, it brought these tendencies to a striking focus, so that his work became the real starting point for a distinctive social-psychological movement in American thought. It will be our purpose in following this movement through in its further development to bring it into relation with the background of American social-psychological thought as it has been traced out so far on the one hand and the modern social-psychological movement in its larger aspects on the other.[2]

II. CHARLES H. COOLEY (1864-1929)

The attempt at specific formulation of social-psychological theory which was definitely begun in this country by Baldwin was carried forward in very notable fashion by Cooley. This was more especially the case because Cooley approached the subject chiefly from the sociological rather than from the psychological standpoint, so that his work supplemented Baldwin's in quite a unique way, as will presently appear. In any event, Cooley's work represents the next step in the line of social-psychological advance which we have been tracing out here and can best be considered alongside of Baldwin's work at this point.

Ward's pioneer reinterpretation of the field of sociological thought in this country, it will be recalled,[3] was followed shortly by the early attempts to establish the subject academically, especially by Sumner, Giddings, and Small. Sociology thus began to come into view as an increasingly important factor in defining the background of American social-psychological thought. In particular, Ward's work was supported

---

[1] See *ibid.* pp. viii, 15, 521 and Appendices E and H; also *supra*, p. 280, note 1.

[2] For a further consideration of Baldwin's social psychology see BRETT, *A History of Psychology*, pp. 296–298; VILLA, *Contemporary Psychology*, pp. 48, 154, 171; WOODWORTH, *Dynamic Psychology*, pp. 182ff.; PARK and BURGESS, *An Introduction to the Science of Sociology*, pp. 41, 85, 423, etc.; DAVIS, *Psychological Interpretation of Society*, pp. 53–54; BRISTOL, *Social Adaptation*, pp. 192–199; BARNES, *Sociol. Rev.*, vol. 13, pp. 204–211, 1921; BOGARDUS, *A History of Social Thought*, pp. 368–388; ELLWOOD, *Sociology in Its Psychological Aspects*, Chap. XIII; GIDDINGS, *Studies in the Theory of Human Society*, pp. 161ff.; COOLEY, *Human Nature and the Social Order*, note, p. 125.

[3] *Supra*, p. 245.

in its social-psychological implications by such other early sociological works as Small and Vincent's *Introduction to the Study of Society* and Giddings' *Principles of Sociology*, both of which have already been referred to here in conjunction with our discussion of Ward. These works appeared respectively in 1894 and 1896, about the same time as Baldwin's two major works. It was in this early setting of American sociological thought that Cooley's first work, his *Human Nature and the Social Order*, took form, and it is this work which provides the basis of our discussion here.

Cooley did not identify this work with social psychology outright, as did Baldwin in the case of his *Social and Ethical Interpretations*, but it has become peculiarly identified with this field of thought, nevertheless, through its subject matter as well as through the general setting of Cooley's social theory as a whole. Formal identification seemed hardly necessary at the time, since social psychology had not yet differentiated itself from sociology in this country. At any rate, Cooley's work has seemingly been even clearer in its social-psychological influence than Baldwin's, for his exposition of social-psychological theory, besides being very much more readable than Baldwin's, is freed from confusing involvement with such questionable elements of Baldwin's presentation as his recapitulation doctrine and his distinctive view of imitation as a social-psychological process. Cooley's three works, his *Human Nature and the Social Order* (1902), *Social Organization* (1909), and *The Social Process* (1918), remain, in fact, one of the most compelling defenses and elaborations of the social-psychological point of view which have yet appeared in this country, certainly of that all-round point of view which has come to be so prominently associated here with Cooley's name.[1]

It is not surprising, therefore, that Cooley's contributions to social-psychological thought should be among the most generally recognized in this country and among the most frequently commented upon in various connections.[2] In so far as recent sociological literature in this country is concerned, more particularly, few writers are as frequently and as confidently quoted in reference to the social-psychological point of view. It will be especially to the point, therefore, to follow out the essen-

---

[1] *Cf.* BOGARDUS, *Essentials of Social Psychology*, p. 24; *A History of Social Thought*, p. 389; also BODENHAFER, *Amer. Jour. Sociol.*, vol. 26, pp. 498–499, 1921; PARK and BURGESS, *Introduction to the Science of Sociology*, p. 67; BARNES, *Sociol. Rev.*, vol. 14, pp. 194–195, 1922.

[2] See in this connection, Bodenhafer's survey of Cooley's thought, *Amer. Jour. Sociol.*, vol. 26, pp. 454*ff.*, 1921; also BARNES, *Sociol. Rev.*, vol. 14, pp. 194–205, 1922; PARK and BURGESS, *Introduction to the Science of Sociology*, pp. 56, 67, 70, etc.; BOGARDUS, *Essentials of Social Psychology*, pp. 23–24; *A History of Social Thought*, pp. 389–395; ALLPORT, *Social Psychology*, p. 325; DAVIS, *Psychological Interpretations of Society*, pp. 59–60; ELLWOOD, *Introduction to Social Psychology*, pp. 51*ff.*, 118, 131, etc.

tial setting of Cooley's thought here and to bring it into relation with the general trend of social-psychological development as it has been traced out so far.

Cooley's social-psychological theory, like Baldwin's, is basically grounded in the observed facts of child development as they presented themselves from the standpoint of the broadened conception of the evolutionary process which had established itself in this country at the time.[1] But it was Cooley's expressed aim to bring these facts into closer relationship with the world of social forms and processes from the sociological standpoint than he felt had been done by previous writers.[2]

Acknowledging freely the influence of Baldwin and James in this connection,[3] Cooley started out in this undertaking with the central thesis of the inseparability of the individual and the social in human life. This basic thesis is reiterated over and over in various connections in the course of the three volumes mentioned above, but perhaps nowhere does it appear more clearly stated in its all-round bearing than in *The Social Process*, where Cooley relates it to the "organic view" of the world of human facts and relations, of which he became one of the most prominent exponents in American thought. He there says:

We see around us in the world of men an onward movement of life. There seems to be a vital impulse of unknown origin, that tends to work ahead in innumerable directions and manners, each continuous with something of the same sort in the past. The whole thing appears to be a kind of growth, and we might add that it is an *adaptive* growth, meaning by this that the forms of life we see— men, associations of men, traditions, institutions, conventions, theories, ideals— are not separate or independent, but that the growth of each takes place in contact and interaction with that of others. Thus any one phase of the movement may be regarded as a series of adaptations to other phases.[4]

Following out this train of thought further, he continues:

That the growth of persons is adaptive is apparent to everyone. Each of us has energy and character, but not for an hour do these develop except by communication and adjustment with the persons and conditions about us. And the case is not different with a social group, or with the ideas which live in the common medium of communicative thought. Human life is thus all a growing whole, unified, by ceaseless currents of interaction, but at the same time differ-

[1] Like Baldwin, Cooley sought to lead out in his theory from observations of child growth and development, both his own and those reported by other investigators (see, for instance, *Human Nature and the Social Order*, 2d ed., pp. 56*ff.*, 81*ff.*, 97*ff.*, 189*ff.*, etc.; *supra*, p. 273).

[2] See *Human Nature and the Social Order*, Preface to 2d. ed.

[3] See *ibid.*, note p. 90 (this and the following references to this work, except where otherwise indicated, are to the first edition).

[4] *The Social Process*, p. 3. Quotations from this work are reprinted by permission of Charles Scribner's Sons, publishers.

entiated into those diverse forms of energy which we see as men, factions, tendencies, doctrines, and institutions.[1]

Such, according to Cooley, are the concrete results of the process of adaptive growth in the world of human relations. All the varied complexities of human life and thought are organized by it into a unified and interdependent whole, in which everything is part of everything else in the sense of the all-embracing conception of interrelation made familiar by modern evolutionary thought, as applied to the realm of psychic and social fact.[2]

This is the significance that the terms "organic," "organization," and "organism" have when referring to the realm of psycho-social interpretation, according to Cooley. These terms are applicable, he explains, "in the sense that influences may be and are transmitted from one part to any other part so that all parts are bound together into an interdependent whole."[3] He says:

If then we say that society is an organism, we mean, I suppose, that it is a complex of forms or processes each of which is living and growing by interaction with the others, the whole being so unified that what takes place in one part affects all the rest. It is a vast tissue of reciprocal activity, differentiated into innumerable systems, some of them quite distinct, others not readily traceable, and all interwoven to such a degree that you see different systems according to the point of view you take.[4]

This general view, from the standpoint of which Cooley approaches all the special problems of his concern, is to be placed in this broad setting of evolutionary thought. It is the aim of this view, says Cooley in familiar terms, "to 'see life whole,' or at least as largely as our limitations permit."[5] It is thus opposed, he points out, to the various "particularistic" explanations of human behavior, whether they be religious, political, economic, or whatever.[6] Such, for example, according to Cooley, are the theories that regard "the personal wills of individual men, supplemented, perhaps, by the similar will of a personal God, as the originative factor in life from which all else comes"; or, again, by contrast, the theories "which find the originative impulse in external conditions of life, such as climate, soil, flora, and fauna, and regard intellectual and social activities merely as the result of the physiological needs of men seeking gratification under these conditions." A well-known example of

[1] *Ibid.*, pp. 3–4.
[2] *Ibid.*, pp. 8*ff.*, 19*ff.*
[3] *Ibid.*, p. 26.
[4] *Ibid.*, p. 28.
[5] *Ibid.*, p. 48.
[6] *Ibid.*, pp. 43 *ff.*

this type of theory having rather wide acceptance, Cooley calls to mind, is "economic determinism."[1] He says:

The fallacy of all such ideas lies in supposing that life is built up from some one point, instead of being an organic whole which is developing as a whole now and, so far as we know, always has done so in the past. Nothing is fixed or independent, everything is plastic and takes influence as well as gives it. No factor of life can exist for men except as it is merged in the organic system and becomes an effect as much as a cause of the total development. If you insist that there is a center from which the influence comes, all flowing in one direction, you fly in the face of fact. What observation shows is a universal interaction, in which no factor appears antecedent to the rest.[2]

The individual is a very real and active thing, but so is the group or general tendency; it is true that you can see life from the standpoint of imitation (several writers have centered upon this) but so you can from the standpoint of competition or organization. The economic process is as vital as anything can be, and there is nothing in life that does not change when it changes; but the same is true of the ideal processes; geography is important, but not more so than the technical institutions through which we react upon it; and so on.[3]

There is no beginning; we know nothing about beginnings; there is always continuity with the past, and not with any one element only of the past, but with the whole interacting organism of men.[4]

Applied to the consideration of the special problems of Cooley's concern in his above-mentioned three works, this general point of view translates itself into a more or less definite conception of procedure which Cooley outlines at some length at the outset of his *Human Nature*.

The subject of that work, he explains, is really the subject of its first chapter, "Society and the Individual." "It is my general aim," he says, "to set forth, from various points of view, what the individual is, considered as a member of a social whole"; while the special purpose of the opening chapter is "to offer a preliminary statement of the matter, as I conceive it, afterward to be unfolded at some length and variously illustrated."[5] This, in its respective aspects, it may be added, is likewise the subject of Cooley's later two volumes which are to be regarded, in accordance with his outlook as outlined above, as merely a continuation of the discussion from the new "points of light" of *organization* and *process* instead of *human nature*.[6] It is thus the more important to follow through Cooley's formulation of his viewpoint in his earlier work.

[1] *Ibid.*, pp. 43–44.
[2] *Ibid.*, pp. 44–45.
[3] *Ibid.*, p. 51.
[4] *Ibid.*, p. 46.
[5] *Human Nature and the Social Order*, p. 1 (see *supra*, note 3, p. 293).
[6] See Preface to his *Social Organization*, also p. 57. It is significant that Cooley's *Social Organization* carries the subtitle "A Study of the Larger Mind."

In explanation of his above-stated purpose, as epitomized by the title of his first work and especially by the subject of its first chapter, Cooley goes on to say:

A separate individual is an abstraction unknown to experience, and so likewise is society when regarded as something apart from individuals. The real thing is Human Life, which may be considered either in an individual aspect or in a social, that is to say a general, aspect; but is always, as a matter of fact, both individual and general. In other words, "society" and "individuals" do not denote separable phenomena, but are simply collective and distributive aspects of the same thing, the relation between them being like that between other expressions one of which denotes a group as a whole and the other the members of the group, such as the army and the soldiers, the class and the student, and so on. This holds true of any social aggregate, great or small; of a family, a city, a nation, a race, of mankind as a whole: no matter how extensive, complex, or enduring a group may be, no good reason can be given for regarding it as essentially different in this respect from the smallest, simplest, or most transient.[1]

So far, then, as there is any difference between the two, it is rather in our point of view than in the object we are looking at: when we speak of society, or use any other collective term, we fix our minds upon some general view of the people concerned, while when we speak of individuals we disregard the general aspect and think of them as if they were separate. Thus "the Cabinet" may consist of President Lincoln, Secretary Stanton, Secretary Seward, and so on; but when I say "the Cabinet" I do not suggest the same idea as when I enumerate these gentlemen separately. Society, or any complex group, may, to ordinary observation, be a very different thing from all of its members, viewed one by one—as a man who beheld General Grant's army from Mississippi Ridge would have seen something other than he would by approaching every soldier in it. In the same way a picture is made up of so many square inches of painted canvas; but if you should look at these one at a time, covering the others, until you had seen them all, you would still not have seen the picture. There may, in all such cases, be a system or organization in the whole that is not apparent in the parts. In this sense, and in no other, is there a difference between society and the individuals of which it is composed; a difference not residing in the facts themselves but existing to the observer on account of the limits of his perception. A *complete* view of society would also be a complete view of all the individuals, and *vice versa;* there would be no difference between them.[2]

Summarizing this introductory statement, Cooley says:

And just as there is no society or group that is not a collective view of persons, so there is no individual who may not be regarded as a particular view of social groups. He has no separate existence; through both the hereditary and the social factors in his life a man is bound into the whole of which he is a member,

[1] *Human Nature and the Social Order*, pp. 1–2. Quotations from this work are reprinted by permission of Charles Scribner's Sons, publishers.
[2] *Ibid.*, pp. 2–3.

and to consider him apart from it is quite as artificial as to consider society apart from individuals.[1]

If this be a true statement of the situation, obviously, then, Cooley goes on to point out as had Baldwin, there is a fallacy "in that not uncommon manner of speaking which sets the social and the individual over against each other as separate and antagonistic." All the well-known expressions which are associated in common usage with this type of antithesis, as individualism and socialism, particularism and collectivism, free will and determinism, egoism and altruism, and their various derivatives, are, according to him, based on the same thoroughgoing misconception of relation between the individual and the social in human life.[2] He observes:

I do not see that life presents two distinct and opposing tendencies that can properly be called individualism and socialism, any more than that there are two distinct and opposing entities, society and the individual, to embody these tendencies. The phenomena usually called individualistic are always socialistic in the sense that they are expressive of tendencies growing out of the general life, and, contrariwise, the so-called socialistic phenomena have always an obvious individual aspect.[3]

These and similar expressions, declares Cooley, may be used conveniently enough in common speech, but whether they are suitable for purposes of careful study and description appears very doubtful. If used at all, according to him, they ought to receive more adequate definition than they have at present, for there is always "some confusion of terms in speaking of opposition between an individual and society in general, even when the writer's meaning is obvious enough." It would be more accurate and less objectionable to say, he points out, "either that one individual is opposing many, or that one part of society is opposing other parts," in order to "avoid confusing the two aspects of life in the same expression."[4] He suggests in this connection:

When Emerson says that society is in a conspiracy against the independence of each of its members, we are to understand that any peculiar tendency represented by one person finds itself more or less at variance with the general current of tendencies organized in other persons. It is no more individual, nor any less social, in a large sense, than other tendencies represented by more persons. A thousand persons are just as truly individual as one, and the man who seems to stand alone draws his being from the general stream of life just as truly and inevitably as if he were one of a thousand. Innovation is just as social as conformity, genius as mediocrity. These distinctions are not between what is

[1] *Ibid.*, p. 3.
[2] *Ibid.*, pp. 4 *ff.*
[3] *Ibid.*, p. 5.
[4] *Ibid.*, pp. 5–6.

individual and what is social, but between what is usual or established and what is exceptional or novel.   In other words, wherever you find life as society there you will find life as individuality, and *vice versa*.[1]

Accordingly, he says in conclusion on this point:

I think, then, that the antithesis, society *versus* the individual, is false and hollow whenever used as a general or philosophical statement of human relations. Whatever idea may be in the minds of those who set these words and their derivatives over against each other, the notion conveyed is that of two separable entities or forces; and certainly such a notion is untrue to fact.[2]

Cooley was keenly aware that this view was opposed to deeply ingrained habits of thought which are reflected in well-established views and theories of conduct.   Thus, he points out:

Most people not only think of individuals and society as more or less separate and antithetical, but they look upon the former as antecedent to the latter. That persons make society would be generally admitted as a matter of course; but that society makes persons would strike many as a startling notion, though I know of no good reason for looking upon the distributive aspect of life as more primary or causative than the collective aspect.   The reason for the common impression appears to be that we think most naturally and easily of the individual phase of life, simply because it is a tangible one, the phase under which men appear to the senses, while the actuality of groups, of nations, of mankind at large, is realized only by the active and instructed imagination.   We ordinarily regard society, so far as we conceive it at all, in a vaguely material aspect, as an aggregate of physical bodies, not as the vital whole which it is; and so, of course, we do not see that it may be as original or causative as anything else.   Indeed many look upon "society" and other general terms as somewhat mystical, and are inclined to doubt whether there is any reality back of them.[3]

Since "this naïve individualism of thought" which, according to Cooley, "does not truly see the individual any more than it does society" is reinforced "by traditions in which all of us are brought up" and is thereby very hard to shake off, he feels it is necessary to point out more definitely "some of the prevalent ways of conceiving life which are permeated by it, and which anyone who agrees with what has just been said may regard as fallacious."[4]

He thus discusses, from the standpoint outlined, what he terms *mere individualism* in which, according to him, "the distributive aspect is almost exclusively regarded, collective phases being looked upon as quite secondary and incidental"; *double causation* or the "partition of power between society and the individual, thought of as separate causes";

[1] *Ibid.*, p. 6.
[2] *Ibid.*, p. 7.
[3] *Ibid.*, pp. 7–8.
[4] *Ibid.*, p. 8.

primitive individualism or the view "that sociality follows individuality
in time, as a later and additional product of development"; and, finally,
the *social faculty view*, by which he means to designate the tendency to
regard "the social as including only a part, often a rather definite part,
of the individual." Human nature, he explains, is divided "into individualistic or non-social tendencies or faculties, and those that are social."
Thus, he points out, certain emotions, such as love, are regarded as
social, while others, such as fear or anger, are regarded as unsocial or
individualistic; or again intelligence is treated as an individualistic
faculty, sociality being attributed to some sort of emotion or sentiment.[1]
By way of contrast, he says:

> Of course the view which I regard as sound, is that individuality is neither
> prior in time nor lower in moral rank than sociality; but that the two have
> always existed side by side as complementary aspects of the same thing, and that
> the line of progress is from a lower to a higher type of both, not from the one to
> the other. If the word social is applied only to the higher forms of mental life it
> should, as already suggested, be opposed not to individual, but to animal, sensual,
> or some other word implying mental or moral inferiority. If we go back to a
> time when the state of our remote ancestors was such that we are not willing to
> call it social, then it must have been equally undeserving to be described as
> individual or personal; that is to say, they must have been just as inferior to us
> when viewed separately as when viewed collectively. To question this is to
> question the vital unity of human life.[2]
>
> At any rate the opinion I hold, and expect to explain more fully . . . is
> that man's psychical outfit is not divisible into the social and the non-social; but
> that he is all social in a large sense, is all a part of the common life, and that his
> social or moral progress consists less in the aggrandizement of particular faculties
> or instincts and the suppression of others, than in the discipline of all with refer-
> ence to a progressive organization of life which we know in thought as conscience.[3]

From his position as thus elaborated, Cooley leads out, much as
Baldwin did, to a reconsideration of such topics as appeared to him to be
especially relevant to his subject matter or to require restatement from
the new point of view. We thus get a discussion and restatement of such
topics of interest as suggestion and choice, sociability, sympathy, the
social self, hostility, emulation, leadership, conscience, freedom, etc. In
his two later volumes, Cooley continued this treatment of relevant
subject matter but, as already suggested, with a central emphasis on
organization and *process*. All in all, he brought his point of view to bear
on a wide range of important material with a cumulative effect that is the
more striking because it seems to flow so naturally from his rather
informal procedure. Cooley's most familiar contributions to modern

[1] *Ibid.*, pp. 8–12.
[2] *Ibid.*, pp. 10–11.
[3] *Ibid.*, p. 12.

thought were made in the treatment of some of these special topics, for example, his discussion of the social self and more especially that part of the social self which he suggestively termed "the looking-glass self" in his *Human Nature;* his classic treatment of primary group life and ideals in his *Social Organization;* his analysis of valuation[1] in his *Social Process.* The following passages from his important discussion of primary group life will suffice to illustrate his characteristic mode of procedure in the treatment of these special topics:

By primary groups I mean those characterized by intimate face-to-face association and cooperation. They are primary in several senses, but chiefly in that they are fundamental in forming the social nature and ideals of the individual. The result of intimate association, psychologically, is a certain fusion of individualities in a common whole, so that one's very self, for many purposes at least, is the common life and purpose of the group. Perhaps the simplest way of describing this wholeness is by saying that it is a "we"; it involves the sort of sympathy and mutual identification for which "we" is the natural expression. One lives in the feeling of the whole and finds the chief aims of his will in that feeling.[2]

The most important spheres of this intimate association and cooperation—though by no means the only ones—are the family, the play-group of children, and the neighborhood or community group of elders. These are practically universal, belonging to all times and all stages of development; and are accordingly a chief basis of what is universal in human nature and human ideals.[3]

Besides these almost universal kinds of primary association, there are many others whose form depends upon the particular state of civilization; the only essential thing, as I have said, being a certain intimacy and fusion of personalities. In our own society, being little bound by place, people easily form clubs, fraternal societies and the like, based on congeniality, which may give rise to real intimacy. Many such relations are formed at school and college, and among men and women brought together in the first instance by their occupations—as workmen in the same trade, or the like. Where there is a little common interest and activity, kindness grows like weeds by the roadside.

But the fact that the family and neighborhood groups are ascendant in the open and plastic time of childhood makes them even now incomparably more influential than all the rest.[4]

These groups, then, are springs of life, not only for the individual but for social institutions. They are only in part moulded by special traditions, and, in

---

[1] Here Cooley made a notable attempt to carry his point of view over into a highly individualistic phase of economic doctrine. For a discussion of this part of his theory see ANDERSON, *Social Value;* BODENHAFER, *Amer. Jour. Soc.*, vol. 26, pp. 461–463, 598, 726 *ff.*, 1921; PARK and BURGESS, *Introduction to the Science of Sociology*, pp. 708–712.

[2] *Social Organization*, p. 23. Quotations from this work are reprinted by permission of Charles Scribner's Sons, publishers.

[3] *Ibid.*, p. 24.

[4] *Ibid.*, p. 26.

larger degree express a universal nature. The religion or government of other civilizations may seem alien to us, but the children or the family group wear the common life, and with them we can always make ourselves at home.[1]

To return to primary groups: the view here maintained is that human nature is not something existing separately in the individual, but a *group nature or primary phase of society*, a relatively simple and general condition of the social mind. It is something more, on the one hand, than the mere instinct that is born in us—though that enters into it—and something less, on the other, than the more elaborate development of ideas and sentiments that makes up institutions. It is the nature which is developed and expressed in those simple, face-to-face groups that are somewhat alike in all societies; groups of the family, the playground, and the neighborhood. In the essential similarity of these is to be found the basis, in experience, for similar ideas and sentiments in the human mind. In these, everywhere, human nature comes into existence. Man does not have it at birth; he cannot acquire it except through fellowship, and it decays in isolation.

If this view does not recommend itself to common-sense I do not know that elaboration will be of much avail. It simply means the application at this point of the idea that society and individuals are inseparable phases of a common whole, so that wherever we find an individual fact we may look for a social fact to go with it. If there is a universal nature in persons there must be something universal in association to correspond to it.[2]

Here [that is, in the discussion of primary group life] as everywhere in the study of society we must learn to see mankind in psychical wholes, rather than in artificial separation. We must see and feel the communal life of family and local groups as immediate facts, not as combinations of something else. And perhaps we shall do this best by recalling our own experience and extending it through sympathetic observation. What, in our life, is the family and the fellowship; what do we know of the we-feeling? Thought of this kind may help us to get a concrete perception of that primary group-nature of which everything social is the outgrowth.[3]

The composite conception of human nature and social life which Cooley thus by stages develops, like the composite picture of the Gothic cathedral which, by analogy, we should get, according to him, were we to view it as a work of organic art ("from many points, and at our leisure, now the front and now the apse, now taking in the whole from a distance, now lingering near at hand over the details, living with it, if we can for months, until gradually there arises a conception of it which is confined to no one aspect, but is, so far as the limits of our mind permit, the image of the whole in all its unity and richness"[4]) contains the following essential and frequently repeated elements:

[1] *Ibid.*, pp. 27–28.
[2] *Ibid.*, pp. 29–30.
[3] *Ibid.*, p. 31.
[4] *The Social Process*, p. 49.

The individual and the social are reciprocal and inseparable aspects of human reality.[1] They are interrelated each with each in those fundamental processes of interaction and communication in which alone they come to expression and development, so that at no time can they in a concrete sense be set over against each other.[2] In this connection, the face-to-face social groups in which contact is of the most intimate character—the family, the play group, the neighborhood, etc.—are of the utmost importance. They are to be regarded as "the nursery" of human nature and social life, and in this sense "primary" as over against the more impersonal or derived groupings in which contact is likely to be much more casual and superficial.[3] Here are developed the primary virtues and ideals—love, freedom, justice, loyalty, sympathy, service, kindness, truth, lawfulness, etc.—which constitute the chief basis of all that is universal in "human" nature and enduring in our common life together.[4] Upon the effective organization of these basic human qualities on the ever widening scale made possible by the improved means of communication in modern life depends that extension and enlargement of the moral order which, according to Cooley, "is the great historical task of mankind."[5] The increasing magnitude of this task has been part of the growing complexity of social life, a fact which explains, in Cooley's opinion, the many shortcomings of its accomplishment. Especially during the nineteenth century have the possibilities of communication, due to the rapid advance of mechanical invention and the "*enlargement* and *animation*" of life which followed, enabled social contact to run clear beyond the ability of social organization to keep the pace.[6] The inevitable result has been that partial breakdown of effective social control which has left our modern life, with its humanizing and democratizing tendencies on the one hand and its superficiality and strain on the other, socially uncoordinated at its points of greatest stress.[7]

Such, in barest outline, are some of the important observations around which Cooley developed his theory and which, added to his lucid conversational style and the stimulating moral quality of his thought, have made his works among the most popular and influential in American social science literature.

But despite this, and despite the wholesome closeness to the concrete facts of social life which Cooley's observations bespeak and which leave the impression, as one writer has said, that "even the casual reader could

---

[1] *Human Nature and the Social Order*, pp. 1*ff*
[2] *Social Organization*, Chap. VI; *The Social Process*, pp. 3*ff*.
[3] *Social Organization*, Chap. III.
[4] *Ibid.*, Chap. IV.
[5] *Ibid.*, Chap. V.
[6] *Ibid.*, Chap. VIII.
[7] *Ibid.*, Chap. X.

hardly run over one of his pages selected at random without a sense of being in somewhat novel contact with life as it is,"[1] perhaps because of these high qualities, it is inescapable that his theorizing is, even more strikingly than that of most writers in his field of interest, essentially of the nature of what Cooley himself more recently termed "arm-chair philosophy."[2] His work is broadly critical and analytical, not narrowly specialized and scientific. He appeals quite as much to general literature for support and illustration of his position as to scientific fact and principle, and his whole procedure is rather directed toward the formulation and illustration of an illuminating point of view than toward the development of a program of scientific investigation.[3] But the latter stage of social-psychological development is in any event only just beginning to come seriously into view; and meanwhile Cooley's work stands out in this country as one of the high-spots in the preliminary formulation of social-psychological theory.

In the second edition of his *Human Nature* (1922), Cooley added a chapter on "Heredity and Instinct" with the object in view of bringing his theory into relation with recent social-psychological discussion, which has centered so conspicuously about these topics. And since he thus brings his point of view into clear contrast with opposing views, some of which are at the present time very widely held, especially as practical expedients in the treatment of personality, it is worth while, in summary, to follow out his brief restatement of his position in this connection. He says in part:

When our individual life begins the two elements of history from which it is drawn, the hereditary and the social, merge in the new whole and cease to exist as separable forces. Nothing that the individual is or does can be ascribed to either alone, because everything is based on habits and experiences in which the

---

[1] SMALL, review of *The Social Process, Amer. Jour. Soc.*, vol. 24, p. 315, 1918–1919.

[2] Address at meetings of The American Sociological Society, 1923, and published *Jour. Appl. Sociol.*, vol. 8, pp. 259–262, 1924.

[3] Cooley himself realized during the recent period of intensified interest in research technique in the field of psycho-social investigation, that his work lacked in respect to its total unconcern with methodology, and in the last few years he set about heroically to translate his point of view into a definitely formulated research approach. Unfortunately, this part of his work was interrupted before it could lead to very clear-cut results. But with his usual suggestiveness, Cooley set a whole group of students to thinking about the implications of established research methods in the field of psycho-social investigation, so that even in this respect, his point of view may have very far-reaching consequences (see in this connection COOLEY, "The Roots of Social Knowledge," *Amer. Jour. Sociol.*, vol. 32, pp. 59–80, 1926; "Case Study of Small Institutions as a Method of Research," *Pub. Amer. Sociol. Soc.*, vol. 22, pp. 133–143, 1928; "The Life-study Method as Applied to Rural Social Research," *ibid.*, vol. 23, pp. 249–254, 1929; also BURGESS, "Statistics and Case Studies," *Sociol. and Soc. Res.*, vol. 12, pp. 103–121, 1927–1928; THOMAS, "The Behavior Pattern and the Situation," *Pub. Amer. Sociol. Soc.*, vol. 22, pp. 1–13, 1928).

two are inextricably mingled. Heredity and environment, as applied to the present life of a human being, are, in fact, abstractions; the real thing is a total organic process not separable into parts. What heredity is, in its practical working at a given time, depends upon the process itself, which develops some potentialities and represses others. And in like manner the effective environment depends upon the selective and assimilating activities of the growing organism. If you wish to understand it, the main thing to do is to study its life-history back to its beginning in the conception and birth of the individual; beyond that you may, if you wish, pursue still farther the germ-plasm and the social inheritance from which it sprang. These give us a background, like the accounts of a man's ancestry and early surroundings in the first chapters of his autobiography. But the life of William Sykes is a thing you must study directly, and no knowledge of heredity and environment can be more than a help to this.[1]

Any socially active human impulse may be appealed to, according to Cooley, to illustrate this "inextricable union of the animal and social heritages." Speech, for instance, serves as a good example, and he says in respect to it:

It springs in part from the native structure of the vocal organs and from a hereditary impulse to use them which we see at work in the chattering of idiots and of the deaf and dumb. A natural sensibility to other persons and need to communicate with them also enters into it. But all articulate utterance comes by communication; it is learned from others, varies with the environment and has its source in tradition. Speech is thus a socio-biologic function. And so it is with ambition and all our socially active impulses. We are born with the need to assert ourselves, but whether we do so as hunters, warriors, fishermen, traders, politicians, or scholars, depends upon the opportunities offered us in the social process.[2]

Heredity and social environment can thus be regarded normally, only as complementary, "each having its own work to do and neither of any use without the other." Which is stronger? Which is more important? As referring to general theory, these are, he declares, "silly questions, the asking of which is sufficient proof that the asker has no clear idea of the matter in hand." It is precisely, he explains, "as if one should ask, Which is the more important member of the family, the father or the mother?" In each case, according to him, the answer may be said to be that both are "infinitely important, since each is

---

[1] Introduction to *Human Nature and the Social Order*, 2d ed., p. 15. It is an old fallacy but one constantly recurring, according to Cooley, which proceeds on the theory that we can in some way measure the hereditary factor in the human mind apart from the social or acquired factor, as is assumed, for example, in some cases of intelligence testing. Since the growth of the mind "is altogether a social process," says he, "it is unreasonable to suppose that the outcome can be in any way independent of that process" (note, pp. 15–16).

[2] *Ibid.*, p. 16.

indispensable; and their functions being different in kind cannot be compared in amount."[1]

There is in this respect, he points out, a notable difference between man and the other animals in terms of teachability and plasticity which is of the utmost importance for the understanding of human behavior. He says:

Although the transmission of heredity through the germ-plasm is much the same in man as in the other animals, there is a notable difference in the kind of traits that are transmitted, and are found to exist at birth. This difference is in teachability or plasticity. The mental outfit of the human child is above all things teachable, and therefore, of course, indefinite, consisting not of tendencies to do particular things that life calls for, but of vague aptitudes or lines of teachability that are of no practical use until they are educated. The mental outfit of the animal, on the other hand, is relatively definite and fixed, giving rise to activities which are useful with little or no teaching.

This difference is fundamental to any understanding of the relation of man to the evolutionary process, or of the relation of human nature and human life to animal nature and animal life. We need to see it with all possible clearness and to follow out its implications.[2]

The situation may be suggestively outlined, according to him, in terms of the following analogy:

Roughly speaking, then, the heredity of the other animals is a mechanism like that of a hand-organ; it is made to play a few tunes; you can play these tunes at once, with little or no training; and you can never play any others. The heredity of man, on the other hand, is a mechanism more like that of a piano: it is not made to play particular tunes; you can do nothing at all on it without training; but a trained player can draw from it an infinite variety of music.[2]

The implications of this difference in heredity are most far-reaching, even recognizing that there is no sharp line of division here, as indeed there never is in the world of nature viewed as a whole, according to him. He explains:

I see a flycatcher sitting on a dead branch, where there are no leaves to interrupt his view. Presently he darts toward a passing insect, hovers over him a few seconds, catches him, or fails to do so, and returns to his perch. That is his way of getting a living: he has done it all his life and will go on doing it to the end. Millions of other flycatchers on millions of other dead branches are doing precisely the same. And this has been the life of the species for unknown thousands of years. They have, through the germ-plasm, a definite capacity for this— the keen eye, the swift, fluttering movement to follow the insect, the quick, sure

[1] *Ibid.*, pp. 16–17.
[2] *Ibid.*, p. 19.

action of the neck and bill to seize him—all effective with no instruction and very little practice.

Man [too] has a natural hunger, like the flycatcher, and a natural mechanism of tasting, chewing, swallowing, and digestion; but his way of getting the food varies widely at different times of his life, is not the same with different individuals, and often changes completely from one generation to another. The great majority of us gain our food, after we have left the parental nest, through what we call a job, and a job is any activity whatever that a complex and shifting society esteems sufficiently to pay us for. It is very likely, nowadays, to last only part of our lives and to be something our ancestors never heard of. Thus [says Cooley] whatever is most distinctively human, our adaptability, our power of growth, our arts and sciences, our social institutions and progress, is bound up with the indeterminate character of human heredity.[1]

As regards the seemingly very important question of the place of the instinctive factor in human behavior, Cooley accordingly has the following to say:

Although instinctive emotion probably enters into everything we do, it enters in such a way that we can rarely or never explain human behavior by it alone. In human life it is not, in any considerable degree, a motive to specific behavior at all, but an impulse whose definite expression depends upon education and social situations. It does not act except through a complex, socially determined organism of thought and sentiment.

If, for example, we say "War is due to an instinct of pugnacity," we say something that includes so little of the truth and ignores so much that it is practically false. War is rooted in many instinctive tendencies, all of which have been transformed by education, tradition, and organization, so that to study its sources is to study the whole process of society. This calls, above all things, for detailed historical and sociological analysis: there could hardly be anything more inimical to real knowledge or rational conduct regarding it than to ascribe it to pugnacity and let the question go at that.[2]

Much the same, he suggests, may be said "of the employment of a supposed gregarious instinct, or 'instinct of the herd,' to explain a multiplicity of phenomena, including mob-excitement, dread of isolation, conformity to fads and fashions, subservience to leaders and control by propaganda; which require, like war, a detailed study of social antecedents." "This is," he approvingly quotes a contemporary writer, "'an easy, dogmatic way of explaining phenomena whose causes and effects are far more complicated than these authors would admit.'" Questioning the evidence in favor of the existence of a gregarious instinct altogether, he says: "It seems to me to be the postulate of an individualistic psychology in search of some special motive to explain collective behavior. If you regard human nature as primarily social you need no such special motive."[3]

[1] *Ibid.*, pp. 21–22.
[2] *Ibid.*, pp. 27–28.
[3] *Ibid.*, p. 28.

All such attempts on the part of certain psychologists, psychoanalysts, biologists, economists, writers on education, etc., to "short-circuit" the current of human causation in terms of instinct Cooley regards as but another instance of that common fallacy of "particularism" against which his "organic view" is a protest.[1] It is important to recall in this connection, according to him, that human history, in distinction from animal history, is a natural outcome of those traits of human psychology which distinguish man from the animal world and one group of men from the other. More concretely, he says:

The hereditary basis, the instinctive but teachable capacities, are relatively constant, and, so far as these are concerned, there is little or no reason to think that the Teutonic stocks from which most of us are sprung are appreciably different now from what they were when Caesar met and fought and described them. If we could substitute a thousand babies from that time for those in our own cradles, it would probably make no perceptible difference. They would grow up in our ways, driving automobiles instead of war chariots, reading the newspapers, and, in general, playing the human game as it is played today quite like the rest of us.[2]

If we would understand the complexities of social life which human history discloses, then, we must turn to the study of the complex human conditions and processes which produce them. The study of heredity and instinct in themselves cannot take us very far.

Perhaps the commonest fallacy which we meet with in discussions of human behavior from the one-sided standpoint of heredity and instinct, suggests Cooley in conclusion, "is that which assumes that human nature does not change, points out respects in which it has worked deplorably, and concludes that it will always work so. An unchanging human nature, it is said, has given us wars and economic greed; it always will."[3] Much depends, of course, he points out in this connection, on the sense in which such an indefinite term as "human nature" is used, but if it is used substantially in the sense of his own usage, as referring to the nature which man develops in the intimate contacts of primary group life, human nature must, according to him, be understood to be decidedly changeable. "It is a nature," he says, "whose primary trait is teachability, and so does not need to change in order to be an inexhaustible source of changing conduct and institutions. We can make it work," from his standpoint, "in almost any way, if we understand it, as a clever mechanic can mould to his will the universal laws of mass and motion."[4]

[1] *Ibid.*, p. 29.
[2] *Ibid.*, p. 31.
[3] *Ibid.*, p. 33.
[4] *Ibid.*, p. 34.

CHAPTER VII

THE EMERGENCE OF A DIFFERENTIATED SOCIAL PSYCHOLOGY

I. Edward A. Ross (1866)

It was inevitable that Ward's social theory, once his influence began to establish itself, should produce more definite social-psychological results than have so far been reflected in this part of our survey. Ward's popularization of Comtean thought in particular had possibilities in this direction which could not long be overlooked. For aside from the social-psychological suggestiveness of Comtean thought itself, this popularization served but as an introduction to French psycho-social thought following Comte, which, as we have seen, was certainly among the most potent influences in the modern social-psychological movement. Besides, French psycho-social thought, especially Tarde's theory, was beginning increasingly to affect the situation in this country directly. A translation of Tarde's *Les lois sociales* (1898) appeared in this country the year following its publication in French with a preface by J. Mark Baldwin. In 1903 there also appeared a translation of his *Les lois de l'imitation* (1890) with a notable introduction by Franklin H. Giddings. It is hardly surprising, therefore, that some of the early American followers of Ward should have turned to French thought appreciatively and with the expectation that the synthesis of French and American psycho-social theory which Ward so fruitfully began could be carried on in important new directions.

Among these, the most prominent from the standpoint of social psychology was E. A. Ross, whose name is important in the history of modern social-psychological thought in several connections but chiefly, perhaps, because he was the author of one of the two first treatises which were identified outright in their titles as "social psychology." His *Social Psychology* (1908), as has already been noted, appeared about the same time as McDougall's *Introduction to Social Psychology* (1908), and together these two works did much to popularize the conception of social psychology as a unified field of endeavor, distinct from general psychology on the one hand and general sociology on the other.

Ross presented his *Social Psychology* as "the pioneer treatise, in any language, professing to deal systematically with the subject of social psychology."[1] He however made ready acknowledgement of indebted-

[1] *Social Psychology*, Preface, p. vii.

ness to Tarde in particular, as his predecessor in the line of thought which he sought to develop, but also by citation, comment, and restatement to many other writers, among them Le Bon, Cooley, Baldwin, Bagehot, and a considerable number of contemporary writers on the psychology of suggestion. Ross accordingly looked upon his work as a venture into unexplored territory chiefly from the standpoint of the conception and organization of his material as "social psychology" rather than from the standpoint of the essential novelty of his theory as such. And in this view, he was certainly for the most part justified, previous treatments of the subject matter having generally been looked upon merely as extensions of one or another of the related and better established fields of investigation, which could thereby require little or no specialized consideration apart from these better established fields.

While, therefore, social psychology had definitely been in view for some time even in this country before the appearance of Ross' work,[1] it was a definite step ahead in the direction of establishing the subject to conceive it as of sufficient importance and development to require systematic consideration on its own account. It is in this sense that Ross' *Social Psychology* was "the pioneer treatise, in any language, professing to deal systematically with the subject of social psychology." And in this sense it continued to remain the pioneer treatise for some time except for McDougall's simultaneously appearing work which, however, was later defined by its author, after it had established itself as an alternative approach to the subject, as a psychological introduction to social psychology and not as social psychology itself.[2]

As regards the relation of Ross' *Social Psychology* and McDougall's *Introduction to Social Psychology*, it has been pointedly remarked that these two treatises have very little more in common than their titles.[3] Ross' work, written essentially from the sociological standpoint, follows up the approach of the French psycho-sociological school, particularly that of Tarde. It is essentially a treatise on the suggestion-imitation theory of the social process as made famous by Tarde and by certain writers on the psychology of social suggestion. McDougall's work

---

[1] Among previous attempts to develop the subject matter of social psychology, identified as such in this country, we have noted especially the work of Baldwin. But the more modest attempt on the part of Small and Vincent to introduce the subject and even Ross' own exploitation of an important aspect of the field of social psychology in his *Social Control* (1901) are likewise notable in this connection (see *supra*, pp. 245, 278; *infra*, p. 310). The term "social psychology," as we have seen, had furthermore been in use in continental literature in related connections for a quarter of a century and more (see *supra*, pp. 42*ff*., 67*ff*.).

[2] See *supra*, pp. 177, 189.

[3] See Review of Ross' work, *Amer. Jour. Sociol.*, vol. 14, p. 681, 1908–1909; also BRETT, *A History of Psychology*, vol. III, p. 295; BOGARDUS, *Essentials of Social Psychology*, p. 25.

on the other hand, as we have seen, was written primarily from the psychological standpoint and followed up directly the biological-evolutionary approach that was central in English psychological and social theory at the time and that tended to emphasize especially the Spencerian individualistic rendering of evolutionary doctrine.[1]

In one fundamental respect, however, Ross was decidedly at one with the approach which McDougall's work represents—much more at one, for instance, than any of the American social psychologists of the Baldwin-Cooley approach, who might otherwise seem to be so much closer to McDougall's conception of the subject—and that was in his ready acceptance of the basic biological implications of McDougall's work.[2] In common with instinct psychology generally, for example, Ross accepts the individual as a biologically given datum.[3] He is not concerned at all, therefore, with the problem of central emphasis in the last chapter— with the problem, that is, of the social development of the self and the social nature of human personality. He is rather concerned, as all biologically orientated social-psychological thought has been historically, with the problem of accounting for human sociality and of describing the manner by which society molds the biologically assumed individual into social conformity. Hence the significance of Ross' earlier social-psychological work, his *Social Control* (1901), in which he views social control as against the individual to be controlled in the more or less formal terms of the French "constraint" notion.[4] But the question of this fundamental difference of basic standpoint apart, his *Social Control* remains one of the outstanding contributions to the sociological foundation of American social-psychological thought, and since it represents Ross' own first approach to social psychology, it will be considered briefly here as an introduction to the more detailed consideration of his *Social Psychology*.

[1] Ross took note of the difference of focus in his work and McDougall's, but he remained strong in the defense of his own point of view (see his article on "What Is Social Psychology," *Psychol. Bull.*, vol. 6, pp. 409–411, 1909).

[2] *Cf.* MEAD, "Social Psychology as a Counterpart to Physiological Psychology," *Psychol. Bull.*, vol. 6, p. 401, 1909.

[3] Ross' whole procedure is based on the implied acceptance of a basic biological view of social behavior on which his more characteristic theory is superimposed. In his *Principles of Sociology*, where he presents the foundations of his thought more systematically than elsewhere, this is brought out clearly (see Chaps. IV–V and especially his statement that the "original social forces are instincts," p. 42, 1920 ed.; also *The Foundations of Sociology*, Chap. VII). This is further brought out in the biological prepossessions which Ross reveals in some of his more popular works (*cf.*, for instance, Ross, *The Old World in the New*, and McDOUGALL, *Is America Safe for Democracy?*). Only very recently has Ross begun to shift to a basically more positive social and cultural viewpoint. See the revised edition of his *Principles of Sociology* (1930), Part II, especially discussions of "Human Nature" and "Culture."

[4] A comparison of Ross' "social-control" point of view with the "social growth" conception developed by Cooley, for instance, is revealing in this connection.

The general subject of social psychology, Ross tells us in this work, and at the time he thought of social psychology as "one narrow tract in the province of Sociology,"[1] falls into two main subdivisions: social ascendency and individual ascendency. The first of these "deals with the domination of society over the individual"; the second—"embracing such topics as invention, leadership, the role of great men—deals with the domination of the individual over society." Social ascendency may be further divided, Ross goes on to say, into social influence—mob mind, fashion, convention, custom, public opinion, and the like—and social control. The former, he explains, "is occupied with the social domination which is without intention or purpose; the latter is concerned with the domination which is intended and which fulfils a function in the life of society." His *Social Control* supposedly deals, therefore, with the latter of these subdivisions of the field of social psychology in its larger aspects as conceived of by him.[2]

This schematism may appear somewhat artificial, and Ross himself did not observe it too closely in the actual treatment of his subject matter, but it indicates clearly enough the setting of Ross' earlier social-psychological work and his leaning toward the sort of antithetical conception of the individual and the social in human life into which the basic biological orientation of his thought inevitably led him. Ross describes the purpose of his *Social Control* further as follows:

In this book I seek to determine how far the order we see all about us is due to influences that reach men and women from without, that is *social* influences. I began the work . . . with the idea that nearly all the goodness and conscientiousness by which a social group is enabled to hold together can be traced to such influences. It seemed to me then that the individual contributed very little to social order, while society contributed almost everything. Further investigation, however, appears to show that the personality freely unfolding under conditions of healthy fellowship may arrive at a goodness all its own, and that order is explained partly by this streak in human nature and partly by the influence of social surroundings. As I now conceive it my task is, therefore, first, to separate the individual's contribution to social order from that of society, and, second, to bring to light everything that is contained in this social contribution.[3]

In more specific terms, he tells us later that "it is the purpose of this inquiry to ascertain how men of the West-European breed are brought to live closely together, and to associate their efforts with that degree of harmony we see about us." He explains:

[1] See *Social Control*, Preface, p. vii; *cf. Social Psychology*, p. 2; *Psychol. Bull.*, vol. 6, pp. 409–411, 1909; *infra*, pp. 314–315.

[2] *Social Control*, Preface, pp. vii–viii; see also *Proc. Intern. Congress Arts Sci.*, vol. 5, pp. 869–880, 1904.

[3] *Social Control*, Preface, p. viii. Quotations from this work are reprinted by permission of The Macmillan Company, publishers.

Social order, even among the passive, unambitious Hindoos, presents a problem for solution. But it is a much more serious problem among the dolichocephalic blonds of the West. The restless, striving, doing Aryan, with his personal ambition, his lust for power, his longing to wreak himself, his willingness to turn the world upside down to get the fame, or the fortune, or the woman, he wants, is under no easy discipline. The existence of order among men of this daring and disobedient breed challenges explanation. Especially is this true of the European man in America or Australia. The same selective migrations that made the Teuton more self-assertive than the docile Slav or the quiescent Hindoo, have made the American more strongwilled and unmanageable than even the West European.[1]

One cannot, therefore, take social order for granted, according to Ross. On the contrary, the problem of its foundations must be frankly faced if we are to understand the processes and mechanisms involved. "Most of us," says Ross, "take order for granted, and are hardly more aware of it than we are of the air we breathe. Order being the universal and indispensable condition of all our social structures, we give no more thought to it than to the force of cohesion that keeps our machinery from flying into bits." However, he suggests:

But it would be, in truth, much juster to assume a state of disorder. We ought to take for granted that men living in propinquity will continually fall afoul of one another. We ought to expect in the normal person, not it is true, the malice, lust, or ferocity of the born criminal, but certainly a natural unwillingness to be checked in the hot pursuit of his ends . . . [2]

Proceeding to explain this point, he says:

Whenever men swarm in new places,—Dutch Flat, Kimberly, Siberia, Skagway,—the man-to-man struggle stands out naked and clear, and the slow emergence of order out of disorder and violence presents itself as the attainment of a difficult and artificial condition. Could we abstract from such communities the training received in older societies, the thrift that recognizes disorder as a blight upon prosperity, and the ready revolver which discourages aggression by equalizing men, we might arrive at a notion of the state in which the men of to-day, despite their high facial angle, would find themselves, if they were remanded to the zero point of social development.[2]

We are thus face to face with the problem of social control in its most elementary aspects. Ross states it in general terms as follows:

By what means is the human struggle narrowed and limited? How has violence been purged away from it? How has the once brawling torrent of conflicting personal desires been induced to flow smoothly in the channels of legitimate rivalry, or even for a time to vanish underground in those numerous cooperations where conflict is absent until it comes to dividing the results?[3]

[1] *Ibid.*, p. 3.
[2] *Ibid.*, p. 4.
[3] *Ibid.*, pp. 4–5.

With this conception of his task in view, he starts out with a pre-liminary survey aiming "to take stock of the moral capital of the person" so as to determine "what human nature can furnish in the cause of social harmony."[1] Under the heading of "The Grounds of Control," he thus discusses such topics as the role of sympathy, of sociability, of the sense of justice, and of individual reaction. Having then considered "what abutments and spans are provided by the individual himself" toward bridging "the gulf between private ends and public ends, between the aims of the individual and the aims of his fellows," he directs himself to his major problem which, as he tells us, is "to measure the extent of the moral engineering that must be undertaken by society."[1] Here under the heading of "The Means of Control," Ross considers in order the following topics: public opinion, law, belief, social suggestion, social religion, personal ideals, ceremony, art, personality, enlightenment, illusion, social valuations. It was this latter part of his discussion, presenting as it did for the first time a unified picture and description of so wide a range of the instruments of social control viewed from the standpoint of their common function as agencies of social order, that constituted Ross' work an outstanding contribution to the sociological foundation of American social-psychological thought.[2] In this respect, in fact, Ross' *Social Control* holds rank with Cooley's *Social Organization* and Sumner's *Folkways*,[3] as one of the foremost products of the earlier

[1] *Ibid.*, pp. 5–6.

[2] See PARK and BURGESS, *Introduction to the Science of Sociology*, p. 849.

[3] Since Ross' *Social Control* and Cooley's *Social Organization* have already been commented upon in some detail here in conjunction with our consideration of Ross' and Cooley's social-psychological positions generally, it remains only to indicate more specifically the social-psychological import of Sumner's *Folkways* in this connection. This work, as the title suggests, was directed to a detailed analysis of one important aspect of the field of social control. The effect of this work, with its notable use of ethnological material and its exceptionally forceful style, was most striking alongside of Sumner's characteristic individualistic standpoint and his defense of classical *laissez-faire* doctrine in its most extreme Spencerian form of interpretation (see *supra*, p. 244). The fact that the terms "folkways" and "mores" are today invariably associated with Sumner's work may be taken as something of an index of the effectiveness with which his treatment of these phenomena has impressed itself upon American psycho-social thought and, incidentally, of the important role which his *Folkways* has played as an offsetting influence to the purely biological conception of human behavior, which, through instinct psychology, was coming into such prominence at the time. "Social control," "folkways and mores," "primary groups," these, in the concrete manner in which they were worked out by the three writers under consideration here, were among the most powerful sociological concepts operative during the earlier period of American social-psychological thought (see in this connection also *supra*, p. 247 and BARNES, *Amer. Jour. Sociol.*, vol. 25, pp. 3–23, 1919–1920; *Sociol. Rev.*, vol. 14, pp. 209–212; 1922; BRISTOL, *Social Adaptation*, pp. 152–153; BOGARDUS, *A History of Social Thought*, pp. 196, 306–315; SMALL, *Amer. Jour. Sociol.*, vol. 21, pp. 732–733, 1915–1916; PARK and BURGESS, *Introduction to the Science of Sociology*, p. 849; COOLEY, *Sociol. Soc. Res.*, vol. 12, pp. 303–306, 1928).

period of American sociological development.   The very notion of "social control" when placed in the setting of Ross' thought as a whole as outlined above and, beyond that, in the setting of the contemporary biological standpoint as it has already been reflected here in various connections, is suggestive along social-psychological lines, much as was the French "constraint" view.   It certainly must be kept in view here as basic to Ross' own standpoint as it was later developed in his *Social Psychology*.

Passing on, then, to Ross' conception of social psychology in its larger aspects, he tells us in general that he applies this term "to the branch of knowledge that deals with the psychic interplay between man and his environing society."[1]   In his *Social Psychology*, he develops this statement in more familiar manner.   He there says:

Social psychology, as the writer conceives it, studies the psychic planes and currents that come into existence among men in consequence of their association.   It seeks to understand and account for those uniformities in feeling, belief, or volition—and hence in action—which are due to the interaction of human beings, *i.e.*, to *social* causes . . . [2]

By way of explaining this conception, he says:

No two persons have just the same endowment.   Looking at their heredity, we should expect people to be far more dissimilar and individual than we actually find them to be.   The aligning power of association triumphs over diversity of temperament and experience.   There ought to be as many religious creeds as there are human beings; but we find people ranged under a few great religions. It is the same in respect to dress, diet, pastimes, or moral ideas.   The individuality each has received from the hand of nature is largely effaced, and we find people gathered into great planes of uniformity.

In shifting attention from the agreements in which men rest, such as languages, religions, and cultures, to the agitations into which they are drawn, it is natural to change the metaphor from *plane* to *current*.   The spread of the lynching spirit through a crowd in the presence of an atrocious criminal, the contagion of panic in a beaten army, an epidemic of religious emotion, and the sympathetic extension of a strike call up the thought of a *current*, which bears people along for a time and then ceases.[3]

Seeking to delimit social psychology as thus conceived from some of the more important borderline fields of investigation, Ross proceeds:

Social psychology pays no attention to the non-psychic parallelisms among human beings (an epidemic of disease or the prevalence of chills and fever among the early settlers of river-bottom lands), or to the psychic parallelisms that result therefrom (melancholia or belief in eternal punishment).   It neglects the uniformities among people that are produced by the direct action of a common physical environment (superstitiousness of sailors, gayety of open-air peoples, sug-

[1] *Social Control*, p. vii.

[2] *Social Psychology*, p. 1.   Quotations from this work are reprinted by permission of The Macmillan Company, publishers.

[3] *Ibid.*, pp. 1–2.

gestibility of dwellers on monotonous plains, independent spirit of mountaineers), or by the subjection to similar conditions of life (dissipatedness of tramp printers, recklessness of cowboys, preciseness of elderly school teachers, suspiciousness of farmers).

Social psychology ignores uniformities arising directly or indirectly out of race endowment—negro volubility, gypsy nomadism, Malay vindictiveness, Singhalese treachery, Magyar passion for music, Slavic mysticism, Teutonic venturesomeness, American restlessness . . . [1]

Social psychology deals only with uniformities due to *social* causes, *i.e.*, to *mental contacts* or *mental interactions*. In each case, we must ask, "Are these human beings aligned by their common instincts and temperament, their common geographical situation, their identical conditions of life, or by their *interpsychology*, *i.e.*, the influences they have received from one another or from a common human source?" The fact that a mental agreement extends through society bringing into a common plane great numbers of men does not make it *social*. It is *social* only in so far as it arises out of the interplay of minds.[2]

As thus viewed, social psychology "seeks to enlarge our knowledge of *society* by explaining how so many planes in feeling, belief, or purpose have established themselves among men and supplied a basis for their groupings, their cooperations, and their conflicts." It "seeks to enlarge our knowledge of the *individual* by ascertaining how much of his mental content and choice is derived from his social surroundings." The subject thus falls, Ross suggests, "into two very unequal divisions, *viz.*, *Social Ascendency* and *Individual Ascendency*, the determination of the one by the many and the determination of the many by the one; the moulding of the ordinary person by his social environment and the moulding of the social environment by the extraordinary person." "The knightly pattern, the ideal of romantic love, the Westminster Catechism, and the belief in public education are," for example, according to Ross, "at once achievements of superior persons, and elements in the social environment of innumerable ordinary persons." Social psychology is concerned with such facts from both of the indicated angles of approach in so far as these facts are a matter of interpsychology.[3]

Ross' organization of his *Social Psychology* in accordance with this conception, with what he describes as Tarde's "two great construction lines—conventionality and custom—yielded by his incomparable *Lois de l'imitation*"[4] as a basis, is too familiar to even the casual American reader in the field of social psychology to require detailed description here.

---

[1] *Ibid.*, pp. 1–2.

The daring generalization and leaning toward literary phrasing which have made Ross' work widely popular on the one hand, and not infrequently subject to unfavorable scientific comment on the other, are well illustrated in these passages.

[2] *Ibid.*, pp. 2–3.

[3] *Ibid.*, pp. 3–5.

[4] *Ibid.*, Preface, p. viii. Ross' statement of indebtedness to Tarde is notable here in its entirety. He says: "At the moment of launching this work, I pause to pay

His discussion of such topics as suggestibility, the crowd, mob mind, fashion, conventionality, custom, and rational imitation, interference and conflict, union and accumulation, etc., constitutes a brilliant reinterpretation and adaptation of Tarde's doctrine of imitation as the central principle of social life, superimposed on a basic background of contemporary biological views regarding human nature and combined with certain other important elements, such as the theory of social suggestion developed by Le Bon and other writers on mob psychology. Throughout, his discussion is enlivened by the sort of sparkling exposition and challenging generalization which recall Tarde's own brilliant exposition in the above-mentioned work. These qualities have carried Ross' work on a wave of popular interest which became an important factor in establishing social psychology in this country and in gaining for it its present-day level of recognition. The fact that the suggestion-imitation theory around which Ross built his treatment of social psychology has been losing scientific ground constantly and that his exposition was not always as consistent in the formulation of the social-psychological consequences of this doctrine as might be, were no more serious factors in curtailing the important role which his work has played in the social-psychological movement than they were in the case of Tarde. In any event, Ross' influence stands out prominently during the earlier period of social-psychological development in this country alongside of the other important influences which have been noted here, the importance of his work in popularizing the notion of social psychology as a distinct field of investigation and in associating it definitely with certain elements of psycho-social thought which strongly suggest his Tardean outlook being particularly in evidence.

One distinguishing feature of Ross' social-psychological theory must be noted here in closing. It has to do with his conception of the basic process of suggestion-imitation and his restatement of imitation doctrine as originally formulated by Tarde and others, in terms of this conception. The following passages from his discussion of suggestibility, which lays the foundation for his more detailed analysis, will serve to bring this conception and the characteristic orientation of Ross' theory as a whole more clearly into view here.

The older psychology was individualistic in its interpretations. The contents of the mind were looked upon as elaborations out of personal experience. It

heartfelt homage to the genius of Gabriel Tarde. Solicitous as I have been to give him due credit in the text, no wealth of excerpt and citation can reveal the full measure of my indebtedness to that profound and original thinker. While my system has swung wide of his, I am not sure I should ever have wrought out a social psychology but for the initial stimulus and the two great construction lines—conventionality and custom—yielded by his incomparable *Lois de l'imitation*. If only this expression of my gratitude could reach him!'' (Preface, p. viii.)

sought to show how from the primary sense perceptions are built up ideas, at first simple, then more and more complex—ideas of space, time, number, cause, etc. The upper stories of personality, framed on beliefs, standards, valuations, and ideals, were comparatively neglected. The psychologist failed to note that for these highly elaborated products we are more indebted to our fellow-men than to our individual experience, that they are wrought out, as it were, collectively, and not by each for himself.

The newer psychology in accounting for the contents of the mind gives great prominence to the social factor. It insists that without interaction with other minds the psychic development of the child would be arrested at a stage not far above idiocy. Such interaction arises necessarily from the suggestibility of human nature. A person cannot unswervingly follow the orbit prescribed by his heredity or his private experience. He does not sit serene at the centre of things and coolly decide which of the examples and ideas that present themselves he shall adopt. Much of what impinges on his consciousness comes with some force. It has momentum, and if he does not yield to it, it is because his mind resists with a greater force . . . Many a man thinks he makes up his mind, whereas, in truth, it is made up for him by some masterful associate or by the man who talked with him last.

Stimuli welling up from within may be termed *impulses*, whereas those reaching us directly from without may be termed *suggestions*. The latter may be defined as "the abrupt entrance from without into consciousness of an idea or image which becomes a part of the stream of thought and tends to produce the muscular and volitional effects which ordinarily follow upon its presence . . . "

Suggestions are true forces and enact themselves unless they meet resistance. The power to withstand, ignore, or throw off suggestions is one form of *inhibition*, *i.e.*, will power. Suggestion and imitation are merely two aspects of the same thing, the one being cause, the other effect.[1]

This conception of the role and the cause-and-effect relation of suggestion and imitation enabled Ross to weave the several parts of his theory, as developed in the discussion of the varied subject matter outlined above, into a more or less unified presentation. It also provided the basis for the prominence which his theory gives to psycho-social thought relating to social contagion, mob mind, and the like, alongside of what might be viewed as his underlying imitation approach, and for the manner in which he combined the views of a large number of early writers who emphasized the more formal and more spectacular aspects of social-psychological theory. His conception of the subject limited his attempt at synthesis to this side of social-psychological thought. His treatment was therefore particularistic in the sense of most of the other early approaches to social psychology. A beginning was now however definitely made in the direction of what he set forth as an attempt at the systematic treatment of social psychology, and the more

[1] *Social Psychology*, pp. 11–13.

balanced execution of the task, as he himself recognized,[1] was inevitably a question of time and the further development of the field.[2]

II. George H. Mead (1863–1931)

Ross' work outlines a conception of social psychology which was very prominent if not predominant during the earlier part of the modern social-psychological movement. In the work of Baldwin and Cooley, however, we get the emergence of another conception which has been growing in importance in this country ever since its first formulation. This latter conception, which, as we have seen, centered about the analysis of the social self and the social nature of personality, was developed further in important directions by George H. Mead.[3] While Mead approached the subject of social psychology in a frankly philosophical manner, for reasons which will appear presently, he has been an outstanding figure in American social-psychological thought alongside of the other writers so far considered here. At any rate, it is necessary to view his social-psychological theory here as supplementing some of the other formulations, despite some altogether unusual difficulties.

For Mead's influence upon American social-psychological thought has been exerted chiefly by way of the classroom and only secondarily by way of his published writings. The latter are fragmentary in the first place and both involved and obscure, and hence limited in their appeal, in the second place. A survey of Mead's published discussions of social-psychological material would, therefore, be peculiarly inadequate as an index of the importance of his social-psychological theory. It is necessary to link these discussions of scattered aspects of his theory with his point of view as a whole, and this is to date not available in published form. The following summary is accordingly based on an unpublished outline of Mead's social-psychological theory[4] and on his class presentation of the material, as well as on some of his published articles. The reader who would follow out this brief summary is neces-

---

[1] See *ibid.*, Preface.

[2] For a further discussion of Ross' social-psychological position see Bodenhafer, *Amer. Jour. Sociol.*, vol. 26, pp. 436–443, 1921; Barnes, *Sociol. Rev.*, vol. 15, pp. 120–131, 1923; Bogardus, *A History of Social Thought*, pp. 395–406; Ellwood, "Professor Ross's Conception of Social Psychology," *Psychol. Bull.*, vol. 5, pp. 381–384, 1908; *Sociology in Its Psychological Aspects*, Chap. XIII; Bristol, *Social Adaptation*, pp. 291–297.

[3] The particular directions of analysis which he chiefly sought to follow out have been suggestively indicated by Mead himself in connection with his discussion of Cooley's social-psychological theory (see "Cooley's Contribution to American Social Thought," *Amer. Jour. Sociol.*, vol. 35, pp. 693–706, 1930).

[4] Available at the University of Chicago library in manuscript form and to be published shortly.

sarily limited to the latter source.[1]   It must at least be borne in mind, however, that Mead's social-psychological theory is really a part of a larger situation which includes Dewey's psychology on the one hand and some of the social-psychological formulations of Thomas, Faris, and others of the group associated with them on the other.   For it is only as his theory is viewed in the light of this larger setting that its real importance as a factor in American social-psychological thought begins to appear.[2]

Mead addressed himself in particular to the careful analysis of the process by which the social unfolding of human personality takes place. Both Baldwin and Cooley had made their distinctive contributions here, but with the developing experimental study of the role of imitation in mental life a serious gap was left, at any rate in Baldwin's side of the analysis, which it seemed, from Mead's standpoint, most important to bridge.[3]   In fact, current social-psychological thought as a whole was so conspicuously associated with the imitation theory of social life that the weakening of this specific theory seemed for the time being to be a weakening also of the social-psychological point of view in general. In directing his attention to a careful re-analysis of the process of social interaction, Mead was thereby attacking a problem which at the time was of fundamental social-psychological importance.   Just when the imitation basis of modern social-psychological thought was beginning to give way, he shifted the center of social-psychological interest, so that imitation became a mere incident in the analysis of the basic process by which personality develops and social interaction is carried on.[4] Mead also went the step beyond current social-psychological thought in this country of extending the social-psychological point of view more directly into the field of what had been looked upon as general psychology proper and of restating from his own standpoint such of its characteristic concepts as, for instance, consciousness, imagination, meaning, mind, thought, impulse, emotion, attention, etc.   His theory accordingly appears to be especially challenging on the side of traditional psychological thought, as we shall see.   In fact, his theory is among the most revolutionary in this respect of any of the formulations which we have so far had occasion to consider.[5]

[1] For a partial list of Mead's relevant articles and an attempt to give them place in relation to current social-psychological thought see *Amer. Jour. Sociol.*, vol. 33, pp. 625, 629, 1927; also ALLPORT, *Social Psychology*, pp. 432–433.

[2] See *infra*, pp. 326–327, 381.

[3] For Mead's criticism of Baldwin's imitation theory see *Psychol. Bull.*, vol. 6, pp. 404–406, 1909; see also BODENHAFER, *Amer. Jour. Soc.*, vol. 26, p. 721, 1921.

[4] See "Social Psychology as a Counterpart to Physiological Psychology," *Psychol. Bull.*, vol. 6, p. 406, 1909; "The Social Self," *Jour. Phil. Psychol. Sci. Meth.*, vol. 10, p. 377, 1913; "The Behavioristic Account of the Significant Symbol," *Jour. Phil.*, vol. 19, p. 160, 1922; "The Genesis of the Self and Social Control," *Intern. Jour. Ethics*, vol. 35, p. 269, 1925.

[5] See *infra*, p. 324.

Though broadly inclusive of related thought, especially of that of James, Baldwin, and Cooley, Mead's approach is chiefly from the activistic and functional view of mental life which Dewey more particularly brought into focus in this country and the genetic and behavioristic movements in modern psychology as represented prominently by Darwin's work on *The Expression of the Emotions* and Wundt's treatment of language in his *Völkerpsychologie*.[1] He starts out with the "social act" as the primitive unit in social psychology, this unit being regarded by him as "social" in no mere secondary or delimiting sense but in the fundamental sense that human psychology in its most distinctive aspects is, according to him, basically social in both origin and function. Conceiving of social psychology "as the counterpart" of physiological psychology in the fundamental sense which recalls the classic defense of this position by Comte and Tarde,[2] Mead proceeded to build up the essential structure of his social-psychological theory about his behavioristic account of the process of interaction in the social act, very aptly and very suggestively designated by him as a "conversation" of attitudes and gestures.[3]

This approach implies, in conformity with the spirit of Mead's social-psychological thought as a whole, that the basic data of human psychology in its social aspects are not "sensations" or "ideas" or "instincts" or any other such abstracted element but rather "acts" or "behavior" as it is directly observable in concrete human conduct. It is in this broad sense, it should be noted, and not in the narrowly technical sense that Mead's approach is *behavioristic* and linked with the behavioristic movement in modern thought, especially as represented by Darwin and Wundt. This approach remained impossible, according to him, as long as psychology continued to deal with entities which were referable to the soul, the mind, or the body, as in the case of the atomistic standpoints suggested above. It came into view only with the organic standpoint which the theory of evolution introduced into modern psychology. In its social-psychological implications, Mead associated this standpoint especially with the above-mentioned works of Darwin and

---

[1] See in this connection "Social Psychology as the Counterpart to Physiological Psychology," *Psych. Bull.*, vol. 6, pp. 401–402, 406, 1909; "What Social Objects Must Psychology Presuppose?" *Jour. Phil. Psychol.*, *Sci. Meth.*, vol. 7, pp. 174, 176–177, 179, 1910; "The Social Self," *ibid*, vol. 10, p. 375, 1913.

[2] *Cf. supra*, pp. 15–17, 96; also *infra*, p. 331.

[3] See, for instance, "Social Psychology as the Counterpart to Physiological Psychology," *Psychol. Bull.*, vol. 6, pp. 406–407, 1909; "Social Consciousness and the Consciousness of Meaning," *ibid.*, pp. 397 *ff.*; "What Social Objects Must Psychology Presuppose?" *Jour. Phil. Psychol. Sci. Meth.*, vol. 7, pp. 176–179, 1910; "The Mechanism of Social Consciousness," *ibid.*, vol. 9, pp. 401 *ff.*, 1912; "The Social Self," *ibid.*, vol. 10, pp. 375–377, 1913; "The Behavioristic Account of the Significant Symbol," *Jour. Phil.*, vol. 19, pp. 160 *ff.*, 1922; "The Genesis of the Self and Social Control," *Intern. Jour. Ethics*, vol. 35, pp. 251–252, 262–264, 286 *ff.*, 1925.

Wundt, so that he naturally sought to lead out from them as points of departure.[1]

The social act, according to Mead, is an act, "in which one individual serves in his action as a stimulus to a response from another individual."[2] Its important character, he maintained, is not imitation but the process of interstimulation in which the participating forms in a social act engage and which links them functionally together in a common social situation. "The important character of the social organization of conduct," says Mead, "is not that one form in a social group does what the others do, but that the conduct of one form is a stimulus to another to a certain act, and that this act again becomes a stimulus to the first to a certain reaction, and so on in ceaseless interaction," as suggested by the distinctive phrase "conversation of attitudes."[3]

In developing this conception of the social act, Mead is led into an attempt to distinguish between what he regards as the world of social objects and relations generally and the physical world. This distinction cannot, according to him, be set up once and for all in physical terms. It is a matter of functional relationship. Thus, a social object, according to him, is one that calls forth a social response and results in social conduct, while a physical object is one that does not elicit such conduct but is acted toward in a characteristically impersonal and mechanical manner.[4]

The child's world is at first entirely a social world, according to Mead, the world of physical objects and relationships being, from his standpoint, an acquisition which the child arrives at as a construct of its experience and by a process of abstraction. The child gradually learns, he suggests, following out the strain of thought which had been previously outlined by Baldwin, that some objects do not respond to it in the manner that people do. It gradually notices, also, that these same objects are treated

---

[1] See *ibid.*, p. 251; also references *supra*, note 1, p. 320.

[2] "Social Consciousness and the Consciousness of Meaning," *Psychol. Bull.*, vol. 7, p. 397, 1910.

[3] "Social Psychology as the Counterpart to Physiological Psychology," *Psychol. Bull.*, vol. 6, p. 406, 1909.

Mead practically limits imitation to conscious copying. "Imitation becomes comprehensible," he says, "when there is a consciousness of other selves, and not before." "Social consciousness is the presupposition of imitation." For the rest, he would restate the situation fundamentally. He says: "The conception of imitation as it has functioned in social psychology, needs to be developed into a theory of social stimulation and response, and of the social situations which these stimulations and responses create" (see *ibid.*, pp. 405–406; also Park and Burgess, *Introduction to the Science of Sociology*, p. 424).

[4] See "The Mechanism of Social Consciousness," *Jour. Phil. Psychol. Sci. Meth.*, vol. 9, pp. 401–403, 1912; "The Behavioristic Account of the Significant Symbol," *Jour. Phil.*, vol. 19, p. 159, 1922; "The Genesis of the Self and Social Control," *Intern. Jour. Ethics*, vol. 35, pp. 255–256, 1925.

with comparative indifference by those about it.   In our society, too, this experience begins to get itself early organized in terms of the knowledge of physics to which the child of our day falls heir.   This knowledge, Mead however calls to mind, is one of our comparatively recent acquisitions, dating back in its modern form only to the beginning of philosophical thought in Greece and in considerable part only to the beginning of the modern scientific movement in Western Europe.   In primitive communities, at any rate, the child's heritage is supposedly quite different in this respect, and its resulting physical world is also supposedly quite different.   Usually it is very much narrowed by the predominant magical attitude toward the world of nature, which the primitive child takes over from its social *milieu*, just as the child in our society takes over our scientifically impersonal attitudes.[1]

Whatever its socially defined boundaries, however, the physical world eventually does become distinguished from the basic world of social objects and relations by its poorer emotional content.   There is in the case of the latter a constant play of responsive adjustment and readjustment, involving inhibition, emotion, and gesture, as there is not in the physical world.[2]   Thus it is, according to Mead, that emotional expression and gesture, as first described in behavioristic terms by Darwin in his *Expression of the Emotions*, are peculiarly the phenomena of the world of social conduct.   They have a special importance, according to him, in the early stages of the social act, for they serve as indications to other forms to adjust appropriately to the stimulus presented, and as a result they set going the play of social stimulation and response characteristic of social conduct.[3]

Thus, for instance, if *A* expresses anger, *B* responds in an appropriate manner.   The adjustment on the part of *B* becomes in turn a stimulus to *A* to readjust, and *A*'s new attitude the occasion for a new readjustment on the part of *B*.   This play of social stimulation and response continues back and forth in the manner suggested by the phrase "conversation of attitudes," until the social act in view is finally brought to a close. Almost any aspect of social interaction can serve as an illustration of the process.   The development of a dog fight, the progress of a fencing match, and the course of conversation on a specific topic all bring it clearly into view.   An illustration from genetic psychology which is more directly to the point here is the play of stimulation and response that goes on

[1] See "Social Psychology as the Counterpart to Physiological Psychology," *Psychol. Bull.*, vol. 6, pp. 403–404, 1909; "Social Consciousness and the Consciousness of Meaning," *ibid.*, vol. 7, pp. 397 *ff.*, 1910; also references in preceding note.

[2] "Social Consciousness and the Consciousness of Meaning," *Psychol. Bull.*, vol. 7, pp. 397, 403–404, 1910.

[3] *Ibid.*, pp. 397 *ff.*; "What Social Objects Must Psychology Presuppose?" *Jour. Phil. Psychol. Sci. Meth.*, vol. 7, p. 177, 1910; "The Mechanism of Social Consciousness," *ibid.*, vol. 9, p. 402, 1912.

continually between mother and child. The child's cry of discomfort serves as a stimulus to call forth a response from the mother which, if it be successful in its effort at relief, probably results in some sort of expression of satisfaction on the part of the child. The latter then tends to become a stimulus to the mother to another response, and so on back and forth until, perhaps, the social act here under consideration resolves itself in the intimate caressing which so frequently climaxes such situations.[1]

This give-and-take of social conduct, this "conversation" of social stimulation and response, may be carried on on an immediate stimulus-response level; and in the case of the lower animals it is carried on largely also on the instinctive level. In the case of the human being, however, according to Mead, "meaning" in terms of anticipated response soon enters in as a mediating factor and, along with it, the whole complex of higher mental processes associated with meaning, thought, and the organized self. The child gradually begins to be in a position, as regards its mental equipment, to "image" the effect of social stimulus and response, and thereby it gradually begins to be in a position, also, to build up the material of its higher mental life as a guide to social conduct.[2]

The child acquires the social imagery on the basis of which it can build up the more complex processes of its mental life as a guide to its social conduct by "taking the role of the other" and by "stimulating itself as it stimulates others," as it constantly does in play and whenever it rehearses its social role in imagination.[3] Vocal gesture in particular plays an important part in this aspect of development, according to Mead, though in a lesser degree those of one's gestures that one can see or feel may make for the same result. "The vocal gesture," he says, "is of peculiar importance because it reacts upon the individual who makes

---

[1] "Social Psychology as the Counterpart to Physiological Psychology," *Psychol. Bull.*, vol. 6, pp. 406–407, 1909; "Social Consciousness and the Consciousness of Meaning," *ibid.*, pp. 397–398; "The Mechanism of Social Consciousness," *Jour. Phil. Psychol. Sci. Meth.*, vol. 9, p. 402, 1912; "The Social Self," *ibid.*, vol. 10, pp. 375–377, 1913; "The Behavioristic Account of the Significant Symbol," *Jour. Phil.*, vol. 19, p. 160, 1922.

The phrase "conversation of attitudes," as Mead uses it, is doubly social in reference, attitudes and gestures themselves being, according to him, "truncated acts" which signify a social situation. Genetically as well as functionally, therefore, attitudes and gestures in the sense of his usage are social in reference (see *Psychol. Bull.*, vol. 6, p. 406, 1909; also *infra*, p. 325).

[2] See references *supra*, p. 320, note 3.

[3] "What Social Objects Must Psychology Presuppose?" *Jour. Phil. Psychol. and Sci. Meth.*, vol. 7, pp. 178–179, 1910; "Social Consciousness and the Consciousness of Meaning," *Psychol. Bull.*, vol. 7, pp. 399 ff., 1910; "The Mechanism of Social Consciousness," *Jour. Phil. Psychol. Sci. Meth.*, vol. 9, pp. 404–405, 1912; "The Social Self," *ibid.*, vol. 10, pp. 375–377; 1913; "The Behavioristic Account of the Significant Symbol," *Jour. Phil.*, vol. 19, pp. 161–163, 1922.

it in the same fashion that it reacts upon another."[1]   "While one feels but imperfectly the value of his own facial expression or bodily attitude for another, his ears reveal to him his own vocal gesture in the same form that it assumes to his neighbor."[2]   The child talks to itself, therefore, and its ear reveals to it its own vocal gesture in substantially the form in which it strikes its associates.   It is thus in a position to affect itself as it affects others and thereby to respond to its own stimulation as others would respond to it.   This mechanism enables the child to reflect its social world upon itself and to mirror its conduct with respect to it and as a part of it in a manner which is of basic importance, according to Mead, at once for its social efficiency and for its highest mental growth.[3]

In any event, Mead finds in this "double stimulation" aspect of social conduct the basis for all those distinctively human qualities of mind and action—self-consciousness, rationality, foresight, planfulness, social consciousness, morality etc.—which have been the objects of special psychological and philosophical consideration down the ages and also for most of the observed uniformities of social conduct which are generally attributed to imitation.   He thus draws the whole scope of these human phenomena, as also their underlying conditions of development in imagination, meaning, thought, and consciousness, into the realm of social conduct and social psychology, so that he gives to some of the supposedly most individual aspects of the human mind a thoroughgoing social setting and interpretation.

This part of his theory, as Mead points out, is intimately linked with Wundt's formulation of the relation of language to gesture.[4]   The manner in which he leads out from Wundt's treatment of language and beyond that, as has already been noted above, from Darwin's background study of emotion is suggestively outlined in the following passage.   Proceeding from a discussion of the instinct standpoint in modern social psychology to a description of his own approach as it leads into this part of his theory, Mead says:

The . . . position to which I wish to call attention, and whose implications I wish to discuss, is that the consciousness of meaning is social in its origin.   The dominant theory at present, that which is most elaborately stated by Wundt in

[1] *Ibid.*, p. 160.

[2] "The Mechanism of Social Consciousness," *Jour. Phil. Psychol. Sci. Meth.*, vol. 9, p. 403, 1912.

[3] See *ibid.*, pp. 403 *ff.*; "The Genesis of the Self and Social Control," *Intern. Jour. Ethics*, vol. 35, pp. 262 *ff.*, 1925; "The Social Self," *Jour. Phil. Psychol. Sci. Meth.*, vol. 10, p. 377, 1913; "The Behavioristic Account of the Significant Symbol," *Jour. Phil.*, vol. 19, pp. 160–163, 1922; "Social Psychology as the Counterpart to Physiological Psychology," *Psychol. Bull.*, vol. 6, pp. 401–402, 1909.

[4] "What Social Objects Must Psychology Presuppose?" *Jour. Phil. Psychol. Sci. Meth.*, vol. 7, p. 177, 1910; "Social Psychology as the Counterpart to Physiological Psychology," *Psychol. Bull.*, vol. 6, p. 406, 1909.

the first volume of his *Völkerpsychologie*, regards language as the outgrowth of gesture, the vocal gesture. As a gesture, it is primarily an expression of emotion. But the gesture itself is a syncopated act, one that has been cut short, a torso which conveys the emotional import of the act. Out of the emotional signification has grown the intellectual signification. It is evident that but for the original situation of social interaction the bodily and vocal gestures could never have attained their signification. It is their reference to other individuals that has turned expression, as a mere outflow of nervous excitement, into meaning, and this meaning was the value of the act for the other individual, and his response to the expression of the emotion, in terms of another syncopated act, with its social signification, gave the first basis for communication, for common understanding, for the recognition of the attitudes which men mutually held toward each other within a field of social interaction. Attitudes had meanings when they reflected possible acts. And the acts could have meanings when they called out definite reactions which call out still other appropriate responses; that is, when the common content of the act is reflected by the different parts played by individuals, through gestures—truncated acts. Here is the birth of the symbol, and the possibility of thought. Still, thought remains in its abstract form sublimated conversation. Thus reflective consciousness implies a social situation which has been its precondition. Antecedent to the reflective consciousness within which we exist, in the beginnings of the society of men and in the life of every child that arises to reflective consciousness, there must have been this condition of interrelation by acts springing from social instincts.[1]

And in another connection he says:

Human conduct is distinguished primarily from animal conduct by that increase in inhibition which is an essential phase of voluntary attention, and increased inhibition means an increase in gesture, in the signs of activities which are not carried out; in the assumptions of attitudes whose values in conduct fail to get complete expression. If we recognize language as a differentiation of gesture, the conduct of no other form can compare with that of man in the abundance of gesture.

The fundamental importance of gesture lies in the development of the consciousness of meaning—in reflective consciousness. As long as one individual responds simply to the gesture of another by the appropriate response, there is no necessary consciousness of meaning. The situation is still on a level of that of two growling dogs walking around each other, with tense limbs, bristly hair, and uncovered teeth. It is not until an image arises of the response, which the gesture of the one form will bring out in another, that a consciousness of meaning can attach to his own gesture. The meaning can appear only in imagining the consequence of the gesture. To cry out in fear is an immediate instinctive act, but to scream with an image of another individual turning an attentive ear, taking on a sympathetic expression and an attitude of coming to help, is at least a favorable condition for the development of consciousness of meaning.

Of course the mere influence of the image, stimulating to reaction, has no more meaning value than the effect of an external stimulus, but in this converse

[1] *Ibid.*, pp. 406–407. Quotations from this journal are reprinted by permission of the Psychological Review Company, publishers.

of gestures, there is also a consciousness of attitude, of readiness to act in the manner which the gesture implies. In the instance given the cry is part of the attitude of flight. The cry calls out the image of a friendly individual. The image is not merely a stimulus to run toward the friend, but is merged in the consciousness of inhibited flight. If meaning is consciousness of attitude, as Dewey, Royce, and Angell among others maintain, then, consciousness of meaning arose only when some gesture that was part of an inhibited act itself called up the image of the gesture of another individual. Then the image of the gesture means the inhibited act to which the first gesture belonged. In a word, the response to the cry has the meaning of inhibited flight.

One's own gestures could not take on meaning directly. The gestures aroused by them in others would be that upon which attention is centered. And these gestures become identified with the content of one's own emotion and attitude. It is only through the response that consciousness of meaning appears, a response which involves the consciousness of another self as the presupposition of the meaning of one's own attitude. Other selves in a social environment logically antedate the consciousness of self which introspection analyzes. They must be admitted as there, as given, in the same sense in which psychology accepts the given reality of physical organisms as a condition of individual consciousness.[1]

Whatever may be said for the details of this theory and for the basis of child observation and introspective analysis upon which it supposedly rests, all in all its effect has been both profound and far-reaching. This has been due partly to the fact that for the reasons suggested above, Mead's social-psychological theory has itself been very illuminating and partly to the fact that it has been so closely associated with other important formulations of American social-psychological theory. Especially important in this connection is the consideration that Mead's social psychology is one of the notable products of the Dewey school of pragmatic thought, for this consideration suggests immediately channels of social-psychological relationship and influence which are widely significant here, as will readily appear from the following sections of this chapter. But in any event, that Mead's theory has been an important factor in American social-psychological thought is evident enough from the direct testimony of an increasing number of writers.[2] We close this brief

[1] "What Social Objects Must Psychology Presuppose?" *Jour. Phil. Psychol. Sci. Meth.* vol. 7, pp. 178–179, 1910. Quotations from this journal are reprinted by permission of *The Journal of Philosophy.*

[2] See in this connection, for instance, THURSTONE, *The Nature of Intelligence,* Preface, p. xvi; FARIS, "Current Trends in Social Psychology," *Essays in Philosophy,* ed. by Smith and Wright, pp. 122, 132; *Amer. Jour. Sociol.,* vol. 32, pp. 625, 629, 1927; QUEEN, *Social Work in the Light of History,* pp. 68, 308 *ff.*; BODENHAFER, *Amer. Jour. Sociol.,* vol. 26, p. 721, 1921; ALLPORT, *Social Psychology,* pp. 148–149, 416, 432–433; YOUNG, *Source Book for Social Psychology,* pp. 303, 341–348; BOGARDUS, *A History of Social Thought,* p. 409; PARK and BURGESS, *Introduction to the Science of Sociology,* p. 424.

outline of his theory with a single passage from one of these writers who has become the outstanding interpreter of Mead's social psychology.

To Professor Mead, according to him, "American scholars are indebted for some invaluable and wholly unique contributions."

Nowhere can be found a comparable analysis of the psychology of meaning, the nature of symbolism, and the distinction between the significant symbol which makes human experience possible and the inferior development which accounts for the limitations of the lower animals. Mead's doctrine of the histrionic tendency which runs through all normal human imaginative experiences, very happily designated as the tendency to "take the role of the other," has, in the opinion of the writer, been one of the major contributions in this generation to our knowledge of how the personality develops and the consciousness of self arises. Mead has set forth the process by means of which the spontaneous and meaningless gesture is defined by the responses of the other so that while our ideas are our own and the symbol is private, yet the soul of the symbol is its meaning, and the meaning is the contribution of others.[1]

It will be helpful, in following out the remaining formulations of social-psychological theory in this chapter, to bear this statement in view, and especially in conjunction with our later consideration of Faris' social-psychological position.[2]

III. JOHN DEWEY (1859)

Dewey could have been considered almost at any point in this survey of American social-psychological thought, for he has been a very prominent factor in the situation throughout the period of American social-psychological development. It will be recalled that in the opening chapter of this part of our survey, Dewey's *Psychology* was mentioned along with James' *Principles* as the two outstanding psychological works on the horizon of early American social-psychological thought.[3] We did not consider his psychological theory at that point, in order to leave the ground clear for the consideration of James' *Principles* in that connection and also because Dewey has since concerned himself with social psychology more directly, and we naturally wished to direct our attention chiefly to this special aspect of his work in due order from the standpoint of related developments. Thus it is that detailed consideration of Dewey's position has been postponed to this point, when his theory is directly of importance in connection with the social-psychological positions of Cooley, Mead, Thomas, Faris, and other writers who came under his immediate influence.

[1] FARIS, "Current Trends in Social Psychology," *Essays in Philosophy*, ed. by Smith and Wright, p. 132.
[2] See *infra*, p. 380.
[3] *Supra*, p. 248; also BRETT, *A History of Psychology*, vol. III, pp. 259–261.

It should, however, be borne in mind that Dewey's social-psychological significance extends back to the first publication of his *Psychology* (1886) and that all along he has been a central figure in the American social-psychological movement. After his first important work, which, in introducing into American psychology the synthetic and activistic approach of contemporary German and English thought, was not unlike James' *Principles* in its general effect, Dewey continued, as Brett says, "to make history" in American psychological thought.[1] Especially notable here among Dewey's earlier psychological writings are his articles on "The Theory of Emotion,"[2] on "The Reflex Arc Concept in Psychology,"[3] the preliminary articles dealing with the subject matter later incorporated in *How We Think* (1910),[4] and his article on the "Interpretation of Savage Mind."[5] As thus formulated in his earlier writings, Dewey's psychology became the nucleus for the more systematic elaboration of "functional" psychology by J. R. Angell[6] and other members of the Dewey group immediately associated with him at Chicago. And functional psychology, with its emphasis on mental activity and the functional and genetic aspects of mind, was prominently before American social-psychological thought during its early period of development alongside of some of the other background developments which have been considered here, especially James' psychology. Being organic and behavioristic in the sense of Mead's and Cooley's social-psychological theory and directed, at least by implication, to the consideration of the environment as well as the organism, as an essential part of the functional situation,[7] it naturally ran closer to the interests of social psychology than more traditional formulations of psychological theory. This was more especially the case since Dewey himself was from the first concerned with the social implications of his thought, though it was not until considerably later that he actually turned his attention to the formulation of a definite social psychology. But in any event functional psychology, especially as associated with Dewey's own early writings, is clearly in evidence as an important influence not only in the case of the writers

---

[1] See *ibid.*, p. 261; *supra*, p. 248; also RILEY, *American Thought*, pp. 289 *ff.*; ROGERS, *English and American Philosophy since 1800*, pp. 388 *ff.*; OTTO, "Instrumentalism," *Philosophy Today*, ed. by Schaub, pp. 37 *ff.*; BOGARDUS, *A History of Social Thought*, pp. 444–447; PARK and BURGESS, *Introduction to the Science of Sociology*, pp. 36–38, 200, 424, 964.

[2] *Psychol. Rev.*, vol. 1, pp. 553–569, 1894, vol. 2, pp. 13–32, 1895.

[3] *University of Chicago Contributions to Philosophy*, vol. 1, pp. 39–52, 1896; also *Psychol. Rev.*, vol. 3, pp. 357–370, 1896.

[4] See Preface and *Studies in Logical Theory* (1903), Chaps. I–IV.

[5] *Psychol. Rev.*, vol. 9, pp. 217–230, 1902.

[6] *Psychology* (1904); also *Psychologies of 1930*, pp. 59–80, 115–127.

[7] See in this connection, for example, JUDD, *Psychology* (1907), discussion of language; also his *Psychology of Social Institutions* (1926).

mentioned above but also in most of the formulations still to be considered in this part of our survey. In the case of some writers, it served as a direct basis of approach into the field of social and social-psychological thought. Among these, we may mention C. A. Ellwood, whose approach to social psychology, which to him was psychological sociology, was in the first place definitely through an attempt to develop the social implications of Dewey's psychology. In connection with his conception of social-psychological procedure, Ellwood has summarized Dewey's psychology as reflected in his earlier writings in reference to its social bearings, and the following passages are quoted from his summary by way of introduction to our consideration of Dewey's own later formulation of his social-psychological position.

Professor Dewey's psychological point of view may be put somewhat schematically as follows: The fundamental fact in the psychical life, according to him, is not the sensation, but the coordination of the living organism in some activity—the act. We cannot get back of the coordination in psychology. Wherever we begin, we must begin with a living organism doing something. The unit of psychical activity, therefore, is the act or coordination. In reality there is only one large coordination—the act of living or the life-process. But within this supreme coordination there arise minor coordinations in the adapting of one part of the organism to another, or of one portion of the life-process to another portion. Or, looking at the process from the opposite standpoint, we may say particular acts are coordinated, unified, into larger coordinations which control the smaller acts; and all are finally unified into, and controlled by, the general life-process of the organism. Thus the psychical life is to be regarded and interpreted as a function of the general life-process. Function, then, rather than organism or environment, is the thing to be considered in psychology. From this point of view all forms of psychical activity can be reduced to two types: coordination and adaptation. All the phenomena of psychical life group themselves about these two fundamental forms—are the outgrowth of them, and are functionally explained by their reference to them. Thus a coordination which has once been successfully established tends to persist, or becomes a habit. The necessity of adjustment, however, arising from some variation in the organism or environment, causes the old coordination or habit to break up, and sensation results. Sensation, then, is the sign of the interruption of a habit, and represents the point at which an activity is reconstructed. The old coordination in breaking up, however, must yield the material for the new coordination; that is, it must be used as means for the construction of a new coordination. The processes of discrimination, attention, and association come in to build up the new coordination. They are all processes which arise only through the transition from one coordination to another. The discriminative process, for example, represents the breakdown of the old coordination, and what we call association represents the building up of the new coordination. Attention represents the conflict of two or more activities involved in the building up of the new coordination; it is the attempt, on the part of the organism, to discover, select, the adequate stimulus for the construction of the new coordination. These illustrations will suffice for our purposes.   In the same manner all psychical processes may be interpreted—as referring either to the coordination or to the transition from one coordination to another.   The coordination is, therefore, the fundamental and central fact of the psychical life.   All other psychical facts are functional expressions of the coordination, or of the relation of one coordination to another within the life-process.   Thus the psychical life presents itself as a system of means and ends, whose unity finds expression in the general end of control over the means of existence, that is, over the conditions of survival.   Summarizing, then, we may say that Professor Dewey's psychological point of view is that of a life-process, or life-activity, functioning to secure control over its own life-conditions, and thereby its own development.   The resulting interpretation of the facts of the psychical life yields a psychology whose chief categories are coordination, adaptation, habit, instinct, selection, evaluation, and the like; in brief, an *evolutionary* psychology.[1]

That such a psychology had a significance for social science which the non-functional psychologies of the past did not have was widely recognized even before Dewey had himself begun to work out this aspect of his thought specifically.   Ellwood says in this connection:

The value of such a psychology to the social sciences must be evident, even from such a schematic and fragmentary statement as we have given.   Such a psychology comes into contact with life at every point and interprets functionally the processes of life; it is no formal, over-abstracted science, but shows us the actual workings of the psychic reality.   The question at once suggests itself: Are not these categories, which have been so successfully applied to the interpretation of the psychical life of the individual, also applicable to the interpretation of the life of society on its psychical side?   Cannot the fundamental principles of such a functional psychology be transferred at once from the interpretation of the life of the individual to that of society?[2]

The direction of applicability suggested here is peculiar to Ellwood's conception of psychological sociology and social psychology.   But it clearly indicates the appeal of Dewey's functional psychology as a point of departure in social interpretation during the earlier period of American social-psychological thought.

Dewey's more specific social-psychological thinking crystallized gradually along with the development of social-psychological thought in this country generally.   His earliest formulations were made incidentally in connection with his treatment of specific problems within the fields of

---

[1] *Prolegomena to Social Psychology*, pp. 12–14.   *Evolutionary*, that is, as Ellwood explains, in the thoroughgoing sense of Dewey's pragmatic point of view, according to which traditional evolutionary and genetic psychology was evolutionary only as regards its material, but not at all as regards its method or interpretation (see KING, *Psychology of Child Development*, Introduction by Dewey, p. xii).

Quotations from the above work are reprinted by permission of the University of Chicago Press, publishers.

[2] *Prolegomena to Social Psychology*, p. 14.

his major earlier interests—in connection, that is, with his treatment of logic, education, ethics, etc.[1] His first treatment of the subject of social psychology directly is to be found in his article on "The Need for Social Psychology."[2] This preliminary discussion of the subject was then followed by his more exhaustive discussion of specific problems of social-psychological interest in his more recent work on *Human Nature and Conduct* (1922), the subtitle of which reads: "An Introduction to Social Psychology." It is with this one of Dewey's works that we shall be chiefly concerned here.

In the above-mentioned article on "The Need for Social Psychology,"[3] which is very important from the standpoint of getting his own social-psychological position in larger perspective, Dewey reviews some of the important developments in the field of social-psychological thought and he brings his own point of view as it appeared to him at the time into relation with them. After an introductory statement on the social-psychological importance of James' *Principles of Psychology*, in which he remarks on "the depth and breadth of the influence of James," he proceeds to consider the work of Tarde and his followers, among whom he notes especially Baldwin and Ross. After commenting on the theory of imitation as the outstanding characteristic of this first period of social-psychological development and on the general importance of this period of social-psychological thought in popularizing the idea of social psychology and in bringing into view some of its basic considerations and problems, Dewey orientates his own social-psychological point of view in the underlying conception which he attributes to Tarde, namely, that "all psychology is either biological or social psychology."[4] He says in this connection:

Tarde himself was certainly one of the most stimulating and varied of writers, and I do not think we shall ever outgrow some of his contributions, although to

[1] See, for instance, "Psychology and Social Practice," *Psychol. Rev.*, vol. 7, pp 105–124, 1900; *The School and Society* (1900), Chaps. I, V; DEWEY and TUFTS. *Ethics* (1910), Chap. XX; *Schools of Tomorrow* (1915), Chap. VII; *Essays in Experimental Logic* (1916), especially Chap. I; *Democracy and Education* (1916), especially Chaps. I, II, XXII; *Reconstruction in Philosophy* (1920), Chap. VIII.

[2] *Psychol. Rev.*, vol. 24, pp. 266–277, 1917, address on the occasion of the twenty-fifth anniversary of the American Psychological Association, December, 1916.

[3] This article may be said to mark the real beginning of psychological interest in the subject of social psychology in this country, American psychologists, with the exception of Baldwin, having been conspicuously disregardful of social psychology until Dewey thus directed their attention to the subject.

[4] *Psychol. Rev.*, vol. 24, pp. 267–276, 1917. Quotations from this journal are reprinted by permission of the Psychological Review Company, publishers.

This position, it will be recalled, was developed by Mead in his article on "Social Psychology as a Counterpart of Physiological Psychology," *Psychol. Bull.*, vol. 6, pp. 401–408, 1909.

my mind they are found rather in logic than in psychology—such as the necessity for reducing the gross phenomena of social life into minuter events which may then be analyzed one by one. The most fruitful of his psychological conceptions was ahead of his time and went almost unnoted. It was that all psychological phenomena can be divided into the physiological and the social, and that when we have relegated elementary sensation and appetite to the former head, all that is left of our mental life, our beliefs, ideas and desires, falls within the scope of social psychology.[1]

Citing next the work of McDougall and Thorndike, and on the social side such writings as those of Graham Wallas, as representative of the next stage of social-psychological development, during which, according to him, social psychology was recalled "from the wrong track in which the Imitation and Suggestibility schools had set it going" and the misleading antithesis between the individual and the social to which these theories led by setting up "two independent and even contrary sciences—individual and social psychology"[2]—he says:

From the root of all such aberrations we were recalled the very moment the problem was presented not as one of the relationship of a mythical psychology of an isolated individual mind to the even more mythical psychology of a mass or crowd or public mind, but as the problem of the relationship of original or native activities to acquired capacities and habits.[3]

Continuing his comment on the significance of this shift of focus he says further:

. . . for those who have learned the lesson of recourse to fundamental responses, the way is opened for emancipation from the greatest foe with which social science has had to contend—which I shall take the liberty of calling the monistic. How often have we been invited to build up our social, political, and ethical explanations in terms of some single and supposedly dominant mental constituent! How often discussions and disputes have been, at bottom, only a question as to which of rival single claimants we shall yield allegiance. Instincts to power, to control others, fear of authority, sex, love of pleasure, of ease, all have been appealed to, and explanations constructed in terms of one or another exclusively. Henceforth it is, I submit, pure wilfulness if any one pretending to a scientific treatment starts from any other than a pluralistic basis; the complexity and specific variety of the factors of human nature, each operating in response to its own highly specific stimulus, and each subject to almost infinite shadings and modulations as it enters into combination and competition with others.[4]

The conception of social psychology in which this outlook results is outlined by Dewey in the words of W. I. Thomas[5] as follows:

---

[1] *Psychol. Rev.*, vol. 24, p. 267, 1917.
[2] *Ibid.*, pp. 267–268.
[3] *Ibid.*, p. 268.
[4] *Ibid.*, p. 268–269.
[5] *Proc. Intern. Congress Arts Sci.*, vol. 5, pp. 860–868, 1904 (see *infra*, p. 353).

On the one hand our problem is to know the modifications wrought in the native constitution of man by the fact that the elements of his endowment operate in this or that social medium; on the other hand, we want to know how control of the environment may be better secured by means of the operation of this or that native capacity. Under these general heads are summed up the infinity of special and difficult problems relating to education on the one hand and to constructive modification of our social institutions on the other. To form a mind out of certain native instincts by selecting an environment which evokes them and directs their course; to reform social institutions by breaking up habits and giving peculiar intensity and scope to some impulse is the problem of social control in its two phases. To describe how such changes take place is the task of social psychology stated in generalized terms.[1]

Such, then, was Dewey's conception of social psychology in 1916 when the instinct theory of human conduct was at the height of its popularity in this country. With the developing attack upon instinct psychology which followed, however, and the clarification of the implications which it held for social-psychological thought, Dewey gradually shifted ground from emphasis on instinct to habit as a basis of attack in social psychology (a position which in any event is more in line with his point of view as a whole) and thereby he arrived at the position which he outlines in his *Human Nature and Conduct.*

Before passing on to the consideration of the latter, it is notable here, especially in view of some of our previous considerations relating to method, that Dewey mentions the application of the statistical procedure to psychological research and the behavioristic movement as most important factors in the positive development of social psychology on the methodological side at this time. Neither of these, he points out, was devised primarily in the interest of social psychology, but both have made themselves felt in bringing to the fore the experimental attitude and the interest in control, and these Dewey regards as all-important in respect to the decisive problem of method in social psychology.[2]

Dewey's final summation of the situation as he saw it at the time is especially to be noted here as background for his later treatment of social psychology in his *Human Nature and Conduct.* He says:

I foresee a great reflex wave from social psychology back into general psychology. An important conclusion in the psychology of native activities does not seem to have been drawn as yet by those who would base a scientific psychology upon this foundation. The conclusion seems inevitable that since "mind" does not appear in the original list of instincts, it represents something acquired. It represents a reorganization of original activities through their operation in a given environment. It is a formation, not a datum; a product, and a cause only after it has been produced.[3]

[1] *Psychol. Rev.*, vol. 24, p. 269, 1917.
[2] *Ibid.*, pp. 269–270 274–275.
[3] *Ibid.*, p. 271.

Theoretically, according to him, it is "possible that the reorganization of native activities which constitute mind may occur through their exercise within a purely physical medium"—a condition assumed by the older individualistic psychology. Empirically, however, "a consideration of the dependence in infancy of the organization of the native activities into intelligence upon the presence of others, upon sharing in joint activities and upon language, makes it obvious that the sort of mind capable of development through the operation of native endowment in a non-social environment is of the moron order, and is practically, if not theoretically, negligible."[1]

The net outcome of the newer movements in psychology, he maintains, has been, "an unexpected confirmation of the insight of Tarde that what we call 'mind' means essentially the working of certain beliefs and desires; and that these in the concrete—in the only sense in which mind may be said to *exist*—are functions of associated behavior, varying with the structure and operation of social groups." The conviction "that anything which may properly be called mind or intelligence is not an original possession but is a consequence of the manifestation of instincts under the conditions supplied by associated life in the family, the school, the market place and the forum," he says further, "is no remote inference from a speculative reconstruction of the mind of primitive man; it is a conclusion confirmed by the development of specific beliefs, ideas and purposes in the life of every infant now observable."[1]

In his more recent work on *Human Nature and Conduct*, Dewey elaborated these preliminary remarks in the discussion of his well-known emphasis upon the social psychology of habit. In explanation of this emphasis and its relation to the subtitle of the work which, as was stated above, reads "An Introduction to Social Psychology," Dewey says:

Perhaps the sub-title requires a word of explanation. The book does not purport to be a treatment of social psychology. But it seriously sets forth a belief that an understanding of habit and of different types of habit is the key to social psychology, while the operation of impulse and intelligence gives the key to individualized mental activity. But they are secondary to habit so that mind can be understood in the concrete only as a system of beliefs, desires and purposes which are formed in the interaction of biological aptitudes with a social environment.[2]

The full social-psychological significance of this statement can appear only when it is viewed in the light of Dewey's point of view as a whole as it is developed here and the particular sense in which he uses the term

[1] *Ibid.*, p. 272.
[2] *Human Nature and Conduct*, Preface. Quotations from this work are reprinted by permission of Henry Holt & Company, publishers.

habit in this connection. We must therefore follow out at some length his conception of the role of habit in mental life and note how he brings this conception into relation with the other important aspects of his theory. He proceeds to point out:

Habits may be profitably compared to physiological functions, like breathing, digesting. The latter are, to be sure, involuntary, while habits are acquired. But important as is this difference for many purposes it should not conceal the fact that habits are like functions in many respects, and especially in requiring the cooperation of organism and environment. Breathing is an affair of the air as truly as of the lungs; digesting an affair of food as truly as of tissues of stomach. Seeing involves light just as certainly as it does the eye and optic nerve. Walking implicates the ground as well as the legs; speech demands physical air and human companionship and audience as well as vocal organs. We may shift from the biological to the mathematical use of the word function, and say that natural operations like breathing and digesting, acquired ones like speech and honesty, are functions of the surroundings as truly as of a person. They are things done *by* the environment by means of organic structures or acquired dispositions. The same air that under certain conditions ruffles the pool or wrecks buildings, under other conditions purifies the blood and conveys thought. The outcome depends upon what air acts upon.[1]

Continuing, he suggests in this connection:

There are specific good reasons for the usual attribution of acts to the persons from whom they immediately proceed. But to convert the special reference into a belief of exclusive ownership is as misleading as to suppose that breathing and digesting are complete within the human body. To get a rational basis for moral discussion [Dewey directs his discussion to this problem constantly in this work by specific reference to the particular problem of moral conduct with which it chiefly deals] we must begin with recognizing that functions and habits are ways of using and incorporating the environment in which the latter has its say as surely as the former.

We may borrow words from a context less technical than that of biology, and convey the same idea by saying that habits are arts. They involve skill of sensory and motor organs, cunning or craft, and objective materials. They assimilate objective energies, and eventuate in command of environment. They require order, discipline, and manifest technique. They have a beginning, middle and end. Each stage marks progress in dealing with materials and tools, an advance in converting material to active use.[2]

The implications of this conception of habit for social psychology are far-reaching. We should laugh, observes Dewey, "at anyone who said that he was master of stone working, but that the art was cooped up within himself and in no wise dependent upon support from objects and assistance from tools." Yet in the field of morals we are "quite accus-

[1] *Ibid.*, pp. 14–15.
[2] *Ibid.*, p. 15.

tomed to such fatuity." Moral dispositions are, according to him, thought of as belonging exclusively to a self and the self is at the same time isolated from its natural and social surroundings.

A whole school of morals flourishes upon capital drawn from restricting morals to character and then separating character from conduct, motives from actual deeds. Recognition of the analogy of moral action with functions and arts uproots the causes which have made morals subjective and "individualistic." It brings morals to earth, and if they still aspire to heaven it is to the heavens of the earth, and not to another world. Honesty, chastity, malice, peevishness, courage, triviality, industry, irresponsibility are not private possessions of a person. They are working adaptations of personal capacities with environing forces. All virtues and vices are habits which incorporate objective forces. They are interactions of elements contributed by the make-up of an individual with elements supplied by the out-door world. They can be studied as objectively as physiological functions, and they can be modified by change of either personal or social elements.[1]

It is precisely this dual aspect of habit which makes it peculiarly significant for social psychology from Dewey's point of view. And since this significance has been traditionally obscured by the tendency of psychological individualism to treat habit as though it were a possession of the individual formed in a social vacuum, it becomes his task to emphasize particularly the social element involved in it.

Since habits imply, he argues, "the support of environing conditions, a society or some specific group of fellow-men, is always accessory before and after the fact." He explains:

Some activity proceeds from a man; then it sets up reactions in the surroundings. Others approve, disapprove, protest, encourage, share and resist. Even letting a man alone is a definite response. Envy, admiration and imitation are complicities. Neutrality is non-existent. Conduct is always shared; this is the difference between it and the physiological process. It is not an ethical "ought" that conduct *should* be social. It *is* social, whether bad or good.[2]

In practical life, according to Dewey, there are many recognitions of the part played by social factors in generating personal traits. One of them, he suggests, is our habit of making social classifications. "We attribute," he says, "distinctive characteristics to rich and poor, slum-dweller and captain of industry, rustic and suburbanite, officials, politicians, professors, to members of races, sets and parties." And while these judgments are, according to him, usually too coarse to be of much use, they show our practical awareness that personal traits are functions of social situations. The significance of this point is suggested by him as follows:

[1] *Ibid.*, p. 16.
[2] *Ibid.*, pp. 16–17.

When we generalize this perception and act upon it intelligently, we are committed by it to recognize that we change character from worse to better only by changing conditions—among which, once more, are our own ways of dealing with the one we judge. We cannot change habit directly; that notion is magic. But we can change it indirectly by modifying conditions, by an intelligent selecting and weighting of the objects which engage attention and which influence the fulfilment of desires.[1]

Refusal to recognize this is responsible, according to him, for a tremendous waste of human energy in the field of social reform. He observes:

We may desire abolition of war, industrial justice, greater equality of opportunity for all. But no amount of preaching good will or the golden rule or cultivation of sentiments of love and equity will accomplish the results. There must be change in objective arrangements and institutions. We must work on the environment, not merely on the hearts of men. To think otherwise is to suppose that flowers can be raised in a desert or motor cars run in a jungle. Both things can happen and without miracle. But only by first changing the jungle and desert.[2]

It is a significant fact, Dewey further suggests in this connection, that in order to appreciate the peculiar place of habit in activity we have to betake ourselves to bad habits, idling, gambling, addiction to liquor and drugs.

When we think of such habits, the union of habit with desire and with propulsive power is forced upon us. When we think of habits in terms of walking, playing a musical instrument, typewriting, we are much given to thinking of habits as technical abilities existing apart from our likings and as lacking in urgent impulsion. We think of them as passive tools waiting to be called into action from without. A bad habit suggests an inherent tendency to action and also a hold, command over us. It makes us do things we are ashamed of, things which we tell ourselves we prefer not to do. It overrides our formal resolutions, our conscious decisions. When we are honest with ourselves we acknowledge that a habit has this power because it is so intimately a part of ourselves. It has a hold upon us because we are the habit.[3]

These traits of a bad habit are precisely the things which are most instructive about all habits and about ourselves. They teach us that all habits are affections, that all have projectile power, and that a predisposition formed by a number of specific acts is an immensely more intimate and fundamental part of ourselves than are vague, general, conscious choices. All habits are demands for certain kinds of activity; and they constitute the self. In any intelligible sense of the word will, they *are* will. They form our effective desires and they furnish us with our working capacities. They rule our thoughts, determining which shall appear and be strong and which shall pass from light into obscurity.[4]

[1] *Ibid.*, pp. 19–20.
[2] *Ibid.*, pp. 21–22, also pp. 9–11.
[3] *Ibid.*, p. 24.
[4] *Ibid.*, p. 25.

"We may think of habits," says Dewey, "as means, waiting, like tools in a box, to be used by conscious resolve. But they are something more than that. They are active means, means that project themselves, energetic and dominating ways of acting." We need, according to him, to distinguish in this connection between materials, tools, and means proper. Nails and boards are not strictly speaking means of a box, he points out. They are only materials for making it. Even the saw and hammer are means only when they are employed in some actual making. Otherwise they are tools, or potential means. "They are actual means," he says, "only when brought in conjunction with eye, arm and hand in some specific operation. And eye, arm and hand are, correspondingly, means proper only when they are in active operation. And whenever they are in action they are cooperating with external materials and energies. Without support from beyond themselves the eye stares blankly and the hand moves fumblingly. They are means only when they enter into organization with things which independently accomplish definite results. These organizations are habits."[1]

This conception of habit is, according to Dewey, double-edged in its social-psychological consequences. Except in a contingent sense neither external materials nor bodily and mental organs are in themselves means. They have to be employed "in coordinated conjunction with one another" to be actual means or habits. "This statement," he suggests, "may seem like the formulation in technical language of a commonplace." But belief in magic, he recalls, has played a large part in human history, and it did not wholly cease with the passing of the coarser forms of superstitious practice. "And the essence of all hocus-pocus," according to him, "is the supposition that results can be accomplished without the joint adaptation to each other of human powers and physical conditions." Such expectations still prevail among us, he points out, in particular in the fields of morals and politics, and in so far, the most important phases of human action are still under the control of the magical attitude.[2] He says further in this connection:

We think that by feeling strongly enough about something, by wishing hard enough, we can get a desirable result, such as virtuous execution of a good resolve, or peace among nations, or good will in industry. We slur over the necessity of the cooperative action of objective conditions, and the fact that this cooperation is assured only by persistent and close study. Or, on the other hand, we fancy we can get these results by external machinery, by tools or potential means, without a corresponding functioning of human desires and capacities. Often times these two false and contradictory beliefs are combined in the same person. The man who feels that *his* virtues are his own personal accomplishments is likely to be also the one who thinks that by passing laws he can throw

[1] *Ibid.*, pp. 25–26.
[2] *Ibid.*, pp. 26–27.

the fear of God into others and make them virtuous by edict and prohibitory mandate.[1]

An example of such superstition, he suggestively notes, is the notion current among even cultivated people that if the right *end* is pointed out, all that is required in order to bring about the right act is will on the part of the one who is to act. As a matter of fact, he maintains, the implication that habit is merely negative, a mere failure to do the right thing which can be made good by an order of the will, is nothing short of being absurd. By way of illustration he observes:

> One might as well suppose that the man who is a slave of whiskey-drinking is merely one who fails to drink water. Conditions have been formed for producing a bad result, and the bad result will occur as long as those conditions exist. They can no more be dismissed by a direct effort of will than the conditions which create drought can be dispelled by whistling for wind. It is as reasonable to expect a fire to go out when it is ordered to stop burning as to suppose that a man can stand straight in consequence of a direct action of thought and desire. The fire can be put out only by changing objective conditions; it is the same with rectification of bad posture.[2]

When we realize this, we are likely to suppose, suggests Dewey, that posture involves difficulties because control of the *body* is physical and hence external to mind and will. "Transfer the command inside character and mind, and it is fancied that an idea of an end and the desire to realize it will take immediate effect. After we get to the point of recognizing that habits must intervene between wish and execution in the case of bodily acts," he explains, "we still cherish the illusion that they can be dispensed with in the case of mental and moral acts." But in fact, from his point of view, formation of ideas as well as their execution depends on habit. "The act must come before the thought, and a habit before an ability to evoke the thought at will." Ordinary psychology, according to him, reverses the actual state of affairs.[3]

It thus follows, as Dewey proceeds to point out, that meaning, purpose, reason, ideas, even sensations are all alike functions of experience and habit. "The medium of habit filters all the material that reaches our perception and thought," according to him. Distinct and independent sensory qualities, for instance, "far from being original elements, are the products of a highly skilled analysis which disposes of immense technical scientific resources." That it is not such a simple matter to have a clear-cut sensation as the older psychology assumed, a moderate amount of observation of a child, suggests Dewey, will suffice to reveal. Even such gross discriminations as black, white, red, green are the result, it will appear, of training, skill, and habit. The psychology of illusion

[1] *Ibid.*, p. 27.
[2] *Ibid.*, p. 29.
[3] *Ibid.*, p. 30.

of perception and of intuitive judgment is full of telling illustrations of this point, according to him.[1]

The term "habit," Dewey recognized, may seem twisted somewhat from its customary use when employed in this way. But a word is needed to express, he explains, "that kind of human activity which is influenced by prior activity and in that sense acquired; which contains within itself a certain ordering or systematization of minor elements of action; which is projective, dynamic in quality, ready for overt manifestation; and which is operative in some subdued subordinate form even when not obviously dominating activity."[2] And habit, he felt, comes nearer to denoting these qualities than any other word. Alternative terms would be "attitude" and "disposition," but these terms appeared to him to hold more misleading suggestions than habit, unless the facts are recognized in advance. The facts involved are, however, the only important consideration, and if these are perceived in their proper relation, the term employed to designate them is a matter of no very great importance, according to him.[3] But in defense and clarification of his own preference for the term habit, he says in summary:

> While it is admitted that the word *habit* has been used in a somewhat broader sense than is usual, we must protest against the tendency in psychological literature to limit its meaning to repetition. This usage is much less in accord with popular usage than is the wider way in which we have used the word. It assumes from the start the identity of habit with routine. Repetition is in no sense the essence of habit. Tendency to repeat acts is an incident of many habits but not of all. A man with the habit of giving way to anger may show his habit by a murderous attack upon some one who has offended. His act is none the less due to habit because it occurs only once in his life. The essence of habit is an acquired predisposition to ways or modes of response, not to particular acts except as, under special conditions, these express a way of behaving. Habit means special sensitiveness or accessibility to certain classes of stimuli, standing predilections and aversions, rather than bare recurrence of specific acts. It means will.[4]

It is in this broad sense that habit is, according to Dewey, the basis of character and conduct, of motive and act, of will and deed, of custom and social organization—in short, "the key to social psychology."[5] In terms of the traditional formula, man is, from his standpoint, "a creature of habit, not of reason nor yet of instinct."[6] The latter, treated by

---

[1] *Ibid.*, pp. 30–33.

[2] *Ibid.*, p. 40.

[3] *Ibid.*, pp. 40–41. W. I. Thomas, as we shall see, has shown a preference for the term "attitude" (see *infra*, pp. 351*ff.*), and a number of writers, for example Graham Wallas, have made use of the term "disposition" in contrast to the biologically orientated term "predisposition" (*supra* p. 202).

[4] *Human Nature and Conduct*, pp. 41–42.

[5] *Ibid.*, Preface, pp. 43*ff.*

[6] *Ibid.*, p. 125.

him respectively in terms of "the place of intelligence in conduct" and "the place of impulse in conduct," in correspondence with his treatment of "the place of habit in conduct," are important, to be sure, but they are, according to him, "secondary" to habit in the understanding of human behavior, since they are, from his point of view, in a real sense functions of habit.[1] This position, Dewey recognized, requires explanation in view of the traditional trend of psychological thought and especially in view of instinct psychology and psychoanalytic theory, and he attempted to meet this requirement, somewhat after the manner of Baldwin and Cooley, through a rehearsal of some of the significant considerations relating to the conditions of infant life and human development.

When the human individual comes into the world, helpless and dependent, Dewey recalls in this connection, the activities of the group are already there, and some assimilation of his own acts to their pattern is a prerequisite for his life and well-being.[2] He says:

Each person is born an infant, and every infant is subject from the first breath he draws and the first cry he utters to the attentions and demands of others. These others are not just persons in general with minds in general. They are beings with habits . . . [and the] nature of habit is to be assertive, insistent, self-perpetuating.[3]

There is thus no miracle in the fact, according to him, that a child learns the language of those about him or that it takes over their morality and group customs. This is, from his point of view, the inevitable result of the facts of infancy, and sex, and the elementary conditions of human life. The child "inherits" these things from the social life of which it must be a part to live and attain mental development in the normal course of events. Furthermore, "few persons," Dewey observes, "have either the energy or the wealth to build private roads to travel upon. They find it convenient, 'natural,' to use the roads that are already there; while unless their private roads connect at some point with the high-way they cannot build them even if they would."[4]

But in any event, it is from the social-psychological standpoint, he recalls, an all-important fact that all children are born into a family, and that the family into which one is born is, as he suggests, "a family in a village or city which interacts with other more or less integrated systems of activity, and which includes a diversity of groupings within itself, say, churches, political parties, clubs, cliques, partnerships, trade-unions, corporations, etc."[5] For it is clear from a consideration of these

[1] *Ibid.*, Preface, pp. 14, 32, 69, 84, etc.
[2] *Ibid.*, pp. 58, 84.
[3] *Ibid.*, p. 58.
[4] *Ibid.*, p. 59.
[5] *Ibid.*, p. 61.

elementary facts that the human individual is plunged into the social life about him perforce and from the very first. The net result of these inescapable conditions of life "is that what can be called distinctively individual in behavior and mind is not, contrary to traditional theory, an original datum" but a quality of habit involving adjustments to social environment in time and place. "In short," he says, "the primary facts of social psychology center about collective habit, custom." Otherwise stated, the psychology of habit is in the first place, as Dewey maintains, "an objective and social psychology."[1]

And yet, "habits as organized activities are secondary and acquired," he calls to mind. "They are outgrowths of unlearned activities which are part of man's endowment at birth." Why, then, he asks, "did we not set out with an examination of those instinctive activities upon which the acquisition of habits is conditioned?" This query, he admits, is a natural one, but it tempts to flinging forth a paradox. Thus he says:

In conduct the acquired is the primitive. Impulses although first in time are never primary in fact; they are secondary and dependent . . . In the life of the individual, instinctive activity comes first. But an individual begins life as a baby, and babies are dependent beings. Their activities could continue at most for only a few hours were it not for the presence and aid of adults with their formed habits. And babies owe to adults more than procreation, more than the continued food and protection which preserve life. They owe to adults the opportunity to express their native activities in ways which have meaning. Even if by some miracle original activity could continue without assistance from the organized skill and art of adults, it would not amount to anything. It would be mere sound and fury.

In short, the *meaning* of native activities is not native; it is acquired. It depends upon interaction with a matured social medium. In the case of a tiger or eagle, anger may be identified with a serviceable life-activity, with attack and defense. With a human being it is as meaningless as a gust of wind on a mud-puddle apart from a direction given it by the presence of other persons, apart from the responses they make to it. It is a physical spasm, a blind dispersive burst of wasteful energy. It gets quality, significance, when it becomes a smouldering sullenness, an annoying interruption, a peevish irritation, a murderous revenge, a blazing indignation. And although these phenomena which have a meaning spring from original native reactions to stimuli, yet they depend also upon the responsive behavior of others. They and all similar human displays of anger are not pure impulses; they are habits formed under the influence of association with others who have habits already and who show their habits in the treatment which converts a blind physical discharge into a significant anger.[2]

As regards the important role which has been assigned to instinct in recent social-psychological theory, Dewey accordingly says:

[1] *Ibid.*, pp. 63, 84.
[2] *Ibid.*, pp. 89–90.

After ignoring impulses for a long time in behalf of sensations, modern psychology now tends to start out with an inventory and description of instinctive activities. This is an undoubted improvement. But when it tries to explain complicated events in personal and social life by direct reference to these native powers, the explanation becomes hazy and forced. It is like saying the flea and the elephant, the lichen and the redwood, the timid hare and the ravening wolf, the plant with the most inconspicuous blossom and the plant with the most glaring color are alike products of natural selection. There may be a sense in which the statement is true; but till we know the specific environing conditions under which selection took place we really know nothing. And so we need to know about the social conditions which have educated original activities into definite and significant dispositions before we can discuss the psychological element in society. This is the true meaning of social psychology.[1]

At some place on the globe, at some time, Dewey calls to mind in defending this position, every kind of practice seems to have been tolerated or even praised. How, he asks, is this diversity of behavior to be accounted for in terms of native equipment, in view of the evidence to the effect that the native stock of instincts is practically the same everywhere?

The wholesale human sacrifices of Peru and the tenderness of St. Francis, the cruelties of pirates and the philanthropies of Howard, the practice of Suttee and the cult of the Virgin, the war and peace dances of the Comanches and the parliamentary institutions of the British, the communism of the southsea islander and the proprietary thrift of the Yankee, the magic of the medicine man and the experiments of the chemist in his laboratory, the non-resistance of Chinese and the aggressive militarism of an imperial Prussia, monarchy by divine right and government by the people; the countless diversity of habits suggested by such a random list springs from practically the same capital-stock of native instincts.[2]

The same original fears, angers, loves, and hates are hopelessly entangled in the most opposite practices and institutions. What avails it, then, to speak of "instinct"? "Exaggerate," says he, "as much as we like the native differences of Patagonians and Greeks, Sioux Indians and Hindoos, Bushmen and Chinese, their original differences will bear no comparison to the amount of difference found in custom and culture." In the course of the further consideration of such facts, Dewey finally leads to the conclusion that "the development of native impulse must be stated in terms of acquired habits, not the growth of customs in terms of instincts." "The thing we need to know," he says, "is how a native stock has been modified by interaction with different environments"; "how different customs, established interacting arrangements, form and

[1] *Ibid.*, pp. 85, 90–91. See *infra*, p. 348, for a comment on this seeming departure from his previous position.

[2] *Ibid.*, p. 92.

nurture different minds"; how social conditions educate "original activities into definite and significant dispositions."[1]

A combination of traditional individualism with the recent interest in progress explains, in Dewey's opinion, "why the discovery of the scope and force of instincts has led many psychologists to think of them as the fountainhead of all conduct, as occupying a place before instead of after that of habits." The orthodox tradition in psychology, he points out, was built upon isolation of individuals from their surroundings. The soul or mind or consciousness was thought of as self-contained and self-enclosed. "Now in the career of an individual if it is regarded as complete in itself instincts clearly come before habits," he observes. "Generalize this individualistic view, and we have an assumption that all customs, all significant episodes in the life of individuals can be carried directly back to the operation of instincts."[2]

But the artificiality of this point of view appears immediately, he suggests, when we recognize that "if an individual be isolated in this fashion, along with the fact of primacy of instinct we find also the fact of death."[3] And if we abandon such "an impossible individualistic psychology," instinct in any concrete and intelligible sense must be regarded as a function of habit, as a product and not a datum, as "filtered" by the social environment.[4] As "instincts" merely, they simply do not exist in human conduct.

Such attempts as have been made, therefore, to define separate instincts and to classify them in sharply demarcated groupings must thus be frankly looked upon, according to Dewey, as attempts to deal with abstracted elements of conduct, and as such they should be judged in terms of the "purpose" which they are intended to accomplish; that is, generally speaking, "to facilitate our dealing with unique individuals and changing events." And, most important of all, one must be careful not to confuse the results of such abstraction with the reality of human conduct itself. "When we assume that our clefts and bunches represent fixed separations and collections *in rerum natura*," he says in this connection, "we obstruct rather than aid our transactions with things. We are guilty of a presumption which nature promptly punishes. We are rendered incompetent to deal effectively with the delicacies and novelties of nature and life. Our thought is hard where facts are mobile; bunched and chunky where events are fluid, dissolving."[5] And because this type of assumption was becoming something of a real obstruction in current psychological thought, Dewey

[1] *Ibid.*, pp. 60, 61, 63, 91–92.
[2] *Ibid.*, pp. 85, 93–94.
[3] *Ibid.*, p. 94.
[4] *Ibid.*, pp. 32, 69, 94.
[5] *Ibid.*, p. 131.

throws out the challenge of "no separate instincts" in his discussion of the subject.[1] He says:

The tendency to forget the office of distinctions and classifications, and to take them as marking things in themselves, is the current fallacy of scientific specialism. It is one of the conspicuous traits of highbrowism, the essence of false abstractionism. This attitude which once flourished in physical science now governs theorizing about human nature. Man has been resolved into a definite collection of primary instincts which may be numbered, catalogued and exhaustively described one by one. Theories differ only or chiefly as to their number and ranking. Some say one, self-love; some two, egoism and altruism; some three, greed, fear and glory; while today writers of a more empirical turn run the number up to fifty and sixty. But in fact there are as many specific reactions to differing stimulating conditions as there is time for, and our lists are only classifications for a purpose.[2]

One of the great evils of this artificial simplification in psychology, he points out, is its influence upon social science. "Complicated provinces of life have been assigned to the jurisdiction of some special instinct or group of instincts, which has reigned despotically with the usual consequences of despotism." Fear, the so-called self-seeking impulse, imitation, invention, cooperation, conflict, sympathy, benevolence, the economic interest, have each in turn held this sort of despotic sway, according to him. "It is surprising," he states, "that men can engage in these enterprises without being reminded of their exact similarity to natural science before scientific method was discovered in the seventeenth century." Just now another of these oversimplifications has become current, he recalls. "All instincts go back to the sexual, so that *cherchez la femme* (under multitudinous symbolic disguises) is the last word of science with respect to the analysis of conduct."[3]

In their practical effect, too, these theories have been injurious, according to Dewey, for they have seemed to lend scientific support to the notion of the "practical unalterability of human nature," the age-old refuge of the opponent to progressive social change.[4] In point of fact, as it seemed to him, native impulse, besides being the raw material of habit, is also the motive-force of progressive adjustment and control, of reorganization and readjustment. "The hen precedes the egg," he says. "But nevertheless this particular egg may be so treated as to modify the future type of hen." It is no accident, therefore, according to him, "that men became interested in the psychology of savages and babies when they became interested in doing away with old institutions."[5]

[1] *Ibid.*, Chaps. V–VI.
[2] *Ibid.*, pp. 131–132.
[3] *Ibid.*, pp. 132–133.
[4] *Ibid.*, p. 107.
[5] *Ibid.*, pp. 93–94, also p. 59.

"The direction of native activity depends upon acquired habits, and yet acquired habits can be modified only by redirection of impulses"[1] is the way Dewey states the issue involved in the above statement. Here, then, is the field of function of intelligence in his scheme.[2] The position of impulse in the habit-impulse-intelligence complex is intermediary.[3] Habit implies, according to him, a balance of organism and environment so that stimulus and response can be mechanically linked together in an unbroken chain. A complete balance, however, never exists, for life flows on beyond established adjustments. In consequence, though habit control the greater part of behavior, life is still a series of interruptions and recoveries. Success in achieving a ruthless and dull life of habit is constantly thwarted by untoward circumstances. "The most skillful aptitude," says Dewey, "bumps at times into the unexpected," from which only the renewing function of impulse and the reconstructing activity of thought can extricate it.[4]

Normally, according to him, the environment remains sufficiently in harmony with the body of organized activities to sustain most of them in active function. But novel situations arise which release conflicting impulses and throw the organism for the time being into a state of confusion and inhibition. The disturbed flow of established habit provokes conscious feeling and thought, the function of which it is to bring to terms the stock of old habits and the newly released impulses, in such a way as to reconstruct the balance of action and adjustment between organism and environment.[5] The manner in which habit, impulse, and intelligence interact in this process of readjustment is suggestively described by Dewey in the following passage:

In this period of redistribution impulse determines the direction of movement. It furnishes the focus about which reorganization swirls. Our attention in short is always directed forward to bring to notice something which is imminent but which as yet escapes us. Impulse defines the peering, the search, the inquiry. It is, in logical language, the movement into the unknown, not into the immense inane of the unknown at large, but into that special unknown which when it is hit upon restores an ordered, unified action. During this search, old habit applies content, filling, definite, recognizable, subject-matter. It begins as vague presentiment of what we are going towards. As organized habits are definitely deployed and focused, the confused situation takes on form, it is "cleared up"—the essential function of intelligence. Processes become objects. Without habit there is only irritation and confused hesitation. With habit alone there is a machine-like repetition, a duplicating recur-

[1] *Ibid.*, p. 126.
[2] *Ibid.*, pp. 169*ff.*
[3] *Ibid.*, p. 169.
[4] *Ibid.*, p. 173.
[5] *Ibid.*, pp. 178–179, 190.

rence of old acts. With conflict of habits and release of impulse there is conscious search.[1]

We may compare life to a traveler faring forth, suggests Dewey, in order to bring out more clearly the functional interrelation between these three basic aspects of mental life. He says:

We may consider him [the traveler] first at a moment where his activity is confident, straightforward, organized. He marches on, giving no direct attention to his path, nor thinking of his destination. Abruptly he is pulled up, arrested. Something is going wrong in his activity. From the standpoint of an onlooker, he has met an obstacle which must be overcome before his behavior can be unified into a successful ongoing. From his own standpoint, there is shock, confusion, perturbation, uncertainty. For the moment he doesn't know what hit him, as we say, nor where he is going. But a new impulse is stirred which becomes the starting point of an investigation, a looking into things, a trying to see them, to find out what is going on. Habits which were interfered with begin to get a new direction as they cluster about the impulse to look and see. The blocked habits of locomotion give him a sense of where he *was* going, of what he had set out to do, and of the ground already traversed. As he looks, he sees definite things which are not just things at large but which are related to his course of action. The momentum of the activity entered upon persists as a sense of direction, of aim; it is an anticipatory project. In short, he recollects, observes and plans.[2]

The trinity of these forecasts, perceptions and remembrances form a subject-matter of discriminated and identified objects. These objects represent habits turned inside out. They exhibit both the onward tendency of habit and the objective conditions which have been incorporated within it. Sensations in immediate consciousness are elements of action dislocated through the shock of interruption. They never, however, completely monopolize the scene; for there is a body of residual and undisturbed habits which is reflected in remembered and perceived objects having a meaning. Thus out of shock and puzzlement there gradually emerges a figured framework of objects, past, present, future. These shade off variously into a vast penumbra of vague, unfigured things, a setting which is taken for granted and not at all explicitly presented. The complexity of the figured scene in its scope and refinement of contents depends wholly upon prior habits and their organization.[3]

In this picture, thought is "eventual, not a source," as was so long supposed. Dewey explains:

Its occurrence marks a peculiarly delicate connection between highly organized habits and unorganized impulses. Its contents or objects, observed, recollected, projected and generalized into principles, represent the incorporated material of habits coming to the surface, because habits are disintegrating at

[1] *Ibid.*, p. 180.
[2] *Ibid.*, pp. 181–182.
[3] *Ibid.*, pp. 181–182, also pp. 169–173, 177.

the touch of conflicting impulses. But they also gather themselves together to comprehend impulse and make it effective.[1]

This psychology "of the dependence of mind upon habit and of habit upon social conditions"[2] is central in Dewey's more recent formulation of his thought on the subject of social psychology. His position as thus outlined, as McDougall, for instance, has taken occasion to point out,[3] is neither altogether consistently carried out nor entirely in line with his previous pronouncements on the subject. It may to some extent even appear to be a reversal from his previously expressed convictions. In a deeper sense, however, it is to be viewed as a growth, corresponding to the development of social-psychological thought generally in this country. For in its essential implications, his social-psychological position as outlined follows more or less directly even from his early thought,[4] so that what appears at first to be a reversal of position is really rather a clarification of point of view on the basis of new and accumulating evidence. At any rate, the main import of Dewey's thought for social psychology is clear enough, and its practical bearing, as an expression of the pragmatic spirit and interest which are characteristic of Dewey's position in every field of thought, is of the deepest significance. This the author has himself taken pains to point out at various times and in various connections.

On the face of it, he says in his article on "The Need for Social Psychology," in contrasting his point of view with other social-psychological positions, the point of view described has implications only for the theory of psychology. Slight scrutiny, however, makes obvious its practical consequences, "for the struggle to gain control of the forces forming society." In an important and very influential passage, Dewey thus explains the import of this statement:

The ultimate refuge of the standpatter in every field, education, religion, politics, industrial and domestic life, has been the notion of an alleged fixed structure of mind. As long as mind is conceived as an antecedent and ready-made thing, institutions and customs may be regarded as its offspring. By its own nature the ready-made mind works to produce them as they have existed and now exist. There is no use in kicking against necessity. The most powerful apologetics for any arrangement or institution is the conception that it is an inevitable result of fixed conditions of human nature. Consequently, in one disguise or another, directly or by extreme and elaborate indirection, we find the assumed constitution of an antecedently given mind appealed to in justification of the established order as to the family, the school, the government, indus-

---

[1] *Ibid.*, p. 183.

[2] *Ibid.*, pp. 86–87.

[3] See his article on "Can Sociology and Social Psychology Dispense with Instincts?" *Amer. Jour. Sociol.*, vol. 29, pp. 657–666, 1924.

[4] See *supra*, p. 330.

try, commerce and every other institution. Our increased knowledge of the past of man has, indeed, given this complacent assumption a certain shock, but it has not as yet seriously modified it. Evolution in the sense of a progressive unfolding of original potencies latent in a ready-made mind has been used to reconcile the conception of mind as an original datum with the historic facts of social change which can no longer be ignored. The effect on the effort at deliberate social control and construction remained the same. All man could do was to wait and watch the panorama of a ready-formed mind unroll. The French school of imitation, and its present successor, the Durkheim school of collective mind, has practically the same outcome as the German school of Volk-geist in this respect. All are engaged in explaining the past and present, and (if they predict at all) in predicting the future on the basis of the past. The new point of view treats social facts as the material of an experimental science, where the problem is that of modifying belief and desire—that is to say mind—by enacting specific changes in the social environment. Until this experimental attitude is established, the historical method, in spite of all the proof of past change which it adduces, will remain in effect a bulwark of conservatism. For, I repeat, it reduces the role of mind to that of beholding and recording the operations of man after they have happened. The historic method may give emotional inspiration or consolation in arousing the belief that a lot more changes are still to happen, but it does not show man how his mind is to take part in giving these changes one direction rather than another.[1]

The new point of view, in bringing with itself the experimental attitude, tends definitely to substitute for the first time, according to Dewey, "the interest in control for the interest in merely recording and what is called 'explaining.' If mind," he says, "in any definitely concrete sense of that word, is an offspring of the life of association, intercourse, transmission, and accumulation rather than a ready-made antecedent cause of these things, then the attitude of polite aloofness or condescending justification as to social institutions has its nerve cut, and with this the intellectual resources of sanctified conservatism disappear." Mind becomes a function of the "shared life of the place and time," and the kind of mind that develops "depends upon the kind of objects of attention and affection which the specific social conditions supply." These conditions being controllable and modifiable, the point of view described becomes at once an incentive to and a challenge for the development of a technique of positive social control.[2]

Here, then, is where Dewey's social psychology passes into his theory of education as the aspect of social control in which Dewey is especially interested, and where it links up intimately with his notable doctrine of social progress, which in its emphasis upon knowledge, education, the democratic ideal, and the positive control of human welfare is so strongly reminiscent of Ward (it is possible to draw some very interesting parallels

[1] *Psychol. Rev.*, vol. 24, pp. 273–274, 1917.
[2] *Ibid.*, p. 274.

between these two otherwise very different writers) that it fairly seems to bring Ward's pioneer social doctrines to a natural and eloquent climax. In respect to these aspects of his thought, Dewey has been so important an influence in this country that they might be said to deserve extended treatment in their bearing on the social-psychological situation here. But for our purposes at this point, it will be sufficient to quote, in closing, the following very brief passages in illustration of this larger setting of his social-psychological theory from his article on "The Need for Social Psychology:"[1]

There is a genuine modesty, and there is a stupid simulation of modesty which is only a mask for lazy complacency. No science has so much cause to be humble about its actual achievements as has social science, including social psychology. But in prospect, in possibility, social science seems to me to stand about where physical science stood three centuries ago in the early years of the seventeenth century . . . The experimental method in physical matters brought with it a technique of control—a technique of invention and construction. Specific desired ends can be formulated in specifically analyzed terms; the conditions of their attainment stated; these conditions subdivided into known and unknown factors, and some definite estimate made as to the practicability, at the given time, of attacking the problem. That we are without any such technique in social matters is self-evident. That the attainment within reasonable time of a similar technique stands and falls with the possibility of developing a human psychology which shall be experimentally applicable to the understanding of social affairs is not, however, self-evident, and is my excuse for reiteration.

Physical science has got to the point of bringing even the ends of the earth into physical, forceful relations with one another, and to the point of mobilizing all its resources for a contest in aggression and endurance. We are overwhelmed by the consequences of the very sciences into which have gone our best thought and energy for these last few hundred years. We apparently do not control them; they control us and wreak their vengeance upon us. Yet how infantile and pusillanimous are those who talk about the bankruptcy of science and who blame the increase of knowledge for our situation. Physical knowledge, and the consequent technique of control of physical forces, has far out-run social knowledge and its technique. The recourse of a courageous humanity is to press forward in the latter until we have a control of human nature comparable to our control of physical nature.

"We are not called upon [says he in conclusion, quoting a previous statement of his] to be either boasters or sentimentalists regarding the possibilities of our science . . . But we are entitled in our daily work to be sustained by the conviction that we are not working in indifference to or at cross purposes with the practical strivings of a common humanity. The psychologist in his most remote and technical occupation with mechanism may be contributing his bit to that ordered knowledge which alone enables mankind to secure a larger and to direct a more equal flow of the values of life.[2]"

[1] See *supra*, p. 243.

[2] *Psychol. Rev.*, vol. 24, pp. 275–277, 1917. For a further consideration of these larger aspects of Dewey's thought, see also *Human Nature and Conduct*, pp. 95–96,

IV. WILLIAM I. THOMAS (1863), ELLSWORTH FARIS (1874), AND OTHERS ASSOCIATED WITH THEIR SOCIAL-PSYCHOLOGICAL VIEWPOINTS

The direction of social-psychological development which has been traced out here, more especially through the work of Cooley, Mead, and Dewey, leads next to the important social-psychological work of W. I. Thomas, who has made a most notable contribution to American social-psychological thought in conjunction with his monographic study of the Polish group, made together with Florian Znaniecki.[1] Thomas' theory has importance here from the standpoint of the advance of American social-psychological thought in several respects, but above all because the methodological form of his exposition has tended to direct attention to social psychology as a research technique and not merely as a point of view and basis of criticism of traditional social and psychological thought, as it for the most part appeared to be in the case of these other writers. In this respect, Thomas supplements the formulations of these other writers very strikingly and, in fact, his work rather tends to link social psychology with the detailed research that is at present increasingly being carried on in the fields of psychology, sociology, and anthropology than with the more abstract and generalized type of discussion which has traditionally so largely occupied these fields of endeavor.

The methodological setting which Thomas gives his social-psychological theory as outlined in conjunction with his monographic study of the Polish group is, however, notable here also in another connection, in that it sets his position off so decisively from conflicting positions and tends to bring the issues of social-psychological thought, as Thomas sees them, to a focus in a way in which they appear nowhere else in recent social-psychological literature. Nowhere else do we get such a clear-cut statement of social-psychological thought from the standpoint of its implications for actual research and investigation, and nowhere else, therefore, do we get such a challenging presentation of the social-psychological position viewed as a definite procedure alongside of psy-

---

106 ff., 127–130, 281, 319 ff.; *Democracy and Education*, pp. 1 ff., 49 ff., 261 ff.; *Experience and Nature*, Chap. V; *The Public And Its Problems*, Chap. VI; especially "Progress," *Intern. Jour. Ethics*, vol. 26, pp. 312–318, 1916; "Pragmatic America," *The New Republic*, Apr. 12, 1922, repr. in *Characters and Events*, vol. II, pp. 542–547; "The New Social Science," *The New Republic*, Apr. 6, 1918, repr. in *Characters and Events*, vol. II, pp. 733–738; also references, *supra*, pp. 212–213.

[1] THOMAS and ZNANIECKI, *The Polish Peasant in Europe and America*, 5 vols. (1918–1920), 2 vols. (1927). The five-volume edition has been used for the purposes of this analysis.

For convenience this study will be referred to hereafter under the name of Thomas, but clearly the discussion has reference to both authors. Znaniecki has elaborated his position in his *Cultural Reality* (1919) and his *Laws of Social Psychology* (1925), which indicate his leanings as compared with those of Thomas.

chology and biology on the one hand and sociology and anthropology on the other. It is for this reason, no doubt, that Thomas' work has brought forth a very considerable following which, despite important differences of interest and emphasis, is conspicuously unified in general viewpoint.[1] In his work we accordingly reach one of the important points of concentration which the research interest in recent American social psychology is precipitating. Others will be noted in the course of this and the remaining parts of our discussion.

Formal methodological discussions in the field of science which are so prominent in Germany are comparatively rare in this country. And those that appear are for the most part quickly forgotten and neglected. There is a feeling here that such discussions are on the whole futile and that science develops, if at all, rather in spite than because of them. Thomas' work represents an exception to the rule in this respect, for in his case interest has centered in his methodological exposition to such an extent that even his concrete study of the Polish group has seemed to take on real meaning and significance only in the light of it. And while this has doubtless been due to the fact that his methodological discussion is developed as an integral part of his monographic study and is supported and illustrated all along in terms of the concrete materials and findings of this study, the fact remains that it is the methodological formulation of his position which has become the common meeting ground of the expanding group of writers associated with his social-psychological theory. It will be important, therefore, to follow out this part of Thomas' work in some detail here as the necessary background upon which the concrete aspects of his study as well as his work as a whole, and in large part also the work of the other writers to be considered in this section, must be projected.[2] First, however, as in the

---

[1] The common ground maintained by these writers is indicated in a recent volume by some of the members of the group, which is dedicated "To William I. Thomas whose concept of social attitudes has been so significant in the contemporary analysis of human behavior." "The present volume," the editor explains, "represents a collection of varied papers written from a point of view similar to that of Mr. Thomas. The authors were all at one time associated with Mr. Thomas either as graduate students or as collaborators in his research. These men have developed divergent interests in the subsequent years and yet they remain essentially fairly close together in their conception of sociology. They stand for a certain viewpoint. In common with Mr. Thomas they recognize the need of a conceptual framework in their research and teaching which takes into account the interaction of the personality and its environment—physical, social, and cultural" (*Social Attitudes*, 1931, ed. by Young, Introductory Note, p. vii).

[2] The work of this group of writers is so intimately interlinked that it is difficult to determine just where the contribution of one ends and that of the other begins. On this account it has seemed best to consider them together in the manner suggested in the title of this section. It should be borne in mind, however, that this is merely a matter of convenience in treatment.

case of other writers considered, we must lead up to this part of Thomas' work through a preliminary consideration of some of his earlier views, such as have relevance here and will help to bring his position as later outlined into proper social-psychological perspective.

Thomas' social-psychological thinking like Dewey's, in whose psychology it was to a considerable extent grounded,[1] presents a striking process of growth corresponding to Dewey's shift of emphasis from instinct to habit as a mode of approach in social psychology. He started out in this field of thought with an expression of interest in the point of view of folk-psychology, from which field Thomas apparently carried over the notion of the closeness of relation between social-psychological theory and ethnological material which he consistently stressed in his work up to the time of his change of viewpoint in this regard in his *Polish Peasant* (1918).[2] This expression of interest was superimposed on an essentially biological orientation of thought and a thoroughgoing individualistic conception of the dynamics of human conduct as represented by instinct psychology in its extremer forms and somatic anthropology.[3] His emphasis at this time fell on "food" and "sex" as the motivating forces of human life and associated with these underlying principles of explanation the so-called "gaming instinct" and the "pursuit pattern of interest" as logical corollaries of this conception. In an early article Thomas said:

A statement of life in terms of food and sex is as crass, when applied to culture conditions, as the chemical definition of man as "forty pounds of carbon and nitrogen scattered through five pailfuls of water." But it is important to recognize that food and sex are the irreducible factors of social life; and that beginning with these, we may hope to understand the meaning of the different variables of society: ideas, institutions, beliefs, sentiments, language, arts, literature—and to trace the "red thread" of consciousness through them.[4]

Food and sex, Thomas felt at the time, "like the foci of an ellipse," are the points about which the whole process of social behavior turns. These were the great original stimuli to action and culture, he argued, and in accordance with the broad principles of evolutionary development,

[1] See especially his article on "The Province of Social Psychology," *Proc. Intern. Congress Arts Sci.*, vol. 5, pp. 860–868, 1904, and his Introductory Note in his *Source Book for Social Origins* (1909).

[2] See *infra*, pp. 357–358.

[3] See his articles on the "Scope and Method of Folk Psychology," *Amer. Jour. Sociol.*, vol. 1, pp. 434–445, 1895–1896, and on "The Gaming Instinct," *ibid.*, vol. 6, pp. 750–763, 1900–1901; also his *Sex and Society* (1907), which is a collection of some of Thomas' early articles given out under the subtitle "Studies in the Social Psychology of Sex."

[4] "Scope and Method of Folk Psychology," *Amer. Jour. Sociol.*, vol. 1, p. 446, 1895–1896. Quotations from this journal are reprinted by permission of The University of Chicago Press, publishers.

they have so ingrained themselves into our innermost physical and mental being as to remain permanently the fundamental motive springs of our nature.[1]

Food and sex, he accordingly held, are at the basis of our most deeply seated cravings and tendencies, of our pleasures and pains, our aversions and enthusiasms, our natural interests and disinclinations. Only by reference to them, for instance, can we get at the underlying reasons as to why we find—as he asserted that we do—war, sport, and the conflict pattern of activity generally interesting, while most of our highly organized industrial and occupational activities are dull and irksome; also as to what the elemental motivation is of such social types as the tramp, the vagabond, and the so-called "sporting" person. For these interesting phenomena all have root, he held at the time, in the elemental struggle for existence which the evolutionary process imposes, and which seemed to him to be ultimately reducible to food and sex, as a minimum formula of the process.[2]

From this standpoint, the chief problem of social psychology, as Thomas pointed out, "is not so much to account for the gambler as to account for the business man." The gaming instinct being part of the original endowment of all normal persons, the gambler, the vagabond, and the like simply express their impulses in reference to this instinct, in the most spontaneous fashion. There is no need, therefore, of a complex social psychology to explain the behavior of this group; it is explainable along simple biological lines. It is the business man on the contrary, according to him, the socially controlled and conventional person, that challenges social-psychological explanation.[3] This, reduced to essentials, has of course always been the conception of social psychology when the subject has been approached from the biological and individualistic standpoint. Thus far, then, Thomas' position was substantially in keeping with the prevalent biological and individualistic rendering of the field of psycho-social interpretation.

A single additional passage will suffice to illustrate this aspect of Thomas' thought and to link it with its proper intellectual setting as already previously developed here.

The human mind was formed and fixed once for all in very early times, through a life of action and emergency, when the species was fighting, contriving, and inventing its way up from the sub-human conditions; and the ground-patterns of interest have never been, and probably never will be, fundamentally changed.

[1] *Ibid.*, p. 445.

[2] "The Gaming Instinct," *Amer. Jour. Sociol.*, vol. 6, pp. 750*ff.*, 1900–1901; *Sex and Society*, pp. 97*ff.*, 243*ff.*

[3] "The Gaming Instinct," *Amer. Jour. Sociol.*, vol. 6, pp. 760–763, 1900–1901; *Sex and Society*, pp. 243*ff.*

Consequently, all pursuits are irksome unless they are able, so to speak, to assume the guise of this early conflict for life in connection with which interest and modes of attention were developed. As a matter of fact, however, anything in the nature of a problem or a pursuit stimulates the emotional centers, and is interesting, because it is of the same general pattern, as these primitive pursuits and problems. Scientific and artistic pursuits, business, and the various occupational callings are analogues of the hunting, flight, pursuit, courtship and capture of early racial life, and the problems they present may, and do become, all-absorbing. The moral and educational problem has been, indeed to stimulate for the simple, co-ordinative killing, escaping, charming, deceiving activities of early life, analogues which are increasingly serviceable to society, and to expand into a general social feeling the affection developed first in connection with courtship, the rearing of children, and joint predatory and defensive enterprises.[1]

From the first, however, Thomas felt the need of supplementing this biological and individualistic standpoint, and he leaned increasingly to the Dewey type of psychology as a basis of interpretation of human conduct and social life. This latter basis of interpretation, with its emphasis on the concepts of habit, attention, crisis, control,[2] gradually led Thomas, as it led Dewey, to the formulation of a more characteristic social-psychological position. Thomas' first transition, consistently with his interest in ethnological material as source material for social psychology, was through a position similar to that of the Boas school of anthropological thought in this country, at any rate in so far as the explanation of cultural and achievement differences among human groups and classes is concerned,[3] a central problem in the folk-psychological conception of social psychology, in which, as was said above, Thomas early became interested.

It was Thomas' position, in general, on the matter of cultural and achievement differences, that the inherited basis of mind, in its essential aspects, is a possession of all mankind and that the observed differences of the present are to be accounted for chiefly in terms of the laws of habit and attention and the accidents of history rather than in terms of biological differences and evolutionary stages of development.[4] Accord-

---

[1] *Ibid.*, pp. 243–244.

[2] See, for instance, his article on "The Province of Social Psychology," *Proc. Intern. Congress Arts Sci.*, vol. 5, pp. 861*ff.*, 1904, his *Sex and Society*, pp. 175*ff.*, and especially his Introductory Note in his *Source Book for Social Origins*, pp. 13*ff.*

[3] See especially in this connection his *Sex and Society*, pp. 233*ff.*, 251*ff.*, and his *Source Book for Social Origins*, Part II.

[4] See foregoing reference. Thomas says in defining his position in his *Source Book for Social Origins*: "Different groups take steps in culture in a different order, and the order depends on the general environmental situation, the nature of the crises arising, and the operation of the attention . . . we have every reason to think that the mind of the savage and the mind of the civilized are fundamentally alike" (pp. 25–26).

ingly, he began to shift emphasis, first in respect to this specific problem and later, more generally, from the food and sex basis of interpretation to this other psycho-historical basis. In this way, he gradually passed on to the position which he outlines in detail in *The Polish Peasant* and in which we are chiefly interested here.[1]

It is upon this formulation of his social-psychological theory in terms of "attitudes," "values," and "wishes" and the concrete investigation which he carried on in conjunction with it that Thomas' position as a social psychologist of note chiefly rests.[2] For the reasons outlined above, the methodological setting which Thomas gives his social-psychological theory here has a special importance when viewed in relation to his monographic study of the Polish group of which it is a part and upon which it supposedly rests, as more or less of an inductive product.[3] This will appear in detail as our analysis of Thomas' position progresses. But in the meantime, his own preliminary description of *The Polish Peasant* is directly of interest in this connection. He says:

The present study was not, in fact, undertaken exclusively or even primarily as an expression of interest in the Polish peasant . . . but the Polish peasant was selected rather as a convenient object for the exemplification of a standpoint and method outlined in the methodological note forming the first pages of the

[1] That Thomas never quite gave up thinking in terms of his earlier basis of interpretation, however, is abundantly evident even in his later work (see his article in *Suggestions of Modern Science Concerning Education* by Jennings, Watson, Meyer, and Thomas, for a summary of his theory as developed in *The Polish Peasant* and a clearer presentation of it in connection with his food and sex principles of explanation. See also here his statement of the wishes in *The Polish Peasant* itself, vol. I, p. 73, vol. III, pp. 33 ff., 56 ff., and in *The Unadjusted Girl*, pp. 4ff., and *infra*, pp. 369, 381).

[2] See in this connection note on Thomas and Znaniecki, p. 351.

[3] *The Polish Peasant in Europe and America*, vol. I, pp. 74–76. Thomas describes the several parts of his concrete study as follows: "The work consists of five volumes, largely documentary in their character. Volumes I and II comprise a study of the organization of the peasant primary groups (family and community), and of the partial evolution of this system of organization under the influence of the new industrial system and of immigration to America and Germany. Volume III is the autobiography (with critical treatment) of an immigrant of peasant origin but belonging by occupation to the lower city class, and illustrates the tendency to disorganization of the individual under the conditions involved in a rapid transition from one type of social organization to another. Volume IV treats the dissolution of the primary group and the social and political reorganization and the unification of peasant communities in Poland on the new ground of rational cooperation. Volume V is based on studies of the Polish immigrant in America and shows the degrees and forms of disorganization associated with a too-rapid and inadequately mediated individualization, with a sketch of the beginnings of reorganization."

The methodological parts of Thomas' work would in themselves comprise a good-sized volume. They are to be found chiefly in the introductions to the first and third volumes. The large two-volume edition of this work which has recently appeared (1927) incorporates some changes in the organization of the material. The references here are all to the original five-volume edition.

present [first] volume. The scope of our study will be best appreciated by having this fact in mind.[1]

Bearing this statement regarding the relation between the methodological and the descriptive parts of Thomas' work in view on the one hand, then, and on the other hand the fact that the real force and import of his methodological argument issue from the supposition that it is essentially a formulation and explanation of the procedure actually incorporated in the concrete part of his work, we may proceed to the analysis of his position as developed in this connection.[2]

Thomas starts out in his *Polish Peasant* by calling attention to the urgent present-day need of a rational and scientific technique of dealing with human affairs and by pointing out the inadequacy, in our present-day complex and rapidly changing social world, of what he terms the "ordering-and-forbidding" and "common-sense" methods of dealing with human situations, which are the methods in use, according to him, in the absence of a scientific basis of procedure. In the interest of stimulating the development of the latter, he proceeds to outline, after a critical consideration of some of the more glaring fallacies inherent in social practice as based upon the ordering-and-forbidding and common-sense procedures, what from his point of view should be the direction of social science development if it is to be able to meet the need of a scientific social technique more adequately than it has in the past.[3] Taking up first the general questions of standpoint and perspective, he says:

If we attempt now to determine what should be the object-matter and the method of a social theory that would be able to satisfy the demands of modern social practice, it is evident that its main object should be the actual civilized society in its full development and with all its complexity of situations, for it is the control of the actual civilized society that is sought in most endeavors of rational practice. But here, as in every other science, a determined body of material assumes its full significance only if we can use comparison freely, in order to distinguish the essential from the accidental, the simple from the com-

---

[1] *The Polish Peasant in Europe and America*, vol. I, pp. vii–viii, also p. 74.

[2] It of course remains as open question on which Thomas has thrown very little light as to just how and to what extent his theory as outlined in his methodological discussion is actually an outgrowth of the concrete part of his study. But the very association of his theory with the imposing collection of concrete source material which this part of his study introduces was in itself a step in advance of the usual type of discussion of social-psychological subject matter, so that in any event his work has a special interest here from the research standpoint. A similar research interest, though in another direction, as we shall see, attaches to Allport's treatment of the subject. These two prominent writers in the field represent, in fact, the vanguard of present-day interest in this country in two very important lines of concrete social-psychological research (see *infra*, p. 377).

[3] It is in this connection that Thomas discusses the methodology of social psychology.

plex, the primary from the derived. And fortunately social life gives us favorable conditions for comparative studies, particularly at the present stage of evolution, in the coexistence of a certain number of civilized societies sufficiently alike in their fundamental cultural problems to make comparison possible, and differing sufficiently in their traditions, customs, and general national spirit to make comparison fruitful. And from the list of these civilized societies we should by no means exclude those non-white societies, like the Chinese, whose organization and attitudes differ profoundly from our own, but which interest us both as social experiments and as situations with which we have to reconcile our own future.

In contrast with this study of the various present civilized societies, the lines along which most of the purely scientific sociological work has been done up to the present—that is, ethnography of primitive societies and social history—have a secondary, though by no means a negligible importance. Their relation to social practice is only mediate; they can help the practitioner to solve actual cultural problems only to the degree that they help the scientist to understand actual cultural life; they are auxiliary, and their own scientific value will increase with the progress of the main sphere of studies. In all the endeavors to understand and interpret the past and the savage we must use, consciously or not, our knowledge of our civilized present life, which remains always a basis of comparison, whether the past and the primitive are conceived as analogous with, or as different from, the present and the civilized. The less objective and critical our knowledge of the present, the more subjective and unmethodical is our interpretation of the past and the primitive; unable to see the relative and limited character of the culture within which we live, we unconsciously bend every unfamiliar phenomenon to the limitations of our own social personality. A really objective understanding of history and ethnography can therefore be expected only as a result of a methodical knowledge of present cultural societies.[1]

This statement represents substantially a reversal of Thomas' position as reflected in his earlier writings, among which his *Source Book for Social Origins* stands out conspicuously, and it is notable here especially because it registers in methodological terms the reaction against the traditional evolutionary approach which dominated psycho-social thought under the influence, more particularly, of Spencer's work and that of the evolutionary anthropologists. It is notable here also because it links up directly with the other point which Thomas emphasizes in his discussion of the object matter of social theory and which is perhaps more immediately suggestive here in its social-psychological bearing, namely, "the necessity of taking into account the whole life of a given society instead of arbitrarily selecting and isolating beforehand certain particular groups of facts."[2] He says in this connection:

We have seen already that the contrary procedure constitutes one of the fallacies of the common-sense sociology. It is also a fallacy usually committed

---

[1] *The Polish Peasant in Europe and America*, vol. I, pp. 17–18. Quotations from this work are reprinted by permission of and special arrangement with Alfred A. Knopf, Inc., authorized publishers.

[2] *Ibid.*, p. 18.

by the observers of their own or of other societies—*litterateurs*, journalists, travelers, popular psychologists, etc. In describing a given society they pick out the most prominent situations, the most evident problems, thinking to characterize thereby the life of the given group. Still more harmful for the development of science is this fallacy when used in the comparative sociology which studies an institution, an idea, a myth, a legal or moral norm, a form of art, etc., by simply comparing its content in various societies without studying it in the whole meaning which it has in a particular society and then comparing this with the whole meaning which it has in the various societies. We are all more or less guilty of this fault, but it pleases us to attribute it mainly to Herbert Spencer.[1]

In order to avoid such arbitrary limitations and subjective interpretations in social theory, there are, according to Thomas, only two possible courses open. "We can study monographically," says he, "whole concrete societies with the total complexity of problems and situations which constitute their cultural life; or we can work on special social problems, following the problem in a certain limited number of concrete social groups and studying it in every group with regard to the particular form which it assumes under the influence of the conditions prevailing in this society, taking into account the complex meaning which a concrete cultural phenomenon has in a determined cultural environment." In the one case, he suggests, we go from the whole social context to the problem, and in the other, we go from the problem to the whole social context.[2] Continuing with this preliminary statement of valid procedure, Thomas says further:

And in both types of work the only safe method is to start with the assumption that we know absolutely nothing about the group or the problem we are to investigate except such purely formal criteria as enable us to distinguish materials belonging to our sphere of interest from those which do not belong there. But this attitude of indiscriminate receptivity toward any concrete data should mark only the first stage of investigation—that of limiting the field. As soon as we become acquainted with the materials we begin to select them with the help of criteria which involve certain methodological generalizations and scientific hypotheses. This must be done, since the whole empirical concreteness cannot be introduced into science, cannot be described or explained. We have to limit ourselves to certain theoretically important data, but we must know how to distinguish the data which are important. And every further step of the investigation will bring with it new methodological problems—analysis of the complete concrete data into elements, systematization of these elements, definition of social facts, establishing of social laws. All these stages of scientific procedure must be exactly and carefully defined if social theory is to become a science conscious of its own methods and able to apply them with precision, as is the case with the more mature and advanced physical and biological sciences.[3]

[1] *Ibid.*, pp. 18–19.
[2] *Ibid.*, p. 19.
[3] *The Polish Peasant in Europe and America*, vol. I, pp. 19–20. It is unfortunate that these steps in social research procedure and the concrete techniques in which

On the basis of this preliminary statement, Thomas proceeds to the consideration of the more detailed content of a social theory that would be able to satisfy the requirements of a scientific social technique. There are, he suggests, two fundamental practical problems which have constituted the center of attention of reflective social practice in all times: (1) the problem of the dependence of the individual upon social organization and culture and (2) the problem of the dependence of social organization and culture upon the individual. Practically, according to him, these two problems express themselves in the following two questions: "How shall we produce with the help of the existing social organization and culture the desirable mental and moral characteristics in the individuals constituting the social group?" and "How shall we produce, with the help of the existing mental and moral characteristics of the individual members of the group, the desirable type of social organization and culture?"[1]

Approaching these fundamental problems and questions, therefore, from the standpoint of social theory viewed as a basis for a scientific social technique, Thomas says by way of introduction to his own central thesis:

> If social theory is to become the basis of social technique and to solve these problems really, it is evident that it must include both kinds of data involved in them,—namely, the objective cultural elements of social life and the subjective characteristics of the members of the social group—and that the two kinds of data must be taken as correlated.

That is, in order to solve these and similar problems, social theory must, according to him, correlate what he technically speaks of as the "social values" and the "social attitudes" involved in a given social situation.[2]

---

they might be incorporated have so long been neglected or rather that they were taken for granted. Social research might have been considerably advanced if more attention had been paid to them. The fact that this aspect of social research method has increasingly begun to come under review during the last few years is one of the notable evidences that psycho-social thought is becoming research conscious in this country. Thomas performed a service in pointing out this need in the above context. Under the influence of his work, too, the Department of Sociology at the University of Chicago has recently been concentrating on the problem. *Field Studies in Sociology* (1928), by Vivien M. Palmer, represents a first step in the direction of its treatment on the basis of actual experience with field research carried on, very largely, from the standpoint which Thomas outlines. See also in this connection BOGARDUS, *The New Social Research* (1926), and the case materials in *Methods in Social Science* (1931), ed. by Rice. For differently orientated works in this field see Chapin, *Field Work and Social Research* (1920); Giddings, *The Scientific Study of Human Society* (1924); Rice, *Quantitative Methods in Politics* (1928); Lundberg, *Social Research* (1929).

[1] *The Polish Peasant in Europe and America*, vol. I, p. 20; *cf. supra*, p. 333.
[2] *The Polish Peasant in Europe and America*, vol. I, pp. 20-21.

These terms, which Thomas introduced into recent psycho-social theory with a distinctive social-psychological significance, he defines as follows:

By a social value we understand any datum having an empirical content accessible to the members of some social group and a meaning with regard to which it is or may be an object of activity. Thus, a foodstuff, an instrument, a coin, a piece of poetry, a university, a myth, a scientific theory, are social values. Each of them has a content that is sensual in the case of the foodstuff, the instrument, the coin; partly sensual, partly imaginary in the piece of poetry, whose content is constituted, not only by the written or spoken words, but also by the images which they evoke, and in the case of the university, whose content is the whole complex of men, buildings, material accessories, and images representing its activity; or, finally only imaginary in the case of a mythical personality or a scientific theory. The meaning of these values becomes explicit when we take them in connection with human actions. The meaning of the foodstuff is its reference to its eventual consumption; that of an instrument, its reference to the work for which it is designed; that of a coin, the possibilities of buying and selling or the pleasures of spending which it involves; that of the piece of poetry, the sentimental and intellectual reactions which it arouses; that of the university, the social activities which it performs; that of the mythical personality, the cult of which it is the object and the actions of which it is supposed to be the author; that of the scientific theory, the possibilities of control of experience by idea or action which it permits. The social value is thus opposed to the natural thing, which has a content but, as a part of nature, has no meaning for human activity, is treated as "valueless"; when the natural thing assumes a meaning, it becomes thereby a social value. And naturally a social value may have many meanings, for it may refer to many different kinds of activity.[1]

By attitude we understand a process of individual consciousness which determines real or possible activity of the individual in the social world. Thus, hunger that compels the consumption of the foodstuff; the workman's decision to use the tool; the tendency of the spendthrift to spend the coin; the poet's feelings and ideas expressed in the poem and the reader's sympathy and admiration; the needs which the institution tries to satisfy and the response it provokes; the fear and devotion manifested in the cult of the divinity; the interest in creating, understanding, or applying a scientific theory and the ways of thinking implied in it—all these are attitudes. The attitude is thus the individual counterpart of the social value; activity, in whatever form, is the bond between them.[2]

Attitudes as thus defined are to be distinguished from psychical states, according to Thomas, just as values are to be distinguished from natural objects, in order to indicate their importance for social psychology. He says on this point:

By its reference to activity and thereby to individual consciousness the value is distinguished from the natural thing. By its reference to activity and thereby to the social world the attitude is distinguished from the psychical state. In the examples quoted above we were obliged to use with reference to ideas and

[1] *Ibid.*, pp. 21–22.
[2] *Ibid.*, p. 22.

volitions words that have become terms of individual psychology by being abstracted from the objective social reality to which they apply, but originally they were designed to express attitudes, not psychological processes. A psychological process is an attitude treated as an object in itself, isolated by a reflective act of attention, and taken first of all in connection with other states of the same individual. An attitude is a psychological process treated as primarily manifested in its reference to the social world and taken first of all in connection with some social value.[1]

"The psychological process," he says in summary, "remains always fundamentally a *state of somebody;* the attitude remains always fundamentally an attitude *toward something.*" And this difference of standpoint, according to Thomas, determines a corresponding difference of methods appropriate to the study of these two types of fact—appropriate, that is, to individual psychology on the one hand and to social psychology viewed by him as a part of social theory on the other.[2]

This statement requires elaboration, inasmuch as attitudes and values are, according to him, the data of all the sciences that deal with human culture and not only of social theory, under which heading, as he tells us later, he seeks to discuss the common methodological aspects of both social psychology and sociology.[3] The limitation of the field of social theory arises quite naturally, however, he suggests, "from the necessity of choosing between attitudes or values as fundamental data—that is, as data whose characters will serve as a basis for scientific generalization."[4] This division of interest is, according to him, a methodological necessity, for there is, he says, "no possibility of giving to attitudes and values the same importance in a methodical scientific investigation; either attitudes must be subordinated to values or the contrary."[5]

Now all of the sciences that deal with separate domains of culture, like the sciences of language, art, economics, etc., subordinate attitudes to the study of values, while social theory, that is in the form of social psychology, tends to subordinate values to the study of attitudes. Social psychology, then, as "precisely the science of attitudes" has thus, Thomas believes, "to perform the part of a general science of the subjective side of social culture." "It may claim," he says, "to be *the* science of consciousness as manifested in culture, and its function is to render service, as a general auxiliary science, to all the special sciences dealing with various spheres of social values."[6]

[1] *Ibid.*
[2] *Ibid.*, pp. 23, 25 *ff.*
[3] *Ibid.*, p. 33.
[4] *Ibid.*, p. 23.
[5] *Ibid.*, p. 24.
[6] *Ibid.*, p. 31.

We see, then, what the importance of social psychology as conceived of by Thomas is from the standpoint of his interest in the larger problem of the relation between social theory and scientific social practice, and we can follow out the elaboration of his position further with this larger problem in view.

As defined above, social psychology is, according to him, a unified field of investigation in its own right, separable alike from "psychology in general" or individual psychology as well as from sociology. As regards his conception of the relation between social psychology and individual psychology, little need be said, since he felt that these two fields of investigation were so different in both standpoint and method that "if it were not for the traditional use of the term 'psychology' for both types of research, it would be even advisable to emphasize this difference by a distinct terminology."[1] In these as well as in other important respects, social psychology is much more closely related to sociology, according to Thomas, though at least theoretically, sociology "as the theory of social organization" is separable from social psychology on the same ground as the other special sciences of culture, namely, that in directing itself primarily to the study of social organization, it must subordinate the study of attitudes.[2] Social psychology and sociology in being "both concerned with the relation between the individual and the concrete social group," are, however, both, according to his view, embraced under the general term of social theory, and their methodology can to a considerable extent be discussed on common ground. It is with this common bearing upon social psychology and sociology that his methodological standpoint is further developed here.[3]

With this common reference in view, then, Thomas proceeds to develop his position as follows: The chief problems of modern science, he recalls, are problems of causal explanation. The aim is always to lay the foundation of a technique and to understand and control the process of *becoming*. If social theory is to become the basis of a scientific social technique, it too must direct itself to this task, and there is, according to him, only one way of fulfilling it.

Social becoming, like natural becoming, must be analyzed into a plurality of facts, each of which represents a succession of cause and effect. The idea of social theory is the analysis of the totality of social becoming into such causal processes and a systematization permitting us to understand the connections between these processes. No arguments a priori trying to demonstrate the impossibility of application of the principle of causality to conscious human life in general can or should halt social theory in tending to this idea, whatever difficulties there may be in the way, because as a matter of fact we continually do

[1] *Ibid.*
[2] *Ibid.*, pp. 31*ff.*
[3] *Ibid.*, pp. 33–36.

apply the principle of causality to the social world in our activity and in our thought, and we shall always do this as long as we try to control social becoming in any form. So, instead of fruitlessly discussing the justification of this application in the abstract, social theory must simply strive to make it more methodical and perfect in the concrete—by the actual process of investigation.[1]

Accepting the above as a statement of goal, therefore, Thomas suggests first of all that "if we want to reach scientific explanations, we must keep in mind that our facts must be determined in such a way as to permit of their subordination to general laws," for, as he says, "a fact which cannot be treated as a manifestation of one or several laws is inexplicable causally."[2] In the past, according to him, the chief error of both social practice and social theory has been that they determined, consciously or unconsciously, social facts in a way which excluded in advance the possibility of their subordination to any laws. "The implicit or explicit assumption," he explains, "was that a social fact is composed of two elements, a cause which is either a social phenomenon or an individual act, and an effect which is either an individual act or a social phenomenon." In this, social theory and social practice have followed uncritically the example of the physical sciences, "which always tend to find the one determined phenomenon which is the necessary and sufficient condition of another phenomenon." Thereby they have forgotten to take into account one essential difference between physical and social reality, "which is that, while the effect of a physical phenomenon depends exclusively on the objective nature of this phenomenon and can be calculated on the ground of the latter's empirical content, the effect of a social phenomenon depends in addition on the subjective standpoint taken by the individual or the group toward this phenomenon and can be calculated only if we know, not only the objective content of the assumed cause, but also the meaning which it has at the given moment for the given conscious beings." This simple consideration should have shown to the social theorist or technician, he suggests, "that a social cause cannot be simple, like a physical cause, but is compound, and must include both an objective and a subjective element, a value *and* an attitude."[3]

Thomas accordingly lays down the following principle, already alluded to in preliminary form above, as basic.

The fundamental methodological principle of both social psychology and sociology—the principle without which they can never reach scientific explanation —is therefore the following one:

The cause of a social or individual phenomenon is never another social or individual phenomenon alone, but always a combination of a social and an individual phenomenon.

[1] *Ibid.*, pp. 36–37.
[2] *Ibid.*, pp. 37–38.
[3] *Ibid.*, pp. 38–39.

Or, in more exact terms:

The cause of a value or of an attitude is never an attitude or a value alone, but always a combination of an attitude and a value.[1]

Elaborating somewhat on the methodological significance of this important principle, he says:

If we wish to explain the appearance of a new attitude—whether in one individual or in a whole group—we know that this attitude appeared as a consequence of the influence of a social value upon the indiviudal or the group, but we know also that this influence itself would have been impossible unless there had been some pre-existing attitude, some wish, emotional habit, or intellectual tendency, to which this value has in some way appealed, favoring it, contradicting it, giving it a new direction, or stabilizing its hesitating expressions. Our problem is therefore to find both the value and the pre-existing attitude upon which it has acted and get in their combination the necessary and sufficient cause of the new attitude . . . [2]

If now we have to explain the appearance of a social value, we know that this value is a product of the activity of an individual or a number of individuals, and in so far dependent on the attitude of which this activity is the expression. But we know also that this result is inexplicable unless we take into consideration the value (or complex of values) which was the starting-point and the social material of activity and which has conditioned the result as much as did the attitude itself. The new value is the result of the solution of a problem set by the pre-existing value and the active attitude together; it is the common effect of both of them.[3]

Examples of the disastrous results which follow the violation of these methodological rules in the field of social theory and practice can be multiplied indefinitely, according to Thomas, and he himself cites some very striking situations by direct reference to the concrete materials of his study of the Polish group in illustration of the practical import and bearing of such violation.[4] We fail so frequently in our attempts to understand and to deal with social problems, he suggests, because we direct our efforts toward one or the other important aspects of a social situation, toward the attitude or value aspect, to the neglect of the other aspect, never realizing that each of these is a function of the other and hence cannot be successfully dealt with in isolation. The confidence which we have in the "legislation" and "moral suasion" techniques, as in themselves effective methods of social control, suffers under this limitation, and the failures which they so frequently result in are precisely the effects which we should expect from their one-sided mode of procedure.

The common practice of reformers, according to him, "is to construct a rational scheme of the social institution they wish to see produced or

---

[1] *Ibid.*, p. 44.
[2] *Ibid.*, p. 45.
[3] *Ibid.*, pp. 47–48.
[4] *Ibid.*, pp. 45*ff.*, 58*ff.*

abolished, and then to formulate an ideal plan of social activities which would perhaps lead to a realization of their scheme if social life were merely a sum of individual actions." But inasmuch "as social reality contains not only individual acts, but also social institutions, not only attitudes, but also values fixed by tradition and conditioning the attitudes, these values cooperate in the production of the final effect quite independently, and often in spite of the intentions of the social reformer."[1]

There is here and quite generally, he suggests, a tendency to overlook what figures as the *tertium quid* in his statement of the basic principles of valid procedure. Hence it is that social programs so frequently fail of their intended purpose or that, at least, their successes are so frequently counterbalanced by their failures that they foster the impression that social behavior is in the main unpredictable and uncontrollable.[2]

It must not of course be concluded, according to Thomas, "that the proper way of formulating social facts is never used by social theory or reflective social practice." The point is that the proper formula has never been applied with any consistency either in social theory or in social practice, while the wrong formula is in widespread use in both of these fields of endeavor. He says:

At every step we try to enforce certain attitudes upon other individuals without stopping to consider what are their dominant attitudes in general or their prevailing attitudes at the given moment; at every step we try to produce certain social values without taking into account the values which are already there and upon which the result of our efforts will depend as much as upon our intention and persistence.[3]

A systematic application and development of the methodological rules stated above would, however, according to Thomas, necessarily lead in a completely different direction. He explains:

Its final result would not be a system of definitions, like law and special parts of political science, nor a system of the philosophical determination of the essence of certain data, like philosophy of law, the general parts of political science, ethics, and many sociological works, nor a general outline of social evolution, like the sociology of the Spencerian school or the philosophies of history, but a system of laws of social becoming, in which definitions, philosophical determinations of essence, and outlines of evolution would play the same part as they do in physical science—that is, would constitute either instruments helping to analyze reality and to find laws, or conclusions helping to understand the general scientific meaning and the connection of laws.[4]

Such an achievement, it is evident, Thomas points out, can, in the natural course of events, be attained only by a long and persistent

[1] *Ibid.*, pp. 50–51
[2] *Ibid.*, pp. 51, 58*ff.*
[3] *Ibid.*, p. 52.
[4] *Ibid.*, pp. 52–53.

cooperation of social science. But this, he takes pains to make clear, is a necessity resulting from the fact of specialization and subjective attitude and is quite apart from the common notion of the complexity of the social world as such which, in his opinion, has been entirely too often and too unreflectively overemphasized. He says very significantly in this connection:

Complexity is a relative characteristic; it depends on the method and the purpose of analysis. Neither the social nor the natural world presents any ready and absolutely simple elements, and in this sense they are both equally complex, because they are both infinitely complex. But this complexity is a metaphysical, not a scientific, problem. In science we treat any datum as a simple element if it behaves as such in all the combinations in which we find it, and any fact is a simple fact which can indefinitely repeat itself—that is, in which the relation between cause and effect can be assumed to be permanent and necessary. And in this respect it is still a problem whether the social world will not prove much less complex than the natural world if only we analyze its data and determine its facts by proper methods. The prepossession of complexity is due to the naturalistic way of treating the social reality. If it is maintained that the social world has to be treated as an expression or a product of the psychological, physiological, or biological nature of human beings, then, of course, it appears as incomparably more complex than the natural world, because to the already inexhaustibly complex conscious human organism as a part of nature is added the fact that in a social group there are numerous and various human beings interacting in the most various ways. But if we study the social world, without any naturalistic prepossessions, simply as a plurality of specific data, causally interconnected in a process of becoming, the question of complexity is no more baffling for social theory, and may even prove less so, than it is for physical science.[1]

The search for social laws, which is precisely the problem at issue in discussions of the complexity of the social world, does not as a matter of fact, Thomas maintains, present any special difficulties if our facts are adequately determined. The process is in all respects parallel, according to him, to the necessary procedure in other fields of scientific investigation. He says in elaboration of this point:

When we have found that a certain effect is produced by a certain cause, the formulation of this causal dependence has in itself the character of a law; that is, we assume that whenever this cause repeats itself the effect will necessarily follow. The further need is to explain apparent exceptions. But this need of explanation, which is the stumbling-block of a theory that has defined its facts inadequately, becomes, on the contrary, a factor of progress when the proper method is employed. For when we know that a certain cause can have only one determined effect, when we have assumed, for example, that the attitude of A + the value B is the cause of the attitude C, then if the presumed cause $A + B$ is there and the expected effect C does not appear, this means either that we have been mistaken in assuming that $A + B$ was the cause of C, or that the action of

[1] *Ibid.*, pp. 53–54.

$A + B$ was interfered with by the action of some other cause . . . In the first case the exception gives us the possibility of correcting our error; in the second case it permits us to extend our knowledge by finding a new causal connection, by determining the partly or totally unknown cause . . . which has interfered with the action of our known case $A + B$ and brought a complex effect, D . . . instead of the expected C. And thus the exception from a law becomes the starting point for the discovery of a new law.[1]

And so all along, according to Thomas, the problem of laws, *i.e.*, "nomothetic" social science, is essentially not unlike, and it remains questionable whether it is more complex than, the corresponding phases of other fields of scientific investigation. Such being the case, and the problem of laws being, as he argues, the most important one of scientific methodology from the standpoint of the control of the process of *becoming*, the ground is cleared for his aggressive attitude toward the development of a technique of scientific social control. Social generalization is of course under the limitation, he recognizes, that it is not so easily subjectable to experimental verification as some other fields of generalization. But this fact must not, according to him, be permitted to discourage aggressive social investigation or to justify laxity of procedure. Rather must it be accepted as a challenge for the exercise of exceptional caution in the use of other safeguards to scientific validity, for example, the methodic use of systematic *observation* in the search for contradictory as well as corroboratory evidence. It is because social theory has not in the past been sufficiently aware of the need of these exceptional cautions that so many of its works, suggests Thomas, "bear a character of composition, intermediary between philosophy and science and fulfilling the demands of neither."[2]

As in other important connections, Thomas elaborates these points concretely and at some length by reference to the concrete materials of his study of the Polish group.[3] In the end he leads to the following conclusion: "There are no obstacles in the nature of the social world or in the nature of the human mind which would essentially prevent social practice from obtaining gradually the same degree of efficiency as that of industrial practice. The only obstacles are of a subjective kind."[4] And these, it is presumed, will gradually give way just as they gave way in the case of other fields of scientific investigation, when they became surer of their ground and really effective in demonstrating their possibilities of success.

Throughout his discussions, Thomas accordingly assumes, in the spirit of this part of his argument, "that if an adequate technique is

[1] *Ibid.*, pp. 54–55.
[2] *Ibid.*, pp. 53, 62.
[3] *Ibid.*, pp. 56 *ff.*
[4] *Ibid.*, p. 66.

developed it is possible to produce any desirable attitudes and values."
This assumption is practically justified in fact, according to him, because
we find in the individual attitudes "which cannot avoid response to the
class of stimulations which society is able to apply to him." In pursuance
of this point, Thomas formulates his now widely known theory of the
fundamental human wishes. And in view of the popularity of this part
of his theory on the one hand and the fact that it defines an important
point of difference between some of the prominent members of the group
of writers associated with Thomas on the other, the form of his statement on this matter is particularly notable here. He says:

> Every individual has a vast variety of wishes which can be satisfied only by
> his incorporation in a society. Among his general patterns of wishes we may
> enumerate: (1) the desire for new experience, for fresh stimulations; (2) the
> desire for recognition, including, for example, sexual response and general social
> appreciation, and secured by devices ranging from the display of ornament to
> the demonstration of worth through scientific attainment; (3) the desire for
> mastery, or the "will to power," exemplified by ownership, domestic tyranny,
> political despotism, based on the instinct of hate, but capable of being sublimated
> to laudable ambition; (4) the desire for security, based on the instinct of fear
> and exemplified negatively by the wretchedness of the individual in perpetual
> solitude or under social taboo.[1]

These four "general patterns of wishes" as defined, indicate at the
same time, then, fundamental directions of human desire and basic lines
of personal dependence on social *milieu* and hence of effective social
control. Thomas explains:

> Society is, indeed, an agent for the repression of many of the wishes in the
> individual; it demands that he shall be moral by repressing at least the wishes

[1] *Ibid.*, vol. I, pp. 72–73, *cf.* vol. III, pp. 33*ff.*, 56*ff.*

It is notable that Thomas says "among his general patterns of wishes." Also
in his restatement of this part of his theory in volume III of his study, the classification as given here is changed to the more familiar form usually quoted (see *infra*,
p. 375). From this it would seem that Thomas himself, at any rate in *The Polish
Peasant*, rather meant to leave this part of his theory more fluid than it is sometimes
made out to be. One is reminded here of the relevancy of Dewey's discussion of the
function of classification as it applies to the current schematizations of instinct
theory (see *supra*, p. 344). But in any event, this part of Thomas' theory defines an
important point of difference among some of the group of writers here under consideration. In particular, Professor Faris has held that Thomas' theory of the wishes is a
hold-over from his earlier instinct approach and that it is at once logically distinct
from his more recent attitudes-values approach and tends to obscure the importance
of the latter contribution. In his own formulations, he has accordingly aimed to
steer clear of this phase of Thomas' theory (see his article on "The Concept of Social
Attitudes," *Jour. Appl. Sociol.*, vol. 9, pp. 404–409, 1925; also his discussion of the
subject in *Social Attitudes*, ed. by Young, Chap. I; "Attitudes and Behavior," *Amer.
Jour. Sociol.*, vol. 34, pp. 271–281, 1928. See in this connection also *supra*, p. 356,
note 1, and the attempt to restate this part of Thomas' theory in PARK and BURGESS,
Introduction to the Science of Sociology, Chap. VII).

which are irreconcilable with the welfare of the group, but nevertheless it provides the only medium within which any of his schemes or wishes can be gratified. And it would be superfluous to point out by examples the degree to which society has in the past been able to impose its schemes of attitudes and values on the individual. Professor Sumner's volume, *Folkways*, is practically a collection of such examples, and, far from discouraging us as they discourage Professor Sumner, they should be regarded as proofs of the ability of the individual to conform to any definition, to accept any attitude, provided it is an expression of the public will or represents the appreciation of even a limited group. And even if we find that the attitudes are not so tractable as we have assumed, that it is not possible to provoke all the desirable ones, we shall still be in the same situation as, let us say, physics and mechanics: we shall have the problem of securing the highest degree of control possible in view of the nature of our materials.[1]

Any further statement on this matter must obviously be based on the detailed study of particular cases. Thomas accordingly leaves this important subject at this point, in order to come back to it in a later more specific connection. In his Introduction to volume III of his study, in accordance with the character of the concrete material which he introduces in this volume, he carries his methodological discussion forward to the consideration of the problems involved in the application of his point of view as so far outlined to the study of an "evolving human personality."[2] This, he explains, is a problem of scientific social *synthesis* corresponding to the problem of social *analysis* and generalization heretofore emphasized in his discussion.[3] In this connection, he outlines his view regarding the value of life histories as source material for sociological and social-psychological purposes. He says:

We are safe in saying that personal life-records, as complete as possible, constitute the *perfect* type of sociological materials, and that if social science has to use other materials at all it is only because of the practical difficulty of obtaining at the moment a sufficient number of such records to cover the totality of sociological problems, and of the enormous amount of work demanded for an adequate analysis of all the personal materials necessary to characterize the life of a social group. If we are forced to use mass-phenomena as material, or any kind of happenings—taken without regard to the life-histories of the individuals who participate in them, it is a defect, not an advantage, of our present sociological method.[4]

[1] *The Polish Peasant in Europe and America*, vol. I, pp. 73–74.

[2] *Ibid.*, vol. III, p. 5.

[3] *Ibid.*, pp. 5–6, 10–11.

[4] *Ibid.*, pp. 6–7. *The Polish Peasant* constitutes the outstanding attempt to use personal documents—letters, life-history material, etc., for sociological and social-psychological purposes. Life-history material had of course been previously used as source material for the study of human behavior in the fields of medicine, psychiatry, and psychoanalysis but never with the methodological implications of this work (see PARK and BURGESS, *Introduction to the Science of Sociology*, pp. 144–145; also BOGARDUS, *The New Social Research*, Chaps. VI–IX).

But in order to be able to use life records for its purposes, social theory must, according to Thomas, have criteria on the basis of which to select from the mass of concrete human documents those which are likely to be scientifically valuable for the solution of a given social problem. "We cannot," he points out, "study the life-histories of all the individuals participating in a certain social happening, for then our task would be inexhaustible. We must limit ourselves, just as the natural scientist does, to a few *representative* cases whose thorough study will yield results as nearly applicable as possible to all other cases concerned."[1] Such criteria can be arrived at, according to him, only by a theory of human individuals as social personalities. This means, he explains, that "the use of individual life-records as material for the determination of abstract social laws must be supplemented by a sociological study of those individuals themselves in their entire personal evolution, as concrete components of the social world."[2]

This sort of synthetic approach to the study of personality is, however, still in its infancy, from his standpoint. The scientific description and classification of social personalities, as a whole, he points out, despite the widespread interest that has at all times attached to the subject of biography and to discussions of temperament and character, shows a striking lack of progress from the level which they reached in antiquity. The reason for this lack of progress is, according to him, evident. It is that almost all the studies of temperament and character have proceeded on the ground of individual rather than social psychology. "Since personal evolution," he says, "can be understood only in connection with social life these theories were unable to take into adequate consideration the whole wealth of important problems bearing on personal evolution, and had to limit themselves to a mere abstract description and classification of statically considered formal types."[3]

With the end in view, therefore, of at least illustrating methodologically the social-psychological approach to the subject, Thomas suggests here his well-known classification of ideal personality types into the "Philistine," the "Bohemian," and the "creative individual."[4] This classification, as he tells us, "based upon relations between the individual and his social environment whose essential features are the same in all societies, whatever may be the content of the personal and social life," is purely formal and tentative, claiming to be "only a starting-point for researches whose aim must consist in a synthetic characterization of human types precisely with regard to the content of the attitudes and values which constitute their social personalities."[5] To be really useful,

[1] *The Polish Peasant in Europe and America*, vol. III, pp. 8–9.
[2] *Ibid.*, pp. 9–10.
[3] *Ibid.*, p. 10.
[4] *Ibid.*, pp. 27–28.
[5] *Ibid.*, p. 11.

he explains, such a characterization must be made from the standpoint of the problem of further development, *i.e.*, from the standpoint of the problem of *becoming* which he throughout emphasizes. The aim, according to him, is to determine *dynamic* types as types of development.[1] He states in respect to this matter:

> The essential points, which cannot be here sufficiently emphasized, are that the social personality as a whole manifests itself only in the course of its total life and not at any particular moment of its life, and that its life is not a mere empirical manifestation of a timeless metaphysical essence, always the same, but is a continuous evolution in which nothing remains unchanged. This evolution often tends toward a stabilization as its ultimate limit, but never attains this limit completely; and even then it is not this limit as such, but the very course of evolution tending to this limit, that constitutes the main object-matter of socio-psychological synthesis.[2]

Methodologically this means, as Thomas notes, the extension of the concept of type to the process of personal evolution, "for the concept of type plays the same part in social synthesis as the concept of causal fact plays in social analysis." And this involves, in turn, according to him, the recognition of the fact that not only single attitudes and values but more or less well-organized combinations of attitudes and values present a certain similarity from individual to individual—in other words, that there are *typical lines of genesis* in personal evolution. The similarity with which we are here concerned, he thus points out, is always only approximate and common only to a limited group, for it is not a matter of a single abstract law that we are dealing with here, but of a concrete cooperation of many laws. The concept of type, however, unlike the concept of law, "needs only an approximate identity of individual cases," according to him, "and class is supposed to possess only a relative generality."[3] Elaborating upon his suggested threefold classification of personality types from this standpoint, he says:

> The definiteness of attitudes attained in character and the corresponding schematization of social data in life-organization admit, however, a wide scale of gradation with regard to one point of fundamental importance,—the range of possibilities of further development remaining open to the individual after the stabilization. This depends on the nature of the attitudes involved in the character and of the schemes of life-organization, and also on the way in which both are unified and systematized. And here three typical cases can be distinguished.
> The set of attitudes constituting the character may be such as practically to exclude the development of any new attitude in the given conditions of life, because the reflective attitudes of an individual have attained so great a fixity

[1] *Ibid.*, pp. 11–12, 17.
[2] *Ibid.*, pp. 11–12.
[3] *Ibid.*, pp. 12–13.

that he is accessible to only a certain class of influences—those constituting the most permanent part of his social milieu. The only possibilities of evolution then remaining open to the individual are the slow changes brought by age in himself and by time in his social milieu, or a change of conditions so radical as to destroy at once the values to whose influence he was adapted and presumably his own character. This is the type which has found its expression in literature as the "Philistine." It is opposed to the "Bohemian," whose possibilities of evolution are not closed, simply because his character has remained unformed. Some of his temperamental attitudes are in their primary form, others may have become intellectualized but remain unrelated to each other, do not constitute a stable and systematized set, and do not exclude any new attitude, so that the individual remains open to any and all influences. As opposed to both these types we find the third type of individual whose character is settled and organized but involves the possibility and even the necessity of evolution, because the reflective attitudes constituting it include a tendency to change, regulated by plans of productive activity, and the individual remains open to such influences as will be in line of his preconceived development. This is the type of the creative individual.[1]

A parallel distinction, suggests Thomas, holds with respect to the schemes of social integration constituting life organization. We range here again, according to him, from the Philistine conformist type, characterized by the ability to define every situation in terms of the most stable elements of social tradition; to the Bohemian type, whose choice of a scheme depends on his momentary standpoint; and again to the creative type, characterized by adaptability and diversity of interest and an ability to adapt his purposes to a continually increasing sphere of social reality.[2]

This threefold classification of types has been justifiably criticized on the ground that it is not mutually exclusive and not free from the implications of subjective valuation. The attempt is, however, highly suggestive from the social-psychological standpoint. Besides, Thomas frankly offers it only as an illustrative scheme which he suggests as a starting point for continued concrete investigation on the problem, and he himself calls attention to the fact that the types defined are not exclusive of each other. Thus he points out in this connection:

The Philistine, the Bohemian and the creative man are the three fundamental forms of personal determination toward which social personalities tend in their evolution. None of these forms is ever completely and absolutely realized by a human individual in all lines of activity; there is no Philistine who lacks completely Bohemian tendencies, no Bohemian who is not a Philistine in certain respects, no creative man who is fully and exclusively creative and does not need some Philistine routine in certain lines to make creation in other lines practically possible, and some Bohemianism in order to be able to reject occasionally such

[1] *Ibid.*, pp. 27–28.
[2] *Ibid.*, pp. 28–30.

fixed attitudes and social regulations as hinder his progress, even if he should be unable at the time to substitute for them any positive organization in the given line. But while pure Philistinism, pure Bohemianism and pure creativeness represent only ideal limits of personal evolution, the process of personal evolution grows to be more and more definite as it progresses, so that, while the form which a human personality will assume is not determined in advance, either by the individual's temperament or by his social milieu, his future becomes more and more determined by the very course of his development; he approaches more and more to Philistinism, Bohemianism or creativeness and thereby his possibilities of becoming something else continually diminish.[1]

The social-psychological suggestiveness of Thomas' classification of personality types as given follows of course from the fact that it links the phenomenon of temperament (a term which he uses in the sense of differential original equipment) and social organization in a unified view of concrete social personality. His classification thus connects up this part of his discussion with his earlier discussion of attitudes and values, social-psychological procedure being thus consistently defined by him, in both its analytical and its synthetic aspects, as a matter of socio-psychic material and method. The following statement on the process of personal evolution is directly of interest here in this respect.

Every process of personal evolution consists, therefore, in a complex evolutionary series in which social schemes, acting upon pre-existing attitudes, produce new attitudes in such a way that the latter represent a determination of the temperamental tendencies with regard to the social world, a realization in a conscious form of the character-possibilities which the individual brings with him; and these new attitudes, with their intellectual continuity, acting upon pre-existing sets of social values in the sphere of individual experiences produce new values in such a way that every production of a value represents at the same time a definition of some vague situation, and this is a step toward the constitution of some consistent scheme of behavior. In the continual interaction between the individual and his environment we can say neither that the individual is the product of his milieu nor that he produces his milieu; or rather, we can say both. For the individual can indeed develop only under the influence of his environment, but on the other hand during his development he modifies this environment by defining situations and solving them according to his wishes and tendencies. His influence upon the environment may be scarcely noticeable socially, may have little importance for others, but it is important for himself, since, as we have said, the world in which he lives is not the world as society or the scientific observer sees it but as he sees it himself. In various cases we may find various degrees of dependence upon the environment, conditioned by the primary qualities of the individual and the type of social organization. The individual is relatively dependent upon society in his evolution if he develops mainly such attitudes as lead to dependence, which is then due both to his temperamental disposition and to the fact that the organization of society is such as to enforce by

[1] *Ibid.*, pp. 30–31.

various means individual subjection; he is relatively independent if in his evolution he develops attitudes producing independence, which again result from certain primary tendencies determined by a social organization which favors individual spontaneity. And thus both dependence and independence are gradually products of an evolution which is due originally to reciprocal interaction; the individual cannot become exclusively dependent upon society without the help of his own disposition, nor become independent of society without the help of social influences. The fundamental principles of personal evolution must be sought therefore both in the individual's own nature and in his social milieu.[1]

Following up this general standpoint, Thomas goes on to indicate the relation of personal evolution to the fundamental human wishes as the concrete organizations of original traits and tendencies on the one hand, and to social organization on the other. In this connection he restates the fundamental wishes in their more familiar form as consisting of the *desire for new experience*, the *desire for stability*, the *desire for response*, and the *desire for recognition*, and he attempts to reflect them upon the basic background of social organization in primary group life.[2] The latter becomes concretely effective in personal evolution, of course, through the processes of social control, which, in the case of personal evolution, as Thomas suggests, may be more appropriately termed "social education." Social education being, then, the crucial point from the standpoint of the possible control and direction of the process of personal evolution, Thomas' theory thus naturally leads him, as indeed the social-psychological point of view has so frequently led American writers since the time of Ward, to a consideration of the social-psychological aspects of education. And his discussion of this subject is particularly interesting because of the suggestive manner in which he interlinks it with his theory of personality types as above outlined.

There is a maximum of social efficiency between stability and flexibility, according to him, which the creative type of person represents, and it is the task of social education to bring about that proper balance of forces which will be most favorable for his development. More than ever, furthermore, the creative type is a social need of the present day, Thomas points out, for the other types are proving themselves increasingly inconsistent with the shifting demands of the present complex social order. From the standpoint of personal efficiency in modern society, in fact, according to him, Philistinism and Bohemianism must alike be regarded as complete educational failures.[3]

Yet under the present conditions of social life and organized education, he recalls, Philistinism and Bohemianism are the most frequent products of personal evolution. The insistence upon a static and narrow

[1] *Ibid.*, pp. 31–33.
[2] *Ibid.*, pp. 33*ff.*, 56*ff.*
[3] *Ibid.*, pp. 65*ff.*

primary-group conformity in education when our complex social life demands dynamic and inclusive standards, forces the great majority of modern individuals, in the opinion of Thomas, into the one or the other of these social types. The individual who succeeds in producing for himself such a life organization as is adapted to the complex demands of present-day life, he suggests, has to do it "by his own devices." He is forced to invent step by step the methods of education which he needs without the help of an organized social technique based upon the past experience of others, and he must even "consider himself lucky," Thomas adds, "if his environment does not interfere with him too efficiently by trying to impose upon him a stable character" too soon. "Under such conditions, the appearance of a really efficient, creative personality is actually a very exceptional social happening, for it needs a very high personal ability and persistence to develop a dynamic individual organization for efficiency instead of adopting a static social organization for stability, when social education has exclusively the second purpose in view." In addition it is, according to him, only by a rare concurrence of circumstances that individuals who have this high ability of developing without proper educational help happen to be left in peace to pursue their own self-made lines. Thus it is, suggests Thomas, that the scarcity of creative individuals in modern society has led to the concept of "genius" and that high efficiency is viewed as something extraordinary.[1]

This situation cannot however long continue, it seems to him. The direction which social evolution has been assuming in modern times tends to put a premium on efficiency and creativeness even at the cost of conformity, and the pressure of these new social tendencies must inevitably bear fruit for the reconstruction of our notions of a desirable life organization.[2] Summarizing his position on this point, Thomas declares:

It is clear that these new characters of modern social evolution require an entirely new standpoint with reference to individual life-organization. The individual must be trained not for conformity, but for efficiency, not for stability, but for creative evolution . . . The best that society has ever done for its members was to put at their disposal materials for creative development by preserving values produced by the past. The task of future society will be not only to remove obstacles preventing spontaneous personal development, but to give positive help, to furnish every individual with proper methods for spontaneous personal development, to teach him how to become not a static character and a conformist, but a dynamic, continually growing and continually creative personality. And such methods, can be found only by socio-psychological studies of human individuals.[3]

[1] *Ibid.*, p. 77.
[2] *Ibid.*, pp. 77*ff.*
[3] *Ibid.*, pp. 80–81.

The study of such typical life records of the culturally passive mass as is presented in volume III of *The Polish Peasant* is, in Thomas' opinion, a first step in this direction. "Only the study of the common-place man," he says, "can make us understand why there are common-place men." Such study "will make us realize also that the greatest defect of our entire civilization has been precisely the existence of a culturally passive mass, that every non-creative personality is an educational failure. It will show the sources of such failures and thus open the way for a more successful social education in the future. It will be the deepest and the most efficient criticism of our social organization as inherited from the past." Particularly at this time, according to him, "when we are facing the greatest historical change that has ever taken place—a general democratization of the world—" is this an important consideration. "The growing recognition that democracy is the only order compatible with our highest humanitarian ideals," he thus says in conclusion at this point, "must be accompanied by a growing understanding that the removal of political obstacles is only the first step toward this order, that what we call democracy has been mainly ochlocracy, and will be until the culturally passive mass becomes a thing of the past."[1]

His point of view as thus outlined Thomas illustrates and elaborates in the course of his treatment of the various aspects of Polish life noted in his description of the concrete part of his study.[2] His treatment of this subject matter, based as it is on his novel use of the somewhat novel source material which this part of his study introduces and which makes up the bulk of his imposing work,[3] is both original and extremely suggestive. But all in all, it leaves many loose ends and raises many troubling questions of procedure, which for all of Thomas' lengthy methodological notes and comments remain unanswered in so far as his own work is concerned. Without stopping on more detailed questions of point of view and position, some of which have already been noted in previous connections,[4] there is, above all, the basic question raised at the outset of our survey of his theory[5] as to just how and to what extent he used the concrete material of his study inductively and to what extent merely illustratively. In the absence of a definite statement on this matter, and in the absence of any description of definite technique and procedure, what reliance can we place on his various conclusions and generalizations over and above the theory of dozens of other writers in the field?

Such statements as Thomas makes touching on this important point, being, for the most part, not specific accounts of actual procedure but

[1] *Ibid.*, pp. 81–82.

[2] See *supra*, p. 356, note 3.

[3] This consists of about twenty thousand personal letters appropriately arranged and organized and the lengthy autobiographical record already referred to above.

[4] See, for example, *supra*, note p. 369.

[5] *Supra*, p. 357, note 2.

general comments on the inductive method, the concrete approach, and the value of the monographic method, are quite inadequate and altogether inconclusive. Some of the more notable of these statements are the following:

As to the present work, it evidently cannot in any sense pretend to establish social theory on a definitely scientific basis. It is clear from the preceding discussion that many workers and much time will be needed before we free ourselves from the traditional ways of thinking, develop a completely efficient and exact working method, and reach a system of scientifically correct generalizations. Our present very limited task is the preparation of a certain body of materials, even if we occasionally go beyond it and attempt to reach some generalizations.

We use in this work the inductive method in a form which gives the least possible place for any arbitrary statements. The basis of the work is concrete materials, and only in the selection of these materials some necessary discrimination has been used. But even here we have tried to proceed in the most cautious way possible . . .

The general character of the work is mainly that of a systematization and classification of attitudes and values prevailing in a concrete group. Every attitude and every value, as we have said above, can be really understood only in connection with the whole social life of which it is an element, and therefore this method is the only one that gives us a full and systematic acquaintance with all the complexity of social life. But it is evident that this monograph must be followed by many others if we want our acquaintance with social reality to be complete . . . Naturally, the value of every monograph will increase with the development of the work, for not only will the method continually improve, but every social group will help to understand every other.

In selecting the monographic method for the present work and in urging the desirability of the further preparation of large bodies of materials representing the total life of different social groups, we do not ignore the other method of approaching a scientific social theory and practice—the study of special problems, of isolated aspects of social life . . .

Now we are ourselves primarily interested in these [special] problems, but we are convinced of the necessity of approaching these and other social problems by isolating given societies and studying them, first, in the totality of their objective complexity, and then comparatively.[1]

These and similar statements leave one with the impression that Thomas' interest was primarily directed to the inductive development of the field of social theory, and yet nowhere does he provide the basis for actually following his theory through in that way. It would seem, everything considered, that his use of his materials was so informal that the need of a definite statement in explanation of his procedure never suggested itself. The whole question of the status of his theory, and beyond that also the more important question of the wider scientific usability of his source material, are thus left hanging in the air, and to

[1] *The Polish Peasant in Europe and America*, vol. I, pp. 74–78, preface, p. vii.

date neither Thomas himself in his later works[1] nor any of his followers have met the challenge of those who remain skeptical of his approach on this account. But precisely because of this, as it would seem, Thomas' work has stimulated the sort of discussion of research technique and procedure which was most needed for the advance of the research interest in the fields of sociology and social psychology. In any event, his work has been prominently in the foreground as a factor during the last decade or so in directing attention to the research approach in these fields of endeavor and in helping to bring about that intensification of interest in research and investigation generally which is so notable a feature of psycho-social thought in this country since the World War.

In large part this has no doubt been due to the fact that Thomas' theory, as was noted at the outset of this section, has been made the basis of further operations by an influential group of colleagues, associates, students, and followers who have themselves been actively interested in furthering the research approach in the fields of sociology and social psychology. The group includes, besides the members of the Department of Sociology at the University of Chicago who were immediately associated with Thomas, a widening circle of younger writers influenced by them. The recent volume in honor of Thomas, to which reference has already been made,[2] presents the following group of contributors, described by the editor as collaborators and students who write from a viewpoint similar to that of Thomas: L. L. Bernard, Emory S. Bogardus, Ernest W. Burgess, Ellsworth Faris, R. D. McKenzie, Herbert A. Miller, Robert E. Park, Stuart A. Queen, E. B. Reuter, J. F. Steiner, E. H. Sutherland, Frederic M. Thrasher, Erle Fiske Young, Kimball Young, Florian Znaniecki. And there is in addition, as stated above, a growing number of other writers less directly associated with Thomas himself who have become identified with the point of view. Altogether, therefore, we are concerned here, certainly with one of the most prominent American groupings of present-day sociological and social-psychological writers and investigators. As a result of their combined effort, Thomas' point of view has been applied to the study of a large number of concrete research problems and kept before American sociological and social-psychological thought as one of the foremost issues of recent years.

Above all, it is necessary to mention here along with Thomas' own work the recent research activities of the Department of Sociology at the University of Chicago, which for the last few years has been in the foreground in applying Thomas' theory in a comprehensive program of concrete community research.[3] In particular the work of Ellsworth

---

[1] *Old World Traits Transplanted* (1921) by Park and Miller; *The Unadjusted Girl* (1923); *The Child in America* (1928) with Dorothy Swaine Thomas.

[2] *Supra*, p. 352, note 1.

[3] For an account of this community research program see *The City* (1925) by Park, Burgess etc. and *Chicago, An Experiment in Social Science Research* (1931), ed. by

Faris, Robert E. Park, and Ernest W. Burgess, in developing, supplementing, and adapting Thomas' point of view to the testimony of accumulating evidence and research experience, has been so intimately a part of Thomas' own work as to be practically inseparable from it. Notable in this connection, especially, is the restatement of Thomas' theory by Park and Burgess in their *Introduction to the Science of Sociology* (1921), where it is brought into proper historical perspective and relation with previous sociological thought, and the reinterpretation of important aspects of his theory by Ellsworth Faris in various articles dealing with the subject matter.[1]

Some of the most challenging and critical formulations of the position under consideration have been the work of the latter writer, who differs from Thomas chiefly in his closer identification with the social-psychological theory of Dewey and Mead and in his more aggressive criticism of the position underlying instinct psychology.[2] In this connection, as well as in his frequent reconsideration of Thomas' position itself, Faris has tended to stress especially the testimony of ethnology, upon which he places a greater reliance than most American social psychologists. In his formulations, therefore, the Thomas point of view is most frequently brought into relation with cultural anthropology and set off against the background of current instinct psychology. The distinguishing characteristics of the viewpoint thus appear more clearly than in the case of most formulations of the position. It is on this account and also because Faris' formulations are at the present time in themselves a very important part of the situation that it is illuminating, in closing this

---

Smith and White.   The nature of this research program appears quite clearly from the following studies already published: PARK, BURGESS, etc., *The City* (1925); THRASHER, *The Gang* (1927); MOWRER, *Family Disorganization* (1927); BURGESS, "Factors Determining Success or Failure on Parole," *Parole and the Indeterminate Sentence* (1928) rept. to Hon. Hinton Q. Clabaugh, chairman, Parole Board of Illinois; WIRTH, *The Ghetto* (1928); PALMER, *Field Studies in Sociology* (1928); CAVAN, *Suicide* (1928); ZORBAUGH, *The Gold Coast and the Slum* (1929); SHAW, *Delinquency Areas* (1929), *The Jack-Roller* (1930); *The Natural History of a Delinquent Career* (1931).

[1] See the following, for example: "Ethnological Light on Psychological Problems," *Pub. Amer. Sociol. Soc.*, vol. 16, pp. 113–120, 1921; "Are Instincts Data or Hypotheses?" *Amer. Jour. Sociol.*, vol. 27, pp. 184–196, 1921; "The Concept of Social Attitudes," *Jour. App. Sociol.*, vol. 9, pp. 404–409, 1924–1925; "The Subjective Aspect of Culture," *Pub. Amer. Sociol. Soc.*, vol. 19, pp. 37–46, 1925; "The Nature of Human Nature," *ibid.*, vol. 20, pp. 15–29, 1926. See also a suggestive discussion of the problem of delinquency from this point of view: BURGESS, "The Study of the Delinquent as a Person," *Amer. Jour. Sociol.*, vol. 28, pp. 657–680, 1922–1923, and various articles in *Social Attitudes*, ed. by Young. An interesting early use of the concept "sentiment-attitude" in connection with the analysis of social behavior in contrast to the concept "instinct-emotion," appears in a pamphlet by Park entitled *Principles of Human Behavior* (1915).

[2] See, for example, his important article on "Are Instincts Data or Hypotheses?" (note 1, above).

section of our survey, to note how he reflects the Thomas point of view upon the background of related social-psychological thought.[1]

The general point of view of Thomas and the others associated with his social-psychological position, says Faris for example in one connection after enumerating various other approaches to the study of human nature and social behavior, among them the imitation doctrine, instinct psychology, orthodox behaviorism, psychoanalysis, etc.

. . . differs essentially from the preceding formulations in the emphasis on the social group or matrix in which the personality takes shape, and in the emphasis on the social nature of individual personality. When Thomas speaks of "social attitudes" he refers to the attitudes of individuals which are the result of social influencing. Dewey wrote: "Institutions cause the instincts." Cooley has written convincingly concerning society and the individual as different aspects or phases of the seamless fabric of human life. Personality appears from this point of view as the subjective aspect of culture. Social psychology so considered draws heavily on anthropology and finds itself closely related to sociology. This explains why so many sociologists have been interested in the subject of social psychology.[2]

Faris has applied this point of view to the criticism of Thomas' position itself in so far as it incorporates elements of the instinct approach, as it strikingly does, he has pointed out, in its theory of the wishes and especially "the four wishes," which have come to be used by some of Thomas' followers as a convenient substitute for the usual list of instincts and with much the same objectionable results. This part of Thomas' theory, Faris has suggested, is a hold-over of his earlier instinct approach. Furthermore, according to him, it is out of harmony with his basic attitudes-values approach and tends to obscure the importance of the latter contribution which, he has maintained, can stand on its own merit as a fundamental shift of focus in modern social-psychological thought corresponding to the alliance of social psychology with the study of concrete social behavior rather than with some assumed abstract elements of

[1] Not unlike Mead, of whose position in reference to social psychology he has become the outstanding sociological interpreter (see *supra*, pp. 526–527), Faris has exercised his influence largely by way of the classroom. For the same reasons, it is therefore difficult to lay hold of his social-psychological theory as a whole for those who are dependent upon his published discussions. But his formulations of the Thomas point of view are reflected in a series of telling, critical and interpretive articles dealing with the subject matter, which have come to be looked upon as among the most authoritative expressions of the position here under consideration.

[2] "Current Trends in Social Psychology," *Essays in Philosophy*, edited by Smith and Wright, pp. 121, 128. This statement explains also why social psychology so conceived should have stimulated the formulation of an antagonistic position by those who seek to link the subject not with sociology and cultural anthropology but with physiology and individual psychology. In particular, it explains the antagonistic position of Floyd H. Allport, who has been the outstanding spokesman of the latter point of view in this country during the last few years (see *infra*, p. 403).

behavior, as in the case of instinct psychology. It is on this account, according to him, that Thomas' point of view has been so valuable as a research approach. "The instinct controversy," says Faris, "is a matter of the last seven or eight years and the subject is at present under discussion with a number of foremost authors still defending the conception as having value, but with an increasing tendency on the part of most writers to be apologetic and tentative in their use of the term . . . A reconciling formula is still in the future, but it seems accurate to say that the concept of instinct plays little or no part in any present researches. It belongs to the realm of 'explanation.'"[1]

It is in this respect that the concept of attitudes represents a most conspicuous step in advance, according to Faris. "The concrete and factual nature of the concept," he says, "has already resulted in valuable researches. This is in marked contrast with the paralyzing sterility of the instinct concept which dominated this field for so long but which is, fortunately, being very rapidly discarded."[2]

In further explanation of this point, he says again in another connection: "The discussion has not reached an end and there is no warrant for asserting unanimity but the trend seems clearly in the direction of complete emancipation from the necessity of discovering or even the possibility of admitting any essential and definite elementary constituents in the developing individual." And this, he points out, would have consequences of the first importance for the study of personality and social behavior. "For it would place the social group in a new perspective and enable us to find in the mores and institutions of a time and area those elements which were formerly asserted to exist in the psychophysical organism."[3]

This emphasis upon the group approach and "the mores and institutions of a time and area" as a necessary setting for social-psychological investigation may be taken as formulative of the essential characteristic of the point of view under review, especially as it has been put into effect in the Chicago research program mentioned. It is in accord with other recent formulations of the point of view, including Thomas' own more recent restatements of his position,[4] and interpretive of what is most

---

[1] "Current Trends in Social Psychology," *Essays in Philosophy*, ed. by Smith and Wright, pp. 124–125; also *Social Attitudes*, ed. by Young, pp. 3–4; "Borderline Trends in Social Psychology," *Pub. Amer. Sociol. Soc.*, vol. 25, pp. 38–40, 1931.

[2] "The Concept of Social Attitudes," *Jour. Appl. Sociol.*, vol. 9, p. 409, 1924–1925; See also Reuter, "The Social Attitude," *ibid.*, vol. 8, pp. 97–101, 1923–1924.

[3] "Borderline Trends in Social Psychology," *Pub. Amer. Sociol. Soc.*, vol. 25, p. 39, 1931.

[4] See in this connection "The Configuration of Personality," *The Unconscious*, ed. by Dummer; "The Behavior Pattern and the Situation," *Pub. Amer. Sociol. Soc.*, vol. 22, pp. 1–15, 1928; *The Child in America*, especially Chaps. XII–XIII; see also statements by Park and Burgess in *The City*, and *Chicago, An Experiment in Social Science Research* (*supra*, p. 380, note 1).

distinctive in the activities of the group of writers enumerated in this discussion.[1]

So far the studies in which this point of view has been incorporated have been largely non-quantitative in character. While some of the most recent of these studies incorporate quantitative procedures and while ultimately most of the investigators associated with the point of view hope to develop significant quantitative presentations and treatments of their materials, for the present the latter are held subordinate to the descriptive technique illustrated in *The Polish Peasant*, the feeling in general being that in the present stage of sociological and social-psychological knowledge and investigation, the quantitative approach is not especially significant in so far as the advance of a genuine science of human behavior is concerned.[2] In this respect, therefore, as well as in respect to the definite alliance of the point of view with anthropology and sociology, as appears from Faris' statement, the direction of social-psychological development represented by the group of writers here under consideration is thus supplemented by another important direction

---

[1] For a highly suggestive further treatment of this point, developed in historical perspective, see Bodenhafer's series of articles on "The Comparative Role of the Group Concept in Ward's Dynamic Sociology and Contemporary American Sociology," *Amer. Jour Sociol.*, vol. 26, pp. 273–314, 425–474, 588–600, 716–743, 1920–1921.

[2] This appears clearly in such attempts as have been made to formulate the research procedure of the group—for example, PALMER, *Field Studies in Sociology* and BOGARDUS, *The New Social Research;* see in this connection also Introductory Note to *Social Attitudes*, ed. by Young, p. vii; also statements by Park and Burgess in *Chicago, An Experiment in Social Science Research*, ed. by Smith and White, and in *The City*, by Park, Burgess etc.; also references *supra*, p. 303, note 3.

That the group is not opposed to the quantitative approach, as is sometimes supposed, but merely finds it inexpedient to concentrate upon the quantitative approach at the present time is evident enough from the spirit of their work as a whole as well as from various studies in the investigation of delinquency and crime which it has recently been carrying on (see, in this connection especially, BURGESS, "Factors Determining Success or Failure on Parole" and SHAW, *Delinquency Areas, supra*, p. 379, note 3).   The work of L. L. Thurstone and others in attempting to adapt quantitative methods to the treatment of materials made significant by the viewpoint outlined is also notable in this connection (see especially THURSTONE, "Attitudes Can Be Measured," *Amer. Jour. Sociol.*, vol. 33, pp. 529–554, 1928; "Theory of Attitude Measurement," *Psychol. Rev.*, vol. 36, pp. 222–241, 1929).

Most of the studies mentioned in this section, and in particular the Department of Sociology community studies of the University of Chicago, have been chiefly concerned with the investigation of urban life.   But in the work of Williams, *Our Rural Heritage, The Social Psychology of Rural Development*, and *The Expansion of Rural Life*, a beginning has been made also toward the study of rural life from a similar standpoint; and in *Middletown* by Lynd and Lynd, we have a study of a different level of city life carried out again from a somewhat similar standpoint.   Williams and especially the Lynds have for the most part worked independently of Thomas and his associates but under the influence apparently of cultural anthropology have arrived at a substantially similar outlook and procedure.

of social-psychological development which has recently been gaining ground rapidly in this country and which by contrast stresses the quantitative approach of statistics and laboratory psychology. This other direction of social-psychological development, to which preliminary reference has already been made in the opening chapter of this part of our survey and which has been associated chiefly with the physiological viewpoint of individual psychology instead of the socio-cultural viewpoints of anthropology and sociology,[1] has until recently lacked social-psychological spokesmen in this country corresponding to those associated with the other viewpoints considered. In Allport's *Social Psychology* (1924) and, increasingly following upon this work, in other treatments of the subject, it has however gained a very decided prominence. This may be judged from such an imposing survey of the quantitative aspects of social psychology as that of Murphy and Murphy in their *Experimental Social Psychology* (1931). It will be considered here further in the next chapter in conjunction with some of these works.[2]

[1] See *supra*, pp. 247, note 1, 266.

[2] For a further discussion of Thomas' social-psychological theory see PARK and BURGESS, *Introduction to the Science of Sociology*, pp. 144, 438*ff*., 497, etc.; BOGARDUS, *A History of Social Thought*, pp. 322–324; *Fundamentals of Social Psychology*, Chap. V; BARNES, *Sociol. Rev.*, vol. 16, pp. 1–19, 1924; BERNARD, *Introduction to Social Psychology*, Chap. XVI; HOUSE, *The Range of Social Theory*, Chap. XV; YOUNG, *Social Psychology*, Chap. I; SOROKIN, *Contemporary Sociological Theories*, Chap. XI; KRUEGER and RECKLESS, *Social Psychology, passim;* and especially *Social Attitudes*, ed. by Young.

For a spirited criticism of the Thomas point of view see, for instance, SOROKIN, *Contemporary Sociological Theories*, pp. 619–627, 644*ff*.; ELLWOOD, *The Psychology of Human Society*, pp. 16, 286*ff*.; also ALLPORT, *infra*, p. 400.

CHAPTER VIII

THE EMERGENCE OF A DIFFERENTIATED SOCIAL PSYCHOLOGY (*Continued*)

ATTEMPTS AT SYSTEMATIC TREATMENT

I. CHARLES A. ELLWOOD (1873)

In the case of social psychology, as in other fields of investigation, the growing complexity of material and the wider popularization of the subject, especially as a department of university instruction, have been accompanied by a parallel development of attempts at organization and systematic treatment. In particular, the simultaneous appearance in 1908 of the two early works on social psychology by Ross and McDougall had the effect of bringing the interest in social-psychological synthesis prominently into view. For these two works tended to bring the difference between the psychological and the sociological approaches to the subject so conspicuously into evidence as to suggest the immediate need of a more comprehensive treatment which would give expression to both of these widely popular conceptions. From this time on, therefore, as will appear in the course of this chapter, interest in the synthetic treatment of social psychology has been intimately a part of American social-psychological thought. Accordingly, along with the development of social-psychological thought in this country, as so far outlined, it is necessary to consider some of the attempts at organization and synthesis which are especially important in filling out the picture thus far presented.

In this connection, Ellwood's social-psychological work stands out with special prominence, not only because of his long-standing interest in this approach to the subject,[1] but also because in his case this approach takes on a special significance which is notable here as an expression of his basic conception of social psychology and social-psychological procedure. His treatment of social psychology will therefore be considered briefly from this standpoint and also as an illuminating basis for the further consideration of the subject matter of this chapter.

According to Ellwood, it should be noted at the outset, social psychology is just another name for psycho-sociology or psychological sociol-

---

[1] His *Prolegomena to Social Psychology* (1901) appeared originally in the *Amer. Jour. Sociol.* in 1899. See also his views on social psychology as expressed in the *Proc. Intern. Congress Arts Sci.*, vol. 5, 1904.

ogy. As such, according to him, social psychology constitutes the greater part of sociology, the other important part being social biology. Consistently with this view, he has favored the designation "psychological sociology" as more suggestive of the actual content of the subject and as more indicative of its essential aim and purpose than the more popular term "social psychology."[1]

It is clear, then, that Ellwood's conception of social psychology is intimately a part of his conception of sociology more generally. And the latter, being considerably at variance with most of the other conceptions touched upon in this part of our survey,[2] it is necessary to note it here in very broad outline as essential background upon which to reflect his more specific social-psychological views.

Ellwood, it is thus notable in this connection, has remained sponsor in this country, more especially in his earlier works, to a view of sociology and thereby also of social psychology which, though not so widely popular today as it was during the earlier period of the modern social-psychological movement when he first began to concern himself with social-psychological theory, is nevertheless of considerable historical importance, namely, that instead of being essentially a technique of first-hand investigation corresponding to the other psychological and social sciences, sociology is essentially a synthetic discipline whose aim it is to arrive at "an all-sided generalization" of social life in accordance with the conception that it is the "general science of society." Sociology is enabled to arrive at this sort of generalization, according to him, by coordinating the results of the special social sciences and interpreting them in terms of the basic principles of social behavior set forth in the "antecedent sciences," especially biology and psychology.[3]

Pursuing this view, Ellwood made sociology depend on biology and psychology to such an extent that, in effect, social psychology as the psychological part of the subject became in large part in his case what it so largely was in the case of the early folk psychologists and organic sociologists, namely, psychology applied to the field of social interpretation. This is fundamentally the case even though, in the final working out of his procedure, he has interpreted the psychological approach broadly, so as to bring into harmony with it the contributions of the more distinctively sociological and anthropological approaches to the study of

[1] See *Sociology in Its Psychological Aspects*, Preface p. vii; *An Introduction to Social Psychology*, Preface, p. v; *Proc. Intern. Congress Arts Sci.*, vol. 5, p. 859, 1904; *The Psychology of Human Society*, pp. v, 15.

[2] It supposedly leads out from the early view of the subject held by A. W. Small and developed in Small and Vincent, *Introduction to the Study of Society*, which has already been referred to here in several connections.

[3] *Sociology in Its Psychological Aspects*, Chaps. I–III, especially pp. 29–31, 55–63; *An Introduction to Social Psychology*, Chap. I; *The Psychology of Human Society*, Chap. I.

social life.[1] Quite naturally, therefore, he placed emphasis on the deductive method as the one by which social psychology, at any rate in its earlier stages of development, may be most readily built up, this being the method upon which he was chiefly obliged to depend in working out the applications of psychology to the field of social interpretation.[2] Social psychology, he suggests in a characteristic passage in one of his earlier works, "presents itself as mainly an application of psychology to the interpretation of social phenomena."[3] "The psychologist," he explains, "turns over to the social psychologist the principles of human nature and the social psychologist uses these to interpret the interactions, combinations, and organizations of individuals."[4]

In keeping with this view, Ellwood applied himself centrally to the task of adapting and making available for the purposes of social interpretation such of the concepts and principles of psychology as appeared to him to be especially significant for the task in hand. Dewey's functional psychology appealed to him as providing a particularly fruitful outlook and approach. Accordingly he made it his point of departure in building up the psychological basis of his theory.[5]

He started out very naturally, therefore, in his *Prolegomena to Social Psychology* (1901), to which reference has already been made here in a previous connection,[6] with an attempt to work out some of the social applications of Dewey's psychology and to sketch the wider outlines of a social psychology as suggested by Dewey's functional point of view. Continuing this early effort on a much more elaborate scale in his *Sociology in Its Psychological Aspects* (1912),[7] he brought a considerable part of

[1] See *Sociology in Its Psychological Aspects*, Chaps. VI–VII; *An Introduction to Social Psychology*, Chaps. II–III; *The Psychology of Human Society*, Chap. II.

[2] *Sociology in Its Psychological Aspects*, especially pp. 55–66, 82–93; *An Introduction to Social Psychology*, especially pp. 4, 12–19; *The Psychology of Human Society*, especially pp. 9–12, 21–23, 29–38.

[3] *Sociology in Its Psychological Aspects*, pp. 59, 61. Quotations from this work are reprinted by permission of D. Appleton & Company, publishers.

[4] *Ibid.*, p. 59. Psychology, as appears today more clearly than a decade or two ago, being not one but many, the question naturally arises in this connection, What principles of psychology? Ellwood's treatment reflects this question more in his recent than in his earlier works, in which he proceeded on the assumption that there is a scientific psychology which should be made the basis of social interpretation. He thus inevitably introduced the factor of selection very prominently into his treatment. But viewing social psychology as an interpretive technique, the selection of interpretive concepts and principles is necessarily in some measure a matter of subjective evaluation and choice (see *infra*, p. 393). This, furthermore, is a characteristic which is to some extent common to all attempts at organization and synthesis and is unavoidably prominent in a new field like social psychology.

[5] *Sociology in Its Psychological Aspects*, pp. viii–ix; *The Psychology of Human Society*, note p. viii.

[6] See *supra*, pp. 328 ff.

[7] See p. 1, note.

current psychological, sociological, and anthropological theory together under the organizing conception provided by Dewey's psychology. This work, as he tells us,[1] he then systematized, simplified, and revised in the light of developing psychological and social thought, and finally he represented it as his *Introduction to Social Psychology* (1917). More recently in his *Psychology of Human Society* (1925), he felt the need to restate his original position as developed in his earlier works, so as to provide for a more adequate incorporation of recent sociological and anthropological thought in this country which, as we have seen in the foregoing sections, had in the meantime become quite aggressively critical of the psychological approach as it was interpreted by him in these earlier works. The latter work, he thus tells us, is intended to supersede both his *Sociology in Its Psychological Aspects* and his *Introduction to Social Psychology*.[2] It is however only in terms of his position as originally outlined that the change incorporated in this more recent work appears in its full significance. We accordingly quote from his first major work, where his original position is most clearly and characteristically stated. The change incorporated in his more recent work will then be brought into proper perspective by comparison. Ellwood says in his *Sociology in Its Psychological Aspects:*

This book attempts to deal with the psychological aspects of sociology, often called "social psychology," but, in the opinion of the writer, more accurately named "psychological sociology." Accordingly, the book does not aim to furnish a comprehensive view of sociological theory, but only of that section of it which rests immediately upon psychology.[3]

The position of the writer is, as implied, that sociology is a study of the biological and psychological factors in the social life with reference to certain problems, especially the problems of social organization and social evolution. As such a biology and psychology of the social life, sociology is as much a natural science as the foundation sciences on which it rests. A scientific sociology, accordingly, must rest upon the assured results of the other positive sciences, especially modern biology and psychology . . . The sociologist must keep the biological and psychological individual constantly in view, as well as the unity or interdependence of society, if he is to reach a scientific interpretation of the social life. The interpretation of society, in other words, must be in terms of the biological and psychological factors in the individual; but the biological factors find their expression in the social life mainly through the psychological factors.[4]

The chief method of this treatise, accordingly, is that of psychological analysis, the method which has been employed so successfully in the development of theoretical economics. Modern functional psychology—the psychology of such

[1] *An Introduction to Social Psychology*, p. v.

[2] *The Psychology of Human Society*, p. v.

[3] *Sociology in Its Psychological Aspects*, p. vii; *cf. An Introduction to Social Psychology*, p. v, and *The Psychology of Human Society*, pp. 12, 14–18.

[4] *Sociology in Its Psychological Aspects*, pp. vii–viii; *cf. The Psychology of Human Society*, pp. 9–11.

writers as James, Dewey, Thorndike, and Angell—rather than the sensationalistic associational psychology of the Nineteenth Century, however, has been made the instrument of social analysis. The merit which is claimed for a sociology developed upon the basis of functional psychology is that it is both synthetic and practical. Many apparently conflicting theories of the social life fall into their proper places as aspects of the more fundamental view as soon as one takes the functional standpoint. Thus imitation, sympathy, conflict, industry, government, law, religion and even morality itself are all seen to be instruments for the carrying on and perfecting of a collective life-process. The functional point of view, in other words, subordinates social activities and institutions to the social life itself and finds no difficulty in arranging them all harmoniously as aspects or phases of that life. It is not, of course, claimed that functional psychology is of itself adequate to interpret fully the social life of man. It is only claimed that it furnishes a point of view and certain principles of explanation which are indispensable for the right understanding of human interrelations. A practical and functional sociology must be constructed with the aid of functional psychology.[1]

This conception of social psychology, basing itself conspicuously, as it does, upon the use of the deductive psychological method, is brought strikingly to a focus in the following passage from Ellwood's *Introduction to Social Psychology*, which summarizes his discussion of social-psychological methods in use:

The chief and most fruitful method in modern sociology has been to take truths discovered in other sciences and carry them over and apply them to the explanation of social life. There is no reason, indeed, why this should not be done, even though the method may have manifest limitations; for there is no reason why the student of society should have to work out for himself, independently, truths which have already been discovered by investigators in other realms. For whatever may be thought of the doctrine of the unity of nature, it is evident that "the social" is no distinct realm in itself, but is evidently a certain combination of biological and psychological factors. Every social situation is made up of, and may be analyzed into, geographical, biological and psychological elements. Ascertained truths in biology and psychology may be used directly, therefore, to explain certain social phenomena. From this it follows that the chief method of social psychology, or psychological sociology, must be to take ascertained laws and principles of the mental life and apply them to the explanation of phases of the social life in which these laws and principles are manifestly at work. Deduction from ascertained laws and principles of antecedent sciences must then be the prime method of social psychology.[2]

Inductive methods are here made generally supplementary by Ellwood to this use of the deductive method. "Deductions from seemingly established truths of antecedent sciences," he says, "must

---

[1] *Sociology in Its Psychological Aspects*, pp. viii–ix, also pp. 58–63 and Chaps. V–VI, XIX; cf. *An Introduction to Social Psychology*, pp. v, vii–xi, Chaps. I, XIV and *The Psychology of Human Society*, pp. vii–viii, Chaps. I, XV.

[2] *An Introduction to Social Psychology*, p. 12. Quotations from this work are reprinted by permission of D. Appleton & Company, publishers.

. . . be supplemented in the social sciences by the use of many other scientific methods." He mentions especially, as supplementary in this sense, the statistical method, the historical and comparative methods, and observation used in conjunction with the method of "sympathetic introspection." "After deduction from ascertained laws and principles of psychology," he explains, in estimating the relative value of these methods for social psychology, "sympathetic introspection is probably our chief instrument at the present time for the psychological analysis of existing social life."[1]

The change of viewpoint and outlook which Ellwood introduced into his *Psychology of Human Society* corresponds to the changes noted in various previous connections, more particularly in the sections on Dewey and Thomas, and centers about a greater emphasis on the "group" and "culture" aspects of social behavior. The following passages will bring this shift of position more clearly into view:

It is becoming increasingly evident that what has been called the psychological method of studying social problems, namely, by deductions from individual psychology, or original human nature, is inadequate. A too exclusive use of this sort of psychological analysis in the social sciences leads to many serious errors; for the human mind, as we know it, and hence social behavior, are very largely products of historical social conditions. The mind and the conduct of an individual, in other words, are largely products of the social tradition or culture into which the individual is born. The psychology of the individual's social behavior becomes dependent, therefore, upon an understanding of the historical social environment in which the individual lives. To study human institutions exclusively from the standpoint of the mechanism of the individual mind is, accordingly, a grievous blunder. Group behavior especially is far more a historical and cultural product than a product of original human nature. Much more than deduction from individual psychology is, therefore, involved in the psychology of human society. It would be unreasonable to suppose that such complex phenomena could be understood through the work in psychological and biological laboratories, though this work may be of great value toward such an understanding . . .

All modern science is essentially inductive in spirit; that is, it proceeds from facts to theory rather than from theory to facts—from particulars to universals rather than from universals to particulars. This does not preclude all use of deductions from biological and psychological laws and principles in the scientific study of society; for such laws and principles have been built up from the inductive study of facts. It does indicate, however, that the scientific student of human society must study social facts, if he is to proceed according to a sound method. Where, then, shall he get his facts concerning human society? Manifestly there are three sources: first, from anthropology and ethnology, both physical and cultural; second, from written history; third, from the observation and collection of facts regarding present social life.[2]

[1] *Ibid.*, pp. 13–16; see also *Sociology in Its Psychological Aspects*, Chap. V.
[2] *The Psychology of Human Society*, pp. 29–31.

There is, then, here a decided shift from the previous one-sided emphasis upon the basic importance of the biological and psychological approaches and correspondingly from emphasis upon the basic importance of the deductive biological and psychological methods. These methods are still recognized by Ellwood as valid, but instead of being made primary and basic, they are now made parts of a complex procedure which has a first-hand reference to inductive investigation, as will readily appear from the following statement:

Biology and psychology may furnish us with general principles for the interpretation of the facts of social behavior. It is a general rule in the more complex sciences that principles of explanation come from the simpler antecedent sciences. The social is not a realm by itself, but is built up out of the biological and psychological. Hence, ultimate principles of explanation in sociology must be either biological or psychological. It is scarcely ever possible, however, to explain human social phenomena simply and wholly through some biological fact; and the same is true of psychological facts. Biological and psychological facts and principles are at work in human society, but we shall untangle their workings best if we combine a knowledge of biological and psychological principles with an inductive study of collective human behavior. In other words, *a complex science such as sociology demands, for a complete and adequate scientific method, a synthesis of the results of deduction from the principles of antecedent sciences with the facts secured through the inductive study of the social life by means of anthropology, history, observation, and statistics.* All the facts from all these sources must be put together in a constructive synthesis before our psychology of human society is complete.[1]

This change of standpoint is strikingly reflected in the changed view of the relation between psychology and sociology which Ellwood finally arrived at in this work, as indicated in the following brief passage. Commenting upon his general statement that *"psychology . . . studies the individual and his behavior while sociology studies the group and its behavior,"* he says:

But we cannot understand the individual apart from his group, any more than we can understand the group apart from the nature of the individuals who compose it. Thus the dependence between sociology and psychology is reciprocal. Individual psychology must accordingly look to the study of group life for the explanation of much in individual behavior. It depends as much upon the psychology of society as the psychology of society depends upon it.[2]

Again, it is notably reflected in the manner in which he interrelates the individual and the social and in the manner in which he brings in the cultural factor in the following passage, which is taken from his summary restatement of his psychological theory of social life as it is given in his

[1] *The Psychology of Human Society*, p. 35. Quotations from this work are reprinted by permission of D. Appleton & Company, publishers.
[2] *Ibid.*, p. 22.

Psychology of Human Society. "It is a mistake," says Ellwood in this connection, "to seek the full explanation for group behavior either in the individual or in the culture of the group." He explains:

Thus the social life presents itself as a process, but a process made up both of individual psychic elements and of social psychic or cultural, elements; that is, of elements of interstimulation and response among individuals—such as communication, suggestion, imitation, sympathy, conflict—and of cultural elements—such as custom, tradition, conventions, and institutions. All of these processes ultimately enter into, and determine, the form of group behavior. Some of them are individual psychic, others are social psychic. The social psychic, or the cultural, however, can operate only through the individual and hence the individual has a chance to modify it. On the other hand, the individual's psychic life itself is largely determined by the social psychic, or the cultural. Individual behavior, in other words, comes largely from group culture; but culture in the last analysis, as we have said, comes from the individual mind.[1]

The organizing viewpoint which Ellwood thus finally arrived at is summarized by him in the following evolutionary statement of his position, which will serve also to bring his new points of emphasis into more effective relation with social-psychological thought as it has been previously outlined here:

Even before the human stage is reached we find uniformities of action apparently brought about in social groups of animals by such psychic processes as suggestion, imitation, and sympathy. Animal groups, however, are undoubtedly dominated by the hereditary or instinctive element. Human society, on the other hand, is characterized from its earliest beginnings by *acquired* uniformities due to habit. A habit which is acquired by one individual of the group may be communicated to and learned by other members of the group and thus become the common property of all. Mental interstimulation and response, especially in the form of intercommunication, thus assumes new importance. Hence a new type of social life is possible—one built upon the basis of learning and of acquired habit; and the acquirements of one individual may become acquirements of all through mental interstimulation and response. Accordingly, the web of intercommunication through furnishing the social stimulation necessary for the transmission of habit takes the place in human groups of instinct in bringing about relative uniformity of action on the part of all members of the group. This explains why the social life of man shows many complex phases of behavior not shown by animal groups, such as industry, art, government, education, science, morality, and religion. All of these taken collectively form what the anthropologist and the sociologist term "culture" (which is the scientific term for civilization in the broadest sense), and rest upon acquired group habits and go back to man's superior means of social communication through articulate speech, as well as to his superior power of adaptation through abstract thought. They distinguish human groups from animal groups.

[1] *Ibid.*, pp. 464–465, see also pp. 9–12; *cf. Sociology in Its Psychological Aspects*, pp. 388–390 and *An Introduction to Social Psychology*, pp. 321–325.

Culture or civilization is, then, not inborn but acquired by every individual in human groups; but this culture of the group dominates the behavior of the human individual and so the behavior of human groups . . . Human sociology becomes very distinct, therefore, from the psychology of the collective behavior of animal groups. *It is culture and habit, not instinct, which must be the main concern of the sociologist, or of any one who offers a psychological interpretation of collective human behavior; for it is the development of culture which distinguishes the social life of man from the social life of the brutes.*[1]

The details of Ellwood's treatment follow from his conception of social psychology and social-psychological procedure as outlined. It is clear that he was from the first concerned with an interpretive survey of the whole field of psycho-social thought with a view to presenting a more or less unified picture of human nature and social life. His discussion accordingly covers a wide range of relevant subject matter, leading out, through a shifting series of intermediate steps associated with the respective standpoints noted, from a consideration of the role of instinct, emotion, and intellect in the social life to an analysis of social unity, social continuity, social change, social order, and social progress.

In undertaking the consideration of this varied subject matter, Ellwood's treatment of specific topics has necessarily been generalized and incomplete. The strengths and weaknesses of his treatment follow clearly enough from this fact. His theory has on the one hand a comprehensiveness, inclusiveness, and breadth of perspective which more specialized approaches to the subject necessarily lack. But on the other hand it is more than ordinarily open to objection and criticism in respect to details of presentation. Working, in accordance with his conception of the subject, in such a broad field of theory and in a field in which conflict and controversy are at the present time still so prominent, he was often obliged to resort to an oversimplification of the situation which is hardly justified by the detailed consideration of the facts. Above all, his synthetic exposition has tended to obscure differences and difficulties which define some of the crucial problems awaiting further investigation.[2] His treatment, skillful as it is in many respects, has thereby appeared to be particularly inadequate from the research standpoint. It is in this respect most conspicuously, in any event, that his treatment has been supplemented by other treatments of the subject, some of which will now be considered here in the light of this introductory discussion of his conception of the task. For while the above considera-

[1] *The Psychology of Human Society*, pp. 9–11.

[2] His method of citing scientific evidence in generalized terms, through the frequent use of such phrases as "anthropology teaches," "biology declares," "history shows," "the bulk of scientific opinion holds," etc., is especially notable in this connection (see, for example, *An Introduction to Social Psychology*, Chaps. II, IX, and *The Psychology of Human Society*, Chaps. II, III, IX. The above phrases are taken from Chap. II of the former work).

tions are factors in most attempts at organization and synthesis in a field which is still in as fluid a state as social psychology is, they are peculiarly a part of Ellwood's conception of the subject, as will increasingly appear in the course of this chapter.[1]

II. EMORY S. BOGARDUS (1882)

The next writer, in chronological order, to concern himself with the systematic treatment of social psychology in this country has been Bogardus. Having started out in his *Essentials of Social Psychology*[2] (1918, 1920), from a position not unlike Ellwood's—especially in so far as his emphasis upon the biological and instinctive basis of social behavior is concerned,[3] Bogardus gradually passed on in his *Fundamentals of Social Psychology* (1924) to a reformulation of his position based chiefly on Park and Burgess' *Introduction to the Science of Sociology* (1921).[4] In conjunction with this reformulation of his position, Bogardus also undertook in his *New Social Research* (1926) to formulate what he conceived to be essential in the research technique which Park and Burgess and those associated with them have employed in their concrete investigations. Finally, he set about to work out some of the concrete applications of this viewpoint and research procedure in first-hand investigation of his own.[5] In the latter connections, it is thus clear, Bogardus' work links up very intimately with the work of the group of investigators considered in the Thomas-Faris section, and it should accordingly be reflected upon the background of our previous consideration of these activities.[6]

It is notable that in his recent reformulation of his social-psychological position, Bogardus has worked out, like Ellwood, an expansion of point of view in the direction of a greater emphasis on the group aspects of social life. In his case this emphasis also takes on a further significance,

[1] See on Ellwood also BODENHAFER, *Amer. Jour. Sociol.*, vol. 26, pp. 443ff., 1921; BARNES, *Sociol. Rev.*, vol. 15, pp. 286–295, 1923; BOGARDUS, *Essentials of Social Psychology*, p. 26; *A History of Social Thought*, pp. 408–409; SOROKIN, *Contemporary Sociological Theories*, pp. 457, 642.

[2] See Chap. I, pp. 11, 13, Chap. II, especially p. 22 (1st ed., 1918), Chap. I, pp. 10, 13, 18, Chap. II, especially p. 32 (2d ed., 1920).

[3] This work is essentially an attempt to harmonize the previous treatments of Ross, McDougall, and Ellwood.

[4] It is difficult to see why one of these works should be entitled "sociology" and the other "social psychology." Such is the present-day state of psychological, sociological, and social-psychological development, however, that there is at the present time a very decided overlapping of these fields upon each other. The discussion of Ellwood and Bogardus on the one hand and Allport on the other will serve to bring this strikingly into view. There are, of course, also any number of other equally telling illustrations of this point.

[5] See, for example, *The New Social Research*, especially Chap. X; also the reports of research on social distance, *Jour. Appl. Sociol.*, Vol. 9, 1925 and subsequent vols.

[6] See *supra*, especially p. 379; also *The New Social Research*, Preface, Introduction.

not only because he sought to incorporate it methodologically as well as interpretively but also because it is associated in his work with a bipolar conception of social psychology which bears directly on the reinterpretation of individual as well as group behavior and of the psychological as well as the sociological foundations of his thought.[1] The following brief passages will bring these comments more clearly into view and serve to indicate how Bogardus' broadening social-psychological perspective is reflected in his conception of the subject.

Already in the first edition of his *Essentials*, Bogardus said in commenting on the different conceptions of social psychology current at the time:

> To some writers, social psychology ccnsists chiefly of a study of the social nature and the social activities of the individual; to other authors, the subject consists largely of an analysis of the psychic interactions of the members of groups. The first emphasis is essentially subjective, genetic, psychological; the second is chiefly objective and sociological.

Contrasting his own view with both of the above, he stated:

> But the new science of social psychology must develop its own methodology and speak from its own vantage ground. Its sector of the field of the social sciences is that important territory where the activities of psychology and sociology overlap. Instead of allowing its advance to be directed from either psychological or sociological headquarters, it must develop its own methods and programs, but remain subject, of course, to the rules of scientific and of social procedure. It is true that according to another view, social psychology has no distinct field and must be either psychology, or sociology; but the probabilities are that time will prove this conception to have been a mistaken one.[2]

With this conception of the subject in view, he outlined the plan of his work at the time as follows:

> It is the plan of this book . . . to begin the discussion with the psychological bases of social psychology, to analyze the social characteristics of the individual, to consider the social operation of these characteristics, to study the group, the types of groups, and the nature of group conflicts, to investigate the psychology of leadership, as well as the psychology of social control, and to close with an analysis of world progress. The method is inductive, evolutionary, cumulative; it moves from the particular to the general, from the individual to the group, and from the group to mankind, and it culminates in the subject of social progress.[3]

[1] Conceiving of social psychology as psychological sociology, Ellwood could naturally not regard the study of the social aspects of individual behavior as a part of social psychology, as did Bogardus, who aimed from the first to integrate the psychological and the sociological approaches to the subject in a single inclusive view of the subject-matter of social psychology (see on this point, ELLWOOD, *The Psychology of Human Society*, p. 17).

[2] *Essentials of Social Psychology*, 1st ed., pp. 10–11. Quotations from this work are reprinted by permission of the University of Southern California Press, publishers.

[3] *Ibid.*, p. 11.

In his further comment on this plan of procedure, Bogardus suggested that "social psychology as at present considered is based upon the facts and principles of general psychology." "It is necessary, first of all," he explained, "to consider the characteristics of the human mind in action," which involves "an understanding of the nature and types of the instinctive, of the habitual, and of the conscious reactions of the human mind."[1]

Social psychology being thus, according to Bogardus, "based on a knowledge of psychological principles," he proceeded, like Ellwood, to stress the special importance of functional psychology as a starting point for social psychology. "Functional psychology," he stated, "furnishes the principles for interpreting the social nature of individuals and for understanding the interactions in group life."[2]

Consistently with the above views, Bogardus gave the following definition of social psychology at this time:

> Social psychology is the scientific study of the social nature and reactions of the mind, of the interactions of individuals within groups, of group conflicts, of group leadership and control, and of the nature of group and societary progress. Social psychology approaches the problems of life from the psychological viewpoint; it draws conclusions and offers programs with reference to societary ends. Social psychology studies the social phases of personality, the interactions of personalities within groups, and the nature of group control and progress.[3]

The nature of the subject matter with which Bogardus sought to concern himself in his original treatment of social psychology, as well as his organizing viewpoint and conception, are indicated clearly enough in these statements. It is evident that despite formal differences, in the actual working out of his conception, Bogardus was in the first place on much the same ground as Ellwood, his treatment as outlined being obviously in large part modeled upon Ellwood's early social-psychological views. His two-sided conception of social psychology, with its increasing emphasis upon the study of personality and the processes of social interstimulation, led out, however, to a different expansion of his viewpoint from that of Ellwood.

On the basis of the above citations, the modifications of outlook and emphasis which Bogardus introduced into his later work will readily

---

[1] *Ibid.*, p. 13.

[2] *Ibid.*, p. 22. The essential similarity of Bogardus' and Ellwood's original views respecting the dependence of social upon individual psychology is clearly brought out here.

[3] *Ibid.*, p. 14. This is one of the most inclusive definitions of social psychology which we have. It was obviously Bogardus' aim to make his definition broad enough to cover completely the more important conceptions of the subject current in the field at the time.

appear.   The following passages from the second edition of his *Essentials* will give his point of view in transition:

Social psychology is the study of the interactions of personalities in groups . . . Upon the conclusions of functional psychology, the social psychologist builds. The first independent step is to analyze and to understand the traits of human personalities.   In the vocabulary of social psychology, personality is the first outstanding term.[1]

Social psychology approaches the problem of life from its own viewpoint which is psychological in origin and sociological in outlook.   It begins with the socio-functional conclusions of psychology and ends in the presentation of societary principles, which underlie all sound reasoning in sociology.   Social psychology is the scientific study of the social nature and reactions of the human mind, of the interactions of minds, of group conflicts and change, and of social control and progress.   The quintessence of social psychology is found in personalities interacting within groups.[2]

To the writer, social psychology begins with the psychological analyses of human personality.   It centers attention upon the social traits of personality as they express themselves under group stimuli, and upon the resultant group activities.   It concludes its work by evaluating the method of group, or social, control in terms of socialized personalities.   In brief, the interactions of personalities in groups is the interesting and attractive field which the student of social psychology is invited to explore.[3]

From this intermediate position, Bogardus passed on to the following restatement of his conception of the subject in his *Fundamentals of Social Psychology*, where he definitely aligns himself with the Thomas "attitudes-values" view and with the emphasis upon the process of social interaction as a determining consideration in social psychology, which is implied in this and the related views of Mead, Dewey, etc.   He tells us here:

Social psychology is more than an application of the psychology of the individual to collective behavior.   It is more than an imitation theory, an instinct theory, a herd instinct theory, or a conflict theory of social life.   It is developing its own approach, concepts, and laws.   It treats of the processes of intersocial stimulation and their products in the form of social attitudes and values.   It obtains its data by analyzing personal experiences.[4]

The quintessence of social psychology [he tells us again here] is found in the study of intersocial stimulation and response and of the resultant social attitudes, values, and personalities.[5]

In explanation of this reorientation of his thought, Bogardus says:

---

[1] *Ibid.*, 2d ed., p. 13.

[2] *Ibid.*, p. 18.

[3] *Ibid.*, p. 27.

[4] *Fundamentals of Social Psychology*, Preface.   Quotations from this work are reprinted by permission of The Century Company, publishers.

[5] *Ibid.*, Introduction, p. xi.

Human beings begin life as simple organic units and develop into personalities with complex spiritual qualities. From a helpless beginning they grow into spiritual dynamos, capable of mastery of themselves and of their social environment. The process is largely one of *intersocial stimulation* and *response*, and the product is human personalities with their attitudes and values of life. According to this analysis social psychology studies intersocial stimulation and response, social attitudes, values, and personalities. It begins with individual human beings and original human nature and traces their growth through intersocial stimulation into persons with socialized attitudes.[1]

Bogardus accordingly adjusts his treatment of the subject in his *Fundamentals* to a central emphasis upon the consideration of the chief forms and processes of social interstimulation. A large part of his work is directly concerned with this subject, and the other parts are definitely reflected from the standpoint of this central part of his discussion, in the course of which he brings under review the following interaction processes: isolation, stimulation, communication, suggestion, imitation, fashion imitation, custom diffusion, convention diffusion, discrimination, discussion, accommodation, assimilation, socialization.[2]

This procedure necessarily implies a somewhat different view of the relation between the several parts of his previous treatment, and this is brought out suggestively in the following two passages which indicate how his new approach incorporates the respective standpoints represented by his previous bipolar conception of social psychology. Bogardus says in connection with his discussion of human nature:

Human interstimulation plays continually upon original human nature, modifying it beyond recognition and organizing it into social patterns or institutions. It is the *modification* of original human nature by social stimulation that transforms it into the personality traits that we know.[3]

Again he says in connection with his discussion of social groups:

Group life is the medium in which all intersocial stimulation occurs. Human nature, personal attitudes, and social values emerge only out of group life. Groups provide all social contacts and stimuli. Once formed the group is prior to the individual. Into groups all individuals are born; up through them personality emerges; and in turn persons dominate and create groups . . . Group environment is the matrix of all intersocial stimulation.[4]

[1] *Ibid.*, p. 3.

[2] See *ibid.*, Chaps. VIII–XX. This is undoubtedly the most notable part of Bogardus' treatment. It suggests immediately the intimate connection between his work and Park and Burgess, *Introduction to the Science of Sociology*, and through the latter it recalls also the approach to the study of social life which was outlined here especially in connection with our treatment of Simmel.

[3] *Ibid.*, p. 8.

[4] *Ibid.*, p. 241.

With this conception of the relation between organic human nature, social interstimulation, and group life as a basis, Bogardus presents a treatment of human nature and social life in his *Fundamentals*[1] which is clearly in line with the positions traced out by such writers as Cooley, Mead, Dewey, Thomas, Faris, and other representatives of the social-psychological viewpoint which has been followed out here in some detail, particularly in the preceding section. It is this viewpoint which he has projected into his discussion of research technique in his *New Social Research* and which supposedly gives point to his characterization of this discussion as "new." For it is new, if at all, in standpoint of interpretation and not in technical detail.

On the basis of the preliminary approaches to the systematic treatment of social psychology by Ross and McDougall and the later attempts in this direction by Ellwood and Bogardus[2] there has recently been, in conjunction with the intensification of interest in social psychology since the World War,[3] such a pronounced increase in the output of this type of social-psychological literature in this country as to make the further individualized consideration of these works a task entirely beyond the limits of this closing section of our survey. Furthermore, the significance and characteristic features of these works can best be brought out in terms of another mode of approach than the one which has been found to serve our purposes best so far.[4] Accordingly we shall consider this group of works only illustratively here, postponing for another occasion their more detailed treatment and analysis,[5] and confine ourselves to the further consideration only of such of the group as are especially important in filling out the picture of American social-psychological thought as so far presented.

[1] See *ibid.*, especially Chaps. I, IX, XXI.

[2] Ross, *Social Psychology* (1908); McDougall, *Introduction to Social Psychology* (1908); Ellwood, *Introduction to Social Psychology* (1917); Bogardus, *Essentials of Social Psychology* (1918).

Another attempt in this direction which should be mentioned here along with the above, inasmuch as it played a considerable role in this country during the period immediately following upon Ross' work, was the outline organization of the subject made by G. E. Howard in his elaborate analytical reference syllabus, *Social Psychology*, 1910 (see Vincent, "George Elliott Howard Social Psychologist," *Sociol. and Soc. Res.*, vol. 13, pp. 108–118, 1928–1929).

It is notable that of the five works mentioned above, all but McDougall's are developed from the sociological standpoint.

[3] Here, as everywhere, there has been a decided intensification of interest in social and psychological science since the war, and social psychology, like many related fields of investigation, has reflected this new interest.

[4] See *infra*, p. 413.

[5] The writer expects to treat these works, as well as other current developments in the field, in greater detail in a supplementary monograph on *Current Developments in American Social Psychology*.

Among the increasing number of these works which might be chosen
for such illustrative consideration,[1] Allport's *Social Psychology* (1924)
and Bernard's *Introduction to Social Psychology* (1926) seem to have a
special claim, not only because they have been conspicuously in the foreground of recent social-psychological discussion in this country but also
because they present a complementary treatment of the subject from a
somewhat similar starting point, so that together they bring into view a
fairly well-rounded picture of the situation as it is at present taking shape.
We shall therefore close this part of our discussion with a brief consideration of these two works, viewed as representative of the larger group of
works to which reference has been made here, and a few general comments on several others of the group which have a special significance in
respect to this closing part of our discussion.

III. Other Recent Attempts at Systematic Treatment

1. Floyd H. Allport (1890)

Allport may be said to be the first American social psychologist radically to challenge the widely accepted view that if social psychology is
to be linked to one of the better established fields of investigation at all,
it more naturally tends to associate itself with sociology than with
psychology.[2] Heretofore, while American psychologists had been concerning themselves with the subject matter of social psychology all along
they did so for the most part either incidentally only to their more traditional psychological interests, as in the case of James, or through a
recognized extension of these interests into an important field of interpretation, as in the case of Baldwin.[3] Allport, however, definitely

---

[1] The following partial list of these works, in addition to those already previously
mentioned in this part of our survey is suggestive in indicating the recent expansion of
this type of social-psychological literature: WILLIAMS, *Principles of Social Psychology*
(1922); GAULT, *Social Psychology* (1923): ALLPORT, *Social Psychology* (1924); DUNLAP,
Social Psychology (1925); ZNANIECKI, *The Laws of Social Psychology* (1925); BERNARD,
Introduction to Social Psychology (1926); YOUNG, *Source Book for Social Psychology*
(1929); *Social Psychology* (1930); SPROWLS, *Social Psychology Interpreted* (1927);
MURCHISON, *Social Psychology* (1929); KANTOR, *An Outline of Social Psychology*
(1929); KRUEGER, and RECKLESS, *Social Psychology* (1931); FOLSAM, *Social Psychology* (1931); MURPHY and MURPHY, *Experimental Social Psychology* (1931).

[2] See in this connection, for example, *Proc. Intern. Congress Arts Sci.*, vol. 5, p. 859,
1904; also WOODWORTH, *Contemporary Schools of Psychology*, p. 192.

[3] The very title of Baldwin's *Social and Ethical Interpretations* is notable in this
connection.

The seeming exceptions to this statement, such as the social-psychological positions of Mead and Dewey, are really not exceptions in that they are frankly philosophical formulations which fit more readily into the spirit of the sociological than
that of the strictly psychological approach to the subject. In any event, their views
were in the first place taken up and developed by social psychologists who approached
the subject from the sociological standpoint, and it was in the first instance largely

approached the subject from the standpoint that it is not only "a part of the psychology of the individual"[1] but also that it is logically not conceivable in any other terms. This point of view he formulated in opposition to what he has termed "the group fallacy" in social psychology, so that his statement of his position has brought him into clear conflict with the "group" and "culture" approaches and the sociological conception of the subject associated with them, as we shall see. It is on this account, in conjunction with its consequences on the side of method, that his social-psychological theory has been prominently before American social-psychological thought in recent years and that it is of special importance here.

Allport says in introducing his particular treatment of social psychology:

Only within recent years have the psychologists of this country turned their attention seriously toward the social field. With one or two exceptions, the earlier works upon this subject, as well as a number of recent ones, have been written by sociologists. To these writers psychologists owe a debt of gratitude for revealing new and promising opportunities for applying psychological science. Sociological writers, however, have given their attention mainly to the larger aspects, the laws of behavior and consciousness as operative in social groups. In so doing they have naturally adopted as materials the concepts of human nature provided by the older psychologists of good standing. With the recent expansion of psychology and growth of psychological insight, it has become necessary to modify many of these earlier conceptions and to add not a few new ones. Social science has not yet profited by taking account of this advancement, but has lagged behind in its fundamental assumptions regarding human na-

---

through the writings of the latter that their views began to gain widespread social-psychological currency.

However, Allport was doubtless very greatly influenced by the conceptions of social psychology set forth by Mead and Dewey as well as by such a writer as W. I. Thomas, whose outlook on the subject Dewey quoted. Especially suggestive in this connection is it to recall the view set forth by Dewey in 1916 when he delivered his address on "The Need of a Social Psychology" before the psychologists of the country. It was at this time that Dewey developed the notion that all psychological phenomena are either physiological or social "and that when we have relegated elementary sensation and appetite to the former head, all that is left of our mental life, our beliefs, ideas and desires, falls within the scope of social psychology." "I foresee," he said at the time, "a great reflex wave from social psychology [used in the objective sociological sense] back to general psychology" (see *Psychol. Rev.*, vol. 24, pp. 266, 271, 1917; also *supra*, p. 333).

[1] *Social Psychology*, p. 4. Allport's conception of social psychology as "a part of the psychology of the individual" may be set over against Ellwood's view that social psychology is just another name for psychological sociology (see Allport's comment on this point, *Social Psychology*, p. 11). In view of these rival conceptions, an increasing number of writers are approaching common ground in the position that social psychology is neither a part of psychology proper nor a part of sociology proper but a more or less well-defined intermediate field, whose chief significance follows from this fact and the resulting two-sided outlook which it can bring to bear upon the problems of human nature and social behavior.

ture. A need has therefore arisen of bringing to the service of those interested in social relationships the most recent psychological investigation and theory. I have written this book as an attempt in the direction of supplying this need.[1]

Commenting further on the relation between his approach to the subject and previous social-psychological thought as it has developed under the influence of sociology, he suggests that while social psychology has grown up largely through the labors of the sociologists, it is a mistake to suppose that it is a branch of sociology rather than of psychology. In this connection, he takes particular objection to Ellwood's designation of the field as "psychological sociology." "This seems to the present writer," he says, "to minimize unjustly the claims of the psychologist. It is surely a legitimate interest to consider social behavior and consciousness merely as a phase of the psychology of the individual, in relation to a certain portion of his environment, without being concerned about the formation or character of groups resulting from these reactions."[2] It is from this standpoint that he proceeds.

More specifically, Allport explains, there were two main lines of development which he aimed to bring within the scope of his treatment of social psychology—the *behavior viewpoint*[3] and the *experimental method*. Along with these, he mentions in the second place "the Freudian contributions to psychology" as deserving special recognition. With these as major lines of interest,[4] he calls attention to the innovations of organization and treatment in which his conception of the subject resulted. He says in this connection:

There are certain innovations in the treatment of the subject for which it may be well to prepare the reader. To one interested primarily in social relations

[1] *Ibid.*, Preface, p. v. Quotations from this work are reprinted by permission of Houghton Mifflin Company, publishers.

[2] *Ibid.*, p. 11.

[3] The behavior viewpoint, that is, as popularized in this country more particularly through Watson's work in the field of genetic psychology (see *ibid.*, note, p. 50). It is interesting to recall here that the current psychological treatises on social psychology in this country began to appear immediately following the appearance of Watson's *Psychology from the Standpoint of a Behaviorist* (1919). To what extent the challenging nature of Watson's work with infants and the decided social-psychological implications of his findings were responsible for this remains a question. But in the case of Allport, at least, the importance of Watson's work stands out clearly (see his basic treatment of "Fundamental Activities" in Chap. III which defines his "conditioned response" viewpoint.

[4] None of these more specific considerations nor all of them together actually serve to distinguish Allport's treatment, for these elements are part of many of the more recent treatments of the subject. What does set it off is his general standpoint of interpretation presently to be outlined. The above are nevertheless very notable features of his work. In fact, they mark an important turning point in the psychological development of the subject in this country. This is especially true in so far as his emphasis upon the experimental approach in social psychology is concerned (see *infra*, p. 404, 414; also editorial statement *Jour. Abnor. Psychol.*, vol. 16, pp. 3–7, 1921).

it may seem that I give an unusual amount of space to purely individual behavior. This is in accordance with my purpose . . . to adhere to the psychological (that is, the individual) viewpoint. For I believe that only *within the individual* can we find the behavior mechanisms and the consciousness which are fundamental in the interactions between individuals. I have, therefore, postponed until the last chapter almost all the material treated in books which have been written from the sociological viewpoint. If the reader finds that not until the final chapter has he arrived upon familiar ground, I shall venture to hope that his understanding may have been increased through treading the less familiar pathways.[1]

In conjunction with this conception of his task, as already noted above, Allport leads into a criticism of the "group fallacy" in social psychology, which defines his position in especially challenging terms. He says:

Impressed by the closely knit and reciprocal nature of social behavior, some writers have been led to postulate a kind of "collective mind" or "group consciousness" as separate from the minds of the individuals of whom the group is composed. No fallacy is more subtle and misleading than this. It has appeared in the literature under numerous guises; but has everywhere left the reader in a state of mystical confusion.[2]

Seeking to define his own essential position in contrast to the above view, he continues:

The standpoint of this book may be concisely stated as follows. There is no psychology of groups which is not essentially and entirely a psychology of individuals. Social psychology must not be placed in contradistinction to the psychology of the individual; *it is a part of the psychology of the individual*, whose behavior it studies in relation to that section of his environment comprised by his fellows. His biological needs are the ends toward which his social behavior is a developed means. Within his organism are provided all the mechanisms by which social behavior is explained. There is likewise no consciousness except that belonging to individuals. Psychology in all its branches is a science of the individual. To extend its principles to larger units is to destroy their meaning.[3]

After taking up the "group fallacy" for more detailed consideration under the special headings of the "crowd mind," the "collective or class mind," and the "group mind," he finally arrives at the following conclusion:

All theories which partake of the group fallacy have the unfortunate consequence of diverting attention from the true locus of cause and effect, namely, the behavior mechanism of the individual. They place the group prior to this mecha-

---

[1] *Social Psychology*, Preface, p. vi.

[2] *Ibid.*, p. 4.

[3] *Ibid.*, p. 4. The physiological orientation which Allport characteristically gives his social-psychological theory and which provides the basis for his criticism of the group viewpoint appears clearly in this passage.

nism in order of study, and substitute description of social effects in place of true explanation.   On the other hand, if we take care of the individuals, psychologically speaking, the groups will be found to take care of themselves.   The reasons for our repeated insistence upon regarding social psychology as a phase of the psychology of the individual should now be fairly evident.[1]

In the light of these views, he proposes the following working definition of social psychology:

> *Social psychology is the science which studies the behavior of the individual in so far as his behavior stimulates other individuals, or is itself a reaction to their behavior; and which describes the consciousness of the individual in so far as it is a consciousness of social objects and social reactions.*   More briefly stated, social psychology is the study of the social behavior and the social consciousness of the individual.[2]

Consistently with this conception of the subject, Allport directed his attention almost entirely to the consideration of individual behavior, first from a purely physiological standpoint and then under various conditions of social stimulation and group influence.   Starting out with a preliminary discussion of the physiological basis of behavior, he proceeds to develop the psychology of "The Individual in His Social Aspects" through a consideration of the usual topics: instinct, habit, learning, emotion, thought, etc.   And having thus prepared his basis of interpretation, he passes on to the consideration of "Social Behavior" in terms of the standpoint established—in terms, that is, of the physiological mechanisms of individual behavior described, his concern in this connection being such subject matter as social behavior in animals, social stimulation through language and other forms of communication, types and conditions of social response, etc.   Only in the closing chapter dealing with "Social Behavior in Relation to Society," as noted above, does he arrive at what he himself describes as the "familiar ground" of social-psychological discussion, in the consideration of social behavior viewed from the standpoint of social unity, social order, social continuity and social change.

This conception of his task naturally enabled Allport to bring experimental evidence from the field of individual psychology within the scope of his discussion to a greater extent than in most social-psychological treatises.   In addition, he has himself done some very notable work in attempting to apply the experimental, testing, and rating techniques

---

[1] *Ibid.*, p. 9; see in this connection also "The Group Fallacy in Relation to Social Science," *Jour. Abnor. Soc. Psychol.*, vol. 19, pp. 60–73, 1925; "The Group Fallacy in Relation to Culture," *ibid.*, pp. 185–191; "The Nature of Institutions," *Social Forces*, vol. 6, pp. 167–179, 1927; " 'Group' and 'Institution' as Concepts in a Natural Science of Social Phenomena," *Pub. Amer. Sociol. Soc.*, vol. 22, pp. 83–99, 1928; "Social Change: An Analysis of Professor Ogburn's Cultural Theory," *Jour. Social Forces*, vol. 2, pp. 671–676, 1924.

[2] *Social Psychology*, p. 12.

to the investigation of special problems of social-psychological interest, and the report of these studies has the effect of emphasizing this phase of his discussion especially.[1]   Recognition of this aspect of his work as a contribution which is at present having widely significant results for the extension of social-psychological methodology and the advance of concrete social-psychological investigation[2] cannot, however, obscure the fact that for the most part, and especially in so far as his organizing viewpoint is concerned, his treatment is merely analytical and reinterpretive on the same basis as most other current reformulations of social-psychological theory.   For example, he did not for the most part disregard the content material usually included in social-psychological treatises written from the sociological standpoint, but he sought to reinterpret it in his own terms. Likewise, he did not, except as indicated above, introduce new material in his treatment of the psychology of the individual, but he sought to bring to the service of his outlook and standpoint the usual discussions of instinct, emotion, habit, thought, etc.

Altogether, his approach is more like McDougall's in the latter's *Introduction to Social Psychology* than that of any other writer so far considered, except that, centering his discussion about the conditioned reflex notion[3] instead of the instinct notion as used by McDougall, he was able to bring the social factor into play in his treatment more directly as well as more tellingly.   This departure being, in fact, at the very basis of Allport's distinctive social-psychological position, it is necessary to consider it here a little further from the standpoint of its bearing on his outlook and procedure.

It was Allport's aim in this connection, as he tells us, "to combine the virtues and omit the defects of both sides of the controversy" regarding the place of instinct in human behavior—the side which tends to hold to this notion too tenaciously and the side which would reject it as a valid basis of explanation in human psychology altogether.[4]   This he sought to accomplish by introducing the "reflex" concept into his discussion as at once more definite and more specific than the traditional instinct concept and by replacing orthodox instinct theory with a modified form of conditioned reflex theory developed in terms of so-called "prepotent reflexes."   Recognizing six important classes of human prepotent reflexes —starting and withdrawing, rejecting, struggling, hunger reactions, sensitive-zone reactions, sex reactions[5]—he says in regard to them:

[1] *Ibid.*, Chaps. VI, IX, XI.

[2] See in this connection MURPHY and MURPHY, *Experimental Social Psychology*, especially Chap. I.

[3] This was in line with Allport's expressed interest in the behavior viewpoint, more especially as represented by Watson's *Psychology from the Standpoint of a Behaviorist* (see *supra*, p. 402; also *Psychologies of 1925*, ed. by Murchison, Part I).

[4] *Social Psychology*, pp. vi–vii.

[5] *Ibid.*, Chap. III, pp. 50*ff.*

The human being has inherited a number of prepotent reflexes which are fundamental not only in their potency, but in the control which they exert over habit formation throughout life. Ultimately, as well as genetically, they are prepotent.[1]

It is clear even from this single passage that, while Allport is more cautious in his identification of inherited behavior patterns, he proposes to use the classification which he arrives at in much the same spirit as instinct psychology has used its classifications.[2] There is, however, always this difference between his treatment and conventional instinct psychology, namely, that the conditioned reflex theory as used by him and such other behaviorist interpreters of human behavior as Watson[3] is much more adaptable to the increasing emphasis upon the importance of the social environment, which is clearly characteristic of modern social-psychological thought. Instead of the instinct-emotion level of interpretation, at any rate, Allport's treatment tends to lead out toward a habit-attitude level, so that, despite important differences of basic orientation, his theory seems at times to approach more closely the social-psychological formulations of such writers as Dewey and Thomas than those of conventional instinct psychology.[4]

The general principle which underlies this part of Allport's discussion is schematically stated by him as follows:

The prepotent reflexes are subject to modification by synaptic changes in their central portions. The effects of such changes are (1) to extend the range and complexity of the stimuli capable of exciting the response, and (2) to refine and specialize the response itself. The first effect, which may be called an afferent modification, is brought about by the principle of the conditioned response; the second, resulting in an efferent modification, is due to the selection and fixation of successful random movements in the processes of habit formation and thought.[5]

Summarizing his more concrete interpretation of this principle as it applies to the social modification of behavior, he notes especially the following major lines of development:

Social objects such as persons, attitudes, expressions, and language serve as the stimuli to which various prepotent activities may be transferred. Approval and disapproval become the conditions of response. Through contact with others an enormous part of the learning takes place by which the original reflexes are converted into useful habits. The child and youth being docile and responsive to language, many prepotent stimuli need be represented only indirectly;

[1] *Ibid.*, p. 50.

[2] For an elaboration of this point and a thoroughgoing criticism of Allport's position on this account, see FARIS, *Amer. Jour. Sociol.*, vol. 30, pp. 719–722, 1925.

[3] See his *Psychology from the Standpoint of a Behaviorist*, Chaps. VI–IX; also *Psychologies of 1925*, ed. by Murchison, Part I. A well-known intermediate position is developed in Thorndike's *Original Nature of Man* (1913).

[4] See especially *Social Psychology*, Chap. XIII.

[5] *Ibid.*, p. 56.

that is, through admonition and instruction.   Hence many of the cruder errors of the learning process are eliminated in advance.   The more drastic experiences in satisfying the need for protection, and for food and sexual adjustment, are worked out in the history of the race.   The individual begins the modification of his prepotent reflexes where unnumbered generations of his forbears have left off.   Thought itself, in its inseparable connection with language, traditional knowledge and custom, is largely a part of the general social influence.   By the direction through society of the learning process the efferent side of the prepotent reflex arcs are modified from purely individualistic to highly socialized responses.   And finally, the common sanction may so far control the habits formed upon the inborn activities as to substitute for the original biological end a somewhat modified purpose of social origin.[1]

In these general terms, Allport develops his treatment of social behavior as outlined above, his emphasis throughout as previously stated, except for the closing chapter, falling naturally upon the physiological behavior mechanisms of the individual as over against the conditioning situations and developments of the social environment.   More flexible though his treatment is in so far as social considerations are concerned, as compared with the conventional instinct approach, it thus leaves the subject with little advance upon such a standard treatment as McDougall's *Introduction to Social Psychology* as regards the study of these conditioning situations and developments of the social environment.   And unlike McDougall, who considered his work merely as an *introduction* to social psychology proper, which subject in itself he proposed to survey in two supplementary volumes—the first of which was his *Group Mind*—Allport, as we have seen, set forth a view of social psychology corresponding to his one-sided physiological approach, and this view he has defended aggressively against all competing views.[2]

More so even than in the case of McDougall, it is accordingly necessary to supplement his conception of the subject with such conceptions as stress the opposite, that is the socio-cultural approach.   It is for this reason that it seems well to consider briefly, alongside of his *Social Psychology*, such a treatment as that of Bernard's *Introduction to Social Psychology*, which leads out from a somewhat similar starting point to a broadly synthetic but predominantly environmental conception of social psychology.

2. L. L. Bernard (1884)

In view of what has already been said regarding Allport's and Bernard's common starting point, the foregoing consideration of Allport's social-psychological approach can in a measure serve also as an introduction to the consideration of Bernard's organizing viewpoint.   For Ber-

[1] *Ibid.*, pp. 81–82.
[2] See *supra*, pp. 400, and 403.

nard's conception of social psychology is different from Allport's, not so much because it is different in its psychological position, as because it is supplementary on the social side. This, as we shall see, appears not only from Bernard's direct references to Allport's social-psychological theory but also from his description of his own particular outlook and approach.

It is notable in this connection that Bernard came to the more general treatment of social psychology through his important special study of instinct (*Instinct: A Study in Social Psychology*, 1924) and that it is in the consideration of this special subject that he defines, as did Allport, his basic approach to social psychology. Referring specifically to Allport's *Social Psychology* in respect to this subject, Bernard says: "It is not necessary to call attention in detail to the striking similarity of viewpoint regarding instinct and emotion in his book and mine."[1]

In particular, it is because of his basic physiological attack of the problem of instinct and because of his leaning toward the conditioned response theory as an improvement upon the instinct theory in social psychology[2] that Bernard meets Allport on common ground in this way. Bernard has, however, taken much sharper issue with the instinct approach to social psychology than Allport (Bernard has been conspicuous in the recent attack upon the instinct theory of human behavior, especially as represented by McDougall's *Introduction to Social Psychology*), and coming to the subject chiefly from the sociological rather than the psychological standpoint, he has naturally sought to lead out beyond Allport's individualistic considerations to an analysis of the social side of the behavior process. In the practical working out of his approach, this has meant also, as might be expected, that he has emphasized a more decided social attack in the treatment of personality integration than Allport, though, setting forth a synthetic conception of social psychology, he did not follow this emphasis out to the extreme of an essentially one-sided treatment of the subject, as did Allport.

He did, however, maintain on the basis of his study of instinct and his consideration of the nature of man's hereditary equipment for social life on the one hand and of the dynamic character of his social environment on the other, that it is not instinct but habit, in the broad sense in which Dewey has popularized this term, which provides the chief key to an understanding of human conduct and social life.[3] And habit, as it enters into human conduct, being always bipolar in its reference to both the social environment and the factor of biological heredity, this position in respect to the subject of instinct carries over directly into the synthetic

---

[1] *Instinct*, p. vii. Quotations from this work are reprinted by permission of Henry Holt & Company, publishers.

[2] See *An Introduction to Social Psychology*, pp. 29–30, 117–122.

[3] See *Instinct*, Chap. I; *An Introduction to Social Psychology*, pp. 36–37, 122.

approach which he outlines in his *Introduction to Social Psychology,* his own major emphasis, for reasons which he develops in detail,[1] falling naturally upon the study of the psycho-social environment.

Stating this position from the standpoint of his detailed study of instinct, Bernard says:

The real task before the social and educational psychologists with respect to instincts is to discover the mechanisms by means of which the child and the citizen build up their habits upon the basis of the instincts, directly or indirectly, and by means of which one habit or set of habits is transformed into another. Hitherto they have approached this problem from essentially the wrong angle, that of the analysis of instinct, on the assumption that instinct dominates the development of habit. Both the approach and the assumption are erroneous. The sociologist is demonstrating that the environment increasingly dominates both the content and the direction or functioning of habit formation. It is, therefore, from the standpoint of the content and the organization of the psycho-social environment that the control of the growth of human character should be approached, the instincts being regarded primarily as the original—not necessarily the immediate or the only—starting points in the process.[2]

By way of suggesting more concretely the basis for this position and for the viewpoint which he develops further in his *Introduction to Social Psychology,* Bernard outlines the following rather striking analogy:

Modern civilization is like a city of . . . skyscrapers. Organized into blocks and sections of this city, facing along certain streets which we may liken to the avenues of custom and tradition, of public opinion and convention, and the like, they collectively constitute the tremendous social environment divided functionally, if not geographically, into institutions. As each new individual comes into the world he has much the same foundation as others have of native soil upon which to build, varied to be sure here and there by excavations, marsh land, hill, or stone; but whether this individual grows into a towering skyscraper, a dingy tenement house . . . or is arrested in his development as a shanty in the slums, depends not so much upon the character of the soil, as defined above, upon which the superstructure is reared, as upon the environment in which it grows.[3]

While this description, he points out, is in the nature of an analogy rather than of an analysis of the concrete activity processes connected with the development of character, "I believe," he says, "the description is essentially true to the facts."

The instincts are very early overlaid by acquired habits in the process of adapting the individual to his environment, and these habits are in turn overlaid by other tiers or stories of habit in which the native character of instinct ever constantly diminishes in proportion and intensity, until the child who has reached a rational age is reacting in nine-tenths or ninety-nine one-hundredths of his

---

[1] *Ibid.,* Chap. IV.
[2] *Instinct,* pp. 533–534.
[3] *Ibid.,* pp. 523–524.

character directly to environment, and only in the slight residual fraction of his nature directly to instinct.   The influence of environment is cumulative in our lives and the decline of the influence of instinct is progressive.[1]

It is clear, therefore, why Bernard presents a synthetic view of social psychology and why, in developing this view, he places a predominant emphasis on the study of the psycho-social environment.   In describing his treatment of the subject in his *Introduction to Social Psychology*, he says:

The present *Introduction to Social Psychology* represents an attempt at a more synthetic type of treatment of the field than has ordinarily been given . . . The text-books which have so far appeared, although for the most part excellent from their several viewpoints, are nevertheless but partial treatments. So notably true is this that there exists a marked controversy as to what properly constitutes social psychology.[2]

Bernard explains further that his *Introduction to Social Psychology* deals with the subject "from the standpoint of the more objective factors which integrate the personality and its responses in a social environment" and is only the first half of his synthetic treatment as planned, "the more extended treatment of the subjective aspects of personality development" having been reserved by him for a second volume.   The full significance of his conception of the subject does not, therefore, as yet appear, though the synthetic character of the part presented is sufficiently suggestive of the effect.

By way of general orientation and introduction to his view of social psychology as it enters into his treatment of the subject, Bernard takes up the question as to what properly constitutes social psychology for consideration, and he views this question first from the standpoint of the general field of science and then from the standpoint of the specific conceptions which are current in the field of social psychology.   After examining a number of these conceptions, he formulates his own definition of the subject in the following terms:

Social psychology studies the behavior of individuals in a psycho-social situation.   This behavior is valid subject matter for social psychology whether it conditions or is conditioned by other social behavior or responses.   It is also concerned with all collective responses, that is, responses of individuals which mutually and reciprocally condition each other and those which are uniform throughout the group, regardless of what environment they arise from.   Of course the chief source of stimuli of which social psychology takes cognizance is the psycho-social environment, and the chief type of behavior in which it is interested is collective behavior.[3]

---

[1] *Ibid.*, p. 524; see also *An Introduction to Social Psychology*, pp. 38, 46.

[2] *Ibid.*, p v.   Quotations from this work are reprinted by permission of Henry Holt & Company, publishers.

[3] *Ibid.*, p. 18.

He also says in another connection:

Social psychology is interested directly and primarily in human behavior in a social situation. It may concern itself with the inner mechanisms of responses to social stimuli, or it may focus its attention upon collective response to similar or identical or to mutual or supplementary stimuli. In the one case it leans toward psychology and in the other it rests upon sociology. Both interests are legitimate to the field of social psychology and in both cases its theme is human behavior.[1]

Commenting on the inclusiveness of this view and the possible criticisms that might be offered of it on the ground that social psychology as thus conceived extends over a large part of the related fields of both psychology and sociology, he says:

Our viewpoint is that social psychology is an outgrowth of both psychology and sociology and overlaps both fields.[2]

Nevertheless the problem of social psychology is as distinct as that of any other social science, according to him. He explains:

It is to find out how men behave in groups, or, in other words, to study the reactions of individuals to the psycho-social environment and the consequent building up of collective adjustment behavior patterns in the individuals in response to social stimuli. In order to answer these questions it is necessary, on the one hand, for the science of social psychology to have an analysis of the psycho-social environment in terms of the processes operating to provide stimuli to the responding individual, and, on the other hand, to understand the organization of behavior patterns in the individual himself. With these two backgrounds it is possible to give an account of the further integration of behavior patterns of individuals responding individually or collectively to psycho-social stimuli.[3]

At another point, he says again in respect to the problem of social psychology:

The very fact that it is a psychological as well as a social science indicates that its task is the study of the responses of the individual to his social environment. Its task is exactly this of connecting the environment (stimulus-giving objects) with the organism (response mechanisms) . . . This involves both an organized presentation of stimulus controls (environment organization) and of response mechanisms (the organization of the personality). The neglect of the former aspect leaves us psychology; of the latter, sociology. In either case of neglect we have no social psychology.[4]

With this general view of social psychology as a background, Bernard follows out his treatment of the subject in its more objective aspects,

[1] *Ibid.*, p. 107.
[2] *Ibid.*, p. 585.
[3] *Ibid.*, p. 589.
[4] *Ibid.*, p. 45.

as noted above. The synthetic character of his treatment appears immediately from his introductory discussion of such topics as "The Organic Bases of Behavior," "The Environmental Bases of Behavior," "The Inherited and Acquired Equipment of Man" as well as from the organization of his work as a whole and especially his consideration of such subject matter as "Habit Mechanisms and the Adjustment Process," "The Functional Organization of Consciousness," "The Integration of Personality in the Social Environment," etc. Perhaps as suggestive a passage as any in characterizing his treatment of this subject matter is the following statement of its objective in behavioristic terms, since Bernard definitely identified himself as a behaviorist at this time.[1] He suggests:

Watson, in his behavioristic program, states that the ultimate purpose of the science of behavior is to make it possible to predict what will be the probable response when a given stimulus is applied. Such a program involves the ascertainment of two things: the nature of the response mechanisms (the organization of the organism), and the nature of the stimuli (the organization of the environment). Psychology has already gone far in the investigation of the former. The time is more than ripe for the sociologists or others to undertake the systematic study of the latter. Hence the emphasis in this volume upon the organization of the environment . . . [2]

With this emphasis upon the environmental aspect of behavior as a point of departure, Bernard combines what he has, as it would seem, rather unfortunately termed the "environmentalist"[3] type of social psychology of Cooley, Mead, Dewey, and Thomas with the physiological type of Allport. He thus arrived at a broadly inclusive view of the content material of social psychology not unlike that of Bogardus in his earlier formulation, though his approach, as indicated above, is basically orientated in the habit conception of Dewey and the conditioned response theory of Allport and others of the behavioristic school rather than in the "instinctivist" position of the McDougall school of thought.

Notable in particular here in conjunction with the above statement of objective and as indicative of the manner in which Bernard's treat-

[1] *Ibid.*, p. 42.

[2] *Ibid.*, p. 44.

[3] *Ibid.*, pp. 29–30. Surely most of the social psychologists whom he classifies as "environmentalists" would object to this label. For the point, as Cooley has so frequently stated, is not to emphasize "environment" as against "heredity" but to recognize that concrete human behavior is always a combination of both. To pit "environment" against "heredity" is no better than to pit "heredity" against "environment." Of course, Bernard did not actually mean to do this, as both his synthetic approach and his analysis of the "environmentalist" and the "instinctivist" positions show, but the suggestion of his terminology is definitely in this direction, and so are many specific passages dealing with the subject. See in this connection FARIS, review of Bernard's *Introduction to Social Psychology*, *Amer. Jour. Sociol.*, vol. 32, p. 484, 1926; also review of *Instinct*, *ibid.*, vol. 30, pp. 601–602, 1925.

ment of the subject supplements Allport's is his attempt to analyze and classify the "environments," especially the "social environments," including the very important subdivision of "psycho-social environments."[1] Defining the environment as "that set of objective factors which cooperate with the inheritance factors in the integration of behavior patterns through its determination of axes in the organism," Bernard recalls the view that "the social psychologist can . . . no more disregard the environment than he can ignore the heredity of the organism, if he expects to have an adequate understanding of the origins and controls of human behavior."[2] As a matter of fact, however, he points out, "environment has been largely neglected by social scientists generally and particularly by the social psychologists." He says:

In the textbooks of this science the concept scarcely appears with any degree of definiteness. Where the term is used it is employed with a vague and somewhat general reference which is not at all comparable with the concreteness and highly organized character of the treatment of the concept of inheritance; although this concept also is at times handled all too vaguely. There is great need for rendering the concept of environment definite and for analyzing it into its constituent parts, in order that the social psychologist may have a clear notion of the objective as well as of the subjective factors which integrate for individual organisms their patterns of behavior.[2]

It is in the detailed elaboration of this thesis through the consideration of material made familiar by modern sociology and cultural anthropology that Bernard carries his analysis beyond Allport's psychological considerations to a sociological treatment of the subject, similar in its essential import if not in its detailed discussion, to some of the other sociological conceptions of the subject which have been examined here. His attempt at analysis of the environmental factor in social behavior through his treatment of the concrete social environment represents a distinct contribution in the direction of the development of this aspect of social-psychological theory.

3. Kimball Young and Others

Lest it should appear, on the basis of the works so far considered in this section, that social psychology is at present more divided than ever, since there is at present a greater play of difference of viewpoint, interest,

---

[1] *An Introduction to Social Psychology*, Chap. VI, also pp. 21, 45, 65.

[2] *Ibid.*, pp. 69–70. A somewhat similar view of social psychology developed from the psychological standpoint has been outlined by Kantor in his *Outline of Social Psychology* (1929); see also "An Essay Toward an Institutional Conception of Social Psychology," *Amer. Jour. Sociol.*, vol. 27, pp. 611–627, 758–779, 1921–1922; "How Is a Science of Social Psychology Possible?" *Jour. Abn. Psychol. Soc. Psychol.*, vol. 17, pp. 62–78, 1922; "The Institutional Foundation of a Scientific Social Psychology," *Amer. Jour. Sociol.*, vol. 29, pp. 674–685, 1924.

and emphasis, it is necessary to recall at this point that at any rate the last two works considered were chosen for analysis precisely because they represented different conceptions of the subject. Most treatments would fall within the extremes set by these works, and a considerable number would range themselves along with one or the other. On the whole, the situation as regards attempts at systematic treatment in the field of social psychology is not altogether unlike the situation in the related fields of sociology, anthropology, and psychology. All of these fields are still in a very fluid state, and they are furthermore so intimately interlinked that it is impossible for any one of them to take definite form altogether apart from the others.

There are in this respect, however, unifying tendencies in the field of social psychology, just as in the other fields mentioned. In closing this part of our discussion, we may call attention, therefore, to two or three additional works which are especially conspicuous in reflecting these unifying tendencies, for example, Young's *Social Psychology* (1930), Murphy and Murphy's *Experimental Social Psychology* (1931), and Sprowls' *Social Psychology Interpreted* (1927), the first because of its all-round descriptive treatment of the subject, the second because of the emphasis which it places on the investigational aspects of the field, the third because of its frank recognition of existing theoretical differences in the field and of their historical importance in defining current issues and crucial problems awaiting further inquiry.

Recognizing the controversial state of many aspects of present-day social-psychological thought, Young resorts to a descriptive treatment of the subject which is inclusive of most of the important current positions in the field. As a result of this procedure, he loses something in consistency of presentation, social psychology being at present not altogether a consistent structure, but he gains much in representativeness. Altogether, he succeeds in giving a more comprehensive picture of the field in its many-sidedness and complexity than most treatments, his expansion of treatment being especially conspicuous through the inclusion of material from the fields of psychiatry, psychoanalysis, and mental hygiene. This broad approach to the subject provides a thought-provoking basis especially for further research and investigation in the field.

In this respect, his treatment is supplemented strikingly by Murphy and Murphy's survey of experimental social psychology, with its central interest in investigational methods and findings, especially those which are most easily describable and definable. In their attack upon the problem of social-psychological methodology, these authors give expression not only to the growing conviction that systematic research is crucial in social psychology at the present time but also to the concentration of interest, in this connection, upon research techniques and devices.

Crucial problems, especially those embedded in controversy, appear in their complex significance only when viewed in historical perspective. This is the importance of Sprowls' work, which seeks to develop the necessary theoretical background upon which to reflect current social-psychological problems. The viewpoint of this work and its significance from the standpoint of the tendencies in American social-psychological thought here under consideration are clearly formulated in the following statement: "The nature of social psychology is such that it cannot in its present stage of development be known without recourse to history."[1]

In these works, especially taken in conjunction with each other, we definitely see social psychology emerging as a systematic discipline, based on a developing foundation of fact. And this is, after all, the only secure basis of unification open to any field of scientific investigation.

In conjunction with this recent movement in American social psychology, as may well be expected, there has been an expansion of interest in the interpretive applications of social psychology to various fields of related endeavor which are concerned with social behavior. The most ambitious attempt in this direction has recently been projected by J. M. Williams in connection with a series of works which are to deal with special aspects of the subject.[2] Williams' approach is from the standpoint of the problems presented by the social sciences and hence is in the first place somewhat theoretical in orientation, but there are any number of other attempts in this direction which have a distinctively practical orientation, as in the case of recent attempts to work out applications in the fields of education, delinquency, mental hygiene, etc.[3] And applications, being always in some measure a reciprocal process, the effect of this expansion of interest in social-psychological application is further to emphasize the factual and research aspects of social psychology.

Altogether, therefore, despite baffling problems and challenging difficulties, there is at present much in the situation in this country that should be encouraging to anyone interested in the advance of social psychology as a field of scientific endeavor.

[1] SPROWLS, *Social Psychology Interpreted*, Preface, p. ix.

[2] Two general works in this series, *The Foundations of Social Science* (1920) and *Principles of Social Psychology* (1922), and two concrete studies, *Our Rural Heritage* (1925) and *The Expansion of Rural Life* (1926) have already appeared. Williams' approach in the latter studies is somewhat similar to that of W. I. Thomas and so has been commented upon in that connection (see *supra*, p. 383).

[3] The following list of works, for example, is suggestive: FOLLETT, *The New State* (1918); *Creative Experience* (1924); EDMAN, *Human Traits and Their Social Significance* (1920); RICHMOND, *What Is Social Case Work?* (1922); GROVES, *Personality and Social Adjustment* (1923); *Social Problems and Education* (1925); BLANCHARD, *The Child and Society: An Introduction to the Social Psychology of the Child* (1928); BOORMAN, *Developing Personality in Boys: The Social Psychology of Adolescence* (1929); PETERS, *Foundations of Educational Sociology* (1930); KARPF, *The Scientific Basis of Social Work* (1931).

CHAPTER IX

SUMMARY AND CONCLUSIONS

I

This survey of the modern social-psychological movement as viewed from the standpoint of the development of American social-psychological thought has now been brought to a close. We have seen how from its indefinite beginnings in nineteenth century philosophical thought and the incidental conclusions and borrowed conceptions of such related techniques as folk psychology and anthropology on the one hand, and evolutionary biology, introspective psychology, and early sociology on the other, social psychology has gradually been taking on much more definite and distinctive form. It has been passing on gradually from attention chiefly to the spectacular, the striking, and the merely formally conceived in the beginning of its modern scientific career (the objective manifestations of so-called "social mind," mob and crowd behavior, the generalized evolutionary treatment of mental and social development) and by degrees approaching the study of the less apparent but more fundamental aspects of its field of problems (the social-psychological analysis of personality, mind, motivation, etc.). Also, it has been advancing gradually from procedure by common-sense conceptions and methods or those uncritically taken over from other fields to the development of conceptions and methods more or less specifically growing out of its own viewpoint and problems and more or less fitted to its particular needs and purposes. This process of differentiated social-psychological development is still, of course, in its infancy. It has, however, put social psychology in the way of the more carefully considered scientific development upon which it is at present quite clearly beginning to enter, as is evident even from such an incomplete review of current tendencies in the field as has been incorporated here, especially in our survey of American social-psychological thought.

It may be said that the first notable attempt to build up a "social" psychology, in contradistinction to the individualistic general psychology which had held practically undisputed ground during the early nineteenth century, was made in Germany by the folk psychologists. From the founding of the *Zeitschrift für Völkerpsychologie und Sprachwissenschaft* in 1860 by Lazarus and Steinthal to Wundt, it was the aim of the folk psychologists to develop a "social" psychology alongside of and supplementary to the current general psychology. This was because they felt

416

that the methods of the latter were inadequate to deal with the more complex products of human mental life with which they sought chiefly to concern themselves.

The conception of social psychology which the folk psychologists sought to work out tended principally, however, toward the gradual building up of a "history of civilization" rather than toward the development of social psychology as we know it today, more particularly in this country. In any event, folk psychology has become more closely identified with anthropology than with social psychology as specialized fields of investigation. Furthermore, during the early period when we are most concerned with folk psychology as a direct factor in the modern social-psychological movement, it was so far dominated by the presuppositions of Hegelian philosophy and the individualistic conceptions of its associated introspective psychology that it in large measure remained apart from the main current of modern social-psychological development outside of Germany. Nevertheless, folk psychology had some very important results for the modern social-psychological movement as a whole, and even as it has taken form in this country. In the first place, folk psychology brought conspicuous support to the growing dissatisfaction with the traditional purely individualistic psychology and to the resulting interest in the study of human phenomena from more adequate social standpoints. Then, folk psychology was on fundamental social-psychological ground in its attempt to relate the objective elements of culture with the mental development of the individual. In addition, folk psychology was not only a factor in the modern social-psychological movement because, like cultural anthropology and early sociology generally, it was helping to bring the social aspect of mental life more clearly into view but also because its analysis had a distinct psycho-social rather than a merely psychological reference. It thus sought to direct attention to the cultural significance of such collective mental phenomena as it designated by the terms "folk soul," "group mind," "social consciousness," "collective will," etc., phenomena which have ever since occupied psycho-social thought, and the gradual investigation of which must be looked upon as a leading factor in the differentiation of modern social psychology. In all these ways, then, folk psychology introduced a challenging social and collectivistic emphasis into its work, which must be recognized as one of the sources of modern social-psychological development, though for the most part an indirect one in so far as American social psychology in particular is concerned.

The social-psychological aspects of folk psychology were supplemented by the early sociological students of social organization, in Germany and Austria. The term "social psychology" was first widely used by the latter group of students. It was Schäffle, specifically, who first gave wide currency to this term in his *Bau und Leben des socialen*

Körpers (1875-1878), where he used it co-ordinately with the terms "social morphology" and "social physiology" in connection with his analogical treatment of society.

The standpoint of early sociology, more especially of German sociology, was definitely "objective" in the sense that its interest was chiefly directed to the analysis of objective social organization, rather than psychological. Its analysis of society, essentially in objective institutional and group terms, corresponded in a general way, in so far as social psychology is concerned, to the analysis of the individual mind by introspective psychology. Both are logically more or less distinct from social psychology, which came into being primarily as an attempt to bridge these two fields of investigation and which, despite some isolated exceptions, is characteristically psycho-social in its procedure in consequence. Because of the background of individualistic thought upon which social psychology began to take form, the analysis of the objective social environment was, however, historically a necessary step in the development of social psychology. The connection between sociology and social psychology has therefore been very close from the beginning, and German sociology in particular, with its insistence on the group approach and its emphasis upon the reality of social life must thereby be noted as an important factor in bringing the need of a social psychology into recognition. Of greater consequence in this respect than Schäffle's analogical "social psychology" are the less imposing but more substantial contributions to the group analysis of society which were made by Ratzenhofer, Gumplowicz, and, especially for the purposes of this survey, by the more recent psycho-social analyses of Simmel.

More important still, however, for the direct advance of modern social psychology was the development of psychological sociology in France. To the psycho-social theories of Tarde, Durkheim, Le Bon, and Lévy-Bruhl must be attributed much of the forceful impulse of the modern social-psychological movement, both as regards social-psychological criticism of individualistic psychological theory and as regards its more constructive attempts to build up an adequate orientation of psycho-social interpretation.

Certainly the widespread interest and discussion which these theories stimulated could hardly have been called forth by the less spectacular development of social-psychological thought elsewhere. And in order to force a hearing during the early period of its development, social psychology needed just such spectacular support. There is no question here of the complete validity of the special theories in terms of which these writers sought to describe the operation of such basic psycho-social phenomena as custom, convention, control, constraint, etc. The consideration of importance as regards the development of social psychology is that their treatment of these phenomena brought the role of psycho-social interaction so forcefully into evidence that their influence expressed itself in a wave of heightened social-psychological interest, which leads directly into the modern period of more organized endeavor in the field of social psychology.

Nowhere, moreover, has the influence of these writers been more fruitful for the advance of social-psychological thought than in this country. Social psychology as it is represented here by such works as Ross' *Social Psychology* and his *Social Control* and also, though less conspicuously, by Ellwood's *Sociology in Its Psychological Aspects* and his *Introduction to Social Psychology* is in large part a development of the direction of psycho-social analysis which they so prominently brought into view. And these works are in turn intimately connected with the other type of social psychology which has become so popular in this country since the appearance of Cooley's *Human Nature and the Social Order* (1902), and which leads out especially to the consideration of English social-psychological thought as a factor of determining importance in American social psychology. In fact, the connection here is of such a nature that it seems best for our purpose to follow out the next two steps of our restatement in conjunction with each other.

So far, social psychology was very largely receiving a one-sided development from the side of the study of social life. It was practically a synonym for psychological sociology. From this one-sided development social psychology was recalled by the rise into prominence of instinct psychology on the one hand and by the development of the genetic study of personal growth on the other. In the first connection, besides the basic work of Darwin, Spencer, and Bagehot, the more specific social-psychological formulations of McDougall, Shand, Trotter, and Wallas stand out, in the second connection, it is necessary to recall, besides James' suggestive treatment of the "social self," especially the work of Baldwin, Cooley, Mead, Dewey, and Thomas, to say nothing further at this point of the growing number of their more recent followers in this country.

The central impulse for the development of instinct psychology in its modern form came from early English evolutionary thought with its biological emphasis and its phylogenetic outlook, in the light of which the study of the hereditary bases of behavior loomed as the problem of central importance in the investigation of human conduct, while the latter direction of social-psychological development, as already indicated, is intimately connected with social-psychological thought in this country. It has resulted in the formulation of a point of view which might, for the want of a better designation, be termed "interaction" psychology or, rather, "interaction"[1] *social* psychology, since it ought to be made evident

---

[1] This term is suggested by the emphasis which this approach has placed on the determining importance of the process of social interaction in the interpretation of

that this point of view is distinctively and emphatically social-psychological in its emphasis on interaction and not merely psychological or sociological in the usual understanding of these terms.

Instinct psychology, it is today generally recognized even by its severest recent critics, was a most important development from the standpoint of the advance of social-psychological thought. For it was not only in itself a distinct social-psychological advance on the older purely intellectualistic type of psychology, at least by possible implication, but the new outlook which it introduced into psychology provided the essential mechanism even for the more characteristic social-psychological interpretations of human behavior which have recently come into conflict with it. As instinct psychology has been developed by its outstanding exponents, however, it has given expression to the social-psychological motive which it clearly embodies, more through the recognition of the basic role which social life plays in racial evolution than in personal development. Its interpretation of the latter has definitely relegated the social factor to a place of secondary importance as compared with the biological factor. In fact, in this connection, it has practically replaced the old type of intellectualistic individualism with a new type of biological individualism, which it has been the more difficult to dislodge because it has seemed to be so firmly grounded in the most influential current of thought in recent scientific history. The implications for a broader social interpretation of personal development and social conduct, which the trend of thought upon which instinct psychology rests clearly incorporated, have been brought out not by instinct psychology itself but by that variant of the instinct approach in social psychology which has been termed "interaction" social psychology here.

Interaction social psychology may be said to be a synthesis of the currents of thought represented by instinct psychology and psychological sociology as outlined above. It began to take form in an atmosphere of protest against biological determinism and *laissez-faire* doctrine in human affairs. It has incorporated instead as practical social motives an intense interest in education and in the scientific control of human conduct. It took its departure from the orthodox position of the instinct theory of human conduct, in the first place, through a broader social interpretation of the evolutionary process as it bears on human development; but gradually it has been building up its position through the direct functional analysis of the processes and mechanisms of personal growth and social action.

While seeking to give due place to the factor of original nature by recognizing that social environment acts through native equipment,

---

human nature and social behavior and as over against the corresponding characteristic development of folk psychology in Germany, collective psychology in France, and instinct psychology in England.

this approach to the study of human conduct has aimed not to overlook the equally important fact that before biological heredity becomes concretely expressive on the level of social conduct, it incorporates social heredity as a basic component factor. Concrete conduct, it has maintained, is thus basically a complex phenomenon combining both biological and social components. It is basically both original and acquired, both individual and social, both a matter of biological heredity and a matter of social environment. Without necessarily bringing up the question as to which of these factors is the more important in human life, it has insisted that the instinct theory of human conduct does not leave room for this basic role of the social factor and that instinct as it is commonly understood is therefore an inapt tool of analysis in social psychology. Accordingly, it has suggested alternative tools of analysis which have a more distinct social reference: habit, attitude, impulse, wish, desire, etc.

Since interaction social psychology, which, as we have seen, defines so large a part of American social-psychological thought that it may be said to establish its distinctive frame of reference,[1] has recently come into sharply defined conflict with instinct psychology, and controversy in the field of social psychology in this country has in the last few years centered about this conflict, it is worth while to pause long enough here to indicate more clearly the chief line of departure between them. In so far as social psychology is concerned with the analysis of personal behavior, it is centrally concerned, as McDougall more than anyone else has aimed to establish, with the problem of the basic springs to human action. In answer to the question, "What is their essential nature?" instinct psychology has replied that they are innate, *i.e.*, basically a matter of biological heredity and only secondarily a matter of social heredity. As against this view, interaction social psychology has held that they are basically a matter of social as well as biological heredity; that they are social "in the germ," so to speak, in consequence of the fact that they are socially defined, conditioned, and directed and by virtue of the very process of social give-and-take in which they function and come to concrete expression. In the terms suggested by one writer recently, they are social products, not biological data.[2] Or, as the issue has been stated by another writer, human impulses are not first biological and then social; they are "socio-biologic" from the first.[3]

[1] Despite the varied forms and connections in which, it will be recalled, interaction social psychology, as here used, has been worked out from Baldwin and Cooley on, it possesses sufficient common ground as over against instinct psychology, in opposition to which it has chiefly crystallized its position, to enable us to consider it as a more or less unified outlook in this connection. It is in this way and from this standpoint that its position is contrasted here with instinct psychology, which is similarly unified for this purpose (see in this respect also note p. 419).

[2] FARIS, "Are Instincts Data or Hypotheses?" *Amer. Jour. Sociol.*, vol. 27, 1921.

[3] COOLEY, *Human Nature and the Social Order*, 1922 ed., Introduction.

This is not a matter of mere difference in degree of emphasis. On the contrary, we are dealing here with a fundamentally different conception of human nature which is of the most far-reaching social-psychological importance, both theoretically and in its bearing on the practical problems of social control. This has nowhere been brought out more forcefully than in the social-psychological writings of Dewey. We accordingly close this part of our summary with the following short passage, repeated from our previous outline of his social-psychological position:

The ultimate refuge of the standpatter in every field, education, religion, politics, industrial, and domestic life, has been the notion of an alleged fixed structure of mind. As long as mind is conceived as an antecedent and ready-made thing, institutions and customs may be regarded as its offspring. By its own nature the ready-made mind works to produce them as they have existed and now exist. There is no use in kicking against necessity. The most powerful apologetics for any arrangement or institution is the conception that it is an inevitable result of fixed conditions of human nature. Consequently, in one disguise or another, directly or by extreme and elaborate indirection, we find the assumed constitution of an antecedently given mind appealed to in justification of the established order as to the family, the school, the government, industry, commerce, and every other institution. Our increased knowledge of the past of man, has, indeed, given this complacent assumption a certain shock; but it has not as yet seriously modified it. Evolution in the sense of a progressive unfolding of original potencies latent in a ready-made mind has been used to reconcile the conception of mind as an original datum with the historic facts of social change which can no longer be ignored. The effect on the effort at deliberate social control and construction remained the same. All man could do was to wait and watch the panorama of a ready-formed mind unroll . . . The new point of view treats social facts as the material of an experimental science, where the problem is that of modifying belief and desire—that is to say, mind—by enacting specific changes in the social environment. Until this experimental attitude is established, the historical method, in spite of all the proof of past change which it adduces, will remain in effect a bulwark of conservatism. For, I repeat, it reduces the role of mind to that of beholding and recording the operations of man after they have happened. The historic method may give emotional inspiration or consolation in arousing the belief that a lot more changes are still to happen, but it does not show man how his mind is to take part in giving these changes one direction rather than another.[1]

What is necessary for the advance of this type of social psychology are detailed studies of the organization of specific types of reaction patterns in specific types of social situations. This is, of course, not peculiarly true of interaction social psychology, but it is peculiarly evident in its case, since in its criticism of instinct psychology it has constantly stressed the need of such concrete investigation. Also,

[1] *Supra*, p. 348.

refusing to accept the current instinct basis of procedure, it is left practically only with a point of view which has so far been used, except in a very few instances, as a basis for valuable constructive criticism and broad interpretation rather than as a basis for the building up of the factual foundation upon which this position must after all squarely rest. In this, as suggested, interaction social psychology has, however, not been alone, for social psychology as a whole has so far concerned itself more with constructive criticism and generalized reinterpretation than with specific and detailed investigation, and for the most part necessarily. But these considerations explain the recent turn of interest toward research technique among this group of students, as has been noted in due course in the latter part of this survey. This matter, however, will be taken up again for further comment in a later connection. At this point, it is necessary to direct attention to some more general considerations of far-reaching import.

II

It is clear from the foregoing summary as well as from our more detailed survey of the development of modern social-psychological thought, that nothing is as yet settled in the field. Social psychology has not yet had time to reach a settled point of view on any of the basic issues involved in its position. It is still essentially in the stage of "schools" of thought and even, in parts, of pioneer explorations of the field. Only here and there has it begun to enter seriously upon a career of systematic research and investigation. One cannot expect as yet, therefore, to find in the field of social psychology the characteristics of a well-established science or even as solid a scientific foundation as some of the older related sciences present. But to compensate for this still undeveloped state of its theory, social psychology has to offer, as has been noted in detail especially in the second part of this survey, a very meaningful and very hopeful approach in the study of personality and social conduct from the standpoint of our practical interests in them and our possibilities of socially controlling them. It is the growing recognition of this fact which is bringing social psychology into prominence alongside of the better established fields of investigation and which is providing the incentive for the expanding program of research activity upon which it is at the present time quite obviously entering.

Nor is social psychology, even in its present state of development, quite so unorganized as is sometimes likely to appear, when attention is directed chiefly to the state of controversy which at present obtains in the field in connection with certain fundamental questions that bear on the field of psychology and social science in general almost as much as on the field of social psychology in particular and that consequently are of very far-reaching interest. Controversy is, after all, a wholesome and needful condition in a new field of investigation, and it should, therefore, not blind us to the progress which social psychology has made and to the accomplishments to which it can lay claim, even though the latter are rather more significant as a basis for further advance than from the standpoint of their established scientific value in themselves.

And whether we regard the accomplishments of social psychology so far as considerable or as of comparatively little account depends largely on the particular outlook from which we view them. In the light of historical perspective they seem considerable; from the standpoint of our present-day ideal of what social psychology as a science of human nature and social behavior ought to be, it seems as if social psychology were only just becoming conscious of its real task. But from whichever of these standpoints the work of social psychology so far is viewed, the fact cannot be overlooked that it has covered indispensable preliminary and preparatory ground. It has tentatively mapped out the field of social-psychological operations; it has crystallized points of view, defined problems, indicated issues, formulated preliminary hypotheses, theories, and principles; and developed a considerable body of literature, almost all of it of unknown scientific validity, it is true, but yet invaluable as a means of orientation and as a basis on which to proceed. Above all, it has dispossessed us of many disqualifying conceptions, and it has gradually built up a genuine appreciation of the social-psychological approach. In other words, whatever absolute scientific value may be attached to the accomplishments of social psychology so far, from the standpoint of further progress in the field, they alone stand between the undefined and undirected feeling of dissatisfaction with individualistic psychological and social theory a few decades ago and the present more or less secure and many-sided attack upon the problems of social psychology.

III

It is obviously, however, not to be expected at the present time, in view of the still wholly fluid state of social psychology and the not altogether dissimilar state of the fields most intimately related to it, that there should be social-psychological agreement on such matters as the place, scope, methods, and relations of social psychology to the rest of the developing field of psychological and social thought. Indeed, the field reveals in this regard all the divergence of emphasis and conception which the several directions of social-psychological development outlined have made possible. It seems necessary, therefore, in conclusion, since there is a persistent display of interest in these matters, to touch upon them at least very briefly in a more general way than has heretofore been consistent with our treatment.

What is social psychology? This question may be answered in two ways: historically and descriptively, and logically. Logical definitions of the field of science are helpful and often very useful, but they for the most part constitute the orderly superstructure not the foundation of scientific progress. Furthermore, they are largely subjective. One's logical view of what social psychology is depends on his particular conception of the place of social psychology in the system and classification of the sciences, especially of the psychological and social sciences, and these conceptions, as we know from the history of thought, are in large part a matter of philosophical leaning and conviction. In the case of a new field like social psychology, which needs most of all for progress to shift emphasis from philosophical exposition to factual investigation, such definitions tend to set up more or less artificial and irrelevant issues that divert attention from the really significant and determining problems of the field. It is for this reason that we shall rather consider the above question from the historical and descriptive standpoint. And from this standpoint, it is of course evident that social psychology is all that has been included in this survey and much more besides, which, for one reason or another, was regarded as falling without its scope. In this country, for example, there are side by side the views of McDougall and Ross, of Ellwood and Allport, of Mead, Dewey, and Thomas, etc. These writers, it will be recalled, have variously defined social psychology as the science of the social aspects of individual behavior (Allport); as the basic science of human nature and social personality in general, in so far as these phenomena are conceived to be human rather than merely biological products (Mead);[1] as psychological sociology (Ellwood); as the science of the "psychic planes and currents" of human uniformity which are due to specifically social causes (Ross); as the general science of the subjective side of culture (Thomas); as group psychology and the study of the social development of individual behavior from its bases in the native equipment of man (McDougall). The views of these authors on the scope, methods, and relations of social psychology are, of course, correspondingly varied.

But whatever be the diversities of emphasis and conception which thus come to view, there is over and above them an essential unity which brings social psychologists, after all, into a more or less well-defined group in their common emphasis of the "individual-social" as over against the essentially "individual" which biology and psychology for instance emphasize and the essentially "social" which sociology and cultural anthropology primarily emphasize. Were one to attempt to formulate, however, a sufficiently representative and inclusive view of social psy-

---

[1] Dewey's statement that "all psychology is either biological or social psychology" ("The Need for Social Psychology," *Psychol. Rev.*, vol. 24, p. 276, 1917) indicates the general position here.

chology, to give place even to the most current conceptions, as Bogardus
for example attempted especially in his earlier formulations of the subject,[1]
one would find that the resulting broadly conceived view would necessarily make social psychology overlap to a very considerable extent on
both of the related fields of psychology and sociology as commonly
thought of. But this is precisely the situation as it presents itself at the
present time, and it is clearly an inevitable outcome of the diverse course
of modern social-psychological development as it has been traced out here.

Social psychology came into being, as we have seen, in consequence
of the fact that the scientific techniques already on the ground, especially
psychology and early sociology, left uncared for an important field of
human problems. As the social-psychological movement gathered
force, however, it tended both to psychologize the point of view of
sociology and, to a considerable extent, also to socialize the point of
view of psychology and thereby to direct their attention increasingly
to the field of problems with which it was itself concerned and which
originally called it into being. The overlapping of these fields on what
has come to be common territory has thus followed in the natural course
of events.

But this situation, far from giving concern because of the philosophical questions of jurisdiction and possible conflict in approach and
interpretation which it raises, should give encouragement that by combined effort the problems of common interest will be the better illumined.
Such overlapping of effort at points of particular scientific interest is to
be expected. There are similar types of overlapping even in the sciences
which have had a much longer history in working out effective lines of
division of labor than the psychological and social sciences. The concentration of endeavor about the important border-line fields of biophysics
and biochemistry are conspicuous cases in point. And the progress of
recent inquiry in these fields is proof of the value of such concentration
of scientific effort. As regards the complex problems of human conduct,
therefore, it is well to encourage the concentration of as many points of
view and scientific divisions of labor as possible—not only psychology,
sociology, and social psychology, but as many more as can direct themselves to this admittedly most important field of study.

It seems idle and fruitless to attempt to speculate at the present
time, furthermore, on what the outcome is likely to be in the matter of
the division of labor between psychology, sociology, and social psychology. The progress of investigation in these fields will gradually, no
doubt, establish effective lines of cooperation between them, as it has
in the case of other closely related fields of scientific investigation. And

---

[1] See his *Essentials of Social Psychology*, 2d ed., pp. 17–18, and *supra*, pp. 394*ff.*;
also other synthetic views of the subject, such as those of Bernard and Young (*supra*,
pp. 407, 413).

since it is no longer considered necessary to predetermine divisions and relations in science, social psychology can go on developing alongside of psychology, sociology, and the other sciences which are closely related to it and safely leave to the progress of events the more exact determination of its formal relations to these fields.[1]

The same, in substance, may be said in regard to the question of method in social psychology. Here, again, it is fruitless to argue abstractly that either one or the other of the established scientific methods is best adapted to social-psychological investigation. So far, as a matter of fact, experiment, systematic observation, testing and rating techniques, case and monographic study, the statistical method, the historico-genetic and ethnological methods have all been successfully used in the field, and seemingly each is supplementary to the others. Experiment is needed, for instance, for verification; case and monographic study, for the investigation of processes and the setting up of causal hypotheses; statistics, for the establishment of norms; etc. Only the further application of these various methods in the investigation of concrete problems can determine more clearly than appears now what are the most effective lines of cooperation between them in so far as the field of social psychology is concerned.

The question of method is, however, of such basic importance from the standpoint of real advance in the factual upbuilding of the field that it merits careful separate treatment on the basis of concrete problems of research and investigation that are at present social-psychologically in view, and probably no better introduction to social psychology can be had than a careful and detailed study of the field from this standpoint. This, as stated, is however a matter for separate consideration and cannot be gone into in detail here.[2]

But it is clear enough from what has already been said that the need which is at present most in evidence all along the line in the field of social psychology is for more verified fact and experience in concrete investigation. There has been enough abstract theorizing and broad generalization in social psychology, though these have had an important place in the social-psychological movement. What is needed now is more fact. For social-psychological theory has now so overrun reliable fact that further progress demands a compensating emphasis on the

---

[1] Perhaps as good a working definition as any at the present time, in view of the above considerations, is to say in a general way that social psychology studies both the social aspects of individual behavior and the psychic aspects of group behavior and social interstimulation and that a more distinctive determination of its scope is still in process of crystallization.

[2] See in this connection *supra*, p. 399, note 5. The first step in the survey of social psychology from this standpoint has already been taken in Murphy and Murphy, *Experimental Social Psychology*. Other treatments of the subject from this standpoint are bound to follow.

latter. It is, for instance, so much time lost at present to continue expounding abstractly the values of the social-psychological approach, when the demand for applicable social-psychological principles which are not yet available is already being re-echoed from every field of intimately related theoretical and practical endeavor. The day for that sort of social psychologizing is past, and along with it the day of "arm-chair" generalization and made-to-order one-man systems of social-psychological theory. Instead, we are inevitably on the eve of a period of specialized research and investigation; of the rule of fact, proof, and careful scientific procedure; and of the patient and painstaking cooperation of many in the task of the gradual inductive reconstruction of the field of social-psychological theory. This new trend of social-psychological development, this new emphasis on research and investigation according to recognized methods of scientific procedure as over against simple descriptive analysis on the basis of random and unverified personal observation and impression is only just beginning to gain a firm foothold in social psychology. In it lies, however, the sole promise of social psychology as the science of human nature and social conduct, which social psychologists for some decades now, have been anticipating, and the vision of which has gained for this field of thought the expanding interest and popularity which it at present enjoys, especially in this country.

IV

In every department of human endeavor, alert thought is becoming conscious of the ever more pressing problems of social behavior which this age is facing. In consequence, there has been a general intensification of interest, more especially since the World War, in scientific theory that appears to give promise of help in the solution of these problems. Along with this new attitude of receptivity toward psychological and social science in general, there has naturally been a rise of interest in social psychology. Parents, teachers, reformers, social workers are all beginning to turn a sympathetic ear toward the teachings of social psychology. Whether social psychology, by riding on the wave of this new interest in its scientific possibilities, will be able in the next few years to make a measurable degree of progress toward meeting the high expectations which it has aroused remains, of course, to be seen. Very largely, this must naturally depend on the earnestness with which it applies itself to the expanding task of research and investigation which is now clearly before it. And encouraging indications are at present not lacking that social psychology is beginning to enter upon such a period of accelerated scientific research and investigation as the situation demands. Certainly the need for scientific work has never been more pressing in any field, nor the promise of high reward for effort expended, in terms of human benefit, more challenging. Whatever, in fact, be the obstacles against rapid progress in this field of investigation, they are more than compensated for by the importance which attaches to it. What more does a courageous and a scientifically inventive age need as a spur to the highest type of effort?

As regards the present social-psychological situation in this country in particular, there is certainly much that appears hopeful for the consistent advance of social psychology. Nowhere is the positive standpoint more firmly established, or the need for an applicable social psychology more keenly felt, or the variety of material for social-psychological study more easily at hand. It is not surprising, therefore, that this country should be producing a considerable part of present-day social-psychological literature and, more particularly, that social psychology as a specialized endeavor should be more definitely launched here than elsewhere.[1] Seemingly, too, both from the standpoint of general interest and the scientific preparation of the field, we are just at the point of a new pace of social-psychological development here. The most convincing evidence of this is to be found in the concentration of social-psychological activity reflected in the current periodical literature of the field. But even in the more formal literature which has chiefly come under consideration in this survey, there is a notable accumulation of evidence in support of this view. How to put these advantageous features of the situation best to account is the immediate practical consideration before American social-psychological thought.

Perhaps the need that stands out most strikingly at the present time in respect to this consideration as well as in respect to American social-psychological thought more generally is that of securing a broadened outlook on the problems of social psychology. As long as workers in the field proceed as if social psychology begins anew with each one of them and hence in total disregard of related endeavor, as is still so largely the case at the present time, orderly advance in thought and investigation remains impossible, and bias and partisanship have full play. The result is the crystallization of artificial issues which interfere with a coordinated attack on more basic problems.

Social psychology has reached the point of development at which, in its larger outlines at least, it presents a fairly well-defined front. It is highly important that workers in the field view themselves in relation to and as a part of the larger movement. This consideration has been basic to the purpose of this survey. It is the hope of the writer that it will help to bring the present-day problems and tasks of social psychology into more significant social-psychological perspective.

[1] See also *Pub. Amer. Sociol. Soc.*, vol. 21, pp. 71–81, 1927.

BIBLIOGRAPHY

Besides cited references, this bibliography includes some works which are especially important for general historical background.   Also, in the case of some writers, it was found inexpedient to list all of the items referred to in the text and a selection of more important references was made in these instances.   Foreign works discussed in the text are listed both in the original and in translation if any.   When two editions of a work were referred to, both are indicated.

ABEL, THEODORE: *Systematic Sociology in Germany*, Columbia University Press, New York, 1929.
ALLPORT, FLOYD H.: "Behavior and Experiment in Social Psychology," *Jour. Abnor. Psychol.*, vol. 14, pp. 297–306, 1919.
———: " 'Group' and 'Institution' as Concepts in a Natural Science of Social Phenomena," *Pub. Amer. Sociol. Soc.*, vol. 22, pp. 83–99, 1928.
———: *Social Psychology*, Houghton Mifflin Company, Boston, 1924.
———: "The Group Fallacy in Relation to Culture," *Jour. Abnor. Social Psychol.*, vol. 19, pp. 185–191, 1925.
———: "The Group Fallacy in Relation to Social Science," *Jour. Abnor. Social Psychol.*, vol. 19, pp. 60–73, 1925.
———: "The Nature of Institutions," *Social Forces*, vol. 6, pp. 167–179, 1927.
———: "The Present Status of Social Psychology," *Jour. Abnor. Social Psychol.*, vol. 21, pp. 372–383, 1927.
——— and GORDON W. ALLPORT: Personality Traits: Their Classification and Measurement," *Jour. Abnor. Psychol. Social Psychol.*, vol. 16, pp. 1–40, 1921.
ANGELL, JAMES R.: *Psychology*, Henry Holt & Company, New York, 1904.
BAGEHOT, WALTER: *Physics and Politics*, D. Appleton & Company, New York, 1884.
BAIN, READ: "An Attitude on Attitude Research," *Amer. Jour. Sociol.*, vol. 32, pp. 940–957, 1928.
———: "Theory and Measurement of Attitudes and Opinions," *Psychol. Bull.*, vol. 27, pp. 357–379, 1930.
BALDWIN, JAMES M.: *Darwin and the Humanities*, Review Publishing Company, Baltimore, 1909.
———: *Development and Evolution*, The Macmillan Company, New York, 1902.
———: *Fragments in Philosophy and Science*, Charles Scribner's Sons, New York, 1902.
———: *Handbook of Psychology*, Henry Holt & Company, New York, 1889–1891.
———: *History of Psychology*, G. P. Putnam's Sons, New York, 1913.
———: *Mental Development in the Child and the Race*, The Macmillan Company, New York, 1900.
———: "Psychology Past and Present," *Psychol. Rev.*, vol. 1, pp. 363–391, 1894.
———: *Social and Ethical Interpretations in Mental Development*, The Macmillan Company, New York, 1913.
———: *The Individual and Society*, Richard G. Badger, The Gorham Press, Boston, 1911.
BARNES, HARRY E.: "Durkheim's Contribution to the Reconstruction of Political Theory," *Pol. Sci. Quar.*, vol. 35, pp. 236–254, 1920.

————: "Psychology and History: Some Reasons for Predicting Their More Active Cooperation in the Future," *Amer. Jour. Psychol.*, vol. 30, pp. 337–396, 1919.

————: "Sociology before Comte," *Amer. Jour. Sociol.* vol. 23, pp. 174–247, 1917.

————: "Some Contributions of American Psychological Sociology to Social and Political Theory," *Sociol. Rev.*, vol. 14, pp. 202*ff.*, 1922; vol. 15, pp. 35*ff.*, 121*ff.*, 194*ff.*, 286*ff.*, 1923.

————: "Some Contributions of American Psychology to Modern Social and Political Theory," *Sociol. Rev.*, vol. 13, pp. 152–167, 204–227, 1921.

————: "Some Typical Contributions of English Sociology to Political Theory," *Amer. Jour. Sociol.*, vol. 27, pp. 289*ff.*, 442*ff.*, 573*ff.*, 737*ff.*, 1921–1922; vol. 28, pp. 49*ff.*, 179*ff.*, 1922.

————: "The Development of Historical Sociology," *Pub. Amer. Sociol. Soc.*, vol. 16, pp. 17–50, 1921.

————: "The Fate of Sociology in England," *Pub. Amer. Sociol. Soc.*, vol. 21, pp. 26–46, 1927.

———— (ed.): *The History and Prospects of the Social Sciences*, Alfred A. Knopf, New York, 1925.

————: "The Philosophy of the State in the Writings of Gabriel Tarde," *Phil. Rev.*, vol. 28, pp. 248–279, 1919.

————: "Two Representative Contributions of Sociology to Political Theory: The Doctrines of William Graham Sumner and Lester Frank Ward," *Amer. Jour. Sociol.*, vol. 25, pp. 1–23, 150–170, 1919.

BARTH, PAUL: *Die Philosophie der Geschichte als Sociologie*, O. R. Reisland, Leipzig, 1915.

BARTLETT, F. C.: *Psychology and Primitive Culture*, University Press, Cambridge, England, 1923.

BECHTEREW, W. von (BEKHTEREV, V. M.): *Die Bedeutung der Suggestion im sozialen Leben*, J. F. Bergmann, Wiesbaden, 1905.

BENTLEY, M.: "A Preface to Social Psychology," *Psychol. Monogr.*, vol. 21, pp. 1–25, 1916.

BERNARD, L. L.: *An Introduction to Social Psychology*, Henry Holt & Company, New York, 1926.

————: *Instinct: A Study in Social Psychology*, Henry Holt & Company, New York, 1924.

————: "Instinct and Psychoanalysis," *Jour. Abnor. Psychol. Social Psychol.*, vol. 17, pp. 350–366, 1923.

————: "Recent Trends in Social Psychology," *Jour. Social Forces*, vol. 2, pp. 737–743, 1924.

————: "The Misuse of Instincts in the Social Sciences," *Psychol. Rev.*, vol. 28, pp. 96–119, 1921.

BLANCHARD, PHYLLIS M.: *The Child and Society: An Introduction to the Social Psychology of the Child*, Longmans, Green & Co., New York, 1928.

BLONDEL, CHARLES: *La conscience morbide*, F. Alcan, Paris, 1914.

————: *Introduction à la psychologie collective*, A. Colin, Paris, 1928.

BOAS, FRANZ: *Anthropology and Modern Life*, W. W. Norton & Company, Inc., New York, 1928.

————: "Anthropology," *The Encyclopedia of the Social Sciences* vol. 2, pp. 73–110, New York, 1930.

————: "Psychological Problems in Anthropology," *Amer. Jour. Psychol.*, vol. 21, pp. 371–384, 1910.

————: "The History of Anthropology," *Proc. Intern. Congress Arts Sci.*, vol. 5, pp. 468–482, New York, 1906.

————: *The Mind of Primitive Man*, The Macmillan Company, New York, 1911.

BODENHAFER, WALTER B.: "Comte and Psychology," *Pub. Amer. Sociol. Soc.*, vol. 17, pp. 15–26, 1922.

————: The Comparative Role of the Group Concept in Ward's *Dynamic Sociology* and Contemporary American Sociology," *Amer. Jour. Sociol.*, vol. 26, pp., 273*ff.*, 425*ff.*, 588*ff.*, 716*ff.*, 1920–1921.

BOGARDUS, EMORY S.: *A History of Social Thought*, University of Southern California Press, Los Angeles, 1922.

————: *Essentials of Social Psychology*, University of Southern California Press, Los Angeles, 1918, 1920.

————: *Fundamentals of Social Psychology*, Century Company, New York, 1924.

————: "Social Distance and Its Origins," *Jour. Appl. Sociol.*, vol. 9, pp. 216–227, 1925; "Measuring Social Distance," *ibid.*, pp. 299–308; also succeeding articles on this subject.

————: *The New Social Research*, Jesse Ray Miller, Los Angeles, 1926.

BOORMAN, W. R.: *Developing Personality in Boys: The Social Psychology of Adolescence*, The Macmillan Company, New York, 1929.

BOUGLÉ, CÉLESTIN: "The Present Tendency of the Social Sciences in France," *The New Social Science*, ed. by L. D. White, University of Chicago Press, Chicago, 1930.

BRANFORD, VICTOR: "Durkheim: A Brief Memoir," *Sociol. Rev.*, vols. 9–10, pp. 77–82, 1918.

BRETT, G. S.: *A History of Psychology*, The Macmillan Company, New York, 1912–1921.

BRINKMAN, CARL: "The Present Situation of German Sociology," *Pub. Amer. Sociol. Soc.*, vol. 21, pp. 47–56, 1927.

BRINTON, DANIEL G.: *The Basis of Social Relations*, G. P. Putnam's Sons, New York, 1902.

BRISTOL, L. M.: *Social Adaptation*, Harvard University Press, Cambridge, Mass., 1921.

BUCKLE, H. T.: *History of Civilization in England*, J. W. Parker and Son, London, 1861.

BÜHLER, CHARLOTTE: *Kindheit und Jugend*, S. Hirzel, Leipzig, 1928.

BURGESS, ERNEST W.: "Statistics and Case Studies," *Sociol. and Social Res.*, vol. 12, pp. 103–121, 1927.

————: "The Study of the Delinquent as a Person," *Amer. Jour. Sociol.*, vol. 28, pp. 657–680, 1923.

————: (See also PARK, ROBERT E., and.)

BURNHAM, W. H.: *The Normal Mind*, D. Appleton & Company, New York, 1924.

CARR, HARVEY: "Functionalism," *Psychologies of* 1930, ed. by C. Murchison, Worcester, Mass., 1930.

CARTER, HUGH: *The Social Theories of L. T. Hobhouse*, University of North Carolina, Chapel Hill, 1927.

CASE, C. M.: "Toward Gestalt Sociology," *Sociol. and Social Res.*, vol. 15, pp. 3–27, 1930.

CAVAN, RUTH S.: *Suicide*, University of Chicago Press, Chicago, 1928.

CHAPIN, F. S.: *Cultural Change*, Century Company, New York, 1928.

————: *Field Work and Social Research*, Century Company, New York, 1920.

COLLINS, F. HOWARD: *An Epitome of the Synthetic Philosophy*, Williams & Norgate, London, 1889.

COMTE, AUGUSTE: *Cours de philosophie positive*, Paris, 1830–1842, freely trans. and condensed by Harriet Martineau, *The Positive Philosophy of Auguste Comte*, J. Chapman, London, 1853.

————: *Système de politique positive*, Paris, 1851–1854, trans. by J. H. Bridges and others, *System of Positive Polity*, Longmans, Green & Co., London, 1875–1877.

CONWAY, W. M.: *The Crowd in Peace and War*, Longmans, Green, & Co., New York, 1915.

COOLEY, CHARLES H.: "Case Study of Small Institutions as a Method of Research," *Pub. Amer. Sociol. Soc.*, vol. 22, pp. 133–143, 1928.

————: *Human Nature and the Social Order*, Charles Scribner's Sons, New York, 1902, 1922.

————: "Now and Then," *Jour. Appl. Sociol.*, vol. 8, pp. 259–262, 1924.

————: "Reflections upon the Sociology of Herbert Spencer," *Amer. Jour. Sociol.*, vol. 26, pp. 129–145, 1920.

————: *Social Organization*, Charles Scribner's Sons, New York, 1909.

————: "Sumner and Methodology," *Sociol. and Social Res.*, vol. 12, pp. 303–306, 1928.

————: "The Roots of Social Knowledge," *Amer. Jour. Sociol.*, vol. 32, pp. 59–80, 1926.

————: *The Social Process*, Charles Scribner's Sons, New York, 1920.

DARWIN, CHARLES: "Biographical Sketch of an Infant," *Mind*, vol. 2, pp. 285–295, 1877.

————: *The Descent of Man*, D. Appleton & Company, New York, 1906.

————: *The Expression of the Emotions in Man and Animals*, John Murray, London, 1872.

————: *The Origin of Species*, John Murray, London, 1859.

DAVIS, MICHAEL M.: *Psychological Interpretations of Society*, Columbia University Studies in History, Economics, and Public Law, New York, 1909.

DAVY, G.: "La psychologie des primitifs d'après Levy-Bruhl," *Jour. psychol.*, vol. 27, pp. 112–176, 1930.

————: "La sociologie," *Traité de psychologie*, by G. Dumas et al., vol. II, pp. 765–808, F. Alcan, Paris, 1924.

————: "La sociologie de M. Durkheim," *Rev. philos.*, vol. 72, pp. 42–71, 160–185, 1911.

————: "Problèmes de psychologie sociale," *Jour. psychol.*, vol. 20, pp. 734–755, 1923.

————: "Sociology," *Philosophy Today*, collected and ed. by E. L. Schaub, Open Court Publishing Company, Chicago, 1928.

DEALEY, JAMES Q.: "Lester Frank Ward," *American Masters of Social Science*, ed. by Howard W. Odum, Henry Holt & Company, New York, 1926.

————: *et al.* "Lester Frank Ward," *Amer. Jour. Sociol.*, vol. 19, pp. 61–78, 1913.

DESSOIR, MAX: *Outlines of the History of Psychology*, trans. by D. Fisher, The Macmillan Company, New York, 1912.

DEWEY, JOHN: *Democracy and Education*, The Macmillan Company, New York, 1916.

————: *Experience and Nature*, Open Court Publishing Company, Chicago, 1925.

————: *German Philosophy and Politics*, Henry Holt & Company, New York, 1915.

————: *How We Think*, D. C. Heath & Company, Boston, 1910.

————: *Human Nature and Conduct: An Introduction to Social Psychology*, Henry Holt & Company, New York, 1922.

————: "Progress," *Intern. Jour. Ethics*, vol. 26, pp. 312–318, 1916.

————: *Psychology*, Harper & Brothers, New York, 1887.

————: *Reconstruction in Philosophy*, Henry Holt & Company, New York, 1920.

————: *The Influence of Darwin on Philosophy and Other Essays on Contemporary Thought*, Henry Holt & Company, New York, 1910.

————: "Interpretation of Savage Mind," *Psychol. Rev.*, vol. 9, pp. 217–230, 1902.

———: "The Development of American Pragmatism," *Studies in the History of Ideas*, ed. by the Department of Philosophy, Columbia University, vol. II, pp. 353–377, Columbia University Press, New York, 1925.

———: "The Need for Social Psychology," *Psychol. Rev.*, vol. 24, pp. 266–277, 1917.

———: *The Public and Its Problems*, Henry Holt & Company, New York, 1927.

———: "The Reflex Arc Concept in Psychology," *Psychol. Rev.*, vol. 3, pp. 357–370, 1896.

———: "The Theory of Emotions," *Psychol. Rev.*, vol. 1, pp. 553–569, 1894; vol. 2, pp. 13–32, 1895.

——— and JAMES H. TUFTS: *Ethics*, Henry Holt & Company, New York, 1908.

DRAGHICESCO, D.: *Du rôle de l'individu dans le déterminisme social*, F. Alcan, Paris, 1906.

DREVER, JAMES: *Instinct in Man*, University Press, Cambridge, England, 1917.

DUMAS, GEORGES: "L'interpsychologie," *Traité de psychologie*, by G. Dumas et al., vol. II, pp. 739–764, F. Alcan, Paris, 1924.

———: *Nonveau traité de psychologie*, vol. I, F. Alcan, Paris, 1930.

———*et al.*: *Traité de psychologie*, F. Alcan, Paris, 1923–1924.

DUNLAP, KNIGHT: "Are There Any Instincts?" *Jour. Abnor. Psychol.*, vol. 14, pp. 307–311, 1919.

———: "Instinct and Desire," *Jour. Abnor. Social Psychol.*, vol. 20, pp. 170–173, 1925.

———: *Social Psychology*, Williams & Wilkins Co., Baltimore, 1927.

———: "The Foundations of Social Psychology," *Psychol. Rev.*, vol. 30, pp. 81–102, 1923.

———: "The Need for Scientific Social Psychology," *Scientific Monthly*, vol. 11, pp. 502–517, 1920.

DUPRAT, G. L.: *La psychologie sociale*, G. Doin, Paris, 1920.

DURKHEIM, ÉMILE: *De la division du travail social*, F. Alcan, Paris, 1893.

———: *Éducation et sociologie*, F. Alcan, Paris, 1922.

———: *L'éducation morale*, F. Alcan, Paris, 1925.

———: *Le suicide*, F. Alcan, Paris, 1897.

———: *Les formes élémentaires de la vie religieuse*, Paris, 1912, trans. by J. W. Swain, *The Elementary Forms of Religious Life*, The Macmillan Company, New York, 1915.

———: *Les régles de la méthode sociologique*, F. Alcan, Paris, 1895.

———: "Représentations individuelles et représentations collectives," *Rev. de mét. et de mor.*, vol. 6, pp. 273–302, 1898, repr. in *Sociologie et philosophie*, Paris, 1924.

EDMAN, IRWIN: *Human Traits and Their Social Significance*, Houghton Mifflin Company, Boston, 1920.

ELLWOOD, CHARLES A.: *Cultural Evolution*, Century Company, New York, 1927.

———: "Current Sociology: The Development of Sociology in the United States since 1910," *Sociol. Rev.*, vol. 19, pp. 25–34, 1927.

———: *Introduction to Social Psychology*, D. Appleton & Company, New York, 1917.

———: "Mental Patterns in Social Evolution," *Pub. Amer. Sociol. Soc.*, vol. 17, pp. 88–100, 1922.

———: "Social Psychology" (Introductory Statement), *Proc. Intern. Congress Arts Sci.*, vol. 5, p. 859, New York, 1906.

———: *Sociology in Its Psychological Aspects*, D. Appleton & Company, New York, 1912.

———: *Some Prolegomena to Social Psychology*, University of Chicago Press, Chicago, 1901.

———: "The LePlay Method of Social Observation," *Amer. Jour. Sociol.*, vol. 2, pp. 662–680, 1897.

———: *The Psychology of Human Society*, D. Appleton & Company, New York, 1925.

————: "Theories of Cultural Evolution," *Amer. Jour. Sociol.*, vol. 23, pp. 779–800, 1918.

ENGLISH, H. B.: "Emotion as Related to Instinct," *Psychol. Bull.*, vol. 21, pp. 309–326, 1924.

ESSERTIER, DANIEL: *Les formes inférieures de l'explication*, F. Alcan, Paris, 1927.

FARIS, ELLSWORTH: "Are Instincts Data or Hypotheses?" *Amer. Jour. Sociol.*, vol. 27, pp. 184–196, 1921.

————: "Attitudes and Behavior," *Amer. Jour. Sociol.*, vol. 34, pp. 271–281, 1928.

————: "Borderline Trends in Social Psychology," *Pub. Amer. Sociol. Soc.*, vol. 25, pp. 38–40, 1931.

————: "Current Trends in Social Psychology," *Essays in Philosophy*, ed. by T. V. Smith and W. K. Wright, pp. 117–134, Open Court Publishing Company, Chicago, 1929.

————: "Ethnological Light on Psychological Problems," *Pub. Amer. Sociol. Soc.*, vol. 16, pp. 113–120, 1921.

————: "Pre-literate Peoples: Proposing a New Term," *Amer. Jour. Sociol.*, vol. 30, pp. 710–712, 1925.

————: "The Concept of Imitation," *Amer. Jour. Sociol.*, vol. 32, pp. 369–378, 1926.

————: "The Concept of Social Attitudes," *Jour. Appl. Sociol.*, vol. 9, pp. 404–409, 1925.

————: "The Nature of Human Nature," *Pub. Amer. Sociol. Soc.*, vol. 20, pp. 15–29, 1926.

————: "The Subjective Aspect of Culture," *Pub. Amer. Sociol. Soc.*, vol. 19, pp. 37–46, 1924.

————: "Topical Summaries in Current Literature: Social Psychology in America," *Amer. Jour. Sociol.*, vol. 32, pp. 623–630, 1927.

FAUCONNET, PAUL: "Current Sociology: The Durkheim School in France," *Sociol. Rev.*, vol. 19, pp. 15–20, 1927.

———— and MARCEL MAUSS: "Sociologie," *La grande encyclopédie*, Paris, 1901.

Feelings and Emotion: The Wittenberg Symposium, ed. by Martin L. Reymert, Clark University Press, Worcester, Mass., 1928.

"Field of Social Psychology and Its Relation to Abnormal Psychology, The," (editorial) *Jour. Abnor. Psychol. Social Psychol.*, vol. 16, pp. 3–7, 1921.

FLINT, ROBERT: *History of the Philosophy of History*, W. Blackwood & Sons, Edinburgh, 1893.

FISKE, JOHN: *Outlines of Cosmic Philosophy*, Houghton Mifflin Company, New York, 1902.

FOLLETT, MARY P.: *Creative Experience*, Longmans, Green & Co., New York, 1924.

————: *The New State*, Longmans, Green & Co., New York, 1918.

FOLSAM, JOSEPH K.: *Social Psychology*, Harper & Brothers, New York, 1931.

FOUILLÉE, ALFRED: *La psychologie des idées-forces*, F. Alcan, Paris, 1893.

————: *La psychologie du peuple français*, F. Alcan, Paris, 1898.

————: *La science sociale contemporaine*, L. Hachette, Paris, 1885.

FREUD, SIGMUND: *A General Introduction to Psychoanalysis*, authorized trans., Boni & Liveright, New York, 1920.

————: "The Origin and Development of Psychoanalysis," *Amer. Jour. Psychol.*, vol. 21, pp. 181–218, 1910.

GALTON, FRANCIS: *Hereditary Genius*, Macmillan & Co., Ltd., London, 1869.

————: *Inquiries into Human Faculty*, Macmillan & Co., Ltd., London, 1883.

————: *Natural Inheritance*, Macmillan & Co., Ltd., London, 1889.

GAULT, ROBERT H.: "Recent Developments in Psychology Contributory to Social Explanation," *Recent Developments in the Social Sciences,* ed. by E. C. Hayes, pp. 97–153, J. B. Lippincott Company, Philadelphia, 1927.

———: *Social Psychology,* Henry Holt & Company, New York, 1923.

GECK, L. H. AD: "Social Psychology in Germany," *Sociol. and Social Res.,* vol. 13, pp. 504–516, 1929; vol. 14, pp. 108–129, 1929.

———: *Sozialpsychologie im Auslande,* F. Dümmler, Berlin, 1928.

GEHLKE, CHARLES E.: *Emile Durkheim's Contributions to Sociological Theory,* Columbia University Studies in History, Economics, and Public Law, New York, 1915.

GIDDINGS, FRANKLIN H.: *Studies in the Theory of Human Society,* The Macmillan Company, New York, 1922.

———: *The Principles of Sociology,* The Macmillan Company, New York, 1896.

———: *The Scientific Study of Human Society,* University of North Carolina Press, Chapel Hill, 1924.

GILLIN, JOHN L.: "The Development of Sociology in the United States," *Pub. Amer. Sociol. Soc.,* vol. 21, pp. 1–25, 1927.

GINSBERG, MORRIS: *The Psychology of Society,* E. P. Dutton & Co., New York, 1921.

GOLDENWEISER, ALEXANDER A.: "Cultural Anthropology," *The History and Prospects of the Social Sciences,* ed. by Harry E. Barnes, pp. 210–254, Alfred A. Knopf, New York, 1925.

———: "Diffusionism and the American School of Historical Ethnology," *Amer. Jour. Sociol.,* vol. 31, pp. 19–38, 1925.

———: *Early Civilization,* Alfred A. Knopf, New York, 1922.

———: "Four Phases of Anthropological Thought," *Pub. Amer. Sociol. Soc.,* vol. 16, pp. 50–70, 1921.

———: "History, Psychology, and Culture," *Jour. Phil., Psychol., Sci. Meth.,* vol. 15, pp. 589–607, 1918.

———: "Psychology and Culture," *Pub. Amer. Sociol. Soc.,* vol. 19, pp. 15–36, 1925.

GROVES, E. R.: *Personality and Social Adjustment,* Longmans, Green & Co., New York, 1923.

———: *Social Problems and Education,* Longmans, Green & Co., New York, 1926.

GUMPLOWICZ, LUDWIG: *Der Rassenkampf,* Wagner, Innsbruck, 1883.

———: Grundriss der Sociologie, Vienna, 1885, trans. by F. W. Moore, *The Outlines of Sociology,* American Academy of Political and Social Science, Philadelphia, 1899.

HADDON, A. C.: *History of Anthropology,* G. P. Putnam's Sons, New York, 1910.

HAEBERLIN, H. K.: "The Theoretical Foundations of Wundt's Folk Psychology," *Psychol. Rev.,* vol. 23, pp. 279–302, 1916.

HALL, G. STANLEY: *Adolescence,* D. Appleton & Company, New York, 1904.

———: *Founders of Modern Psychology,* D. Appleton & Company, New York, 1912.

———: *Life and Confessions of a Psychologist,* D. Appleton & Company, New York, 1923.

———: *Youth,* D. Appleton & Company, New York, 1907.

HANKINS, FRANK H.: *Adolphe Quetelet as Statistician,* Columbia University Studies in History, Economics, and Public Law, New York, 1908.

———: "Individual Differences: The Galton-Pearson Approach," *Social Forces,* vol. 4, pp. 272–281, 1925.

HAYES, E. C. (ed.): *Recent Developments in the Social Sciences,* J. B. Lippincott Company, Philadelphia, 1927.

———: "Sociological Construction Lines," *Amer. Jour. Sociol.,* vol. 11, pp. 26–48, 1905.

HEALY, W., A. F. BRONNER, and A. M. BOWERS: *The Structure and Meaning of Psychoanalysis,* Alfred A. Knopf, New York, 1930.

HEGEL, G. W. F.: *Grundlinien der Philosophie des Rechts*, Berlin, 1821, trans. by S. W. Dyde, *Hegel's Philosophy of Right*, George Bell & Sons, London, 1896.

———: *Phänomenologie des Geistes*, Berlin, 1807, trans. by J. B. Baillie, *The Phenomenology of Mind*, The Macmillan Company, New York, 1910.

———: *Vorlesungen über die Philosophie der Geschichte*, Berlin, 1837, trans. by J. Sibree, *The Philosophy of History*, Colonial Press, New York, 1900.

HELLPACH, WILLY: *Sozialpsychologische Forschungen*, vol. I, Julius Springer, Berlin, 1922.

HELSON, HARRY: "The Psychology of Gestalt," *Amer. Jour. Psychol.*, vol. 36, pp. 342–370, 494–526, 1925; vol. 37, pp. 25–62, 189–223, 1926.

HERBART, JOHANN F.: *Lehrbuch zur Psychologie*, Leipzig, 1816, trans. by M. K. Smith, *A Textbook in Psychology*, D. Appleton & Company, New York, 1891.

———: *Psychologie als Wissenschaft*, A. W. Unzer, Königsberg, 1824–1825.

———: "Über einige Beziehungen zwischen Psychologie und Staatswissenschaft," *Schriften zur praktischen Philosophie*, L. Voss, Leipzig, 1851.

HERBERTSON, DOROTHY: "Le Play and Social Science," *Sociol. Rev.*, vol. 12, pp. 36–42, 108–112, 1920.

HERDER, JOHANN G.: *Ideen zur Philosophie der Geschichte der Menschheit*, G. Hempel, Berlin, 1876.

HERSKOVITS, M. J.: "Social Pattern: A Methodological Study," *Jour. Social Forces*, vol. 4, pp. 57–69, 1925.

———: (See also WILLEY, M., and.)

HOBHOUSE, L. T.: *Development and Purpose*, The Macmillan Company, New York, 1913.

———: *Mind in Evolution*, The Macmillan Company, New York, 1904.

———: *Morals in Evolution*, Chapman & Hall, Ltd., London, 1906.

———: *Social Development*, Henry Holt & Company, New York, 1924.

———: *Social Evolution and Political Theory*, Columbia University Press, New York, 1911.

HOCKING, W. E.: "The Dilemma in the Conception of Instincts as Applied to Human Psychology," *Jour. Abnor. Psychol. Social Psychol.*, vol. 16, pp. 73–96, 1921.

HOLT, E. B.: *The Freudian Wish and Its Place in Ethics*, Henry Holt & Company, New York, 1915.

HOUSE, FLOYD N.: "The Concept 'Social Forces' in American Sociology," *Amer. Jour. Sociol.*, vol. 31, pp. 145ff., 347ff., 507ff., 1925–1926.

———: *The Range of Social Theory*, Henry Holt & Company, New York, 1929.

HOWARD, GEORGE E.: *Social Psychology: An Analytical Reference Syllabus*, University of Nebraska, Lincoln, Neb., 1910.

HUME, DAVID: *A Treatise of Human Nature*, Longmans, Green & Co., London, 1898.

HUNTER, WALTER S.: "The Modification of Instinct from the Standpoint of Social Psychology," *Psychol. Rev.*, vol. 27, pp. 247–269, 1920.

JACOBS, PHILIP P.: *German Sociology*, Columbia University Thesis, New York, 1909.

JAMES, WILLIAM: *Collected Essays and Reviews*, Longmans, Green & Co., New York, 1920.

———: *Pragmatism*, Longmans, Green & Co., New York, 1908.

———: *Some Problems of Philosophy*, Longmans, Green & Co., New York, 1911.

———: *The Principles of Psychology*, Henry Holt & Company, New York, 1890.

———: *The Will to Believe*, Longmans, Green & Co., New York, 1897.

JONES, H. C., and M. C. JONES: "Genetic Studies of Emotions," *Psychol. Bull.*, vol. 27, pp. 40–64, 1930.

JOSEY, C. C.: *The Social Philosophy of Instinct*, Charles Scribner's Sons, New York, 1922.

JUDD, CHARLES H.: *Psychology*, Charles Scribner's Sons, New York, 1907.

———: "Language, Psychology of," *Cyclopedia of Education*, ed. by Paul Monroe, New York, 1912.

———: "Social Psychology," *Cyclopedia of Education*, ed. by Paul Monroe, New York, 1912.

———: *The Psychology of Social Institutions*, The Macmillan Company, New York, 1926.

JUNG, CARL G.: "The Association Method," *Amer. Jour. Psychol.*, vol. 21, pp. 219–269, 1910.

KANTOR, J. R.: "A Functional View of Human Instincts," *Psychol. Rev.*, vol. 27, pp. 50–72, 1920.

———: "An Attempt toward a Naturalistic Description of Emotions," *Psychol. Rev.*, vol. 27, pp. 19–42, 1921.

———: "An Essay toward an Institutional Conception of Social Psychology," *Amer. Jour. Sociol.*, vol. 27, pp. 611–627, 758–779, 1922.

———: *An Outline of Social Psychology*, Follett Publishing Company, Chicago, 1929.

———: "How Is a Science of Social Psychology Possible?" *Jour. Abnor. Psychol. Social Psychol.*, vol. 17, pp. 62–78, 1922.

———: "The Institutional Foundation of a Scientific Social Psychology," *Amer. Jour. Sociol.*, vol. 29, pp. 674–685, 1924.

———: "The Problem of Instinct and Its Relation to Social Psychology," *Jour. Abnor. Psychol. Social Psychol.*, vol. 18, pp. 50–77, 1923.

KARPF, F. B.: "The Development of Social Psychology," *Pub. Amer. Sociol. Soc.*, vol. 21, pp. 71–81, 1927.

KARPF, M. J.: *The Scientific Basis of Social Work*, Columbia University Press, New York, 1931.

KIDD, BENJAMIN: *Social Evolution*, The Macmillan Company, New York, 1894.

KING, IRVING: *The Psychology of Child Development*, University of Chicago Press, Chicago, 1920.

KIRKPATRICK, E. A.: "Child Study," *Cyclopedia of Education*, ed. by Paul Monroe, New York, 1912.

———: *Fundamentals of Child Study*, The Macmillan Company, New York, 1910.

KLEMM, OTTO: *A History of Psychology*, trans. by E. C. Wilm and R. Pitner, Charles Scribner's Sons, New York, 1914.

KLÜVER, HEINRICH: "Contemporary German Psychology," in G. Murphy, *An Historical Introduction to Modern Psychology*, Harcourt, Brace & Company, New York, 1930.

———: "Weber's 'Ideal Type' in Psychology," *Jour. Phil.*, vol. 33, pp. 29–35, 1926.

KOFFKA, KURT: Part III, *Psychologies of 1925*; Part V, *Psychologies of 1930*, ed. by C. Murchison, Clark University Press, Worcester, Mass., 1926, 1930.

———: "Perception, An Introduction to the Gestalt Theory," *Psychol. Bull.*, vol. 19, pp. 531–585, 1922.

———: *The Growth of the Mind*, trans. by R. M. Ogden, Harcourt, Brace & Company, New York, 1925.

KÖHLER, WOLFGANG: *Gestalt Psychology*, Horace Liveright, New York, 1929.

———: Part III, *Psychologies of 1925*; Part V, *Psychologies of 1930*, ed. by C. Murchison, Clark University Press, Worcester, Mass., 1926, 1930.

———: *The Mentality of Apes*, trans. by Ella Winter, Harcourt, Brace & Company, New York, 1925.

KROEBER, A. L.: *Anthropology*, Harcourt, Brace & Company, New York, 1923.

———: "The Possibility of a Social Psychology," *Amer. Jour. Sociol.*, vol. 23, pp. 633–650, 1917.

———: "The Superorganic," *Amer. Anthrop.*, vol. 19, pp. 163–213, 1917.

KRUEGER, E. T., and W. C. RECKLESS: *Social Psychology*, Longmans, Green & Co., New York, 1931.

KRUEGER, FELIX: *Über Entwicklungspsychologie*, W. Engelmann, Leipzig, 1915.

KUO, Z. Y.: "Giving Up Instincts in Psychology," *Jour. Phil.*, vol. 18, pp. 645–664, 1921.

———: "How Are Our Instincts Acquired?" *Psychol. Rev.*, vol. 29, pp. 344–365, 1922.

LAZARUS, MORITZ: Über das Verhältnis des Einzelnen zur Gesamtheit," *Ztschr. f. Völkerps. u. Sprachw.*, vol. 2, pp. 393–453, 1862.

———: Über die Verdichtung des Denkens in der Geschichte," *Ztschr. f. Völkerps. u. Sprachw.* vol. 2, pp. 54–62, 1862.

——— and HERMANN STEINTHAL: "Einleitende Gedanken zur Völkerpsychologie als Einladung zu einer Zeitschrift für Völkerpsychologie und Sprachwissenschaft," *Ztschr. f. Völkerps. u. Sprachw.*, vol. 1, pp. 1–73, 1860.

LE BON, GUSTAVE: *La révolution française et la psychologie des révolutions*, Paris, 1912, trans. by B. Miall, *The Psychology of Revolution*, T. Fisher Unwin, London, 1913.

———: Les lois psychologiques de l'évolution des peuples, Paris, 1894, trans. *The Psychology of Peoples*, T. Fisher Unwin, London, 1899.

———: *Psychologie des Foules*, Paris, 1895, trans. *The Crowd*, T. Fisher Unwin, London, 1917.

LEPLAY, P. G. F.: *Les ouvriers européens*, A. Mame, Tours, 1878.

LÉVY-BRUHL, LUCIEN: *History of Modern Philosophy in France*, trans. by G. Coblence, Open Court Publishing Company, Chicago, 1899.

———: *L'âme primitive*, Paris, 1927, trans. by Lilian A. Clare, *The Soul of the Primitive*, The Macmillan Company, New York, 1928.

———: La mentalité primitive, Paris, 1922, trans. by Lilian A. Clare, *Primitive Mentality*, The Macmillan Company, New York, 1923.

———: Les fonctions mentales dans les sociétés inférieures, Paris, 1910, trans. by Lilian A. Clare, *How Natives Think*, George Allen & Unwin Ltd., London, 1926.

———: *The Philosophy of Auguste Comte*, trans. by K. DE Beaumont-Klein, G. P. Putnam's Sons, New York, 1903.

LICHTENBERGER, JAMES P.: *The Development of Social Theory*, Century Company, New York, 1923.

LINDNER, GUSTAV A.: *Ideen zur Psychologie der Gesellschaft als Grundlage der Socialwissenschaft*, Carl Gerold's Sohn, Vienna, 1871.

LIPPMANN, WALTER: *Public Opinion*, The Macmillan Company, New York, 1922.

LOWIE, R. H.: *Culture and Ethnology*, Boni & Liveright, New York, 1917.

———: *Primitive Society*, Boni & Liveright, New York, 1920.

———: "Psychology and Sociology," *Amer. Jour. Sociol.*, vol. 21, pp. 217–229, 1915.

LUNDBERG, G. A.: *Social Research*, Longmans, Green & Co., New York, 1929.

LYND, R. S., and H. M. LYND: *Middletown*, Harcourt, Brace & Company, New York, 1929.

McDOUGALL, WILLIAM: *An Introduction to Social Psychology*, John W. Luce & Company, Boston, 1926.

———: "Can Sociology and Social Psychology Dispense with Instincts?" *Amer. Jour. Sociol.*, vol. 29, pp. 657–666, 1924.

———: *Outline of Abnormal Psychology*, Charles Scribner's Sons, New York, 1926.

———: *Outline of Psychology*, Charles Scribner's Sons, New York, 1923.

———: Part IV, *Psychologies of 1925*; Part I, *Psychologies of 1930*, ed. by C. Murchison, Clark University Press, Worcester, Mass., 1926, 1930.

———: *The Group Mind*, G. P. Putnam's Sons, New York, 1920.

————: "The Use and Abuse of Instincts in Social Psychology," *Jour. Abnor. Psychol. Social Psychol.*, vol. 16, pp. 285–333, 1921.

MacIver, Robert M.: "What is Social Psychology?" *Sociol. Rev.*, vol. 6, pp. 147–160, 1913.

Mackenzie, J. S.: *An Introduction to Social Philosophy*, The Macmillan Company, New York, 1895.

Marett, R. R.: *Psychology and Folklore*, Methuen & Co., London, 1920.

Markey, J. F.: *The Symbolic Process and Its Integration in Children*, Harcourt, Brace & Company, New York, 1928.

Martin, E. D.: *The Behavior of Crowds*, Harper & Brothers, New York, 1920.

Matagrin, A.: *La psychologie sociale de Gabriel Tarde*, F. Alcan, Paris, 1910.

Mauss, Marcel: "Rapports réel et pratiques de la psychologie et de la sociologie," *Jour. psychol.*, vol. 21, pp. 892–922, 1924.

————: (See also Fauconnet, Paul, and.)

May, M. A., and H. Hartshorne: "Personality and Character Tests," *Psychol. Bull.*, vol. 23, pp. 395–411, 1926. Also subsequent annual reviews with R. E. Welty.

Mead, George H.: "Cooley's Contribution to American Social Thought," *Amer. Jour. Sociol.*, vol. 35, pp. 693–706, 1930.

————: "Social Consciousness and the Consciousness of Meaning," *Psychol. Bull.*, vol. 7, pp. 397–405, 1910.

————: *Social Psychology* (typed *ms.*), University of Chicago Library, 1924.

————: "Social Psychology as a Counterpart to Physiological Psychology," *Psychol. Bull.*, vol. 6, pp. 401–408, 1909.

————: "The Behavioristic Account of the Significant Symbol," *Jour. Phil.*, vol. 19, pp. 157–163, 1922.

————: "The Genesis of the Self and Social Control," *Intern. Jour. Ethics*, vol. 35, pp. 251–277, 1925.

————: "The Mechanism of Social Consciousness," *Jour. Phil., Psychol., Sci. Meth.*, vol. 9, pp. 401–406, 1912.

————: "The Social Self," *Jour. Phil., Psychol., Sci. Meth.*, vol. 10, pp. 374–380, 1913.

————: "What Social Objects Must Psychology Presuppose?" *Jour. Phil., Psychol., Sci. Meth.*, vol. 7, pp. 174–180, 1910.

Merz, John T.: *A History of European Thought in the Nineteenth Century*, W. Blackwood & Sons, Edinburgh, 1907–1914.

Meyers, C. S., *et al.*: "Instinct and Intelligence" (symposium on) *British Jour. Psychol.*, vol. 3, pp. 209–270, 1910.

Moede, Walther: *Experimentelle Massenpsychologie*, S. Hirzel, Leipzig, 1920.

Morgan, C. Lloyd: *An Introduction to Comparative Psychology*, W. Scott, London, 1894.

————: *Animal Behavior*, E. Arnold, London, 1900.

————: *Animal Life and Intelligence*, E. Arnold, London, 1890–1891.

Mowrer, Ernest R.: *Family Disorganization*, University of Chicago Press, Chicago, 1927.

Muirhead, J. H.: "Hegel," *Encyclopedia Britannica*, 13th ed., vol. 13, pp. 200–207.

Murchison, Carl (ed.): *A History of Psychology in Autobiography*, Clark University Press, Worcester, Mass., 1930, 1932.

————: (ed.) *Psychologies of 1925*, Clark University Press, Worcester, Mass., 1926.

————: (ed.) *Psychologies of 1930*, Clark University Press, Worcester, Mass., 1930.

————: *Social Psychology*, Clark University Press, Worcester, Mass., 1929.

Murphy, Gardner: *An Historical Introduction to Modern Psychology*, Harcourt Brace & Company, New York, 1930.

———— and Lois B. Murphy: *Experimental Social Psychology*, Harper & Brothers, New York, 1931.

Northsworthy, Naomi: "Child Psychology," *Cyclopedia of Education*, ed. by Paul Monroe, New York, 1912.

Odum, Howard W. (ed.): *American Masters of Social Science*, Henry Holt & Company, New York, 1927.

Ogburn, William F.: "Bias, Psychoanalysis, and the Subjective in Relation to the Social Sciences," *Pub. Amer. Sociol. Soc.*, vol. 17, pp. 62–74, 1922.

————: *Social Change*, B. W. Huebsch, New York, 1923.

————: "The Historical Method in the Analysis of Social Phenomena," *Pub. Amer. Sociol. Soc.*, vol. 16, pp. 70–83, 1921.

Ogden, C. K., and I. S. Richards: *The Meaning of Meaning*, Harcourt, Brace & Company, New York, 1927.

Osborn, Henry F.: *From the Greeks to Darwin*, The Macmillan Company, New York, 1913.

Otto, M. C.: "Instrumentalism," *Philosophy Today*, collected and ed. by E. L. Schaub, Open Court Publishing Company, Chicago, 1928.

Palmer, Vivien M.: *Field Studies in Sociology*, University of Chicago Press, Chicago, 1928.

Park, Robert E.: *Masse und Publikum*, Lack & Grunau, Bern, 1904.

————: *The Principles of Human Behavior*, The Zalaz Corporation, Chicago, 1915.

———— and Ernest W. Burgess: *Introduction to the Science of Sociology*, University of Chicago Press, Chicago, 1921.

———— and ————: *The City*, University of Chicago Press, Chicago, 1925.

———— and H. A. Miller: *Old World Traits Transplanted*, Harper & Brothers, New York, 1921.

Parrington, V. L.: *Main Currents in American Thought*, vol. I, Harcourt, Brace & Company, New York, 1927.

Partridge, G. E.: *Genetic Philosophy of Education*, Sturgis & Walton, New York, 1912.

Patrick, G. T. W.: *The Psychology of Social Reconstruction*, Houghton Mifflin Company, Boston, 1920.

Patten, S. N.: *The Development of English Thought*, The Macmillan Company, New York, 1899.

Pearson, Karl: *The Grammar of Science*, A. & C. Black, London, 1911.

Peters, C. C.: *Foundations of Educational Sociology*, The Macmillan Company, New York, 1930.

Piaget, Jean: "Psychology," *Philosophy Today*, collected and ed. by E. L. Schaub, Open Court Publishing Company, Chicago, 1928.

Problems of Personality, Studies in Honor of Dr. Morton Prince, Harcourt, Brace & Company, New York, 1925.

Queen, Stuart A.: *Social Work in the Light of History*, J. B. Lippincott Company, Philadelphia, 1922.

Quetelet, L. A. J.: *Anthropométrie, ou, Mesure des différentes facultés de l'homme*, C. Muquardt, Brussels, 1870.

————: *Du système social et des lois qui le régissent*, Guillaumin, Paris, 1848.

————: *Sur l'homme et le développement de ses facultés, ou Essai de physique sociale*, Bachelier, Paris, 1835.

Radin, Paul: *Primitive Man as Philosopher*, D. Appleton and Company, New York, 1927.

Rand, Benjamin: *The Classical Psychologists*, Houghton Mifflin Company, Boston, 1912.

RATZENHOFER, GUSTAV: *Die sociologische Erkenntniss,* F. A. Brockhaus, Leipzig, 1898.

REUTER, E. B.: "The Social Attitude," *Jour. Appl. Sociol.,* vol. 8, pp. 97–101, 1923.

REYMERT, MARTIN L. (ed.): *Feelings and Emotions: The Wittenberg Symposium,* Clark University Press, Worcester, Mass., 1928.

RIBOT, TH. A.: *German Psychology of Today,* trans. by J. M. Baldwin, Charles Scribner's Sons, New York, 1886.

———: *English Psychology,* trans. from the French, H. S. King and Co., London, 1873.

RICE, STUART A. (ed.): *Methods in Social Science,* University of Chicago Press, Chicago, 1931.

———: *Quantitative Methods in Politics,* Alfred A. Knopf, New York, 1928.

RICHMOND, MARY E.: *What Is Social Case Work?,* Russel Sage Foundation, New York, 1922.

RICKERT, HEINRICH: *Kulturwissenschaft und Naturwissenschaft,* J. C. B. Mohr, Tübingen, 1910.

RILEY, I. WOODBRIDGE: *American Philosophy,* Dodd, Mead & Company, Inc., New York, 1907.

———: *American Thought,* Henry Holt & Company, New York, 1915.

RIVERS, W. H. R.: *Instinct and the Unconscious,* University Press, Cambridge, England, 1920.

———: *Psychology and Ethnology,* Harcourt, Brace & Company, New York, 1926.

———: *Psychology and Politics,* Harcourt, Brace & Company, New York, 1923.

———: "Sociology and Psychology," *Sociol. Rev.,* vol. 9, pp. 1–13, 1916.

ROGERS, ARTHUR K.: *English and American Philosophy since 1800,* The Macmillan Company, New York, 1922.

ROMANES, G. J.: *Animal Intelligence,* D. Appleton & Company, New York, 1883.

———: *Mental Evolution in Animals,* D. Appleton & Company, New York, 1884.

———: *Mental Evolution in Man,* D. Appleton & Company, New York, 1902.

ROSS, E. A.: *Social Control,* The Macmillan Company, New York, 1901.

———: *Social Psychology,* The Macmillan Company, New York, 1908.

———: *The Foundations of Sociology,* The Macmillan Company, New York, 1905.

———: "The Present Problems of Social Psychology," *Proc. Intern. Congress Arts Sci.,* vol. 5, pp. 869–880, New York, 1906.

———: *The Principles of Sociology,* Century Company, New York, 1920, 1930.

———: "What Is Social Psychology," *Psychol. Bull.,* vol. 6, pp. 409–411, 1909.

ROYCE, JOSIAH: *Herbert Spencer: An Estimate and Review,* Fox, Duffield & Company, New York, 1904.

———: *Lectures on Modern Idealism,* Yale University Press, New Haven, 1919.

———: *The World and the Individual,* The Macmillan Company, New York, 1901.

SCHÄFFLE, ALBERT: *Abriss der Soziologie,* H. Laupp, Tübingen, 1906.

———: *Bau und Leben des socialen Körpers,* H. Laupp, Tübingen, 1881.

SCHAUB, EDWARD L. (ed.): *Philosophy of Today,* Open Court Publishing Company, Chicago, 1928.

SCHELER, MAX: *Die Wissensformen und die Gesellschaft: Probleme einer Soziologie des Wissens,* Der Neuegeist Verlag, Leipzig, 1926.

———: *Versuche zu einer Soziologie des Wissens,* Duncker & Humblot, Munich, 1924.

SHAND, A. F.: *The Foundations of Character,* Macmillan & Co., Ltd. London, 1914.

SHAW, CLIFFORD R.: *Delinquency Areas,* University of Chicago Press, Chicago, 1929.

SIGHELE SCIPIO: *La foule criminelle,* French trans. by P. Vigny, F. Alcan, Paris, 1892.

———: *Psychologie des sectes,* French trans. by L. Brandin, V. Giard & E. Brière, Paris, 1898.

SIDIS, BORIS: *The Psychology of Suggestion*, D. Appleton & Company, New York, 1898.

SIMMEL, GEORG: *Soziologie*, Duncker & Humblot, Leipzig, 1908. Selected translations by A. W. Small, *Amer. Jour. Sociol.*, vols., 2, 3, 4, 5, 8, 9, 11, 15, 16, 1902–1910.

——: *Soziologische Vorlesungen von Georg Simmel*, Society for Social Research, University of Chicago, Chicago, 1931.

——: *Über sociale Differenzierung*, Duncker & Humblot, Leipzig, 1890.

SMALL, A. W.: "A Comtean Centenary," *Amer. Jour. Sociol.*, vol. 17, pp. 510–513, 1922.

——: "Fifty Years of Sociology in the United States," *Amer. Jour. Soc.*, vol. 21, pp. 721–864, 1916.

——: "General Sociology," *Amer. Jour. Sociol.*, vol. 18, pp. 200–214, 1912.

——: *General Sociology*, University of Chicago Press, Chicago, 1905.

——: *Origins of Sociology*, University of Chicago Press, Chicago, 1924.

——: "Sociology and Plato's Republic," *Amer. Jour. Sociol.*, vol. 30, pp. 513–533, 683–702, 1925.

—— and G. E. VINCENT: *Introduction to the Study of Society*, American Book Company, New York, 1894.

SMITH, ADAM: *The Theory of Moral Sentiments*, George Bell & Sons, London, 1911.

SMITH, T. V.: "The American Doctrine of Equality in the Light of Evolutionism," *Intern. Jour. Ethics*, vol. 35, pp. 377–403, 1925.

——: "The Social Philosophy of George H. Mead." *Amer. Jour. Sociol.*, vol. 37, pp. 368–385, 1931.

—— and D. WHITE, (ed.): *Chicago, an Experiment in Social Science Research*, University of Chicago Press, Chicago, 1929.

Sociological Papers (of the London Sociological Society), London, 1904–1907.

SOROKIN, PITIRIM: *Contemporary Sociological Theories*, Harper & Brothers, New York, 1928.

SPENCER, HERBERT: *First Principles*, D. Appleton & Company, New York, 1892.

——: *Principles of Biology*, D. Appleton & Company, New York, 1900.

——: *Principles of Psychology*, D. Appleton & Company, New York, 1903.

——: *Principles of Sociology*, D. Appleton & Company, New York, 1882.

——: "The Comparative Psychology of Man," *Mind*, vol. 1, pp. 7–20, 1876.

——: *The Man Versus the State*, D. Appleton & Company, New York, 1888.

——: *The Study of Sociology*, D. Appleton & Company, New York, 1893.

SPRANGER, EDUARD: *Types of Men*, trans. by P. J. W. Pigors, M. Niemeyer, Halle, 1928.

SPROWLS, J. W.: "Recent Social Psychology," *Psychol. Bull.*, vol. 27, pp. 380–393, 1930.

——: *Social Psychology Interpreted*, Williams & Wilkins Co., Baltimore, 1927.

SPYKMAN, NICHOLAS J.: *The Social Theory of Georg Simmel*, University of Chicago Press, Chicago, 1925.

STEINTHAL, HERMANN: "An den Leser," *Ztschr. d. Ver. f. Volkskunde*, vol. 1, pp. 10–17, 1891.

——: "Der Begriff der Völkerpsychologie," *Ztschr. f. Völkerps. u. Sprachw.*, vol. 17, pp. 233–264, 1887.

——: *Philologie, Geschichte und Psychologie in ihren gegenseitigen Beziehungen*, Ferdinand Dümmler, Berlin, 1864.

——: (See also LAZARUS, MORITZ, and.)

STERN, WILLIAM: *Die Psychologie und der Personalismus*, J. A. Barth, Leipzig, 1917.

——: *Psychology of Early Childhood*, trans. by Anna Barwell, Henry Holt & Company, New York, 1924.

STOLL, OTTO: *Suggestion und Hypnotismus in der Völkerpsychologie*, Veit & Co., Leipzig, 1904.

STOLTENBERG, H. L.: *Soziopsychologie*, K. Curtius, Marburg, 1914, 1922.

SUMNER, WILLIAM G.: *Folkways*, Ginn & Company, Boston, 1906.

——: *The Forgotten Man and Other Essays*, Yale University Press, New Haven, 1918.

——: *War and Other Essays*, Yale University Press, New Haven, 1911.

——: *What Social Classes Owe to Each Other*, Harper & Brothers, New York, 1883.

SWINNY, S. H.: "Sociology: Its Successes and Its Failures," *Sociol. Rev.*, vol. 11, pp. 1–10, 1919.

SYMONDS, P. M.: "What Is an Attitude?" *Psychol. Bull.*, vol. 24, pp. 200–201, 1927.

TAINE, H. A.: *De l'intelligence*, L. Hachette, Paris, 1906.

——: *History of English Literature*, trans. by H. van Laun, Holt and Williams, New York, 1871.

TARDE, GABRIEL: *Études de psychologie sociale*, V. Giard & E. Briére, Paris, 1898.

——: "Inter-psychology," trans. by C. H. Page, *Intern. Quar.*, vol. 7, pp. 59–69, 1903.

——: *La logique sociale*, F. Alcan, Paris, 1895.

——: *La philosophie pénale*, Paris, 1890, trans. by R. Howell, *Penal Philosophy*, Little, Brown & Company, Boston, 1912.

——: *Les lois de l'imitation*, Paris, 1890, trans. by E. C. Parsons, *The Laws of Imitation*, Henry Holt & Company, New York, 1903.

——: *Les lois sociales*, Paris, 1898, trans. by H. C. Warren, *Social Laws*, The Macmillan Company, New York, 1899.

——: *L'opinion et la foule*, F. Alcan, Paris, 1901.

——: *L'opposition universelle*, F. Alcan, Paris, 1897.

THOMAS, WILLIAM I.: "Scope and Method of Folk Psychology," *Amer. Jour. Sociol.*, vol. 1, pp. 434–445, 1896.

——: *Sex and Society*, University of Chicago Press, Chicago, 1907.

——: *Source Book for Social Origins*, University of Chicago Press, Chicago, 1909.

——: "The Behavior Pattern and the Situation," *Pub. Amer. Sociol. Soc.*, vol. 22, pp. 1–13, 1928.

——: "The Configuration of Personality," *The Unconscious*, ed. by Mrs. W. F. Dummer, Alfred A. Knopf, New York, 1927.

——: "The Gaming Instinct," *Amer. Jour. Sociol.*, vol. 6, pp. 750–763, 1901.

——: "The Persistence of Primary-group Norms in Present-day Society and Their Influence in Our Educational System," *Suggestions of Modern Science concerning Education*, by H. Jennings et al., The Macmillan Company, New York, 1921.

——: "The Province of Social Psychology," *Proc. Intern. Congress Arts Sci.*, vol. 5, pp. 860–868, New York, 1906.

——: *The Unadjusted Girl*, Little, Brown & Company, Boston, 1923.

—— and DOROTHY S. THOMAS: *The Child in America*, Alfred A. Knopf, New York, 1928.

—— and FLORIAN ZNANIECKI: *The Polish Peasant in Europe and America*, University of Chicago Press, Chicago, 1918–1920.

THORNDIKE, EDWARD L.: *Animal Intelligence*, The Macmillan Company, New York, 1911.

——: *The Original Nature of Man*, Teachers College, Columbia University, New York, 1913.

THRASHER, FREDERIC M.: *The Gang*, University of Chicago Press, Chicago, 1927.

THURNWALD, RICHARD: "Die Probleme der empirischen Soziologie," *Ztschr. f. Völkerps. u. Soz.*, vol. 3, pp. 257–273, 1927.

——: "Probleme der Völkerpsychologie und Soziologie," *Ztschr. f. Völkerps. u. Soz.*, vol. 1, pp. 1–20, 1925.

——: "Zum gegenwärtigen Stande der Völkerpsychologie," *Kölner Vier. f. Soz.*, vol. 4, pp. 32–43, 1925.

THURSTONE, L. L.: "Attitudes Can Be Measured," *Amer. Jour. Sociol.*, vol. 33, pp. 529–554, 1928.

——: "The Influence of Freudianism on Theoretical Psychology," *Psychol. Rev.*, vol. 31, pp. 175–183, 1924.

——: *The Nature of Intelligence*, Harcourt, Brace & Company, New York, 1924.

——: "The Stimulus-response Fallacy in Psychology," *Psychol. Rev.*, vol. 30, pp. 354–369, 1923.

——: "Theory of Attitude Measurement," *Psychol. Rev.*, vol. 36, pp. 222–241, 1929.

TODD, ARTHUR J.: *Theories of Social Progress*, The Macmillan Company, New York, 1918.

TOLMAN E. C.: "Can Instincts Be Given Up in Psychology?" *Jour. Abnor. Psychol. Social Psychol.*, vol. 17, pp. 139–152, 1922.

——: "The Nature of Instinct," *Psychol. Bull.*, vol. 20, pp. 200–218, 1923.

TOSTI, GUSTAVO: "Social Psychology and Sociology," *Psychol. Rev.*, vol. 5, pp. 347–361, 1898.

——: "Tarde's Sociological Theories," *Pol. Sci. Quar.*, vol. 12, pp. 490–511, 1897.

TRIDON, ANDRÉ: *Psychoanalysis and Behavior*, Alfred A. Knopf, New York, 1920.

TROTTER, W.: *Instincts of the Herd in Peace and War*, The Macmillan Company, New York, 1916.

TYLOR, E. B.: *Primitive Culture*, John Murray, London, 1871.

VIERKANDT, ALFRED: "Die Überwindung des Positivismus in der dentschen Soziologie der Gegenwart," *Jahrbuch f. Soz.*, vol. 2, pp. 66–90, 1926.

——: *Gesellschaftslehre, Hauptprobleme der philosophischen Soziologie*, Ferdinand Enke, Stuttgart, 1926.

——: *Naturvölker und Kulturvölker, Ein Beitrag zur Sozialpsychologie*, Duncker & Humblot, Leipzig, 1896.

VILLA, GUIDO: *Contemporary Psychology*, trans. by H. Manacorda, The Macmillan Company, New York, 1903.

VINCENT, G. E.: "George Elliott Howard, Social Psychologist," *Sociol. and Social Res.*, vol. 13, pp. 108–118, 1928–1929.

——: (See also SMALL, A. W., and.)

VON WIESE, LEOPOLD: *Allgemeine Soziologie*, Duncker & Humblot, Munich, 1924–1929.

——: "Current Sociology: Germany," *Sociol. Rev.*, vol. 19, pp. 21–25, 1927.

——: "Systematic Sociology: Science of Interhuman Behavior," *Sociol. and Social Res.*, vol. 15, pp. 103–115, 1930.

WADDLE, CHARLES W.: *Introduction to Child Psychology*, Houghton Mifflin Company, Boston, 1918.

WALLAS, GRAHAM: *Human Nature in Politics*, Archibald Constable & Co. Ltd., London, 1908.

——: *Our Social Heritage*, Yale University Press, New Haven, 1921.

——: *The Great Society*, The Macmillan Company, New York, 1914.

WALLIS, W. D.: "Mental Patterns in Relation to Culture," *Jour. Abnor. Social Psychol.*, vol. 19, pp. 179–184, 1925.

——: "The Analysis of Culture," *Pub. Amer. Sociol. Soc.*, vol. 21, pp. 158–164, 1925.

——: "The Independence of Social Psychology," *Jour. Abnor. Social Psychol.*, vol. 20, pp. 147–150, 1925.

WALTHER, ANDREAS: "The Present Position of Sociology in Germany," *Jour. Appl. Sociol.*, vol. 10, pp. 229–238, 1926.

———— et al.: "Soziologisches Symposium," *Ztschr. f. Völkerps. u. Soz.*, vol. 5, pp. 131*ff.*, 257*ff.*, 385*ff.*, 1929.

WARD, LESTER F.: *Applied Sociology*, Ginn & Company, Boston, 1906.

————: *Dynamic Sociology*, D. Appleton & Company, New York, 1883.

————: *Pure Sociology*, The Macmillan Company, New York, 1903.

————: *The Psychic Factors of Civilization*, Ginn & Company, Boston, 1893.

WATSON, JOHN B.: *Behavior: An Introduction to Comparative Psychology*, Henry Holt & Company, New York, 1914.

————: *Behaviorism*, W. W. Norton & Company, New York, 1925.

————: Part I, *Psychologies of 1925*, ed. by C. Murchison, Clark University Press, Worcester, Mass., 1926.

————: *Psychology from the Standpoint of a Behaviorist*, J. B. Lippincott Company, Philadelphia, 1919.

WEBER, MAX: *Gesammelte Aufsätze zur Religionssoziologie*, J. C. B. Mohr, Tübingen, 1922–1923.

WELLS, W. R.: "The Anti-instinct Fallacy," *Psychol. Rev.*, vol. 30, pp. 228–234, 1923.

————: "The Value for Social Psychology of the Concept of Instinct," *Jour. Abnor. Psychol. Social Psychol.*, vol. 16, pp. 334–343, 1922.

WENZL, A.: "Psychology," *Philosophy Today*, collected and ed. by E. L. Schaub, pp. 486–524, Open Court Publishing Company, Chicago, 1928.

WESTERMARCK, EDWARD: *The History of Human Marriage*, Macmillan & Co., Ltd., London, 1894.

————: *The Origin and Development of Moral Ideas*, Macmillan & Co., Ltd., London, 1906–1908.

WHITE, LEONARD, D. (ed.): *The New Social Science*, University of Chicago Press, Chicago, 1930.

————: (See also SMITH, T. V., and.)

WHITE, W. A.: *The Mechanisms of Character Formation*, The Macmillan Company, New York, 1916.

WILLEY, M., and M. J. HERSKOVITS: "Psychology and Culture," *Psychol. Bull.*, vol. 24, pp. 253–284, 1927.

WILLIAMS, JAMES M.: *Our Rural Heritage*, Alfred A. Knopf, New York, 1925.

————: *Principles of Social Psychology*, Alfred A. Knopf, New York, 1922.

————: *The Expansion of Rural Life*, Alfred A. Knopf, New York, 1926.

————: *The Foundations of Social Science*, Alfred A. Knopf, New York, 1920.

WILSON, L. N.: *G. Stanley Hall*, G. E. Stechert & Company, New York, 1914.

WINDELBAND, WILHELM: *A History of Philosophy*, trans. by J. H. Tufts, The Macmillan Company, New York, 1919.

WIRTH, LOUIS: *The Ghetto*, University of Chicago Press, Chicago, 1928.

————: "Topical Summaries of Current Literature: Modern German Conceptions of Sociology," *Amer. Jour. Sociol.*, vol. 32, pp. 461–470, 1926.

WISSLER, CLARK: *An Introduction to Social Anthropology*, Henry Holt & Company, New York, 1927.

————: *Man and Culture*, Thomas Y. Crowell Company, New York, 1923.

————: "Psychological and Historical Interpretations for Culture," *Science*, vol. 43, pp. 193–201, 1916.

————: "Recent Developments in Anthropology," *Recent Developments in the Social Sciences*, ed. by E. C. Hayes, J. B. Lippincott Company, Philadelphia, 1927.

————: "The Culture Area Concept in Social Anthropology," *Amer. Jour. Sociol.*, vol. 32, pp. 881–891, 1927.

WOODWORTH, ROBERT S.: *Contemporary Schools of Psychology*, Ronald Press Company, New York, 1931.

———: *Dynamic Psychology*, Columbia University Press, New York, 1918.

WUNDT, WILHELM: *Elemente der Völkerpsychologie*, Leipzig 1912, trans. by E. L. Schaub, *Elements of Folk Psychology*, The Macmillan Company, New York, 1916.

———: *Outlines of Psychology*, trans. by C. H. Judd, W. Engelmann, Leipzig, 1907.

———: "Über Ziele und Wege der Völkerpsychologie," *Philosophische Studien*, vol. 4, pp. 1–27, 1888.

———: *Völkerpsychologie: Eine Untersuchung der Entwicklungsgesetze von Sprache, Mythus und Sitte*, W. Engelmann, Leipzig, 1911–1920.

WYATT, H. G.: "The Recent Anti-instinctivistic Attitude in Social Psychology," *Psychol. Rev.*, vol. 34, pp. 126–134, 1927.

YOUNG, KIMBALL (ed.): *Social Attitudes*, Henry Holt & Company, New York, 1931.

———: *Social Psychology*, F. S. Crofts & Co., New York, 1930.

———: "Social Psychology," *The History and Prospects of the Social Sciences*, ed. by Harry E. Barnes, pp. 156–209, Alfred A. Knopf, New York, 1925.

———: *Source Book for Social Psychology*, Alfred A. Knopf, New York, 1927.

———: "The Field of Social Psychology," *Psychol. Bull.*, vol. 24, pp. 661–691, 1927.

———: "The Contributions of Psychiatry to Social Psychology," *Pub. Amer. Sociol. Soc.*, vol. 21, pp. 82–91, 1927.

———: "The Measurement of Personal and Social Traits," *Pub. Amer. Sociol. Soc.*, vol. 21, pp. 92–105, 1927.

ZNANIECKI, FLORIAN: *Cultural Reality*, University of Chicago Press, Chicago, 1919.

———: *The Laws of Social Psychology*, University of Chicago Press, Chicago, 1925.

———: (See also THOMAS, WILLIAM I., and.)

ZORBAUGH, H. W.: *The Gold Coast and the Slum*, University of Chicago Press, Chicago, 1929.

INDEX

449

POSTSCRIPT

Since the original publication of this book, American social psychology has naturally continued to develop in a number of important directions, in addition to the background approaches to the subject outlined in *American Social Psychology*. Most important has been the gradual accumulation of an impressive quantity of concrete research, most of it specialized, limited and unintegrated with the field as a whole. It nevertheless provides a factual and verifiable base for new procedures in interpretive and integrative theory, along with its contributions to the practical import of social psychology.

More generally, social psychology has expanded its boundaries markedly, with continuing contributions not only from psychology, sociology and cultural anthropology—the disciplines historically most directly concerned with the development of social psychology—but also from the allied applied fields of psychiatry, psychoanalysis and education, as well as from some of the other social sciences, such as economics and political science. The result has been a complex of supposedly relevant but not always consistent material of differing and at times conflicting orientation and perspective, suggesting selective eclecticism as the most manageable method of ordering it.

Altogether, then, the situation is ripe for new organizing and integrating effort. There has therefore been a renewed interest in historical backgrounds as a basis for forward attempts at the formulation of new empirically grounded and supported interpretive and integrative theory. The reissue of *American Social Psychology* is in line with these considerations.

Fay B. Karpf

BEVERLY HILLS, CALIFORNIA
October, 1971